Comm Studies

Stuart Price

...TS AND TECHNOLOGY

LONGMAN

Addison Wesley Longman Limited,
Edinburgh Gate, Harlow, Essex CM20 2JE

© Addison Wesley Longman Ltd. 1996

First published 1996

ISBN 0582 27795 7

Set in 10.5/12.5 pt New Century Schoolbook
Produced by Longman Singapore Publishers Pte Ltd
Printed in Singapore

The Publisher's policy is to use paper manufactured from sustainable forests.

Contents

Acknowledgements

Communication Studies was written over a period of some eighteen months, during full-time teaching on a variety of courses. Almost all of the material it contains was produced specifically for this publication, though some of the work on address in the media emerged from PhD research. Substantial excerpts from the text were presented to A-level, Access and Degree students, before the book went into print.

My thanks go first to Lucy Byrne for her consideration and support, and to Edward and Huw Price for their patience during the revision of the text. Within the Media Education section at Somerset College, Rivers Barry provided an example of prescience and boldness in the field of communication teaching, directing attention to neglected areas of inquiry such as intonation and significance. Anita Abrams's support in the delivery of Media Studies and Media Arts is also greatly appreciated.

Extensive resources were required during this project; I am grateful to those members of the Somerset College LRC who helped in processing books, and wish to thank in particular the staff member who procured a rogue library card with an unusually high capacity. Raoul Wedge-Thomas's flair for representing diagrams to such a high standard, together with his irrepressible cheerfulness, must be acknowledged, together with Mick Garland's hard work in producing many photographs throughout the text. Charlie Davies showed particular kindness in allowing the use of a number of Exeter College projects, while Lorna Cocking and Catherine Allison at Longman, and Ian Little at Pitman, were most helpful during the various stages of the exercise. Although officially 'anonymous', the comments of Patrick Brereton were both thorough and encouraging.

My thanks to the following people and organisations for permission to use illustrations, transcripts and other material:

Mick Garland for photos on pages 217, 269, 388, 432, 433, 526–8; *The Guardian* and Guardian News Service Ltd, for Amy Raphael's article 'Not Just an Asian Babe'; Kippa Matthews for photographs of Sonya Aurora-Madan
The Daily Express for the front page 'Why We Had to Talk to the IRA'
The *Daily Mail* and the Solo Syndication & Literary Agency for the front page 'Criminals and Cheats Beware'.

The Associated Examining Board for the 'Thomas Eslopp Trust' case study
D.C. Thompson & Co. Ltd. and *The Beano* for the 'Dennis the Menace' cartoon
The BBC and Hat-trick productions for the extract from *Have I Got News for You*; Andrew Parker for the photograph of Tidenham Tunnel.
Hush Puppy for the advertisement 'A Dog's Not Just for Christmas'.
Andersen Press Limited, Red Fox and Random House Children's Books for permission to reproduce David McKee's *Not Now Bernard*, first published in full colour by the Andersen Press Limited, London, ISBN 0905478711.
Suzy Mullins for transcripts and, with Rachel House, for speech events in Chapter 3; Pascale Garrod, Lucy Pitt and Theresa Wistaw for appearing in photographs, and Fiona Jenkinson for speech events in the activities section of Chapter 3; Simon Lewis for 'modelling' illustrations of body language; Liz Ayres for extracts from project work; Zoe Watson for permission to reproduce the cover from The Guarder.

For my mother, Jean Price

Preface

This book attempts to provide a comprehensive reference and learning resource for teachers and students of Communication Studies. It was produced in the belief that the subject encourages a critical perspective on a variety of disciplines, offering a number of important insights into the study of language, culture and power.

It is often said that the characteristic strengths of this subject are best revealed through the practical investigations made by its students. Such undertakings will always require access to contemporary theory if they are to make, in their turn, original contributions to the field. It is in support of this view that a thorough account of the different strands of communication theory, together with an overview of research, is given in this text. Extracts from student projects also appear, so the reader may gain an idea of the practical potential of a range of investigations. In order to demonstrate the worth of the various interpretative methodologies available to students, the analysis of textual material is allowed a prominent position in a number of chapters.

Communication Studies: problems and challenges

A major problem faced by teachers and students of Communication Studies has been that its wide remit has encouraged the assumption that the subject is merely a convenient 'hold-all'. Related to this is the concern that, while its openness and breadth of content have sustained intellectual freedom, it may also at times have allowed students to subsist on a diet of speculation.

My aim has been to work towards solutions to those problems caused by the great range of topics and approaches which Communication Studies embraces. If careful and intelligent inquiry can be allied to the freedom of discussion and action which this discipline encourages, then the task of making links between theory, practical work, personal experience, and research into communication events should be made easier. The outcome may eventually be a true communication 'practice', in which students not only understand the practical and theoretical aspects of all branches of the subject, but are able to produce an integrated expression of these in their own work.

Introduction

Communication Studies: direction vs. diversity?

There are two closely related problems which exist in the field of Communication Studies; both emerge from the exceptional breadth of the subject. In the first place, each area of work appears to require access to a wide variety of published sources. This makes great demands upon teachers and students, though it does provide the opportunity to study materials which would be difficult to introduce in other, more restrictive disciplines. Secondly, a separate *method* of inquiry seems to be required for individual topics. It is hardly surprising that, at one point in its history, Communication Studies appeared to be the classic case of multi-disciplinary confusion.

One of the enduring arguments in the subject is over the degree of **direction** which may be required to make a course of study coherent, and the extent to which a **diversity** of approach brings its own rewards. Another way of looking at the problem is offered by John Corner and Jeremy Hawthorn in the fourth edition of *Communication Studies: An Introductory Reader.* *Corner and Hawthorne describe the difference between an **interdisciplinary** and a **multi-disciplinary** approach to the subject.

The first approach sees Communication Studies as (p. 1) 'operating *across and between* disciplines,' while the second would recognise the 'range of distinctive disciplinary inputs' which exist. The use of an *interdisciplinary* perspective would suggest that there is a specific principle or goal which directs work in the subject, while a *multi-disciplinary* view would seem to regard the study as a less strictly focused inquiry.

While it is clear that Communication Studies encompasses parts of many other disciplines, this book favours an interdisciplinary approach, based upon a clear sense of purpose. The next part of this Introduction attempts to bring this purpose into sharper focus. It begins with a brief overview of those perspectives which have become most closely associated with the subject, and ends by suggesting a revised agenda for its future development.

*Full details of publications mentioned in the text are given in the Bibliography at the end of this book.

Communication Studies: a sense of purpose

Orthodox approaches

Often, when certain topics within Communication Studies are investigated, established or 'time-honoured' perspectives are used to explain their significance. During the last decade, some approaches among the different traditions which inform the subject have encouraged the emergence of what could be called *orthodox* positions.

A few examples may illustrate this point. It seems that human interaction, including non-verbal communication, has most usually been studied from the viewpoint of behavioural psychology, a 'scientific' tradition which emphasises the importance of observable behaviour. A number of North American writers represent this tradition. Another typical perspective may be seen in the field of organisational communication, where a Business Studies approach is often applied. The problem in this case is that communication is studied only in order to calculate its efficiency. Media institutions, however, have been investigated using theories borrowed from sociology, while a rather ornate semiology is used to interpret the various 'texts' the media produce. (Semiology is the systematic study of signs and their meaning.)

The approaches mentioned above do not make up a complete list of those inherited by the subject. They do, however, represent some of the dominant perspectives still in use. Although these traditions might be accused of having failed to provide a coherent overview of the field of communication, it was never reasonable to imagine that they should do so, considering the diversity of material to which each refers. A more serious charge is that such perspectives have not always provided convincing descriptions of the *individual* fields of inquiry they were supposed to explain.

Criticism of established perspectives

I am not suggesting that all established theories and methods are worthless, rather that to continue to allow them precedence may act as a brake on the development of the subject. In recent years, a number of writers and commentators have expressed doubts about the ability of the dominant agenda to make sense of public culture and communication. For example, David Buckingham, following the work of Carmen Luke (see *Children Talking Television*, p. 16), argues that psychological approaches to television make the *social* context of its consumption intelligible only 'in terms of the psychological reactions and experiences of individuals'. Hanno Hardt, in *Critical Communication Studies*, describes mainstream American communication research as (p. 5) 'ahistorical and unreflective'. Other critics have turned their attention to the shortcomings of interpretative systems. In *Television Form and Public Address* (p. 3), John Corner notes the feeling that semiology 'has frequently become over-elaborate in its terminology ... failing to "catch" the subleties of what it is addressing'.

New directions

Faced with the shortcomings of orthodox ideas, theorists are beginning to draw upon alternative currents of research emerging from media, linguistic and cultural studies. Part of this revision entails a move away from the 'personal' and developmental models which were so popular at the genesis of the subject. Concepts of the *social* and *contextual* (see next section) have now been applied to areas of study which were once regarded as having little in common. Crowley and Mitchell, in *Communication Theory Today*, identify this trend (p. 2), together with 'a growing emphasis on meaning creation and human agency'. Some currents of thought have rejected the 'objective' model of research, where experts interpret the behaviour of human subjects, and have turned to investigate the meanings which people attribute to their own actions.

The tendency to give more space to audience studies, and to the analysis of *reception* theory in particular, is usually taken to be a healthy sign in cultural inquiry. The impact of the 'new media technologies', for example, demands that we pay attention to those influences which, some argue, make for a more fragmented public culture.

The aims of a 'reformed' Communication Studies

Attempts to create a 'reformed' Communication Studies could begin by placing the *social subject* (the human being in society) at the centre of the entire investigation. Less emphasis would be placed upon theories of personality, and more on the collective dimensions of existence, especially those communication events expressed through *language*. This would imply a critical analysis of *discourse*, which, simply defined, means conversation or public speech. Theories of *contextual* meaning, where a communication event is interpreted in the light of its material circumstances, would also assume particular significance. Approaches which depend upon investigating cognition, (the faculty of understanding), and intellectual processing would have to be considered in conjunction with research into *emotional* responses.

Using this agenda, it may eventually be possible to construct a Communication Studies which is able to interpret texts, events and human interaction in their social and historical contexts, paying close attention to the meanings which contemporary individuals and groups attach to them. Those strands of theory and research which seem to assist this project will be strongly represented in this book, but will appear within the context of a detailed presentation of established communication approaches.

Communication practice: investigation and practical expression

The type of reformation just described clearly implies a turn to a critical and contextual theory able to investigate the creation, circulation and interpretation of meaning as it occurs in exchanges between 'text', audience and institution.

Investigation, however, makes up only half the purpose of Communication Studies; the other essential element is each student's **expression** of what has been learned. The importance of this point cannot be over-emphasised.

The various components of Communication Studies (theory, research and practical production) are brought together in project work, an inquiry which eventually produces an artefact aimed at a specific audience. It is sometimes argued that the purpose of the AEB project is to create 'links' between theory, research and production. If we use the concept of *practice* (a term I used in the Preface), then it will become clear that our goal could be more ambitious. Communication practice refers to the practical *expression* of a student's *understanding* of the internal dynamics of 'text' (the interplay between form and content in a photograph, an article, a piece of music, a conversation, etc.) and of any text's relationship to theories of institution, address, audience and reception.

In simple terms, this means that everyone involved in the subject should be able not only to *interpret* the different forms in which public meanings are expressed (speech, press articles, magazine covers, television advertisements, or whatever) but also that they must be able to *create* their own artefacts (films, displays, audio programmes, magazines and so on). Within communication practice, theory must provide tools (rather than 'rules') for interpretation, so that the purposes and structures of all types of symbolic exchange may be studied.

It follows that all practical experiments in the subject should help students recognise how codes and conventions are employed, thus allowing them to make an informed choice about whether or not to make, in their own work, departures from established forms. Chapter 6 explores the challenge of research and project work in more detail.

Organisation of the book

The structure of this book is set out in the list of contents. It may be useful, however, to provide a brief introduction to the major concerns of each chapter.

Chapter 1 starts with definitions of communication, and introduces some of the major approaches to the study of the subject. It then uses elements of the AEB syllabus (forms, categories, uses and purposes) to guide students through the basic approaches to the subject. This would be the most appropriate place to begin study. The first chapter also considers the methods used to interpret textual material (see the section on 'Text and context'), before moving on to describe models of communication. Theories of representation and reality, and descriptions of sensory perception, form an important aspect of the first chapter's approach.

Chapter 2 concentrates on ideas about the social subject (moving from what is usually known as *intra*personal communication to theories and examples of the *inter*personal). It examines concepts of mind, thought and expression, and the ways in which human identity is constructed. Ideas about the presentation of self are introduced, before the chapter ends with examples of everyday speech.

Against the background of communication and power, Chapter 3 offers a description of the social *process*, referring to the pivotal role of language. Categorisation, stereotyping, social identification and group communication also form part of its concerns.

Chapter 4 studies formal organisations and communication in hierarchical or graded structures, and includes reference to issues such as bureaucracy, authority and subordination in the workplace. It also describes the development of communication and the birth of the 'mass' media. It concludes with a study of new or 'interactive' technology. Chapter 5 deals with critical theory, beginning with written communication and the discourses of art, and moving on to an extended analysis of the major perspectives on culture and cultural production. Chapter 6 presents an assessment of research methodology and examines the practical application of knowledge through project work.

Each chapter is illustrated with a wide range of material and carries a summary of content. Chapters 2 to 5 also include student activities. The book ends with a full Bibliography and an Index.

CHAPTER I

Descriptions and definitions

The challenge of definition

Books on communication often begin by stating that the concept is hard to define. There is certainly some truth in this, not only because communication encompasses a wide field, but because we are forced to describe a feature of human experience through the very processes which are the object of study. This is quite a challenge, especially when there does not seem to be an 'objective' standpoint from which to pass judgement on communication events. Attempts to describe communication are bound, therefore, to unearth definitions which appear to be at variance with one another.

Despite the differences between the various definitions of the concept, each attempt at description has its uses, offering students, academics and professional communicators a variety of positions from which to explore the social construction of meaning. This means that, while some of the definitions listed below may not attain the accuracy or descriptive power of the best explanations, none is likely to disappear completely from the communication agenda. I would also propose that the reproduction of the whole range of descriptions is useful because it allows an insight into the development of communication theory.

Furthermore, it may be possible to imagine the various definitions as part of a *continuum*, a structure containing individual but *related* elements. From this standpoint, an understanding of communication could be said to emerge from the relationship between the five 'components' described in outline below, which I have called **transmission**, **exchange**, the **generation of meaning**, **context** and **discourse**.

Theories of transmission

Some writers have defined communication as the *transmission* of various types of data from one individual to another, or from an institution to an audience. Transmission means, essentially, the transfer of information from a source to a receiver. At its simplest, this implies that the purpose of communication is to deliver messages. A message may consist of 'a thought, an instruction, a wish, an idea, a feeling' (see Gurevitch and Roberts, *Issues in the Study of Mass Communication and Society*, p. 12). So, for example, a phrase such as 'Please remain in your seats' could be seen as the transmission of information from A to B.

Transmission also implies that *reception* will occur at some point. Although communication does involve the movement of data, a definition which posits no more than a single act of transfer will be unable to convey the full complexity of real events. Another problem with this definition, according to Denis McQuail (see *Communication*, p. 14), is that it 'implies an underlying rationality and purposefulness about communication'. The idea of a rational and purposeful 'act' of communication may suggest that 'it is the intention of the communicator which defines the meaning of a communication event'. This leads to notions of successful transfer, reinforcing those positions which are concerned with the *efficiency* of communication.

In practice, the person who *initiates* an act of communication may be the original 'source' of the event, but is unlikely to monopolise the role of sender; there is usually a reply and therefore an *exchange*. Raymond Williams, in *Keywords*, notes that the term 'communication' itself is ambiguous, referring both to a 'one-way process' and to the sharing of information.

Material produced and circulated by the media conforms more closely to the transmission model, at least in the sense that the mode of communication allows the process to be dominated by the source (the media institution). The extent to which the 'new' or 'interactive' media encourage a breakdown of this relationship is examined at the end of Chapter 4.

From transmission to exchange

An idea which makes a clear advance on theories of transmission may be found in those definitions which stress the constant *exchange* within a society (and between societies) of words, images, signs, gestures and other forms. This can take place in a number of ways, and at different levels. The usual term for the process of exchange is *interaction* – the action and reaction which take place between the different parties involved.

Whether intentional or unintentional, all interaction must be accompanied by some sort of impact. This is an emotional or cognitive response which may or may not result in an observable physical outcome, but which will entail a change of state in those individuals or groups involved in communication. Returning to the example used before, the expression of a plea to remain seated would become an exchange if it prompted a reply or an action which confirmed the relevance or force of the request. For instance, a spoken refusal to be seated, or alternatively a ready compliance with the request, would constitute an exchange and show that the request was meaningful.

The generation of meaning: symbolic form and content

There is, however, a danger in concentrating exclusively upon the concept of exchange; in our eagerness to examine the mechanics of interaction, we may lose sight of the *purpose* of communication. The more sophisticated definitions of communication direct our attention to the generation of *meaning*, concentrating on the use of **symbolic forms** by human beings.

Symbolic forms include the spoken and written language, as well as other modes of communication which are recognised within a specific culture (though some forms, like music, are often said to transcend cultural boundaries). A request such as 'Please remain in your seats' is meaningful because it employs a specific example of symbolic content (a complete 'unit' of meaning) drawn from a recognised symbolic form (current usage of the English language). The content and form in this case are said to be *symbolic* because they refer to, or stand for, some thing or concept or state of affairs in the real world. According to this approach, communication is essentially social, growing from the personal, economic, cultural and political needs of individuals and groups located in a particular time and place.

Some symbolic forms are thought to be 'systematic' or *formal* – language, as I indicated above, is the primary example. Other modes of communication – the signs, gestures and even noises used by human beings to refer to their experience of the world – are sometimes described as *informal* modes of communication.

Communication as contextual meaning

In recent years, the idea that meaning emerges when communication takes place within a specific *context* has become more popular. Using, once again, the example already employed ('Please remain in your seats'), we may discover that the exact nature of the sentence's meaning will depend upon a number of 'influences', such as the *intention* of the communicators, the *relationship* between the participants, and the *location* or *setting* in which the phrase is used. These are the primary contextual factors in any interaction. In addition, there are elements which supplement or give context to spoken language; 'body language', gesture and intonation provide important 'clues' to meaning for an onlooker or audience.

If we imagine our phrase occurring in a primary-school classroom, the request may be part of the repertoire of control used by a teacher; the relationship between the class and the teacher makes the sentence a typical part of everyday interaction. Alternatively, it could be uttered in the same setting by a pupil, during a game in which children imitate the discourses of authority. Or, to use another (rather unlikely) example, 'Please remain in your seats' may be used by a politician who, overcome with modesty, genuinely wishes to refuse the acclaim offered by a meeting of party delegates.

It is important to realise that 'context' does not always refer merely to physical location, since quite different events may occur in similar places. (For a complete description of contextual variables, see the reference to Hymes in this chapter's section on 'Text and context'.)

Communication as discourse

The idea that communication is the utterance of meaningful *discourse* emerged from the more practical branches of linguistics, and began with the idea that spoken language is the primary mode of human interaction. The term 'discourse' originally referred to an utterance larger than a sentence, but was extended to include any coherent expression of ideas. Communication theorists have adopted the term to describe the *social* process of creating meaning, through the use of language and other symbolic forms.

The public nature of communication and the inevitable competition between ideas have led some writers to use 'discourse' in a more specific way, to mean the expression of a specific ideology (a system of belief) through spoken, written and other means. It is certainly true that many types of public discourse, from political speeches to painting, are used to express ideas about the world, but whenever attempts are made to put organised or *systematic* belief into a coherent form, the result is never entirely 'pure'. That is, all belief and ideology draw upon ideas which already circulate in social life, and will therefore have to find expression in ways which are familiar to an audience or 'target group'. It is probably more useful to imagine the existence of overlapping *discourses*, which specific ideologies try to use for their own purposes.

When a message is constructed, its content is chosen from within the recognised scope of a symbolic form; every language, for instance, offers a certain range of meaning. Although the creation of meaning occurs as a natural process (whenever, for example, an individual or group exercises the faculty of language), there are always constraints on what may be expressed. The selection which is made from contemporary *usage* will be influenced by those discourses or 'ways of speaking' which are currently 'fashionable', and which are therefore regarded as *appropriate* within a specific context. The general capabilities of public language or other symbolic forms, and the types of expression thought appropriate in practice, together make up the *discursive* context of an event.

To appreciate this point, imagine an election briefing for journalists, called by one of the mainstream political parties. Near the end of the meeting, the representatives of various newspapers and networks rise from their places to leave. At this point, an unexpected development prompts the organisers to broadcast a request to extend the briefing. The assembled correspondents are therefore exhorted: 'Please remain in your seats.' The request to remain seated is drawn from the public 'store' of language, and yet also obeys, in its formality and politeness, discourses regarded as suitable to the occasion.

The successful reproduction of meaning depends, therefore, on the use of a specific *repertoire* of communicative devices drawn from the general *range* of language. It is worth noting that it is in the interests of the hypothetical political party to conduct itself in a reasonable way, and so to use a conventional mode of address. It would hardly be appropriate for the organisers to *demand* that the correspondents keep still, or for abusive language to be directed at those who begin to drift away.

Definition: a summary

From the material covered so far, communication may be defined as **an activity in which *symbolic content* is not merely *transmitted* from one source to another, but *exchanged* between human agents, who interact within a shared situational and/or discursive *context*.** Although we have arrived at a definition, this does not obliterate the differences between the individual descriptions which helped in its formation. The existence of competing definitions reveals not simply the complexity of the subject, but also the variety of *perspectives* on and *approaches* to communication.

Communication Studies: perspectives and approaches

The word **perspective** is used to describe human perception of the relative positions of solid objects on a plane surface; it suggests that something is seen from an objective or fixed viewpoint. A perspective *on* something means the way in which a particular subject or issue is understood or valued. Used in an academic context, the term refers to *a point of view* held regarding the worth or function of a discipline or an aspect of study.

An **approach**, on the other hand, means a way of *dealing with* or getting to grips with a subject. In this context, it describes how theorists and researchers (those individuals who hold perspectives or views) initiate or carry out their studies in a certain field.

It is possible to combine the concept of *perspective* with that of *approach*, since most people involved in academic study will hold certain views which are connected to the way they carry out research. It should be made clear, however, that while a preference for a particular perspective may suggest some allegiance to a related approach, it does not necessarily mean that a writer will show an exclusive devotion to one 'angle' on communication. An interest in models of transmission does not, for example, imply that a theorist will neglect ideas about the *context* of that process.

It is possible, nevertheless, to identify some consistent positions in Communication Studies. The section below combines 'Perspectives and approaches' in order to summarise those ideas generally associated with the five definitions explained earlier. (A section called 'Communication Studies: traditions' appears later in this chapter, and provides an expanded introduction to the schools of thought which exist within Communication theory.)

Perspectives and approaches

Research which concentrates on **transmission** is often criticised for showing a preoccupation with the *efficiency* of the communication process, over and above other considerations. This attitude is often linked with a *functionalist* perspective (see the section on functionalism, below). In *Key Concepts in Communication* (see p. 43), Tim O'Sullivan and his co-authors note that this viewpoint has been attacked for attempting to 'increase the ability of the communicator to intervene within, or control, the life of the "receiver"'. An absorption in the process of transmitting messages also suggests, according to O'Sullivan, that meaning and social context are likely to suffer neglect. However, transmission theory is still valued for its practical view of the communication process. (For a positive reassessment of Shannon and Weaver's 1949 process model, see the work on models later in this chapter.)

A preoccupation with **exchange**, on the other hand, could indicate a number of different approaches, depending on which elements in the process are thought most worthy of attention. Where a study of turn-taking in conversation takes precedence, an analyst might be interested in the 'moves' made or the strategies adopted by the participants. Some researchers, following the tradition of *transactional analysis*, spend their time trying to discover the psychological 'attitude' which lies behind an utterance, attributing particular 'ego states' to individual speakers. This means that each speaker adopts a psychological 'role' during interaction, which may supplement or clash with that used by the speaker's opposite number. The weakness of this approach lies in its inability to provide supporting evidence to justify linking speech acts (self-contained units of speech) with specific, and supposedly hidden, states of mind. Traditions which place interpersonal and *subjective* human factors at the centre of communication research are examined in the next few pages.

Theorists whose studies deal with the **generation of meaning** may belong to a variety of 'schools', but are likely to have inherited some of their methods from *structuralism*. This is a type of critical inquiry which proposes that the individual elements of a text or communication event create meaning only when contrasted with other 'units' belonging to the same structure. So, for example, a heroic act in a story will be recognised as such only because it is set beside unheroic events.

Some branches of structuralism have been criticised for over-emphasising the idea that meaning is to be found exclusively 'inside' books, films, paintings and other forms. The relationship between the text, its producer and its audience has been brought into sharper focus in later currents of structuralist thought (see the section on 'structuralism' later in this chapter).

Research into **context** is popular among academics who want to emphasise the *social* nature of the communication process, and wish to stress other variables besides those associated with textual elements. Context may refer to the immediate or *situational* features which surround an event, or to what O'Sullivan calls (p. 53) the 'wider social, political and historical circumstances' which give meaning to events in general. I would argue that the aim of advanced contextual theory should be to examine the relationship between 'immediate' circumstances and the broader forces which influence the structure of interaction. One danger is that unimaginative reference to context will devalue the spontaneous and creative aspects of communication.

Discourse *analysis* is used by linguists who wish to examine the ordinary modes of speech used in conversation, while theories of *discourse and power* have emerged from the work of post-structuralist writers like Michel Foucault. He advanced the idea that all arguments about truth are characterised by 'a will to power'. Foucault believed that power is not found simply in governments, or armies, or other institutions. It has rather, in the words of Madan Sarup, 'the character of a network; its threads extend everywhere' (see *An Introductory Guide to Post-structuralism and Postmodernism*, p. 82). In communication and cultural studies, 'discourse' is sometimes used to refer to the expression of dominant ideas, but means more usually 'the social process of making and reproducing sense' (see O'Sullivan, cited above).

One drawback of a very general definition of discourse is that it might lead us to think that all the ideas produced in society carry equal weight. In fact, certain discourses achieve considerable prominence, while others attain a much more restricted circulation. On the other hand, a very precise description of discourse as the 'pure' expression of ideology suggests that the concept is somehow removed from the ordinary conversations and arguments which have provided such useful insights into everyday expressions of belief. A helpful way of defining discourses, in my opinion, would be to describe them as 'social narratives', stories which offer broadly plausible explanations for events in the world.

Organising the subject

Social vs. communication phenomena

Ultimately, the role of all communication theorists, whatever their individual perspective, is to investigate no less than the production, circulation and interpretation of meaning within a society. At the same time, a distinction has to be made between *social* phenomena and communication. As McQuail says (*Communication*, p. 20), 'all communication relationships [are] social relationships [but] the reverse is not true'. In other words, social relationships do not need to be communicative. McQuail gives the example of the cinema-goer, who does not communicate with the actors seen during the course of a film, but does share in the social or institutional process we might call 'the cinema'.

Making choices

Even a brief study of the material set out above will show the extent of the challenge faced by attempts to organise Communication Studies. How might a meaningful structure be built when we are confronted with a seemingly overwhelming amount of data, together with a number of competing academic perspectives? According to some theorists, the field of study is never-ending and has no identifiable beginning. Clearly, some choices have to be made; otherwise, it would be impossible to handle the raw material found in the subject. At the same time, however, the process of selection will always reveal the particular standpoint of the individual theorist. I would suggest that the following list should form the basis for organisation. The first three points are drawn from the AEB syllabus:

- Acceptable boundaries between different *forms* of communication must be drawn.
- Broad *categories* of communication should be recognised.
- The various *uses* and *purposes* of communication need to be described.
- Definite points should be set in time and space where specific examples of communication – usually called *acts* or events – can be said to begin and end.
- Broad *conventions* (and their associated *codes*), growing from the social practice of communication, must be acknowledged.
- The diverse methods of *interpreting* written, spoken and visual material ought to be described, applied and evaluated.

These points are discussed in detail in the sections that follow.

In essence, this method of organisation treats communication as though it is *divisible* (able to be divided into recognised units) and *finite* (limited in size and duration). This might sound highly artificial, but it is a practice in which we all engage in our everyday lives. The fact that we are used to defining and categorising things in our world suggests that the basic approaches of academic inquiry are not as far removed from common experience as some imagine. Of course, this will not solve all the problems encountered in the subject, and there are problems inherent in making strict divisions between different areas, as we shall see below when we consider *categories* of communication.

Forms of communication

Forms are the ways in which communication manifests itself. They can be organised as follows:

- **oral** – the spoken expression of ideas and events through verbal language and expressive sound;
- **written** – the accepted and codified symbols of a language, reproduced in a variety of styles and traditions by individuals;
- **printed** – the codified symbols of languages as above, presented on paper in forms of type or 'fonts';
- **non-verbal** – expressive gesture belonging to individuals, whether intentional or unintentional;
- **pictorial** – such as representational drawing and fine art;
- **graphical/symbolic** – diagrammatic and non-representational;
- **technological** – the methods and perspectives used by a range of institutions and individuals to disseminate communication acts, some of which have increased the impact of mass communication, while others have found more strictly interpersonal uses (see the section on 'Categories' below).

Categories of communication

The term *categories* as it is used in this context refers to the most basic divisions between types of communication. Identifying categories of communication is useful as a starting point, but once real examples of communication are studied, efforts to fit them into a particular category can be counterproductive. In practice, many communication 'events' will belong to more than one category.

Intrapersonal

Intrapersonal communication, described as that which occurs *within* and therefore *with the self*, is usually placed first in the list of categories. Although it is often regarded as the category from which the other divisions emerge, not all theorists find this acceptable. While it is true that there must be individual intelligence and perception before any form of exchange takes place, some writers (see Burgoon *et al.* in *Human Communication*, p. 20) insist that communication can be said to happen only when at least two individuals interact. Such a view would exclude those processes which take place *within* the individual.

The beginning of Chapter 2 is devoted to the question of the 'intrapersonal' and proposes a solution to the problem of its status. In the meantime, the intrapersonal may be said to include:

- perception;
- cognitive and reflective thought processes;
- emotional responses;

- attitudes, values and beliefs;
- subjectivity and self-concept;
- the creation and interpretation of meaning.

These are not, however, exclusively 'internal' elements or processes. Every one of these elements depends upon the individual's action within and reaction to a specific social context. The intrapersonal may in fact be *externalised* quite easily, without anyone else necessarily receiving the 'messages' created – people talk to themselves, write notes to themselves, and so on.

Most forms of expression, however, even those usually regarded as private, are produced with a sense of audience in mind. Diary entries, for example, have sometimes a very powerful sense of the audience they intend ultimately to address, and can be a convenient disguise for the creation of records which are really intended to transcend the personal mode. (Chapter 2 contains a study of diary entries.)

Cronen (see Myers and Myers' *The Dynamics of Human Communication*, p. 8) believed that the intrapersonal is concerned with *meaning*, while the interpersonal (see below) is connected with the realm of *action*. The trouble with this division, internal/meaning and external/action, is that it does not recognise that the internal and external influence one another, or that meaning and action are interdependent.

We have only to think of the main communicative faculty exercised by human beings, language, to see how meaning and action are linked. For instance, it is not uncommon for politicians to offer *explanations* of political events (an example of the creation of meaning), and then to describe the *practical* steps they think necessary to shape future occurrences. Self-contained units of speech are often called 'acts' because they perform material functions. In simple terms, language use has a real impact on the way life is conducted and understood. The whole point of intrapersonal communication, in general, is that it is closely linked to action; it not only prepares individuals for activity, it guides them during interaction. Action is not, therefore, the exclusive property of interpersonal communication.

Interpersonal

Interpersonal communication is often defined as that which occurs when *two people* are engaged in some form of *communicative exchange*. This definition is useful because it provides one hard and fast distinction between this category and group communication, but 'interpersonal' is used by some writers to describe an exchange between two *or more* people.

Interpersonal communication includes, in my judgement, the following elements:

- mutual recognition;
- reciprocal exchange using available codes;
- the creation and interpretation of meaning;
- awareness of physical and social context;
- the assumption of personal and social roles;
- some change of state, whether intellectual, emotional or physical.

Some writers insist that interpersonal communication takes place only when the participants are in close physical proximity. Others disagree, including one-to-one communication mediated by electronic links (such as the telephone system) in the general definition.

In most cases of interpersonal communication, an exchange may be effected through more than one 'channel' (non-verbal and verbal, including the use of intonation). The interpersonal sphere is often presented as the primary means through which we confirm or question our sense of self.

Group

Group communication requires *a collection of individuals* who share some *common attributes, goals or interests*. The individuals concerned will interact within the context of the group and will share or at least display *common values* or *norms of behaviour*.

The idea of 'the group' is based ultimately on the idea that its members will share recognisable attributes, and that they will be able to identify specific differences in individuals who are members of other groups. McQuail (see *Communication*, p. 4) describes the idea of belonging in the following way:

'To belong to a social group, a society, a culture is to share a common denominator of frames of reference, significant objects, systems for describing the world and facilitating interaction with each other.'

The familiar argument that group communication exists only where participants are able to address one another *face to face*, and not through the agency of some other individual or medium, implies that there is a point at which viable communication breaks down. (Chapter 3 examines this question in more depth.) Of course, we must also recognise those theories which draw attention to *social* groups, collectives which exist without requiring contact between their members. As we shall see in Chapter 3, the question of who *defines* the criteria for group membership is of particular significance, because groups are sometimes categorised by people or institutions who observe them from the outside. Some groups, described or 'identified' by outsiders, may reject the label provided for them.

Despite the problems with specific cases of 'belonging' and categorisation, all group *communication* must be founded on the following elements:

- a perception of the group's identity, broadly common to its members;
- the ability to differentiate between the group and its allies or rivals;
- a knowledge of aims and objectives within the group, whether those aims are agreed or imposed;
- participation in interpersonal exchange using available codes and channels of communication, both formal and informal;
- the assumption of formal and informal roles.

Group theory also recognises divisions between *large* and *small* groups, between *formal* and *informal* groups, and between groups which people join voluntarily and those to which individuals belong without advance consent. The latter includes groups such as family and class. There are, unsurprisingly, difficulties in drawing boundaries between some of the sub-divisions recognised above.

If we begin with the example of group size, a sub-group of scores of people, within a corporate body of many thousands, may be defined as small in comparison to the overall dimensions of the organisation, but outside this context might be described as quite large.

The formal/informal distinction between groups also creates difficulties, since in practice all groups contain elements of both. Governments, for example, use 'kitchen cabinets' (informal groups of close friends, allies and aides) in order to supplement formal groupings, within which there is anyway a variety of informal alliances.

When groups are actively chosen by individuals, they are selected for a variety of purposes. These may vary widely, from the desire to establish solidarity to the pursuit of a leisure activity. Whatever the reason for the choice, we may expect the member concerned to be able to describe the criteria for membership. The issue of social identification has prompted a number of studies of 'in-groups' (collectives with which people identify) and 'out-groups' (groups seen as undesirable, for whatever reason).

Other studies are concerned to analyse the breakdowns and misunderstandings in communication occurring between different groups of people, particularly where ethnic and/or cultural differences exist. In *Bridging Differences*, the American author William Gudykunst identifies inter-group hatred and stereo-typing as examples of (p. 2) 'polarised communication', where each group is convinced that it is in the right and its rivals mistaken.

We do not always need, perhaps, to be quite so dramatic in our assessment of group identity, since group identification inevitably entails *differentiation* from other groups and therefore also involves, to some degree, the negative characterisation of those others. Chapter 3 examines, at some length, the issue of categorisation and stereotyping.

Mass

The media are usually identified as those *formal bodies* engaged in *the industrial production and circulation of meaning*. **Mass** communication is a category which includes all the *institutional practices* of the mass media, and which also refers to the *scale of communication* supposedly achieved by the media. Scale here means the actual or potential capacity to create a significant impact on large numbers of the public.

Mass communication possesses these essential features:

- high levels of industrial activity;
- formal, centralised organisation;
- institutionalised values and practices;
- the mediation of authority;
- large scale of operation;
- a 'standardised' product directed to a mass audience;
- the possibility of simultaneous reception of messages by audiences.

It is important to realise that mass *communication* is never imagined as an interaction between one mass of *people* and another. Rather, it is seen as the transmission of cultural 'material' from an *institutional* source to a mass *audience*.

Even so, the idea that there is a mass audience for mass communication depends upon how we are prepared to conceptualise audiences, whether the texts produced for them are actually received, and whether or not media content has a significant impact. The idea of a docile audience in receipt of one type of mass communication is highly problematic, as is the easy assertion that audiences are too wily to let the media influence their political or social outlook. Much of the debate on this issue is prompted by attempts to understand the power relationships established between the media, the state, and the audiences which receive media 'products'.

It is useful to note the difference between notions of mass communication and what is ordinarily meant by 'mass' society. In 1939, Herbert Blumer distinguished between the 'mass' and other forms of human collectivity, by creating four categories. These are the *group*, the *public*, the *crowd* and the *mass*. Each was then characterised as possessing different levels of interaction, separate purposes, contrasting modes of organisation and control, and different levels of consciousness.

The 'mass' collectivity as it is imagined by Blumer, has a low degree of inter-action, is prone to having its attention directed by outside forces, is subject to external manipulation, and possesses a low level of consciousness. Such a description stands in stark contrast to the socialist idealisation of the mass as a positive and creative force in history, yet it does find an echo in the work of those 'pessimists' (of the right and of the left) who describe mass society as particularly vulnerable to direction from above. (See the analysis of power in Chapter 3, and the study of the mass media in Chapter 4.)

Although the media may be of a considerable size, public and private bodies involved in 'mass' communication often imitate *personal* modes of address, a strategy which is useful when they wish to appear approachable, and which anyway reflects the fact that all institutions are created and sustained by a series of relationships between authority and its 'public'. After all, the natural instinct of all individuals and groups is to frame an address in a way which will have an impact on those they intend to address. Paddy Scannell, writing in the Introduction to *Broadcast Talk*, notes that (p. 3):

> 'Broadcasting could not speak to its audience as a crowd. It had to speak to them as individuals.'

It may be, with the advent of 'interactive' media, that the relationship between human and mass communication will receive more attention.

Extrapersonal

Extrapersonal communication can be described as communication *between machines*. It does not, strictly speaking, include communication between individual *humans* and machines, but only that between machines which supposedly require little human intervention. Communication between human individuals and computers is really an instance of intrapersonal processing, while communication between two operators at different terminals may actually be a form of interpersonal communication using an electronic *channel*.

'Extrapersonal' as a category should perhaps be reserved for communication which is genuinely 'extra' or outside the self. Communication between machines without extended human interference would therefore be the only true example of this type, though even this requires an initial programme and thus some connection with a human operator.

Research into 'artificial intelligence' (attempts to make a machine behave as if it had human powers of reasoning) covers a number of fields. Geoffrey James of the Honeywell computer group, describes these as robotics, language processing, vision and speech, and expert systems (see Barrett *Text, Context, and Hypertext*, p. 15). *Expert systems* (p. 17) 'simulate the behaviour of an expert, reproducing the logic that the expert applies to a routine situation'.

The salient feature of the extrapersonal may be summarised as:

- the processing of some form of meaningful or potentially meaningful signal between machines, requiring human input but little supervision during the duration of the process itself.

Uses and purposes

Uses and purposes are usually discussed under one heading. Use refers to how communication, in whatever form, is employed, while **purpose** means the end result intended when a communication act is planned. In practice, this means examining the *hows* and *whys* of communicative practice; uses and purposes will therefore appear together as one category.

For the purposes of clarity, I have organised the list which follows under five main headings (some authors employ eight or more distinctions). These headings are:

- **socialisation**;
- the **social functional or ritual**;
- the **instrumental**;
- the **persuasive**;
- the **expressive**.

They are all in fact closely related, at least in the sense that the social order is maintained through the functions associated with each of these sub-divisions. People are, for example, 'controlled' as much and perhaps more so by their own socialisation as they are by the direct intervention of the state. Or, to take another example, apparently neutral or purely instrumental functions of communication may be part of the repertoire of social control. Some communication events will encompass a number of purposes and will therefore fulfil more than one of the uses listed above and described below.

An important point to bear in mind when reading the explanation which follows is that the uses and functions of communication will alter according to the intention, position and outlook of the individual, group or institution producing the 'message'. In addition, it is not unusual for those who receive a particular communication to misunderstand the intention behind it.

Socialisation

The *uses* and *purposes* of communication include **socialisation**, where human subjects acquire values, roles and norms through a variety of influences. These include upbringing, the mediation of culture through language, and various group and institutional practices, including those of the mass media.

One of the most important aspects of socialisation is interaction with and dependence on other individuals. From the perspective of those who exercise authority, the purpose of socialisation is the dissemination of values able to be represented as 'universal'. For example, political discourse may emphasise ideas about responsibility or good citizenship. This may on occasion be no more than a smokescreen, which obscures the real dynamics of power by making the values of those in authority seem 'natural' instead of questionable.

The social functional or ritual

Closely related to socialisation is the **social functional** or **ritual**, whose purpose is to help 'affiliate' people to other individuals, institutions or societies. Ritual *behaviour* is essentially a formalised type of communicative behaviour. Civil and religious ritual share a number of similar features, including the use of *symbols* which are supposed to prompt feelings of awe or reverence in the onlooker. In this respect, religious objects serve a similar function to the flags and icons of the nation-state.

Ritual *uses* of communication include attempts to establish psychological unity within a group or society, and may be seen in those ceremonies of universal significance (marriages, funerals, initiations). These are often conducted in specialised forms of language. Most use ritual forms of discourse in order to help initiate human subjects into a wider social group or institution.

These ceremonies often involve the use of *ideological* modes of communication. Ideology is a term which usually refers to *systems* of belief. To 'qualify' as ideology, the beliefs concerned must form some kind of coherent system, and must be connected in some way to the use of *power* in social life. The state usually feels bound to intervene in ritual proceedings, and where it does not, representatives of other established authority usually preside over the event.

The **phatic** uses of communication may be included in this category. They encompass those apparently conventional or ordinary exchanges whose content is considerably less important than their function as the *reinforcement* of social contact and social status. The term 'hello' may be a fairly unimaginative greeting, but establishes a channel of communication. Whole conversations, the *content* of which appears largely insignificant, may in fact have clear *social* uses. Phatic communication is in my opinion much more than mere sociability.

Some communication is *role-based*. If we consider formal roles, like those fulfilled in the workplace, then it seems that some communication is generated by the *situation* or *context* in which we are placed.

The instrumental

One of the most basic uses of communication is the **instrumental**, meaning quite simply the deployment of content in order to achieve or obtain something. In all deliberate communication, the person or persons involved in framing the 'message' will have some conscious aims in mind. These aims may be intended to benefit the individuals or groups concerned, or may be intended to achieve wider *social* benefits.

Affective communication may be included under this heading, as that which is designed to make an impact on an individual or a group. Instrumental uses also include the **informative**, where elaborate terms and rhetorical flourishes are irrelevant or detrimental to the goal of clarity. The warnings embossed on the outside of fuse boxes, for example, are meant to be purely informative.

The persuasive

The **persuasive** function of communication is sometimes described as that of 'control', but really constitutes *structures which are used to manipulate* the actions or cognitions of individuals, groups or institutions. This may be done for one of two reasons, either for the *mutual* benefit of the persuader and the persuadee, or to attain some exclusive advantage for one of the parties involved.

By contrast to the phatic and the social, the **interpellative** function of communication grows purely from the relations of power in society. It is understood as the address made by authority to any subordinate group or individual, where that group or individual *recognises* the relationship of power and responds accordingly. It is therefore a specialised and direct form of *ideological* communication, the production of meaning drawn from a particular system of belief.

The idea of a completely successful interpellative address, in which the human subject automatically acknowledges his or her 'subject position', has to be treated with some caution. People's responses are usually more complex.

The expressive

When described as a *use* of communication, the **expressive** is the representation of personal or aesthetic feelings. It is linked with the idea of creativity and is sometimes thought to be typical of an emotional rather than a cognitive state.

Expressive acts are in fact not necessarily intentionally communicative at all, and the creation of influence or the achievement of specific effects is not their primary aim. Expressive forms are associated with artistic endeavour; some appear to suit didactic purposes, but others seem less adaptable to the construction of instrumental messages. Some writers, for example, use verse as a form because it allows them to represent feelings without relying upon a purely intellectual process.

Narrative uses of communication are an interesting sub-division of expressive form. Narratives are more than a specialised mode employed for public storytelling; they are one of the most basic methods people use to organise and represent their experience. (Narrative approaches to cinema appear in Chapter 5.)

Communication: acts and events

Problems of definition

There is a difference between a communication **act** and a communication **event**. An act is usually regarded as a single deed, a deliberate action on the part of an individual or collective source. An event, on the other hand, is conceived as something which happens without necessarily requiring human intervention. An event is thought to possess a clear beginning and a definite end, and is supposed to be identified by virtue of its *difference* to other occurrences.

An act is usually imagined as lasting for only a brief period, but may in fact refer to a *process*. Denis McQuail describes any communication act as a sequence of occurrences (*Communication*, p. 14), from 'a decision to transmit meaning' to 'the formulation of the intended message into a language or code', followed by the reception of the message together with a new transmission, made by the receiver.

McQuail summarises the problems which arise from this formulation. In the first place (p. 14), it 'implies an underlying rationality and purposefulness about communication', suggesting a concern with efficiency. (See the work on communication efficiency and functionalism later in this chapter.) It also suggests that it is 'the intention of the communicator which defines the meaning of a communication event'. At this point, McQuail has moved from considering an act to describing an event.

Another problem with this description is the reference to the formulation of messages into codes. It suggests a process of 'translation' of concept or idea into symbolic form, whereas some theorists argue that the form used is chosen instantaneously, and is essentially indistinguishable from the idea itself.

Acts and events: genre and performance

Malcolm Coulthard, writing in *An Introduction to Discourse Analysis*, provides another approach to the problem of distinguishing between an *event* and an *act*. He refers to the linguist Hymes, and his description of speech events as **genre** and speech acts as the 'doing' of a genre, or performance. A genre is understood as (p. 43) 'a unique combination of stylistic structure and mode'. Coulthard gives the example of conversation, which can be used in a wide variety of situations, and prayer, the use of which is by comparison highly restricted. It might be useful to think of these individual genres as 'available' to speakers, whose particular choices make up the specific act.

Hymes's distinction could be extended to communication in general, but it is desirable not to lose the idea of event as an occurrence, and as *larger* than an act, involving a number of exchanges or units of meaning. We should, however, heed McQuail's warning, when he notes that (p. 32):

'Social scientific views of phenomena are selective, and different perspectives produce different versions of what is going on.'

This is a useful reminder that the criteria for judging communication events, and indeed the decision as to whether certain incidents count as events at all, are often decided by forces which stand outside the genres or actions described.

Conventions and codes

In *Communication* (p. 6), McQuail argues that 'communication necessitates the conscious manipulation of physical forces and objects according to agreed rules and conventions'. All communicative forms, including speech, gesture, writing, graphic design, music, film, broadcast talk and so on, have **codes** and **conventions** which have become established through use, but which in some cases, such as language, appear to be based on *innate* abilities. (I noted above the drawback of imagining that ideas have to be 'translated' into symbolic content, which seems to separate language or code from *thought*.)

This is not to say that communication is *entirely* conventional, since individuals will experiment a great deal, testing a variety of forms in different contexts. It is true, however, that a range of values and a history of meanings attach themselves to each act of communication. If someone wishes to convey any kind of coherent message, that person must make choices from within an established set of practices. In conclusion, we might say that there are endless numbers of individual choices which may be made within broad conventions.

With reference to the *conscious* manipulation of physical forces which McQuail identifies, individuals may be unaware of some of the meanings their choice of phrase or style of dress suggests, and any number of signals may be misread. Human beings in general, however, use a variety of methods to ensure that they achieve their communication goals.

Codes and conventions should not be thought of as rules. No system of rules could explain the subtlety of human interaction, depending as it does on a variety of *styles* and *registers*. We know, for example, that intonation and pitch in speech are employed as essential guides to the way we want our verbal messages to be received.

Methods of interpretation

This section provides a short introduction to the different methods which are used for interpreting communication. It uses the hypothetical example of a political speech and examines the various approaches which, taken together, may provide an understanding of the event.

From 'units of meaning' to rhetoric

Methods of interpretation are many and varied, but the techniques of analysis actually employed are usually suggested by the *form* of the communication event or text being studied. For instance, the printed text of a political speech (on, say, the Health Service) may be interpreted using linguistic approaches. The speech might be examined from the point of view of *sentence construction*, though more basic **units of meaning** could be identified. The study of language would provide a reasonable insight into the technical and expressive abilities of the writer (who is not usually the person who delivers the speech).

In addition, it may be useful to extend this approach, by noting whether there are any **rhetorical** devices the writer has used to persuade an audience to support a particular policy. This would allow the use of rhetorical analysis or inquiry into *strategies of speech*. These may include the repetition of certain key points, the deployment of concepts such as 'the rule of three', and the use of antithesis as a device. (See Chapter 3 for an account of rhetoric.)

Content and structural analysis

Another approach might be to make a thorough investigation of **content**, in the sense that statements, assertions, allusions to external events and so on could all be listed and their generic references sorted into groups. These groups would be examined in order to gauge what the writer appears to regard as important. An evaluative judgement, assessing the worth of the writer's views, is not the purpose of content analysis. Similarly, a **structural analysis** would ask how the internal elements of the speech are arranged in order to create meaning.

Empirical comparison

Our speech on the Health Service might contain six references to increased resources, four attacks on the policies of opposition parties, and no hint about imminent hospital closures. Content analysis may then provide the basis for an **empirical** study, which observes the real conditions to which the speech refers. If there is evidence that resources are being directed to administration rather than patient care and that there is an extensive programme of hospital closures in full swing, then it will be possible to judge the value of the statements which have been made. Clearly, departures have now been made from a purely textual analysis.

Ideological analysis

Essentially, all methods of interpretation mentioned so far prepare the ground for an **ideological analysis** of public discourse. This would examine the ways in which an audience is addressed, the ideas which are expressed, and even what remains unsaid. The aim would be to understand the belief systems which are suggested during public expression.

Ideological analysis is based on the assumption that power, far from being evenly distributed in society, is concentrated in the hands of a ruling class or coalition. Public discourses will therefore reflect the material struggle over influence and resources, so that any utterance will carry clues as to the real relations of power within the social formation. Some ideological perspectives pay close attention to the ways in which an audience is *addressed* by the powerful. They often refer to external reality, in attempts to prove the inherent bias in events like political broadcasts. This approach will also include ideas about the *shared knowledge* already held by the recipients of any political message.

Role and expression

If we have heard the speech on audio tape, as well as having read a transcript, then we are no longer dealing simply with a text, but are moving towards the analysis of an event. New factors come into play. Something will be learned about the identity of the speaker. An insight will be gained into the accent, age and sex of the speaker, and thus how regional, age and *gender* **roles** are used or adapted by the individual concerned. Some aspects of *context* will come into clearer focus, especially those devices, like *intonation*, which provide the vital information required to estimate how far semantic meaning has been judged accurately.

Contextual analysis

If our public speech is actually witnessed or recorded on video tape, then situational and discursive **context** (referred to earlier in this chapter) will become more apparent. The *body language* and the *dress codes* of the speaker can be evaluated, the responses of an audience may be noted, and the events which come before and after the speech, and which may be said to *frame* the event, can be added to the equation.

Media analysis

If the speech is broadcast or reported by the media, then supplementary methods of interpretation will be required. An understanding of the principle of *mediation* would be helpful, including some knowledge of the *news values* (established ways of 'grading' events) which the press and television seem to use to interpret reality.

Content analysis might reveal what agenda the media have brought to the event – that is their assumptions and aims – revealed in what aspects of the speech they have chosen to question, or promote, or ignore. The discursive frame set up by the particular format of a programme, or by the personality of a political correspondent, could also be considered.

In a newspaper report of the speech, the balance between image and text would call for a combined *semiological* and discursive analysis, and in addition some appreciation of design. Semiology is a method which examines symbolic meaning and signification. It explores the connotations of speech, image and text, based on the idea that the associations called to mind by words or imagery will always provide an insight into the cultural preoccupations of social groups.

Narrative approaches

Narrative theory is produced in the belief that all but the simplest symbolic expression is structured as narrative, and that the construction of stories is an essential method of people organising and representing experience. (See Chapter 5 on narrative theory and film.) Various currents run through this tradition, many of which owe a great deal to structuralist interpretations of novels and films, but are also applied to the tales and fables circulated by politicians.

Text and context

This section will examine how a variety of analytical approaches may grow from the study of a printed text. It presents an extended analysis of a short conversation or exchange between two unnamed individuals, which means of course that a study of the **language** used will form the primary frame of reference. In order to concentrate on a linguistic approach, the reader will for now be told nothing about the source of the extract which follows.

The conversation

A Why don't you ask George, the Colonel's son, to go with you – I'm sure he'd like it!

B No – he never seems to have time for me – besides – I like long lonely walks.

This is a fairly ordinary conversation. It appears to be easy to understand. Asked to summarise what has happened, we might say no more than 'a suggestion put forward by one individual is rejected by another'. Our ability to read and understand this piece without much trouble may lead us to dismiss the passage as trivial. Or we might regard the knowledge and skill needed to interpret it as insignificant. It is only on those occasions when we stop to consider the many nuances we gain from these few printed signs (an example of *symbolic content*) that the degree of complexity in even a short passage begins to emerge.

Whatever else A and B may say while they are together, the extract printed above makes up a distinct, self-contained unit of meaning. How would teachers of language or communication describe this text? The linguist Hymes had two basic divisions which he used to label examples of speech, though other writers on the subject have proposed as many as six categories for analysis. Hymes described a speech event, the largest unit in which structure can be identified, and a speech act, the simplest form of utterance, which might be no more than a request or a command (we saw earlier that an event is also known as *genre* and an act as *performance*). Since the extract above is not a single or unfinished utterance and is 'free-standing' in terms of sense, despite its brevity, it may be described as a **speech event**.

Other linguists would use descriptions ranging from *pair* to *exchange* or *sequence*. In addition to the term **event**, I have selected **exchange** as an alternative and equally accurate description of this short piece. For the sake of variety, it will also be referred to as a **conversation**.

Interpersonal communication

An exchange of this type is clearly an example of **interpersonal** communication. Interpersonal communication consists of an *interaction* which takes place between two people. An interaction must consist of at least an *action* and a *reaction*. In this case we have only a printed record of the words spoken. We cannot see the speakers, or hear their tone of voice; we have no knowledge of their identities, or the setting in which the event takes place. However, we still manage to construct meaning from the evidence we have. This is because, in many aspects of our daily lives, we are used to making sense of (and acting upon) incomplete information, using experience and intuition to reach what are often reasonably successful conclusions.

Rules of meaning

As we read, we make judgements about meaning, based on the text and the possibilities the text offers. These judgements may be refined later on, but emerge in the first place through a natural process of interpretation. Although we may not be able to describe how we reach our conclusions, we probably realise that any written expression which expects to be understood must obey certain rules. These are the rules of *morphology* (word formation), *syntax* (sentence formation) and *semantics* (the system of meaning). These are not the kinds of rule which users of English or any other language need to learn by heart, if the language is their mother tongue or first language. They are already known from experience and applied in practice.

Basic units of meaning: morphemes

The most basic unit of meaning is the **morpheme**. This word derives from the Greek meaning *form*. A single word may be made up of one or more morphemes. In the conversation presented above all but one of the words (besides those like 'don't' which are contractions) are composed of one morpheme. Some morphemes constitute words by themselves. *Son* or *time* are examples in the conversation studied here. The one word to be made up of two units of meaning is 'lonely'. *Lone* makes one morpheme, and *ly* makes the other. Morphemes such as *ly* can only ever make up part of larger words.

The combination of morphemes into larger units may create new words, while the grammatical combination of words creates phrases and sentences. Some linguists have concentrated their investigations on the smallest units of meaning, while others have examined everything from brief speech acts to quite lengthy speech events.

Syntax: structure and language

The component of grammar that refers to a writer's or speaker's knowledge of language structure (whether of phrases or sentences) is called *syntax*. Words alone do not create meaning. The **structure** of a sentence or a phrase is of vital importance. A change in word order can produce quite different readings. An example might be the sentence 'Why don't you ask George?' A new meaning may be produced if the word order is changed as follows: 'You don't ask why George.' Both examples are also perfectly grammatical. The first is addressed to B (an unknown 'you'), while the second is addressed to George.

Grammaticality

Anyone reading this book will realise that there is a limit to the number of ways the same words can be rearranged and still make sense. 'George you why ask don't' does not produce much immediate meaning. The words themselves are capable of communicating something, but it would be impossible to know whether a request or command or inquiry was intended, or how, for example, the word 'you' is meant to operate.

This is not to say that an extensive knowledge of grammar is required in order to recognise a sequence that is ungrammatical. Mother-tongue or native speakers of English or any other language carry notions of 'grammaticality' with them; they do not have to refer to some kind of rule-book. Nor is a complete knowledge of specific sentences necessary. No one could possibly remember every grammatical sentence he or she had encountered. It is the experience of syntax and our innate ability to create meaning in general, rather than a knowledge of 'correct' examples, which allows both the recognition of meaningful sequences and the creation of new examples.

Green Ideas

However, the linguist Noam Chomsky showed that the creation of a *grammatical* sequence does not depend on whether or not a sentence is actually intelligible. He produced the sentence, 'Colourless green ideas sleep furiously.' It is completely satisfactory as a piece of syntax (the words are placed in an acceptable order, subject followed by predicate), but meaningless as a guide to events in the world we know.

Semantics

Once a reader has arrived at the end of the conversation held between A and B, he or she has probably reached a settled interpretation of the whole speech event. What readers in general may have less conscious awareness of is the ways in which they arrived at that meaning. In addition, it is also possible to forget the *provisional* meanings which were suggested during the course of reading, before a conclusion or *closure* was reached.

The process of discovering 'deeper' meaning in this or any speech event or conversation is often described by the phrase 'reading between the lines'. Some exploration of semantics as it operates on readers during the course of reading may help to reveal how the process of comprehension works.

Clues in the text: words, readers and meaning

The user of English will know the words belonging to the language, through recognition of the **form** of the word (the physical appearance or sound) and the **meaning** which belongs to that form. In any passage, individual words may make sense when taken alone but, as we have already seen, will achieve new distinctions of meaning according to their place in the text (when they are set beside other words).

Of course, the eye will flick across the *design* of a page (the way that words are *set out*), and most readers would see our example as a record of some type of speech. This perception of *overall form* or **genre** (in this case a record of speech) has considerable power to influence the range of meaning a reader will expect, and should not be under-estimated.

Approaches to analysis: 1 – units of meaning

The first part of this analysis will concern itself with a study of what may be learned from morphemes, words, phrases and sentences. Making this kind of study does not imply that reading a text is actually undertaken in mechanical stages, with small units of meaning being deciphered one by one before the reader moves to the next stage (the interpretation of phrases and sentences). In practice, the precise understanding of small units is simply modified, as the passage is read, by the larger units in which the smaller occur. Units of meaning are mutually dependent. One 'type' is not more important than the other, though some forms of linguistic research may have led people to this conclusion.

Here is the conversation again:

A Why don't you ask George, the Colonel's son, to go with you – I'm sure he'd like it!

B No – he never seems to have time for me – besides – I like long lonely walks.

If we return to the idea set out above, that it is our knowledge of the *form* and *meaning* of words which indicates the intention behind their use, then the 'why' at the beginning of the interaction may be recognised as the start of a question, in this case, 'why don't you'. This must then be followed by other words which will frame a more specific inquiry. Clearly, a speech event cannot begin and end with 'why don't you'; we must allow a reasonable chance to suggest meaning.

This kind of study means stating what sounds obvious, but which may otherwise be taken for granted. The word *son* is a useful illustration of basic meaning. *Son* refers to a particular example of male offspring, and implies a relationship in the past or present to one or more parent. It is interesting to note that the word *son* often leads a reader to expect the individual so described to be reasonably youthful, even where there is no evidence for the supposition.

Another useful example of the sense we pick up from individual units of meaning is the word *walks*, which on its own might impress the reader either as a plural noun (describing established paths and/or the practice of taking one kind of exercise), or as part of a verb indicating an action (such as the third person singular 'she walks'). Its appearance in this extract as a noun is confirmed by its place and function in the sentence.

Approaches to analysis: 2 – address

Studies of the ways in which a reader is 'positioned' or 'spoken to' by the text being read have become increasingly popular in recent years, particularly when the issue of power and influence is raised. As we read the first complete part of this interaction (which begins, 'why don't you ask George'), we may realise that this is an **address** which seems to be directed towards someone besides ourselves. We appear to occupy the role of a witness. The word 'you' cannot refer to the person who reads the text, because he or she is not expecting to be quizzed about a male individual called 'George', even if someone of that name is known to the reader. If the opening sequence of words had read, 'Why don't you take out a mortgage with us', then the reader would indeed feel that a direct address had been made. Now, although it is true in this case that a *direct* address is not made to the reader, it may yet turn out that the extract we are using has some designs on us. (There is more on address in 'Mass communication: questions of address' in Chapter 4 and at the beginning of Chapter 5.)

Approaches to analysis: 3 – 'shared knowledge'

One of the most important aspects of conversation is the *shared knowledge* that the participants must be able to call upon. When A suggests that B ask George out, referring to 'George, the Colonel's son', it is clear that the individual named must be known to B. The reader, however, may wonder why such a precise description is being used. Are there a number of friends called George, so that A must provide more detail to avoid confusion? The reader does not know the status of the relationships, and is excluded from the knowledge the speakers share. Who are these two individuals? Is it possible to make a guess at their gender from either the form or content of their speech? These questions will be re-examined before the end of this chapter.

Approaches to analysis: 4 – strategies of speech

This section is intended to investigate the strategies used by A and B in their attempts to present coherent ideas to one another. Many studies of what I would call **strategic speech** have appeared in recent years, under the title of 'deceptive', 'equivocal' or 'misleading' communication. Some of the forms of speech commonly used by all speakers are recognisable as *open* attempts at persuasion or influence, while other forms involve some type of *hidden* or *masked* intention. The intention of a speaker is often difficult to discover; this will be one of the central questions for study when we take a closer look at the concept of discourse.

When A suggests to B that George 'go with you', the rider which follows ('I'm sure he'd like it!') is intended to increase the chances of a positive response. This seems to be an open attempt at persuasion. We may at this point think that the central function of the whole interaction is simply to establish whether or not B will accept George as a companion on this particular occasion. It is the nature of B's response which reveals that something more significant is at stake.

Although B rejects the suggestion, offering two reasons for turning it down, the *content* of these statements contrasts with their apparent negativity. The first reason offered is that George 'never seems to have time for me'. Any reader may recognise that this phrase is often used to elicit sympathy and concern. It carries a hint of regret and the suggestion of some regard for George. It is in fact possible to discover some aspects of a text's meaning by paying attention to what is *not* in the text, through examining reasonably likely choices which have not been selected. B does not say 'No – George is a bore', for example. (In longer pieces of literary composition, obvious avoidance of uncomfortable ideas or neglect of the text's own internal logic are known as 'silences in the text'.)

The second response, 'besides – I like long lonely walks', is presented by B as an alternative to the first reason offered, but is also used to reinforce the underlying refusal. Of the two adjectives which describe 'walks', *long* is relatively neutral. The second adjective, *lonely*, contradicts the whole assertion that B is content to go out alone. It is possible from this to conclude that B would actually like George's company and is providing just enough evidence, whether intentionally or not, for A to discover the truth.

Departures from the text? Social context

Although the four approaches indicated above have concentrated on language, it is in fact impossible to talk about 'pure' linguistic analysis. When any language is brought under scrutiny, so too is the culture from which that language grows. A culture's attitudes, histories and practices are revealed in its language use. Rules about language cannot operate without considering the wider social context in which they are supposed to work. The briefest exchange must be understood in the discursive and ideological frames all speech must occupy.

In *An Introduction to Discourse Analysis* (p. 3), Malcolm Coulthard cites Labov's argument that:

> 'in order to predict correctly the applicability of many rules one must be able to refer to assumptions about the social context of an utterance, as well as to other implicit assumptions made by the participants in a discourse'.

Coulthard recognises that inquiry into spoken language has compelled researchers, however limited their approach, to consider wider social issues:

> 'the results of empirical investigation have forced many transformational linguists to recognise the importance of context and to join a series of disciplines converging on the study of situated speech'.

It is this 'situated speech' which must now be re-examined.

Situational context

Earlier, I noted that we have only a printed record of the conversation studied, and therefore cannot see the speakers, or hear their tone of voice; also that we lack knowledge of their identities and the setting in which the interaction takes place. Although we have seen that it is possible to learn a great deal through textual analysis alone, exactly because cultural practices are revealed through language, a greater degree of knowledge may be achieved. For a fuller understanding we need more than the printed record, or text. We require all those elements which together produce an external or **situational** context.

A list of contextual elements

We can see how little we know about the context of the 'lonely walks' conversation when all the contextual elements required for study are listed.

According to the linguist Hymes, anyone engaged in the collection of data about a speech event should be able to provide information on the following elements:

- structure;
- setting;
- participants;
- purposes;
- key;
- topic;
- channel;
- message form.

Structure is the form of the event (reunion, press announcement, lecture, and so on).

Setting refers to the fact that all events occur in time and space; certain events are more *likely* to occur in particular places and times. Events have a *psychological* setting, which Coulthard calls (p. 45) 'the cultural definition of an occasion as formal or informal, serious or festive'. The structure or form of an event may be the same in two societies (a lawsuit, for example), yet *from the viewpoint of the participants* the meaning and thus the style of the event may be quite different. Setting remains entirely obscure in our example.

Participants will normally be the *addressor* and the *addressee*, but may also include an *audience* and a *speaker*. In some cases, roles are allocated to specific individuals, whose subject position will allow them to qualify as participants. For example, the role of chief in a Native American tribe demands that only males of a certain age and status (all of which make up subject position) may qualify. In other instances, there are fewer restrictions on who may fulfil a role. We have so far been able to identify the roles adopted in our conversation, but cannot attribute identity to the speakers.

Purpose would be that which brings the participants together, for example to discuss something, to celebrate an event, and so on. It is difficult to be sure of the purpose in the case of the 'lonely walks' speech event. The purpose which brought A and B together might be entirely different to the purpose we might guess from their words. The two might have come together to celebrate a birthday, or review plans for decorating a room.

Key is the *spirit* in which the speech event is conducted; for example a spirit of mockery, or jest, or as a serious public or private inquiry. Key is obviously influenced by structure, setting and purpose.

Topic is the subject matter; so, for example, the event may be a wedding, but the subject matter may actually be the question of romance.

Channel refers to the choice of medium for transmitting messages, including speech, or song, or written notes. It is not even clear whether our event was spoken or written down; either might be the case, since we have no contextual information.

Message form refers to the conscious attempt on behalf of the speakers involved to *present* their messages in a way which will have a significant impact on the other parties involved. This may include a variety of 'speech strategies'. Temporary agreement with opponents may in fact be part of a long-term strategy to convince them of one's own case.

Characters in a frame

This (Figure 1.1) is the original source of the speech event or exchange printed at the beginning of this chapter. It consists of a sketch of the two characters I have referred to so far as A and B. Their conversation is written out using the convention of speech bubbles, which suggests the comic or cartoon form.

Figure 1.1   'Why don't you ask George?'

It is now seen for what it is, a deliberate *re-presentation* of human speech and the physical attitudes or **body language** which may accompany it. Acting on preconceptions of what kinds of relationship and speech use are 'appropriate' to different genders, some readers might have suspected that at least one of the speakers (B) was a heterosexual female, purely because of the suggested relationship to George. If this was simply assumed from the start, then we have obtained evidence of a heterosexist tendency in our cultural make-up.

However much the exact status of the whole example may now have altered, it must be emphasised that the *linguistic* analysis given above remains valid. But why use a piece which some readers will now feel is simply not 'true'? Why lose the goodwill of people who might think that they too, like the characters above, have been manipulated or 'set up' (the temptation is to use the term 'framed')? If my purpose had been to analyse speech alone, then it would of course be perfectly easy to find real speech events which closely parallel the extract used, either in terms of structure or perhaps even in content.

In fact my intention is to do more than analyse speech. In line with the introductory material to this book, the purpose of every chapter is to make links between the various areas of the subject. Here, we may see the conjunction of speech analysis, graphic communication, the re-presentation of body language, narration and ultimately ideological analysis. In the work which follows, **form**, **content** and **context** will be reconsidered in the light of the historical and ideological frame which gave birth to the drawing we now see as the source of the 'lonely walks' exchange. The characters shown may not have life, but they have been created by a person or persons who knew very well the conventional heterosexual behaviours of their own society, and how to represent those behaviours effectively.

Intention and context

I have said that the linguistic approaches used remain correct, but there are two vital qualifications to be made. The first is that we are no longer dealing with the real *intentions* of two distinct speakers. Those elements of analysis which dealt with the *intentionality* of the speakers must acknowledge that there is another figure behind the characters we see drawn here. This is the artist and/or writer. What were the intentions of those who produced this cartoon drawing? This question must now come to the forefront of our debates.

The second qualification is that we will not be able to apply the study of **context** in the same way, since these characters inhabit the historical context of their creators, rather than having an independent existence of their own. The intention behind the curiously precise reference to 'George, the Colonel's son' may now be shown to be the provision of information for the reader, and not for B.

Appearance and body language: the context of speech

I began the linguistic analysis by summarising the short speech chosen. A summary of the drawing may also be useful. The older woman (A) is seen in profile and carries a book. The younger of the two women (B) stands by an open door, scarf around her neck, a sign that she is ready to leave the house.

A number of ideas now become much clearer. The way the characters are drawn is intended to show an age difference to the reader, so that it is as easy as possible to infer that these two are related, and are probably mother and daughter. (A number of students who were shown the drawing believed the older woman to be a housekeeper.) The hints we picked up about B's frame of mind are reinforced by the way her physical attitude is represented; the inclination of her body and her downcast eyes. This is a clear attempt to illustrate body language, shown here in order to act as a vital contextual clue for the words. (The group of students referred to above thought the younger woman's body language indicated not depression or shyness but arrogance.) The style of the characters' clothes and hair also provides clues about the historical era in which this little drama appears to be taking place. Pictures and words act to reinforce one another, so that a clear message is offered to an audience.

The next question concerns the purpose of this drawing, which is clearly either some decades old or has been purposely drawn in an archaic style. Is it designed to inform, or to entertain? Is it a single image, or part of a series? What kind of group is it intended to reach? From the evidence we have so far, it may once have been part of a romantic narrative intended for a young audience.

The second frame

The second frame in this series (Figure 1.2), which shows the older woman thinking or musing aloud, reveals the purpose of the whole communication. It is to advertise a crispbread called 'Vita-Weat'. The 'plot' that has been suggested, which turns on Joan's (B's) attitude to George, is revealed as a device, a problem which 'Vita-Weat' can solve. Joan's tiredness, her listlessness, is the result of an affliction called 'starch-heaviness'. The solution, which has the approval of 'the doctor' (an expert), is a commercial product.

But what is 'starch-heaviness' and why have we never heard of it? Either it has been eradicated through the use of 'Vita-Weat', or else it was merely a convenient fiction, like Joan, Joan's mother, and poor George.

Figure 1.2   The second frame

The complete advertisement

This advertisement (Figure 1.3), taken from the *Picture Post* of 4 February 1939, uses a number of methods to suggest the effectiveness of the product it is advertising; linguistic certainly, but also graphic and narrative. We began by treating the first exchange as a short speech event in its own right. The status of all written material, including that which is directed at the reader, may now be seen as part of a **persuasive address**. However, the techniques of persuasion in this case cannot be studied in isolation from the narrative that *carries* the message.

Narrative: the representation of experience

Narrative is essentially a way of organising material. It consists of both the plot or story-line used by the storyteller, and the methods employed to tell that story. Narrative should not be seen as simply a 'fictional' practice. Human beings report everyday events and encounters in the form of narrative, often with the express intention of showing how 'true to life' their experiences are.

In *Narrative Comprehension and Film* (p. 1), Edward Branigan explains how:

> 'making narratives is a strategy for making our world of experiences and desires intelligible. It is a fundamental way of organising data.'

Branigan believes that narrative is directly related to the way in which human beings perceive their environment: it is 'a perceptual activity that organises data into a special pattern which represents and explains experience'. If this is true, then the use of narrative methods by advertisers will be able to create a *positive response* in an audience, not necessarily because of the *content*, but because the intended audience will recognise a familiar structure. In other words, we accept the advertising address not because we feel sorry for Joan and her terrible afflictions, but because we encounter an experience that we ourselves are used to reproducing – the *narrative* experience.

The 'Vita-Weat' narrative is contained within a larger set of narratives; that of the other advertisements which surround it on p. 9 of this edition of *Picture Post*, of similar material which appears throughout the magazine, and ultimately of the discourses set up by the entire publication. The issue concerned carries an article on 'the Tragedy of Spain' (including photographs of refugees fleeing the fascist armies of General Franco), general features on foreign affairs and hobbies, and a study of the National Unemployed Workers' Movement.

Narrative transformation

The narrative of this advertisement may be represented as follows: a problem is posed, a solution is sought, and a resolution is reached. This is in fact the structure that most narratives follow. Theories which have grown from studies

Figure 1.3   The complete advertisement

of literature and folklore may be applied successfully to any forms which employ narrative structures, including advertising.

Todorov, a Russian critic, identified a process through which all narratives appear to pass. A simplified version of his method would be to note that, in all stories, there is usually some state of *equilibrium* – all in the social world is as it should be. This is followed by a *disruption* of this state, leading to *disequilibrium*. In turn, there must be some *recognition* that things are not as they were, followed by an attempt to repair the damage caused by the disruption. The final phase sees a return to some kind of *equilibrium*.

This applies to the starch-heaviness saga, with the exception that, in common with many narratives, it begins with disruption. The reader or viewer is left to imagine the original state of order which contrasts with the problem that is introduced.

Why do so many narratives have the same structure? The theorist Wallace Martin (see Branigan, p.10), writes that:

> 'Identification of universal narrative patterns would seem to tell us not just about literature but about the nature of the mind and/or universal features of culture.'

In other words, narratives are similar in structure because they all grow from human culture and reflect the ways in which the human mind operates when faced with the need to organise and re-present experience.

Narrative and address

The concept of **address** is quite simple. A communicator directs a statement or request or admonition to a specific person or group of people, taking into account the suitability or *register* of the words, phrases and sentences used. What might be the right kind of address for one audience may be completely unsuitable for another. The philosopher Althusser described a specialised form of address called **interpellation**, where human beings are subject to a simple force in our society, that of being 'hailed' or called to order by some form of authority. The example used by Althusser is that of a citizen being 'hailed' by a police officer, as in 'Hey, you there!' (see *Essays on Ideology*, p. 48). The point is that interpellation works because the citizen *recognises* that the address made by authority is indeed directed at him or her. Althusser's conception of the power of address seems to allow for little manoeuvre.

How far would the concept of address, and particularly its authoritarian variant, be useful to an understanding of the Vita-Weat advertisement? There is no face-to-face communication involved in the address from advertiser to reader. The advertiser does not have the same type of social power as a police officer. But there is evidence that the advertiser has a clear conception of some of the **values** held by readers; the use of these values, through language and the graphical representation of certain 'types' of individual, is intended to *position* consumers, to lead them to a point where their values seem to coincide with those displayed by the advertiser. This is not to say that an address will always succeed.

Types of address

The first exchange is intended to set out the problem which Vita-Weat will solve. The reader is in the position of an eavesdropper, but in fact the drama is laid on for his or her benefit. Joan is drawn as young, neatly turned out, and attractive. Her mother appears as a concerned and considerate adult, drawn as a mature female of middle years. She finds a solution for Joan's listlessness, but her musings in the second frame are not merely an internal monologue, though they certainly stand in that tradition.

Starch-heaviness in general, and not just the digestive problems of one individual, must be defeated by Vita-Weat. The transformation comes once Joan has been shown consuming the crispbread. With the final frame ('one month later'), the rewards are set out; Joan has made an impression on the tall and broad-shouldered George, who makes the perfectly correct suggestion that Joan return for tea with 'us', presumably members of his family, perhaps including the Colonel himself. There is a suggestion that George may belong to a social class a little above that of Joan.

The dramatic, narrative mode of the cartoon frames contrasts with the direct address of the explanatory box. This tells the reader about something that is supposed to exist in a real environment:

'Starch-heaviness comes when your stomach has too much half-raw starch to deal with, and is protesting to you about it.'

Notice that the reader is addressed directly. 'Your' stomach is protesting to 'you'. Personal modes of address are being copied in an attempt to get closer to the consumer. The passage continues:

'In normal, everyday foods there *is* this excess of starch. In Vita-Weat, the sensible modern crispbread, the starch is already broken down.'

Here, the 'everyday' is inadequate, yet Vita-Weat is both sensible *and* modern. These words are therefore designed to appeal to values founded on good sense but also on the benefits of modernity. The last two sentences read:

'Vita-Weat gives you a great deal more than old-fashioned bread, with a good deal less strain. Buy Vita-Weat and see.'

'Old-fashioned' bread is denigrated. The old advertising sleight of hand is exercised to promise 'more' benefits with 'less' effort. The practical step suggested by consuming the crispbread is linked to the romantic denouement set out in the final frame.

Magical agents and fairy Godmothers?

Another narrative approach was outlined in the 1920s by Vladimir Propp, who analysed the narrative functions of character in fairy-tales. He identified some eight 'character-roles' in any narrative, including Hero, Princess, Donor, Dispatcher, Helper, Villain, False Hero and Father. These roles are sometimes taken by more than one person in the narrative and can overlap. Propp's system, although difficult to apply exactly to specific narratives, sheds light on how what we often take to be 'character' is in fact a function of narrative.

The role of Hero in this case would be taken both by Vita-Weat (which doubles up as a Magical Agent) and by Joan, though she could be seen as the Princess who acts as the reward for George, the Hero/Prince. The roles of Helper, Donor and Dispatcher would all be taken by Joan's mother. The Villain is clearly Starch-heaviness. False Heroes and Fathers are kept out of sight.

The narrative that has been established through the cartoon form reaches a satisfactory conclusion; George and Joan are united in mutual affection thanks to Joan's mother and the agency of Vita-Weat.

Structuralist approaches

Propp and Todorov may be described as structuralist thinkers, concerned as they are with the internal arrangement of textual elements. As Edward Branigan writes (p. 4), in openly structuralist terms:

> 'In a narrative, some person, object, or situation undergoes a particular type of change ... Narrative is a way of experiencing a group of sentences or pictures (or gestures or dance movements, etc.) which together attribute a beginning, middle, and end to something ... the first sentence of a novel is not itself "the beginning". It acquires that status in relationship to certain other sentences ... the elements themselves are *not* the pattern.'

Content analysis and gender role

A method which sheds light on the **gender** roles assumed by any figures in advertising (whether seen on television or in two-dimensional displays) is simply to record who is shown doing what. In this example, women are largely shown in the domestic sphere, concerned with the practicalities of diet, or shown speculating on the actions of an active male. Joan, influenced by the other characters, is unable to act without the good offices of her mother, who puts her on a diet of crispbread. ('This is good mum – it's so light and crisp', she says, advertising the product to the reader.) George gives his approval when she has shaken off her starch-heaviness ('I love these walks with you').

The reader is thus able to look back on the title 'She said she <u>liked</u> long lonely walks' in the confidence that this assertion was never true. She wanted to be with George. Romance is offered as a suitable reward for the sensible course chosen.

The cast of three keeps the interactions simple and the message clear. There are some individuals we never see, and may wonder about; there is no male figure in Joan's household, while George's parent, 'the Colonel', remains no more than a verbal reference. However, absent or dysfunctional parents are a signal in many narratives for the onset of an adventure.

Models of communication

The following section offers an analysis of some of the models of communication which are used to assist the study of process and context in human interaction. It includes an original model based on an analysis made by Denis McQuail.

Descriptions of reality?

A model of a communication process is 'a consciously *simplified description* in *graphic form* of a piece of reality' (*Communication Models*, McQuail and Windahl, p. 2). This means that an idea about communication is expressed in a drawing or design, which is kept as simple as possible; the purpose is to make communication theory more accessible. The most commonly used term for such a diagram is a 'model', though sometimes the word 'model' is used interchangeably with 'theory'.

Structural and functional models

McQuail and Windahl propose that models are able to provide 'images of wholes' which we might otherwise be unable to perceive, allowing us to appreciate general features of a range of circumstances. The construction of a good model may also help to predict specific communication events.

The basic distinction between types of model are those which are **structural** (usually representing the static components of an *object*) and those described as **functional**. The functional type is supposed to show the forces involved in an *event*, as well as the parts, actors or contexts involved in communication, and must represent dynamic elements such as the direction taken by messages and responses.

Mechanical models?

The simplest models of communication involve message, sender and receiver. The famous Lasswell 'formula' of 1948 (Figure 1.4) asks a number of simple questions which may be applied to any communication act: **who** says **what**, in which **channel**, to **whom**, with what **effect**? Lasswell, interested at the time

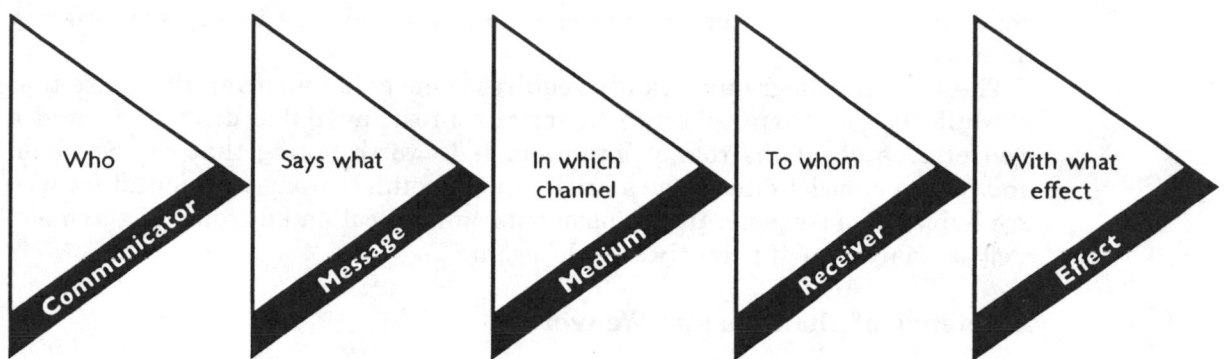

Figure 1.4   After Lasswell, 1948: a model of a communication act

in political persuasion and propaganda, was anxious to investigate ideas about effect. The 'says' used here needs to be taken not as a literal indicator of speech, but rather as referring to any form of human expression.

Shannon and Weaver, in a model intended as a scientific or objective guide to the factors governing the act of communication (Figure 1.5), included an *information source*, the *message*, the sender or *transmitter* who supplies the message, the *signal*, a *receiver* of the message, and the *received signal*. Along the route, there might be external interference of some sort, which was at one time called *noise*. The concept of 'noise' was offered as an explanation for the mechanical interruptions and other difficulties communication must face. This model has given rise to a number of other graphic representations of communication, and has also exerted influence on the way that communication in general is theorised.

Criticisms of transmission models

The most common criticism of the two models illustrated above is that they represent a linear, one-way process. Most writers, as we saw earlier in this

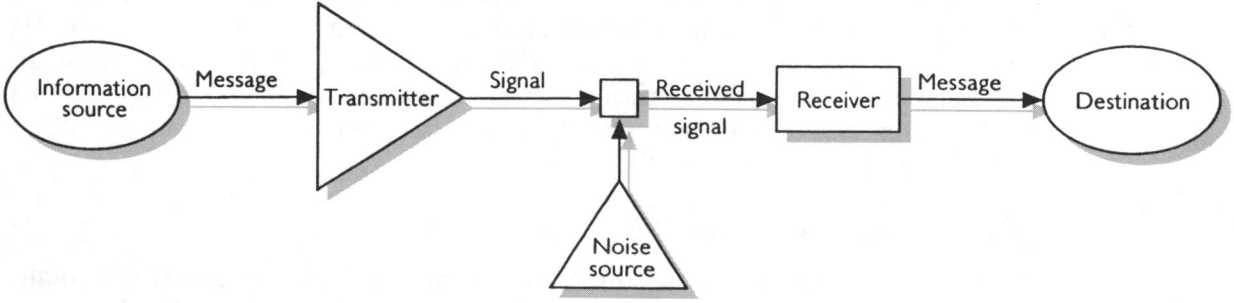

Figure 1.5   After Shannon and Weaver: a model of the communication process

chapter, insist that interpersonal communication always involves a two-way interaction.

The Lasswell diagram certainly requires some adjustment, in the sense that it would benefit from reference to social context, available discourses, and a clearer idea about the role of intention. It is worth noting that the Shannon and Weaver model often draws criticism, sometimes from commentators who are happy to make generalisations about communication but reluctant to make a close analysis of apparently 'simple' events.

A defence of Shannon and Weaver

We should ask what this particular model helps to explain, as well as criticising it for what it neglects. It is not really the case, in my opinion, that its failings are due to its being mathematical or mechanical, and therefore unsuitable for use in human communication. In fact, it is exactly its 'mechanical' nature that might help remind us of the *physiological* factors involved in human communication, allowing insight into, for example, the mechanical reproduction of speech. If we imagine this model to represent a case of interpersonal communication, then:

- The *information source* could be the human mind.
- The *message* would refer to content.
- The *transmitter* might in this case be the larynx of an individual.
- *Signal* could refer here to the human voice.
- *Noise source*, as always, would refer to interruption or interference from an external source.
- The idea of a *received signal* is actually an important distinction to make, reminding us that the original signal is subject to distortion and alteration.
- Finally, *destination* would be the mind of the receiver.

The Shannon and Weaver model remains useful, therefore, in helping us to think clearly about the various origins, stages and operations of basic types of communication. For example, the difference between source and transmitter is worth investigating. Other features may be retained; for example, although the mind and voice would appear to work together, their separation in this model helps to explore ideas about the relationship between human understanding and the actual use of language.

The message and its handlers

A more creative criticism of the 'process' we have just encountered might examine the idea that communication mishaps are not only caused when *clear messages* are distorted by external interference, as the Shannon and Weaver diagram suggests. The 'signal' itself, and the way in which it is expressed, often carry the seeds of any misunderstandings which may occur. While the *content* of the message is usually regarded as the most important factor in creating meaning, its *form* often provides the vital clues to interpretation.

We need also to understand, where possible, the purpose behind the message, whether it is, for instance, informational or persuasive. This implies that we need to examine the *intention* of the sender. McQuail mentions this factor in his simplified overview of the communication process (see below). The study of intention looks at the known and unknown, the free and hidden elements which go to the the the formation of messages. Finally, the tradition which allocates the role of sender to one participant, and receiver to another, needs eventually to be revised, since interpersonal communication implies that these roles will be assumed by both participants (see the section 'From transmission to exchange', at the beginning of this chapter).

Communication practices

In the case of communication **form**, individuals use a battery of devices to create meaning. For example, speech will be accompanied by non-verbal signals, while writing and graphical communication may be employed together in order to create a more powerful impact on an audience.

People are also adept at signalling to others how they wish their communication to be understood; for instance, a verbal statement may be delivered using a variety of *contextual devices* which may either reinforce or undermine the apparent *content*. The entire meaning of an utterance, for example, may change depending on the intonation used by the speaker, or because of the deployment of non-verbal elements. The mass media, in turn, use known generic codes (like specific sounds or evocative passages of music in television and film) to signal to their audiences how they are supposed to react to a particular text.

All individual communications must of course be **finite**. When communication events are in progress, people use a variety of methods to produce *demarcations* between phases of an event. Human beings mark out the places where a *specific* communication will start and finish. For example, non-verbal signals may be employed in the process of withdrawing from a conversation. The practices of the mass media reflect the habitual need to signal where a particular communication begins or ends, in for instance the internal structure of a news bulletin. These abilities to mark out where communication begins and ends, and to say what type of communication is taking place, emphasise the idea introduced under the earlier section entitled 'Organising the subject'; the creation of distinct communication *events*.

Communication: acts, actors and events

Denis McQuail, writing in *Communication* (pp. 1–2), offers 'a simple way of regarding human communication', which is:

'to consider it as the sending from one person to another of meaningful messages'.

The *messages* sent in this process are *meaningful* – they are constructed according to a known pattern or code, and may therefore be successfully interpreted.

McQuail believes there are some common features to all communication, and his basic definition presupposes not only 'a communicator and a receiver', but a relationship between the two. McQuail sees this relationship as 'a mutual awareness, or orientation of one to another'. This awareness or *orientation* will presumably exist alongside some kind of knowledge of the general environment in which the communication event is taking place.

According to McQuail (*Communication*, p. 2), human communication must also involve the following elements:

'an intention, especially on the part of the communicator; an external referent – what the message is about; a common language and some sharing of experience. Finally, it indicates some activity and change of state as a result of the act.'

This introduces a model of communication based essentially on a straight-forward and limited encounter between two individuals. It involves a **message** which has a *clear form* and *unambiguous content*. The **intention** of the sender is noted, as is the shared experience of the two participants but, for the purposes of simplicity, McQuail does not treat these areas as problematic.

Communication in context

Everything McQuail says in this passage points towards the fact that communication must take place in some kind of context. *Context* and the concept of the *social* are perhaps the most useful terms we could reintroduce at this point. If a message is meaningful, this is because it emerges from a code which the two participants or *actors* in this event share. The code, language or para-language which is shared emerges from the social order; not merely from the immediate setting (the time and place in which the actors find themselves) but from the discursive possibilities the participants are able to perceive.

What I would call the 'cultural range' of language presents a number of choices to the communicator. These choices are *circumscribed* first by what is grammatically meaningful and what is not, and then by the range of appropriate meanings which may be generated in the context of interaction. (See the definitions of communication at the beginning of this chapter, particularly the sections on 'The generation of meaning: symbolic form and content' and 'Communication as discourse').

Simple and more complex models from McQuail

Version 1

In this model (Figure 1.6) adapted from McQuail's written description (outlined above), the communicator A has become the sender, a more appropriate title for the simple process shown.

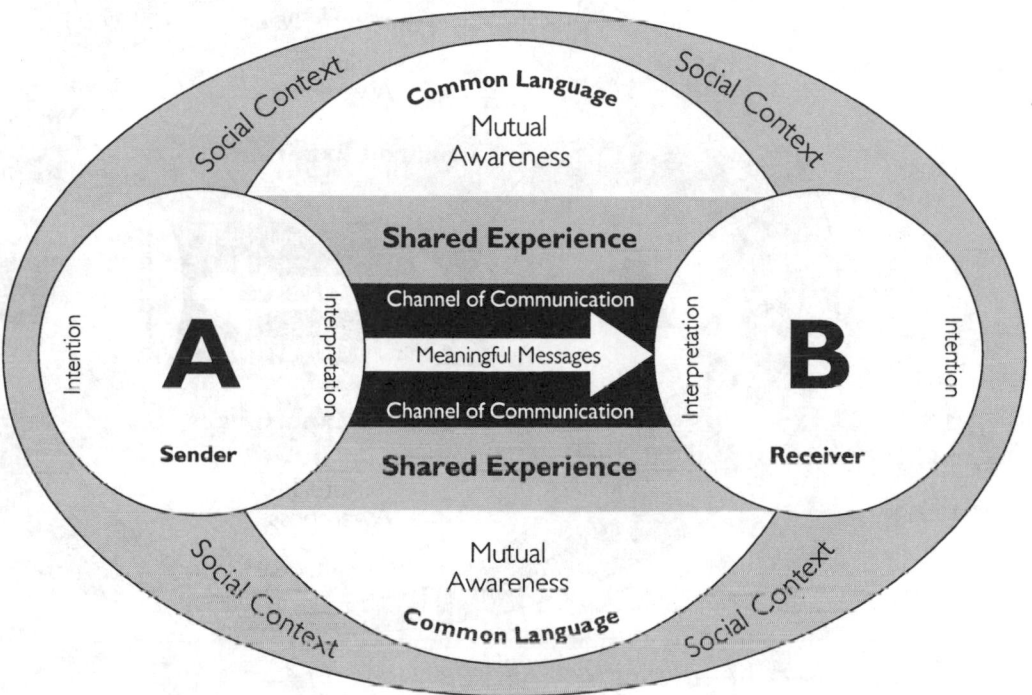

Figure 1.6   After McQuail's description: version 1

It seems clear that the type of process shown here is also **one-way**, a 'single-shot' communication. **Interactive** communication, on the other hand, requires not simply an *act* on the part of one person, but a recognised *reaction* or response from the other. Most writers argue that a true communication 'event' will only take place when a response is elicited from the party which receives the initial message; in their view communication must be interactive. (See the section 'From transmission to exchange' earlier in this chapter.) This might, in effect, exclude the mass media from the study we have undertaken. In this model, issues of intentionality, social context and mutual awareness have all been emphasised in the diagram.

Version 2

In Figure 1.7, the messages sent now travel in two directions, and the intention of each participant has been divided into two areas – *exposed* and *concealed*.

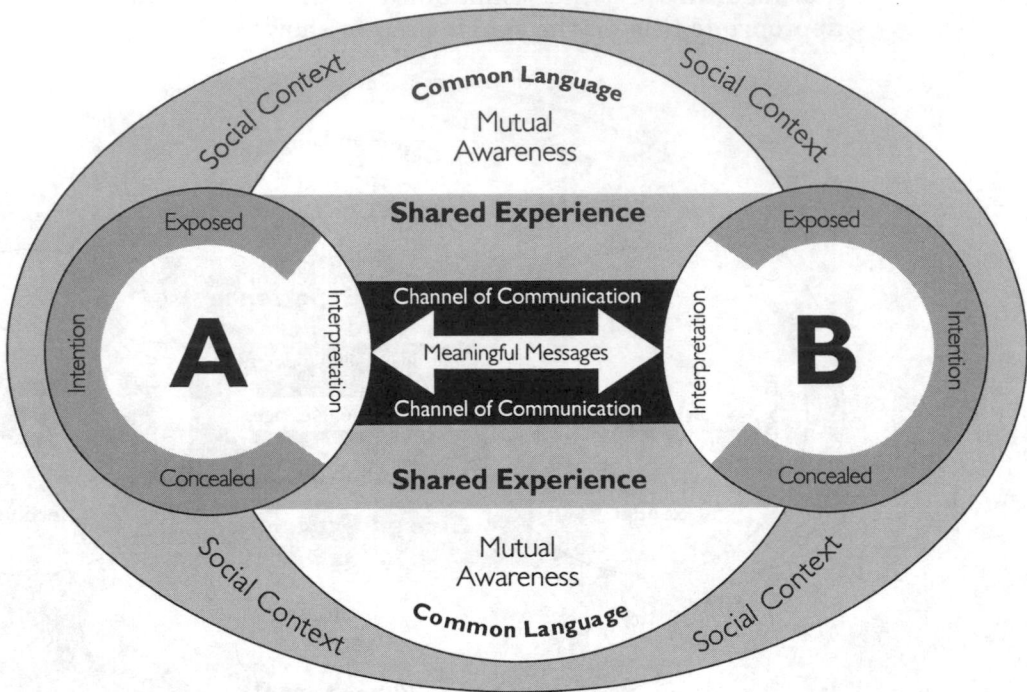

Figure 1.7   After McQuail's description: version 2

Communication: natural process or art?

The capacity of human beings to produce meaning has led some writers to draw particular attention to the 'art' of communication. Dimbleby and Burton, in the Preface to *More than Words* (p. xii), express their belief that;

> 'the art of communication is not a natural process or an ability we are born with. We learn how to communicate.'

'Art' in this context means a human skill, an ability which is developed or acquired. It may be studied, learned and then applied to new situations. It is not clear whether these authors regard the whole of human communication as an art, or are referring to a particular branch which requires special skill or training, but the *practice* of communication may indeed be artful; rhetoric, for example, is the study of methods which can be applied to situations requiring persuasive forms of public address.

When Dimbleby and Burton use the term 'art' to signify the opposite of 'a natural process or an ability we are born with', they are arguing that the 'art' of communication is not **innate**. However, all the evidence points to the idea that the ability to communicate (artful or not) is innate, that it is there from birth, and that human beings are predisposed to express themselves as part of what it means to be human.

For example, pre-speech infants are able to communicate hunger and distress as part of their mechanism for survival. In other words, infants communicate through a genetic mechanism, and it is this innate ability which *continues to prompt* our communication. Of course, human beings are not born with all the skills they eventually acquire, but the fundamental ability already exists. When we acquire an 'art' or skill, we undergo a *natural* process of learning – exactly the idea that Dimbleby and Burton are anxious to deny.

To prove this point, we may employ evidence taken from the study of rhetoric, mentioned above. Highly polished rhetorical skills grow from **ordinary contexts** which require a certain form of persuasive speech. We all encounter such situations at one time or another. Perhaps the tricks or arts of rhetoric are after all part of a process which remains fundamentally natural, and not that far removed from ordinary patterns of speech. If the predilection to speak is innate, then the dramatic or heightened elements of speech must also be natural and to some extent inborn.

Although people do learn how to communicate in more sophisticated ways, refining their skills and abilities through experience and by reflection on that experience, the reason for the complexity we encounter in everyday communication is exactly that it is a natural and *not* an artificial phenomenon. In some respects, deliberately artful examples of communication are easier to study than those interactions which are unplanned. Not all the messages produced by those in authority will be highly polished, and the communication of 'ordinary' people should not be seen as straightforward or so easy to read that it is somehow 'transparent'.

Reference to the world

What comes first: content or structure?

Denis McQuail, (in *Communication*, p. 58) argues that:

'for people to co-operate, or simply to cope with environmental facts, agreed ways of denoting experience must be arrived at'.

We should not imagine from this that members of a tribe or group must at some time have sat down together to agree on a system for describing and interpreting experience; this would of course be impossible without the existence of a shared communicative system in the first place.

This leads to one of the most important questions we might ask in any study of communication. How are symbolic systems put together and used? This suggests that we need to know how human subjects make sense of the world. The opposing approaches to this could be summarised in two fundamental questions:

- Are symbolic systems made by inventing basic 'units' of meaning, building blocks upon which complete systems are then founded? Using human language as an example, we might ask if words (or more accurately *morphemes*) are the basic elements from which languages are created.
- Alternatively, do human beings carry in their minds symbolic systems, structures which are able to generate individual ideas? This would imply that linguistic **structure** gives rise to individual units of meaning, and not the other way about.

Universal structures?

If we understand communication as the generation of meaning through symbols, this might suggest that understanding is available only to members of the same culture. After all, different language groups have significant difficulty in understanding one another's native tongue. However, the idea of 'culture-specific' *meanings* may obscure some very important ideas about how languages and other symbolic systems are formed and used.

On the basis of evidence suggesting that all infants acquire language in a similar way, and that all languages contain similar structures, the celebrated linguist and critic Noam Chomsky suggested that the human species is genetically predisposed to acquire language systems. He also pointed out that people seem to know instinctively when a sentence is ungrammatical, even when that sentence has never before been encountered. Most theorists are beginning to accept the idea that the human brain is specifically equipped to acquire language. An increasing amount of research is being assembled which appears to support the idea of a 'universal grammar'.

The argument that communication is really only meaningful within a specific culture also looks shaky when we consider that some types of symbolic content, such as body language or music, seem to have the ability to carry meaning *beyond* the boundaries of the particular group which produces them. The meanings produced by this type of symbolic content are sometimes regarded as being 'universal'.

If some systems are useful for communicating ideas across cultural boundaries, it may be worth asking if such a discipline as Communication Studies can be adequately represented through print and graphic means alone, without recourse to the human voice or to music, or without reference to the sounds of the natural world.

Forms of communication

To be able to *report* our awareness of the external world, to produce meaning about things, about other individuals and events, we employ communicative systems which manipulate signs or symbols. These systems are commonly thought to have recognised rules and established practices, and are usually taken to include speech, writing, mathematical calculation and other formal systems. In other words, in order to communicate what has been perceived, and to respond to the messages delivered by others, the human subject must use a recognised form of communication.

Mental replicas?

Mainstream theorists argue that the agreed symbol for an idea or thing or concept will, when it is perceived, prompt us to recall the idea, thing or concept itself. As Glass and Holyoak say in *Cognition* (p. 59):

'a printed word automatically activates representations of its pronunciation and meaning'.

This idea depends on the belief that the human subject must be able to *recognise* different features in his or her environment before any communication can take place. It would imply that each person must be able to store, recall and then 're-use' information. According to this theory, no human being could describe any object or event or idea found in the world without first being able to 'call to mind' either the thing or notion that he or she wished to express, using a sort of 'mental replica'.

However, the actual links we make between symbols and real things may be a little less straightforward than the neat process suggested in Glass and Holyoak's example. A single word is capable of doing more than provoking a recollection of formal elements; it might also create a *feeling*, since words are bound to carry an emotive charge. This kind of link with the real is a little more untidy, and much more difficult to define, because it does not fit easily into the kind of rational system proposed in most theories of human understanding.

Internal symbolisation?

The term *symbolic content* was employed earlier to refer to the basic material used in the representation of human experience. At its most simple, this would mean that a tree, for example, could be represented by a photograph or a drawing which *shows* a tree, or by the word 'tree' which *symbolises* the tree itself. The existence of symbolic content has led some writers to argue that there is also a process called 'internal symbolisation' or the production of sets of mental *representations*. This could be explained as the existence of a 'fund' of images and symbols, collected together as memories, and used whenever the occasion requires that we refer to an aspect of experience.

The established theory states that the capacity for communication calls for:

> 'the communicator to construct an internal representation of the external world, and then to carry out some symbolic behaviour that conveys the content of that representation'. (Johnson-Laird in Mellor, *Ways of Communicating*, p. 4)

This sounds perfectly rational, but seems to refer to the sort of 'symbolic behaviour' which is usually expressed in *formal* systems of communication. Theories which propose that we depend for meaning-creation upon formal systems take the route of cognitive psychology, where **cognition** means 'knowing' and refers to all the ways in which knowledge of the world is attained, retained and then used.

The theory of representation: 'internal' and 'external'

At this point we must examine the meaning of the term **representation**. It is used by communication theorists, psychologists and biologists alike to describe both the process of creating **internal** or mental versions of the real, and the mobilisation of these internal versions for **external** use. In other words, the concept of representation states *first* that individuals in societies retain or remember symbols which stand for real experiences, and *second* that they are able successfully to refer to real things by expressing themselves through the symbols they have learned.

Fables of communication

As we may have guessed, ideas about *internal* representation have begun to cause some disquiet, on the grounds that the systems imagined in most scenarios are a little too neatly arranged. The notion of internal representation is still, however, one of the staple concepts of communication theory.

Johnson-Laird, writing in *Ways of Communicating* (p. 2), uses the example of insects to argue that symbolisation and external representation occur in some creatures but not in others. He begins with the case of the fire ant.

When this insect returns to the nest from an abundant food source, it leaves a chemical trail (a 'pheromone') which other workers are able to track. Johnson-Laird does not believe that such behaviours constitute communication. The ants simply follow a smell. We may suppose that they do not necessarily connect the chemical signal with food, no matter how many times they may have followed it before. Since this is an entirely *physiological* response, there is (p. 3):

'no need for the ant's nervous system to construct an internal representation of some rudimentary "idea" of food that lights up in the insect's mind as soon as it smells the pheromone'.

Johnson-Laird goes on to argue that the 'dance' of the bee, performed at the hive by bees which have found food elsewhere, is significantly different from the long march of the ant. He cites experiments carried out by von Frisch, which appeared to demonstrate that bees are capable of indicating the direction in which food is located. Food was placed on one side of a mountain range, forcing the bees to take an indirect route to the source. The route was displayed to members of the hive through a *representation* (in the 'dance').

Johnson-Laird calls the bees' dance symbolic, in the sense that its purpose is to represent the distance and direction of food. It does seem reasonable to assume that the bees' dance is an *external* representation, but Johnson-Laird decides in addition that the nervous systems of bees are able to construct an *internal* or *symbolic* representation of the world.

Informal meanings?

Many aspects of *human* communication, which are vital to the creation of meaning, do not appear to function in the tidy way that some theorists imagine. For example, meaning is often created through methods which are not usually thought of as particularly systematic or rule-bound. Gestures, dance, mime, music, visual and three-dimensional art, and even expressive sounds (especially intonation) all appear to create specific meaning in certain contexts. The formal meanings found in written language, for instance, are not reproduced in precisely the same way in speech, where meaning is partially generated through less formal means, including body language and intonation.

The philosopher Wittgenstein believed that meaning is not found in systems at all, but is simply the *use* to which we put the signs at our disposal. In the words of Harré and Gillett, he came to realise that (*The Discursive Mind*, p. 19):

'mental activity is not [an] . . . inner set of processes but a range of moves or techniques defined against a background of human activity and governed by informal rules'.

It is the informal 'move', working either in conjunction with or in opposition to our more obviously systematic communicative practices, which suggests that understanding involves the emotional as well as the cognitive attributes of human beings. It may also suggest that the idea of a 'store' of mental experience, which is supposedly used to assist expression, is an inadequate explanation for the fact that the human subject is able to create meaning in situations which lie outside his or her experience. It is the theory of *internal* symbolisation which is unconvincing, while a concept of external representation or *presentation* may still provide us with a sensible description of human communication.

The power of emotions: informal processes

When McQuail (in *Communication*, p. 10) argues that:

> 'sounds become associated with certain experiences and can be said to have meanings, [and] as a result of this association their utterance gives rise to the image of the experienced object',

we may question his dependence upon visual reference, by asking if the 'experiences' we carry in our minds call upon stored images alone. In fact, people are able to link a sound most easily to an emotional quality, and perhaps less easily to a specific object. While much human memory mobilises 'visions' of the past, such visualisations often include memories of sound. In fact, memories are really only meaningful insofar as they call up emotional states associated with past experience.

The preoccupation with exploring the intellectual processes of understanding (the cognitive processes used by human beings) has led a number of authors to the conclusion that the *emotional* factors in human understanding have been neglected. Jaak Panksepp, writing in an essay called 'Gray zones at the Emotion/Cognition Interface' (p. 289), points out that:

> 'emotions have a power of their own in directing and disrupting behavioural options, thinking processes, and bodily states'.

He opposes the 'fashionable [idea] that a cognitive analysis can shed penetrating new light on the nature of emotions'. Emotions, according to Panksepp, are created from the activities of 'specific types of neural circuits' in the brain, which are quite different to the centres of intellectual processing.

This is not to say that emotions do not have some cognitive or behavioural features, rather that they are not concerned primarily with 'forms of information processing which focus on relationships about external events'. Panksepp sees human emotions as 'instinctual' operating systems of the brain which promote a coherent individual response to 'basic survival needs'.

Naming and categorising

The most fundamental part of the shared knowledge possessed by any society or group must be what people are able to agree exists, including the ideas and objects which individuals name. The activity of **naming** or labelling things involves the use of ideas about the *significance* or importance of what is experienced, as we shall see in Chapter 3.

The first stage of categorisation is naming; the second is the placing of what is named in groups or **categories**, which are supposed to share some common features or elements. The act of placing things in either broad or exclusive groups and categories does more than simply help us to describe the world. It directs and shapes our understanding of social reality.

Questions of reality

Is the world 'made' by communication?

The central role played by communication in making sense of the world has encouraged a variety of writers to produce admiring descriptions of its power. James W. Carey, in *Communication as Culture*, goes so far as to claim that (p. 25):

'reality is brought into existence, is produced, by communication'.

At first sight, this appears to be a curious statement. How could reality be manufactured by the communicative practices of human beings? In order to answer this question, we need to reach an acceptable definition of reality and the real.

Definitions of reality

The real is defined in the *Concise Oxford Dictionary* as: 'actually existing as a thing or occurring in fact'. There is a close relationship between *thing* and *fact*. A **thing** is whatever may be thought about or perceived, whether that is animate (living) or inanimate (an object). A **fact** is something that is known to have occurred or which is true. The same dictionary defines **reality** as:

'property of being real ... real existence, what is real, what underlies appearances'.

When Carey writes that 'reality is brought into existence, is produced, by communication', his statement may now be tested against definitions of the real just explored. If the real includes *things* which are perceived by people, then the natural features of the landscape (mountains, rivers and forests, for example), could hardly be 'brought into existence' by communication. We usually assume that such things have to exist *before* they can be perceived, and before any communication takes place. (Even 'man-made structures', which depend on interaction in order to get built, are not produced by communication alone, but by human activity also.) If reality is assumed to exist before perception, with perception coming before representation, reality cannot be created directly by people.

Shared knowledge and social reality

In my opinion, what human beings actually 'create' and share through communication is a shared understanding of reality, where reality is that which has the potential first to be perceived or thought about, and then to be represented. I would suggest that the term social reality should be used to describe the understandings of the real circulated within human societies.

The reluctance of some communication theorists to keep the terms *reality* and *social reality* separate continues to suggest contradictory positions in the same texts, and even at times in the same paragraph. Stuart Sigman's essay on 'Social Communication', in the fourth edition of *Communication Studies: An Introductory Reader*, states that (p. 125):

> 'Communication is the means by which social reality is created, lived through, sustained, and/or altered.'

This is essentially similar to the argument expressed above, that communication creates *social reality*. Social reality, as we have seen, must be a reality which is shared, otherwise the word 'social' may as well be dropped. Sigman believes that communication is more than a private exchange between individuals; it is the process of handling information within a social system.

However, he then goes on to argue that:

> 'Rather than a process whereby information about an external, "real" world is shared *by* individuals, [communication] is the mechanism whereby information is used to construct reality *for* individuals.'

In this passage, the communication process is not the sharing of information about external reality. It is now presented as a mechanism in which information creates *reality* itself, a reality which seems to be presented to individuals without requiring their participation. In addition, the inverted commas around the word *real* seem to suggest some doubt about the existence of an external world upon which any notion of reality could be based in the first place.

Questioning the real

Philosophers have, in every age, investigated a number of problems concerning the human condition, and it is hardly surprising that one of the most persistent has concerned the status of the real. From our point of view, if communication is the *presentation* of knowledge about the environment we inhabit, then it would be useful briefly to identify the arguments which:

- attempt either to support or contradict the notion that the world is there in the first place to be represented;
- support or contradict the idea that our perception of the world is broadly accurate.

Realism and anti-realism

Any philosophical position may be called **realist** if it argues in favour of the actual existence, whether perceived by human beings or not, of material things and objects. **Anti-realist** positions include those which either question the actual existence of things and objects, or state that we are only able to perceive the existence of symbolic systems, or logical structures, or ideas.

Platonic realism: universals and particulars

The Ancient Greek philosopher Plato thought that knowledge consisted of the apprehension of universal 'forms', which contained the true meanings of all general terms. This idea will become especially important when we consider how people put objects, ideas or living things into classes or groups.

Plato had faith in the reality of the world, deciding that any object, idea or creature which could be perceived belonged to a particular class or category. However, the way in which Plato imagined the categorisation of real things seems to confuse the issue. A dog, for example, would belong to the class 'dog', because it shares in the *universal form* 'Dog'. The **universals** are supposed to be real, but our senses are unable to perceive them. We perceive only the *particular* object, idea or creature.

This philosophy of the real has a number of problems associated with it. In the first place, the nature of the connection between particular and universal form is unclear. Does the universal form 'Dog' somehow produce a member of the class or category 'dog'? If not, how are individual or particular instances of 'dog' linked to the universal? Secondly, anyone reading Plato's account is bound to feel irritated that the reality of the universal form is beyond the range of our senses. It may prompt some to ask, not unreasonably, where exactly these forms are hidden away.

In fact, Plato was a realist before he developed his theory of universals or 'forms', and his realist perspective does not depend on the notion of universals at all. He was particularly concerned to oppose the idea that notions like truth and justice are merely whatever an *individual* might either assert or believe. Plato was convinced that truth is capable of proof, and that both truth and justice are more important than the political machinations of the powerful.

Anti-realist positions: idealism, nominalism, phenomenologism

Idealism may be understood as the doctrine that reality is in fact a mental phenomenon, based on ideas (and not, as some suppose, 'ideals'). The more extreme form of idealism is the belief that (A.J. Ayer, *A Dictionary of Philosophy*, p. 97):

'matter does not exist except in the form of ideas in the mind, or as a manifestation of mental activity. The "mind" in question may be one's own mind, minds in general, or the mind of God.'

Nominalism promotes the idea that all we are actually able to know is the names or classes of things in the world, taking the view that there are no such things as the Platonic 'universals', but rather *paradigms*, reliable examples of a particular class of thing or creature, to which others may be compared. The problem here is where to draw the line between examples of things, and indeed how the choice of the paradigm is made.

Phenomenologism is an approach which begins with the study of appearances, involving the belief that things have an essence which may be discovered through description. The appearances which form the basis of inquiry are *phenomena*, what Ayer calls 'the objects of experience', brought into being by the activities of the human mind.

Human senses and the real: sensory deception?

Some cultural theorists and philosophers believe that there is a 'weak link' in the chain of what makes up the real. They argue that if the real can only be perceived by human senses, then all we can know for sure is the *data gathered by the senses* through perception, not the reality which lies behind it. The philosopher Kant, for example, was interested in the idea that there might be a difference between the real and *reality as it is known* by human beings. He believed that reality existed independently but that its appearance was shaped by the structures of the mind.

Some **postmodernists** take this a step further, arguing that we are even further from those notions of reality we have accepted since the Enlightenment of the eighteenth century, and that we now inhabit a world dominated by media-generated images and concepts. These forms of data are supposed no longer to bear a direct relationship to the real at all, but instead are meant to refer merely to another set of images or ideas. The result is that reality is supposed to have become 'suspended' and consequently our judgements about our lives must now take account of this change in our conceptual environment (see the section on 'Postmodernism' below).

Realist responses

It makes sense to argue that there is no *exact* correlation between the world and the ways in which it is perceived. This does not mean that a realist would need to abandon the idea that real objects do exist. Some writers argue that the real and the basic categories of human experience may not coincide exactly, but do correspond very closely. In *Thought and Language* (p. 9), the American academic J.M. Moravcsik argues in favour of realism by indicating 'the success of the human mind in coming to understand reality', and by noting that human beings use categories which are close to the reality they identify.

Certainly, *individual* human beings would cause chaos on a much grander scale than they do at present if their perceptions of the real were not so close to the real itself. However, it may be that the human species taken *collectively* has a distorted understanding of some very important aspects of reality. An example would be its inadequate conceptualisation of the dangers posed to the natural world by the human race.

In response to postmodernism (which will be considered more fully in later chapters), there are realist positions which accept many of the questions postmodern thinkers have raised about the ways in which we have traditionally described ourselves and the society we inhabit. I believe, however, that communication theorists need to look critically at one of the central tenets of postmodern thought, that which suggests we live in a world dominated by meanings created by media technologies.

Descartes: the search for reliable knowledge

René Descartes was a mathematician and philosopher who was born in the closing years of the sixteenth century. His 'world' or environment was certainly one of significant and uncomfortable change. At the time, there was sharp conflict between various branches of philosophy. Many thinkers were attracted towards *scepticism*, a position which questions whether any human belief can be supported by evidence.

Some philosophers went further than the sceptics, declaring that 'man is the measure of all things' and that there was no other standard against which to judge actions in the world. The implication would therefore be that human beings should concern themselves only with the most selfish of personal goals. Such thinkers based their ideas on the *Sophist* philosophers of Ancient Greece.

Descartes decided to test received ideas about knowledge and truth, in an attempt to isolate only that knowledge which could be regarded as completely reliable. He avoided investigating the status of single instances of belief or opinion, looking instead at general categories of belief. If there was any flaw in the broad category, then the individual examples belonging to it could be jettisoned.

Descartes and the certainty of existence

After the process of investigation was complete, the only fact that Descartes felt to be completely reliable was that he himself existed. The notion that the whole world may be little more than an illusion, a deception invented by some malicious agency or demon, would fail to shake the conviction of the philosopher in his own existence. In order to doubt the reality of the world, Descartes would have to go through some process of thought. The act of thinking would prove his own status as a real and independent being. This gave rise to the famous declaration, 'I think, therefore I am.' Descartes wrote (see *An Introduction to Philosophy*, p. 185):

'No matter how hard I try to disprove the statement "I think therefore I am", as soon as *I think*, the truth of the statement has been demonstrated again.'

The major disadvantage of Descartes's philosophy, from the perspective of the discursive theory explored in this book, is the propagation of the 'mind/body split', a form of dualism which holds 'mental' and 'material' experience apart, and which has been responsible for the development of theories which suggest that mental life is 'internal' while behaviour is 'external' (see my criticism of theories of *meaning and action* in the 'Intrapersonal' section earlier in this chapter). This split led in turn to the type of research project which seeks to discover the 'internal' causes which produce various types of human behaviour. A number of modern theorists, in contrast to Descartes, have sought to demonstrate that there is no 'hidden' side to human existence.

Empiricism: the primacy of experience

Some philosophers have asked whether we require or use absolutely certain knowledge. For most ordinary purposes, they argue that all we need to possess is *probable* knowledge (see *An Introduction to Philosophy*, p. 192):

'Instead of seeking absolutely true knowledge about an alleged real world, they have tried to discover where we do *in fact* get our information from, and what degree of reliability it actually possesses.'

This is known as **empiricism**.

Locke, an English philosopher who was active at the end of the seventeenth century, believed that ideas came only from experience, arguing that there were two sources of knowledge: sensation and reflection. He distinguished between a primary or scientific description of an object, and a secondary category based on ordinary experience. His arguments (see *An Introduction to Philosophy*, p. 199) assert that:

'our knowledge of our own ideas is more than just our own imagination, and there is a conformity between our ideas and the real nature of things . . . all simple ideas represent something real'.

However, this approach to defining reality led to an insistence that the human mind is unable to invent those ideas regarded as 'simple'. Locke's attack on scepticism relied on the idea that objects are real because they exist in the mind of God.

More questions on representation

As we have seen, some writers have turned their attention from interrogating the status of the real to questioning the Western tradition, which has for so long made a distinction between an external world and the internal 'version' of reality which is supposedly located in the human mind. John Shotter, in *Conversational Realities*, notes that (p. 4):

> 'we take it for granted that we are self-contained individuals, having minds that contain "inner mental representations" of possible "outer" circumstances'.

Shotter argues that this conceptualisation of ourselves is not universally shared among the peoples of the world. He refers to the work of anthropologists like Geertz and Lienhardt. They discovered that some cultures do not construct a version of the internal 'mind', positioned between people and their immediate experience of the external world, and used to evaluate or filter external influences. This may be taken as an attack on some theories of representation, as outlined earlier when I set out Johnson-Laird's description of communication as an exchange of meanings based on *symbolic behaviour*.

Shotter is interested in language and speech less as systems which (p. 11) refer to real 'things and substances' than as practices which refer to 'a world of activities and events'. Shotter in effect rejects the 'realist' approaches to representation, using what he calls the *community*, instead of an external world, as the only reliable test of truth and accuracy in human communication.

However, Shotter's sense of this community is rather vaguely formed, based on describing a variety of shared human activities, some formal and others informal (including 'playful discussion and gossip'), but all of which involve the idea of mutual obligation and the concepts of belonging and citizenship. He searches, in his own way, for a *referential* frame for his work, even if this is not offered as a certainty.

The anxiety to find frames of reference features prominently in the work of many writers on communication and social reality, including those who reject the status of the real. The touchstone offered instead may be variously the media, the individual, God, or different types of human collective. Ideas about referentiality proper will be examined again, when we explore the relative strengths and weaknesses of realist, 'ritual' and postmodernist descriptions of communication and social life (see Chapter 5).

Representation and structures

As I argued in the sections above on representation, it may not be necessary to reject representation as a concept, even if we are reluctant to accept the existence of mental structures or 'schemas' of representation. In *Thought and Language*, Moravcsik notes that some objects of thought, like chess, mathematics and logic (p. 80), 'are made up partly of constitutive rules'. He deduces from this that:

> 'it is reasonable to assume that we must have a cognitive representation of a system of rules'.

The existence of a cognitive system would, as Moravcsik says, suggest that representational thought exists. The question we have explored is, can representational thought be anything besides logical and schematic? Although not widely accepted, the idea of a form of human thought that is spontaneous may suggest (as Moravcsik recognises) that cognition and information processing are inadequate explanations.

Moravcsik proposes that (p. 266) 'human thought is projective'. If this is true, then it presents a picture of human communicative capability which is more promising than the models which insist that the mind relies purely upon assessing and sorting through experience. 'Projection' involves the imaginative use of language to describe new possibilities in the arrangement of social life. Communication Studies has yet to embark on an analysis of what a 'projective' model would look like, but it remains one of the important tasks which faces the subject.

Human communication and society

While some communication theorists forget that society as a whole is created through economic activity, and not simply through communication, it is still true that the sense we have of our 'place' in the world depends on (McQuail, *Communication*, p. 4) 'a set of understandings, a framework of shared meanings' which 'enables people to orient themselves to each other and inhabit a common environment'.

According to McQuail, society is sustained through what he calls 'reaffirmation' and 're-creation'. This means that the elements of social life are emphasised and renewed in forms of ritual and through language. In turn, this implies that human groups and societies must share common ideas and some kind of common outlook.

Societies must of course change, but this constant evolution should be reflected in both the form and content of communication. Since it is the case that the 'knowledge' which people have of their society, and of the changes which take place within it, must be (in McQuail's words) 'acquired, maintained and altered by communication', the perception people have of their surroundings may be seriously distorted by any restrictions which are placed on the freedom to communicate.

Inherited meanings

McQuail argues that 'the common understandings' we share encompass more than simply the perception and naming of physical events and objects. They include the 'obligations, rules and views of what is desirable'. This is similar to the position held by Shotter, when he uses the 'community' as his touchstone.

However, since the descriptions or 'labels' used in representing things in reality are inherited from the culture people inhabit (including social processes, and especially 'rules and views of what is desirable'), it is possible that some descriptions may fail to reflect change in society, or may act to limit some forms of thought and consequently some types of interaction. Not only do the labels we attach to things (and the categories we use to 'place' these things) carry the values, positive and negative, of our society, they also retain the traces of historical values, attitudes and beliefs.

Is it possible that the language we receive from the past threatens to frame our understanding of the present? Language is important because it grows from the real and has in turn a material effect on life. Language *use* causes argument because it is a struggle over how we define the world and our place in it. Rebellions against authority are often expressed in a form of language which deliberately creates distance between itself and the old order.

It is also clear that no language stands still. Words and phrases change their meaning noticeably not just within lifetimes but in the space of a few years. For example, the term 'political radical', once used exclusively to signify someone of left-wing persuasion, is now applied to individuals on the further reaches of the right. Another example may be the deliberate use of different terms and words to describe the same basic condition of life, made so often by authority to soften the reception of an event. An economic 'depression' becomes a 'recession', for example.

The extent to which it is possible to force a *change* in society through the use of language will be studied briefly in Chapter 3 when I consider the notion of 'political correctness'. While McQuail believes that (p. 4):

'we are most aware of our dependence on shared understandings and on communication, at points of change or discontinuity in time or space and in situations of conflict',

it could be said that the exact opposite is also sometimes the case; that we are especially aware of *differences* between ourselves and others at those times when the social order is under pressure.

Communication Studies: traditions

In the sections which follow, a number of established approaches to the study of communication are described. Some of these have emerged from the subject itself, but most are taken from major currents of theory which have affected all branches of critical inquiry, including media, cultural and political studies. Together, these make up some of the traditions which inform research and colour debate in the subject.

These traditions have not all, of course, attained the same *status* as theory; some have been minor influences on the direction of the subject, or are better known as examples of practice. We should, nevertheless, remember that the practice of communication is usually connected, however indirectly, to dominant trends of thought. In addition, it is not unnusual for one 'movement' to grow from an earlier body of knowledge.

A summary of traditions

The list begins with the *student-centred* approach and those *skills-based* traditions which are often closely associated with it. The concept of *effectiveness in communication* includes discussion of *individualist* approaches and those perspectives which emphasise *interpersonal relations*. Theories of society and communication are provided, from *functionalism* and *symbolic interactionism* to *Marxism, feminism, structuralism*, and *post-structuralism* and *deconstruction*. *Postmodernist* theories of meaning are described at the end of the section.

A more extensive examination of critical theory is given in Chapter 5.

The 'student-centred' approach

Many texts, quite understandably, make large claims for Communication Studies as a discipline. For example, in *What is Communication Studies?*, James Watson describes the subject as a 'process of exploration' and contrasts it with most other academic disciplines. In his opinion these are (p. 2):

'information-centred. There is a body of knowledge which has to be absorbed before that knowledge can be acted upon. This gives lecturers a great advantage over their students.'

By contrast, according to Watson, Communication Studies operates through a different set of values:

'the relationship between the student and the subject, and the student and the teacher is arguably of a different order. Facts are important, but perception of those facts is open to debate.'

Those involved in the subject will certainly recognise two of the central tenets which inform their work: the positive encouragement of rapport between staff and students, and the underlying principle which allows productive interaction between each group to take place. This principle holds that all theories and categories of information, however exalted or well-established, are subject to revision in the light of experience and debate. Watson goes further, offering the view that at its best, study will involve 'a multi-way discourse between students and teacher' where 'students have an enormous store of personal experience to draw upon' and teachers act as 'facilitators of learning'.

The virtues of Communication Studies are many and varied, but we should perhaps be more circumspect about the claims we are prepared to make on behalf of the subject. We may wonder if our discipline is really the only one where facts and ideas are subject to rigorous inquiry. Other subjects could also lay claim to this principle. In addition, we cannot rely upon good intentions alone; has the value placed on students' own experience of communication always translated into good practice?

The 'student-centred' approach does have certain strengths. At its best, when linked to practical exploration and adventurous research, it encourages students to take control of many areas of the subject, emphasising the practical experience of learning.

The 'skills' tradition

An important part of most communication courses is the promotion of a variety of **skills**. Instruction and practice in public speaking, in interview techniques, in the use of appropriate verbal and written 'registers', and in the construction of essays may all be described as practical abilities in communication. The skills 'tradition', however, has often become divorced from the academic core of the discipline. The separation between theory and practical application has arisen partly because the cultural and political *context* of communication skills has been neglected. Indeed, some courses have concentrated purely on a form of 'training'.

In an attempt to give a proper context to the acquisition of skills, Dimbleby and Burton (see *Teaching Communication*, p. 12) propose a four-fold division of the concept, into **intellectual**, **functional**, **interpersonal** and **group**. Intellectual skills, according to these authors, are mostly concerned with acquiring, deciphering and using information. Functional skills are, by contrast, those which refer to the ability to produce different forms of communication, such as letters, charts, posters and so on. The interpersonal includes social and perceptual abilities, while group skills are seen in the way that tasks are carried out and roles are maintained.

Recent attempts to present Communication Studies as wholly vocational are misleading. The point is that it is supposed to supply a wider perspective on vocational studies, while *at the same time* being of considerable practical use in all aspects of everyday existence. The tradition of practical and critical inquiry found in Communication Studies makes it an ideal subject to offer students engaged in both academic and vocational courses, but it may cease to be of value to either group if it tries to disguise itself as a general course in 'life skills'.

Effectiveness in communication

'Individualist' approaches

The 'student-centred' perspective outlined at the beginning of this section leads naturally to the study of a closely related tradition, that which promotes personal effectiveness in communication, and which places the **individual** at the centre of its concerns. *The Dynamics of Human Communication*, for example, first produced in the United States by Myers and Myers in 1973, has a reputation for promoting liberal attitudes and discourses, offering the reader the opportunity to (p. xvi, 1985 edition):

'detect unhealthy use of language in others and make your own words more effective'.

There are two aims here. The first is the detection of 'unhealthy' language use. This presumably refers to a whole range of techniques, including manipulative or misleading forms of speech employed by the unscrupulous. The second part of the sentence encourages the reader to become an 'effective' communicator. The drawback to this approach begins if we recognise that there must come a point where the moral imperative ('detect unhealthy use of language') clashes with the goal of efficacy which is also presented.

Other books addressed to a student readership emphasise the goal of improved competence in communication. In the Preface to *More than Words*, Dimbleby and Burton explain their assumption that their readers will be (p. xi) 'interested in learning how to communicate more effectively'. Communication appears once again as more than an ordinary study; in an attempt to encourage the idea that the student stands at the centre of the project, the prize of personal enhancement is offered.

While it is certainly possible to improve some aspects of personal communication, there are dangers to be avoided. The first is the idea that there is such a thing as a completely reliable 'system' for teaching people how to be good communicators. Formal programmes which promise to improve personal or organisational effectiveness through communication ('neuro-linguistic programming', for example) isolate individual features of human behaviour and speech, employing them in the service of personal improvement.

The difference between such programmes of self-enhancement and the major functionalist approaches (see below) is one of scale. It must also be acknowledged that improved ability in communication is often a worthwhile aim, when it benefits groups which have traditionally been excluded from political power.

However, any goal concerned with purely *individual* advancement may significantly distort the communicative relationships we are able to establish with others, and might detract from the essentially *social* project which draws many students to Communication Studies in the first place. Any endeavour which aims to tidy up or narrow down human communication will result in the neglect of some of the most significant parts of interaction, those which are *spontaneous*. Spontaneity may be regarded as one attribute which it is impossible to teach.

Interpersonal relations

The well-known American studies of **interpersonal relations**, including the work of Myers and Myers in the various editions of *The Dynamics of Human*

Communication (1973 to 1985, mentioned above) and Patton and Giffin in *Interpersonal Communication in Action* (1981), emerge from the individualist approach, examined in the preceding paragraphs.

While the goal of effectiveness features in this perspective, the aim is chiefly to show how better relationships between individuals might be established. The relative success or failure of individual exchanges is examined with the aid of psychological models of human interaction. Research into interpersonal communication becomes, therefore, more than a study; it is seen as a moral imperative. This tradition amounts to the study of *interpersonal relations*, without the use of *interactionist* perspectives.

Within the books mentioned above, material is consciously directed to a client group imagined as receptive to the project of improved interaction. Patton and Giffin, the editors of *Interpersonal Communication in Action*, write (p. 9):

'communication is the foundation for all of our interpersonal relationships; its relevance to and significance for our lives can hardly be overemphasised. Yet only recently have attempts been made to translate behavioural theories into research-based foundations for personalised growth and development.'

Here, questions of individual competence are regarded as centrally important, but the authors do not present a study of real interactions. Instead, Patton and Giffin encourage their co-writers to search for those underlying principles which they believe must govern communicative competence. It seems odd that real speech events do not feature in the studies made by authors who claim to be interested in improving personal relations.

The captions to photographs used in different chapters in *Interpersonal Communication in Action* illustrate the central values of the book: 'physical contact communicates attitudes and inner emotional states'; 'people who look for happiness and success are likely to find it'; 'fences may serve as symbolic gaps between neighbours'; 'people must be authentic if their relationship is to grow'; 'by self-disclosure to trusted others, a person can achieve a healthier personality'. Patton and Giffin's volume ends with a Postscript arguing that 'people of good faith' should not have to accept 'the alienations, the undue hostilities, the misunderstandings' so common in life.

The major criticism of this approach is that the propagation of 'good' communication may at times lead merely to more sophisticated and devious forms of communicative behaviour. In contrast to this tradition, some currents of theory which value human interaction have studied real verbal exchanges ('pragmatics' or discourse analysis).

Communication and society

Functionalism

Research into public communication has been particularly strong in the United States, where a number of competing schools of thought have flourished.

Within the North American tradition, **functionalism** has formed one of the most significant sociological approaches to communication.

Functionalism is the idea that events, including communication events, can best be understood in terms of the functions or purposes they serve within a society. Anthony Giddens, writing in the second edition of *Sociology*, explains that the study of the function of a social practice or institution is (p. 711):

> 'to analyse the contribution which that practice makes to the continuation of the society as a whole'.

One of the most influential of the American functionalists was Robert K. Merton, whose research in the late 1950s included studies of large-scale industrial societies, marking a departure from the work of anthropologists like A.R. Radcliffe-Brown, a British writer who studied the Andaman islanders of Burma.

In the study of communication, a functionalist approach would emphasise the role played by public communication, in establishing and maintaining social cohesion. The weakness of traditional functionalism lies in its tendency to emphasise social unity while neglecting those factors which lead to conflict. Other shortcomings include its attribution of 'purposes' to a society, and its relative lack of interest in the meanings that human actors give to the events in which they participate. Merton, however, understood the limitations of the established approaches, which he believed grew from the smaller and more integrated societies studied by his predecessors. Merton distinguished between functions and 'dysfunctions', the latter being those events or types of social activity which threaten to destabilise societies.

Hanno Hardt, in *Critical Communication Studies: Communication, History and Theory in America*, argues that the preoccupation with functionalism in the United States emerged from 'a Western utilitarian culture', citing Alvin Gouldner's description of the values underlying this type of research. Gouldner noticed (p. 15):

> 'a great stress upon winning or losing, upon success or failure as such, rather than upon the character of the intention that shapes a person's action, or upon the conformity of his intention with a pre-established rule'.

In Hardt's view, the functionalist tradition in communication defines communication (p. 16) 'in terms of its effectiveness or efficiency'. Although functionalism, as a theory of society, deals with large-scale or *sociological* perspectives on communication, it can be linked, therefore, with the goal of efficiency (see the preceding section).

Symbolic interactionism

This tradition, which emerged from the work of George Herbert Mead (1863–1931), an American philosopher and sociologist, places language at the centre of human communication. Language, as we have already seen, is a *symbolic form*; hence the use of the term *symbolic* in Mead's description of social *interaction*.

Unlike the functionalist approach, interaction was seen by Mead and his pupil Herbert Blumer (in Blumer's words) as 'the collective and concerted actions of individuals seeking to meet their life situations' and not as a function of 'a system either in a state of balance or trying to achieve balance' (see McQuail, *Communication*, p. 46). In other words, symbolic interactionism concentrates upon the human perspective on events, emphasising 'the active, creative components of human behaviour', while many other approaches stress 'the constraining nature of social influences on our actions' (Anthony Giddens, *Sociology*, p. 718).

The other important tenet of this tradition is that, in carrying out acts of communication, the individual is making an impact not only on others but on him or herself. Through communication, a person is able to gain an objective view of his or her own personality and social role. Mead used the term 'other' to refer to the general notion of the 'not self', an awareness of which he regarded as vital in the creation of self. (Chapter 2 pursues this theory in more detail.) In sending messages, the individual is thus engaged in a form of social reinforcement, in which he or she stands at the centre of both continuity and change.

The Marxist tradition

Marxism is often treated as though it is one system of thought. Although all Marxists share a number of basic ideas, concerning the need for a class analysis of society and culture, and the desirability of positive action on behalf of the oppressed, there are many different variants within the broad tradition.

Marxism began as one current of revolutionary thought in nineteeenth-century Europe. Rival philosophies included anarchism, represented by contemporaries of Marx such as Michael Bakunin. The *Communist Manifesto* of 1848, written by Karl Marx and Frederick Engels, saw the working class in developed nations (England was a prime example) as the key to the liberation of society from poverty and wage-slavery. The workers were supposed to require the services of a centralised revolutionary party in order to advance their cause. Despite revolutionary upsurges in 1848 and 1871 (the Paris Commune), workers in the advanced industrial nations failed to create organisations of sufficient strength to challenge established institutions (including reformist trade unions).

In the years leading up to the First World War, a number of political groups worked to undermine the decaying Russian empire. In 1917, a revolution took place in the industrial centres and Leninism, a ruthless philosophy originally based on Marxist principles, was established in what became the Soviet Union. Other Marxist groups attempted to seize power, in Germany for example, but were defeated. Soviet Communism worked to export its world-view in the years between the two world wars, meeting some resistance when it met other left-wing currents, most notably in Spain during the Civil War of 1936–9.

Early versions of Marxism, usually described as *classical* Marxism, held a fairly straightforward view of communication in a capitalist society. The media were seen as the tools of the ruling class, disseminating ideas designed to keep other groups in society in a position of subservience. Quite simple theories of cause and effect were used to explain the dominance of 'ruling ideas'. The working class was seen as the prisoner of the 'false' ideology propagated by the state. *Political economic* theory is a label revived by Denis McQuail (see *Mass Communication Theory*, p. 64) to describe an approach which concentrates upon the structures of ownership and control which operate within the media. The economic 'base' of society is thought to determine the ideas which circulate within it, so that information is supposedly valued according to the degree of profitability it is able to generate.

The *Frankfurt School* was composed of a number of academics and theorists who began work in 1923 in Weimar Germany. With the advent of the Nazi era, the school (properly known as the Frankfurt Institute for Social Research) was dispersed, most of its members seeking refuge in the United States. It was then re-established in post-war Germany. Its leading thinkers were Max Horkheimer, Theodor Adorno and Herbert Marcuse. These individuals tried to understand the defeat of working-class radicalism and the advent of fascism in Europe.

One theory advanced by this group was that monopoly capitalism had produced a 'mass culture', in which the widespread provision of goods and services, together with the propagation of a myth of equality and classlessness, had together produced wide acceptance of the system. To some degree, this implies that the working class had been somehow 'duped' by mass culture and seduced by the material rewards of consumer society. In the post-war years, Horkheimer and Adorno relinquished their political approach, while Marcuse (who remained in America) produced an analysis of the consumer society called *One-Dimensional Man*.

Theories of *hegemony* represented an attempt to come to terms with the power of culture, emerging from the work of the Italian Marxist Antonio Gramsci, who had been associated with the Factory Councils of Turin during the heyday of working-class self-organisation. Imprisoned by Mussolini, Gramsci produced a series of *Prison Notebooks* which expressed, in somewhat guarded terms, a theory of society which sought to explain the dominance of ruling elites. This approach looked closely at the way in which subordinate groups in society consent to the rule of the powerful. Gramsci was interested, therefore, in how the ideas of the ruling class reproduced themselves in the minds of the oppressed. (See 'Hegemony: Gramsci's theory of power' in Chapter 3.)

What McQuail calls the *social-cultural* approach, and which is sometimes known as *British cultural studies*, probably marks a significant departure from many of the central tenets of classical Marxism. It looked instead to a particular interpretation of Gramsci (see above). Throughout the 1970s, the Centre for Contemporary Cultural Studies (CCCS) in Birmingham produced a number of studies of popular culture which displayed a positive approach to 'mass' media texts. Led by Stuart Hall, the CCCS was particularly concerned to discover the *uses* to which mass communication is put, and how subordinate groups are drawn into the social formation through the consumption of texts.

A number of theorists see the work of the CCCS as a model for their own work. Hanno Hardt, in her attempts to advance the cause of 'critical' communication studies in the United States (see *Critical Communication Studies*, p. 173), describes British cultural studies as a 'political response [to] traditional American communication research and its ideological context'. Hardt's book appeared in 1992, while similar enthusiasm for the CCCS was expressed in the 1995 text *Gender, Race and Class in Media*. The editors, Dines and Humez (Preface, p. xix), talk of its 'progressive politics ... [its] broader and more democratic definition of culture ... and its research methodology, which is more flexible than that of the ... social-scientific research of traditional U.S. communications studies'.

It is interesting to note that some currents of thought within cultural studies do not display such unqualified support for the CCCS. The 'Gramscian' tradition associated with Hall and his colleagues has come under attack from David Harris (see *From Class Struggle to the Politics of Pleasure*), who has criticised its tendency to produce a selective reading of Gramsci's theories. He notes, for example (p. 17), 'Gramsci's advocacy of traditional education [which] can seem dreadfully elitist and "unfortunate" ... Gramscians simply have had to ignore much of his work here'. Martin Barker and Anne Beezer, in *Reading into Cultural Studies* (p. 8), believe that 'early cultural studies work' and explore 'the potential for resistance and revolt against ... dominatory forces'. In their opinion, more recent projects undertaken by writers associated with the CCCS constitute a wholesale reteat from a critical perspective, and ignore in particular the importance of class analysis.

Feminist approaches

Writing in the second edition of *Sociology*, Anthony Giddens identifies (p. 718):

> 'a basic dilemma of theory which hardly figures at all in orthodox traditions of sociology, but which can no longer be ignored'.

This is the problem of 'incorporating' a satisfactory understanding of gender into sociological analysis. An immediate response may be that *incorporation* may not be the best method for appreciating the significance of feminism for studies of culture and communication, since feminism may call into question the very categories with which it is supposed to merge. As Giddens points out, sociology has been produced about human subjects who are treated as though they are (p. 719) "neuter" ... abstract "actors" rather than differentiated women and men'. (See Chapter 2 on identity.)

Marx believed that gender differences can be traced to class divisions, in which women had over time become the 'property' of men. Therefore, with the collapse or destruction of capitalist society, the liberation of women would follow with the establishment of socialism. Other writers have used the tools of Marxism to produce a closer analysis of the role of women in society.

Iris Young (1981), for example (see Sargent, *The Unhappy Marriage of Marxism and Feminism*, p. 50), used the concept of 'the division of labour' to argue that:

> 'the labour of women occupies a central place in any system of production, and ... sexual hierarchy is a crucial element in any system of domination'.

Young examines the inadequacy of classical Marxist theory from a socialist-feminist perspective (p. 52):

> 'Using the category of production or labour to designate *only* the making of concrete material objects in a modern factory, has been one of the unnecessary tragedies of Marxian theory.'

According to this theory, the traditional women's tasks such as child rearing should also be considered part of the *gendered* division of labour, just as the production of goods allows us to study how one class works while another reaps the rewards of ownership.

Katie Stewart (1981) investigates the social rituals associated with the creation of male identity, in a society she believes to be (Sargent, *The Unhappy Marriage*, p. 288):

> 'individualistic. Both equality and achievement depend, however, on competition, and individual differences must be constantly asserted and re-asserted.'

In all their 'bonding' activities, particularly in the realm of sport, men are caught in the conflict between individual and team achievement. Fraternal societies are seen as attempts to resolve the contradiction between *achieved* masculinity (that won in competition) and *ascribed* masculinity, that gained from the bonding between groups of men.

Any survey of feminist cultural inquiry must acknowledge that there are different currents within the broader movement. E. Ann Kaplan (1992), in *Channels of Discourse, Reassembled*, (edited by Robert C. Allen), points to the difference between *political* and *philosophical* approaches to feminism. The *philosophical* category includes 'essentialist' and 'anti-essentialist' approaches, the first of which regards the difference between the sexes as ultimately biological in origin, while the second is more interested in investigating how notions of 'the feminine' are constructed in patriarchal society. *Political* feminism is divided by Kaplan into four groups or outlooks: *bourgeois* feminism, which concentrates on achieving equal rights within the constraints of the system; *Marxist* feminism, which examines the oppression of women within a class-based analysis of power; *radical* feminism, largely separatist in its aims; and *post-structuralist* feminism, which investigates the structures of language to discover how women are excluded from the 'symbolic order'.

Feminist approaches to communication have found a number of priorities for analysis. The question of difference in *language use* has been investigated by Jennifer Coates in 1986 and 1993 (see *Women, Men and Language*). Coates advances the idea that women use language in co-operative rather than competitive ways. Some feminists go further, advancing the idea that women have been excluded from the symbolic form of language. One response has been to 'correct' the inherent bias of 'man-made' language, by altering the symbolic structure of words like 'women' so that they suggest quite different ideas ('wymyn' is one form which forces the reader to reconsider the nature of the group which is under discussion, though the term has failed to become generic and therefore seems to indicate a *faction* based on political activism). Another, perhaps more profound response, has been to explore those branches of psychology which offer ways of investigating how the female subject is created. (See references to the work of Bronwyn Davies in Chapter 2.)

Criticism of popular culture and the ways in which women are portrayed in forms like television, as well as studies of the *gendered* patterns of television consumption within the family, have appeared in the work of various authors. Kath Davies and her co-editors produced a collection in 1987 called *Out of Focus*, in which media representations of women were compared with how women perceived their own identities (see the work on gender and identity in Chapter 2). Diana Meehan made an exhaustive study of women's roles and actions in television (see *Channels of Discourse, Reassembled*). Lillian Robinson used content analysis and empirical research to discover the difference between women's real work roles and the representation of female labour through television.

Some writers, such as Tania Modleski, have concentrated upon what have become known as 'women's genres' in popular culture, in the belief that forms such as soap opera break down the distance which is maintained between spectator and text. Angela McRobbie explored the uses to which young women put popular culture, while one of the most influential film theories emerged from Laura Mulvey's conception of 'the male gaze', in which male spectators of film were thought to undergo identification with the male hero, thus exercising a controlling gaze over the female characters.

Information technology and the *gendered* use of communication has produced a range of studies; Liesbet van Zoonen (1992) has written material on feminist theory as it applies to the new media technologies, at the same time as a number of researchers have begun to investigate the domestic consumption of mass media forms.

Structuralism

Structuralism has exerted considerable influence on academic perceptions of society, culture and communication. The Swiss linguist Ferdinand de Saussure (1857–1913) argued that the true characteristics of language, its *structures*, could only be discovered by examining the rules of grammar that lie behind ordinary speech. Saussure believed that the meaning of words did not depend on their ability to refer to real objects in the world, but was created through the *differences* between closely related concepts. The meaning of the term 'knife' is found, therefore, in its relationship to other utensils such as 'spoon' and 'fork'. Saussure argued that language could be studied along two axes, one concerned with time (temporal) and the other with space (spatial). He called the first of these **diachronic** and the second **synchronic**. The investigation of language, in the structuralist sense, is an *abstract* study, one concerned with systems and structures.

Saussure also divided the study of language into **langue**, the system of rules underlying speech, and **parole**, the speech of individuals, regarded as the infinitely variable expression of those abstract rules. Langue may be translated as 'language', while parole can be defined as 'speech'. Some modern versions tend to replace langue and parole with 'code' and 'message', but these terms lack the same resonance and are actually more limited in the range of their application; 'message' in particular may reduce our appreciation of the diversity of human expression.

According to Saussure, the **sign** is made up of two aspects: the **signifier** (a physical representation of something in the real world), and the **signified** (the mental concept called to mind by the signifier). Some theorists (see Hodge and Kress in *Social Semiotics*, p. 24) consider that Saussure has failed to recognise that signifier and signified are both equally *material*, and that the result has been to create an unnecessary split between *concepts* on the one hand, and *reality* on the other.

Earlier, structuralism was described as a method of analysing textual material, in which the relationship between elements is seen as the chief factor in the creation of meaning. The structuralist approach does not, therefore, attempt to estimate the *value* of what is studied. Since the sense of any narrative form (the novel, television drama, or whatever) does not reside in individual details, similar events or characters may be substituted for the original elements, and the same basic meaning will emerge. As Terry Eagleton writes, in his book *Literary Theory* (p. 96):

> 'if the particular contents of the text are replaceable, there is a sense in which one can say that the "content" of the narrative is its own structure . . .

the narrative is in a way about itself; its "subject" is its own internal relations'.

Anyone who regularly watches a television series may notice the repetition, from week to week, of identical themes and elements. A series is often based on a central character and the typical actions that character performs. Structuralist analysis is a useful way of gaining insight into textual meaning, though some measurement of audience response is also required.

Post-structuralism and deconstruction

A thing or event which carries the prefix 'post' means a phenomenon which comes **after** something else. There are a number of currents running through post-structuralism, but it is characterised by its hostility to what it sees as the illusions of absolute truth and the fixed meanings described in structuralist thought.

Some post-structuralist thinkers, like Deleuze and Guattari (who produced a book called *Anti-Oedipus: Capitalism and Schizophrenia* in 1977), express an interest in notions of the 'pre-symbolic' human being, an individual supposedly more in touch with fundamental truths. They point to children, primitive peoples, and the mad as examples of pre-symbolic individuals. Madness is regarded not as an alien experience but as the source of spontaneous behaviour, in which desire is pure and there is no such thing as the 'whole' person; instead, madness recognises the fragmented nature of the human personality. Other writers associated with the post-structuralist tradition include Lyotard, Foucault and Derrida.

Jean-Francois Lyotard was for many years a member of a small left-wing group, and for much of his career his work was informed by a Marxist outlook. His departure from this perspective was signalled by his increasing hostility towards what he saw as the restrictive rationalism of leftist thought.

In the 1960s, Michel Foucault's work was focused upon language and how the human subject was created discursively. In his later work, Foucault turned to consider how people are 'constituted' by the relationships of power. Foucault is therefore an important source for those interested in the relationship between discourse and politics.

Jacques Derrida produced a number of influential books in the late 1960s, which drew attention to the shortcomings of structuralist theory. He is now regarded as the foremost exponent of 'deconstruction', a technique of close textual analysis designed to reveal how writers use concepts in an inconsistent way, and therefore how a text can fail to make sense on its own terms.

While the mathematician C.S. Peirce had introduced the idea of the importance of context, insisting that a sign (a word, an image, a sound) should be *interpretable* in accordance with prevailing conventions, Derrida argued that the relationship between *signifier* and *signified* was not as straightforward as structuralists believed. It is not fixed; new meanings keep arising. In the words of Madan Sarup (see *An Introductory Guide to Post-structuralism and Postmodernism*, p. 36):

> 'Meaning is scattered or dispersed along the whole chain of signifiers; it cannot be easily nailed down, it is never fully present in one sign alone.'

At first sight, the idea that meaning is not 'fully present' in a sign can seem quite strange. Derrida believed, however, that the sign's relationship to 'the present ... to a present reality ... is always deferred' (see *Positions*, pp. 28–9). The reason for this deferment lies in the notion that reality is never *immediate* or 'present' because it is always *mediated* by language.

Derrida opposed the belief that the human individual is able to grasp meaning *intuitively*, and argued that human consciousness has to use signs in order to understand any event. He advanced the idea of 'differentiality', or *differance*, which means both 'differing' and 'deferring'. In his view, every new signifier is also a signified, so that we are faced with a never-ending chain of references, each of which 'puts off' final interpretation; every sign is therefore supposed to carry a 'trace' of other signs.

Derrida appears, up to a point, as the champion of free interpretation, standing against the rather mechanical outlook of traditional structuralist practice. We should not forget, however, that Derrida is more likely to argue for the impossibility of discovering meaning at all than simply for a more 'liberal' approach to analysis. Stuart Sim poses the problem in the following way (*Beyond Aesthetics*, p. 40):

> 'It is when we come to ask ourselves what is being offered positively in the wake of the negative critique that the problems begin in earnest with Derrida's post-structuralism.'

John Sturrock (see *Structuralism*) notes Derrida's preference for the written over the spoken word. Derrida believed that the study of writing had been neglected in semiology, and that the 'intimacy' of speech, where the individual imagines his or her own words to be an immediate and true representation of meaning, was a misleading illusion. Derrida was more concerned to demonstrate the 'impersonality' of the sign, and did so most easily through the study of written language. He was opposed to the 'phonocentrism' of linguistic studies (the emphasis on sound as meaning). Sturrock explains Derrida's preference thus (p. 141):

> 'it is when sequences of words are written and thus made permanent that we are easily able to think of them as somehow existing simultaneously'.

This would of course be possible; if we read a phrase instead of hearing it spoken, we are perhaps more inclined to notice its abstract qualities. Derrida's rejection of speech in favour of the written text suggests that it is precisely the immediacy of speech which may pose a challenge to his theory. Chapter 5 pursues this idea in greater detail.

Postmodernism

Like modernism, postmodernism appears in a variety of guises. In architecture it makes itself felt as a deliberately disordered and 'ahistorical' amalgam of styles. In theories of capitalist production it is presented as a 'post-industrial' and anti-monolithic trend. In critical theory, it is expressed as a hostile response to all 'totalising' discourses, by which it means any philosophies which attempt to offer a 'closed' or even systematic critique of the social, political and moral order. Writers associated with postmodernism include Lyotard, Derrida and Jean Baudrillard (whose thought is described in Chapter 5).

Postmodernism not only distrusts all 'meta-narratives' (any large-scale theories which attempt to provide a 'total' critique of society) but also marks a departure from every aspect of 'enlightenment' thinking (social theories characterised by their pursuit of rationality). Where materialists like Adorno and Horkheimer warned against the dangers of the capitalist 'enlightenment', postmodernism calls into question the whole purpose of systematic inquiry and the various perspectives upon which it is based.

Liberalism, Marxism, structuralism – any systems in fact which appear to advance a rational critique of human society – have, according to postmodernism, simply been engaged in the perpetuation of fantasy or myth. Some extreme forms of postmodernism take this a stage further, attacking any critical theory which even attempts coherence or which argues that it is still necessary to establish a dividing line between truth and fiction. Engaging with postmodernist argument is therefore made difficult by its tendency to assume that anyone using a particular kind of 'discourse', based on a supposedly 'defunct' system of thought, must inevitably produce observations which amount to no more than misunderstandings, delusions or attempts to force social life into a strait-jacket of theory.

One of the major reasons given for the onset of the 'postmodern' is the rise of the mass media and the 'information society'. Postmodernist thinkers consider that this marks a radical departure from the past and that older systems of thought and inquiry are unable to make sense of the new sort of society we inhabit. Another tenet of postmodernist thought is the idea that the 'chain' of signification has been broken, that images and ideas no longer have links to a real state of affairs, but instead refer only to other sets of images, other discourses within society. The 'floating' signifier is often attributed to the cultural dominance of the media industry; within this concept lies the possibility of creating a radical critique of its practices.

David Harvey, in *The Condition of Postmodernity*, believes that postmodernism has the potential for creating certain positive effects, largely based upon its (p. 113) 'concern for difference, for the complexity and nuances of interests, cultures, places'. A number of other commentators also draw attention to this potential. Stuart Sim, for example (see *Beyond Aesthetics*), notes that postmodern theory is useful in so far as it reminds philosophers of the weakness of 'total' systems, but that it is less helpful when it takes this challenge to extremes (p. 136):

> 'It becomes questionable only when the transition is made from theories . . . to theory, and the theoretical imperative, *in general*.'

It is worth noting that many postmodernist tendencies seem to echo some of the 'post-industrial' strategies of governments and large corporations. David Harvey recognises that there are various *tendencies* (organised directions of thought) within postmodernism, including one which appears to celebrate the chaos of the capitalist marketplace.

SUMMARY

● COMMUNICATION: DESCRIPTION AND DEFINITIONS

Despite the differences between the various definitions of communication, each attempt at description has its uses, offering those who study the subject a variety of positions from which to explore the social construction of meaning. An understanding of communication emerges from the relationship between the following five 'components': **transmission**, **exchange**, the **generation of meaning**, **context** and **discourse**.

● Theories of transmission

Communication may be defined as the **transmission** of various types of data from one individual to another, or from an institution to an audience. Transmission means the transfer of information from a source to a receiver. This implies that the purpose of communication is to deliver messages.

● From transmission to exchange

An advance on theories of transmission may be found in definitions which stress the constant **exchange** within a society (and between societies) of words, images, signs, gestures and other forms. The usual term for the process of exchange is **interaction** (the action and reaction which takes place between the different parties involved).

● The generation of meaning: symbolic form and content

More sophisticated definitions of communication direct our attention to the generation of **meaning**, concentrating on the use of **symbolic forms** by human beings. Symbolic forms include the spoken and written language, as well as other modes of communication which are recognised within a specific culture

● Communication as contextual meaning

The idea that meaning emerges when communication takes place within a specific **context** has become increasingly popular. For example, the exact nature of a speech event's meaning will depend upon a number of 'influences' such as the *intention* of the communicators, the *relationship* between the participants, and the location or setting in which the utterance is used.

● Communication as discourse

The idea that communication is the utterance of meaningful **discourse** emerged from linguistics. The term 'discourse' originally referred to an utterance larger than a sentence, but was extended to include any coherent expression of ideas. Communication theorists use the term to describe the *social* process of creating meaning, through the use of language and other symbolic forms.

● Definition: a summary

Communication may be defined as **an activity in which *symbolic content* is not merely *transmitted* from one source to another, but *exchanged* between human agents, who interact within a shared situational and/or discursive *context*.**

COMMUNICATION STUDIES: PERSPECTIVES AND APPROACHES

A **perspective** on something means the way in which a particular subject or issue is understood or valued. Used in an academic context, the term refers to *a point of view* held regarding the worth or function of a discipline or an aspect of study. An **approach** means a way of *dealing with* or getting to grips with a subject.

Research which concentrates on **transmission** is often criticised for showing a preoccupation with the *efficiency* of the communication process, over and above other considerations, so that meaning and social context are likely to suffer neglect.

A preoccupation with **exchange** could indicate a number of different approaches, depending on which elements in the process are thought most worthy of attention. These approaches might include *transactional analysis* and other *subjective* methods.

Theorists whose studies deal with the **generation of meaning** are likely to have inherited some of their methods from structuralism, a type of critical inquiry which proposes that the individual elements of a text or communication event create meaning only when contrasted with other 'units' belonging to the same structure.

Research into **context** is popular among academics who want to emphasise the *social* nature of the communication process, and wish to stress other variables besides those associated with textual elements. Context may refer to the immediate or *situational* features which surround an event, or to the wider social, political and historical circumstances which give meaning to events.

Discourse *analysis* is used by linguists who wish to examine the ordinary modes of speech used in conversation, while theories of *discourse and power* have emerged from the work of post-structuralist writers like Michel Foucault.

● ORGANISING THE SUBJECT
● Social vs. communication phenomena

Ultimately, the role of all communication theorists, whatever their individual perspective, is to investigate no less than the production, circulation and interpretation of meaning within a society, but a distinction has to be made between **social** phenomena and communication.

● Making choices

Clearly, some choices in organising content have to be made, otherwise it would be impossible to handle the raw material found in the subject. At the same time, however, the process of selection will always reveal the particular standpoint of the individual theorist. The following list is used to organise the subject:

- Acceptable boundaries between different *forms* of communication must be drawn.
- Broad *categories* of communication should be recognised.
- The various *uses* and *purposes* of communication need to be described.
- Definite points should be set in time and space where specific examples of communication – usually called *acts* or *events* – can be said to begin and end.
- Broad *conventions* (and their associated *codes*), growing from the social practice of communication, must be acknowledged.

- The diverse methods of *interpreting* written, spoken and visual material ought to be described, applied and evaluated.

In essence, this method of organisation treats communication as though it is *divisible* (able to be divided into recognised units) and *finite* (limited in size and duration).

FORMS OF COMMUNICATION

Forms are the ways in which communication manifests itself. They can be organised as follows:

- **oral** – the spoken expression of ideas and events through verbal language and expressive sound;
- **written** – the accepted and codified symbols of a language, reproduced in a variety of styles and traditions by individuals;
- **printed** – the codified symbols of languages as above, presented on paper in forms of type or 'fonts';
- **non-verbal** – expressive gesture belonging to individuals, whether intentional or unintentional;
- **pictorial** – such as representational drawing and fine art;
- **graphical/symbolic** – (diagrammatic and non-representational);
- **technological** – the methods and perspectives used by a range of institutions and individuals to reproduce communication acts.

CATEGORIES OF COMMUNICATION

The term **categories** as it is used in this context refers to the most basic divisions between types of communication.

Intrapersonal

Intrapersonal communication, described as that which occurs *within* and therefore *with the self*, is usually placed first in the list of categories. Although it is often regarded as the category from which the other divisions emerge, not all theorists find this acceptable. The beginning of Chapter 2 is devoted to the question of the 'intrapersonal' and proposes a solution to the problem of its status.

In the meantime, the intrapersonal may be said to include:

- perception;
- cognitive and reflective thought processes;
- emotional responses;
- attitudes, values and beliefs;
- subjectivity and self-concept;
- the creation and interpretation of meaning.

These are not, however, exclusively 'internal' elements or processes. Every one of these elements depends upon the individual's action within and reaction to a specific social context.

Interpersonal

Interpersonal communication is often defined as that which occurs when *two people* are engaged in some form of *communicative exchange*. Interpersonal communication includes the following elements:

- mutual recognition;
- reciprocal exchange using available codes;
- the creation and interpretation of meaning;
- awareness of physical and social context;
- the assumption of personal and social roles;
- some change of state, whether intellectual, emotional or physical.

Group

Group communication requires *a collection of individuals* who share some *common attributes, goals or interests*. The individuals concerned will interact within the context of the group and will share or at least display *common values* or *norms of behaviour*. All group *communication* must be founded on the following elements:

- a perception of the group's identity, broadly common to its members;
- the ability to differentiate between the group and its allies or rivals;

- a knowledge of aims and objectives within the group, whether those aims are agreed or imposed;
- participation in interpersonal exchange using available codes and channels of communication, both formal and informal;
- the assumption of formal and informal roles.

Group theory also recognises divisions between *large* and *small* groups, between *formal* and *informal* groups, and between groups which people join voluntarily and those to which individuals belong without advance consent.

Mass

The media are usually identified as those *formal bodies engaged in the industrial production and circulation of meaning*. **Mass** communication is a category which includes all the *institutional practices* of the mass media, and which also refers to the *scale of communication* supposedly achieved by the media. Mass communication possesses these essential features:

- high levels of industrial activity;
- formal, centralised organisation;
- institutionalised values and practices;
- the mediation of authority;
- large scale of operation;
- a 'standardised' product directed to a mass audience;
- the possibility of simultaneous reception of messages by audiences.

Extrapersonal

Extrapersonal communication can be described as communication *between machines*. It does not, strictly speaking, include communication between individual *humans* and machines, but only that between machines which supposedly require little human intervention. The salient feature of the extrapersonal may be summarised as:

- the processing of some form of meaningful or potentially meaningful signal, between machines requiring human input but little supervision during the duration of the process itself.

USES AND PURPOSES

Uses and purposes are usually discussed under one heading. **Use** refers to how communication, in whatever form, is employed, while **purpose** means the end result intended when a communication act is planned. Uses and purposes include:

- **socialisation**;
- the **social functional or ritual**;
- the **instrumental**;
- the **persuasive**;
- the **expressive**.

Socialisation

The *uses* and *purposes* of communication include **socialisation**, where human subjects acquire values, roles and norms through a variety of influences.

The social functional or ritual

Closely related to socialisation is the **social functional or ritual**, whose purpose is to help 'affiliate' people to other individuals, institutions or societies. Ritual *behaviour* is essentially a formalised type of communicative behaviour. The phatic uses of communication may be included in this category.

The instrumental

One of the most basic uses of communication is the **instrumental**, meaning quite simply the deployment of content in order to achieve or obtain something. **Affective** communication may be included under this heading, as that which is designed to make an impact on an individual or a group. Instrumental uses also include the **informative**.

The persuasive

The **persuasive** function of communication is sometimes described as that of 'control', but really constitutes *structures which are used to manipulate* the actions or cognitions of individuals, groups or institutions. The **interpellative** function of communication grows purely from the relations of power in society, and is understood as the address made by authority to any subordinate group or individual. **Ideological** communication is the production of meaning drawn from a particular system of belief.

The expressive

When described as a *use* of communication, the **expressive** is the representation of personal or aesthetic feelings. It is linked with the idea of creativity. **Narrative** uses of communication are an interesting sub-division of expressive form.

COMMUNICATION: ACTS AND EVENTS

There is a difference between a communication **act** and a communication **event**. An act is usually regarded as a single deed, a deliberate action on the part of an individual or collective source. An event, on the other hand, is conceived as something which happens without necessarily requiring human intervention. An event is thought to possess a clear beginning and a definite end, and is supposed to be identified by virtue of its difference to other occurrences.

Acts and events: genre and performance

Malcolm Coulthard, writing in *An Introduction to Discourse Analysis*, provides another approach to the problem of distinguishing between an *event* and an *act*. He refers to the linguist Hymes, and his description of speech events as **genre** and speech acts as the 'doing' of a genre, or **performance**.

CONVENTIONS AND CODES

In *Communication* (p. 6), McQuail argues that 'communication necessitates the conscious manipulation of physical forces and objects according to agreed rules and conventions'. All communicative forms, including speech, gesture, writing, graphic design, music, film, broadcast talk and so on, have **codes** and **conven-**

tions which have become established through use, but which in some cases, such as language, appear to be based on *innate* abilities.

METHODS OF INTERPRETATION

Methods of interpretation are many and varied, but the techniques of analysis actually employed are usually suggested by the *form* of the communication event or text being studied. Methods of interpretation include:

- content and structural analysis;
- empirical comparison;
- ideological analysis;
- role and expression;
- contextual analysis;
- media analysis;
- narrative approaches.

TEXT AND CONTEXT

This section explores how a variety of analytical approaches grow from the study of a printed text. It presents an extended analysis of a short conversation or exchange between two unnamed individuals.

MODELS OF COMMUNICATION

A **model** of a communication process is 'a consciously *simplified description* in *graphic form* of a piece of reality'. This means that an idea about communication is expressed in a drawing or design, which is kept as simple as possible; the purpose is to make communication theory more accessible.

Structural and functional models

The basic distinction between types of model are those which are **structural** (usually representing the static components of an *object*) and those described as **functional**. The functional type is supposed to show the forces involved in an *event*, as well as the parts, actors or contexts involved in communication. They must represent dynamic elements like, for example, the direction of messages and responses.

● Mechanical models?

The simplest models of communication involve message, sender and receiver. The famous Lasswell 'formula' of 1948 (Figure 1.4) asks a number of simple questions which may be applied to any communication act; **who** says **what**, in which **channel**, to **whom**, with what **effect**? Lasswell, interested at the time in political persuasion and propaganda, was anxious to establish ideas about effect. The 'says' clearly does not need to be taken as a literal indicator of speech, but of some form of human expression.

Shannon and Weaver, in a model intended as a scientific or objective guide to the possibilities of sending successful messages (Figure 1.5), included an *information source*, the *message*, the sender or *transmitter* who supplies the message, the *signal*, a *receiver* of the message, and the *received signal*. Along the route, there might be external interference of some sort, which was at one time called *noise*.

Criticisms of transmission models

The most common criticism of the two models illustrated above is that they represent a linear, one-way process. Most writers insist that inter-personal communication always involves a two-way interaction.

A defence of Shannon and Weaver

We should ask what this particular model helps to explain, as well as criticising it for what it neglects. It is exactly its 'mechanical' nature that might help remind us of the *physiological* factors involved in human communication, allowing insight into, for example, the mechanical reproduction of speech.

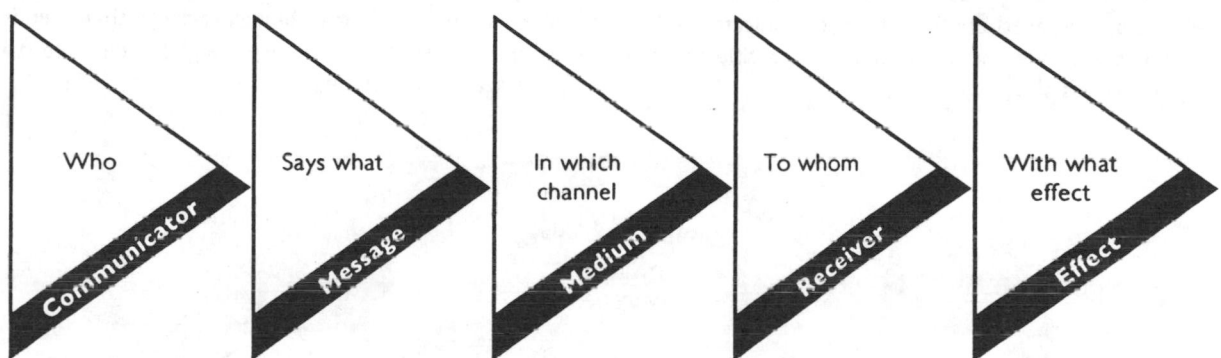

Figure 1.4   After Lasswell, 1948: a model of a communication act

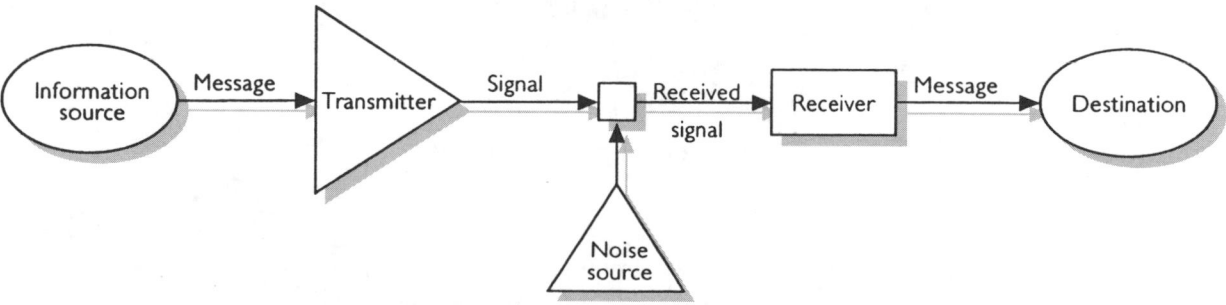

Figure 1.5   After Shannon and Weaver: a model of the communication process

Communication practices

In the case of communication **form**, individuals use a battery of devices to create meaning. Speech will be accompanied by non-verbal signals. Writing and graphical communication will be employed together in order to create a more powerful impact on an audience.

The ability to mark out where communication begins and ends, and to say what type of communication is taking place, emphasises the idea of distinct communication *events*.

Simple and more complex models: from McQuail

Version 1

In this model (Fig. 1.6) adapted from McQuail's written description (detailed above), the communicator A has become the sender, a more appropriate title for the simple process shown.

Version 2

In Figure 1.7, the messages sent now travel in two directions, and the intention of each participant has been divided into two areas – *exposed* and *concealed*.

REFERENCE TO THE WORLD
What comes first: content or structure?

How are symbolic systems put together and used? The opposing approaches to this could be summarised in two fundamental questions:

- Are symbolic systems made by inventing basic 'units' of meaning, building blocks upon which complete systems are then founded?
- Alternatively, do human beings carry in their minds symbolic systems, structures which are able to generate individual ideas?

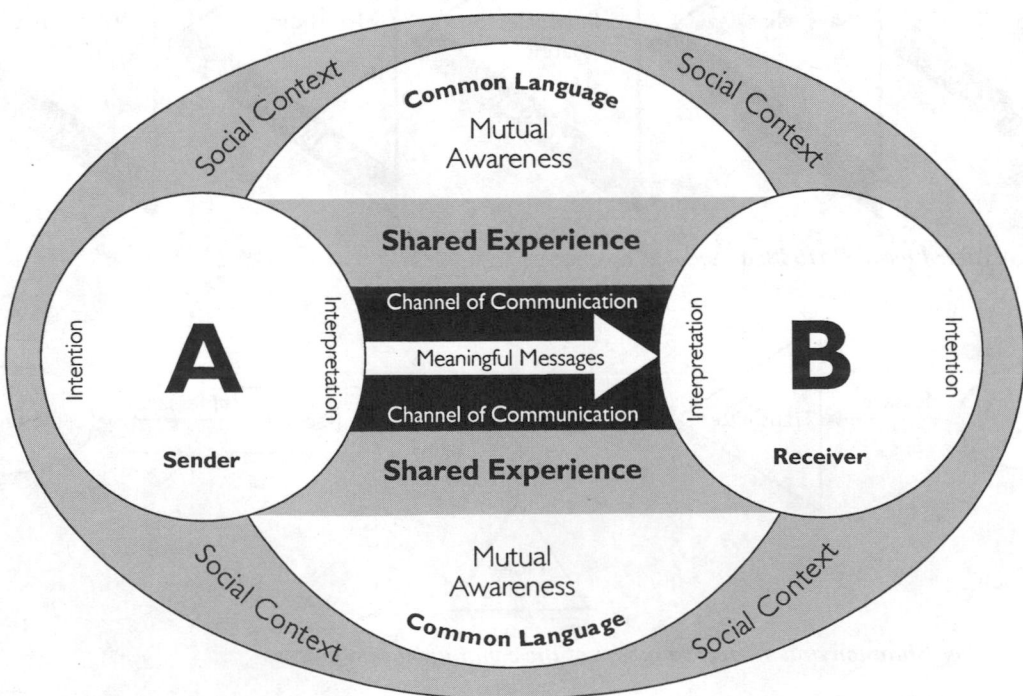

Figure 1.6   After McQuail's description: version 1

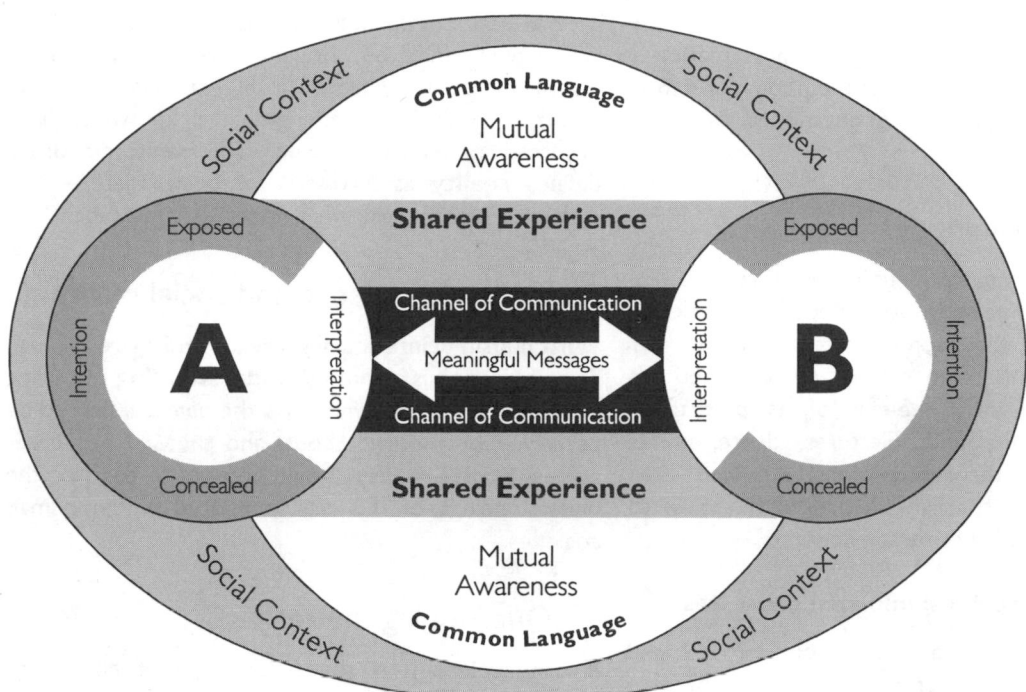

Figure 1.7   After McQuail's description: version 2

● Universal structures?

Noam Chomsky suggested that the human species is genetically predisposed to acquire language systems. He also pointed out that people seem to know instinctively when a sentence is ungrammatical, even when that sentence has never before been encountered. Most theorists are beginning to accept the idea that the human brain is specifically equipped to acquire language.

● Forms of communication

To be able to *report* our awareness of the external world, to produce meaning about things, about other individuals and events, we employ communicative systems which manipulate signs or symbols.

● Mental replicas?

Mainstream theorists argue that the agreed symbol for an idea or thing or concept will, when it is perceived, prompt us to recall the idea, thing or concept itself. However, a single word is capable of doing more than provoking a recollection of formal elements; it might also create a *feeling*, since words are bound to carry an emotive charge.

● Internal symbolisation?

The existence of symbolic content has led some writers to argue that there is also a process called 'internal symbolisation' or the production of sets of mental *representations*. This could be explained as the existence of a 'fund' of images and symbols, collected together as memories, and used whenever the occasion requires that we refer to an aspect of experience.

● The theory of representation: 'internal' and 'external'

Representation is used to describe both the process of creating **internal** or mental versions of the real, and the mobilisation of these internal versions for **external** use. The notion of internal representation is still one of the staple concepts of communication theory, but has begun to be questioned by some theorists.

Informal meanings?

Many aspects of *human* communication, which are vital to the creation of meaning, do not appear to function in the tidy way that some writers imagine. For example, meaning is often created through methods which are not usually thought of as particularly systematic or rule-bound. Gestures, dance, mime, music, visual and three-dimensional art, and even expressive sounds (especially intonation) all appear to create specific meaning in certain contexts.

The power of emotions: informal processes

Are the 'experiences' we carry in our minds based upon stored *images* alone? People seem to be able to link a sound most easily to an emotional quality, and perhaps less easily to a specific object. While much human memory mobilises 'visions' of the past, such visualisations often include memories of sound. Memories are meaningful because they call up emotional states associated with past experience.

Naming and categorising

The most fundamental part of the shared knowledge possessed by any society or group must be what people are able to agree exists, including the ideas and objects which individuals name. The first stage of categorisation is **naming**; the second is the placing of what is named in groups or **categories** which are supposed to share some common features or elements.

QUESTIONS OF REALITY
Definitions of reality

The **real** is defined in the *Concise Oxford Dictionary* as 'actually existing as a thing or occurring in fact'. There is

a close relationship between *thing* and *fact*. A **thing** is whatever may be thought about or perceived, whether that is animate (living) or inanimate (an object). A **fact** is something that is known to have occurred or which is true. The same dictionary defines **reality** as 'property of being real ... real existence, what is real, what underlies appearances'.

Shared knowledge and social reality

What human beings actually 'create' and share through communication is a **shared understanding** of reality, where reality is that which has the *potential* first to be perceived or thought about, and then to be represented. **Social reality** should be used to describe the understandings of the real circulated within human societies.

Questioning the real

If communication is the *presentation* of knowledge about the environment we inhabit, then it would be useful briefly to identify the arguments which:

- attempt either to support or contradict the notion that the world is there in the first place to be represented;
- support or contradict the idea that our perception of the world is broadly accurate.

Realism and anti-realism

Any philosophical position may be called **realist** if it argues in favour of the actual existence, whether perceived by human beings or not, of material things and objects. **Anti-realist** positions include those which either question the actual existence of things and objects, or state that we are only able to perceive the existence of symbolic systems, or logical structures, or ideas.

Platonic realism: universals and particulars

The Ancient Greek philosopher Plato thought that knowledge consisted of the apprehension of universal 'forms' which contained the true meanings of all general terms. The **universals** are supposed to be real, but our senses are unable to perceive them. We perceive only the *particular* object, idea or creature.

Anti-realist positions: idealism, nominalism, phenomenologism

Idealism may be understood as the doctrine that reality is in fact a mental phenomenon, based on ideas (and not, as some suppose, 'ideals'). **Nominalism** promotes the idea that all we are actually able to know is the names or classes of things in the world, taking the view that there are no such things as the Platonic 'universals', but rather *paradigms*, reliable examples of a particular class of thing or creature, to which others may be compared. **Phenomenologism** is an approach which begins with the study of appearances, involving the belief that things have an essence which may be discovered through description.

● Human senses and the real: sensory deception?

Some cultural theorists and philosophers believe that there is a 'weak link' in the chain of what makes up the real. They argue that if the real can only be perceived by human senses, then all we can know for sure is the *data gathered by the senses* through perception, not the reality which lies behind it.

● Realist responses

It makes sense to argue that there is no *exact* correlation between the world and the ways in which it is perceived. This does not mean that a realist would need to abandon the idea that real objects do exist. Some writers argue that the real and the basic categories of human experience may not coincide exactly, but do correspond very closely.

● Descartes: the search for reliable knowledge

René Descartes was a mathematician and philosopher who was born in the closing years of the sixteenth century. Descartes decided to test received ideas about knowledge and truth, in an attempt to isolate only that knowledge which could be regarded as completely reliable.

Descartes and the certainty of existence

After the process of investigation was complete, the only fact that Descartes felt to be reliable was that he himself existed. In order to doubt the reality of the world, Descartes would have to go through some process of thought. The act of thinking would prove his own status as a real and independent being. This gave rise to the famous declaration, 'I think, therefore I am.'

● Empiricism: the primacy of experience

Some philosophers have asked whether we require or use absolutely certain knowledge. For most ordinary purposes, they argue that all we need to possess is *probable* knowledge. This is known as **empiricism**.

● More questions on representation

Some writers have turned their attention from interrogating the status of the real to questioning the Western tradition, which has for so long made a distinction between an external world and the internal 'version' of reality which is supposedly located in the human mind. John Shotter argues that this conceptualisation of ourselves is not universally shared among the peoples of the world, discovering that some cultures do not construct a version of the internal 'mind'.

Representation and structures

In *Thought and Language*, Moravcsik notes that some objects of thought, like chess, mathematics and logic (p. 80), 'are made up partly of constitutive rules'. He deduces from this that 'it is reasonable to assume that we must have a cognitive representation of a system of rules'. The existence of a cognitive system would, as Moravcsik says, suggest that representational thought exists.

● Human communication and society

The sense we have of our 'place' in the world depends on (McQuail, *Communication*, p. 4), 'a set of understandings, a framework of shared meanings' which 'enables people to orient themselves to each other and inhabit a common environment'. McQuail argues that 'the common understandings' we share encompass more than simply the perception and naming of physical events and objects. They include the 'obligations, rules and views of what is desirable'.

● COMMUNICATION STUDIES: TRADITIONS

A number of communication traditions are explored:

- the 'student-centred' approach;
- the 'skills' tradition;
- 'individualist' approaches;
- interpersonal relations;
- functionalism;
- symbolic interactionism;
- the Marxist tradition;
- feminist approaches;
- structuralism;
- post-structuralism and deconstruction;
- postmodernism.

CHAPTER 2

The social subject

Intrapersonal communication?

When **intrapersonal communication** is discussed, two distinct aspects of the subject are usually indicated. One is the common assumption that the activities which take place within the individual (perception, cognition, memory and emotional responses) are indeed types of internal *communication*. Psychologists like G.H. Mead (1934) believed that a person 'interacts' with the self, making an address to self and responding to that address.

The second aspect of the 'intrapersonal' typically concerns the variety of forms (speech, diaries, personal reminders and so on) through which an individual might *express* or record some feature of his or her private experience. Certain of these forms are regularly presented as examples of communication with 'the self'.

However, the idea that some types of expression reveal a world which is somehow entirely 'private' and uniquely individual needs careful scrutiny. In fact, the whole concept of 'internal' communication requires some revision.

Internal processes

The first point to be scrutinised above was the notion that a form of communication occurs within each individual. This idea depends on accepting the traditional view of a 'dual' self, in which the 'core' self and the self which supposedly *reflects* on this core are able to communicate.

In fact, self-awareness is *not* the same as communicating with oneself. For real communication to take place, an *exchange* of meaning, between distinct and separate individuals, must occur. The 'split-self' theory is perhaps an attempt to meet this requirement, but its weakness is shown by the fact that the 'core' self never answers the 'reflective' self! (See the section on 'Identity', later in this chapter.)

When we 'monitor' our own thinking, what we are actually engaged in is the *process of thought*; there is no separate 'communication event'. If we accept the idea that communication properly refers to *interaction between people*, then we must reject the proposition that thought processes have the same status. In other words, we would reach the conclusion that *thought is not communication*.

A less controversial description of the activities and events which take place inside the individual would be **internal processes**.

External expression

The second aspect of our inquiry into the intrapersonal consists of the various means by which individuals represent their internal apprehension of the world. This aspect may now be called **expression**, whether it takes the form of speech, writing, graphics, gesture, or any other recognised mode of communication.

Among those types of expression which are cited as evidence of internal communication, the diary is sometimes given pride of place. Diaries are often presented as a form in which an address is made *to the self*. Such an address is supposedly free from the constraints and demands of public communication, which always involves the presence of an audience. The diary is therefore thought to reveal the true nature of the individual's emotional and cognitive existence. In order to judge the accuracy of this belief, extracts from various diaries will be examined in a later part of this chapter.

Internal/external: a misleading division?

Although it might be convenient to identify *internal* and *external* aspects of human communication, such a distinction may have an unfortunate side-effect. We may begin to imagine a great division between thought and expression, as though one is 'private' and the other 'public'. In fact, thought and expression do appear to use different 'systems' (as we shall see when we examine the difference between expression and mental processing), but both are part of a continuous social process; the production of **meaning**. This process should be recognised as *material*, and should not be seen as belonging to some disconnected 'intellectual' sphere.

Living in a material world

What is meant when we use the term 'material'? Different meanings are intended, depending on whether a speaker is making a reference to everyday life, or is attempting to use the term in the context of academic debate.

An example of 'ordinary' usage is found in Madonna's 1985 single, 'Material Girl'. The lyrics of this song referred to life in 'a material world', where romance and the pursuit of material security are closely linked. Another example of everyday use is found when someone is described as 'materialistic'. This indicates that they are thought to be rather too interested in the value of *things* and, by implication, that they have perhaps neglected other, more important aspects of life. In sum, the concept 'materialism' is widely used to describe an outlook or belief which places the acquisition of money and possessions above all other considerations.

In the study of philosophy and politics, however, 'materialism' means something different. In its extreme form, it describes the belief that nothing exists besides solid matter, which means that there is no room for notions about religion or any reference to an 'unseen' or ideal plane of existence.

Materialism: radical approaches

Some writers, particularly those influenced by Marxism, use the term 'materialism' to refer to the idea that all societies are based upon material or *economic* foundations, and that inequalities between people arise largely because access to economic and social power is unevenly distributed. A common criticism of Marxist and other leftist philosophies is that they appear to suggest that life is capable of being 'reduced' to a material base, as though *all* human endeavour is no more than a reflex action designed to ensure individual or group survival.

In fact, most left-wing theories argue only that life is *ultimately dependent* upon material conditions, and do not suggest that culture is capable of being reduced to economic processes. In addition, very few writers now support the once popular division of society into a 'real' material base and a 'superstructure' of concepts and ideas. Such a division is unhelpful because it suggests that the world of thought and ideology is somehow less real than the world of objects.

Creative interaction

The *use* of language and other expressive systems may be prompted by each person's material interaction with the world (a world in which certain objectives must be attained if individuals are to secure the fundamental requirements of life), but human communication is essentially creative. In other words, expression may emerge from material circumstances, but does more than dwell upon basic needs, showing a tendency to look forward to new forms of social existence and organisation. Language will embody the variety of *perceptions* of human need which circulate within a society.

'Dialectical materialism' is a refinement of materialist theory which insists that matter itself is *dynamic* and subject to change, rather than fixed or static. If it is true that the material world is always in a state of flux, human beings will be forced to adapt to a variety of circumstances. Their expressive abilities will therefore be tested quite extensively, demonstrating a creative response to their environment.

Effects of expression

The idea that expression reflects the material conditions of human life, and that it has certain *effects* on the environment, is not particularly controversial. Various types of utterance, for example, will have material consequences, in the sense that the reality we inhabit may undergo some change as a result of communication. This is a fairly commonplace idea, found whenever we consider simple examples of cause and effect.

For instance, the words or written communiqués of an individual (a *social actor*) may cause some change in the natural or social environment. When one person tells another to carry out some action, and that action is performed, we have an obvious case. Notice, however, that this example does not work through expression alone. Some physical action is also required to achieve the objective. In addition, a successful outcome (the performance of the action) demands that the source of the message possess sufficient social power to make it likely that the utterance will be obeyed.

Material expression

Although the example presented above has certain limitations, the real problem lies in the shortcomings of the theory itself. The idea that language 'sets events in motion' is only part of the story. A more complete argument would be that the use of symbolic content not only influences events, but *emerges* from the conditions of material reality. Speech, for example, could then be described as an **act** because it flows from material necessity and has, in turn, a moral or *social* effect. This means that expressive acts may not always produce an immediate physical change in our surroundings, but that some alteration will nevertheless have taken place at the level of social reality, a change which may, eventually, become apparent.

For example, written instructions sent by a government minister to his or her civil servants, calling for the implementation of spending cuts, will create a set of circumstances which will alter one part of the social reality we inhabit. Sooner or later, the new conditions will have noticeable effects on human lives.

The purpose of expression

What is the *purpose* of expression? It has been variously described. It may be to effect change in the environment, or to alter the actions and attitudes of others; it may be to consolidate something which has already been achieved; or it may be to plan ahead in order to make certain desirable outcomes more likely. Some theorists believe that human communication is always *instrumental*, designed to achieve a specific objective.

Nevertheless, the human subject will often engage in expression for the sake of expression. At first, this does not seem like a very helpful remark, because it brings us back to the original question, which asks us to investigate *purpose*.

The point is, however, that people cannot help but express their thoughts and feelings, and often do so without being driven by a strong instrumental motivation. The human urge to speak is a useful example; if there is no available audience, then humans will often talk to themselves, or to inanimate objects, or to animals. The moment of expression is often the point at which an individual instinctively 'externalises' his or her thoughts.

In the last analysis, the idea that thought and expressive behaviour (despite their differences as *systems*) are part of the *same* public, social or 'discursive' process, marks a departure from not just the old 'intrapersonal' theory of human communication but, as we shall see, from many of the 'individualist' approaches which have flourished within the subject for many years (see Chapter 1). Whether it is competitive or co-operative, purposeful or 'instinctive', human expression occurs in the context of a material reality.

Conventional expression

There are of course differences between what we think, on the one hand, and what we feel it is appropriate to divulge, on the other, because all public expression operates within certain rules and conventions. When an act of communication takes place, the *content* selected for transmission will be closely related to the expressive *form* which all participants regard as suitable to the occasion.

In a court of law, for example, the purpose of speech is to use formal discourses of 'truth' and rational inquiry to work towards a conclusive outcome, the attainment of which marks the end of the event. During the event, respect is shown for due process and established authority. Turn-taking will be formalised and clearly signalled.

On the whole, convention is re-established (and sometimes reinvented) whenever interactions take place within any recognised public context. All those who engage in communication in their own right, rather than on behalf of someone else, will recognise that they may be publicly accountable for what they express. This also helps to maintain the observation of certain rules and conventions. Although individuals occasionally refuse to comply with established practices, this does not mean that they are unaware of how they are *supposed* to act in various contexts.

Meaning and action

The view of the intrapersonal domain advanced by Cronen, that it is concerned with meaning rather than action, has already been described (in Chapter 1) as misleading. Although intrapersonal or mental 'processing' is usually understood as a search for order and meaning (involving perception and interpretation), there would be no point in such functions if they were used solely for 'internal' purposes.

When individuals evaluate past and present experiences, they do so for practical reasons; they are involved in a quest for meaning and explanation. The point of internal processing is not the 'fine-tuning' of the individual psyche, but the preparation of the individual for *action* and *interaction*, for future events and encounters. This means that the purpose of 'internal' processes is really to *orientate the individual to the external or social world*. In one sense, therefore, there is no such thing as an exclusively internal or 'private' existence.

It is in fact impossible to discuss the intrapersonal dimension of communication without referring to the ways in which it is *shaped* by external forces and *expressed* through social codes. To explore this idea, we need to understand something about the systems of thought and expression which are actually used by human beings.

Thought

Descriptions of thought

'Thought' may be variously defined as the process of **cognition**, the power of **reason**, a reflective **state**, or an individual **idea**. As with all definitions, we may observe a difference in usage over time. While rationalist philosophers of the eighteenth century used it to refer to the faculty of reason, it appears in some late eighteenth- and early nineteenth-century literature as the description of a private, *reflective* state. Wordsworth's definition of poetry as 'emotion recollected in tranquillity' comprises part of this tradition. Sometimes, especially in the more dramatic forms of Romantic verse, thought appears as a type of creative agitation which the writer or protagonist seems partly to dread.

Creative thought

The thought process involved in the production of literature, particularly verse, is often characterised as a mysterious process, a kind of mental short-circuit over which no writer has complete control. Ted Hughes's widely anthologised poem 'The Thought-Fox', which first appeared in a collection of 1957, is a well-known description of the creative process;

> 'Something else is alive
> Beside the clock's loneliness
> And this blank page where my fingers move.'

This is the thought-fox, which 'sets neat prints into the snow', moving forward until it suddenly 'enters the dark hole of the head' and 'the page is printed'.

Hughes, in keeping with the subject matter, does not attempt to explain, but rather is able to *reproduce* the sensation of a process which seems to by-pass cognition (notice that the creative impulse is an 'animal', not a person). The most suitable vehicle for an exposition of this act is the verse form itself, because a 'reasoned' analysis would violate the terms of the insight which is offered. As the poem is read, so the process of creation is to some degree experienced by the reader.

The nineteenth-century poet Gerard Manley Hopkins described the production of verse as a process which begins with acute feeling or emotion, producing thought which leads in turn to a long period of gestation. In his sonnet of 1889, 'To R.B.', the metaphor of conception is employed. The moment of inspiration is the 'father', while the mind itself is the 'mother':

> 'The fine delight that fathers thought; the strong
> Spur, live and lancing like the blowpipe flame,
> Breathes once and, quenched faster than it came,
> Leaves yet the mind a mother of immortal song.'

This writer sees the creative impulse as 'a fine delight', an emotional experience which leads to thought. Once again, the initial cause of poetic expression is described as a form of inspiration and not as a deliberate cognitive process.

A place of refuge?

However it is characterised, the seat of thought is popularly regarded as the mind, a place of refuge and the stronghold of human individuality. George Orwell examines this idea in *Nineteen Eighty-Four*, a novel which was for many years held up by right-wing politicians as a warning against any form of socialism. In fact, it grew from Orwell's experiences as an anti-fascist in Republican Spain, where he experienced the conduct of the Spanish Communist Party as well as the actions of the Nationalist rebels.

Assault on the mind

In *Nineteen Eighty-Four*, Winston Smith is surrounded by the propaganda of a totalitarian state. Oceania, a nightmare society led by 'Big Brother', includes the island Airstrip One, once known as England. The political slogans of the party which controls Oceania are heard and seen everywhere, and Big Brother's portrait appears in every possible public context (p. 25):

> 'On coins, on stamps, on the covers of books, on banners, on posters, and on the wrappings of a cigarette packet – everywhere. Always the eyes watching you and the voice enveloping you. Asleep or awake, working or eating, indoors or out of doors, in the bath or in bed – no escape. Nothing was your own except the few cubic centimetres inside your skull.'

'The few cubic centimetres' inside the skull refers of course to the human mind, imagined here as the last bastion against the total control of the state. In such a society, free or critical thought is regarded as dangerous, and the dissenter must take care not to betray any emotion which might reveal his or her true state of mind (p. 53):

'It was terribly dangerous to let your thoughts wander ... The smallest thing could give you away. A nervous tic, an unconscious look of anxiety, a habit of muttering to yourself – anything that carried with it the suggestion of abnormality, of having something to hide.'

By the end of the narrative, the individual mind has fallen to the onslaught of the corporate state (p. 239):

'it was all right, everything was all right, the struggle was finished. He had won the victory over himself. He loved Big Brother.'

Composite conceptions: image, language, abstraction

Thought consists of what Harré and Gillett (see *The Discursive Mind*, p. 47) call 'composite' conceptions, made up of:

- *particular* ideas about specific objects;
- *general* concepts about the world.

These conceptions include **images**, the 'pictures' of things we create in our minds. They also include **linguistic** elements, since it is clear that we also use some features of language in our thought processes. Such processes also involve more **abstract** elements; one example would be when a mathematical property is brought to mind. In addition, thinking about individual sounds or musical notes suggests that the brain has the ability to engage in abstract conceptions.

In sum, it seems clear that not all thought is pictorial or based on linguistic description. Harré and Gillett argue this point when they observe that (p. 46):

'it would be absurd to say that someone was not thinking when they were cogitating about something unpictureable ... or non-linguistic (such as the aroma of coffee)'.

Stephen Pinker, in *The Language Instinct*, argues that thought constitutes an entirely separate system from that used when human beings engage in various forms of expression. 'Mentalese' is the term he employs to describe the system used in thought. This is discussed in more detail later in this chapter.

Purity of thought?

It may be, however, that there are very few thoughts which do not use pictorial or linguistic elements at *some* point in their production. Images are particularly useful. For example, when I think about a supposedly abstract phenomenon, such as the smell of coffee, I find it difficult not to introduce a picture of a cup or a jar (sorry, only images of instant decaffeinated are available in this book). It is equally difficult to use a purely abstract concept when thinking about some mathematical property; words and pictures tend to intrude.

Auditory knowledge

In his contribution to the volume edited by McAdams and Bigand, *Thinking in Sound*, Robert G. Crowder describes experiments in auditory processing and auditory memory. He makes a case for the specific existence of **auditory knowledge**, and outlines his investigations into the ability of the human subject to reproduce sound and retrieve musical sequences from memory.

One of his most interesting observations is that *timbre* in music or speech (the characteristic quality of a particular instrument or voice) is difficult to describe or reproduce, but that we are nevertheless able to distinguish between different timbres. In fact, Crowder regards simple melodies and 'spoken language units' as less reliable examples of 'pure' auditory memory than timbre. He suggests that (p. 135) 'memory for this auditory quality [timbre], ... is not likely to be re-coded into some other format'. The concept of 're-coding' here refers to the ways in which information is stored in the memory.

Thought and expression

From what we have seen above, we may realise that **images** (graphical communication), **language** (speech and text), and other, more **abstract** expressive systems are all used in the process of communication. In addition, more recent accounts of human understanding (particularly the fields known as 'discursive psychology' and 'critical linguistics') argue that both images and linguistic elements are able to generate meaning because human subjects *know how to use them* in real situations. Or, put another way, units of speech, words on a page, or graphical designs are known to carry specific meanings when used in a variety of *contexts*.

The importance of context

Context can refer to the place of one unit within a larger system (a word in a sentence, for example), but more usually means the immediate physical *situation* in which a communicative event takes place, combined with the *form* of the event. In the case of an informal conversation in a public house, for example, the physical situation would be the pub itself and the spatial relationship of those conversing, while the *form* would be the accepted mode of informal behaviour usually displayed by the participants in any speech event which occurs within that situation.

'Context' is also used to indicate the wider *social* context in which an event takes place, which could be described as the 'universal' form of all public discourses. This would include all the freedoms and constraints conferred by society as a whole on the general form of any communication event.

Meaning and events

As we saw in Chapter 1, a full *analysis* of any speech event (and perhaps any instance of communication) must include knowledge of structure, setting, participants, purposes, key, topic, channel and the form and content of a message. Of course, when individuals choose to communicate they do not require knowledge of these divisions, because they are familiar with the contexts in which they must act, and therefore understand the appropriate ways of behaving in those situations.

People engaged in communication also understand the principle that a change of context will alter meaning just as surely as a change of content. Although content and context are usually regarded as separate (for example, the units of meaning in an utterance, and the tone of voice in which those units are delivered), the two are in fact closely related. If we take the situational context of the public-house conversation, the movement of the participants to a formal setting will often mean that certain types of content are unlikely to appear. In this way, context may be seen to be closely linked to the production of content.

Everything we have encountered in this chapter tends to reinforce the idea that expression is a *social* as well as a *creative* act. Expression (speech for example), grows from the same root as internal processing (thought). The common root shared by intrapersonal processing and external communication may be found in their dependence on the same genetic predispositon shared by all humans – the impulse to express themselves. Both thought and expression are shaped by the public events in which individuals participate, although the 'expressive impulse' itself exists independently.

The 'content' of thought is supposed to be constructed from familiar public material. As long ago as 1949, Gilbert Ryle had argued against the idea of a separate 'shadow world' of thought, insisting that there was no hidden psychological process behind what human beings say and do.

The difference lies in the *codes* used in thought and expression. Before this is explored in more detail, it is important to look at the background to contemporary ideas about the acquisition of knowledge, and the closely related debate about language and thought.

Behaviourists and mentalists

The human acquisition of knowledge is an area of study which has caused considerable disagreement among various commentators. The two most clearly opposed positions on this question are called behaviourism and mentalism.

Behaviourists believe that human behaviour is prompted by *learning* a process in which some stimuli (events of some sort) are reinforced, while others are not. The **mentalist** position, on the other hand, turns on the theory that the mental structures of the human subject are already in place, and are simply geared to the acquisiton of certain kinds of knowledge. The first significant defeat of the traditional behaviourist approach came in 1959 when Noam Chomsky (see the reference in Chapter 1) produced an analysis of the work of the behaviourist B.F. Skinner.

Innateness

The ability of people in widely different locations and circumstances to acquire language systems (which all seem to share remarkably similar structures) led Chomsky to advocate a theory of **innateness**. This is the idea that the human organism is 'programmed to speak'. Chomsky noted the 'striking uniformity' of the grammars found throughout the world. He also realised that it was unlikely that humans would ever be able to acquire all the complexities of speech from experience. This prompted him to attack those approaches to language which insisted that it is based purely on a process of learning. He decided that the general features of language structure (see *Aspects of the Theory of Syntax*, 1965):

'reflect, not so much the course of one's experience, but rather the general character of one's capacity to acquire knowledge'.

The majority of linguists now appear to agree with Chomsky's mentalist or innate theory of language. However, some recent research (as we shall see below under 'Theories of mind and brain') may support the notion that a type of mental reinforcement does occur in the early years of life. There is in fact no reason why this should exclude a theory of innate ability. If reinforcement occurs, something has first to exist in order to be selected and strengthened.

Separate parts of mind?

Some academics consider that the intrapersonal processes that we usually recognise are really just convenient labels, and cannot be separated from one another to make distinct 'parts of mind'. D.A. Allport, writing in 1983 (see Harré and Gillet, *The Discursive Mind*, p. 53), argued that:

'there is not some subprocess, nor any collection of subprocesses, called "perception" (for example) that we could separate off from other subprocesses called "memory," "attention," "reasoning," still less from "intelligence" or vice versa. In other words, these descriptive faculties are not parts of mind. They do not partition its structure.'

Allport argues that things like perception and memory are made by the combination of 'overlapping' processes. We may just as usefully conclude that successful human communication depends on a *unified* or *composite* mental ability; in other words, that human beings are able to combine innate abilities with lessons learned from experience, and cognitive processes with emotional responses, all in the same act of communication.

Thought and language

Rather than set up a counter-productive opposition between thought and language, or ask 'which came first', it may be useful to examine the various theories which attempt to explain the relationship between these categories.

In *Psychology, The Science of Mind and Behaviour*, Richard D. Gross sets out contrasting views of the thought-language relationship (see p. 360):

- Some argue that thought is *dependent upon* or *caused by* language. Extreme behaviourists, for example, emphasise the role of external influences upon the individual to such a degree that internal processes are allowed little importance.
- A second view may be represented by the psychologist Piaget, who believed that language was dependent upon the level of cognitive development attained by the individual.
- Vygotsky, who studied language and development, argued that speech and practical activity were two entirely separate modes of behaviour, coming together at about the age of two years to produce verbal thought (language).

Language as the dominant partner

In the first case, it is interesting to note that some writers see the 'dominance' of language as setting **limits** not just on what it is possible to describe but also, by implication, on what it is possible to think. The ability of human beings to generate meaning in different ways (including ways which are *not* based on language) should allow us to reject the work of authors who take this view. Also, if there are limits set by language, we should remember that language *changes* and that it is quite possible that ordinary discourse will supply new descriptive categories to meet the need of communities.

While Edward Sapir, as a **linguistic relativist**, was probably correct when he noted that a community's 'language habits' predispose individuals to make 'certain choices of interpretation' (see Gross, p. 361), the conclusion he went on to reach, that this 'undermines the possibility of man's access to the real world', does not follow from his initial observation. Sapir is wrong, first because we also have access to the real world through non-linguistic systems of interpretation (those based on, for example, pictorial codes and emotional responses), and second because 'language habits' grow from experience of the real, bearing its imprint and providing a fairly reliable guide to the world.

Thought as the dominant partner

Jean Piaget (1896–1980) saw the growth of personal knowledge as a process of interaction involving the individual and his or her environment. Concerned with child psychology and intelligence, Piaget identified a number of cognitive stages which he believed all infants passed through. Each stage was supposed to represent a new level in the development of intelligence. According to this theory, language is the *reflection* of thoughts which themselves emerge from *actions*.

Few theorists now support the idea of hard and fast stages for cognitive development. Piaget himself, in his later years, moved to a theory which conceptualised development as continuous.

Vygotsky

L.S. Vygotsky (1896–1934) exercises influence upon theories of language and mind not because of the division he made between practical activity and speech, but because he insisted upon the *social* nature of speech. This led to a belief in the transformation of interpersonal processes into intrapersonal ones. According to this view, a child witnesses events and discourses and then internalises them.

Language as 'autonomous system'

One version of the thought-language argument (similar to Harré and Gillett's view of discourse as the real source of psychological 'events') may be found in 'Attribution and language as a socio-cognitive environment' (see *Language, Interaction and Social Cognition*, p. 79), where Semin and Fiedler argue that:

> 'many psychological phenomena which are usually conceived as cognitive, motivational or emotional processes within the minds and brains of individual people, are permanently installed in language as an autonomous system above and beyond the individual'.

On the face of it, this may sound as though individuals are at the mercy of systems. However, Fiedler and Semin are not arguing that cognitive and emotional processes are unable to exist outside language, rather that the role of language has been undervalued. They suggest, for example, that language *rules* may supply what have previously been thought to be purely *cognitive* processes, and that the decisions taken by individuals may be structured by the *linguistic* frame in which problems are posed.

Pinker: 'mentalese'

Stephen Pinker's *The Language Instinct* offers an alternative view, dealing with the language-thought dispute by arguing that the 'representations underlying thinking' and 'the sentences in a language' are not the same. He concludes that thought and expression work at cross-purposes. They do so because far more information is generated when human beings think than any known language can reflect.

Pinker questions the idea that 'internal representations' have a close relationship to the individual units of meaning in a language (p. 78):

'if we know that Socrates is a man, is it because we have neural patterns that correspond one-to-one to the English words *Socrates*, *is*, *a*, and *man*, and groups of neurons in the brain that correspond to the subject of an English sentence, the verb, and the object, laid out in that order?'

One way of attempting to answer this question is by examining English sentences and asking if they (p. 78) 'embody the information that a processor would need to perform valid sequences of reasoning'. This means taking the evidence of external expression (sentences) and investigating the possiblity of *working backwards* from such evidence to reach a reliable set of conclusions about meaning. This, in Pinker's opinion, would establish whether or not the units of language match specific patterns of thought.

Ambiguous sentences

Pinker uses a series of ambiguous sentences to show that a language (in this case, English) sometimes fails to convey the meaning intended by its users. For example, the headline:

> 'Queen Mary Having Bottom Scraped'

is used by Pinker to demonstrate that it is possible to read two different meanings into a sentence. The sub-editor who produced this headline, however, presumably intended to convey a single meaning which he or she had clearly in mind. This is offered as proof that thought had not 'translated' successfully into language.

A language of thought?

The Language Instinct also draws attention to a series of other deficiencies found in the English language, including its lack of 'logical explicitness', the way that definite and indefinite articles ('the' and 'a') are used, and the problems of context and synonymy. All of this suggests to Pinker that mental processes are different to language (p. 81):

> 'People do not think in English or Chinese or Apache; they think in a language of thought.'

Pinker describes this language as 'mentalese', a system that is not the same as any of the world's languages, but from which all languages grow. He wonders (p. 56) whether 'mentalese' is:

> 'a silent medium of the brain – a language of thought ... merely clothed in words whenever we need to communicate them to a listener'.

Criticisms of Pinker

When Stephen Pinker considers the difference between the basic structure of 'mentalese' and language, he seems to provide convincing evidence. However, a weakness emerges when he uses arguments based on *intention*. In the second chapter of his book, he argues that there is often a difference between what is said or written and what was originally *meant* by a speaker or writer. He uses the idea of a gap between 'original' meaning and expression as proof that there must be an original intention. Here is the passage which contains this argument (p. 57):

'We have all had the experience of uttering or writing a sentence, then stopping and realising that it wasn't exactly what we meant to say. To have that feeling, there has to be a "what we meant to say" that is different from what we said.'

Although Pinker uses the word 'exactly' in a context which suggests some distance from 'exactness', he means to argue that there really is an *original* meaning which is sometimes not adequately expressed in language.

While it is certainly true that what we mean to express often *seems* not to match the actual written or spoken message we produce, the whole idea of a 'mismatch' between intention and expression needs to be treated with great caution. Just because human beings 'feel' that they have not expressed themselves accurately, it simply does not follow that there is always a definable 'message' or idea which suffers in translation. Or, put another way, it does not prove that the original thought always has a form that language misrepresents.

This is not to say that individuals have no definite purposes in mind until they communicate, but rather that the exact *form* of meaning is found only when expression is made. For instance, it is quite possible that saying or writing the 'wrong' thing is often not really a mistake at all, but a 'trial run' for the production of a discourse which is suitable to the *context* in which expression is made.

It should not be forgotten that, while we sometimes feel that we have not expressed ourselves adequately, at other times we do feel certain that we have said or written what we meant; this is often, in fact, what we feel the situation requires us to produce. If we accept a view of expression as social, then 'what we meant to say' (or our *intention*) will be influenced by our knowledge and expectation of various situations. 'What we meant to say' will become, in most circumstances, *what it is possible to say*. This suggests a theory of **contextual intention**.

Anyone who has experienced a heated argument between friends will be able to testify that the individuals involved usually repent of any harsh words spoken, arguing that they didn't actually mean what they said. This is really a way of recognising that certain utterances cease to be valid when circumstances have altered. Pinker's 'what we meant to say' seems to be wholly individual, suggesting that he believes in a 'pure' intention which somehow exists separately to discourse and interaction.

Getting the gist?

Pinker notes that it is sometimes difficult to find any words 'that properly convey a thought'. From this observation, he goes on to argue that (p. 58):

> 'When we hear or read, we usually remember the gist, not the exact words, so there has to be a gist that is not the same as a bunch of words.'

If thoughts are 'gists' then it is no wonder that language cannot exactly reproduce Pinker's idea of 'original' meaning. The reproduction of the 'gist' of something will always be imperfect, not because language is inadequate, but because the thought, or gist, is vague and imprecise. It is quite likely that Pinker's 'mentalese' or 'language of thought' is always founded on imprecision, in which case I would suggest that it is the context of interaction and the purposes shaped by context which force the human subject to make attempts at *accurate* expression.

A turn to active models: 'explanation seeking'

As we have seen, there has been a great deal of criticism of research into cognition and the 'intellectual' processes of understanding. The major dissatisfaction concerns the fact that cognition has largely been regarded as 'information processing', suggesting a passive model of human understanding. A turn has been made instead towards active models of cognition, in which the human subject does not simply process information, but concerns itself with 'explanation seeking'.

Moravcsik, for example, (see *Thought and Language*, p. 122) suggests a move away from semantics, towards a system of analysis which is capable of dealing with natural languages and everyday speech events (as opposed to the study of formal systems). He argues for a *contextual* understanding of meaning, noting that:

> 'in natural languages meanings are only partially determined, and much of the determination . . . is left to non-linguistic context'.

The 'non-linguistic context' here means features like intonation, the form of the event, non-verbal communication and so on. From this evidence, it seems important to argue both that language is more *important* than it is sometimes thought, and also that it is not the *only* important element in the creation of meaning.

Language and cognition

Terence Moore and Christine Carling, in *Understanding Language: Towards a Post-Chomskyan Linguistics*, are interested in discovering the general characteristics of language, which they believe will emerge (p. 10):

> 'once it is no longer seen as separable from the attitudes, beliefs, expectations and overall experience of language users'.

This agenda could be described as social, because it moves away from the purely abstract project which once sought to understand 'universal' properties of grammar. Moore and Carling argue that an 'understander' does not receive information from an utterance, but rather 'uses the utterance to gain access to information which in some form and to some degree he already possesses'.

These authors call language 'a self-organising complex of interactive processes', and assume that the processing involved in language *use* takes place within a 'complex framework of the knowledge, experience, expectations, attitudes and beliefs' that language users possess.

Limited perceptions?

Curiously enough, for writers who express their theories within a social context, they think that people share apects of this framework to 'a limited extent' only. While they claim to 'shift the emphasis from language to language users', they also appear to believe that individual language users are (p. 11):

> 'trapped within the confines of their own experience and limited in their knowledge of the world and their perception of it'.

This sounds like the counsel of despair, and runs counter to the argument that human beings demonstrate an extraordinary creativity, using information to make intuitive and often accurate predictions about those aspects of the world which lie beyond their immediate experience.

In Moore and Carling, we witness a return to a linguistic variant of cognitive processing (p. 11):

> 'We assume that each individual has what we might crudely refer to as a "knowledge base", representing his accumulated and categorised experience of his environment.'

This 'knowledge base' is not seen as a static 'store of information'. It is rather 'a self-organising and self-regulating system, constantly shifting and modifying as a result of fresh input'. However, if the 'knowledge base' of any individual is *not* a static store of information, then this seems to contradict the idea previously advanced by these authors, that people are 'trapped within the confines of their own experience and limited in their knowledge of the world'.

External expression: evidence of internal states?

It is sometimes assumed that various forms of *external* expression always offer direct evidence of specific *internal* processes. The extract from *Nineteen Eighty-Four*, in which Winston Smith worried about the messages which might be broadcast by unconscious facial expressions, reflects the belief that onlookers may be able to gain an insight into one's private thoughts and deliberations. Although it is possible to observe external evidence of internal processes (for instance, when an emotion is signalled by involuntary signs like tears), this does not necessarily mean that it is always easy to identify the exact process, intention or response which lies behind such signs.

Shakespeare's *Othello*, for instance, contains a passage where Iago is questioned about the meaning of his behaviour. Othello, anxious to discover Iago's true opinion of Cassio, repeatedly attempts to make him provide what we would call a 'straight answer' (Act 3, Sc. 3):

> '*Othello*: And when I told thee he was of my counsel
> In my whole course of wooing, thou criedst "Indeed!"
> And didst contract and purse thy brow together,
> As if thou then hadst shut up in thy brain
> Some horrible conceit.'

Iago wishes to infect his master with jealousy, and so provides him with a series of ambiguous signals which force Othello to ask yet more questions. These signals, such as the cry of 'Indeed!' and the facial expressions which accompany it, draw on conventions of behaviour which are useful exactly because they stop short of outright disagreement or contradiction. Distance is created between Iago's *intention* and *responsibility* for that intention. The use of such conventions allows Iago to appear reluctant to divulge the damaging falsehoods he had always intended to express.

Misreading signals

On many occasions, people are mystified by the expressive signals which are offered by the individuals they meet. An episode of *The Living Soap* (12 August 1994), a programme which followed the fortunes of a group of university students, provides a useful example.

One of the students met an elderly woman at an exhibition commemorating the Holocaust. He was unable to understand why she was smiling when she recounted the fact that her family had died in a concentration camp. His reaction to such distressing information prevented him realising that the woman's smiles were offered as a response to his inquiry; in other words, that they were used as a code designed to encourage social interaction and were thus not indicative of her feelings about the subject under discussion.

Those individuals who claim to be able to match various intellectual or emotional states to specific behaviours, often through 'body language', sometimes fail to appreciate the complexity of the relationship between internal and external states.

Body language and expression

To a large degree, body language is ambiguous. In the first place, it is often difficult to tell what has prompted an individual physical reaction. Secondly, there is no direct correlation between a particular stimulus and the observable outcome. Michael Argyle believes that the only reliable means of establishing meaning is to establish a context for individual examples of physical expression (*Bodily Communication*, p. 294):

> 'to make the meaning of an ambiguous non-verbal signal clear the sequence of events and the structure of the situation needs to be shown. A person raises his finger – the meaning of this signal depends on whether he is an umpire at a cricket match, a bidder at an auction sale, or in some other situation, and on the place of this act in the sequence.'

Attempting to establish 'universal' meanings from non-verbal signals is not a particularly fruitful practice. As Argyle says (p. 294) 'there is nothing like a verbal grammar ruling how the different kinds of units are to be combined'.

Judy Gahagon (see *Interpersonal and Group Behaviour* (Methuen, 1975) argues that there are two functions of non-verbal communication. The first is the expression of emotion, while the second illustrates and supports speech. She calls the second function 'punctuation' (p. 73):

> 'in speech and conversation we use non-verbal signals to help the listener to follow the content of what is being said ... language, fully occupied as it is with carrying the ideational content of the communication, could not carry all the information relating to the mechanics of social interaction as well, and it is non-verbal communication which is used for this purpose.'

Do some types of body language have a 'universal' meaning?

Despite notions of context and 'punctuation', some theories of non-verbal communication stress the supposedly 'universal' meaning of certain types of gesture. There do appear to be some examples of body language which, even if they are unable to generate identical meanings throughout the world, at least make roughly the same impact on all members of a similar culture. Consider, for example, the set of pictures which appear in Figure 2.1–2.3. What state does each seem to express?

Intention and expression

As we have seen, one of the questions which agitates those interested in the different forms of public expression is how close a particular utterance might

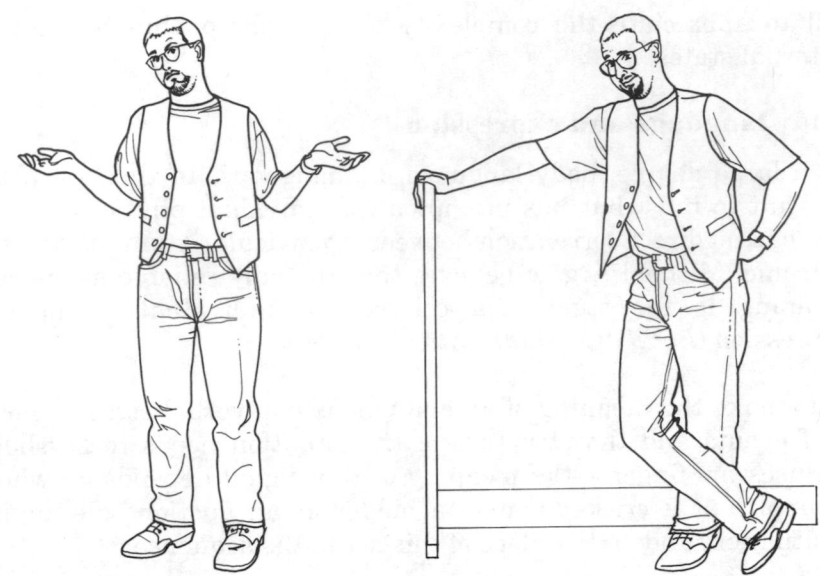

Figure 2.1

Figure 2.2

Figure 2.3

be to the original intention of a speaker. I suggested above that Pinker's notion of intention needs to be treated with caution.

It is worth noting that there are various contextual pressures on individuals when they are required to form or convey public messages including, as we noted earlier, the fact that they may be held responsible for the communicative acts they perform. Since individuals are likely to understand the conventions which operate in any situation, certain 'genres' or types of speech may be produced to meet the occasion.

The production of meaning

The production of meaning always takes place within a specific context. One approach would be to argue that this context will *limit* people's freedom to express exactly what they mean. Another argument may be that the parameters set by context may actually help individuals to produce coherent messages. If a context or situation is known in advance, or is understood during the progress of an interaction, then the appropriate modes of behaviour will also be understood and may act as a guide to expression.

This would suggest that intention is created not by individual determination alone, but by the possible range of circumstances in which people find themselves. We all know examples of people who insist that they will speak their mind, only to discover that their mind changes when they are placed in circumstances for which they are not prepared, or which intimidate them.

Where an individual refuses to *recognise* convention, the refusal itself may act to draw attention to models of individual conduct. These issues will again be examined when we consider examples of public argument and debate.

The moment of expression: 'true' meaning?

So far, our discussion of expression and language has concentrated on the theory that the human subject either strives to create, or attempts to disguise, an accurate *external* insight into the exact *internal* meaning he or she had in mind. In fact, the process of meaning-creation may be quite different. People may only really find an exact meaning when they come to *express* the various ideas and emotions which they experience. Some writers (see the material on **rhetorical psychology** in Chapter 3) argue that the point at which a public expression is made may be the point at which individuals 'make up their minds'.

Internal communication?

In the meantime, it would be mistaken to assume that private expression (for instance, talking to oneself or 'thinking aloud') is really always close to the actual 'content' of thought, or that it reveals precise details of mental processing. After all, someone might express quite complex understanding through a very simple vocalisation, such as 'I see.'

This brings us back to the concern outlined at the beginning of this chapter, that certain forms of personal expression are too readily assumed to provide evidence of a distinct process called 'intrapersonal communication'. As we saw, one of the forms most often chosen to demonstrate that individuals communicate 'within and to themselves' is the *diary* or personal journal.

Words and values

All written forms must obey certain syntactical and semantic rules if they are to be understood. These rules are not merely a set of conventions; they carry a particular emotional force, and are part of the established values of a society. We have only to think of the passions which are aroused when people offend against recognised practices in English grammar to remember how social and cultural values are regarded as inseparable from spoken and written usage.

The integrity of Language?

Dennis Freeborn, in *Varieties of English*, cites the example of a letter to *The Times*, in which a reader called Colville lamented the (p. 3):

> 'mushroom growth of transatlantic grammatical errors . . .
> [and] . . . the infiltration of German constructions into our language'.

The original letter spawned no fewer than twenty-one replies, some in support of, and others in opposition to, the position held by Colville. Clearly, no deviation from English 'norms' would cause such depth of feeling unless some people were convinced that certain positive values lay in the maintenance of its supposed integrity.

Such views are not uncommon and not without historical precedent. Thucydides, the fifth-century BC author of *The Peloponnesian War*, believed that correct use of language was a moral issue. Thucydides argued that true meaning can be distorted during traumatic events like wars. During periods of armed conflict, the opposing parties usually attempt to ensure loyalty to their particular cause. According to Thucydides, political expedience will therefore come before responsible behaviour, and the usual meaning of words will be distorted (see *The Peloponnesian War*, p. 242). In this passage, he writes of a period when civil war raged within the Athenian state:

> 'To fit in with the change of events words, too, had to change their usual meanings. What used to be described as a thoughtless act of aggression was now regarded as the courage one would expect in a party member . . . the idea of moderation was just an attempt to disguise one's unmanly character; ability to understand a question from all sides meant that one was totally unfitted for action.'

Diaries and journals: evidence of individuality?

The act of making a record of thoughts, actions, events and encounters is obviously a *personal* response to daily life. However, a social approach to the study of communication will also be concerned to establish whether there are factors involved which reveal the shared perceptions of a society or social group. Any private journal, since it has to use an established linguistic system, will find itself reproducing not only examples of common phrases, but also the meanings and values which the writer has encountered in public interaction, or has picked up from various written sources.

Notions of individuality

Personal accounts of life will appear whenever the conditions for making such records are favourable. Literacy is obviously the main prerequisite. If we delve a little deeper, we may wonder whether the diary as a form depends on a society having notions of *individuality*, ideas about the special worth of individuals, as opposed to those philosophies which emphasise the significance of collective experiences.

Before the birth of the diary, which became an established form in the seventeenth century, we find examples of self-reference in other established genres, most usually in travel journals, verse, and sometimes works of history. However, these references do not at all resemble expressions of the highly self-conscious idea of the writer as 'unique individual', found in a great deal of modern writing, private or otherwise. Is the reason for the rather self-effacing approach of many 'pre-modern' authors the result of a difference in the way people understood 'individuality', or is it because the forms of writing used – dispassionate and 'objective' accounts – do not lend themselves to detailed revelations about the self?

Perhaps one solution is to suggest that attitudes to individuality, on the one hand, and the forms of expression which are available, on the other, depend on one another. When a society attaches less importance to the supposed uniqueness of an individual's daily activities, it is to be expected that public events might be regarded as more significant, and that histories of events in general will become a significant genre. If the various experiences of personal life are regarded as relatively insignificant, then expressions of individual psychology might emerge in forms like lyric verse.

Voices from the past

Pausanias, a Greek doctor and traveller of the second century AD, produced one of the earliest 'tourist' books, an extensive and detailed work called *Guide to Greece*. In this guide, he uses the first person singular pronoun 'I' for the usual reasons: when he wishes to express a personal opinion about the reliability of a story or report, or when he brings his own knowledge to bear on historical events or places of interest.

He does not, however, write about his *emotional responses* to stimuli. His personality does not intrude. His 'I' is not the highly self-conscious or self-regarding ego we often encounter in print. We might call his 'I' the 'self as verifier', a distinctly rational force which offers opinions and passes judgements on the raw material collected (the *Guide*, p. 89):

> 'they say a musician called Kyknos was king of the Ligurians ... and when he died he was changed into a swan by the will of Apollo. I believe a musician was king of the Ligurians, but find it incredible a man should change into a bird.'

An author like Pausanias is not concerned with self-presentation, and the absence of egocentric writing may be attributable both to his society's view of the individual, and to the established genres available to writers. What, though, is the established genre of which the diary is part? Broadly speaking, it is *journalism*, the creation of a daily record of events.

Questions of address

If we ask *to whom* the diary form is **addressed**, the careless answer might be, 'to the self'. Although a diary may be written for the benefit of its owner, the structures of language tend to encourage each author to address some kind of audience.

On occasion, diaries are addressed to an imaginary friend. This is perhaps a 'device' employed to solve a contradiction which all diarists must face: the tension between the form of expression (written composition, with all its 'public' rules and conventions) and the solitary nature of the activity. Diarists may feel that they are addressing their remarks to some 'other' because of the essentially *reflective* nature of the process. The constant monitoring of their own response to events may create this feeling.

Of course, writers may well have an eye to the future, and this may solve the problem of address. However, the central argument here is that all diarists are forced to make an address which requires them to be self-conscious. Diaries often move between the dramatisation of events and the interrogation of the self.

To sum up, we may see a difference between a private impulse and the fact that any attempt to be coherent means using the publicly recognised genres of language. It may be useful to recognise a distinction between the *personal* mode in which diaries are written and the mistaken attempt to characterise them as entirely *private* expressions, somehow able to reveal exactly the process of individual thought.

The intentions of the diarist

Diaries are kept in order to record more than mere events; they are intended as personal documents, composed in response to a variety of circumstances. They are reasonably immediate, and are usually produced without the virtue of historical hindsight, though they may be 'written up' over a period of time. The correct definition of a diary is, however, a journal which is kept on a daily basis. The degree to which actual diaries are meant to be 'private' depends upon the intentions of the author. As I have said, it is quite possible for writers to have, eventually, some more public intention in mind.

A person of substance

Samuel Pepys, who kept a journal in the 1660s, was a largely unselfconscious diarist who wrote in a form of shorthand or code, in order to ensure that his observations remained secret. He was a well-known figure in seventeenth-century naval administration, a man of substance who composed in an age where the journal was regarded as a private form of writing – few were published. On 6 January 1663, he wrote:

> 'After dinner to the Dukes house and there saw *Twelfth night* acted well, though it be but a silly play and not relating at all to the name or the day. Thence Mr. Battersby (the apothecary) his wife and mine by coach together, and setting him down at his house, he paying his share, my wife and I home and find all well. Only, myself somewhat vexed at my wife's neglect in leaving of her scarfe, waistcoat, and night-dressings in the coach today that brought us from Westminster, though I confess she did give them to me to look after – yet it was her fault not to see that I did take them out of the coach. I believe it might be as good as 25s. loss or thereabouts.'

Here we see a writer interested in recording the 'landmarks' of each day. The passage of time is recognised, and the day divided, by ordinary events like meals and social occasions. Pepys blames the loss of the various garments on his wife, though the irritation expressed seems to grow from recognition of his own neglect. Generally, Pepys's great sociability and interest in other people means that he is not a self-obsessed diarist.

Straitened circumstances

Born into a social location which was neither working-class nor part of the established middle strata, the Brontë sisters faced the problem of many nineteenth-century women who had some education but little money and no 'connections'.

On 30 July 1841, Emily Brontë (the author of *Wuthering Heights*) wrote a diary paper which was sealed and put aside, to be opened four years from the date of composition. It forms part of a series which cannot, strictly speaking, be said to form a true diary (see Winifred Gerin, *Emily Brontë*). Part of the entry concerns the plans the sisters made for the establishment of their own school (p. 114):

> 'A scheme is at present in agitation for setting us up in a school of our own; as yet nothing is determined, but I hope and trust it may go on and prosper and answer our highest expectations. This day four years I wonder whether we shall still be dragging on in our present condition or established to our heart's content.'

A diary is one place where people can mull over what for most individuals is a natural preoccupation; the economic and personal circumstances in which they find themselves. This often involves, as it does here, reference to the straitened circumstances of the present and speculation about future prospects. In this sense at least, diaries represent the way that human subjects think, always casting forward and attempting to plan ahead.

Writers under pressure

In some cases, the diarist does not feel able to escape the environment in which he or she exists, and entries become concerned with the minutiae of immediate and pressing restrictions. In 1934, the French writer and libertarian socialist Simone Weil kept a journal which recorded her experiences as a worker at a factory owned by the Renault company. This is one brief extract (see *Formative Writings*, p. 223), written after a particularly difficult day at work:

> 'Monday, in a bad way. Going back to work infinitely more painful than I would have thought. The days seem an eternity to me. Heat ... Headaches ... These C4 x 16 screws disgust me. It's one of the "cushy jobs"; I would have to do it quickly, and I can't. Barely finished, I think, by 3.30. Prostration, bitterness at stupefying work, disgust. Fear also, all the time, of the cutter coming loose.'

This entry records the isolation felt by the author. The constant worry about the failure of the machinery she had to use was directly linked to the embarrassment she felt at having to ask for the foreman's assistance. The short sentences seem to indicate the pressure felt and despair experienced. It is reasonably easy to sympathise with the plight of such an individual, particularly if readers find an echo of the challenges which they themselves must face.

All is ash

On occasion, it might be rather more difficult to identify with a diarist, particularly when their problems seem to lie outside the common order of events. Alan Clark, a minister in Margaret Thatcher's Conservative administration, once lamented his personal misfortunes in the following manner (see his *Diaries*, Thursday 24 December 1987):

'Christmas Eve. I've got £700,000 in my Abbey National Crazy-High-Interest account. But what's the use? Ash, ash, all is ash. Lay not for thyself treasures on earth. The cars are getting streaked and rust spotted, the books foxed, the furniture dusty. The window panes, all 52,000 of them are *revolting*, so greasily blotched. Translucent only. And there is moth everywhere. My grandfather's great Rothschild coat, bought in Wien in 1906, is terminally degraded ... The whole thing is out of control. And why? I know why. Because I'm not rich enough to have servants.'

Cognition

If intrapersonal functions and abilities are designed to make sense of experience, then it would be useful to know what theories are used to describe them. The traditional approach to thought has emphasised the **cognitive** abilities of human beings. Cognition may be explained as the *action* or *faculty* of understanding.

Research into understanding has included ideas about the existence of 'schemas', which are supposed to be cognitive frameworks or 'mental scaffolds'. Alternatively, schemas may be described as organised collections of information about objects or types of event (see *Social Psychology*, Baron and Byrne, p. 122). Some investigations have been directed towards the search for a centre of logical processing supposed to be present in the brain. This is sometimes called the 'central processing mechanism'.

At this point, some may wonder why students of communication should be presented with a question which appears to have turned into a discussion of biology. The point is that the way communication is *understood* depends ultimately upon the accepted ways of describing the world. Our theories of mind and behaviour grow from scientific *orthodoxy*, from a set of ideas which have become dominant in our culture. Many of our assumptions about communication depend upon these sources.

In recent years, some of these orthodoxies have been questioned. One major target for reassessment is the idea that human development and understanding arise from a strictly *logical* mental process.

Opposition to the cognitive tradition

Objections to those approaches which emphasise cognition may be found in an increasing number of academic perspectives. Some of these theories argue for a new model of cognitive research. Among these critiques, Harré and Gillett's book *The Discursive Mind* is particularly useful. It examines the origin of cognitive theories, noting that (p. 13):

'when cognitive scientists started making up hypotheses about human cognition, they used concepts like ... "logical operation", "processing of information" and so on. Why those?'

The idea which came to dominate much research into cognition was the notion that 'rule-following' typified the way that the human mind worked. Harré and Gillett argue that, rather than searching for evidence of actual processes, researchers imposed a framework of rules and logical structures on the study of human thought:

'Rules were inserted into the hidden recesses of the mind. They appeared in different guises ... scripts ... grammars ... role-rule model[s].'

In sum, human thought was explained by comparing cognitive processes to advanced machine 'intelligence', as though the brain itself operated in the same way as a computer.

Theories of mind and brain

Dissatisfaction with theories which compare mind and thought to the logical operations of computers has grown within a variety of disciplines. In particular, a number of developmental psychologists, linguists and philosophers have found it necessary to move away from the established metaphors employed to describe the workings of the brain.

One of the new investigative approaches has emerged from theories of **selection**.

Gerald Edelman's work on the way that the brain selects and reinforces some physical operations, while weakening or discarding others, coincided with experiments into child development conducted at Indiana University. The Indiana experiments investigated the ways in which infants learn to use their limbs.

Babies who have reached the age of six weeks will almost always make attempts to grasp objects placed within their reach. However, they are unable to co-ordinate or properly direct their movements and therefore fail to seize the objects concerned. Gradually, however, babies learn to grasp objects because they select, over time, those movements which obtain success.

At the next stage, the repertoire of movements possessed by the child is narrowed down and some movements become redundant. The Indiana researchers use this evidence to argue against the existence of genetic 'programming'. There is, however, no reason why theories of selection cannot exist together with the idea of a set of innate abilities, which could be regarded as the ground upon which selection operates.

Structures of the brain

The most important part of Edelman's theory depends on understanding the structure of the brain. The dominant part of the human brain, associated with intellectual function and personality, is the *cerebrum*. This is covered with grey matter – the *cerebral cortex* – which contains *neurons*. These are cells that conduct nerve impulses, and both send and receive a variety of chemical messages.

Each individual cell is connected to thousands of other cells. There are overall some hundred billion cells in the brain and about one million billion connections. The vast number of these 'firing patterns' has led many to the conclusion that a huge number of potential thoughts and actions are available to the human individual.

Value systems

The limbic system, at the base of the brain, is traditionally regarded as the seat of the emotions. The brain stem, around which the limbic system is arranged, is thought by Edelman and his colleagues to contain structures called 'value systems'.

These structures are supposed to have evolved to recognise certain events and occurrences as beneficial or useful, such as actions taken in order to eat, to seize objects, and so on. They are supposed to select only those firing patterns which, through experience, produce useful actions. Ultimately, 'value systems' are supposed to strengthen certain firing patterns which result in beneficial actions, while other actions of less usefulness to the human organism are used increasingly less and consequently become weakened or disappear altogether.

The implication here is that every useful action is suffused with value, so that even the highest and most abstract levels of human thinking are based on more than just logic; they are also based upon emotion. Edelman, speaking in a BBC *Horizon* programme of 1994, said:

> 'We live in a view of science that's highly mechanised ... we've been talking about essentially the machine model of the mind, the computer ... I'm against that ... the facts stand up for individuality, for the fact that ... you can't really prescribe how an individual ... is going to behave in every circumstance.'

It is interesting to note that the philosophy which this scientist offers as a parallel to his theory of mind is a liberal 'individualism', a consequence perhaps of the political context in which all scientific inquiry takes place.

Social construction and theories of the mind

In an attempt to understand the way that the mind actually works, Harré and Gillett begin by examining the 'informal rules' used during everyday speech, in which there are correct and incorrect ways of using words. Instead of imposing a system upon the human mind, they attempt to establish the types of meaning-creation that humans undertake. They are in favour of a less coldly 'objective' approach to human research, one based on (p. 20):

'an empathetic identification with the other that helps the observer make sense of what the other is doing'.

This may also help to support the collectivist outlook which *social* approaches to communication would favour above the 'individualistic' perspective suggested by Edelman.

Against representation?

Harré and Gillett propose a view of the mind which avoids using the theory of representation, in which experience of the world is compared with an inner 'picture' taken from experience. They describe the mind as (p. 22):

'a social construction ... our concepts arise from our discourse and shape the way we think'.

In this view, human subjectivity is created from participation in a number of different discourses (all interactive situations, most of which involve speech events). The mind is therefore dynamic, essentially social, and impossible to define as an isolated phenomenon. The concept of a 'private' world would thus be redundant.

The drawback here, as far as we are concerned, is Harré and Gillett's hostility to the concept of representation. They reject it because they disagree with the idea of 'mental comparison'. As we have seen, this is the theory that people recognise their world because they are able to compare 'sense data' with stored 'versions' of various experiences. The idea of 'mental comparison' is certainly a little over-simplified, especially as it neglects the idea that we recognise *contexts* rather than just objects.

Researchers may disagree about the exact ways in which internal processes work, but the theory of representation is still useful, provided we use it to mean the 're-presentation' of human experience, using a variety of symbolic systems.

Three principles

Harré and Gillett's approach (which they describe rather grandly as the 'Second Cognitive Revolution') gives rise to three principles, which can be summarised as follows:

- Many psychological phenomena are in fact the properties of discourse. Where the discourse is *public*, it is behaviour, and where *private* it is thought.
- Individual uses of symbolic systems are taken from interpersonal discourses.
- The production of emotion, attitudes, decisions and so on depends upon the skill of the actors, their 'moral standing' in the community, and 'the story lines that unfold'.

The conclusion is that 'discursive phenomena', such as remembering (p. 27), 'are not manifestations of hidden subjective, psychological phenomena. They *are* the psychological phenomena.'

Harré and Gillett's theory proposes that thought and language are part of the same system. Instead of speech being understood as a reflection of the speaker's underlying cognitive state, speech events are seen as expressions of a response to situational and therefore discursive context.

Notice, however, that their first principle insists that *behaviour* marks the public appearance of discourse. This means that ideas and ideologies are expressed not just in *language*, but through all the expressive systems available to human beings. Such perspectives mark a significant break with the idea that there is a separate and rather mysterious world of the mind, to which it is impossible to gain access.

Sensory perception: communication and physiology

At this point, an understanding of the range of human perception may help to resolve some of the questions about the extent of our communicative abilities. This suggests that a brief study of human **physiology** – *the science of natural functions* – needs to be undertaken. In other words, any appreciation of the communication *process* depends on asking questions about the physical structures of the human organism and the environment in which it exists. These questions include the following:

- What faculties do we use to perceive our environment?
- How reliable are these faculties?
- Are such faculties always actively deployed?
- How do we communicate our understanding of the world to others?
- What social or environmental constraints are placed on our communication?

Perceiving the environment

The natural and social worlds we inhabit are filled with a vast number of signals and messages, yet we manage with reasonable ease to construct, for most of the time, a manageable and ordered existence. In order to understand how this is possible, we need to ask how humans *interpret* their environment.

Human subjects need first to be able to **perceive** an adequate range of **physical elements**. The elements perceived by human beings are the *external objects* which make an impression on one or other of the *sense organs*, which then relay the stimulus caused by the external object to the brain. The five senses – sight, smell, touch, hearing and taste – provide individuals with a composite understanding or perception of their environment.

Sensory receptors

One of the sensory receptors in the human system is the eye. Light waves reflected from external objects fall upon the eye's retina, which converts light energy into a pattern of active neurons, firing electrical impulses which are then carried to the cerebral cortex. The factors which determine visual response *before* the exercise of conscious control are called the *pre-conscious* factors; they are brightness, dimension (which includes shape and colour) and location. The combined representation of these factors is known as the *visuospatial code*.

Sound, by contrast, is the result of a mechanical disturbance in the environment, which then produces vibrations which travel through a medium such as air. When sound is collected by the pinna (the external part of the ear), it is channelled down the auditory canal. At the end of the auditory canal, the eardrum vibrates when the sound pressure strikes it. Sound then travels to the middle and inner ear respectively. The inner ear or cochlea converts sound into *neural impulses*, which can then be detected by the brain.

Limitations of the senses

One of the problems which always arises in studies of human culture is the reliability of 'sense data' and the relationship which exists between human perception and the external world. As we saw in the discussion of reality in Chapter 1, the degree to which human perception is 'accurate' has wide-ranging implications for any study of communication.

In the first place, it is important to recognise that the senses do have certain limitations. For example, we are unable to hear the range of sound frequencies perceived by many animals, and can see only certain types of light (infra-red and X-rays are invisible to human beings). In fact, when the brain receives whatever information the senses *are* able to detect, it is unable to process it all. The brain lacks the capacity to deal simultaneously with all the elements it is able to collect. Human beings therefore perceive more than they can *identify* and *report* at a conscious level.

Such a 'failure' at this level may have its uses, since the vast amount of information making an impact on an individual may not be relevant to his or her immediate needs. However, the marked discrepancies in evidence obtained from bystanders who have witnessed the same public event indicate some of the disadvantages of limited perception and inaccurate recall.

Our ability to identify what is important, what is worth communicating, will be influenced by more than our immediate circumstances; it will also be shaped by the values and cultural norms which exist within our society.

Selective attention

Considering the great variety of data encountered, it is hardly surprising that people cannot *process* all the communicative 'traffic' which passes before them, and that the human senses act to control the range of things it is possible to notice. There are in fact two ways in which our attention may be specifically concentrated upon certain features in our surroundings.

The first is where attention is drawn by a sudden change in the environment. The second is where the individual concerned *consciously directs* his or her attention to a certain place. A 'selective attention' task (see Glass and Holyoak, *Cognition*, p. 52) is described as:

'one in which you are trying to pay attention to one input (the target) in the presence of other [stimuli]'.

Directing attention to certain environmental features may lead to the relative neglect of other elements. For instance, when we read a book, we are sometimes not fully aware of other aspects of our immediate environment.

Attention and preference

There is a tendency to suppose that the selections we make are based upon the avoidance of any unpleasant or inconvenient events or messages. The authors of *See What I Mean?*, Morgan and Welton, hold this view and argue that (p. 59):

'we pay more attention to, and remember, messages that we like. If we are faced with a message we dislike ... we tend to ignore those parts which make us uncomfortable.'

Although this sounds plausible, and may account for some of our responses, it can only create misunderstandings about the nature of perception and selection. It would be more accurate to say that we pay attention to those features of our surroundings which make an impact on us, whether that impact is positive or negative. Negative events may just as easily demand attention, being noticed exactly because they disturb our equilibrium.

Models of perception

Perception itself is most often understood as an active faculty. The idea of perception as an active process was advanced by the American psychologist J.J. Gibson in 1966. The empiricist thinker, R.L. Gregory, also in 1966, described perception (see Gross *Psychology*, p. 224) as 'a dynamic searching for the best interpretation of the available data'. The 'available data' will obviously affect the conclusions we are able to reach, but the 'best interpretation' is often determined by the *values* which circulate within a society. When people thought that the earth was flat, this was based not only on data that was insufficient, but also on interpretations of evidence which were shaped by specific systems of belief, including religion.

Whatever the constraints placed on what it is possible to perceive, the notion of activity clearly implies choice, or *selection* of aspects of the various physical elements in the environment. This does not exclude the idea of passive *reception*, because a stimulus is sometimes received but not *attended to*. For example, most individuals can recall a time when the spoken word has made little impression and seemed to lose semantic impact, taking on instead the quality of tonal noise. It is worth noting, however, that it is perfectly possible to glean some elements of meaning when we register nothing more than tone.

While sound provides an interesting case study in the debate over the nature of perception, some theorists take the argument further. Albert Bergman, for example (see 'Auditory scene analysis' in *Thinking in Sound*), attempts to demonstrate that understanding of sound is not always *consciously* active, involving in the first instance what he calls the *automatic* activation of 'learned schemas'. Here, there is an activity, even though it is not a conscious one. If we accept Bergman's view, then we have acquired the notion of an *automatic* act (see the section below on 'Theories of the perception of sound').

Awareness: receiving or selecting?

The problems of awareness, reception and selection, prompt Hastorf and his co-authors (in Corner and Hawthorn, *Communication Studies: An Introductory Reader*, p. 119) to note that:

> 'from a myriad of impinging stimuli, we are aware of only certain objects and certain attributes of the objects'.

We have seen, in the previous section, that there are different approaches to the question of perception or awareness. Some theorists believe that the translation of sense data into meaning is essentially passive, governed by the structure of the human senses themselves, and by the physical properties of the various types of event or object which create responses. Others argue that there is also an *active* component to our perception, because our experiences of the world are often selective.

'Bottom-up' or **direct** theories are those used to support the idea that the *processing of information* in humans is essentially determined by the nature of external objects in the world, while those which emphasise the selective and organisational role of the human senses are called 'top-down' or **indirect**.

Psychologists who adhere to the *Gestalt* school of psychology would argue that perception tends towards the construction of overall form. Using a variety of visual tests, it is possible to show that human subjects create a *Gestalt*, or organised whole, from drawings and figures that have some element missing.

Solving the problem?

If we return to the notion of perception as both a *faculty* we possess and as an *act*, it may be possible to avoid a stand-off between 'active' and 'passive' models. The idea of perception as a faculty allows us to accept the idea that individuals possess 'open channels' into which information may flow, while the concept of perception as an act helps to remind us that people also make active choices, involving the detection and the interpretation of information gained from the external world. One complication arises because many who comment on this subject note the difference between 'active' and 'passive', but fail to distinguish between *conscious* and *unconscious* processes. It would appear, for example, that some forms of perception are not fully conscious.

Perception of form: 'visual scales'

The various theories of perception may be examined or interrogated by research into visual response to objects (see *Perception*, Sekuler, R. and Blake, R., p. 139). If we accept the idea that each physical element in the world contains a variety of information, we may apply this to the study of the image. Sekuler and Blake describe the range of visual information as ranging from 'very fine' to 'very coarse'; these diverse types are known as **visual scales**.

Figure 2.4 demonstrates three types of visual scale, emerging from a single picture. The first is *large* scale (the skyline), the second is *intermediate* (that created by individual buildings), and the third *fine* (architectural details belonging to each building). A person looking at the original picture will perceive all available scales, but has also the ability to concentrate on, or search for, one in particular.

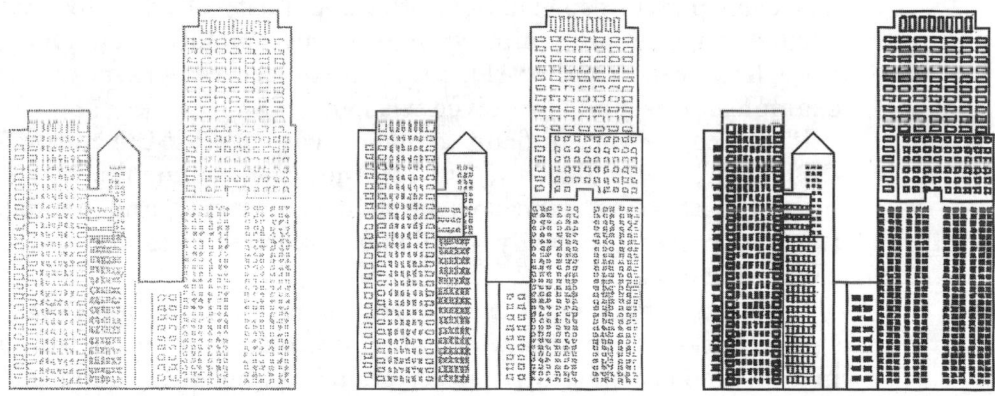

Figure 2.4   Illustration of scale

If someone looks at an image for a period of time, the three 'scales' seem to assume greater and lesser importance in turn, as though the image itself begins to impose form upon the observer. In this case, it is probably the *unevenness* of our concentration, rather than the attempt to direct awareness, which produces the effect.

Experiments using a number of images show that some part of a stimulus always stands out as the **figure** (that which is accepted as the foreground),

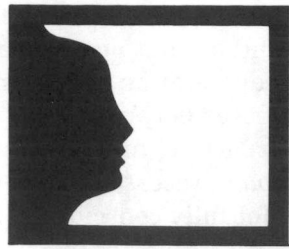

Figure 2.5   Illustration of figure and ground

while the context which gives the figure meaning is known as the **ground** or the background (Figure 2.5). In some examples, figure and ground become interchangeable.

The image vs. sound?

The difference between the impact made in our culture by visual stimuli and that created by sound may be demonstrated through the everyday attitudes expressed towards the two types of data. When an object or a pictorial representation of an object is presented to an audience, it appears to encourage the confident belief that a reasonably direct comparison with previous knowledge can be made. In semiology, the description of the **iconic** sign (that which *looks* like the object it represents) as being particularly close to the real, has been partly responsible for the popularity of this idea. It has long been argued, for example (quite wrongly in my opinion), that photographs have a close link to the real world. The phrase 'the camera never lies' is only one example of this kind of received wisdom.

It is of course very difficult to make a case against the cultural domination of the image, particularly if we consider the common practice of textbooks, including this one, which so often use diagrams and photographs because they represent an easily available supplement to the linguistic mode of communication.

In books which make references to music or other types of sound, the significance of the auditory can only be brought into focus through the use of a high degree of comparative description; references to sound must be mediated through language. Where a symbol is used to represent, for example, a musical note, the appropriate sound will only register with those able to read music.

'Interactive' books and multi-media presentations made through computers, although often designed for a visual impact, may at least encourage more active experiments with contextual sound.

Theories of the perception of sound

It is unfortunate that theories which examine how individuals distinguish between different sounds have received less publicity than comparable studies of visual perception. However, research into both these areas shares some common ground; most approaches are based on *cognitive* theories, i.e. ideas about the human acquisition of knowledge and understanding.

Some theorists believe that sound is particularly prone to misrepresentation whenever a purely cognitive perspective is used to measure its effects on audiences. If cognitive approaches are unable to explain the range of human responses to sound, then it would appear that a study of its emotional impact is required.

Part of the problem lies in the fact that all sound events are significantly complex; they contain elements which succeed one another in time, sometimes over an extended period. In *Auditory Scene Analysis: Hearing in Complex Environments* (see McAdams and Bigand, *Thinking in Sound*, p. 11), Albert Bergman describes a common response to the problem of sound perception:

'When you describe the problem of mixtures to most people, they are inclined to say that they solve it simply "by paying attention to one of the sounds at a time".'

He observes that subjects imply that the parts of the same sound 'are somehow a coherent bundle that can be selected by the process of attention'. According to Bergman, the act of selection is not as straightforward as this suggests:

'we must remember that the only thing received by the ear is a pattern formed by pressure changes over time'.

When a graph of the wave form of a mixture of sounds is examined, Bergman notes that 'there is nothing obvious in it that labels the sound as a mixture or tells you how to take it apart'.

In order to 'decompose' auditory mixtures, he believes that there are at least two processes which occur in the human listener. The first example he gives is the **automatic** activation of what he calls learned schemas. A *schema* is a mental representation of something in the environment, and in this case would provide a model for the structure of certain sounds. An example of the automatic level of response is the recognition of one's name amongst other sounds. The second example of process Bregman offers is the **active** or deliberate use of schemas to pick out a particular sound.

The limits of a cognitive approach

The sound environment is one which requires careful inquiry since, as we have already seen, 'commonsense' notions of auditory perception may be misleading. Many writers believe that the perception of sound must depend upon the ability to store and compare a series of representations. In general, the theory of 'schemas' can only really explain what has already been learned or experienced. McAdams and Bigand argue that (*Thinking in Sound,* p. 3):

'our perception of the sound world ... greatly surpasses the quality of the sensory information available at each instant: it results from mental processing'.

Cognitive approaches to human understanding, however, cannot always explain responses that appear to be innate. Stephen McAdams, for instance, notes the difference between theories based on a model of cognition or information processing, where the series of sounds heard by the human subject is compared with an abstract representation in memory, and a newer strand of theory known as **ecological psychology**.

Ecological psychology states that the 'sounding object' and the function it serves for the listener are perceived *directly*. In other words, perception does not 'pass through an analysis of the elements composing the sound event', and there is no necessary comparison with an idea or a schema held in the memory (see *Thinking in Sound*, p. 147).

Perception: the dominance of the visual?

I indicated that material on visual perception is allowed a pre-eminent place in many books on communication. There are, as I mentioned before, practical reasons for this, together with a tradition within semiology which has concentrated on the image (a bias which persists in postmodernism: see Chapter 1). However, we might still wonder why references to sight are so often used to define perception in general. In language also, descriptions of human understanding and perception often use *metaphors which refer to sight*.

One reason which might in part explain why the visual has received more attention than the auditory may be the tendency of the brain to give greater credence to information gained from the eyes – in other words, the domination of vision in the human organism itself. For example, experiments carried out by cognitive psychologists like Egeth and Sager (1977) have shown that, when a light source and a noise are presented to a human subject at the same moment, the light is likely to be detected first.

The dominance of visual data in this limited cognitive sense results in more than simply greater speed of processing. It has other effects; *mislocalisation* is the term used to describe the phenomenon where information received by the eyes prevails over auditory data, with the result that the human subject imagines sounds emanating from the wrong source. An example of this tendency is cited by Sekuler and Blake in their book *Perception*: a person watching a film in the cinema perceives that sound comes from (p. 348) 'the appropriate sources on the screen', whereas it is in fact usually produced by electronic speakers on either side of the projected image.

Human development and visual perception

Some believe that the predominance of the visual stems from its role in human development. John Berger, in *Ways of Seeing* (p. 7), argues that:

'Seeing comes before words ... the child looks and recognises before it can speak.'

While the child may not at first 'speak', it is worth asking how its recognition of features in its environment is *communicated*. An infant communicates its experiences and essential needs through the use of expressive sounds and cries. Seeing may come before words, but the production of noise which *another will find meaningful* may well be the first step in communication.

Identity: theories of self

The human environment

Human beings are born into a complex world, which can be divided into three elements:

- a natural environment;
- a social world of people, values and events;
- those artificial objects and structures produced by human exploitation of the first element.

This does not mean that these three aspects of life act separately on the human subject; they combine to shape its growth and existence. For example, the geography of the natural world determines many of the material decisions made by human collectives. A settlement, for instance, will grow on the banks of a river, or a hill may form the centrepiece for a set of defences. In this way, we might say that the basic social outline of human communities is drawn by the natural environment, which continues to form the overall context in which human endeavour is made.

In order to survive in what are sometimes uncomfortable or chaotic circumstances, organised human groups create social systems. Within these systems they produce structures and artefacts. However, nothing made or said or done is ever purely *functional*, because all human activity is also *expressive*. The artefacts people make, the behaviours they recognise, and the events they organise will express both universal and particular features of the human condition.

The 'split' self

According to the psychologist Murphy (1947), the *self* is supposed to be 'the individual known to the individual', while R.B. Burns (1980) defines it as 'the set of attitudes a person holds towards himself' (see Gross, *Psychology: The Science of Mind and Behaviour*, p. 607). Many psychologists argue that there is a difference between the *knowing*, reflective self and the self that is *known*.

In the poem **'The Face in the Mirror'**, Robert Graves describes a moment when his own reflection makes him pause for thought (see *Selected Poems*, p. 177):

> 'Grey haunted eyes, absent-mindedly glaring
> From wide, uneven orbits . . .
> I pause with razor poised, scowling derision
> At the mirrored man whose beard needs my attention.'

The feeling of alienation from self is expressed in the idea that it is the beard of the 'mirrored man' which the author is required to shave. References to the experience of seeing oneself in a mirror have become a commonplace in psychology. Gross refers to the individual who sees his or her own reflection (p. 607):

> 'When you look in the mirror at your face, you are both the person who is looking and that which is looked at.'

He moves on to argue that 'when you think about the kind of person you are . . . you are both the person doing the thinking and what is being thought about'. This theory suggests that the individual is capable of being both the *subject* (thinker) and *object* (what is being thought about).

Another way of making this distinction is by using the terms 'I' and 'me', where *I* refers to the subject and *me* to the object. Such approaches could be described as theories of the **'split' self**, one part of the individual being the conscious monitor, the other being the element that is monitored.

Against the 'split-self' theory

Some writers take issue with the split between conscious self and self as object. (The later parts of Chapter 1 expressed reservations about such a division.) Although, for example, the philosopher Gilbert Ryle believed that:

> '[it is] certainly true that when I do, feel, or witness something, I . . . frequently do pay swift retrospective heed to what I have just done, felt or witnessed'

(see *The Concept of Mind*, p. 153), he did not believe that this constitutes evidence of a split, because he argued that such self-checking is *part of* the usual mental process and not something separate which happens outside it.

Furthermore, Ryle indicates that 'self-reflection' (thinking about the self) is not *always* a feature of individual behaviour. There are some states of mind (p. 159):

'which cannot be cooly scrutinized, since the fact that we are in those states involves that we are not cool ... no-one could introspectively scrutinize the state of panic or fury, since the dispassionateness exercised in scientific observation is, by the definition of "panic" and "fury", not the state of mind of the victim of those turbulences'.

Ryle uses these examples to argue that, since self-reflection is *not always* present, there are not really separate parts of mind. Therefore, reflection should not be awarded a special status as a kind of superior 'monitor'.

A sense of self: theories of location

Rom Harré and Grant Gillett, writing in *The Discursive Mind*, also object (p. 101) to the 'implication of reference to an inner entity'. They argue that, in order to have a sense of self, a human subject must also have a sense of *place*. This may be explained as follows: in the first instance, it is essential to have a sense of one's place in **space** and in **time**. In addition, an awareness of one's moral responsibility or status as a moral **actor**, together with knowledge of the **social** place one inhabits (constructed by age, ethnicity, class and so on), are also necessary. The four 'locations' are therefore:

- a location in space;
- a location in time;
- a location as a responsible actor or agent;
- a location as a subject, including features like age, ethnicity, gender, class and so on.

These authors, following the principles of discursive psychology, do not think the mind is made up of some kind of 'mental substance', but believe instead (p. 104) that it is composed of the 'discourses that [people] are involved in, private and public'. An understanding of mind would therefore, according to this theory, be achieved through the study of discourse, particularly those aspects that involve first- and second-person pronouns. In simple terms, we might be able to learn a great deal about 'self' if we were to study the way that 'I,' 'me' and 'you' are used in ordinary conversation.

Finding 'location' in utterance

Harré and Gillett's contention (p. 103) that 'to have a sense of one's personal individuality is to have a sense of having a place or places in various ... systems of locations' is supported by reference to ordinary situations.

One of their examples is the use of the phrase 'I can feel a draught.' It is possible to gain information about the world from this statement, in the sense that the draught (p. 107) 'is to be felt at the place at which the speaker is presently located'. However, another of the four locations comes into play, because the reliability of this (or any) statement will depend upon the 'speaker's "position" or standing in the local moral order'. An individual's identity is his or her sense of being located in space *and* of possessing a position in the 'moral order'.

One disagreement with this idea comes to mind: a speaker's location in the moral order may actually be quite low, but he or she may inhabit a position of *authority* which allows a statement to go unchallenged. Harré and Gillett do not discuss the question of *power*, which suggests that we will need to turn to other authors for this vital factor in the creation of human identity (see Goran Therborn in the section on 'subjection/qualification: human potential', below). They are more successful in demonstrating that human interactions produce a sense of identity, and that individual identity is constructed through language, particularly through the use of **indexical** terms. These are terms whose reference depends upon the context in which they are used, like 'I', 'you', 'here', 'now' or 'tomorrow'.

Gross notes that (p. 619) 'when children refer to themselves as "I" (or "me") and others as "you", they are having to reverse the labels that are normally used to refer to them by others ("you", "he", "she")'. The challenge they face is one of *shifting reference*. Their sense of self and of *location* allows most children to use the hypothesis that 'I' means whoever is speaking and 'you' refers to the person to whom speech is addressed. Children do not usually select the incorrect hypothesis that 'I' means an adult who is speaking and 'you' means the child.

The divided self?

Freud: three categories of self

Sigmund Freud (1856–1939) is sometimes castigated for the complexity of the terms he used for the various aspects of 'self'. These are **id**, **ego** and **superego**. Freud had originally made three rather less pretentious-sounding divisions, using the ordinary German words for the 'it', the 'I' and the 'over I'. Apparently, these categories attained their familiar and more difficult Latin names when Freud's work was translated into other languages.

The *id* is supposed to be the part of the personality which responds purely to instinct, and which is governed by the **pleasure principle**. It is said to be the 'pre-socialised' part of the human identity, associated with infantile behaviour and desires (see Maslow in the section on 'Motivation and needs', below).

The *ego* is that part of the original personality (the *id*) thought by Freudians to be logical or rational, and to be determined by the **reality principle**. It has, however, no *moral* superiority to the **id**. The *superego*, by contrast, provides the 'special agency' in which the parental influence is maintained, and it is here that judgements about right and wrong are made.

Jung and the elements of the psyche

Carl Gustav Jung (1875–1961) thought that the totality of the personality (all its elements, whether conscious or unconscious) could be called the **psyche**, which has three separate parts. These are **consciousness**, the **personal unconscious**, and finally the **collective unconscious**.

Consciousness is described as the only part known to the individual, and consists of thinking, feeling, sensing and intuiting. Jung believed that the development of consciousness is the beginning of individuation, the process by which a person becomes psychologically 'individual', as an indivisible unity or whole. From Jung's perspective, the individual is thus a complete being more or less from birth.

The *personal unconscious* consists of those experiences which are unique to the individual, including what has been forgotten, events or emotions which have been repressed, and those things which have been stored in memory. Certain feelings and ideas in the unconscious may form 'complexes' which prevent the complete individuation of a person from taking place.

The *collective unconscious* is composed of those *inherited* characteristics which affect how a person will respond to the challenges and experiences of life. Jung's theory included the idea that the evolutionary history of human beings provided them with a collective 'store' of *primordial* images, which are actually not pictures as such, but rather predispositions to behave in certain ways. A common example is a fear of the dark, supposedly inherited from our ancestors, though more immediate and practical reasons for such trepidation may suggest themselves. Jung's theory of the collective unconscious has attracted criticism on the grounds that it reinforces fascist ideology, in which the inheritance of an unconscious 'racial' psychology motivates behaviour.

Self-concept and self-esteem

The practice of dividing the self into distinct parts can lead us to believe that there are actually separate mental functions which *determine* our behaviour. The usefulness of such divisions, however, lies in their ability to focus attention on different aspects of social conduct. The conscious part of self is often divided into **self-concept** and **self-esteem**.

The **self-concept**, or the 'cluster' of ideas held about the self, includes the qualities, preferences and shortcomings perceived by an individual as belonging to him or herself. Since self-concept is supposed to be based on the *descriptions* individuals make of themselves, it is clear that there must be some external standard against which people can measure the characteristics they regard as their own. (See 'The group and the individual: social identification' in Chapter 3.) Self-concept is therefore usually thought to be shaped, altered or maintained through interaction with others.

Self-concept is meant to encompass all notions of self, including *realistic* and *ideal* selves. The *realistic* self is individuals' perception of what they take to be their 'true' qualities and shortcomings, while the *ideal* self is that which individuals strive, or believe it is possible, to become. Self-concept includes both social roles and 'personality traits', as well as subjects' assessment of their physical appearance and subjective attributes such as gender identity and class position. Gross makes the observation that 'when we know someone well, part of what we mean is that we know what they think of themselves'.

Self-esteem is *evaluative* where self-concept is *descriptive*. It refers to how far individuals like or approve of themselves. Coopersmith (1967) described it as 'a personal judgement of worthiness' (see Gross, p. 609). A sense of self-esteem is supposed to be tested and readjusted through interaction, but will not in fact be entirely dependent on other people. Many individuals are able to sustain an adequate sense of personal esteem from the actions they perform, or from the interests they pursue, without needing constant reassurance from other people.

Although, as G.H. Mead suggested (see Jorge Larrain's *Ideology and Cultural Identity*, p. 147), 'we divide ourselves up in all sorts of different selves with reference to our acquaintances', some writers suggest that there is a 'complete' self which is an amalgam of the various parts. Jorge Larrain argues that (p. 147) 'the unity and structure of the complete self reflects the unity and structure of the social processes in which the individual participates'. It is exactly the unity and structure, or *completeness*, of both the human individual and the society it inhabits which has been called into question by theorists who value the 'postmodernist' approach. (See Chapter 1.)

Social norms

If we agree that individuals seek approval from others, it suggests the existence of *shared* values and beliefs. The values recognised in any society may be seen in the material practices it undertakes. The term *material practices* refers to more than the organised production of solid things. It includes the recognised and meaningful behaviours in a community, including speech events in a variety of settings (naming ceremonies such as christenings, weddings, funerals, and so on). Therefore, all aspects of the *social* world will express the systems of belief and the norms of behaviour that must at least be *recognised*, even where an individual objects to some aspects of the social order.

Roles: great expectations?

G.H. Mead was interested in developmental theories which stress the way in which individuals are able to get 'outside themselves' by taking on **roles**, or by viewing themselves from the vantage point of *other people*. A straightforward definition of role is given by Dimbleby and Burton in *More than Words*, when they say that (p. 90):

'a role is a way of behaving which is considered to be suitable for a particular situation'.

By 'situation', they mean presumably a variety of public and private events which are recognised as belonging to distinct categories, and which therefore demand different modes of behaviour. Public performances of music (formal and informal concerts) are the examples given by these authors. The individual audience member is supposed to behave in a way regarded as appropriate to the occasion.

Universal and particular expectations

From where, exactly, do social or public expectations come? Is appropriate role behaviour decided by families, the state, individuals or groups? The answer must be that all these influences are involved in the process of role 'description', and that individuals acknowledge **universal** as well as **particular** behavioural expectations in every situation they meet. *Universal* expectations are the generally accepted *range* of actions and declarations which it is usual for any one individual to make in any situation. *Particular* expectations relate to the types of conduct most appropriate to any specific context or 'definable' situation.

Convention and practical necessity

Much of our behaviour is in fact 'conventional' in the sense that it is based upon practical necessity. The different conventions of behaviour that Dimbleby and Burton assign to the formal concert hall and the rock concert will have their origins in the practical requirements of each situation. The quiet attentiveness of individuals at a classical recitation may have *become* a convention, but is clearly suited to the requirements of the event. While Dimbleby and Burton regard role as a fluid concept, Therborn (*The Ideology of Power and the Power of Ideology*, pp. 20–1) sees role as the behaviour 'expected of individuals occupying a particular social position'.

Rude and loud: offending against norms

The norms which operate in a variety of situations are usually clearly understood, but are not always obeyed. Peter Hartley draws attention to this (see p. 89 of *Interpersonal Communication*) when he notes that 'many people do seem to constantly break specific norms and yet this is ignored or even accepted'. This statement contains an irony of which the author seems unaware, since he breaks a grammatical 'norm' by splitting an infinitive!

One of the reasons why people offend against norms of behaviour is that they, or the groups to which they belong, hold other values which they place above those held by society in general. Sometimes, patterns of behaviour are deliberately adopted in order to offend against the requirements of politeness or tradition. However, departures from accepted norms rarely cause catastrophic upsets, probably because the *recognition* that an offence has taken place itself helps to re-establish expected standards of conduct.

In addition, attempts to correct or punish 'deviant' behaviour are fraught with difficulties. In fact, a mild deviation, provided it is followed by a subsequent recognition of its nature, may even reinforce the conformity of those groups or individuals who witness it.

Role as a disguise?

When *roles* are considered in some theories of interpersonal behaviour, the beneficial use of 'role-play' and phatic communication (see Chapter 1) is emphasised. Others consider that the assumption of roles is largely negative. Barnlund, for example (see Patton and Giffin, *Interpersonal Communication in Action*), believes that (p. 43):

> 'it is when men interact in roles, speaking as they believe they should rather than as they feel, that communication is often corrupted'.

Speaking as we 'believe we should' is the whole point of contextual communication; it can refer to our sense of a *moral* obligation to speak, and may include utterances which completely oppose mainstream ideas. Speaking 'as we feel' may have disastrous consequences.

Roles are not merely *disguises*, nor are they simply *masks* which conceal malevolence or dishonesty. They may indeed have negative effects, but they are also able to assist interaction, because people will understand that a speaker is conforming to an accepted role; they will thus know how to respond. Individuals are also able to see beyond role, while apparently agreeing to follow the rules of formal interaction.

The presentation of self in everyday life: Goffman

In *The Presentation of Self in Everyday Life* Erving Goffman explored the ways in which behavioural norms could be used by the individual to manipulate the perceptions of others. He worked on the theory that our shared awareness of what certain behaviours *reveal* about people could be used in an underhand way to present a desired version of the self. This goes further than the idea of 'role as a disguise'.

The first page of Goffman's book presents the basic concept which motivates his study:

> 'observers can glean clues from ... conduct and appearance which allow them to apply their previous experience with individuals roughly similar to the one before them'.

This would depend on the idea that people do indeed observe others and ascribe personality types to specific kinds of appearance. Goffman was convinced that the 'true' or 'real' attitudes, beliefs and emotions of the individual can be ascertained 'only indirectly, through his avowals or through what appears to be involuntary expressive behaviour'.

While *avowals* may be useful indicators of personality and character, Goffman believed that most people are disinclined to take these on trust. Therefore, instead of examining forms of utterance in order to discover what they might disclose, Goffman turned to the study of behaviour. The idea that people in general regard behavioural patterns as more revealing than utterance is, in fact, highly questionable, since people attend to the *combined* impression they receive from one another. Goffman's approach does, however, provide the starting point for some useful analysis.

Natural behaviour?

In Goffman's view, some forms of behaviour are regarded as 'natural' or as an expression of the unconscious. If this is the case, then onlookers use them as a reliable guide to the person they observe (p. 2):

> 'The expressiveness of the individual ... appears to involve two radically different kinds of sign-activity: the expression that he *gives*, and the expression that he *gives off*.'

Goffman notes that 'the first involves verbal symbols or their substitutes' while the second encompasses a wide range of action that others can treat 'as symptomatic of the actor'. He sees the individual as capable of conveying misinformation through both speech and visible behaviours. In the case of speech, this is supposed to involve deceit, while the manipulation of observable behaviour is rather a case of what Goffman calls 'feigning'.

He believes, in fact, that it is perfectly natural for people to convey misinformation. Why should this be? Is Goffman just cynical about human nature?

We cannot begin to appreciate his point unless we realise that, in most situations, there is something 'to play for'. This does not mean that communication always involves huge stakes, or vast possibilities for social and material advancement. It is enough that people wish to make favourable impressions, or that they are anxious not to appear incompetent.

Playing a character

Since all individuals have some awareness of being watched, and will know that others may attempt to 'place' them in specific categories according to their actions and appearance, it may be possible to shape such perceptions. In order to illustrate this point, Goffman used an extract from William Sansom's 1956 novel, *A Contest of Ladies*. The passage cited concerns the public behaviour of an English holidaymaker, Preedy, who performs a variety of actions and strikes a number of attitudes in order to make a deliberate impression on those around him. He is careful to make these behaviours appear natural, in the hope that they will be interpreted as reliable evidence of his character. Preedy appears here on a Mediterranean beach (Goffman, p. 17):

'First of all, he had to make it clear to those potential companions of his holiday that they were of no concern to him whatsoever. He stared through them, round them, over them – eyes lost in space ... If by chance a ball was thrown his way, he looked surprised; then let a smile of amusement lighten his face (Kindly Preedy), looked round dazed to see that there *were* people on the beach, tossed it back with a smile to himself ... and then resumed carelessly his nonchalant survey of space.'

Preedy must also, however, perform more active demonstrations of his personal qualities. In the words of the author, it was 'time to institute a little parade':

'By devious handlings he gave any who wanted to look a chance to see the title of his book – a Spanish translation of Homer, classic thus, but daring, cosmopolitan too – and then gathered his beach-wrap and bag into a neat, sand-resistant pile (Methodical and Sensible Preedy), rose slowly to stretch at ease his huge frame (Big-Cat Preedy), and tossed aside his sandals (Carefree Preedy, after all). The marriage of Preedy and the sea! There were alternative rituals. The first involved the stroll that turns into a run and a dive straight into the water ... the alternative course ... avoided the cold-water shock ... The point was to appear so used to the sea, to the Mediterranean, and this particular beach, that one might as well be in the sea as out of it. It involved a slow stroll down and into the edge of the water – not even noticing his toes were wet, land and water all the same to *him*! – with eyes up at the sky gravely surveying portents, invisible to others, of the weather (Local Fisherman Preedy).'

Of course, the success of such a pantomime depends upon the readiness of others to notice individual examples of behaviour, and on this evidence to ascribe to the performer the character he or she wishes to create.

Motivation and needs

Communication is **motivated** by human **need**. Abraham Maslow, writing in 1954, believed that *unsatisfied* needs motivated behaviour. He organised his description of needs into a hierarchy (Figure 2.6), with the most urgent being *physiological*. These encompass the most basic requirements of life, such as food and water and anything affecting physical survival. The next on the list,

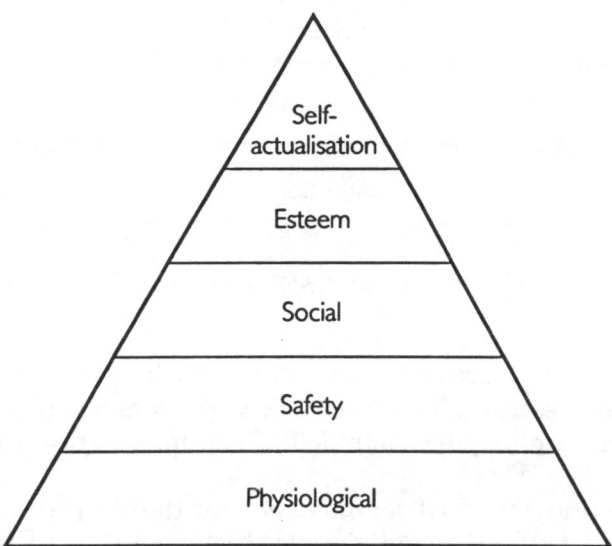

Figure 2.6   Maslow's hierarchy of needs

safety needs, are those whose attainment allows freedom from danger and deprivation. *Social* needs follow, supposedly becoming important when the first two stages are satisfied; companionship, belonging and friendship comprise this level. *Esteem* needs emerge from the desire to achieve self-esteem and to win approval from others (two requirements which are in fact very close to one another). The fifth and last level is that of *self-actualisation*, where individuals may attempt to attain the fullest degree of their potential.

The problem with the theory lies in its hierarchical nature, which suggests that each stage needs to be fulfilled before the next assumes significance. It is obvious that human needs are rather more complex. For example, it is perfectly possible that social needs may remain unfulfilled if self-actualisation is regarded as more important. There are, for example, times when ambitious individuals will place success above the desire for close relationships. Even the most basic requirements of human life may be neglected if they are seen as less important than the fulfilment of a particular aim. The action of the political hunger-striker is a case in point.

If we take the argument further, we might begin to realise that our needs are not always easy to tell apart. For example, while there is a difference between hunger (a physiological need) and ambition (usually thought to be 'psychological'), the latter will often be explained as a *material* feature of personal experience; the term 'hungry' is sometimes applied to those who are eager for success.

Schutz: inclusion, control, affection

William Schutz, in *The Interpersonal Underworld*, describes three needs which give rise to communicative behaviour: **inclusion**, **control** and **affection**

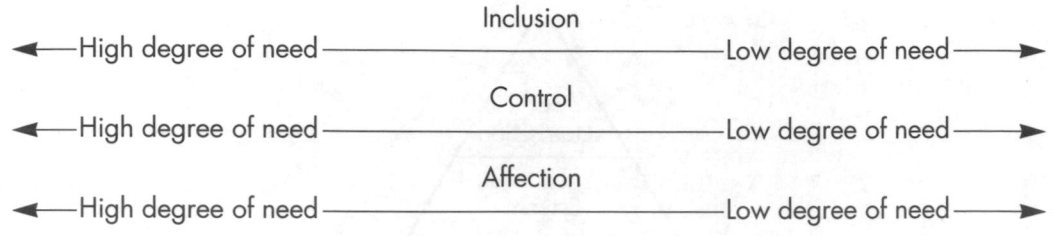

Figure 2.7   Diagrammatic version of Schutz (1966) showing an individual's 'degrees of need'

(Figure 2.7). These needs are social, and do not include the basic survival and physiological needs described by Maslow. However, when we speak of the quest for social 'survival,' we may be reminded of the importance attached to basic social competence.

Schutz argues that the need for *inclusion* is the desire to be seen as an individual, distinct from other individuals. Inclusion is used therefore in the sense of gaining attention, rather than simply being 'accepted' by other people. *Control*, on the other hand, is the desire to exercise power, over oneself but more significantly over one's environment. The idea that inclusion and control can be quite separate is shown in the example of the person who is content to exercise power 'behind the scenes'. *Affection* is the desire to give and receive friendship or love.

Degrees of need

Schutz believed that different individuals possess varying degress of need. For example, one type of individual might regard inclusion and recognition from others as life's most important requirement. According to Myers and Myers (see *The Dynamics of Human Communication*, p. 90), this kind of person feels that 'to be punished is better than to be ignored'. The opposite personality type is usually thought to be the individual who prefers not to be noticed.

Schutz advanced the theory that people belonging to either of these types are motivated by the same fear: the concern that their *individuality* might not be recognised. In the first case, this results in attention seeking. In the second, it motivates the individual to protect his or her privacy. Myers and Myers argue that 'most people are probably somewhere in the middle'.

Needs, norms and theories of dependence

When explanations are sought for the differences which exist between individual needs, the accepted practice of one school of thought (called *individualist* in Chapter 1), has been to attribute such differences to

personality. The assertion that these are *types* of people seems to provide a number of theorists with their chief explanation for human behaviour. For example, Myers and Myers describe any situation where there is a preponderance of the type called the 'recognition seeker' as a recipe for discord: (p. 90)

> 'if all members [of a group] are recognition seekers, chances are they will have a difficult time securing attention from one another'.

The idea that an individual always behaves in accordance with his or her dominant 'trait' is simply not borne out by actual group processes, where mature individuals have at least to alter their behaviour to suit contextual circumstance. Personality type is not always the most essential factor in human interaction. While there is some evidence that the notion of typage is based upon innate differences between people, we need also some sense of the social or historical context to human behaviour.

Myers and Myers do not recognise the discursive and situational context in which people operate. When they produce remarks like the following (p. 91), 'Cold people and warm people do not mix well', it seems they have strayed beyond the bounds of coherent theory.

Communication or the etiquette of personal exchange?

As we have seen above, most communication theory insists that the 'self' is maintained through a relationship with others. This is a useful idea, but has unfortunately encouraged some writers to concentrate solely on *interpersonal* exchanges. The fact that interpersonal communication proper takes place between two people appears to suggest to some commentators that they are merely observing the play of relationships, rather than acts of social construction. Instead of regarding the interpersonal **dyad** as a sub-group of the larger social collective, there is a tendency to regard it as the be-all and end-all of research.

Patton and Giffin, in their 1981 study *Interpersonal Communication in Action*, provide many examples of this approach, arguing that (p. 50):

> 'we depend on other people to confirm our views ... To the extent that our personal interaction with others is successful and confirming, we are able to grow, find our identity, gain self-esteem, and feel we are firmly in touch with reality.'

Although this appears, at least superficially, to have something in common with the *social* model of communication proposed in this book, most of *Interpersonal Communication in Action* is concerned to interpret human *behaviour* from external evidence, essentially that which takes place between two people. The study of communication becomes essentially a plea for better understanding within individual relationships (p. 128):

'If we fear others and their motives, we are likely to respond in a defensive, uncooperative manner. Only when we trust – are willing to rely on people to achieve a desired object in a risky situation – is cooperation possible.'

I would argue that *individualist* or 'psychological' approaches to communication employ a model which has proved popular because they look at interaction from the point of view of the individual, but without the sense of context used in *social* perspectives. In other words, the reader is constantly encouraged to substitute his or her 'I' for any one partner in a printed exchange. Instead of asking students to consider their surroundings and what they have in common with others, it begins from a perspective which dwells on the 'unique' traits of individual subjects.

Trying to fit in?

The central idea which runs through Patton and Giffin's book seems essentially to foster a 'therapeutic' approach to communication. What receives less attention is the idea that the whole of the interpersonal domain has a relationship with *language* as the primary system for the creation of meaning. Instead of a critical analysis of the social order, *Interpersonal Communication in Action* propounds the theory and practice of trying to 'fit in' and court success.

In line with this goal, the concept of **validation** takes the idea that the human subject is essentially social and turns it into a theory of dependence. According to this outlook, each person's self-worth is *primarily* related to how he or she is perceived by other individuals. Barnlund argues that (p. 69):

'almost every time we initiate communication, even on a nonverbal level, we are making an implied request: "Please confirm my viewpoint".'

Patton and Giffin make a similar claim (p. 18):

'Whenever one person attempts to initiate interpersonal communication with another, he or she has made an implicit request: "Please validate me as a person!"'

While these assertions have the virtue of reminding us that human beings seek affirmation, it also reveals a flaw in these authors' understanding of the social. Human beings are not always entirely dependent on other people in the way suggested here. This is not to argue that other people are unnecessary, but rather that a sense of self is not founded solely upon the approval or recognition accorded to the self by others; 'validation' or affirmation may be sought and obtained through other, more 'self-centred' endeavours, or perhaps through conceptualising one's relationship to other elements, including the natural world.

Following their original assertion, Patton and Giffin argue that (p. 18):

'If there is consistent social confirmation, a strong, integrated self-identity will be developed and sustained.'

In fact, social confirmation may not always require constant 'topping up'. It is exactly because this argument puts so much emphasis on *belonging* that it neglects to examine the nature of the society to which individuals are encouraged to belong. Attachment to the shared values of a social group may produce the 'integrated self-identity' mentioned here, but the overall social effect may be entirely negative. Fascism, for example, has been known to produce strong subject positions for individuals to occupy.

In the world of the interpersonal theorist, every attempt at communication may be reduced to a wish for personal approval. In fact, the complete opposite may be the case; we may wish to provoke *disagreement*. In many ways, it is more beneficial to have one's viewpoint challenged. It is worth mentioning that identity is often attained through the process of *differentiating* the self from other individuals and groups. (See theories of self-identification in Chapter 3.) If constant accord and agreement are sought, then the 'self-worth' promoted in so many books may be built upon very shallow foundations.

Behavioural context

Myers and Myers argue that (p. 63):

'as an adult, you behave in a given situation not just on the basis of how you perceive the situation but on the basis of *how you imagine other people in general expect you to act*'.

These authors do not recognise the possibility that the expectation of others counts as a form of context; they split *perception of a situation* from *perception of role*, but of course the two features are very difficult to separate, since they are both elements which go to the creation of communicative context. 'Other people' will expect the individual to act according to the constraints of the situation. I would argue that the notion we have of how others perceive us is partly our awareness of how *any* individual would be judged in a similar situation.

Myers and Myers put the onus for successful communication entirely on the individual (p. 63), and seem to believe that positive thinking has almost magical powers to affect the outcome of communication:

'If you think of yourself in positive terms, you will tend to imagine that others perceive you in a positive light. If you think of yourself in negative terms, you will anticipate negative reactions from others.'

They go on to make the interesting assertion that:

'in both cases you act on the basis of *how you think other people view you* and not on the basis of *how they actually view you*'.

This advances the idea that positive or negative self-regard creates an inaccurate impression of how one is seen by others; but how is such an effect achieved? Is it not possible that the two, self-regard and external impression, might sometimes coincide? Aren't most experienced individuals astute enough to work out roughly how they are thought of by others? If this is not achieved, how then would any useful picture of social reality be constructed? Myers and Myers seem to picture a world of relationships more complex than the one that actually exists, and appear to exaggerate the 'gap' between perception and reality.

Self-fulfilling prophecies

The next stage is the *self-fulfilling* prophecy, where an individual's negative perception of self is revealed through external behaviour. This is noted by observers, who conclude that the individual concerned is inadequate or somehow anti-social. In this scenario, the subject's perception of other people's response leads to more negative feelings and a repetition of the same kind of poor self-display. Once others pick this up, they are then able to confirm their original assessment. In this way, the cycle of self-defeating behaviour continues (see Myers and Myers, p. 63):

'your expectations of how others perceive you leads you to act in such a way that ultimately you may help develop in others the kind of perceptions you thought they had; and you find in their behaviour toward you the final evidence that you were right in the first place'.

Myers and Myers provide a cautionary tale in the form of the 'shy young man', who becomes convinced that he is not of any interest to other individuals (p. 63):

' "No one pays any attention to me; I am unattractive, and I knew it all along", becomes his entrenched philosophy, making it more and more unlikely that he will break out of the vicious circle he helped to create.'

The agenda behind this theory appears to be a belief in the power of improved self-esteem, but it is difficult to know how exactly this will be obtained, since the 'vicious circle' is difficult to break. Will increased self-esteem come from greater exposure to interactive events, and will this, in turn, require the individual to produce a superhuman effort to appear interesting or competent?

The effect of Myers and Myers's approach is to suggest that negative events will remain the responsibility or fault of the individual. To some degree, therefore, it lets the group and the society off the hook, and certainly does not address problems such as the fact that groups are often deliberately intended to be *exclusive* and sustained through the use of negative discrimination.

A sorry tale

Myers and Myers also cite the example of the 'Pygmalion effect', which seems to date from an informal college experiment carried out in the US during the 1930s. This is the tale of five American graduates who set about changing the self-image of a female student. The student concerned was supposed to be 'rather plain'. After a long series of planned interactions, during which the male graduates talked to the young woman and eventually asked her out, some alteration in her behaviour was supposedly discovered (p. 64):

> 'after a couple of months a noticeable change occurred in the young woman. She started wearing more attractive clothes, she did her hair in a more becoming style, she smiled more, and she talked more in class and outside of class.'

The moral of this sorry tale of manipulation is, according to these authors, that the female student became attractive because 'the male students *behaved* to her as though she was attractive and important'. This does not sound like a very good recommendation for a theory of positive reinforcement.

Personality types or discursive choices?

In Patton and Giffin's *Interpersonal Communication in Action*, Virginia Satir identifies 'seemingly universal patterns' in the way people communicate. Satir carried out a series of observations of human interaction. Whenever any form of personal stress was evident in her subjects, she discovered that the individuals concerned employed various **strategies** for coping. She characterised these methods as **placating, blaming, computing** and **distracting**. In itself, this amounts to a plausible series of responses, useful for example in the analysis of speech events.

It is the search Satir makes for psychological states *behind* utterances which is unconvincing. She produces a series of beliefs which are supposed to inform the actions of each type, such as the 'placater's' conviction that 'without him/her I am dead. I am worthless.' The *placater* is able to agree with his or her opposite number (usually a spouse) but only because they feel 'like a nothing'. It would have been more useful to present the four strategies as **discursive choices**, available to all those involved in interaction, rather than offering each as evidence of distinct personality types.

In the 'therapeutic' model of interaction, all behaviours, however temporary or subject to contextual influence, seem to be remorselessly quantified and labelled. Barnlund, another contributor to *Interpersonal Communication in Action*, repeats T.H. Newcom's idea (see *Readings in Social Psychology*) that avoidance of communication is 'autistic hostility'. The seemingly endless invention of different labels for various states of mind appears to have produced a whole quasi-science.

Subjection/qualification

Bringing up baby: instruction, sanction, affirmation

One tradition of communication research regards human identity as a phenomenon which is *confirmed* by social interaction. The question which remains to be examined is: how is identity *created*? Although an infant will be shaped in ways which the adults around it may regard as 'natural', its upbringing will entail many forms of **instruction** and **sanction** designed to ensure it follows the norms of the social group. *Instruction* is the issuing of direct orders, *sanction* is the system of rules which allows the application of penalties or rewards, while **affirmation** is the positive encouragement of certain actions which are regarded as beneficial or morally desirable.

While many of these restrictions are entirely sensible, since the infant must be protected, none will be 'value-free' and all will help to 'place' the child in society. In fact, it is often those restrictions regarded as the most 'natural' which are used by authority in attempts to control the individual. Some writers consider that this 'placing' derives ultimately from the power of the state. Others concentrate on the role of more immediate agencies within the social structure, such as the family.

The psychologist Eleanor Maccoby (1980) defines moral development as the acquisition of rules about right and wrong, and the evolution of an under-standing of the values that regulate behaviour in the social world. However, a sense of right and wrong does not necessarily have to match the 'mainstream' values which are found within a society. In this book, I will refer to the *social order* as that force, including the state, which creates the conditions which 'socialise' the infant and 'monitor' the conduct of the mature subject.

Early influence?

Myers and Myers, in common with many authors, regard the greatest influence on early identity to be the way that children are brought up by their parents (from *The Dynamics of Human Communication*, p. 61):

> 'The way you were treated began to lay the foundations upon which you developed feelings and thoughts about the kind of person you were. If you were lucky, you received messages of warmth and love . . . some children are not so lucky and go ignored and untouched for long periods of time . . . they learn at a most impressionable age that they do not matter, that no-one cares for them, and consequently that they must be no good.'

The deterministic nature of such pronouncements may encourage us to believe that there is no escape from the factors which shaped our original identity, and to regard 'self' as *irrevocably* shaped in the space of a few short years. To accept this idea unreservedly is to neglect the variety of influences which continue to act upon the individual. However, there is no doubt that upbringing remains a central factor in the construction of the self.

Myers and Myers see role-play as the formative stage of the public persona (persona means the character or part 'acted' by an individual). Role-play allows children to rehearse their understanding of the adult world, and modes of behaviour in different situations. The later phase is called **symbolic role-taking**, a period during which individuals incorporate the roles they believe others will expect of them.

My name and I

Robert Graves identified the *naming* of a child as central to identity, and wrote about the distance sometimes felt between the 'true' self and the name one is given (see 'My Name and I' in *Selected Poems*, p. 162):

'The impartial Law enrolled a name
For my especial use:
My rights in it would rest the same
Whether I puffed it into fame
Or sank it in abuse.'

Graves's parents choose his first name and instruct him to ensure that 'Robert Graves' behaves in an exemplary fashion. The poet's true identity does not have the same status because it is unnamed and hidden, though always in evidence; 'I was always I / Illegal and unknown'. Graves 'cannot well repudiate / This noun, this natal star', yet refuses identification with it:

'Yet, understand, I am not he
Either in mind or limb;
My name will take less thought for me,
In worlds of men I cannot see,
Than ever I for him.'

The 'spirit of perversity'

Stevie Davies, in the introduction to her 1994 study of Emily Brontë (*Emily Brontë: Heretic*), notes that 'the spirit of perversity' found in young children is (Preface, p. xi):

'systematically squashed, slapped, smoothed, wheedled and argued out of [them]'.

Davies sees that rebellion lies often in the refusal to acknowledge those norms which appear self-evident, and that the eventual acceptance of 'obvious' truths implies not merely the end of naivety, but also the loss of important insights into the structures of power. Davies invents a 'parable' to demonstrate this point:

> 'A child informs its parents that night is the time to be awake and the day the time to sleep; that God is bad and so-called "naughtiness" is really good; that girls are not different from boys – and furthermore, that ice is blue ... years later, the same child prefers sun to moon, "knows right from wrong", endorses gender difference and the consensus palette of colours.'

However, since negative reinforcement is not sufficient to produce socialised human subjects, there must also be some positive forms of encouragement or *affirmation* (see above), which are designed to encourage conformity.

Specific identities: gender, ethnicity, class

Michael Argyle, in *The Psychology of Interpersonal Behaviour*, distinguishes between self-esteem as it pertains to men and women, noting that (p. 192):

> 'For a man, the job will also be central, unless he is suffering from job alienation. For a woman her family and husband's job may also be central.'

Here, the division of labour is presented as though it always produces the same **role-affiliation**. In other words, the condition of employment appears as a universal litmus test of the *male* psychological condition, while the female individual is characterised as primarily orientated to the family and the concerns of the male. In this scenario, the female does not stand in her own right. The extract reveals the use of certain assumptions which are usually described as *sexist*.

Influences which help 'construct' human subjectivity include religion, education, family, nation, age and the political formation, but questions of ethnicity, class and gender have attracted particular attention in recent years. Theories of the construction of **gendered identity** appear in many textbooks, while a number of research projects in human and mass communication have shown that most academic inquiry treats the human subject as though it is 'neutral' and not endowed with specific identity. In effect, this means that the *dominant* perspective has remained male-dominated, even while academic etiquette demands that the use of terms like 'man' to describe the human race in general is no longer acceptable.

Gender and identity

In physiology, the term *sex* is used to refer to the *biological* status of an individual (whether male or female), while the use of *gender* in an academic discipline means the classification of people as male or female according to *social* factors. The continuing debate over gender concerns the points at which biologically determined characteristics and abilities can be separated from those features of behaviour or performance which are determined by *social* factors.

The research of Maccoby and Jacklin (1974) discovered that some biological differences might exist, such as the superiority of verbal ability in girls, and the more advanced 'visual-spatial' ability ascribed to boys. However, many of the more fundamental questions, such as whether one sex is more physically active than the other, remain unresolved.

The acquisition of *gendered identity* takes place in the early years of childhood development. According to Gross (see *Psychology: The Science of Mind and Behaviour*, p. 681), a number of researchers have discovered that very young children are aware of gender roles and are wary of 'crossing the line' between behaviours regarded as 'male' or 'female'. The findings of Parish and Bryant (1978) showed that children aged five to eleven showed a positive attitude to their own sex and a negative attitude to the opposite sex. (This would fit in with self-identification theory; see Chapter 3). A variety of theories describe the possible reasons for differences between male and female role-behaviour, ranging from those which are purely **biological**, and those **biosocial** perspectives which also take social factors into account, to the **cultural relativism** of Margaret Mead, who produced a book in 1935 which argued that the traits we identify as feminine and masculine are entirely cultural in origin.

Investigating women's subjectivity

Bronwyn Davies, a lecturer at the University of New England, investigated female subjectivity in the following terms (in Ellis and Flaherty, *Investigating Subjectivity*, p. 54), insisting that she was referring not to biological sex, but to:

'the discursive category of female/woman and the experience of being discursively constituted as one who belongs to that category'.

Davies recounts the attempt to produce written material in conjunction with a male colleague who objected to her extensive references to feminism. He argued that her constant reference to her own position (or subject position) as a woman detracted from the validity of her work. Davies notes that this reveals (p. 54):

'the myth of the positionless speaker as the one who speaks the most valuable truths'.

Davies realises that the multiple subject positions females have to occupy might lead some theorists to believe that women are caught in a hopeless dilemma, but believes that women should not attempt to force an artificial division between their various public roles and a private 'self'. She argues that men have been able to act in contradictory ways because they have kept the private 'I' separate from the variety of roles (or variants of 'me') which they display for public consumption. Traditionally, women have been much less comfortable with this division.

Why do individuals, both male and female, experience a 'crisis' in identity at all? Jorge Larrain, in *Ideology and Cultural Identity* (pp. 151–2), points to the increasing *pace* of technological and social change, the 'compression' of relationships between time and space (the speeding up of life and the 'shrinking' of our concepts of space), the growing 'internationalisation' of the economy, and the advent of a mass global culture.

The self and the 'other'

Academics from disciplines concerned with linguistics, social or anthropological theory, classics, ancient history, cultural studies and a host of other fields have shown an eagerness to explore ideas about the 'other'. As we saw in Chapter 1, G.H. Mead used the term to refer to the general notion of the 'not-self', an awareness of which he regarded as vital in the creation of self. The twentieth-century psychologist Jacques Lacan is also associated with 'the other'. In early Lacanian psychology, the 'other' is the individual signified by the term 'you', and the human subject is created through the tension between the opposite poles of 'I' and 'you'. In Lacan's later work, the 'other' is language itself. Bannister and Agnew (1976) also thought that the construction of self depended upon having a concept of 'not-self'. This would imply that we build up a view of our 'self' by contrasting our supposed attributes with those of others.

In *Defining Women*, edited by Linda McDowell and Rosemary Pringle (p. 3), women occupy the role of the 'other':

> 'Women are constantly defined in relation to men. Whether they are similar to men, different from or complementary to them, men, masculinity and male behaviour are always the reference points.'

Women's identity and status 'derive from their relation to the explicitly gendered categories of mothers, daughters and wives'.

David Maybury-Lewis, in the television series and the accompanying book *Millennium: Tribal Wisdom and the Modern World*, notes that identity in an Indonesian tribe (the Sumba) 'is important enough to go beyond the grave'. The tribespeople believe that people will only know their identity when they are asked direct questions. The remains of ancestors are also asked to identify themselves. Unlike the academic perspective, however, which sees the 'other' as either language, or an oppressed group, or a suppressed memory – in essence a conflictual *opposite* which helps to create the self – the Indonesian perspective sees the other or opposite as a *harmonious* supplement. The world is a place where, in the words of a tribal elder (*Millennium*, p. 128, but transcript here from the television series):

> 'Everything is paired, each has its other half, opposite, counterpart. If there is no pair there is nothing, that is the order of things.'

Maybury-Lewis argues that 'we always want to isolate, define the individual, what it is, where it starts, and finishes', whereas in tribal society, identity is 'dependent on relationships . . . identity is who answers your questions'.

Subjection/qualification: human potential

Goran Therborn (see *The Ideology of Power and the Power of Ideology,* p. 17) believes that the 'manifold potentialities of human infants' are shaped by the social order in which they are born, which:

'favours certain drives and capacities, and prohibits or disfavours others'.

The idea here is that **human potential** will be circumscribed by the way that life is both *understood* and *organised*. According to this theory, individuals are given roles which are supposed to ensure that the major relationships of power in the social order continue as before. Therborn's approach is centred on social class, but it does include reference to other forms of subjectivity. Gender roles, for example, are absolutely central to the maintenance of an unequal social order.

Therborn notes that a contradiction often arises between the needs of a society to repress or control individuals (**subjection**) and the requirement to train capable individuals who are autonomous enough to perform certain functions (**qualification**). He argues that it is not unusual for a social order to produce individuals who will turn against the society which has nurtured them, because:

'new kinds of qualification may be required and provided, new skills that clash with the traditional forms of subjection'.

For example, it may be necessary for a society, as it becomes more technologically advanced, to create a class of people able to analyse and reproduce information (computer programmers, for instance). This group may, by virtue of its role and position, begin to alter the traditional 'balance of power'.

A parallel example of the need to increase qualification may be found during the war against Nazi Germany, when Britain and the US required women to work in roles previously allocated to men. The survival of the democracies (each founded on a system of class patriarchy) depended therefore on taking the risk that women could first be successfully mobilised to perform 'men's' work, and would later allow themselves to be moved back into 'traditional' roles. In other words, the social order had to suffer some temporary fracture if it was to stand a chance of being rebuilt after the war.

A society may, on the other hand, create new types of subjection which clash with established patterns of qualification. For instance, exercises in privatisation and cost-cutting may result in the disciplining of a workforce whose existing abilities or skills (qualification) do not alter. As Therborn says (p. 17):

'The effects of a contradiction between subjection and qualification are opposition and revolt or underperformance and withdrawal.'

Contradictions at work

When there is a **contradiction** or clash between the requirements of subjection and qualification, does this mean that one of the two categories has become more important than the other? Might a reduction in qualification amount in practice to the same thing as an an increase in subjection? On the other hand, if employers or the state make expensive investment in training for the sake of long-term benefits, then qualification has been *increased*; does this mean that subjection has to some degree been lessened?

The best way of understanding subjection and qualification is to picture them as part of an interactive process. In practice, human subjects experience the two as a single force in their lives. Subjection and qualification may be compared to the terms described earlier: *sanction* and *affirmation*.

Expression and meaning

Dictionary knowledge?

When the poet Laura Riding began her attempt to produce a dictionary which would provide one exact meaning for every word, she was clearly engaged in a task that would prove impossible. As Moore and Carling point out in *Understanding Language: Towards a Post-Chomskyan Linguistics*, meaning is not an inherent but an *emergent* property of words and sentences. They argue that the function of the dictionary is not 'a store of word meanings' (p. 133):

> 'but rather a list of words with guides as to the area of experience to which they may refer, enabling users to confirm or not ... the way in which particular words are generally used in their culture'.

Although Riding worked on the project for a number of decades, it may come as no surprise to the reader to discover that it was never finished.

Context and use

Katz and Fodor, writing in 1964, also appear to have assumed that speakers use 'dictionary knowledge' in interpreting language. They argue that 'given an accurate dictionary of English, *which he applies by using his linguistic ability*, the fluent speaker can semantically interpret any sentence ... under any of its grammatical derivations'.

Here, at least, there is some reference to linguistic ability, but the meaning of a written or spoken word or phrase is never simply a matter of definition; it is also dependent upon situated context and *use*. This means that a literal interpretation is sometimes only a small part of the meanings native speakers create during an interaction. What other elements are used as conversations unfold? As Chapter 1 argued, these are intonation and body language, elements which are often described as subsidiary but which, certainly in the case of intonation, should be seen as rather more important.

Historical context found in content

Although we often rely upon context to reveal the subtleties of usage, this does not mean that we are *unable* to interpret a phrase or sentence when it appears outside its original context, especially in the case of written language. Historical context, at least, is often *inscribed* in content, in the sense that the literary practices of a period will reveal something about that era's public values. The vocabulary and grammar employed by a writer will also reveal the historical context of composition.

As an example, consider the following short extract from Edmund Burke's 1790 *Reflections on the Revolution in France* (p. 233):

'I do not like to compliment the contrivances of men, with what is due in a great degree to the bounty of Providence.'

The passage from which this is taken discusses the relationship between population and geography, but knowledge of this is not required in order to appreciate the spirit of the extract. The language used is archaic, but not impenetrable. The choice of 'compliment' in this sentence (which could be glossed using forms of the verbs 'credit' or 'attribute') is an example of a now defunct usage. Reference to 'the bounty of Providence' (the generosity of God or nature), made without irony, also helps to place the passage in an era whose public values and practices are to some degree different from our own.

Language function

Michael Halliday (1973) produced a list of no fewer than seven categories of language function, as follows:

- instrumental;
- regulatory;
- representational;
- interactional;
- personal;
- heuristic;
- imaginative.

In *Investigating Language*, Ronald Wardhaugh (see p. 190) explains each of these functions in turn, beginning with **instrumental**. This function allows the human subject to 'manipulate things in the environment'. Although instrumental utterances are often supposed to be **performative**, they may also be expressed through suggestion and persuasion. **Regulatory** functions of language are deployed during attempts to control the consequences of events, or to regulate encounters between people. The **representational** aspect refers to those types of language which are used to communicate or represent events and ideas. **Interactional** elements include the *phatic* or social features revealed in human utterance, while the **personal** function is a reference to language use which is designed to express individual personality. **Heuristic** functions are concerned with the acquisition of knowledge, while the **imaginative** part of language use includes all types of creative expression, from informal musings to extended works of imagination such as novels.

In practice, a single example of linguistic expression may include many of the functions listed above. This is particularly the case during spoken exchange.

Interpretation of speech

In every waking moment, the human subject encounters a great variety of sounds. The interpretation of **speech** depends, in the first place, upon the ability to distinguish between speech sounds and 'non-speech' sounds. The debate about 'active' versus 'passive' models of perception, introduced in Chapter 1, becomes relevant once again. The problem of characterising perception was solved in the first chapter, by suggesting that it is both a *faculty* and an *act*.

In *Investigating Language*, Ronald Wardhaugh argues that listening and understanding, which he calls (p. 104) 'the complete processing of language', requires 'the active involvement of the listener at all stages of what is being said'. This is certainly true, but should not lead us to imagine that understanding is founded purely on a cognitive basis, with meaning emerging solely from the semantic impact of an utterance. The point of paying close attention to an utterance is that all elements, including intonation and speed of delivery, are taken into account. In fact, it may not always be neccessary to attend to the strict semantics of an utterance, since the tone of voice will often provide the necessary clue to understanding.

Semantic vs. grammatical information: forensic discourse analysis

There is evidence to suggest that human beings do not remember **semantic** and **grammatical** information in the same way. Sachs, writing in 1967, demonstrated that the meanings of sentences are easier to recall than their exact 'grammatical shapes' (see Wardhaugh, p. 113). In this case, changes in form will be regarded as unimportant by comparison with changes in meaning. Such findings suggest, in Wardhaugh's words, that:

> 'the exact grammatical form of a sentence is quickly forgotten but ... the information it contains is not'.

The idea that individuals remember information, but not always the exact *form* of an utterance or passage of writing, has important implications for the study of memory, and especially for notions of truthfulness. In *Advances in Spoken Discourse Analysis*, Malcolm Coulthard describes the function of **forensic discourse analysis**, which is the practice of examining interview records or statements in order to reach conclusions about their authenticity. This procedure is usually carried out by a linguist on behalf of the defence.

Coulthard describes the aim of such an inquiry as follows (p. 243):

> 'the first task of the analyst is to point out that discourse analysis can say nothing at all about the truth of what is said *in* the disputed text, but can sometimes comment usefully on the truth of diverging claims made by both sides afterwards *about* the text. In most cases, in demonstrating the inaccuracy, unreliability or impossibility of a claim made about a text, the analyst is able to discredit the text itself as evidence.'

Coulthard notes that, in examining any record of a faked interaction, the analyst is faced with (p. 244) 'the work of an amateur dramatist'. The role of the analyst is to discover 'non-authentic features' in the record of the exchange. One 'non-authentic' feature may be discovered through use of the idea described above, that individuals are unable to recall the precise nature of what they have heard, or indeed have themselves said during an interaction.

The reports of everyday speech delivered by individuals usually offer the impression that they *are* able to recall the exact wording used in an exchange. While in some instances this is indeed possible, it is more usually the case that people fail to produce an accurate reproduction. The difference between original utterance and a subsequent report allows the analyst to treat with caution evidence which shows exact concordance between the two.

Trial of the Birmingham Six

As an example, Coulthard uses the case of the Birmingham Six, a group of men who were wrongfully imprisoned for an IRA bomb attack on a public house. Parts of one defendant's interview record and the statement which followed it were identical. The police claimed that the accused, William Power, had simply retold the story in the same words, while Power insisted that the second text had been copied by police from their record of the first.

Coulthard, as the analyst working for the defence, demonstrated that people cannot, as a rule, remember the exact form of their utterances. Instead, they remember their experience and 'encode' this experience in new forms. During the Birmingham Six trial, the evidence presented was in fact covered twice, because the defence disputed the admissibility of part of the prosecution case. Coulthard, therefore, had access to two versions of the events described by the defendants, each different in form but essentially similar in content. Extracts from the two versions supported the observation that an individual could not, contrary to police evidence, reproduce identical accounts.

Coulthard offers these contrasting versions of Power's testimony as proof of the tendency to encode the same experience differently (p. 247):

'*Power*: They told me there was a mob outside the house and my wife and children would be lynched, only for the Police who were inside ragging it, searching it.'

'*Power*: He told me there was a mob outside my house and they were ready to lynch my wife and children and the only thing that was stopping them was because the Police were outside my house.'

Police evidence, by contrast, looked unconvincing, offering as it did identical versions of Power's experience.

Language and meaning

Wardhaugh describes laboratory experiments which demonstrate that single words, or short sequences of speech, are almost unidentifiable if taken out of context and presented to individual listeners (see *Investigating Language*, p. 104). The inability of subjects to identify small extracts of speech suggests that the basic units of **meaning** in spoken interaction must be larger than was once supposed:

'to achieve ninety per cent intelligibility, [subjects] must hear sequences of seven to eight words produced in no less than about two seconds.'

Meaning must therefore repose in more than *component sounds* alone.

This kind of discovery has led some commentators to challenge the entire basis of traditional approaches to the interpretation of spoken language. The suspicion that current interpretative methodologies do not do justice to the range of meaning which it is possible to generate during an exchange has prompted some to reject what Rivers Barry (*Language and Meaning*, 1994) calls 'systematic' inquiry. By this he means the 'series of logical connections: syntax, semantics, phonology, etc.' which characterise mainstream investigations of spoken language.

Among those elements which Barry believes to have been overlooked or undervalued are *context* and *sound*. What is the reason for the reluctance of theorists to investigate such areas? According to Barry, it is (p. 2):

'the enormous complexity of the subjects. Neither lends itself to scientific scrutiny, simply because they are so full of variables'.

Such variables include the fact that speakers change their language behaviour with 'mood, non-contextual circumstances and personal proccupations'. This means that gathering data which will fit into currently accepted scientific discourses would prove extremely difficult. However, the lack of descriptive categories should not mean that new theories should be dismissed out of hand. Moravcsik, for example, in *Thought and Language*, insists that no progress will be made unless theorists are prepared to consider new forms of analysis, even where they do not yet offer *comprehensive* accounts of their subject matter.

Barry sees the shortcomings of academic interpretation as directly attributable to the use of rationalist approaches (p. 3):

'A more appropriate method may be to see the chaos [of ordinary speech] as a virtue. To look at meaning not as an item of cognition but of emotion may go some way towards this.'

'Meaning' vs. 'significance'

Barry makes a distinction between meaning that is 'semantically demonstratable' and meaning that is 'intuitively recognised'. The method he adopts is to reserve 'meaning' for semantic elements, and to use the term 'significance' for what he calls 'emotional meaning'. He gives the following example (p. 4):

'if a speaker says, "This is pleasant", we know what they mean. But the *significance* of the utterance changes (while the literal meaning stays the same) if the context of the utterance is obviously not pleasant, or if a tone of sarcasm is used, or if rising intonation turns the utterance into a question.'

While recognising that there are problems with a term like 'intuition', he argues that its use should be understood in the Chomskyan sense, as the *recognition* by a native speaker of meaning:

'Our understanding of language is only partly syntactic and semantic. Much of it is based on sound (intonation), phonology (pronunciation) and context (pragmatics).'

In Barry's view, the human system of communication is one that uses our cognitive powers but 'invests them with emotional significance'. In a similar vein, the capacity of the human subject to interpret meaning leads Wardhaugh to conclude that speech is interpreted and evaluated as part of a 'total process of perception', a 'top-down' approach to understanding which, as we saw in Chapter 1, emphasises the selective and organisational role of all the human senses.

Pragmatics

The study of real exchanges which take place in specific situations is known as **pragmatics**. Our investigation of context provides a useful background to this aspect of communication. Whatever the precise reason for engaging in a specific exchange, the overall purpose of making utterances is to carry out *social actions*. This means that social actors are not just saying things, but also at the same time *doing* things.

In *Everyday Conversation*, Robert E. Nofsinger cites the example of a conversation between a district attorney and a public defender in a US court case of 1984:

> '*DA*: Uh I'll give you ninety days with credit for time served.
> *PD*: Nah that's no good.'

Here, the initial utterance is more than just speech; in making the utterance, the district attorney is making an offer. The reply of the other participant constitutes rejection of the offer. When Nofsinger notes that people are able to recognise 'the language game in which they are involved', we may take this as confirmation of *contextual* understanding.

According to Nofsinger, the participants in the plea-bargaining case reproduced above recognise that their conversation has a **formal goal** and understand what 'moves' (social or communicative actions) are required in order to reach that goal. Therefore, when engaged in conversation, a participant will use his or her understanding of certain elements to decide what might be regarded as a suitable response. These elements are:

- what has been done so far;
- what needs to be done;
- what the utterance seems designed to do;
- what alternative actions might have been performed at this point in the conversation.

Nofsinger notes that the particular meaning of the exchange depends on the identity of the participants. Had it taken place between a judge and a *defendant*, then an observer would assume that the response 'Nah that's no good' was intended to be disrespectful. As it is, an exchange between participants who are essentially at the same level, as both are lawyers, means that forms of speech which indicate respect are unnecessary, and may even get in the way of an efficient outcome.

The power of 'everyday talk'

Nofsinger (see p. 1 of *Everyday Conversation*) emphasises the 'immense power of everyday talk', which includes the following functions:

'to contact and influence other people: to enlist their help, to offer them companionship, to protect ourselves from their demands, to establish important relationships with them, and to present ourselves as having the qualities they (and we) admire'.

Conversation is of particular importance, according to this author, because other, more formal systems of spoken communication are actually *dependent* on ordinary exchanges (p. 2):

'We learn conversation first and then apply our conversational skills to other forms of interactive talk.'

Five categories of speech

Likening human interaction to a series of *moves* in a game, Nofsinger examines Searle's division of all speech acts into five categories. These are:

- commissives;
- directives;
- assertives;
- expressives;
- declarations.

The first category, **commissives**, includes promises and other forms of commitment which are undertaken by the speaker. **Directives** are requests as well as commands, since the point of this category is to make an individual comply with the desires of the speaker. **Assertives** are intended to reveal the speaker's belief in the propositional content of an utterance; in other words, that the thing said is actually true. **Expressives** include all those statements which are taken to be expressions of a speaker's psychological state. The last category, **declarations**, is that type of utterance which has a material consequence or effect, such as an announcement to the effect that someone is relieved of his or her post; the declaration makes its own content a reality.

From illocutionary acts to questions and answers

An **illocutionary act** is an utterance which could be understood as a 'move' in a communicative exchange – an 'offering' made by one participant to another. The conventions of language provide the frame in which people speak, but conversational requirements are instinctively understood by individuals during their participation in speech events.

William Labov (1970) identified the following structures for conversation analysis:

- question and answer;
- challenge and response;
- invitation and acceptance.

His ideas about **question and answer** are very important for any study of linguistic power.

Following Labov, we could use a single question to make a point about the range of responses which are available to a speaker. 'Are you going into town?' may elicit the answer 'Yes', which is perfectly straightforward. Such a response is direct and unambiguous, as would be its opposite, 'No'.

Suppose, however, that the answer to this question was, 'It's raining heavily.' This is rather different. Grice (in Coulthard) argued that there is an underlying constraint which acts on all those engaged in conversation; they must produce answers which both participants will recognise as **relevant**. Departures from relevance will be recognised by those who participate in, and those who act as witnesses to, public interaction.

Therefore, the second answer I have provided ('It's raining heavily') depends for its effect upon the questioner recognising that the words are indeed relevant. The reference to heavy rain may imply a negative response, or it may act as a provisional answer which prepares the way for a more complex discussion about the wisdom of venturing out. Either way, if the hearer both recognises and accepts the relevance of the response, then the conversation can proceed.

Shared knowledge

Such recognition depends, as Malcolm Coulthard notes, on the existence of **shared knowledge** of the world, and not just shared *rules* of language usage. Coulthard (*An Introduction to Discourse Analysis*, p. 8) uses an extract from a study made by Labov to explore the idea of relevant response. The participants are both children, Linus the younger of the two:

> '*Linus*: Do you want to play with me?
> *Violet*: You're younger than me (shuts the door).
> *Linus*: (puzzled) She didn't answer my question.'

Here, Linus does not appreciate the significance of the reply; he does not recognise it as being relevant to his question.

In his study of speech events, Nofsinger also reproduces exchanges which turn on the interpretation of an indirect or *implied* answer (see p. 42). In this extract, a boy of about twelve years old is trying to sell a newspaper subscription to a man:

> '*Boy*: G'n afternoon, sir, W'dju be interested in subscribing to the Progress Bulletin t'help me win a trip to Cape Kennedy to see the astronauts on the moon shot . . .

Man: Well I *live* in Los Angeles. I don' live around here but *these* fellas live here, you might ask them.'

The man's reply does not specifically include the word 'no', but it is none the less taken by the boy as a negative response. Unlike Linus, this child has understood the implicit meaning of the answer used.

On many occasions, two participants in a speech event will understand exactly what is really going on behind the ambiguities of language, but will choose to exploit the breadth of interpretation which is available. *Advances in Spoken Discourse Analysis* reprints Coulthard and Sinclair's example of a father who uses the resources of language to draw his son's attention to a misdemeanour (see p. 111):

'*Father*: Is that your coat on the floor again?
Son: Yes (goes on reading).'

Clearly, the son has deliberately chosen to misinterpret his father's utterance, which is in reality a request disguised as a question. Both participants are aware of the significance of the exchange, but the son chooses to recognise only the formal meaning.

Working by the rules?

Labov divides statements into **A-events** and **B-events**, where A-events are things known only to A, and B-events are things known only to B. Labov (see Coulthard, p. 9) argues:

'If A makes a statement about a B-event, it will be heard as a request for confirmation.'

Here we are really interested not in **realisation** rules, which refer to the structures of grammar, but in **interpretive** rules, which allow us to address the question of significance in speech events. In all studies of conversational interaction, attempts to understand exchanges by applying theories of conventional, or 'rule-defined', meaning often fail to arrive at a complete understanding of the material studied. In Nofsinger's view, this is because researchers (p. 33):

'underestimate the extent of meaning that goes beyond what has been said in so many words (or is even contradictory to it)'.

Nofsinger makes the observation that participants in a conversation often supply meanings which are only implicit in what speakers say. This is sometimes very useful for the speakers themselves, because they will often depend on the construction of additional meanings which do not have to be made explicit.

Nofsinger cites the case of a story told about an employee's last day at a branch of McDonald's. The speaker says:

'T'day was Aaron's last day at McDonald's (.) and they gave him a cake.'

One of the hearers responds with the words, 'Oh *did* they: (1) great.' ((.) shows a very brief pause, and (1) a one-second pause.) This reply has clearly reached the desired interpretation, never explicitly pronounced, that the occasion of Aaron's departure and the presentation of a cake are causally linked.

Structures of conversation?

Some research made into conversation has discovered that there are recurring patterns of interaction within speech events, **structures** which occur despite the change of personnel or situation. This appears to lend support to many of the findings of discursive psychology, which emphasise the way that similar structures seem to arise over and above individual control. Heritage, writing in an essay which appeared in *Structures of Social Action*, 1984, found that:

'organised patterns of stable, structural features ... stand independently of the psychological or other characteristics of particular speakers.'

Nofsinger recognises that many communicative actions occur in pairs, such as greeting/greeting and question/answer, while longer conversations maintain coherence through the pursuit of a consistently delineated *topic*.

Features of spoken language

We may now have realised that there are specific **features** which belong to spoken discourse. Individuals involved in a natural transaction will *overlap* each other's speech, will use *repetition*, will *correct* themselves as they speak, will make *false starts* and will *complete* each other's utterances.

The following extract demonstrates some of these points. It is taken from a conversation published in *Varieties of English*, by Freeborn, French and Langford. Pauses for breath are marked as (h), while, again, longer pauses or hesitations are shown with the appropriate number of seconds in the bracket, such as (2), and very brief pauses are represented by (.). 'Non-fluency' elements of speech – and those features which include hesitation and other breaks in flow – are shown in italics, a practice I have reproduced here. The oblique slash / represents the division between complete units of speech. The passage is part of a conversation held between a nine-year-old girl and her father. The girl is explaining how she constructed a model of a marketplace (see *Varieties of English*, p. 89):

'*F.* You've been making what?/a market?/
R. yeah/
F. *so* and you've been using *match*. (.) matchboxes?/
R. and matchsticks/

F. what did you use the box part for?/ (1)
R. that was for the table/
F. oh I see /(.) the stall was it?/
R. yeah/(h) *and* (.) then I made lots of those (h) (3) and later on I'm going to (.) finish it off by making a village square/ (h) *and I make the village square by* (3) (h) *well I'm going to put* I'm going to put er (h) *benches for* (.) benches/ and I'm going to put bins around the place/and bus-stops/ (h) and I'm going to put my market on/(h) (3) *em*

. . . . . .

F. so how did you make (1) the fruit (.) with the plasticine?/
R. I just came to put them in the shape of the fruit/ (3)
F. what rolled them *or s.*?/
R. well it depends what kind of a shape really/ if they're bananas I made them in a long line and curved them/ (h) and if they were apples I made them into a ball/(h) and I had (.) pears what *I* (.) I had quite a trouble making those/ (h)'

When an individual is engaged in speech, at least three functions are being performed at once. Freeborn and his co-authors explain these as (p. 87):

'planning what to say next, saying what you have planned, and monitoring what you are saying in order to check that it is what you meant to say'.

Fulfilling all these objectives means that conversation is marked by hesitations, self-corrections, repetitions and false starts. Such features of speech should not be regarded as mistakes. Although a nine-year-old girl might be expected to make errors, they are often exactly the same kinds of 'non-fluency' found in the speech of her father:

'*F.* You've been making what?/a market?/
R. yeah/
F. *so* and you've been using *match*. (.) matchboxes?/'

The *so* and the *match*. Indicate, first, either a premature move to sum up or a vocalisation which indicates the marking of time and, secondly, a common 'feint', using the first syllable of a word. 'Non-fluency' is an essential part of normal human speech, and in fact can be extremely revealing, showing the way in which the subject forms and reforms *opinion* as well as speech.

Spontaneous speech, like that reproduced above, contains features which would not be discovered in written prose. Freeborn's work is useful because it also includes a written version of the interview given above. The young girl was asked to write out what she had been saying. The result demonstrates a number of points about the different ways in which spoken and written content is organised:

'These are the things I used. I used dead matches and match box's and plasticene. First I stuck the matches at the bottom [*sic*] of the match box's for legs. Then I stuck four at the top of the match box and then made a roof out of paper. later on I painted it black. When it had dried I made the things to go on them. I made fruit, bread, flowers, then I made a material shop by rolling material round matches.'

Notice that the written account shows a retrospective ordering of items into categories. In the spoken account, the problems encountered in constructing the toy marketplace are given in an order which approximates to its construction. The description of time and activity clearly differs in the two accounts.

The immediacy of direct speech

The most noticeable feature of direct speech is its **immediacy**. This means that narrative both unfolds and is *appraised* as the individual proceeds. Here are the words of a black American veteran of World War II, engaged in recounting a narrative direct to camera for an American documentary called *Liberators*. He is describing his unit's advance into Germany:

'We came into this town and . . . eer . . . we stopped the tanks and everybody piled out of the tanks, you know, and we were searching the houses and what-not . . . and eer . . . I hit this house and went in to the door and there were some German people in there . . . and they said "Kamerad, kamerad," you know, they were friendly . . . and eer I happened to glance that this . . . I saw something behind the door, so I slammed the door closed real fast and this big German officer was standing up behind the door, and I stuck my pistol up in his face, and I said . . . eer . . . "surrender," and what-not. He said . . . he spoke very good English, "I don't have to surrender to you damn niggers," and when he said that I slapped him right across the mouth and teeth jumped all over the place.'

The narrative is marked by hesitations to collect thought, by changes of direction when the speaker considers that he is running ahead of himself, and by linguistic idiosyncracies, such as the use of 'what-not' as a generalisation designed to cover detail which the listener can fill in for him or herself.

What cannot be reproduced here are the subleties of intonation. For example, it appears from the written text that the old soldier's assessment of the German civilians was that they were 'friendly'. The original intonation, however, reveals that the statement containing the phrase 'they were friendly' was actually intended to describe the efforts of the Germans to *appear* harmless, and did not mean that the soldier necessarily *believed* them to be genuinely so.

A public address

The following extract from the same programme is part of a public speech made by a black US veteran to a mixed audience of fellow soldiers and Jewish survivors of the Nazi camps. It is not, therefore, directed to an interviewer:

> 'On this day in April 1945, I was to have the shock of my life, you see, because I was going to walk through the gate of a camp called Buchenwald ... I knew that on this day I had seen the face of evil. I'm talking about racism! *Racism*, that would cause one group of people, for some superficial reason, to say that they are superior, they are better than others, and therefore when they become so powerful they can dictate terms of life and death for other people. I saw that at Buchenwald. That was evil. That was racism.'

The public forum and the highly charged atmosphere allow a more dramatic delivery than the previous extract, which was essentially anecdotal, with the camera used to record an interaction between subject and interviewer. Here, the narrative is prepared in advance, not because the audience is unaware of what is to follow, but exactly because it is an event which everyone present has experienced directly.

The camera merely records the address, and does not substantially alter its content or delivery. Notice that the declamatory style serves to emphasise the central theme of the speech, which is not concerned with particular detail, but is more an expression of a collective sense of moral outrage. The use of repetition serves another purpose; it acts to give structure to the speech, allowing the speaker to 'mark time' while he considers the development of his next point.

Public speech

The tendency to employ certain patterns of speech is found wherever individuals make a particular effort to impress an audience. When politicians speak to a prepared text, we encounter a more deliberate selection of **rhetorical devices**. Where a speaker's concern is more to manipulate than to inspire, the emotional force of the *ex tempore* speech, and the natural exuberance of expression, may be lost. Rhetoric will be examined in more detail in Chapter 3.

SUMMARY

● INTRAPERSONAL COMMUNICATION?

The whole theory of **intrapersonal communication** is held up for scrutiny. Two aspects of intrapersonal communication are discussed. One is the common assumption that the activities which take place within the individual are indeed types of internal *communication*. The second aspect of the 'intrapersonal' typically concerns the variety of forms (speech, diaries, personal reminders and so on) through which an individual might *express* or record some feature of his or her private experience.

● Internal processes

If we accept the idea that communication properly refers to *interaction between people*, then we must reject the proposition that thought processes have the same status. In other words, we would reach the conclusion that thought is not communication. A less controversial description of the activities and events which take place inside the individual would be **internal processes**.

● Internal/external: a misleading division?

The distinction between 'internal' and 'external' communication is examined. Although thought and expression use different 'systems', both are part of a continuous social process; the production of **meaning**.

● Materialism

The term 'material' is analysed. The concept 'materialism' is widely used to describe an outlook or belief which places the acquisition of money and possessions above all other considerations, but in the study of philosophy and politics, 'materialism' describes the belief that nothing exists besides solid matter. Some writers, particularly those influenced by Marxism, use the term 'materialism' to refer to the idea that all societies are based upon material or *economic* foundations, and that inequalities between people arise largely because access to economic and social power is unevenly distributed.

● Creative interaction

The *use* of language and other expressive systems may be prompted by each person's material interaction with the world (a world in which certain objectives must be attained if individuals are to secure the fundamental requirements of life), but human communication is essentially creative. In other words, expression may emerge from material circumstances, but does more than dwell upon basic needs, showing a tendency to look forward to new forms of social existence and organisation.

● Material expression

The idea that language 'sets events in motion' is only part of the story. A more complete argument would be that the use of symbolic content not only influences events, but *emerges* from the conditions of material reality. Speech, for example, could then be described as an **act** because it flows from material necessity and has, in turn, a moral or *social* effect. This means that expressive acts may not always produce an immediate physical change in our surroundings, but that some alteration will nevertheless have taken place at the level of social reality, a change which may, eventually, become apparent.

● The purpose of expression

The idea that thought and expressive behaviour (despite their differences as *systems*) are part of the *same* public, social or 'discursive' process marks a departure from not just the old 'intrapersonal' theory of human communication but also from many of the 'individualist' approaches which have flourished within the subject for many years.

Conventional expression

Convention is re-established (and sometimes reinvented) whenever interactions take place within any recognised public context. Although individuals occasionally refuse to comply with established practices, this does not mean that they unaware of how they are *supposed* to act in various contexts.

Meaning and action

The view of the intrapersonal domain advanced by Cronen, that it is concerned with meaning rather than action, was described as misleading in Chapter 1. Intrapersonal or mental 'processing' is usually understood as a search for order and meaning (involving perception and interpretation), but there would be no point in such functions if they were used solely for 'internal' purposes.

THOUGHT
Descriptions of thought

'Thought' may be variously defined as the process of **cognition**, the power of **reason**, a reflective **state**, or an individual **idea. Creative thought** is described and extracts from two poems are reproduced in the text. The seat of thought is popularly regarded as the mind. An extract from *Nineteen Eighty-Four* is used to illustrate the concept of the mind as the last available sanctuary from the power of the repressive state.

Composite conceptions: image, language, abstraction

Thought consists of what Harré and Gillett call 'composite' conceptions, made up of *particular* ideas about specific objects and *general* concepts about the world. These conceptions include **images**, **linguistic** elements, and more **abstract** elements. Stephen Pinker, in *The Language Instinct*, argues that thought constitutes an entirely separate system from that used when human beings engage in various forms of expression. 'Mentalese' is the term he employs to describe the system used in thought.

Auditory knowledge

Robert G. Crowder describes experiments in auditory processing and auditory memory. He makes a case for the specific existence of **auditory knowledge**, and outlines his investigations into the ability of the human subject to reproduce sound and retrieve musical sequences from memory.

THOUGHT AND EXPRESSION

Images (graphical communication), **language** (speech and text), and other, more **abstract** expressive systems are all used in the process of communication. In addition, more recent accounts of human understanding (particularly the fields known as 'discursive psychology' and 'critical linguistics') argue that both images and linguistic elements are able to generate meaning because human subjects *know how to use them* in real situations. Or, put another way, units of speech, words on a page, or graphical designs are known to carry specific meanings when used in a variety of contexts.

The importance of context

Context can refer to the place of one unit within a larger system (a word in a sentence, for example), but more usually means the immediate physical *situation* in which a communicative event takes place, combined with the *form* of the event.

'Context' is also used to indicate the wider *social* context in which an event takes place, which could be described as the 'universal' form of all public discourses. This would include all the freedoms and constraints conferred by society as a whole on the general form of any communication event.

Meaning and events

A full *analysis* of any speech event (and perhaps any instance of communication) must include knowledge of structure, setting, participants, purposes, key, topic, channel and the form and content of a message. When individuals choose to communicate they do not require knowledge of these divisions, because they are familiar with the contexts in which they must act, and therefore understand the appropriate ways of behaving in those situations.

Behaviourists and mentalists

The two most clearly opposed positions on the question of human knowledge are called behaviourism and mentalism. **Behaviourists** believe that human behaviour is prompted by *learning* a process in which some stimuli (events of some sort) are reinforced, while others are not. The **mentalist** position turns on the theory that the mental structures of the human subject are already in place, and are simply geared to the acquisiton of certain kinds of knowledge.

Innateness

The ability of people in widely different locations and circumstances to acquire language systems (which all seem to share remarkably similar structures) led Chomsky to advocate a theory of **innateness**. This is the idea that the human organism is 'programmed to speak'. The majority of linguists now appear to agree with Chomsky's mentalist or innate theory of language. However, some recent research may support the notion that a type of mental reinforcement does occur in the early years of life. There is in fact no reason why this should exclude a theory of innate ability. If reinforcement occurs, something has first to exist in order to be selected and strengthened.

Thought and language

Three contrasting views of the thought–language relationship may be set out as follows:

- Some argue that thought is *dependent upon* or *caused by* language.
- Others believe that language is dependent upon the level of cognitive development attained by the individual.
- Vygotsky argued that speech and practical activity were two entirely separate modes of behaviour, coming together at about the age of two years to produce verbal thought (language).

Language as 'autonomous system'

One version of the thought-language argument (similar to Harré and Gillett's view of discourse as the real source of psychological 'events') may be found in Semin and Fiedler, who argue that, 'many psychological phenomena which are usually conceived as ... processes within the minds and brains of individual people, are permanently installed in language as an autonomous system above and beyond the individual'.

Pinker: 'mentalese'

Stephen Pinker's *The Language Instinct* offers an alternative view, dealing with the language-thought dispute by arguing that the 'representations underlying thinking' and 'the sentences in a language' are not the same. Pinker describes the 'language of the mind' as **mentalese**, a system that is not the same as any of the world's languages, but from which all languages grow.

Criticisms of Pinker

A weakness emerges when Pinker uses arguments based on *intention*. In the second chapter of his book, he argues that there is often a difference between what is said or written and what was originally *meant* by a speaker or writer. If we accept a view of expression as social, then 'what we meant to say' (or our *intention*) will be influenced by our knowledge and expectation of various situations. 'What we meant to say' will become, in most circumstances, *what it is possible to say*. This suggests a theory of **contextual intention**.

Pinker's 'what we meant to say' seems to be wholly individual, suggesting that he believes in a 'pure' intention which somehow exists separately to discourse and interaction.

'Explanation seeking'

Moravcsik, in *Thought and Language*, suggests a move away from semantics, towards a system of analysis which is capable of dealing with natural languages and everyday speech events. He argues for a *contextual* understanding of meaning, noting that, 'in natural languages meanings are only partially determined, and much of the determination ... is left to non-linguistic context'.

The idea that **external expression** provides **evidence of internal states** is examined. The concept of **misreading signals** is introduced, and **body language** is discussed.

The production of meaning

The production of meaning always takes place within a specific context. One approach would be to argue that this context will *limit* people's freedom to express exactly what they mean. Another argument may be that the parameters set by context may actually help individuals to produce coherent messages. If a context or situation is known in advance, or is understood during the progress of an interaction, then the appropriate modes of behaviour will also be understood and may act as a guide to expression.

The moment of expression: 'true' meaning?

The theory that the human subject either strives to create, or attempts to disguise, an accurate *external* insight into the exact *internal* meaning he or she had in mind may be misleading. In fact, the process of meaning-creation may be quite different. People may only really find an exact meaning when they come to *express* the various ideas and emotions which they experience.

Words and values

All written forms must obey certain syntactical and semantic rules if they are to be understood. These rules are not merely a set of conventions; they carry a particular emotional force, and are part of the established values of a society. We have only to think of the passions which are aroused when people offend against recognised practices in English grammar to remember how social and cultural values are regarded as inseparable from spoken and written usage. The **integrity of language** is a perennial feature of much discussion on written and spoken language.

DIARIES AND JOURNALS

The notion of a private journal being able to reveal some internal processes is explored through the use of a number of extracts from actual diaries. **Notions of individuality** also feature within this discussion. In addition, **questions of address** are considered.

COGNITION

The traditional approach to thought has emphasised the **cognitive** abilities of human beings. Cognition may be explained as the *action* or *faculty* of understanding.

The way communication is *understood* depends ultimately upon the accepted ways of describing the world. Our theories of mind and behaviour grow from scientific *orthodoxy*, from a set of ideas which have become dominant in our culture. Many of our assumptions about communication depend upon these sources. In recent years, some of these orthodoxies have been questioned. One major target for reassessment is the idea that human development and understanding arise from a strictly *logical* mental process.

Opposition to the cognitive tradition

Objections to those approaches which emphasise cognition may be found in an increasing number of academic perspectives. Some of these theories argue for a new model of cognitive research. Others have produced new **theories of mind and brain**; Gerald Edelman's work on the way that the brain selects and reinforces some physical operations, while weakening or discarding others, and his investigation of **value systems**, is an important recent development.

Social construction and theories of the mind

Harré and Gillett begin by examining the 'informal rules' used during everyday speech, in which there are correct and incorrect ways of using words. Instead of imposing a system upon the human mind, they attempt to establish the types of meaning-creation that humans undertake. They are in favour of a less coldly 'objective' approach to human research.

Three principles

Harré and Gillett's approach gives rise to three principles, which can be summarised as follows:

- Many psychological phenomena are in fact the properties of discourse. Where the discourse is *public*, it is behaviour, and where *private* it is thought.
- Individual uses of symbolic systems are taken from interpersonal discourses.
- The production of emotion, attitudes, decisions and so on depends upon the skill of the actors, their 'moral standing' in the community, and 'the story lines that unfold'.

Harré and Gillett's theory proposes that thought and language are part of the same system. Instead of understanding speech as a reflection of the speaker's underlying cognitive state, speech events are seen as expressions of a response to situational and therefore discursive context.

● SENSORY PERCEPTION: COMMUNICATION AND PHYSIOLOGY

The first issue examined is the **physiology** of the human subject and its relationship to communication. The questions which must be asked about the individual and the world they inhabit include the following:

- What faculties do we use to perceive our environment?
- How reliable are these faculties?
- Are such faculties always actively deployed?
- How do we communicate our understanding of the world to others?
- What social or environmental constraints are placed on our communication?

● Perception

Human subjects need to be able to **perceive** an adequate range of **physical elements**. The elements perceived by human beings are the *external objects* which make an impression on one or other of the *sense organs*, which then relay the stimulus caused by the external object to the brain. The five senses – sight, smell, touch, hearing and taste – provide individuals with a composite understanding or perception of their environment.

Sensory receptors

The eye and the ear are both used as examples of sensory receptors. The different factors in each case are explained.

● Limitations of the senses

Ideas about the reliability of 'sense data', and the relationship between human perception and the external world, always appear in studies of communication. These issues appear later in the chapter, but it is important to note that the senses do have certain limitations. The brain, for example, lacks the capacity to deal simultaneously with all the elements it is able to collect. Human beings therefore perceive more than they can *identify* and *report* at a conscious level.

Our ability to identify what is worth communicating will be influenced by more than our immediate circumstances; it will also be shaped by the values and cultural norms which exist within our society.

● Perception: active or passive?

Concepts of **selective attention** and ideas about **preference** are examined, and lead to the study of **models of Perception.**

Perception itself is often understood as an active faculty, in which the 'best interpretation' of events is sought (although this is often determined by the *values* which circulate within a society). Some theorists promote the idea of passive *reception*. Theories used to support the idea that the *processing of information* in humans is essentially determined by the nature of external objects in the world are called 'bottom-up' or **direct**, while those which emphasise the selective and organisational role of the human senses are called 'top-down' or **indirect**.

● Solving the problem?

Perception is recognised as both a *faculty* we possess and as an *act*. The idea of perception as a faculty allows us to accept the idea that individuals possess 'open channels' into which information may flow, while the concept of perception as an act helps to remind us that people also make active choices, involving the detection and the interpretation of information gained from the external world.

Perception of form and the idea of **visual scales** are introduced. Experiments using a number of images show that some part of a stimulus always stands out as the **figure** (that which is accepted as the foreground), while the context which gives the figure meaning is known as the *ground* (or the background). In some examples, figure and ground become interchangeable.

● The image vs. sound?

The difference between the impact made in our culture by visual stimuli and that created by sound is debated. **Theories of the perception of sound** are introduced. Research which examines how individuals distinguish between different sounds has received less publicity than comparable studies of visual perception. Research into both these areas share some common ground because most approaches are based on *cognitive* theories, i.e. ideas about the acquisition of knowledge and understanding.

Some theorists believe that sound is particularly prone to misrepresentation whenever a purely cognitive perspective is used to measure its effects on audiences. If cognitive approaches are unable to explain the range of human responses to sound, then it would appear that a study of its emotional impact is required.

● The limits of a cognitive approach

Cognitive approaches to human understanding cannot always explain responses that appear to be innate. Some writers note the difference between theories based on a model of cognition or information processing, where the series of sounds heard by the human subject is compared with an abstract representation in memory, and a newer strand of theory known as **ecological psychology**.

● Perception: the dominance of the visual?

One reason which might in part explain why the visual has received more attention than the auditory may be the tendency of the brain to give greater credence to information gained from the eyes (in other words, the domination of vision in the human organism itself).

● Human development and visual perception

Some believe that the predominance of the visual stems from its central role in human development. However, an infant communicates its experiences and essential needs through the use of expressive sounds and cries. Seeing may come before words, but the production of noise which *another will find meaningful* may well be the first step in communication.

● IDENTITY: THEORIES OF SELF
● The human environment

Human beings are born into a complex world, which can be divided into three elements:

- a natural environment;
- a social world of people, values and events;
- those artificial objects and structures produced by human exploitation of the first element.

● The 'split' self

According to the psychologist Murphy (1947), the *self* is supposed to be 'the individual known to the individual,' while R.B. Burns (1980) defines it as 'the set of attitudes a person holds towards himself'. These theories suggest that the individual is capable of being both the *subject* (thinker) and *object* (what is being thought about). Another way of making this distinction is by using the terms 'I' and 'me', where *I* refers to the subject and *me* to the object. Such approaches could be described as theories of the **'split' self**, one part of the individual being the conscious monitor, the other being the element that is monitored.

Against the 'split-self' theory

Some writers take issue with the split between conscious self and self as object, including the philosopher Gilbert Ryle. Ryle uses examples to argue that, since self-reflection is *not always* present, there are not really separate parts of mind; therefore, reflection should not be awarded a special status as a kind of superior 'monitor'.

A sense of self: theories of location

Rom Harré and Grant Gillett argue that, in order to have a sense of self, a human subject must also have a sense of *place*. This may be summarised as follows:

- a location in *space*;
- a location in *time*;
- a location as a responsible *actor* or agent;
- a location as a *subject*, including features like age, ethnicity, gender, class and so on.

These authors, following the principles of discursive psychology, do not think the mind is made up of some kind of 'mental substance', but believe instead that it is composed of the 'discourses that [people] are involved in, private and public'.

THE DIVIDED SELF?
Freud: three categories of self

Sigmund Freud (1856–1939) used three terms to denote the various aspects of 'self'. These are **id**, **ego** and **superego**. The *id* is supposed to be the part of the personality which responds purely to instinct, and which is governed by the *pleasure principle*. The *ego* is that part of the original personality (the id) thought by Freudians to be logical or rational, and to be determined by the *reality principle*. The *superego*, by contrast, provides the 'special agency' in which the

parental influence is maintained, and it is here that judgements about right and wrong are made.

Jung and the elements of the psyche

Carl Gustav Jung (1875–1961) thought that the totality of the personality (all its elements, whether conscious or unconscious), could be called the **psyche**, which has three separate parts. These are **consciousness**, the **personal unconscious**, and finally the **collective unconscious**.

Self-concept and self-esteem

The **self-concept**, or the 'cluster' of ideas held about the self, includes the qualities, preferences and shortcomings perceived by an individual as belonging to him or herself. Self-concept is usually thought to be shaped, altered or maintained through interaction with others.

Self-esteem is *evaluative* where self-concept is *descriptive*. It refers to how far individuals like or approve of themselves. Coopersmith (1967) described it as 'a personal judgement of worthiness'.

SOCIAL NORMS
Roles: great expectations?

G.H. Mead was interested in developmental theories which stress the way in which individuals are able to get 'outside themselves' by taking on **roles**, or by viewing themselves from the vantage point of *other people*.

Universal and particular expectations

Is appropriate role behaviour decided by families, the state, individuals or groups? The answer must be that all these influences are involved in the process of role 'description', and that individuals acknowledge **universal** as well as **particular** behavioural expectations in every situation they meet.

Convention and practical necessity

Much of our behaviour is in fact 'conventional' in the sense that it is based upon practical necessity. The idea of **offence against norms**, and the concept of **role as a disguise**, are both critically examined.

The presentation of self in everyday life: Goffman

In *The Presentation of Self in Everyday Life* Erving Goffman explored the ways in which behavioural norms could be used by the individual to manipulate the perceptions of others. Since individuals have some awareness of being watched, and will know that others may attempt to 'place' them in specific categories according to their actions and appearance, it may be possible to shape such perceptions.

MOTIVATION AND NEEDS

Communication is motivated by human need. Maslow's system is illustrated in Figure 2.6.

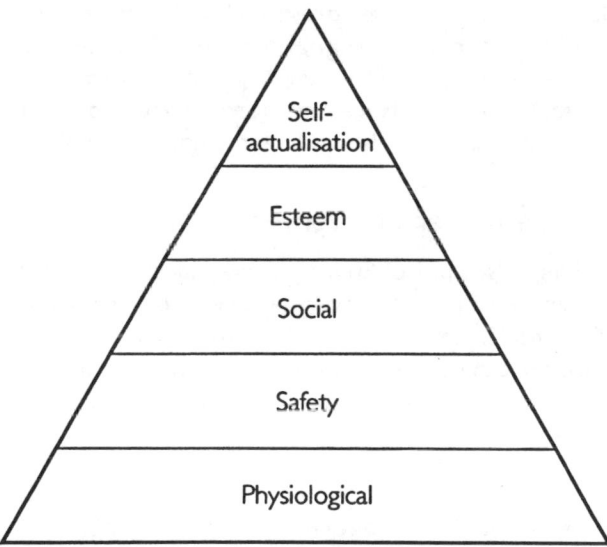

Figure 2.6   Maslow's hierarchy of needs

Schutz's ideas about **inclusion**, **control** and **affection** are also described, and his notion of **degrees of need** are examined.

NEEDS, NORMS AND THEORIES OF DEPENDENCE

A particular tradition in interpersonal studies is examined, in which the social context of interaction is neglected in favour of theories of personality. The assertion that these are *types* of people seems to provide a number of theorists with their chief explanation for human behaviour. Myers and Myers, Patton and Giffin, Virginia Satir and the psychologist Barnlund are identified as belonging to the 'individualist' school of thought.

Personality types or discursive choices?

Virginia Satir identifies 'seemingly universal patterns' in the way people communicate and searches for psychological states which supposedly lie *behind* utterances. An alternative proposal is that the utterances she identifies are not connected to personality type, but are **discursive choices**, available to all those involved in interaction.

Subjection/qualification

Instruction, **sanction** and **affirmation** in the socialisation of children are discussed. Theories on early influence include that offered by Myers and Myers, with their description of **symbolic role-taking**. The consequences of naming children are studied through a poem by Robert Graves, while the '**spirit of perversity**' in infants is covered through a reference to a book by Stevie Davies.

Specific identities, including **gender**, **ethnicity** and **class**, are covered, paying particular attention to the question of **gendered identity** and **female subjectivity**. The concept of the '**other**' is introduced and discussed with reference to a number of sources.

Subjection/qualification: human potential

The idea that human potential will be circumscribed by the way that life is both *understood* and *organised* is taken from the work of Goran Therborn. According to this theory, individuals are given roles which are supposed to ensure that the major relationships of power in the social order continue as before.

EXPRESSION AND MEANING
Dictionary knowledge?

Katz and Fodor, writing in 1964, appear to have assumed that speakers use 'dictionary knowledge' in interpreting language. They argue that 'given an accurate dictionary of English, *which he applies by using his linguistic ability*, the fluent speaker can semantically interpret any sentence ... under any of its grammatical derivations'. However, the meaning of a written or spoken word or phrase is never simply a matter of definition; it is also dependent upon situated context and *use*. This means that a literal interpretation is sometimes only a small part of the meanings native speakers create during an interaction.

Language function

Michael Halliday (1973) produced a list of no fewer than seven categories of language function, as follows:

- instrumental;
- regulatory;
- representational;
- interactional;
- personal;
- heuristic;
- imaginative.

Each of these is explained in turn.

Semantic vs. grammatical information: forensic discourse analysis

There is evidence to suggest that human beings do not remember **semantic** and **grammatical** information in the same way. Sachs, writing in 1967, demonstrated that the meanings of sentences are easier to recall than their exact 'grammatical shapes'.

The idea that individuals remember information, but not always the exact *form* of an utterance or passage

of writing, has important implications for the study of memory, and especially for notions of truthfulness. Malcolm Coulthard describes the function of **forensic discourse analysis**, which is the practice of examining interview records or statements in order to reach conclusions about their authenticity.

Language and meaning

Wardhaugh describes laboratory experiments which demonstrate that single words, or short sequences of speech, are almost unidentifiable if taken out of context and presented to individual listeners. The inability of subjects to identify small extracts of speech, suggests that the basic units of **meaning** in spoken interaction must be larger than was once supposed.

Pragmatics

The study of real exchanges which take place in specific situations is known as **pragmatics**. Whatever the precise reason for engaging in a specific exchange, the overall purpose of making utterances is to carry out *social actions*. This means that social actors are not just saying things, but also at the same time *doing* things.

The power of 'everyday talk'

Nofsinger (see p. 1 of *Everyday Conversation*) emphasises the 'immense power of everyday talk'. Conversation is of particular importance, according to this author, because other, more formal systems of spoken communication are actually *dependent* on ordinary exchanges.

Five categories of speech

Likening human interaction to a series of *moves* in a game, Nofsinger examines Searle's division of all speech acts into five categories. These are:

- commissives;
- directives;
- assertives;
- expressives;
- declarations.

William Labov (1970) identified the following structures for conversation analysis:

- question and answer;
- challenge and response;
- invitation and acceptance.

Recognition depends, as Malcolm Coulthard notes, on the existence of **shared knowledge** of the world, and not just shared *rules* of language usage.

Working by the rules?

Labov divides statements into **A-events** and **B-events**, where A-events are things known only to A,

and B-events are things known only to B. Labov argues: 'If A makes a statement about a B-event, it will be heard as a request for confirmation.'

The typical **structures of conversation** and the recurring patterns of interaction within speech events are described. **Features of spoken language** are examined through the use of a variety of extracts. **The immediacy of direct speech** is contrasted with the type of expression used in more formal types of address. Examples are used from the speech of two black US ex-servicemen who fought in the Second World War.

STUDENT ACTIVITIES

EXPRESSION IN CONTEXT
Revision: Conventional expression

Read the following extract from Chapter 2 and the accompanying piece on humour. Then discuss the questions that follow them.

There are of course differences between what we think, on the one hand, and what we feel it is appropriate to divulge, on the other, because all public expression operates within certain rules and conventions. When an act of communication takes place, the *content* selected for transmission will be closely related to the expressive *form* which all participants regard as suitable to the occasion.

In a court of law, for example, the purpose of speech is to use formal discourses of 'truth' and rational inquiry to work towards a conclusive outcome, the attainment of which marks the end of the event. During the event, respect is shown for due process and established authority. Turn-taking will be formalised and clearly signalled.

On the whole, convention is re-established (and sometimes reinvented) whenever interactions take

place within any recognised public context. All those who engage in communication in their own right, rather than on behalf of someone else, will recognise that they may be publicly accountable for what they express. This also helps to maintain the observation of certain rules and conventions. Although individuals occasionally refuse to comply with established practices, this does not mean that they are unaware of how they are *supposed* to act in various contexts.

Humour: contrasting discourses

Some forms of humour work by 'playing with' discourse, setting up a contrast between the *structure* of an event and the genres of speech which an audience expects to be used within it. The comedians Newman and Baddiel produced a successful sketch called 'History Today', in which two rather ancient professors appeared in a television programme devoted to their subject. The sketch used the codes associated with similar events; in front of a sombre background, two chairs and a low table were set out for the participants. The whole exercise was introduced by a piece of classical music. Here is a typical example of the kind of exchange which occurs between the two academics, A and B:

'A: Good evening (.) Once again I'm joined by Professor F.J. Lewis, emeritus professor of history at All Saint's College, Oxford (I) I understand that some viewers felt that we rather skated over the topic of 'Great Britain 1931–38, the Austerity Years' (.) I can only offer my apologies, and pledge that Professor Lewis and myself will make every endeavour to fully explore tonight's topic of discussion, the 1905 Sebastapol uprising. (I) Professor Lewis, do you feel, as many do, that Sebastapol was indeed the birthplace of the Russian revolution?
B: See people who talk like this (.) *quacking noise* (I) that's you, that is (I) that's you talking your *best*.
A: I see. You see girls running like this *flapping arms* (2) That's you, that is. That's how you run.'

Questions for discussion

1 Is formal turn-taking observed in this extract?

2 Analyse the event using Hymes's list of the factors which shape interaction: structure, setting, participants, purposes, key, topic, channel and message form (see the section on 'Text and context' in Chapter 1).

3 Explain how the joke is created, in terms of the contrast established between the structure of the event and the different genres of speech used.

4 Find two other examples of humour which use conflicting 'styles' of speech.

PERCEPTION AND REALITY
Exercise: Attitudes to perception

Carry out the exercise which follows (based on Myers and Myers's 'agree/disagree' list, *The Dynamics of Human Communication*, p. 366), then read the extracts on perception and reality from Chapter 2, and the material on 'Questions of reality' taken from Chapter 1. Indicate whether you agree or disagree with the statements which follow. Using the left-hand column, make a tick if you agree, and a cross if you disagree. In groups of three or four, discuss each statement and reach a *consensus*. Record the group concensus in the same way as before, but use the right-hand column.

Individual

Group

Agree	Disagree		Agree	Disagree
_____	_____	1 Since perception is unreliable, no one can be sure of having truly perceived the real world.	_____	_____
_____	_____	2 Human subjects see what they wish to see, regardless of reality.	_____	_____
_____	_____	3 The perception of a physical object is shaped more by the object itself than it is by the individual observer.	_____	_____
_____	_____	4 The use of science is a dependable way of overcoming the limits of perception.	_____	_____
_____	_____	5 Human beings perceive reality, but create social reality.	_____	_____

Myers and Myers ask whether, when the group decision goes against an individual, it is difficult for that person to 'give up' an answer previously written down. Do individuals in this situation begin to doubt their original decision? The other major question concerns the *process* of decision making. Did the group reach a true consensus, or were certain opinions disregarded in an effort to force a conclusion?

Revision: Perception and reality

Chapter 2 argued that an understanding of the range of human perception may help to resolve some of the questions about the extent of our communicative abilities. *Physiology* is the science of natural functions. A number of questions were asked about human perception and communication:

- What faculties do we use to perceive our environment?
- How reliable are these faculties?
- Are such faculties always actively deployed?
- How do we communicate our understanding of the world to others?
- What social or environmental constraints are placed on our communication?

Human subjects need to be able to **perceive** an adequate range of **physical elements**. The elements perceived by human beings are the *external objects* which make an impression on one or other of the *sense organs*, which then relay the stimulus caused by the external object to the brain. The five senses – sight, smell, touch, hearing and taste – provide individuals with a composite understanding or perception of their environment.

One of the problems which always arises in studies of human culture, is the reliability of 'sense data' and the relationship which exists between human perception and the external world. As we saw in the discussion of reality in Chapter 1, the degree to which human perception is 'accurate' has wide-ranging implications for any study of communication.

In the first place, it is important to recognise that the senses do have certain limitations. For example, we are unable to hear the range of sound frequencies perceived by many animals, and can see only certain types of light (infra-red and X-rays are invisible to human beings). In fact, when the brain receives whatever information the senses *are* able to detect, it is unable to process it all. The brain lacks the capacity to deal simultaneously with all the elements it is able to collect. Human beings therefore perceive more than they can *identify* and *report* at a conscious level.

Chapter 1 examined the opinion of James W. Carey, who claimed that 'reality is brought into existence, is produced, by communication'. The **real** is defined in the *Concise Oxford Dictionary* as 'actually existing as a thing or occurring in fact'. There is a close relationship between *thing* and *fact*. A **thing** is whatever may be thought about or perceived, whether that is animate (living) or inanimate (an object). A **fact** is something that is known to have occurred or which is true. **Reality** is the 'property of being real ... real existence, what is real, what underlies appearances'. Stuart Sigman, in the fourth edition of Corner and Hawthorn, *Communication Studies: An Introductory Reader*, argued that 'rather than a process whereby information about an external, "real" world is shared *by* individuals, [communication] is the mechanism whereby information is used to construct reality *for* individuals'.

We usually assume that things have to exist *before* they can be perceived, and before any communication takes place. If reality is assumed to exist before perception (with perception coming before representation), reality cannot be created directly by people. What human beings actually 'create' and share through communication is a *shared understanding* of reality, where reality is that which has the *potential* first to be perceived or thought about, and then to be represented. The term **social reality** could be used to describe the understandings of the real circulated within human societies.

Any philosophical position may be called **realist** if it argues in favour of the actual existence, whether perceived by human beings or not, of material things and objects. **Anti-realist** positions include those which either question the actual existence of things and objects, or state that we are only able to perceive the existence of symbolic systems, or logical structures, or ideas.

The Ancient Greek philosopher Plato thought that knowledge consisted of the apprehension of universal 'forms', which contained the true meanings of all general terms. Plato had faith in the reality of the world, deciding that any object, idea or creature which could be perceived belonged to a particular class or category.

Idealism is the doctrine that reality is in fact a mental phenomenon, based on ideas (and not, as some suppose 'ideals'). The more extreme form of idealism is the belief that (A.J. Ayer, *A Dictionary of Philosophy*, p. 97): 'matter does not exist except in the form of ideas in the mind, or as a manifestation of mental activity'.

Nominalism promotes the idea that all we are actually able to know is the names or classes of things in the world, taking the view that there are no such things as the Platonic 'universals', but rather *paradigms,* reliable examples of a particular class of thing or creature, to which others may be compared. The problem here is where to draw the line between examples of things, and indeed how the choice of the paradigm is made.

Phenomenologism is an approach which begins with the study of appearances, involving the belief that things have an essence which may be discovered through description. The appearances which form the basis of inquiry are *phenomena*, what Ayer calls 'the objects of experience', brought into being by the activities of the human mind.

Some philosophers believe that there is a 'weak link' in the chain of what makes up the real. They argue that if the real can only be perceived by human sense, then all we can know for sure is the *data gathered by the senses* through perception, not the reality which lies behind it. The philosopher Kant, for example, was interested in the idea that there might be a difference between the real and *reality as it is known* by human beings. He believed that reality existed independently but that its appearance was shaped by the structures of the mind.

Some **postmodernists** take this a step further, arguing that we are even further from those notions of reality we have accepted since the Enlightenment, and that we now inhabit a world dominated by media-generated images and concepts. These forms of data are supposed no longer to bear a direct relationship to the real at all, but instead are meant to refer merely to another set of images or ideas.

It makes sense to argue that there is no *exact* correlation between the world and the ways in which it is perceived. This does not mean that a realist would need to abandon the idea that real objects do exist. Some writers argue that the real and the basic categories of human experience may not coincide exactly, but do correspond very closely. In *Thought and Language* (p. 9), the American academic J.M. Moravcsik argues in favour of realism by indicating 'the success of the human mind in coming to understand reality', and by noting that human beings use categories which are close to the reality they identify.

IDENTITY
Revision, analysis and discussion: A sense of self

Read the following summary of material from Chapter 2, and *The Guardian* article and questions which follow.

Chapter 2 argued that, in order to have a **sense of self**, a human subject must also have a sense of *place*. Four 'locations' in which individuals exist, were described: a location in **space**, in **time**, as a responsible **actor** or agent and as a **subject**. The last category includes features like age, ethnicity, gender, status and so on.

Harré and Gillett, following the principles of discursive psychology, advance the idea that the mind is composed of the '**discourses** that [people] are involved in, private and public'. Some theories point to the way in which individuals are able to get 'outside themselves' by taking on **roles**, or by viewing themselves from the vantage point of *other people*. Bannister and Agnew (1976) thought that the *construction of self* depended upon having a concept of 'not self'. In *Defining Women*, Linda McDowell and Rosemary Pringle argue that women occupy the role of the 'other' in patriarchal society; 'women are constantly defined in relation to men'. The 'other' is sometimes seen as complementary, sometimes as exotic.

The **self-concept**, or the 'cluster' of ideas held about the self, includes the qualities, preferences and shortcomings perceived by an individual as belonging to him or herself. Since self-concept is supposed to be

Not just an Asian babe

Why Echobelly's frontwoman is fed up with her image

Amy Raphael

Sonya Aurora Madan . . . 'I was an east west casualty'   KIPPA MATTHEWS

SONYA AURORA-MADAN is perched on the arm of a cracked white leather sofa in her west London basement flat. Head resting on knees, hands clasping toes, the former kick boxer turned singer-songwriter is tonight wearing a man's suit and suede Converse; sometimes she pulls on knee-high DMs, camouflage trousers and a customised Union Jack T-shirt with "My Country Too" written across it in black felt pen.

Aurora-Madan, 28, has unwittingly found herself torn between two roles: "exotic " Asian babe and cross-cultural icon. The mainstream press see a photogenic singer; the Asian media expect her to promote traditional values. She fronts guitar pop band Echobelly, part of the Brit pop coalition that also numbers Pulp and Blur, and which has spent this year sticking a finger up at last year's imported grunge bands.

Echobelly (which means "to be hungry for something") are good — "Too good to be true" cried the music press last year upon the release of their first EP, Bellyache. Their debut album, Everyone's Got One (consider the acronym), released on Monday, does not disappoint. The crashing pop is as immediate and passionate as the lyrics: Bellyache explores how a friend went into denial after having an abortion; Give Her A Gun incites Asian women to take control; Father, Ruler, King, Computer rails against Asian marital traditions. Aurora-Madan's voice swaggers between Debbie Harry, Siouxsie and Morrissey (a devoted fan).

Born in India, Aurora-Madan joined her academic parents in London's suburbia aged three. Like everyone born in the mid to late sixties, she grew up addicted to Top Of The Pops; being discerning, she tuned into John Peel's pioneering Radio One show while doing her homework. Similarities with her peers stopped there: her parents tried to stop her having boyfriends because she was being "saved" for an arranged marriage. She had other ideas. At 17, Aurora-Madan took a train to the West End, found a "trendy hairdresser" and had a mohican. Her father wouldn't let her back in the house for hours but she'd made her point.

Thereafter the teen rebel did something different to her hair each week. "It was a bit pathetic really," she says, grinning. "It came from a need to stand out as an individual because I didn't feel I fitted into anything. I wasn't like other Indian girls at school; I didn't listen to bhangra, I didn't have a real sense of community and I wasn't interested in marrying an Indian boy. I was an east-west casualty."

Growing up, Aurora-Madan had no Asian role models to look to. More than a decade on, the singer is finding herself thrust into the precarious role of a mainstream, cross-cultural icon. That Echobelly have nothing to do with traditional Asian music is of little importance; Aurora-Madan has been made a spokeswoman, receiving constant requests to appear on Asian TV programmes and in Asian magazines.

The attention is flattering; the questions are not. "They all want to know the same thing; they talk about marriage agencies — bureaux for arranged marriages — and ask about my ideal man, who I'd like to have as a husband. Obviously they presume that I'm heterosexual; obviously I don't answer."

She pauses. "It's hard because the Asian community puts very high value on getting married and it doesn't matter how successful you are if you haven't got a husband. I suppose I should be flattered by their interest in me but I have no desire to answer those questions."

It is not only the traditional Asian mentality that is alienating. Aurora-Madan has also found it hard to deal with the perceived image of female musicians: she defiantly cut off her long locks last year, saying: "I can't cut my tits off, but I can cut my hair." She feels equally uncomfortable with being the token Asian indie babe in the mainstream press. The boy-bonding nipple 'n' bum mag Loaded recently asked her to pose for a swimwear story. "The problem is, I did an i-D cover in an open white shirt and black bra. When I saw it, I thought: 'Oh God! I'm going to be typecast.' I don't want to fulfil the exotic, Asian beauty stereotype. I'm not interested in selling my sexuality; I want the media to talk about my role as a singer."

It has not, inevitably, proved that simple. When Channel 4's Naked City invited her to join Aki of militant Asian rap group Fun-Da-Mental in a pre-recorded discussion on racism, she accepted without hesitation. The debate lasted just under half an hour, during which time the two musicians argued heatedly. When the programme was broadcast a few days later, Aurora-Madan says their segment had been cut to a few minutes, during which she was reduced to an eye-pleasing fixture. "Most of the camera angles were these very mundane, pretty girlie shots where I wasn't saying anything. You could see me and hear Aki's voice. It was typical censorship. I was totally misrepresented, made into an airhead musician."

Aurora-Madan may be an "east-west casualty", squirming with discomfort when asked about arranged marriages, scowling with disgust when asked to play the exotic beauty, but she knows one thing for sure. She wants success. "Fronting a band, being a strong woman and being Asian, I expect a lot of criticism and misunderstanding," she says, "but at the same time I really believe in what I'm doing. I want every prize existing, I want to be on the cover of every publication. I want to be best at what I do." Who said anything about an ego?

Amy Raphael is features editor of Elle magazine.

Figure 2.8A   From The Guardian, 4 August 1994

Figure 2.8B   Contact sheet by Kippa Matthews

based on the *descriptions* individuals make of themselves, it is clear that there must be some external standard against which people can measure the characteristics they regard as their own. Self-concept is therefore usually thought to be shaped, altered or maintained through interaction with others.

Self-concept is meant to encompass all notions of self, including **realistic** and **ideal** selves. The *realistic* self is an individual's perception of what he or she takes to be their 'true' qualities and shortcomings, while the *ideal* self is that which individuals strive, or believe it is possible, to become. Self-concept includes both social roles and 'personality traits', as well as subjects' assessment of their physical appearance and subjective attributes such as gender identity and class position.

Self-esteem is *evaluative* where self-concept is *descriptive*. It refers to how far individuals like or approve of themselves. Coopersmith (1967) described it as 'a personal judgement of worthiness'. A sense of self-esteem is supposed to be tested and readjusted through interaction, but will not in fact be entirely dependent on other people. Many individuals are able to sustain an adequate sense of personal esteem from the actions they perform, or from the interests they pursue. Jorge Larrain argues that (*Ideology and Cultural Identity*, p. 147) 'the unity and structure of the complete self reflects the unity and structure of the social processes in which the individual participates'.

Norms are those established standards of behaviour and thought which may act to influence the individual as he or she engages in social interaction. **Motivation and needs** refer to those forces and requirements which drive the human subject. Abraham Maslow organised his theory of needs into a hierarchy, moving from the most basic, **physiological** needs, to **safety**, **social** and **esteem** needs, and finishing with **self-actualisation**, where an individual may attempt to attain the fullest degree of his or her potential. William Schutz describes three needs which give rise to communicative behaviour: these are **inclusion**, **control** and **affection**.

From where, exactly, do social or public expectations come? Is appropriate role behaviour decided by families, the state, individuals or groups? The answer must be that all these influences are involved in the process of role 'description', and that individuals acknowledge **universal** as well as **particular** behavioural expectations in every situation they meet. *Universal* expectations are the generally accepted *range* of actions and declarations which it is usual for any one individual to make in any situation. *Particular* expectations relate to the types of conduct most appropriate to any specific context or 'definable' situation.

When you have read the article (Figure 2.8A) 'Not just an Asian babe', use the following questions as a starting point for discussion about 'a sense of self'.

Questions

1 How is the article *designed*? Consider the following visual and linguistic elements:

- the photograph. How is Sonya Aurora-Madan portrayed? Consider the physical stance or pose, her facial expression, clothing and the background against which she appears.
- the title, sub-heading and caption. How are we meant to interpret the title of the piece, 'Not just an Asian babe'? How closely does the caption to the picture, 'I was an east–west casualty', represent the content of the article?

2 In the first paragraph, why is Aurora-Madan's typical style of dress described?

3 The article describes the singer as being 'torn between two roles: "exotic" Asian babe and cross-cultural icon'. How useful is such a contrast in helping to understand the singer's identity?

4 Why is the lack of Asian 'role models' mentioned when the singer's early years are described (paragraph 6)? Are role models essential for young people?

5 How is the singer's *subjectivity* represented? (By subjectivity, I mean individual identity as it is constructed through social relationships.) Consider all the influences, for good or bad, which are mentioned in the article. What roles does the singer refuse? Is a theory of 'not-self' useful in understanding the singer's persona?

6 In terms of content, how much of the article is devoted to material about Aurora-Madan's image/identity, and how much to her music and role in Echobelly?

7 What is the singer's self-esteem based upon? What appears to motivate her? What social pressures does she feel are placed upon her, and what norms does she refuse to obey? Is there an 'ideal' self she wishes to attain?

8 Study Kippa Matthew's contact sheet (Figure 2.8B) for the article. What, in your opinion, influenced the particular choice that was made? Why was the chosen photograph regarded as suited to the piece? Would any of the alternatives have changed the *meaning* of the article?

IDENTITY AND SELF-DESCRIPTION
Research and production: The video diary

Questions

1 Carry out research into the diary as a form (see the section on diaries in Chapter 2). Useful material may be found in the diaries of Samuel Pepys, Che Guevara and Anne Frank, and in the journals of politicians like Tony Benn. If members of the class keep a diary, see whether anyone is prepared to present an extract to the group.

2 Collect a number of examples of **self-description**, either explicit or implicit. The latter kind are often to be found when writers describe the groups to which they belong, or when they contrast themselves with individuals or groups they regard as *unlike* themselves, or as undesirable.

Some films use the central character as narrator. In the American film *Just Another Girl on the IRT*, Chantelle despairs of her parents' squabbling and makes a direct address to camera:

'My parents work from pay cheque to pay cheque. That's not gonna be me. After graduation, I'm straight to college, then med. school. I got it *all* planned out. I ain't never gonna work for nobody, I'm gonna be my own boss. You watch. My life is gonna be *way* different.'

Chantelle's sense of self is created partly by comparison with the lives of her parents.

3 *The Guardian*'s 'Questionnaire' consists of nineteen questions, including the following. Use them to produce information on yourself:

- What is your idea of perfect happiness?
- What is your greatest fear?
- Which living person do you most admire?
- What is your most unappealing habit?
- What is your favourite journey?
- What or who is the greatest love of your life?
- Which living person do you most despise?
- What is your greatest regret?
- What would your motto be?
- How would you like to die?
- How would you like to be remembered?

4 Assemble a number of short extracts from the *Video Diary* series and make transcripts of useful passages. Travel books are also useful sources, because an individual's conception of 'self' is often described as being 'tested' by the privations and dangers of travel.

5 Study *two* documentaries and *two* fictional narratives. Is there a central theme in these films? Is there a central 'character', through whom we perceive events?

Story Board

Production _ Story Board No. _ _ _ _

Picture	Description	Audio & effects

Shot ☐ Cam ☐

Shot ☐ Cam ☐

Shot ☐ Cam ☐

Shot ☐ Cam ☐

Shot ☐ Cam ☐

Shot ☐ Cam ☐

Shot ☐ Cam ☐

Shot ☐ Cam ☐

Shot ☐ Cam ☐

Figure 2.9   Example of a blank story board

List the similarities and differences in the camerawork and editing styles of the material studied.

6 Write a proposal for the production of a video diary, which must be aimed at a specific audience of your choice. Consider the *register* and *address* you wish to employ.

7 Produce a story board detailing the major sequences of the video. (Fig 2.9 shows an example of a blank story board.) Once an initial idea of content has been sketched out, consider the *form* in which the diary is to be cast. The 'documentary' form has, in recent years, taken its inspiration from 'fictional' practices; there is no hard and fast difference between the conventions used by 'factual' and 'fictional' narratives.

8 Produce a short (5-minute) video diary which presents a descrption of yourself, your 'location' in time, space and the social order, your interests, values and beliefs, and your hopes for the future. Shoot the material in a variety of relevant contexts, including perhaps your home and your working environment.

You may wish to produce a montage of images, a clear narrative or a series of impressions, but the visual material must be supported by a coherent voiceover or address to camera.

9 Write an evaluation of your work, under the following headings:

- **Aims of the production**.
- **Research**: describe audience, sources, and investigative methods used.
- **Form and content**: describe how the diary's form and content (mainstream or alternative) was decided.
- **Development**: assess the problems encountered during the production process.
- **Conclusion**: evaluate the strengths and weaknesses of the finished product, and describe its reception by your audience.
- **Appendices**: transcript of diary voiceover/ soundtrack, complete story board, transcripts of individual audience responses, graphs or other data illustrating audience response.

Analysis: qualitative data

Read the following material on qualitative research, then investigate the question which follows.

Carolyn Baker (1982) asks the following questions about the status of qualitative interviews. What is the relation between interviewees' accounts and the world they describe? Are such accounts potentially 'true' or 'false' or is neither concept appropriate?

David Silverman, in *Interpreting Qualitative Data*, provides this definition of the difference between two traditions of research. **Positivism** assumes that interview data gives us access to facts about the world, while **interactionism** believes that subjects

who are interviewed actively 'construct' their social worlds. Silverman (p. 9) describes the variation in the ways in which HIV patients *presented* themselves to medical staff. These types of presentation were as follows: *cool*, where no apparent worry was revealed and patients seemed to accept their fate; *anxious*, a state of mind where any opportunity was taken to express the patients' worries; *objective*, when patients presented themselves as a 'bundle of objective symptoms'; and *theatrical*, a type of self-presentation in which the sufferer downplayed physical symptoms in order to make remarks which acknowledged 'the listening audience'.

Question

Are there certain types of **presentation** and certain **discourses** which appear time and again in subjects' *self-descriptions*? Compare the interviews transcribed by the class and identify the **themes** and **strategies** used by subjects when they are called upon to describe their own personality and autobiographical experience.

NAMES AND IDENTITY
Reading and research

Read the following material on an extract from the science fiction programme *Red Dwarf*, then complete the research assignment which follows.

In one episode of the popular science fiction comedy *Red Dwarf*, the crew are led to believe that all their experiences in space have been generated during an extended 'interactive' computer game, played over a period of three years. Their original identities are seemingly no more than the *roles* they have had to assume during the course of the game. They are forced, therefore, to investigate their 'real' identities. Recovering from the shock of their discovery, they find a number of suitcases in an ante-room, cases which have been stowed away for later collection. They open each case and discover their 'actual' identities (though this, in turn, is later revealed to be have been an hallucination).

Rimmer: Kryten, open the next one.
Kryten: Listen, whoever you are, don't push your luck by ordering whoever I am around, because almost certainly, whoever I am, I'm not the kind of guy who's going to take any crap from whoever you are ...
Lister: Right, this one's you.
Kryten: Oh, who am I?
Lister: *Wow*, you're a detective, in the Cybernautic Division of the police department.
Kryten: Ha! Golly. Really?
Lister: Yeah. This is your badge.
Kryten: A detective, huh? What's my name?
Lister: Jake Bullit.
Kryten: *Jake Bullit*, cybernautic detective. I *like* that. That sounds like the kind of hard-living flatfoot that gets the job done by cutting corners and bucking authority ...
Rimmer: On the other hand, Mr Bullit, perhaps the Cybernautic Division is in charge of traffic and you just happen to have a rather silly macho name.

Another case is opened, which the group at first think belongs to Lister. The name attached is 'Billy Doyle', which prompts Rimmer to speculate on the lowly origin of the person concerned:

Rimmer: Billy Doyle. Well that's a name that came from the wrong side of the tracks isn't it. You can see it all now; a youth spent in and out of corrective institutions, a string of illegitimate children ... has to take up petty crime to cover the court orders for maintenance. Before he knows it, he's standing in a bank with a sawn-off shotgun. Somehow it goes off. An old lady gets both barrels through a crocheted bobble-hat.
Lister: It's yours.
Rimmer: What?
Lister: It's yours, *Bill*.
Rimmer: No.

This discovery leads Rimmer to change his mind about the connotations of the name.

Rimmer: William Doyle ... *William Doyle*. Good old Bill Doyle. You know, that sounds like a hell of a name to me. Probably connected to the Boston Doyles – old money, blue chip stock. You know I think it's all beginning to come back to me now.

Research: Analyse the cast list of any mainstream television or cinematic text and write out the names which are used for the heroes/heroines and villains. Do the names suggest a particular character? Are certain nationalities or ethnic groups cast in particular roles in mainstream texts?

List and analyse the names given to cars and to 'special editions' of such vehicles. What associations are called to mind by different names which are assigned to cars?

LANGUAGE AND EXPRESSION
Analysis: a child playing

Some writers would regard the following as an example of *intrapersonal communication*. It is in fact an example of *dramatised expression*, where the child (a boy who has just had his eighth birthday) creates a narrative as he goes along. He is playing with a number of Lego pirates. The words in italics are 'sound effects', produced to signify battle and other events.

The transcript has been given a structure only through the addition of capitals and the creation of divisions between speech acts. Three dots (...) signify a place where part of the transcript has been cut.

> *ching ching ching ching* aaaah! *whistle explosion*
> whoops eee daisy *pishooo aaaah!*
> Aaarrruh arrr arrr get on me hearties fighting ...
> Arrr *poosh* ah oooh aah *pushoo* aahh ooooh *roar* daar
> I'll kill you
> Who says? *ching ching* yuh you little rat don't call fighting
> *roaring explosions groans* we're under attack we're under attack
> Aha this'll do thanks my gold *shooting* oh *shooting groans shooting groans*
> You OK?
> Yeah I'm OK I dropped my pistol yeah that was pretty close get me out of here
> Anything but that please no *groans shooting*
> You'll pay for this Henry that was (1) hard to expect (1) go back to the boat go back to the boat
> Are you sure you want to chicken out like that sir?
> Shut up and row friend we shall go (1) the pirates are the ones that will be wiped out by us I declare (1) I declare war *shooting*
>
> We've been wiped out totally sir face it
> We didn't make that war no we didn't (.)
> Lets go over and we lost thousands and thousands of men
> You're not harmed man and as for you why you little (.) you could have been robbed by pirates you're lucky you're not dead already you're lucky you're not dead already
> Sadly I can't now because he's already dead
> I hate battle I hate it those priartes goh I hate them
> Sir you be mad let's take
> Who says?
> Well at least did you kill him?
> I'm not sure I think he's suffering right now
> Henry youve got blood all over
> Me hearties take these dying *whisper*
> Dick saved my life before
> I know I know he told me to you and my arms ah
> I've had enough fighting I dont care if our ship gets stuck
> We declare war do you hear me
> Eeer you shot Henry I saw you shooting *agonised roar*
> Steer the ship I will have to *swishing noise* a storm's blowing up
> Ooh it's a dead body it's holding a pistol with fifty shots for a start (...)

Questions

1   How many individual roles requiring speech do there appear to be?

2   William Labov (1970) used the following structures for conversation analysis:

- question and answer;
- challenge and response;
- invitation and acceptance.

Identify and record any examples of these structures in the passage above.

3   Can you identify the *narrative structure* of this event?

4   Is there a reason for the repetition of certain sections, such as 'you're lucky you're not dead already you're lucky you're not dead already'?

5   What perspective on war and conflict does the narrative dramatise?

ESSAY TITLES

1 'The individual subject's self-concept is entirely dependent on the responses he or she gains from other individuals.'

Discuss.

2 'I tell you who I think is the best team in London – Tottenham.'

> *The only things Ray could say genuinely, were exactly those things (like the example above) that anyone else would say sarcastically. (from 'Ray, the man afflicted with a sarcastic tone of voice', Newman and Baddiel, 1994)*

To what extent does the significance of any statement actually reside in the intonation used in its delivery? Use examples from your own observation.

3 Goran Therborn (*The Ideology of Power and the Power of Ideology*) complains that most role theorists see 'social relations as interpersonal relations only'.

Is this an accurate description of the perspective of writers like Myers and Myers, Barnlund, and Patton and Giffin?

Provide evidence to support your opinions.

4 'A speech act is not created by individual intention alone, but by the circumstances in which people find themselves. "What we meant to say" will become, in most circumstances, *what it is possible to say*.'

Discuss with reference to the context of any speech act you have encountered.

5 'The most sinister part of socialisation is exactly that which appears most natural, or most beneficial for the child. It is the reproduction of state control through communication.'

Discuss.

6 'The best theories of communication are those which treat the human subject as *neutral*, and which do not confuse the issue by revealing the identity of the communicators.'

Discuss with reference to models of communication and theories of gender and identity.

CHAPTER 3

The social process

Language, power and human groups

Categorisation

One of the major ways in which people distinguish between the various perceptions they make is through the process of **categorisation**. This means that the 'sense data' collected by individuals is organised into systems of 'belonging'. Categorisation is, therefore, the process of sorting objects, events or living things into a series of *classes* or groups. Categories are used to refer to a variety of elements found in the world, from the fairly specific to the more general features of experience. For example, the category 'dog' has a narrower range of reference than the more inclusive category 'animal'.

Categories in print

Many children's books are clearly concerned to reinforce the process of categorisation. Dick Bruna's *I Know about Shapes*, for example, begins with the class of shape called *round*. From this, we proceed to pictures of the members of the group; a 'round ball', a 'round plate' and 'round wheels'. There may be a hint here, in the different kinds of 'roundness' which feature in Bruna's austere volume, that the process of categorisation is a little more complicated than it first appears.

Traditional views of categorisation

Traditional approaches to categorisation assume that it codifies human experience in terms of *similarity*, or what John R. Taylor (see *Linguistic Categorisation*) calls the 'conjunction of necessary and sufficient features'. In simple terms, the established view is that clear *boundaries* exist between category types. Individual variations between phenomena which belong to the same category are, however, regarded as acceptable, provided such differences do not violate the 'essential' criteria thought necessary for group membership. True members of a category will, according to this perspective, always share the same 'core' features. For instance, an evergreen and a deciduous tree may show marked differences to one another, but would be described as sharing the essential criteria (roots, branches, a trunk, a certain size) for membership of the category *tree*.

'Family resemblance'

The philosopher Wittgenstein (writing in *Philosophical Investigations*) challenged the received wisdom about categories. He used the example of the activities called 'games', to ask what organising principle was actually used to assign various phenomena to the same category (*Linguistic Categorisation*, p. 39):

> 'Consider for example the proceedings that we call "games". I mean board-games, card-games, ball-games, Olympic games, and so on. What is common to them all? – Don't say: "There must be something common, or they would not be called 'games'" – but look and see whether there is anything common to all. For if you look at them you will not see something that is common to *all*, but similarities, relationships.'

Wittgenstein examined a great variety of games, demonstrating that the differences between the purposes and conduct of various examples makes it difficult to find a set of criteria which apply to each and every one. Instead of trying to find hard and fast credentials, or clear-cut boundaries between what is a game and what is not, Wittgenstein used the example of **'family resemblances'**, where there exists a series of relationships between the members, each sharing a number of features but none encompassing all the possible criteria for membership.

When is a cup not a cup?

An alternative to the 'classical' theory was also proposed by William Labov in 1973. Labov is probably most famous for his work on ethnic speech communities in the United States. In this case, he studied the linguistic categorisation of household objects such as vases, bowls, glasses, mugs and cups.

In one experiment, he presented a series of pictures of various receptacles to a group of students (Figure 3.1). The appearance of the containers showed quite considerable variation (some were represented as wider or taller than others), but all shared important features like handles, and thus bore some broad similarity to the category 'cup'.

Labov wished to discover whether there would be variations in the way each pictorial representation was named once different *uses* of the objects were suggested to the students. In the first instance, he asked his students to imagine each artefact in someone's hand. In the second, he required them to picture the objects standing on a table with mashed potato inside. In the third and final instance, he told his subjects to think of the receptacles placed on a shelf, holding flowers.

Figure 3.1   Varieties of receptacle, after Labov

In the first and most 'neutral' context, the term *cup* was readily applied by the students, except for the widest examples of receptacle, which were more usually called *bowl*. In the second, the frequency of choices of *bowl* became somewhat higher, and included those items which were of only medium width. Finally, where subjects had been asked to imagine the container holding flowers, the same pattern emerged; the choice of *vase* rose at the expense of the category *cup*.

Types of category: superordinate and basic

Despite the various criticisms of the established theory of categorisation, the basic idea of increasingly inclusive *stages* or levels remains useful. Taylor, writing in *Linguistic Categorisation*, points out the difference between **superordinate** and **basic** categories, examples of which we have already encountered. A superordinate category is one which refers to the *general* class of whatever is being described, whether these are concepts, objects, events or living things. 'Fruit' is one example of a superordinate category. An example of a *basic*-level category, which belongs to the general class of 'fruit', might be an 'orange'. Of course, oranges are not the only fruit, so other basic categories will include apple, banana, peach and so on.

Categories are organised on more than just two levels, however. Taylor shows that things may be categorised in a number of different ways, and that this

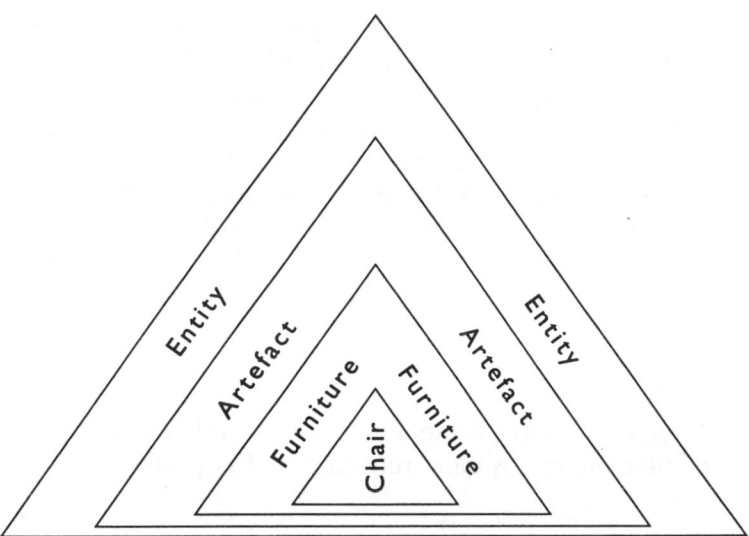

Figure 3.2   Hierarchy of categories, after Taylor's examples

creates a *hierarchy* of descriptive classes. Using the example of an ordinary chair, he demonstrates that the object can belong to the following categories: *chair*, *furniture*, *artefact* and *entity* (Figure 3.2). As the list of categories grows, each in succession indicates a greater range of significance. Each is more *inclusive* than the previous category on the list.

It is the *basic* level, however, which Taylor sees as the most commonly used in everyday speech. He demonstrates this observation with the following example (p. 49):

> 'If a foreigner were to point to the object I am now sitting on and ask "What do you call that in English?", I would almost certainly answer, "It's a chair". I would not reply "It's an artefact", or "It's a piece of furniture", even though these alternative answers would be equally "correct".'

Basic-level terms can be identified because they are usually short and have simple linguistic structures, and occur frequently in the ordinary usages of language.

Innocent parts of language?

Basic-level terms may appear to be the most natural and innocent parts of language. However, some theories of ideology assume that it is exactly the *ordinary* names given to aspects of experience, and the *basic* divisions made between 'things in the world', that reflect a society's values and beliefs.

For example, some supposedly neutral and 'scientific' categories actually function in a discriminatory way. A 'descriptive' term like *white*, applied to *people* rather than to objects, has often promoted discrimination against those placed outside its rather arbitrary and subjective boundaries. Indeed, many societies have built vast wealth on the simple practice of using physical or 'racial' characteristics as the mark of high or low status; in such cases, categories are nearly synonymous with social class.

It is also possible that certain categories may *restrict* what it is possible to say about various aspects of experience. G.W. Allport, writing in 1954 (see *The Nature of Prejudice*), said that some labels tend to prevent alternative classification, acting 'like shrieking sirens, deafening us to all finer discriminations that we might otherwise perceive'. If this is true, then a category we may use quite casually to describe an everyday phenomenon has the ability to influence our perception of an object or event. This is not to argue that categories are always somehow *sinister*, rather that they are not entirely *innocent* in their effects. Allport recognised this problem when he argued that (p. 20):

> 'The human mind must think with the aid of categories ... once formed, categories are the basis for normal prejudgement. We cannot possibly avoid this process. Orderly living depends upon it.'

Although the process of categorisation is inevitable, it is still possible to criticise the undesirable effects it occasionally entails. The feeling that certain categories encourage a negative attitude to particular aspects of existence has led to a number of attempts to 're-categorise' things, people and events. For example, the use of the term 'mankind' seemed to ignore the existence of women, and was eventually replaced by 'humankind'.

The growth of new labels for established concepts has been particularly noticeable in the United States, where a number of alternative terms have become enshrined in, for example, parts of the educational system. The fashion for 'political correctness' has prompted a number of humorous ripostes. Henry Beard and Christopher Cerf, two American authors, produced *The Official Politically Correct Dictionary and Handbook*, delighting in the replacement of redundant terms like 'housewife' with absurdities such as *domestic incarceration survivor*. 'Political correctness' has also, however, provided an opportunity for the political right to attack genuine attempts to promote a critical awareness of discriminatory attitudes and practices.

Categorisation and language acquisition

Learning about categories is a basic part of **language acquisition** and also, therefore, a feature of socialisation. As the infant learns how the world is described, it grows to understand the *value* attached to those descriptions. By *value*, I mean both the moral, social and political worth accorded to different things through language, and the strength or degree of *effect* likely to be achieved by the *use* of specific linguistic 'labels'. The growing child will, however, learn about more than just names and categories; through the combination of apparently simple and uncontroversial terms, it will encounter a whole system of values. Above all, it will come to know which discourses produce an effective change in its environment. In other words, it will learn how to use the power of language.

Appeals to shared values

While early acquisition of knowledge about the world probably means that the basic moral values of a culture are *known* to all individuals who share and use symbolic codes (such as language), this does not mean that people will necessarily behave in the ways that convention dictates. In other words, there is quite a difference between understanding moral precepts (in the sense that individuals are able to *identify* them correctly) and choosing to act in accordance with the values from which they emerge.

In the light of this tendency, it is worth noting that no corporate, public or political authority is guaranteed absolute success when it exhorts people to conduct their lives according to established models of behaviour. There are many reasons why such failures occur, including weakness in the structure of the messages themselves, but one of the most significant is connected with the attitudes held towards the *source* of these appeals. There is a belief, quite commonly held, that double standards operate in public life. When, for example, government ministers call for a return to 'basic' moral values, such appeals are unlikely to succeed when the politicians concerned behave in ways which contradict their own words.

Making sense of experience?

Some writers consider that the reason the human subject tends to categorise its perceptions is that it must find a way of coping with all the different events which occur in life. Our species would otherwise, they argue, be faced with the problem of having to construct an infinite number of *unique* representations of things in the world, in order to be able to recognise each separate experience. Glass and Holyoak (see *Cognition*, p. 149) are two authors who hold this view, arguing that:

'if each experience were given a unique mental representation, we would be quickly overwhelmed ... By encoding experiences into an organised system of categories, we are able to recognise significant commonalities in different experiences.'

It seems clear that people would indeed feel bewildered by their own mental processes, if they were forced to create new representations for every single thing encountered; but in fact there is never any danger of this happening. Glass and Holyoak have simply conjured up the threat of mental chaos to support their theory that the process of categorisation saves individuals a lot of work.

Essentially, they see categorisation as a process which *limits* or *controls* the amount of mental processing humans are required to undertake. In response to this view, it should be noted that people are actually engaged in a great deal of 'processing' anyway; presented with a variety of experiences, which occur in a number of different contexts, individuals have constantly to update or re-evaluate their perceptions. Categories do not automatically solve all the challenges of interpretation and understanding. The simple process of everyday living tests the accuracy of the categories which individuals have at their disposal.

It is also important to remember that, while categories may appear to refer always to the same things or concepts, two points should be borne in mind. In the first place, categories will change their meaning over time. Secondly, individual experience of categories will differ, according to the intensity of the experience and the *subject position* of the individual concerned. The human subject is 'placed' in society through a number of factors, including biological sex, gender roles, class, ethnicity, age and so on. (See the section on 'Women as a social group?' later in this chapter.)

Redrawing boundaries

The second point Glass and Holyoak make, that people only recognise similar aspects of life because they have the ability to organise their experiences into classes, implies that recognition of such similarities *follows* the process of categorisation. While our perception of the significance of an event, or our interpretation of the meaning of an action, is often influenced by our knowledge of the class to which it 'belongs', we are also capable of perceiving similarities in things which are traditionally placed in quite different classes, suggesting that categories are not straitjackets for the mind and that it is possible to redraw their boundaries.

Recognising context

Individuals are often assisted in their identification of objects, events and persons by the general nature of the situation in which each phenomenon is found. In other words, our knowledge of the *use* and *place* of things in the world helps us assign them to categories. For example, an object we had perhaps never seen before would not neccessarily be identified until its *relationship* to other things could be established. Presented with an exotic vegetable, with no knowledge of its category status, we might not be sure that we were really meant to eat it. We would feel more certain about its status if we could see it being prepared as part of a meal in which other, more familiar types of food were present.

It is only when things are in use, or when events are seen to have certain consequences, or when individuals prove they are what they claim, that we should feel satisfied that identification has been made correctly. In the meantime, we should realise that the *precise* category membership of an individual thing may change according to the circumstances in which it is found, or the uses to which it is put. As Hastorf and his colleagues show ('The perceptual process' Corner and Hawthorn, in *Communication Studies: An Introductory Reader*, p. 120):

'there are occasions when all of us change categories in perceiving objects. Instead of size and colour, we may see things in terms of function: the large blue pen and small green pencil are suddenly similar when we want only to jot down a telephone number.'

If people regard objects in a variety of ways, according to the *perceived use* of the artefacts concerned, then as Taylor puts it (p. 41), there might not be an exact description available for each artefact:

'attributes might sometimes be functional (they concern the use to which an object is put) or interactional (they concern the way people handle the object)'.

Taylor argues that the attributes of an object are not entirely based on the 'inherent properties' of the object itself, but emerge from 'the role of the object within a particular culture'. Of course, once that role is understood, then the object will be recognised for what it is, even in a different context. In the same way that objects may be understood through their role, so too are linguistic categories understood through their function in discourse.

Collective perceptions

Although category membership alters according to context, it cannot change to the extent that it makes nonsense of the conventions of language. 'Dog' will never belong to the category 'plant', for example. It is important to realise that categories are established in the material practice of language use, and are therefore an important part of the *social process*, providing evidence of *collective* rather than merely individual perceptions. Categories should be understood as part of the 'outlook' of entire cultures and subcultures at any given moment in their history.

Prototypes

The theory of **prototypes** states that there are certain phenomena in various societies which are always regarded as belonging to a certain category, and which may therefore be described as the 'originals' for the categories which are constructed around them. In Western culture, for instance, the category *cup* is understood as referring to an object of a certain size, of a certain appearance, possessing a clear function and use.

It is sometimes said that a prototype, rather than having an existence as an actual object, is a 'schematic representation' of what Taylor (p. 58) calls the 'conceptual core' of a category. The conceptual core would be the *idea* of the category based on an abstraction of all its agreed features. The danger with the idea of the prototype is that we may end up by creating another version of the Platonic 'ideal form', where there is supposed to be one 'true' version of each category, from which all other related phenomena take their characteristics. (See Chapter 1 for a brief discussion of Plato's forms.)

Rather than retreat from our emphasis on the social and contextual frame of meaning, it would be better to observe how people, located in their material circumstances, decide category membership. This would mean accepting that a prototype would alter not only as a result of the place and time in which the selection is made, but also according to the groups or individuals concerned.

Creative expression

Despite the restrictions it encounters, human expression remains essentially **creative**; when events cannot be explained through the available terminology, new labels and categories are invented. At the same time, the human subject is usually able to recognise the true nature of those things which words are intended to disguise. For example, the substitution of the term 'Ministry of Defence' for the older 'Ministry for War' does not mean that the essential functions of the institution itself are hidden from view.

As we grow up in a particular 'speech community', we are bound to inherit the attitudes and values carried not just in the language as a whole, but in the particular idiosyncrasies of that community's *habits of speech*. Our access to the 'standard' language used in the wider society is mediated at various levels. In fact standard language is, more than anything, a theoretical proposition built from culturally biased perceptions of which *dialect* is most respectable.

The act of naming

On some occasions, the existing names or labels we use are unable to describe an unexpected phenonemon, and new terms (or more likely, new combinations of old terms) have to be found. The discovery in Vietnam in June 1994 of a creature previously unknown to science brought an immediate problem: how should it be *categorised*? A newspaper report described it as 'a large ox-like mammal' and provided descriptions of its physical characteristics. Familiar labels such as 'ox' and 'mammal' are used here, yet are qualified in order to indicate difference. The animal was given two names, one scientific and the other intended for wider use: *Pseudoryx nghetinhensis* and Vu Quang ox. Neither will provide a completely reliable conceptualisation of the animal until its appearance and habits become more widely understood. Only then will the terms used to describe it begin to seem 'natural'.

The act of *naming* is always regarded as important. In *An Introduction to Language*, Victoria Fromkin and Robert Rodman describe the practice of some African tribes who do not name their newborn children until they grow to acquire knowledge (p. 3):

'a newborn child is a kuntu, a "thing", not yet a muntu, a "person". Only by the act of learning does the child become a human being.'

Careful consideration goes into the process of choosing children's names. Certain names are considered to be more attractive than others. Gross (*Psychology*, p. 483) reports an experiment in which a group of American teachers gave more favourable grades to essays which carried names previously characterised (by other teachers) as attractive.

Categorisation of people

It is usually felt that there is a significant difference between labelling objects or animals and classifying people, whether as individuals or in groups. As soon as we turn to consider people, we are dealing even more obviously with concepts of *the social*. An insight into the way that 'labels' are attached to different groups will help towards an understanding of the **social power** which is exercised through language.

If, for example, we apply the label 'king' to a person, the usual response it entails will include a host of ideas about social deference and the 'special' status of an individual. Whether or not we mean to indicate approval, there remains an agreed range of meaning which attaches to the term. In the last analysis, it cannot do anything other than indicate an unusual degree of personal and social status. The term carries this power even at the moment when a society decides to depose, or otherwise dispense with, an individual member of the category.

Typage in verse

Semonides, an early Greek writer of the seventh century BC, produced a satire in verse called *An Essay on Women* in which he described the various types of women created by the gods from different animals. Each 'type' in the series of categories presented by Semonides bears some resemblance to the animal from which it is supposed to come. The poem concerns itself with the suitability of women as wives, and so analyses virtues and shortcomings entirely in the light of what are supposed to be male requirements. It also assumes that appearance bears a close relationship to character, providing one of the earliest examples of mostly negative stereotyping to be found in literature. The extracts which follow are taken from Richmond Lattimore's *Greek Lyrics* (pp. 8–9):

'One was a donkey, dusty-gray and obstinate.
It's hard to make her work. You have to curse and tug to make her do it.'

The most suitable wife is, according to this ancient writer, the one who is most thoughtful, the one most like:

'a bee. The man is lucky who gets her.
She is the only one no blame can settle on.'

Even so, the conclusion of the *Essay* is a list of the miseries of married life, in which all wrong-doing is laid at the door of the female.

This form of typage has survived in modern advertising. The McCann Erikson 'Woman Study' of 1985, designed to provide companies with a guide to habits of consumption, divided the female population of Britain into eight distinct types, each allocated a character and an animal supposedly suited to that character. The details of this study include the 'typical' purchases made by each group, together with the suggestion that psychological type is closely linked to social class (see Price, *Media Studies*, p. 126).

Apartheid: classification by the state

What used to be known as 'petty' apartheid in South Africa – the practice of dividing public space and public facilities between 'ethnic' groups identified by the government – was in fact very far from trivial. Rather than a sign of mere bigotry, it was an act of racial categorisation to which all had to submit. By complying with signs which read 'whites only', or 'black employees' or 'coloureds only', the population acknowledged the material power of language and address. These were indeed labels which acted like Allport's 'shrieking sirens', not just preventing alternative classification but reinforcing divisions in status and thus determining access to resources.

The principle of racial classification produced the most ridiculous consequences. On some occasions, when it discovered different shades of skin colour within the same family, the apartheid regime declared siblings to be members of different racial groups. There were also cases where individuals were reclassified and thus found to have 'changed' their racial identity.

Categorisation: scare tactics

In the political sphere, a tried and trusted method of undermining the moral status of any opponents or rival group is to declare that they belong to a category which will inspire fear or dislike in the minds of neutral observers. Such tactics are also employed in addressing an audience known to be susceptible to prejudices which can be triggered by the mere mention of certain groups.

For example, *The Daily Telegraph* of 10 May 1982 carried a report on a demonstration called in London to oppose the Falklands War. Describing the speeches made at the end of the march, the *Telegraph* characterised the assembly as follows:

> 'The audience appeared to consist mainly of Communists and other left-wing activists, CND [Campaign for Nuclear Disarmament] supporters, Irish Republicans and Iranian students.'

Of course, the anti-war lobby at this time included a variety of groups, such as liberal socialists and Christians of various denominations, which are simply not mentioned in this report; there were also individuals who owed allegiance to no group in particular. However, the list given by the *Telegraph* seems designed to strike a particular chord amongst its readers.

Notice that the categories mentioned here might appear as though they are all groups to which individuals belong through choice, implying perhaps that the members of each category deserve any disapproval they may encounter. It is the inclusion of 'Irish Republicans' and 'Iranian students' which suggests that the reader is meant to disapprove of certain people partly on the basis of nationality.

Damned through association

Another way of condemning those who do not meet one's approval is to link them with other groups which are supposedly universally reviled. An organisation called 'Peace Through Security' (reminiscent of the titles of Orwell's state ministries in *Nineteen Eighty-Four*), was sporadically active during the Falklands War. It issued a pro-war leaflet during the very march described above by the *Telegraph*, characterising CND as 'Communists, Neutralists, Defeatists'. Part of the text reads:

> 'The scare propaganda about nuclear war churned out by CND is extraordinarily similar to the scare tactics used by the Appeasers during the 1930s. Those people too tried to persuade the public that defending ourselves against the Nazis was both useless and a provocation.'

Here, history is not examined too closely. Who were the appeasers? A substantial number owed their allegiance to right-wing organisations and causes, but this would not suit the purposes of this group, supported at the time by a number of Young Conservatives. The Argentinian military is by implication the equivalent of the 'Nazis' mentioned in the leaflet.

Categories designed to mislead: a case from history

The use of negative categorisation has a long pedigree in the twentieth century. Its use is not confined to the political right, though it is often associated with authoritarian philosophies of one sort or another.

In February 1921, after a long civil war, the Leninist administration in Russia faced a difficult situation. Widespread deprivation amongst the populace led to a wave of strikes in the cities. Many of the Communists' own party members were thoroughly disillusioned. Led by Communist sailors, the entire Baltic fleet, based at Kronstadt, called for a return to direct democracy and for policies which would ease the economic situation (see Maurice Brinton, *The Bolsheviks and Workers' Control*, p. 77 onwards).

Trotsky, who at the time held the post of people's commissar for war, issued an ultimatum to the entire city of Kronstadt, choosing to describe the rebels as 'White guard insurrectionists', a term designed to indicate that the rebellion was led by the same right-wing forces which had opposed Bolshevism during the civil war. Trotsky went on to issue other communiqués, insisting that the revolt was inspired by French counter-intelligence and led by anti-Bolshevik generals. After a struggle lasting just over two weeks, which saw the defection to the rebels of many units of Red Army troops, the uprising was crushed. Those who could not escape were shot, or imprisoned and executed in the months which followed the uprising.

Categorisation as name-calling

In 1938, looking back on the Kronstadt events, Trotsky no longer maintained that the rebels of 1921 had been right-wing agitators inspired by foreign powers. Instead of a struggle against dangerous reactionaries and foreign governments, the suppression of the Kronstadters had become 'a tragic necessity'. If the insurgents could no longer be described as right-wing, then they could instead be characterised as misguided. In 'Hue and cry over Kronstadt' (see Lenin and Trotsky, *Kronstadt*, p. 87), Trotsky dismissed the Kronstadt sailors as:

> 'completely demoralised elements, wearing showy bell-bottom pants and sporty haircuts'.

It would appear that, when history revealed his earlier accusation to be an untidy fiction, Trotsky decided to categorise his opponents as fashion victims!

In the late 1930s, the Soviet leadership under Stalin was using the same techniques of repression against 'Trotskyist counter-revolutionaries', executing all who might represent a threat to the regime (including a number of those who had led the action against Kronstadt).

Mutually exclusive categories

One of the consequences of placing people in a particular category is the difficulty faced when they are found to 'belong' to more than one. 'Irish Republicans' caused the *Daily Telegraph* no problems because the two terms, in that newspaper's view, were complementary, or explained one another. However, as Rothbart and Taylor discovered (see 'Category labels and social reality' in Semin and Fiedler, p. 29), powerful social categories 'may dominate the psychological field' in a way that 'inhibits multiple classification'. In other words, some social classifications will 'dominate' others, leading to a situation where an onlooker may have (p. 29):

'difficulty in seeing a single object or person as simultaneously belonging to more than one category'.

Rothbart and Taylor found evidence for this tendency in a statement made by Raymond Barre, then prime minister of France. A synagogue on the Rue Copernic in Paris was bombed as part of a terrorist campaign against the state of Israel. Barre declared that:

'the criminal attack killed Jews as well as innocent Frenchmen'.

The implication was clear that, in Barre's mind, being Jewish placed some of the victims outside the categories 'innocent' and 'French'.

Research evidence: categories which clash?

Research undertaken by Saltz and his colleagues in the late 1960s and early 1970s showed that young children demonstrate what is called the 'strong form' of mutual exclusivity, which takes the form of denial that an individual can belong at one and the same time to certain types of category. Those found to be mutually exclusive in the children's minds included *father* and *doctor*, and *mother* and *teacher*. In a survey conducted in 1967, it was found that 63 per cent of 5-year-old children reported that a father who studied until he became a doctor would no longer be a father. This line of research also seemed to indicate that (p. 30):

'When the valence of the two categories differs (for example, doctor and thief), even eight-year-olds tend to claim that a single person cannot belong to both categories.'

In addition, the degree of *conventionality* displayed in the combination of descriptive categories sometimes leads mature individuals, and not just children, to make category choices which may appear strange. Rothbart refers to her own research, in which she found that people who believe that women are unscientific, and who are thrown into a dilemma by meeting a female scientist, are likely to resolve the difficulty by categorising the individual concerned as a *scientist* rather than as a *woman*!

The power of contrast

Social categories work by indicating what they are not, as much as what they are. They are essentially **contrastive**, implicitly drawing attention to differences. As Hogg and Abrams note (in *Social Identifications*, p. 14):

> 'the social category *Black* is meaningless unless it serves to differentiate those who are *Black* and those who are not – that is, it is a contrasting category'.

Since the social structure undergoes change, new social categories appear, while others alter in terms of the status or power they are able to mobilise. The nature of the link between social categorisation and stereotyping has long been the subject of debate, as we shall see in more detail in the following pages.

'Natural kind', 'human artefact' and 'social' categories

Reviewing the types of category used to describe the social reality we inhabit, Myron Rothbart and Marjorie Taylor make a distinction between **natural kind** and **human artefact** categories. They also refer to **social** categories (see Semin and Fiedler, *Language, Interaction and Social Cognition*, p. 11).

The examples they give of *natural kind* categories are birds, fish, gold and daffodils. These are all seen as having a significant degree of independence from the human sphere. Instances of *human artefact* categories given by these authors include chair, bicycle, sweater and house. *Social* categories are the divisions used to make distinctions between 'types' of people, based on characteristics like ethnicity, or occupation, or personality, or on any of the variety of 'subjectivities' people possess.

Essential attributes?

Rothbart and Taylor discovered that people are inclined to view categories of natural kinds as 'less arbitrary' than those of artefact kinds, because (p. 12):

> 'natural kinds are believed to possess underlying essences that make one category different from another'.

In plain terms, they are saying that things in the natural world are treated as though they have *essential* attributes that *cannot be changed*, so that the distinction between each category is thought to reflect some unchangeable truth about the thing which is categorised. In contrast, the names attached to human artefact categories are thought *not* to express *essence* or essential qualities.

These authors argue that, in many cases, we allow experts the freedom to place types of natural phenomena in the correct categories, so for example gold may be distinguished from (p. 12) 'other yellow metals' and diamonds will be shown to be different from cut glass.

Social categories

The next stage of Rothbart and Taylor's argument is that social categories (those used to describe individuals or groups) are in reality very close to human artefact categories (those reserved for the *things* people have made). Social and artefact categories are similar because both are used, by human subjects, to organise *social* reality. The problem, as these authors see it, is that social categories are treated by most people as though they have more in common with natural kind categories. For example, this theory would mean that the social category 'teacher' may be invested with a certain degree of power because it is thought somehow to reflect a *natural* state, just as any natural kind category would be regarded as containing some essence which cannot be denied or ignored.

This has important implications. If Rothbart and Taylor are right, it suggests that we have a tendency to treat social categories as trustworthy or correct because they are thought to reflect an aspect of the *real*. Categorisation of this sort may therefore both reflect and sustain a certain rigidity in our ideas about social existence. It may also mean that human subjects will display a variety of behaviours (favourable or unfavourable) towards other individuals, which are based on the belief that such categories really express the *truth* about those others.

Physical appearance

Some of the most powerful acts of social categorisation are based on very simple aspects of human experience. This includes the idea (see Semin and Fiedler, *Language, Interaction and Social Cognition*, p. 26) that 'deep, underlying attributes are inferred from appearance', implying that the presence of **physical** differences may 'have a ... special status in intergroup attitudes'. This leads Rothbart and Taylor to the conclusion that:

> 'the imposition of natural kind structure onto our thinking about social categories gives disproportionate strength to category differences correlated with physical appearance. This prediction seems consistent with what we know about the ubiquity and power of stereotypes based on race and gender.'

In this scenario, individuals' physical appearance leads to the creation of a great many assumptions about their character and category membership. The widespread power of the form of characterisation called **stereotyping** is felt by these authors to grow from the tendency to regard the 'social' labels attached to people as though they reflect the essence of the individuals or groups concerned.

This theory seems to strike a fairly pessimistic chord. People, in this scenario, appear to take inherited social meanings on trust and, since they are content to allow experts to determine the boundaries which should be placed between things in the natural environment, are perhaps also inclined to allow other 'experts' (sociologists, market researchers) to decide how human beings should be classified.

The exercise of judgement?

However, we must remember that the uses of categorisation described above are *tendencies*, rather than effects which will always inevitably arise. Human beings are able to question the established social order and the categories it recognises. Individuals also exercise scepticism about their own judgements, and caution with regard to actions based on their perceptions, partly because perception is not always regarded as reliable.

Familiarity and expertise

Despite the healthy scepticism that is part of our human make-up, it is interesting to note that people are more likely to trust *their own* judgement when they are faced with what Rothbart and Taylor call '*familiar* artefact categories' (my emphasis). They quote Schwartz (1978), who argued that:

> 'If a scientist were interested in chairs as a subject of scientific study and got himself a good specimen and started to examine it closely in order to discover the nature of chairs, we would think he was crazy. Compare this with a zoologist interested in snakes, who obtains a fine specimen and begins to dissect it.'

Is there evidence to suggest that people trust their own perceptions when faced with familiar artefacts, but allow experts to judge natural phenomena (and even some aspects of the social)? Malt, working in 1989, carried out experiments to test the contrast between artefact and natural categories, and appeared to discover some support for this view.

Describing the unfamiliar

Some of the natural kind examples employed by Rothbart and Taylor are distinctly unfamiliar and exotic, lying beyond the direct or usual experience of many individuals (tigers are mentioned, for example). Other instances of natural kind categories might have *economic* value attached to them, so that individuals might well hesitate when they consider the market price a certain object or substance might be able to fetch. Gold would be one example of this type of category, while diamonds would be another. Pursuing this line of thought, Rothbart and Taylor (p. 11) mention one of the issues introduced in the early part of this chapter (see the section on 'Innocent parts of language?' p. 185):

'it is often quite difficult in practice to determine whether our perception of an object is disproportionately influenced by our knowledge of the object's category membership.'

A good example of our *collective* perceptions suffering 'disproportionate influence' because we 'know' the category to which an object belongs may be found when we consider the case of the diamond. Most people would agree that the diamond belongs to the category 'precious stone'. Diamonds fetch a high market price. The reason for the price they are able to command is their relative scarcity, compared to substances like coal, another form of carbon. However, the cause of this relative scarcity is that the number of diamonds entering the market is strictly controlled. In a free market, they would fail to create the value currently ascribed to them.

What is interesting about this case is that it shows how category membership may be manipulated, and that categorisation is above all a material practice. We 'know' that diamonds are precious, but it turns out that what we know is actually the *social* rather than simply the *natural* attributes of the substance. In fact, it is possible to take the argument further, by noting that all 'natural' categories alter their range of social significance depending upon the uses to which the things themselves are put, and the rules which are invented to govern their use.

Categorisation and the stereotype

As we saw earlier, Allport insisted that 'the human mind must think with the aid of categories' and that once they have been formed, categories become 'the basis for normal pre-judgement' (see *The Nature of Prejudice*, p. 20). **Stereotypes**, also associated with pre-judgement, are generally regarded as a form of negative categorisation, and are thus most often understood as a type of *prejudice*. Prejudice may be defined as an extreme attitude which can be found in the *cognitive*, *emotional* and *behavioural* attributes of human subjects.

Although it is sometimes argued that the stereotype is a 'neutral' form of descriptive category, and that prejudice may be either 'positive' or 'negative' (prejudice *for*, as well as prejudice *against*), most case-studies involving such theories concentrate upon their negative associations. As early as 1942, Zawadzski declared that (Oakes, Haslam and Turner 'Stereotyping and Social Reality' p. 21):

'traits are selected, not because they are actually most found among members of the group, but because they serve best the malicious intent of ridiculing or discrediting the group.'

In everyday speech, terms like 'prejudice' are nearly always employed to indicate the existence of negative values.

I would therefore describe the *established* definition of stereotyping as:

> the practice of making simplistic and usually negative social identifications of certain groups, in which the supposed attributes of the group are applied to all those identified (rightly or wrongly) as group members.

In other words, the process of stereotyping is said to work by taking the traits and characteristics thought to belong to specific groups, and reapplying them to individuals.

Stereotyping: flawed understanding?

The traditional approach to the question of stereotyping not only regards it as negative but also embraces the idea that it is *inaccurate*, or in some way flawed or inadequate. The notion which lies behind this view is that the people who are 'labelled' do not really resemble their stereotypes. While there is no doubt, as Oakes, Haslam and Turner point out (see *Stereotyping and Social Reality*, p. 2), that 'groups are part of social reality', many theorists continue to argue that our perception of *group characteristics* is by and large a distortion of reality.

Doubts about the accuracy of perception of *groups*, and the tendency to regard group behaviour as somehow a distortion of true conduct, have been responsible for the belief that *interpersonal* communication and studies of individual psychology reveal a more accurate picture of human character. Evidence of this tendency may be found in those communication textbooks which dwell on interaction in 'dyads' and which make pleas for people to be appreciated as individuals, and not as 'members of a crowd'.

The fact that many researchers have taken the view that stereotyping arises from a warped process, resulting in a mistaken conception of both individuals and groups, has meant that vast efforts have been expended in trying to find what Oakes and her colleagues (see *Stereotyping and Social Reality*) call 'the psychological basis of that deficiency'.

Sociotypes

Some who have worked on the problem of stereotyping have examined the possibility of constructing accurate or 'objective' theories of individual characteristics. The work of Bogardus (1950), for example, is notable in this respect. He proposed that an objective and 'sociologically valid' set of categories should be constructed, which he called **sociotypes**. The drawback here is that such inquiries do not investigate the ways in which people *experience* and *explain* their own subjectivity. There is often a considerable difference between the 'types' identified by sociologists and the ways in which individuals identify themselves.

Alternative views of stereotyping

A number of theorists have made a stand against the tide of 'deficiency' theorists. Fishman, writing in 1956, believed stereotypes to be valid to the extent that they reflected the actual *interactions* which take place between groups, both those groups which were categorised and those which were responsible for applying the stereotype concerned. Sherif (1967) also argued that stereotypes reflected the reality of *intergroup relations*. Frederick Glen, writing in *The Social Psychology of Organisations* (1975), noted that (p. 26):

> 'The stereotype has frequently been described and discussed as if it was a form of ideational malfunction with associated undesirable characteristics of bias and prejudice ... the process involved in stereotyping is rather more general than this view would suggest, based on the tendency to use a form of categorisation as part of our perceptual processes.'

It is worth looking at each of these arguments in turn. The idea that stereotypes reflect the *reality* of intergroup relations does not mean that the groups concerned are always *equally* responsible for the *use* of stereotypes. One aspect which is usually neglected or under-valued is the fact that there is often an inequality of *power* between the groups, with the stronger being able to deploy negative characterisations with more effect. It is not the stereotype itself which is most dangerous, but the imbalance of power which allows the dissemination of negative views.

The idea that stereotyping is a 'malfunction' does indeed require some revision. At the same time, we should exercise caution; it would be a mistake to decide, just because stereotypes emerge from the 'natural' process of categorisation, that they should be exempt from close scrutiny into their *effects*. If the difficulty with a 'negative' view of stereotyping is that it fails to examine the roots of the process, the problem created by 'neutral' approaches is that they are unlikely to provide a critical perspective on discriminatory forms of *behaviour*.

Stereotyping as differentiation

Asch, as an early critic of the 'negative' perspective, argued (1952) that the behaviour of individuals is often determined by their group membership and that, as a result, the stereotypical representation of individuals is an important aspect of the social reality which people inhabit. At this point, we should perhaps re-examine Zawadzski's belief that stereotyping is actually based upon a 'malicious intent'.

There is no doubt that there is intent behind the use of stereotyping, but it is not necessarily malicious. If we accept the idea that stereotyping is really about **differentiating** between one group and another, then it is not surprising that much of it is, after all, at least *contrastive* and also on occasion negative. The purpose would seem to be the need to create distinctions between the group to which one belongs and other groups. As we shall see, the intention behind this may be primarily to create *identities for the self*. Negative judgements about others would therefore be a kind of side effect rather than the primary objective of the process.

Stereotypes and group membership

One of the most enduring concepts used when group theory is applied to the process of stereotyping is found in the notion of **in-groups** and **out-groups**. An 'in-group' is the collective with which the subject identifies, while an 'out-group' is a body which possesses contrasting and supposedly less desirable characteristics.

The problem with this approach is that it creates the impression that such groups are permanent. The crux of the issue is that change in society, and the material or ideological interests of each person, will affect the attitudes which are held by individuals towards groups. Allport made this point in *The Nature of Prejudice* (p. 35):

'Not only do the strength and definition of ingroups change over the years in a given culture, but a single individual, too, may have occasion at one time to affirm one group loyalty and at a different time another ... Ingroup memberships are not permanently fixed. For certain purposes an individual may affirm one category of membership, for other purposes a slightly larger category.'

The importance of this statement for a *rhetorical* approach to understanding public declarations of allegiance cannot be overestimated. We may find that we characterise ourselves in certain ways at certain times in order to gain the best advantage from different situations.

Stereotypes from categorisation

Tajfel argued that the negative and positive aspects of stereotyping grow from the process of categorisation itself (see his 1969 article 'Cognitive aspects of prejudice'). The need to identify oneself in a reasonably positive way is therefore presumably a *social* need, involving the wish to find something in common with groups thought desirable. The group need not necessarily be physically present. Immediate physical proximity is not a prerequisite for categorising the self.

Positive identities

An example of conflicting categorisation may be supplied from an incident witnessed during a meeting of media educators, made up of teachers from further and higher education. During the meeting, one university lecturer declared that he and his colleagues saw themselves as 'practitioners'; in other words, that they worked on their own media projects, such as photography and film, and therefore possessed a real insight into the subject.

Challenged to describe the further education group, a spokesperson for the college lecturers replied by saying that, for their part, they were happy to be known first and foremost as teachers, a title they valued highly. The status accorded by the first speaker to practice, intended to elevate his own self-description above possible alternatives, led to a response which suited the purposes of resistance and differentiation. The status of *teacher* was therefore presented as a *positive* alternative, and perhaps as a veiled criticism of the values held by the university group. In a different context, this response might have been less pronounced or even altogether different.

Descriptions of the self

At the 1976 trial of Steve Biko, the black consciousness leader who eventually died in the custody of the South African police, the judge conducting the case questioned Biko's attachment to the term 'black' as a description of the indigenous peoples of South Africa (see Oakes *et al.*, *Stereotyping and Social Reality*, p. 157):

> '*Judge*: But now why do you refer to you people as blacks? Why not brown people? I mean you people are more brown than black.
> *Biko*: In the same way as I think white people are more pink and yellow and pale than white.
> *Judge*: Quite ... but why do you not use the word brown then?
> *Biko*: No, I think really, historically, we have been defined as black people, and when we reject the term non-white and take upon ourselves the right to call ourselves what we think we are, we have got available in front of us a whole number of alternatives ... and we choose this one precisely because we feel it is most accommodating.'

Oakes and her colleagues use this example to demonstrate that certain choices are made in order to create a positive self-identification. The nature of the real may indeed dictate that Biko and his supporters were 'brown', but the social reality Biko inhabited ensured that *black* was the most suitable and accurate description (Oakes, p. 157):

> 'Biko argued ... that the ... representation of his own group as "black" ... was the most valid, meaningful and appropriate representation, *even though* in an individualistic, decontextualised sense it might appear wrong.'

The recuperation of negative categories

On some occasions, the negative characterisation of groups by their rivals may have the opposite effect to the one intended. In the Second World War, during the North Africa campaign, the German Field-Marshal Rommel called the British Eighth Army 'desert rats'. The British soldiers assumed the title as a mark of positive self-evaluation. The same process occurred during the 1984–85 miners' strike, when a small group of Nottinghamshire strikers was dubbed the 'Dirty Thirty' by their working colleagues. It was not long before the striking miners appeared on the picket line wearing badges inscribed with the very epithet that had been intended as an insult.

These examples suggest that it is possible to 'recuperate' negative categories, turning them to a positive use. Such acts of defiance are also possible at an individual level. Nancy Mairs, writing in McDowell and Pringle, *Defining Women*, explores her motivation for using the term 'cripple' as an act of positive self-description (p. 56):

> 'People – crippled or not – wince at the word "cripple" as they do not at "handicapped" or "disabled". Perhaps I want them to wince. I want them to see me as a tough customer, one to whom the fates/gods/viruses have not been kind, but who can face the brutal truth of her existence squarely.'

Mairs combines this attitude with distaste for what she sees as the dishonesty of euphemisms like 'disabled', which she considers to be either inaccurate or deliberately imprecise, used to soften the bluntness of more uncomfortable terms. Therefore, not only does she embrace the negative category, but she rejects those labels which are clearly intended to be positive or progressive. She argues that euphemisms:

> 'seem to be moving away from my condition, to be widening the gap between word and reality. Most remote is the recently coined ... "differently abled" ... which strikes me as pure verbal garbage.'

Mairs recognises that her choice is personal, and (p. 57) points out that she 'would never refer to another person as a cripple'.

It is important not only that researchers recognise the *existence* of self-identification, but also that they investigate the *reasons* individuals give for the particular choices which are made. Without such insights, studies of audience will fail to represent an important aspect of social reality, remaining 'objective' but also far removed from discovering the meanings which real social groups attribute to their own actions.

Group solidarity

Asch wrote about the nature of **group solidarity**, arguing that (Oakes, p. 28):

> 'A picket line in front of a plant has a quality of unity that is a product of its organisation ... the group property cannot be rediscovered in the individuals taken singly.'

This means that the social organisation in which individuals find themselves will determine aspects of individual behaviour. However, it should still be possible to discover aspects of the group property within individuals, even if its true *expression* can only be observed once the group action has begun. In other words, the action of picketing may both create and reinforce forms of solidarity, but once people have gained positive experience of collective behaviour, the *principle* of solidarity and group cohesion may well reside within those individuals.

Stereotypes as a contextual factor

Stereotypes are able to achieve a wide circulation even where the group itself is not directly known to those who pass on the stereotype. This circulation takes place through the use of jokes, and appears in other elements of popular culture.

Where a group decides to stereotype or satirise its *own* habits and foibles, this is usually regarded as more acceptable than similar jokes created by an 'out-group'. BBC 2's *The Real McCoy* was devoted to black comedians, with an audience drawn largely from the black community. One comedian put his audience in a serious frame of mind by referring to the oppression of his people:

'We've suffered 500 years of slavery . . .'

only to redirect their attention by adding:

'. . . and three years of Clyde and Hattie on *EASTENDERS*'.

When the gaze of an 'in-group' is turned on other communities, the effect can be quite revealing. Here, another comedian refers to the British 'punter's' fondness for lurid tabloid stories about the royal family:

'Why do they want to see their royal family naked? I don't want to see Nelson Mandela in the nude.'

Holding back?

Despite our access to what could be called a 'fund' of stereotypical characterisations, it is often the case that we do not choose to apply the stereotype at our disposal. S.E. Taylor (see Oakes, p. 64), makes this point in work dating from 1981:

'there appear to be contextual dimensions that facilitate or inhibit the imputation of stereotypes to individuals.'

In other words, the *context* in which people are encountered may lead to a variety of responses. This means that, in some situations, characteristics we regard with little enthusiasm may not meet with our disapproval because other considerations outweigh the need to draw atention to them. For example, if we are familiar with the stereotypical view of leading executives as 'ruthless', we may find that our attachment to one particular individual, or our need in a *particular situation* to emphasise more positive features (which for the moment elude my powers of description), will mean that the stereotype is not applied.

Where stereotypes *are* employed, one reason for their use is exactly their familiarity. There would be no point in inventing a human type which was not considered to be appropriate, or which was not able to prompt feelings of recognition in an audience.

Sticks and stones?

Some writers believe that stereotyping amounts to no more than a refusal to treat individuals as unique, in which case they feel that the process should not be described as a distortion of reality. Indeed, most people will have witnessed, or will themselves have made, negative remarks which are not very deeply felt. A convenient resort to stereotypical categorisation may act to disguise disapproval of quite another kind; for example, the abuse directed against some aspect of a person's physical appearance may be triggered by *behaviour* that the abuser finds annoying. The attribution or otherwise of negative characteristics to individuals may also depend on whether or not the people concerned are known and liked. If stereotypes are used in such a case, they are often applied without great vehemence or real hostility.

One interesting point is that the 'psychological deficiency' theory of prejudice may be more dangerous than those approaches which argue that negative stereotyping has real links to ordinary social behaviour. If the basis of prejudice can simply be attributed to small numbers of people who are in no way typical of the general population, then it is possible that it will not be seen as a serious problem. It is also the case that a psychological perspective does not address the question of *power*, and thus may fail to make the link between prejudice and acts of discrimination. When racism, for example, is expressed as public discourse, it *enacts* certain inequalities of power which exist in society. Racist discourses have *material* effects. The point at which racism is publicly expressed is, in my view, the point at which it is *acted upon*.

Displacement of aggression

Some perspectives have stressed that stereotyping is the displacement of frustration and aggression from oneself to an 'out-group'. Such an approach is often applied to cases of racism or attachment to fascist ideology. In such instances, the rage felt against the subject's own social or economic deprivation is supposedly transferred to some innocent group, which is then characterised as having caused all the problems which are endured. However, this theory would not explain the rise of fascist groups whose membership includes a large proportion of prosperous individuals. Le Pen's neo-fascist Front National is an obvious example.

Some sections of the radical left, on the other hand, have for many years attempted to turn economic discontent against a different 'out-group': the state or the capitalist class. Some radical groups, finding such alternatives rather too abstract and unexciting, have targeted individual members of 'out-groups' such as the police force or 'the rich'. The newspaper *Class War* gained some notoriety for its invective against individual aristocrats, royalty, policemen and business people. The particular target of its disapproval was the yuppie, a species of middle-class professional which moved into residential areas once regarded as the domain of the proletarian. For the anarchists of *Class War*, the concept of class was not so much *relational* as *positional*. The existence of certain 'out-groups' served, in this case, to reinforce the chosen identity of the group's supporters.

Group communication

Criteria for identifying a group

We have already encountered some aspects of group theory through the study of categories and stereotypes. It is important, however, to understand how groups are usually conceptualised, since it seems to be impossible to describe individuals without referring to the groups to which they belong. In 1951, G.C. Homans (see *The Human Group*, p. 12) defined a group as:

> 'a number of persons who communicate with each other often enough over a span of time and who are few enough so that each person is able to communicate with all the others, not at second hand through other people but face to face'.

The central features here are **frequency** of contact over **time**, the idea that the group is manageable in **size**, and the importance given to direct **interpersonal** or 'face-to-face' communication.

There are, however, some questions which arise from this definition. For instance, the reference to individuals who interact 'often enough' and who remain 'few enough' for personal communication to occur, seems at first sight unhelpfully vague. Secondly, a comprehensive description of group communication usually includes some reference to the **goals** and **values** which are supposed to be shared by groups, and (as we have seen above) to the ways in which groups categorise themselves and others.

Strict definitions?

In defence of Homans, it must be said that an exact description of the point at which a collection of communicative individuals *ceases* to be a group is simply not necessary, even if it were possible to make. Homans's definition works by setting out criteria which allow us to recognise the principle that truly interactive communication can only take place when a group avoids becoming too large or unwieldy.

According to this view, a group will presumably expand to a point at which it either ceases to function as a group, or else splits into smaller, more manageable units. These may then, from Homans's perspective, be described as true groups. In fact, groups of all types are constantly in the process of formation, decay, and reformation.

Homans stressed the central role of communication in defining a group. This is important, because it is quite easy to neglect communication when investigating group *structure*. Group communication will inevitably involve interaction between individuals, but it also contains other features which a purely interpersonal approach will not reveal. McQuail (in *Communication*) notes that it is in fact difficult to separate communication as *a distinct element for analysis*, because all interaction within a group is in some sense 'communication'.

Group size: primary and secondary groups

In 1909, the American researcher C.H. Cooley produced a book called *Social Organisation*, in which he proposed the classification of two major *types* of group. One of these is called a **primary** group, which is small in size and whose members have frequent face-to-face contact. The other is known as a **secondary** group, more extended in size and less able to provide an opportunity for personal contact between all its members. (Homans would probably have denied that the 'secondary' collective qualified as a group at all.)

The membership of a secondary group is often widely dispersed in location, but, provided a system of communication exists, quite close relationships may be established and maintained. R.F. Bales, however, writing in 1951, argued that inequality of participation among group members increases as the group grows in size.

Frederick Glen, in *The Social Psychology of Organisations* (p. 18), provides examples of two groups at the opposite ends of the scale; the 'primitive tribal group' and the 'complex technological society'. The tribe is primary, while the technological society is clearly secondary. Glen's choice of example is perhaps unfortunate; the distinction between 'primitive' and 'advanced' depends as much on the degree of social and environmental awareness displayed within each group as it does on the technologies at their disposal.

Group structure: formal and informal groups

Groups may also be either **formal** or **informal**. The first type includes groups which possess a formal set of aims and objectives, laid out in advance of any tasks it undertakes. These aims and objectives may not be fully apparent to outsiders. In fact, depending on their position within the group, some members may not be fully aware of all aspects of the group's aims.

Informal groups are those which arise more naturally and spontaneously, and include friendship and peer groups.

Combinations

From Figure 3.3, it should become clear that it is possible for groups to be, for example, both primary in size and formal in structure, or secondary in size and informal in structure (the shaded areas indicate the possible relationships). An example of primary/formal would be a small consumer group which sets out in advance a set of rules for the conduct of its campaign. A secondary/informal group might be a network of anti-road protesters, extensive in number yet reliant upon general political principles rather than a detailed structure or programme created in advance.

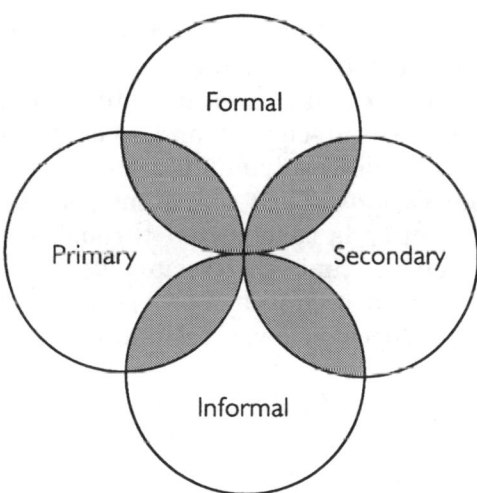

Figure 3.3   Diagram demonstrating possible composition of groups

It seems quite usual for people to assume that large groups are always 'formal' in all respects. In fact, many have a formal structure which functions poorly, forcing alternative structures to provide direction and support.

A question of belonging: groups chosen and not chosen

Part of the problem in defining groups lies in the question of choice. Some groups are deliberately chosen, while in other cases individuals find that membership is less than voluntary. The child who insists that it has no wish to belong to the particular family it finds itself born into will remain frustrated in its wish to escape the category. Relatives, and the wider society the child inhabits, will usually continue to define the child as a member of the family in question.

Women as a social group?

Jennifer Coates (see *Women, Men and Language*) advocates the idea that women constitute a distinct social group. She mentions some of those groups traditionally regarded as worthy of sociological analysis, including these examples (p. 7): 'working class people in Belfast, Afro-Caribbeans in London ... adolescents in Reading'. Such groups, despite their differences, have a number of characteristics in common. Coates lists these as:

'[living] near each other in a recognised neighbourhood ... or [having] recognised meeting places ... a recognisable and distinctive sub-culture ... [and] ... group identity'.

Women, by comparison, 'constitute a very unusual social group'. They do not of course live together as a single identifiable group, but according to Coates share a 'recognisable and distinctive sub-culture' and a positive social identity.

In 1978, J.A. Williams and H. Giles contributed a chapter to Henri Tajfel's *Differentiation between Social Groups*. They see women as a *disadvantaged* gender group, whose social identity is constructed through *comparison* with men. Williams and Giles believe that the social identity of women is unavoidably negative, because men occupy a more powerful social position, and comparison with them produces a lower estimation of self-worth. The consequence of their disadvantaged position is that women must take action in order to develop a more positive sense of their own distinctiveness.

According to these authors, the kinds of action taken by women may be either individual or collective in nature. Individual action is where a woman attempts to improve her status by devoting herself to the interests of a partner or spouse, attempting to enhance her self-image in that way. Collective action occurs where groups of women try to establish a positive identity for women as a whole.

Although Williams and Giles's work was influential, other writers have criticised the limitations of the perspective described above. Suzanne Skevington and Deborah Baker (see *The Social Identity of Women*) outline some of the problems. They believe that (p. 5):

'Williams and Giles are describing the ideological intergroup relations between men and women from a theoretical rather than an empirical stance. In doing so, they make the mistake of assuming that womanhood is perceived by all women in the same way, using the consensual (and unfavourable) dimensions when comparing themselves with men.'

In 1979, G.M. Breakwell (in *Women: Group and Identity?*) suggested that there is actually no agreed view of women's identity, and that women suffer the experience of being marginalised because no consensus on identity has been achieved. Breakwell distinguishes between *external* and *internal* criteria for group membership. External criteria are supposed to emerge from social norms and are found in stereotypes, while internal criteria grow out of personal knowledge and beliefs about group experience. The clash between self-concept and the expectations held by society results in marginalisation. For example, a woman may see herself as a mother, but her personal view of that role may be contradicted by the expectations held by society. The problem here is not simply that a person's 'internal' understanding of role is always shaped by 'external' factors; individual perspectives are made up from the various ideas about role found in society.

Returning to Williams and Giles's theory, Skevington and Baker point to another flaw in their scenario. The idea that only women who reject traditional sex roles are able to carry out collective action ignores research evidence, which shows that 'traditional women' are also able to express solidarity with their peers. Such women may accept the existence of established views on gender identity, and will perhaps believe in co-operation with men, but may also feel that their own roles are preferable to those which are available to men.

Class, sexuality and ethnicity in women's identity

Feminist writers in particular have helped to focus attention on the *subjective* elements of social research. They have asked how gendered individuals actually experience inequality in society. However, just as it is misleading to treat the individual (the social subject) as 'neutral' in terms of gender, so it is also a mistake to imagine that all the members of a particular sex will perceive their position and experiences in the same way. A number of other subjective factors will come into play, including ethnicity, class, personality, age, political belief and spatial location, to name a few. If we examine these factors, it will become obvious that women do not constitute a completely unified social group.

In *Women and Social Class*, for example, Pamela Abbott and Roger Sapsford ask (p. 89):

'do women married to working-class men have the same social imagery as working-class men?'.

They identify the two 'basic' issues in class-based research as investigations of **class** *consciousness* (the identification of class and the sense of 'belonging') and questions about the extent to which people 'see society as structured into bounded classes (i.e. middle-class, working-class) or as a continuous status hierarchy' (see p. 90). Unfortunately, as Abbott and Sapsford point out, much research into *objective* social class has taken the occupation of a male 'head of household' as the major determinant of the class position of women. Such studies include married and single women *where they have some connection to men*. So, for example, women who are single are placed in the class position held by their fathers.

The experience of many women is, however, completely excluded in these inquiries. For instance, those who are unmarried and have no close connection to their fathers, or those whose **sexuality** precludes relations with men, will become 'invisible' using these approaches. Christine Riddiough's essay in Sargent, *The Unhappy Marriage of Marxism and Feminism* (see p. 74), points out that some feminist theory actually ignores lesbian women, insisting that:

> 'The goal of feminism is the liberation of women, and included in this is sexual self-determination for all people, and the liberation of gay men and lesbians.'

If we take the study of groups seriously, we must examine *self-identification*, because many individuals are not prepared to accept the labels which are foisted on them by other – usually more powerful – forces. The study of how self-identification is made must extend to all the aspects of human identity, including, as Riddiough argues, the question of sexuality.

It is interesting to note that, despite the radicalism of many critiques of capitalism and patriarchy, 'race' – or more usefully, **ethnicity** – has often been left out of the equation. We saw above that it is not enough to believe that women will embrace a straightforward class identity; equally, it is no use assuming that gender will determine *every* aspect of a woman's life experiences. Gloria Joseph (see Sargent, *The Unhappy Marriage*) argues (p. 93) that:

> 'Both marxist and feminist analysis do gross injustice to Black women whose historical experiences of slavery have left them with a most peculiar legacy of scars.'

Joseph is anxious to record the fact that a black feminist approach is necessary, because the relationship between black men and black women generally occurs in a quite different set of cultural and economic conditions from that experienced by white men and white women. In the United States, the legacy of slavery continues to define the self-identification of the black or African-American population. Indeed, the very transition from the term 'black' to the historically and geographically specific 'African-American' shows the importance placed on the original social location as a vital element of identity.

Groups: ascribed and free

Clearly, one problem faced in defining groups turns on the question of who does the 'labelling' or classification, and whether or not those described as members agree with the category ascribed to them. For instance, the term 'juvenile delinquent' was once applied to a variety of individuals, creating the sense that there was an identifiable group of people involved in the reproduction of the *same* type of anti-social behaviour. In fact, the range of behaviours included under the heading was extremely wide.

On many occasions, the use of a general category may obscure the very different types of conduct which occur within the 'group' itself. Some groups, especially those described or 'identified' by outsiders who do not belong to them, may reject the definition provided, as we have already seen. A group considering itself to be dedicated to 'national liberation' would baulk at accepting the label 'terrorist group', for example.

Groups can have their *status* changed by the way in which their activities are interpreted. A clear contemporary example would be people who co-operate to organise free parties and festivals. The individuals concerned may see their membership of such groups as perfectly innocent, but find that their activities have been 'labelled' as criminal under new laws. Their actions would therefore have been reinterpreted in the light of criteria over which they have no control (see the leaflet from the campaign against the Criminal Justice Bill in Figure 3.4). There is a vast difference between belonging to a group through active choice, and being 'allocated' a place by other individuals or institutions.

Formation of groups

The reasons for the **formation** of a group are many and varied, but may be seen to emerge from two basic purposes; the need to achieve a *specific material goal*, and the desire to acquire or reinforce a *shared social identity*. As an example of the first case, a number of individuals may form a local branch of a trade union in order to improve their conditions of work. As an instance of the second, individuals may come together in a social setting because of a shared interest in music, finding that they gain a positive reinforcement of personal identity from the experience. In many cases, the two aspects of collective purpose will be combined in one group.

Development of groups

In 1965, B.W. Tuckman proposed that the 'life' of a group goes through four stages before it reaches maturity. The first stage is **forming**, during which the prospective members display tentative forms of behaviour, experience feelings of anxiety, seek to understand the nature of the situation and the rules of interaction, and rely upon a leader. The second is known as **rebellion**, where there is supposed to be a degree of conflict, resistance to rules and a struggle

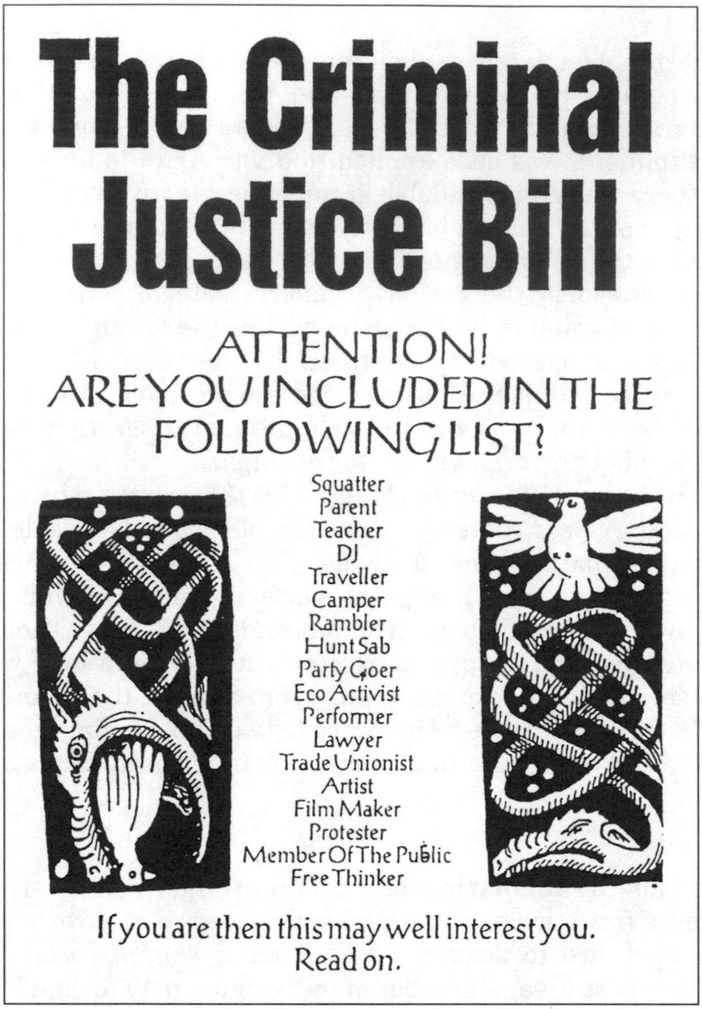

Figure 3.4   Leaflet protesting against the Criminal Justice Bill (now law)

for position. The third stage is usually described by the ugly title **norming**, in which conflicts are resolved, and roles and tasks are agreed upon. The fourth and final part of the developmental sequence is called **co-operation** or **performing**: this sees the beginnings of a cohesive group identity and the direction of energies towards the completion of group tasks.

However, more recent research has discovered that groups do not necessarily obey this pattern of development, showing instead that they *alternate* between different phases. This suggests that they may revert to the earlier and more disorganised types of behaviour which Tuckman described. At certain times, groups will concentrate on *functional* tasks, while at others *social* reinforcement will be at the top of the agenda.

The group and the individual: social identification

Hogg and Abrams, in *Social Identifications*, argue that groups have 'a profound impact on individuals' identity'. The groups they identify include national, religious, political, ethnic, sex, tribal and youth. They believe that (p. 20):

'the groups to which people belong will be massively significant in determining their life experiences'.

These authors complain about the lack of direction in many group investigations carried out by professional researchers. In their opinion, this has been caused by attempting to understand the social group in terms of the characteristics of the individual. The result has been that the concept 'group' no longer carries any distinct meaning. Hogg and Abrams set out to explore (p. 13) 'the dynamic relationship between individual and society'.

Of course, it is not unusual to believe that social categories lead to differences in status, power and therefore attitudes and behaviour. These authors, however, are also interested in how individuals express their own sense of belonging or *identification*. Hogg and Abrams search for evidence of how an individual's identity is acquired through membership of groups, while writers like Oakes, Haslam and Turner investigate the way that group character is created through the interaction of individual and group identity. Oakes and her co-writers (see *Stereotyping and Social Reality*, p. 93) cite Turner, who argues that:

'The identity perspective ... reinstates the group as a psychological reality and not merely a convenient label for describing the outcome of interpersonal processes and relationships.'

Social identity: a matter of choice

The approach Hogg and Abrams suggest is called **social identity**. Social identity is a reference not simply to the fact that the individual knows that he or she belongs to a group, but also is the fact that the person concerned attaches some value to his or her membership of the group, feeling some emotional attachment to it. They define a group (p. 7) as two or more individuals who 'perceive themselves to be members of the same social category'. This means that **self-description** would be the most important aspect of the attachment an individual feels for a group, reinforcing the ideas about self-categorisation suggested by Oakes and her co-authors. The idea here is that the individual feels a positive sense of self-worth from the attachment to the group, which is, as Hogg and Abrams point out (p. 7):

'very different from merely being designated as falling into one social category or another'.

In this case, group membership is chosen, and is not imposed or merely accidental.

The 'psychological' group

In effect, a **'psychological' group** is one which fulfils the true criteria for cohesive group identity. The idea is similar to that of 'social identity' described above: both approaches put emphasis on the positive feeling of identity generated by identification. Neither describes the 'accidental' collection of individuals, the usual example of which is the bus queue.

The psychological group is one in which individual members have a high degree of awareness of other people in the group. Interactions develop to the point at which it is possible to identify set exchanges or patterns of communicative behaviour. A 'group boundary' is erected, while the group itself possesses clear goals and shared norms. It also encourages affective relationships (emotional attachments) between members.

Groups formed to combat a threat

There are many examples of groups which are formed in order to meet a threat to themselves or to the wider community. Groups which protest against road-building may be motivated by local conditions, but may also justify their actions by drawing attention to the condition of the nation or of the planet in general. The formation of anti-fascist groups in Germany, after the Rostov bombings carried out by neo-Nazis in 1991, drew support from individuals determined to oppose the growth of violence and racism. The two photographs in Figure 3.5 were taken during an anti-Nazi demonstration in Germany in 1992.

Groups: goals and values

At the beginning of this chapter, I touched upon the question of shared goals and values. We have seen that some writers believe that true groups exist only where individuals consciously share a goal and a system of values. The extent to which goals and values are actually held in common depends on whether individuals:

- join a group willingly;
- have full knowledge of the aims and objectives of the group;
- sincerely accept the goals, values, and models of behaviour which the group appears to value.

McQuail notes that (*Communication*, p. 102) communicative activity in *formal* organisations is:

Figure 3.5A   Hanover, 1992. German anti-fascists assemble for a demonstration

Figure 3.5B   Hanover, 1992: gathering of anti-fascists

'structured and planned for independently of the spontaneous wishes and interests of participants'.

There is an important difference between joining a group because of economic necessity, and belonging to an organisation whose aims and objectives an individual wishes positively to support. Where individuals feel some attachment to a group, they may be prepared to endure all sorts of inconvenience and even discomfort in pursuit of its aims. However, where no such attachment exists, the common goals of the group may produce no more than weary compliance and lip service. This is particularly the case in those workplaces where management fails to address the real concerns of their staff.

Gang membership: values

A great deal has been written about **gangs** and the reasons which prompt young people to join them. A number of sociological studies have been carried out into organised groups, from youth 'cults' like Mods and Rockers in the 1960s to the football hooligans who flourished during the 1970s and 1980s. Much of this research has assumed such groups are 'deviant', not simply because their *behaviour* is out of the ordinary but in the sense that the gang or criminal association is thought to hold values which run counter to those held by conventional society. According to the sociologists Shaw and McKay (see Haralambos, p. 596), crime in low-income areas is:

'one of the means employed by people to acquire . . . the economic and social values generally idealised in our culture, which persons in other circumstances acquire by conventional means'.

On occasion, gang members are themselves able to express their views. Such events are particularly useful because they allow an insight into the expression of *self-identification*, so often missing from 'objective' social inquiry.

In August 1994, Channel 4 broadcast a programme in which a prominent member of the Los Angeles 'Crips' was interviewed. The first encounter with Kershaun 'L'il Monster' Scott took place in 1989, while the subsequent material was assembled in 1992. The early, rather brief interview showed 'L'il Monster' repeating one of the sayings of Malcolm X, then going on to declare:

'I hate everything that America stands for, I hate the Establishment, and I hate the damn Flag.'

On the face of it, this would appear to support those sociologists who have characterised gang membership as a deviation from accepted social norms. However, many of the other statements made by this particular gangster reveal a more complex relationship to conventional society. When the subject under discussion turns to the family, gangsters are shown to share the same values as mainstream groups. It is just that their concept of family is extended to include their 'homeboys' and 'homegirls', and features a defensive posture which promises violent mobilisation against perceived threats.

Two discourses

Two **discourses** seem to run through many of the topics raised by Kershaun Scott. One is clearly political, in line with the Crips' origins as a political group. The group is identified in the first instance by differentiating itself from the wider society, using the discourse of militant black self-determination. The other discourse is concerned with violent vendettas and gangsterism.

Using one speech genre, 'L'il Monster' Scott is able to refer to his role as a 'community activist', and makes a point of justifying the possession of weapons in *political* terms:

> 'Once you disarm the community you're throwing rocks at tanks like the brothers and sisters in Palestine and South Africa. We will never disarm . . . we have the right to bear arms.'

The radicalism of such a stance often leads towards a form of separatism. In this instance, Scott declares that 'I want total independence from the American government . . . it's a struggle that I'm going to hand down to my son.'

In contrast to this perspective, the enemies he actually confronts are rival gang members, individuals with whom he has more in common than with the mainstream society he claims to oppose. When Scott speaks of gangster activity, he does not use the 'gangland' speech genre we might expect. Instead, he uses military phrases to describe the drive-by shootings which he leads:

> 'Once the sun went down, the mission was in action. We started on our journey into enemy territory . . . we combed each block looking for any sign of movement.'

Reasons for gang membership

The pressures on individuals to conform are particularly strong where social conditions offer few avenues for alternative lifestyles, and where there are real dangers in remaining isolated. Scott's older brother Cody revealed what happened when his family arrived in the South Central area of Los Angeles:

> 'We ceased being children as soon as we hit South Central . . . we just had to go with the flow . . . or just be eliminated.'

He gave this description of the gang society he encountered:

> 'I knew that they had the power, that alluring power . . . in that particular area, everybody was a gang member . . . the gang gravitated as centre-earth,

nothing was important outside of that, so to be a part of that was to be *in*, and then you had the power, and you weren't a victim no more.'

The pride and confidence engendered by membership of a powerful 'in-group' causes its members to express themselves through a number of forms: the use of a specialist language, the employment of non-verbal signs made with the hands, the wearing of certain clothes which act as a badge of identity, and the acquisition of tattoos. Cody Scott explained that 'we have pride. I got 8-tray [the gang title] on my neck.' By contrast, Cody said, 'you never seen George Bush with "capitalism" on *his* neck'. Cody's view was that the outside world must understand what motivates the gangster, particularly that the gang provides the social cohesion sought in other ways by 'straight' society:

'you have to understand the mind set of the gang member. Nothing outside of the gang is important. The gang is your religion, the gang is your corporation, the gang is your college, the gang is everything that any civilian holds dear, the gang is all that, it's your family, it's everything, so nothing outside that exists.'

Group cohesion and 'negative stereotyping'

It has become a commonplace that human beings have 'a tendency to infer deep essential qualities on the basis of surface appearance' (Rothbart and Taylor, p.1). If this tendency exists, then we may have discovered one reason for the 'negative stereotyping' which is present in so many cultures. However, some forms of social categorisation may be intended primarily as positive reinforcement for group members, as we saw above. The negative face turned to others may in some cases be a side effect of positive group cohesion.

Social identification: acceptable behaviour

Hogg and Abrams ask how human beings can behave so badly towards groups of people regarded as different from themselves, yet be at the same time (p. 1), 'the most sociable of all creatures'. The answer, according to these authors, may be found in the social identity of groups. Since people are the 'products of history, culture and society', whose 'views, opinions, values, activities, and means of communication are learnt or acquired from others', then Hogg and Abrams believe it must follow that (p. 1):

'behaviour is governed by norms, or agreements between people, concerning appropriate or acceptable ways to behave and opinions to hold under particular circumstances'.

The one mistake here is to assume that norms are arrived at through agreement instead of through *precedent*. Yet it is also true that norms and models of appropriate behaviour are not simply imposed upon individuals; they are *re-established* through interaction.

Group conflict

There has, in recent years, been much debate over the causes of inter-group conflict. This discussion is not confined to groups of academics. It is often readily supposed that group conflict starts at an individual level; siblings who bicker and argue are told 'that's the way that wars start'.

A number of writers have emphasised the notion that conflict can arise for quite trivial reasons. Rothbart and Taylor produce their own argument for this approach, providing a list of what they call (p. 23) 'naturally occurring, protracted conflicts'. These conflicts include 'the Middle East, South Africa, [and] Northern Ireland'. (Each of these conflicts has now reached an 'official' conclusion.)

Rothbart and Taylor go on to attack what they call:

'a tendency to view the particular dimensions underlying a conflict as *inherently* conflict-inducing. For example, in those conflicts where differences in religion are paramount, there is an assumption that those differences inexorably lead to conflict. This bias ignores the fact that the same differences in other contexts may be considered insubstantial, and that meaningless differences in one's own society may be associated with profound conflict elsewhere.'

It is true that differences which may cause intense conflict in one context will not produce a similar effect in another situation. Many commentators, however, would argue that the essential requirement for civil strife boils down eventually to material rivalry between groups.

Trivial reasons for conflict?

Although Rothbart and Taylor may be right when they say that some differences are meaningful only within a particular context, they do not ask what factor is *shared* by the real conflicts to which they draw attention. Instead, they go on to argue that trivial differences are capable of sparking serious dissension. In support of this view, they refer to the 'powerful insight' provided by Jonathan Swift in *Gulliver's Travels*, where the conflict between Protestants and Catholics is satirized in the tale of two warring sects, the Little-Endians and the Big-Endians. The Little-Endians ate boiled eggs by breaking into the small end, while the Big-Endians breached the large end.

Does this really provide the powerful insight sought by theorists who believe that conflict can be essentially 'meaningless'? It does not reveal the *material* struggle between Catholicism and the Protestant Church. Just because the outward forms of religion seem to suggest a trivial difference, the fact remains that the struggle turned on international rivalries between countries like England and Spain, and was based on a fight over land, money and hegemonic power.

Reasons for competition

In 1961, Sherif argued that there was no need for a long *history* of value conflict or belief conflict to create hostility between two groups. He did, unlike Rothbart and Taylor, state that there was a need for competition over limited resources, though the groups themselves could be 'self-defined'.

According to Rothbart and Taylor, one does need 'real' differences, such as cultural, linguistic or physical ones, to establish conflict. All that is required is collectives – groups which may be formed for arbitrary reasons. They cite various experiments where individuals are placed in groups which have no real clash of interests. They go on to claim that hostility between such groups must come from the mere fact that they have been labelled or categorised differently (p. 24):

> 'competition is not a necessary condition for bias against the outgroup, but mere categorisation is'.

In their opinion, 'what makes competition so powerful ... is that it continually activates the use of *us versus them* distinction, given the zero sum nature of the interaction'.

But this begs the whole question. The purpose of categorisation in cases like this is to identify the self and the 'in-group' against some other, and then to *prepare* for some kind of action or interaction. Categorisation is never merely the process of labelling.

More criticisms of Rothbart and Taylor

Some of the research Rothbart and Taylor use to support their case needs closer scrutiny. The Robber's Cave experiment of 1961, where white middle-class boys were randomly divided into two groups (the groups named themselves), and then told that inter-group relations were either competitive or co-operative, does not prove that conflict or its opposite flow from trivial causes. Nor does it show, as Rothbart and Taylor argue, that *competition* is unnecessary for the creation of conflict and rivalry. These authors believe that *categorisation* alone is sufficient to create rivalry. If it is, then it is the *starting point* for the polarisation or co-operation of groups.

Categorisation is a material practice, carried out in a world where competition and co-operation make up an important part of everyday life. In fact, the very terms *conflict* and *co-operation* must prompt us to ask: conflict and co-operation over what exactly? Material resources and material *activity* turn out to feature in all the evidence Rothbart and Taylor produce. In addition, it is worth noting that the *geography* or location of the two groups is a neglected factor in the whole analysis. Ultimately, any experiment of this kind must recognise that the behaviour patterns discovered are consistent with ordinary conduct in advanced capitalist societies like the United States.

Jumping to conclusions

The fact that some researchers thought that they were witnessing motiveless conflict means that they failed to identify the social process of competition and its corollary, co-operation. Such experiments allow *rehearsals* for real-life situations. The idea of the 'minimal group paradigm', in which trivial labels or preferences create serious divisions, needs to be treated with caution. Preference for one type of ice cream, for one colour over another, or for one painter over another make a perfectly sound basis for beginning *group actions*, and are therefore very far from being meaningless. Rothbart and Taylor's belief in the principle that (p. 24) 'virtually any basis for separating individuals into mutually exclusive groups can produce the same effects' does at least lead them to acknowledge that 'superficial' differences may be 'diagnostic' of more important underlying conflicts, though the material nature of this conflict is not examined.

Analysis of group interaction

Primitive models

One method for recording group interaction is to design a simple 'tally' system (Figure 3.6A), in which each participant is represented by a labelled circle, and a mark is placed inside the appropriate circle each time a person speaks. This system is quite primitive, creating a record of frequency of intervention, but providing no insight whatsoever into duration, impact, style or form of the contributions made. For instance, a high degree of intervention will not necessarily indicate that the speaker will be influential.

Another method of analysis is to reproduce the same system of representation, with the use of lines which indicate to whom remarks are addressed. This is known as a **sociogram**, and an example is reproduced in Figure 3.6B.

Such a model also has considerable drawbacks. It does not indicate what each interaction *means*, so that high levels of contact between individuals could indicate either accord or discord.

Interaction process analysis

This system was proposed by R.F. Bales in 1950, and was built on the notion that all communicative behaviours within groups may be divided into four main areas:

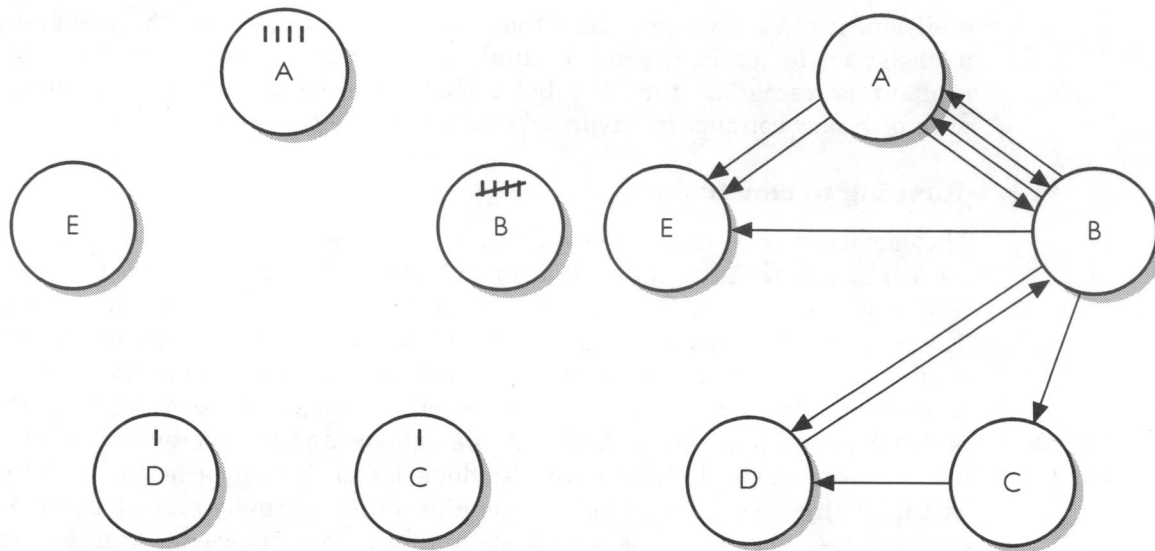

Figure 3.6A Diagram showing the tally method of counting the number of contributions

Figure 3.6B Sociogram of participation in a group context

- **positive** socio-emotional behaviour;
- **negative** socio-emotional behaviour;
- **information giving**;
- **information receiving**.

Positive behaviour is that which shows solidarity, allows group tensions to be relieved and produces agreement. *Negative* behaviour is supposed to include disagreement, the expression of stress and shows of antagonism. It is unfortunate that this division has been made, since the *outcome* of an individual's 'positive' behaviour may be entirely negative for the group, or may have unfortunate effects in the wider society. Equally, 'negative' behaviour very often has positive effects. Study of these behavioural forms is often made without proper attention to context. The danger is that Bale's system might lend itself only to the analysis of individual communicative styles.

The notion of *information giving* involves making suggestions, giving opinions and offering information. *Information receiving* includes requests for information, opinion and direction. Bales supports the idea of integration within the group, implying that progress is only made when differences are eliminated; as such, his system is more concerned with the mechanics of group function than with the moral and political role of the group in society. Bales has a clear though limited agenda, which obviously acts to restrict the kinds of meaning it is possible to discover.

Discourse analysis and visual observation

The most useful contemporary methods of analysing group communication are probably found in **discourse analysis** and the possibilities presented by the use of audio or video tape.

Some ethical and practical questions arise as soon as the use of tape is considered. In the first place, permission must be sought to use the material, but some researchers insist that this must be requested after the speech event itself takes place, since they believe that consciousness of the presence of an electronic device would distort the exchange; this implies that the recording must, in the first place, be obtained secretly. Other approaches attempt to familiarise groups, over a period of many months, with the presence of a camera or tape-recorder, in the hope that the subjects will forget the presence of the equipment. Some involved in this field consider that the presence of recording machines has little effect, since tendencies to dramatic exaggeration exist in all group situations anyway. (Video tape is sometimes useful for making records of non-verbal communication in its proper context.)

Discourse analysis provides a series of criteria for describing the acts of everyday conversation. The first point must be to establish the general range of possible acts within an exchange. These, following the work of Labov, were described in Chapter 2 as question and answer, challenge and response, and invitation and acceptance. In addition, the analyst would have to recognise **turn-taking**, **alignment**, the difference between **interruption** and **collaborative completion**, and examples of **repair** and **repetition**. Gill Francis and Susan Hunston (see Coulthard, *Advances in Spoken Discourse Analysis*, p. 123) propose no fewer than thirty-two identifiable acts of everyday conversation. For our purposes, we require the exercise of intelligent interpretation of what is often decontextualised material.

Group speech events

Formal exchange

In some contexts, a group speech event will actually consist of a reasonably **formal** set of exchanges between *two* people at a time. In other words, what is essentially an interpersonal exchange is made within a group context. The following is taken from the end of a tape made (in 1993) by a teacher during a lecture. The tape was intended as a record of the session's content, but the lecturer forgot to turn it off as he began interrogating students about work which was due in that day. A is a male lecturer, while B and C are both female students.

'**A**: How many leaflets have we got now? *Finished* leaflets.
B: I haven't done (.) um (.)

> **A**: You haven't done anything about it.
> **B**: I *did* do it, it's not my fault.
> **A**: You *didn't* (.) well (.) it's not your fault? Why not?
> **B**: It's not my fault, 'cos I couldn't write, 'cos I nearly broke my arm.
> **A**: Nearly broke your arm.
> **B**: I fell down the stairs and I cut my arm (.) they've only just straightened things out and so I couldn't write (.) and I can't write right-handed.
> **A**: OK (1) pass those up.
> **C**: I haven't finished mine but I've started it, 'cos I didn't know what you had to write in it.
> **A**: I'm getting depressed (.) have you done *any* work on leaflets?'

Here, the lecturer has set the criteria for the exchange; it will not be a free-for-all, as each student is supposed to supply the written assignment, or else a proper reason for its absence. In essence, we find two separate interpersonal exchanges occurring. The students, who have not produced the work required, are in fact content to be questioned in turn, since they are slightly embarrassed and are probably preparing excuses. There is no interruption or background noise. Institutional and situational context allows the adoption of tried and tested roles.

The low expectation of the lecturer is shown when he qualifies his request by asking for *'finished* leaflets'. He also completes the first student's sentence. In this case, it is not a 'co-operative' completion, but a hostile one:

> '**B**: I haven't done (.) um (.)
> **A**: You haven't done anything about it'.

The next exchange reveals a clash between the two, but also a hesitation where the lecturer seems to take account of the plea made by the student:

> '**B**: I *did* do it, it's not my fault.
> **A**: You *didn't* (.) well (.) it's not your fault? Why not?'

The story which follows this exchange seems a little far-fetched but is accepted, probably because the effort required to pursue the matter is too great; when the second failure is made evident, the lecturer addresses the whole group through the second-person singular. The actual intention appears to have been to ask 'Have *any* of you done any work?'.

Informal exchange

On some occasions, the concerns of one speaker are not taken up by other participants. For example, it may be quite difficult in some **informal** group situations to guarantee that listeners will respond to one's agenda. All participants in the following transcript are female:

'**A**: My voice is a bit croggy.

B: Listen to Bash then (.) he's like (1) a little bloke that's got his voice broken . . .

A: In the morning it's bad and when I go to bed it's bad (.) all last week it's been like that.

C: Yeah.

A: My voice is always bad in the week at night (2) but when I get up in the morning I'm alright.

C: We're goin' down town.

B: Just rose – roam the streets at night.

C: Yeah, get some smokes, yeah get some smokes.'

In this extract, A makes an attempt to achieve a response to her problems, but the conversation moves on to other topics. B does reply to A's opening remark, but C's response to a later comment ('Yeah') is much more perfunctory, and may be a way of avoiding having to take a full turn in the exchange. Notice that A is offering a general picture of her unhealthy state, which does not depend on the accuracy of precise detail; she includes one contradictory statement when she asserts that her throat is both bad and 'alright' in the mornings. B and C are preoccupied with their trip into town, and the projected purchase of cigarettes, which might imply some insensitivity to the content of A's discourse. Notice the correction B is forced to make, when she begins to say 'just rose' for 'just roam'.

Shared narratives

Native or mother-tongue speakers belonging to the same family often engage in exchanges which review well-worn themes, and reveal awareness of one another's typical behaviour and character. In this exchange, A is the daughter, B the father and C the mother:

'**A**: How far have you gone with the silaging?

B: Three days (.) so far we've had so many breakdowns (1) the wheel fell off with grandad yesterday.

A: That's typical of grandad (.) everything he touches breaks or goes wrong (.) he's bloody useless (2). give him a fork and he's happy.

C: Don't be tight (.) he can't help it (1). I'd like to see you mow a field.

B: Rach wouldn't even know which field is ours (.) or what to use.

A: Yeah right.

B: Pick up Chris from youth club (.) on your return from work.

A: Yeah OK (.) I think I can just about manage that without too much hassle.'

The aspersions cast on the manual prowess of the grandfather are turned back upon the daughter, who is characterised not as impractical as such, but rather as completely ignorant of the first principles of farming. Her response to the accusation that she does not even recognise the family's field, 'Yeah right', is in fact mildly sarcastic and does not indicate actual agreement. The end of the exchange shows that she recognises the status she has been accorded; 'I think I can just about manage that without too much hassle.'

Communication and power

Communication occurs in a variety of different circumstances, and for a number of different reasons. McQuail believes that communication takes place most usually in various **institutional settings**, between those who have a close physical and social **proximity**, and between those who have certain **interests** in common. In all these cases, communication is (McQuail, p.6) 'an integral part of the exercise of power'.

Although *communication* as described by McQuail may well occur most typically in situations where contact is close and interests are similar, it would be a mistake to imagine that the same principles could be transferred to the study of power. The exercise of power, in contrast to McQuail's description of the communication process, often takes place where there is considerable social or physical distance between source and 'receiver'. In addition, power works in situations where there is *no* commonality of interest. The existence of these differences leads to the question: what is understood by the term 'power' in communication and other studies?

Descriptions of power: capacity and use

The philosopher and mathematician Bertrand Russell described **power** as 'the production of intended effects' (see Stephen Lukes, *Power*, p. 1). In fact, the term signifies more than this. Power means both the **capacity** to do something and the active **use** of that capacity. For example, it can refer to the economic wealth of a nation, as well as to the actual *use* of that wealth to dominate a weaker neighbour. The two meanings of power are also sometimes expressed as the difference between 'power to' and 'power over'. It is possible to make distinctions between personal or *subjective* power, *group* power, *institutional* power and *state* power. Where then is power to be found? It is a phenomenon which is seen in the *relationships* and the *actions* existing or occurring within human societies.

Power: intended effects?

Some authors question Russell's description of power as having *intended* effects, since in some cases power may be exercised without deliberate intent.

A form of personal power, for example, could be said to exist when someone is considered particularly attractive; the effect on other individuals may be unintentional. In addition, it is worth asking if the ability to produce 'trivial' effects is a reliable indication of the possession of power (see Stephen Lukes's Introduction to *Power*). Communication research is usually devoted to calculating the effect of deliberate messages formed by individuals or collectives with the intention of attaining a specific result.

In 1947, the German economist and sociologist Max Weber produced a definition *combining* the notion of power as capacity and power as use. Ng and Bradac (*Power in Language*, p. 4) provide this interpretation of Weber's position:

> 'Power (*macht*) is the probability that one actor within a social relationship will be in a position to carry out his or her own will despite resistance, regardless of the basis on which this probability exists.'

The 'social relationship' mentioned here refers to the personal and institutional circumstances in which individuals find themselves. Notice that this description refers to 'an actor'; all human beings have to act in the sense that they carry out actions, but they are also forced by circumstance to perform these actions in a variety of roles. Goffman (see *The Presentation of Self in Everyday Life*) described the human capacity for 'dramaturgical performance' in ordinary situations.

Power 'at rest'?

There are times when power is 'at rest', in the sense that it is not being actively deployed. This brings us to an interesting question: does power continue to affect people when it is not in obvious use? If the *structures* of power are first established (in, for example, an institution such as a private company), and the kinds of relationship which ensue are recognised by all participants, then the constant *display* or use of power is unnecessary.

If power exists, and its strength is known from past experience, then individuals will be mindful of its possible effects. They will have to take the existence of power into account, and their behaviour will include some *consciousness* of its force. This may lead to a situation where individuals 'police' themselves, ensuring that their behaviour is appropriate to the situation in which they find themselves.

Burgoon talks of the 'structural attributes' of power, using as an example the job interview, where the employer has (*Human Communication*, p. 56) 'relatively little to lose from engaging in this transaction' while the prospective employee is dependent upon the goodwill of the employer. The structural power in this situation is plain to see. If and when the post is awarded to the candidate, then an important precedent has been set for the future. I would suggest that other events which place the employee in a similar situation, such as disciplinary action or a change in conditions of work, will mark a return to the basic condition upon which such employment ultimately depends – inequality of power.

Power: negative or positive effects?

Since power is both the capacity to affect the natural and social environment, and the exercise of forms of domination by societies, institutions, groups or individuals over any other social category, various writers have argued whether power should be seen as generally **negative** or **positive** in its effects. Clearly, certain instances of power carry extraordinary promise for the positive development of the human race, while others entail the most appalling dangers. The difficulty lies in obtaining universal agreement about what constitutes good and bad uses of power.

Distribution of power

There are a number of perspectives on the subject of power as it manifests itself in our society, but all commentators acknowledge the fact that there are certain inequalities in its distribution. Not all 'social actors' have access to the same number of props and few carry out their actions on a particularly big stage (which makes the sight of powerful individuals standing on soapboxes particularly distasteful).

Theories of power: authoritarianism, pluralism, functionalism and leftism

The basic divisions on the issue of power are between:

- those who argue that established institutional or state power is legitimate, and that inequality between leaders and led is a necessary and desirable condition;
- theorists who believe that the existence and present use of power in the 'democracies' is on the whole legitimate, since it is to some degree shared among the various interest groups which comprise society;
- individuals who think that, legitimate or not, power has an important *function* to perform in society;
- those who argue that the present social order is fundamentally unjust and founded ultimately upon coercion. (In this case, a variety of solutions has been advanced to solve the problem of injustice, ranging from political reform to social revolution.

The first school of thought concerned with the issue of power could be described as **authoritarian**, and is usually found either in situations where some form of dictatorship (regional, national or institutional) has been established, or else in the propaganda of extremist groups. It is possible, however, for strong authoritarian currents to emerge within democratic structures. As a *theory* of power, undiluted authoritarianism rarely appears in its natural state. Tyrannical individuals or regimes are often anxious to disguise the true relations of power by using more liberal discourses. The Thatcher government in Britain, and the Reagan administration in the United States, were noted for their ability to mobilise populist and anti-bureaucratic rhetoric in the service of quite marked authoritarianism.

The **pluralist** approach to power promotes the idea that the state in democratic nations acts in the interests of its citizens, who by and large accept the legitimate authority of their leaders. Pluralists do, however, recognise sectional interests and the idea that different aspects of an individual's background and experience will produce a variety of responses to political events. Modern pluralists come from a variety of political traditions within 'liberal democracy', which includes most of the 'centre' as well as the reformist left in British society, including the 'modernisers', the traditional right and the 'soft left' of the Labour party. One wing of the Conservative party is broadly pluralist in spirit.

However, a note of caution must be sounded at this point. Political groups will not necessarily rely upon a single perspective to represent their philosophy; all parties committed to electoral politics must consider how to achieve influence in public life, and therefore will seek to discover which ideas will assist in attaining this goal.

The social theorist Talcott Parsons took a **functionalist** view of power (officially, functionalism is a form of pluralism). According to this outlook, society as a whole is supposed to benefit from the increased power produced by the economic system. Parsons regarded differences in access to power as necessary for the effective pursuit of collective goals (see Haralambos, *Sociology*, p. 122). He argued (see *Power*, p. 99) that:

> 'the political control of productivity makes it possible ... to produce a surplus above the monetary funds committed'.

This surplus could not be attained, according to Parsons, without the conscious use of power. From a functionalist perspective, power itself is defined as (p. 101) 'a circulating medium' rather like money; Parsons seems to regard it as a necessary, effective but uncontroversial element of society, rather like oil in an engine. It is (p. 103) 'a generalised capacity to secure the performance of binding obligations by units in a system of collective organisation'.

The alternative to different forms of pluralism is the tradition of radical, **leftist** or Marxist critiques of power. Karl Marx argued that economic power had been acquired and effectively centralised by one class, the modern bourgeoisie. This group replaced the aristocracy as the leading political force, coming to prominence during the Industrial Revolution and gradually strengthening its control of political institutions. Unlike Parsons, Marx did not see economic power as 'neutral', but as a force which consolidates and concentrates the rule of the bourgeoisie, at home and abroad. At home this class (*Bottomore* and Rubel, *Karl Marx: Selected Writings*, p. 146):

> 'keeps more and more doing away with the scattered state of the population . . . it has agglomerated [brought together] population, centralised means of production, and has concentrated property in a few hands'.

The consequence of this process, according to Marx, was *political centralisation*. The imperialism of the bourgeoisie is felt abroad not simply through military adventure, but through the power of production (p. 146):

> 'The bourgeoisie, by the rapid improvement of all instruments of production, by the immensely facilitated means of communication, draws all, even the most barbarian nations, into civilisation. The cheap prices of its commodities are the heavy artillery with which it batters down all Chinese walls.'

Marxists developed a theory of revolution, which was to take place in the advanced industrial countries where the political power of the working class was at its strongest. Having centralised the population and having created an urban proletariat, capitalism was thus supposed to have ensured its own eventual downfall. As the predicted revolutions failed to materialise, Marxism began to develop a variety of explanations for the supposed docility of the oppressed. These often stressed the dominance of ruling *ideas*, rather than just the coercive force which capitalism had at its disposal. The following section is devoted to exploring the development of ideas which grew from radical and Marxist perspectives on power.

Hegemony: Gramsci's theory of power

The first successful revolution which took much of its inspiration from Marxist precepts took place in Russia in 1917 (see 'The Marxist tradition' in Chapter 1). This revolution was expected to spread, but hopes for a world revolution suffered a setback when post-war revolts in Germany were crushed by reactionaries. Instead of witnessing the triumph of Communism, the left saw extreme forms of nationalism and racism grow in strength. A stand was made against fascism in Spain in 1936, when a host of radical parties and groups fought alongside the increasingly authoritarian (and Stalinist) Spanish Communist party.

Before the Spanish calamity, the first fascist state had been established in Italy in 1922. Four years later, in 1926, the Italian dictator Mussolini used the pretext of an alleged attempt on his life to extinguish the last elements of resistance to his rule. Among the vast numbers of people arrested by the regime was the Communist Antonio Gramsci, who was also a member of parliament. Gramsci suffered greatly during his imprisonment; he had been born with a malformed spine and was subject to other disorders. Despite these trials, Gramsci produced an extensive series of political musings in the *Prison Notebooks*, which were smuggled out of Italy at his death in 1937.

Gramsci pointed to the apparent willingness of the working class to accept the ideas of their rulers as one explanation for the failure of revolutionary politics. Gramsci did not, however, simply argue that ruling ideas had indoctrinated the working class. He believed the process of domination was based on two principles (*Selections from Prison Notebooks*, p. 12):

'1. The "spontaneous" consent given by the great masses of the population to the general direction imposed on social life by the dominant fundamental group; this consent is ... caused by the prestige ... which the dominant group enjoys because of its position and function in the world of production.

2. The apparatus of state coercive power which "legally" enforces discipline on those groups who do not "consent" either actively or passively. This apparatus is ... in anticipation of moments of crisis of command and direction when spontaneous consent has failed.'

Gramsci's conception of **hegemony**, in which the ruling class manages to obtain active consent for its world-view, emerges from the combined action of these two aspects of domination. Thus, in an era which saw the decline of radicalism, a theory like hegemony, which stressed the importance of the power of ideas *supported* by the 'legalised' threat of force, was seized upon as a plausible explanation for working-class quietism, and gave rise to a number of studies of ideology.

The Frankfurt School

As we discovered in Chapter 1, the Frankfurt School began work in 1923 in Weimar Germany, the year after fascism seized power in Italy, and three years before Gramsci's arrest. Horkheimer, Adorno and later Marcuse also tried to understand the reasons for the defeat of working-class radicalism. Horkheimer and Adorno's perspective became known as 'Critical Theory', and made a significant departure from Marx's theories of rational progress towards socialism.

Critical Theory recognised that Marx had unmasked the real relations of power supposedly hidden by the 'neutral' appearance of market forces, and agreed that the working class was oppressed. However, the split with traditional Marxism occurred because the Frankfurt School disagreed with Marx's belief that the growth of economic production would lead towards a more rational society, one whose natural outcome would be socialism. Horkheimer and Adorno saw only the subjugation of individuals and the growth of new myths, this time of rationality and progress.

Jurgen Habermas (see Larrain's *Ideology and Cultural Identity*, p. 55) argued that these authors' suspicion of ideology became total, and was 'turned not only against the irrational function of bourgeois ideals, but against the rational potential of bourgeois culture itself'. Another of the School's central tenets was the existence of a 'mass culture', in which the easy availablity of commodities, together with the myth of equality and classnessness, had helped to ensure acceptance of capitalist society.

Power: new radical departures?

The movement away from models of a unified, monolithic power holding sway over a docile population may be seen in the work of a number of writers. Nicos Poulantzas, for example, argued that the dominant economic class, the capitalist class, did not rule directly through the organ of the state. The state itself had some degree of autonomy, or freedom of action, which it was able to exercise on behalf of capitalism. This conception is useful because it moves away from the idea of direct and absolute rule, although some feel that it is contradictory to argue that the state has 'relative autonomy' and yet still in essence serves the ruling class. In *State, Power, Socialism*, Poulantzas explains that the state is not a 'thing' but rather (p. 148):

> 'the strategic site of organisation of the dominant class in its relationship to the dominated classes. It is a site and a *centre* of the exercise of power, but it possesses no power of its own.'

Poulantzas's ultimate concern was the strengthening of democratic socialism in the context of advanced liberal democracy.

State fractions

Since physical and ideological authority often converge at times of extreme dislocation, such as during major strikes and other forms of unrest, the study of crises is often favoured by those theorists who see the state as speaking essentially with one voice (see Masterman on the miner's strike in his *Television Mythologies*, 1984). The operation of crisis management seems to reveal a *permanent political* allegiance at the level of the state, but this is actually manifested through a *temporary ideological* cohesion. The sociologist David Coates (see Haralambos, p. 158) observed that the ruling class is composed of different 'fractions', to the extent that the state will at times act against the interests of one fraction as it works to favour another. This happens because the state itself is made up of different factions.

David Tetzlaff of Miami University (see 'Divide and conquer') advanced the idea that the citizens of modern nation-states are controlled not by attempting to make them think or do the same thing, as traditional Marxism had believed, but by allowing a high degree of *diversity*. The culture industry, for example, may produce a variety of messages which a number of different groups are able to take as representing their interests. Thus power works to some extent by allowing access to culture, but it is this very culture whose function Tetzlaff considers to be (p. 31) 'to reconcile capital's subordinates to their position within the economy'. This does not, however, examine how these subordinates use popular culture.

A more sophisticated version of theories of 'divide and rule' is advanced by Jurgen Habermas, who argues that our society 'increasingly functionalises its citizens for various public purposes, but it privatises them in their consciousness' (see William Outhwaite's *Habermas*, p. 7). Habermas, in his most recent work, has attempted to construct a theory of law and civil obligation which will provide a model of equal rights for life in a liberal democracy.

Power and discourse

The French writer Michel Foucault understood the problems involved in trying to maintain a 'monolithic' view of power. By 'monolithic' he meant the kind of impersonal, abstract structure which stands above and beyond the individual. He saw that power was something which all individuals experienced, and more importantly produced. He saw that the relationship of power existed between individuals and was carried in *discourse*, or what we may call for the moment *socially constructed* speech exchanges. He was interested less in the supposed *intentions* of the powerful than in the actual places where power was *applied*. In *Disciplinary Power and Subjection*, he wrote that (Lukes, *Power*, p. 232):

> 'one should try to locate power at the extreme points of its exercise, where it is always less legal in character'.

In fact, some of the most clear examples of the exercise of power come from perfectly legal sources. Foucault has been criticised for neglecting the project which theorists of power have traditionally pursued, the study of state power, and retreating instead into a characterisation of power as 'a war of all against all' (see *Power/Knowledge*, p. 123).

Power as a relationship

Power is often *institutionalised* or established in the structures of various public and private bodies. A corporation or public body may take certain functions as its own by right and may then eventually exercise power through the precedent of use. Institutional power is often organised in a hierarchical structure. All public and private organisations, for example, contain *hierarchies* –

graded divisions of groups of people. Such divisions are established at a series of levels, where each level has a different degree of access to power.

I would suggest therefore that some of the problems surrounding the nature of power can be solved if it is understood as a **relationship**. If we use the example of wealth, its possession is only meaningful in our society because there is such a thing as poverty; since wealth is not universal and can only be created where others experience its deficiency, merely to possess it is to enter into a power relationship.

The relationships of power are numerous. Power can exist between individuals, between individuals and groups, and between groups and other collective forms such as whole societies. Its operation is both internal and external. It exists, for example, in the form of intra-group power (a relationship between the members of a single group) and in the form of inter-group power (a relationship between distinct groups).

The operation of power: authority and solidarity

The operation of power may be represented by the diagram in Figure 3.7.

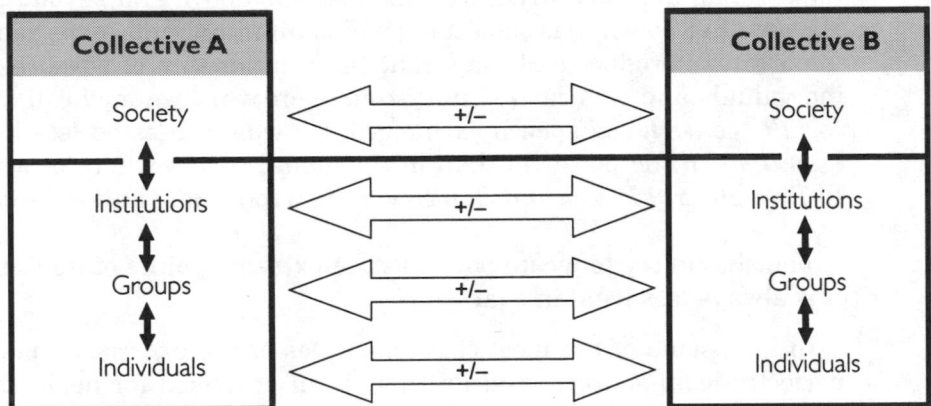

Figure 3.7   Operation of power

This diagram represents two collectives, where relationships of power are established internally between the components of each collective (seen in the vertical plane) and externally between elements of both collectives (shown in the horizontal plane). The double-headed arrows along the side and between elements indicate the ways in which each level may interact with another, whether that interaction takes the form of domination, acquiescence, co-operation, competition or resistance. In each case, the *individuals* shown experience their subjective positions as members of a specific society.

Power operates along the vertical plane, and also along the lateral or horizontal plane, involving the same range of possible relationships. The collectives A and B represent two societies, but if we use the diagram below the line, then the elements on each side may be seen as part of a single society.

Each element may enter into a relationship with any other. For example, an *institution* from collective A may exercise **authority** over an *individual* from the same collective. Alternatively, there are cases where an *individual* would appear to dominate an *institution* or even a *society*, as in the case of a dictator, elected or otherwise. A single element may also seek or express **solidarity** with another; an *individual* may attempt to support the actions of a *group* from the same collective.

Equally, as I indicated above, any of these relationships may occur between elements taken from different collectives. For instance, a *group* in collective B may compete with an *institution* in collective A; or an individual may find him or herself subjected to the laws or customs of a foreign *society*.

The term 'solidarity' usually has a positive meaning, but I use it here to indicate simply the act of combination between any of the forces listed above. Two fascist dictatorships are quite capable of expressing a form of mutual solidarity.

Types of authority

We have seen above that 'authority' is a factor in the configuration of power, but the precise range of its meaning requires explanation. The word 'authority' comes from *author*, which means the originator of an event or a message. To recognise authorship is to recognise a degree of originality in the message of the author. **Formal authority** is the condition in which individuals or groups hold recognised office in some institution. **Moral authority** is the type which draws upon the ability to set an example of conduct. Max Weber went beyond this, to distinguish between three types of authority. These were (see Haralambos, p. 118):

- **charismatic authority**, where a leader is supposed to possess, or actually displays, qualities which provoke the admiration of rivals and subordinates;
- **traditional authority**, in which the power of domination rests on belief in the inherent correctness of established relationships;
- **rational-legal authority**, where control emerges from consensus over an agreed framework of supposedly impersonal rules, such as those found in the legal system.

Of course, these types may often be combined, and are intended only as paradigms of the types of authority which exist in the real world.

Coercive power: back to the state

There is no doubt that some political groups regard the use of coercive power merely as a question of expedience. The use of power is either praised or condemned depending upon the groups which exercise it, and the purposes to which it is put. Many nation-states regard their own use of economic or political power as justified, while attacking the exercise of power by their rivals. Authoritarian Marxism, particularly the Leninist variant, seemed to regard the power exercised by a revolutionary vanguard as wholly legitimate, while the power of the capitalist state and non-Bolshevik organisations was regarded as largely contemptible. Lenin (see *Left-Wing Communism, an Infantile Disorder*, p. 76) argued that older socialist bodies like the Second International, a 'moderate' socialist organisation, were incapable of creating:

> 'a really centralised and really leading centre capable of directing the international tactics of the revolutionary proletariat'.

Poachers turned gamekeepers

When the Bolsheviks came to govern, their fear of any dissension allowed them to exercise state power quite ruthlessly. This power was often deployed against those groups which had taken the rhetoric of revolution seriously, and had seized factories and other workplaces. Direct workers' control was soon ended, often by decrees which dissolved those 'soviets' created by the rank and file.

By December 1918, the Bolshevik Lozovsky protested against his own government's use of violence – a form of direct coercive power – to suppress strikes. In April 1918, increasing centralisation of power prompted another party member (Osinsky, executed by Stalin in 1938) to warn Lenin that Bolshevism would eventually create 'state capitalism' instead of socialism (see Brinton, *The Bolsheviks and Workers' Control*, p. 39).

Hostility to centralised power

Other forms of Marxism, particularly those with a libertarian perspective, took a different position on the question of power. Rosa Luxemburg (see *Leninism and Marxism*, p. 88) perceived as early as 1904 the Bolshevik tendency to require:

> 'the blind subordination, in the smallest detail, of all party organs, to the party centre, which alone thinks, guides, and decides for all'.

A similar view was taken by the Dutch Marxist Pannekoek, who argued that:

> 'the struggle of the proletariat is not merely a struggle against the bourgeoisie *for* state power, but a struggle *against* state power'.

Lenin had at one time been broadly sympathetic to this position (in *State and Revolution*, p. 136), but abandoned it when his party came to dominate the political landscape.

Some philosophies, however, particularly the various currents of anarchism, have always expressed hostility to all forms of state power. According to such approaches, state power cannot be seized, because it is actively harmful to those revolutionary societies which attempt to employ it. The anarchist Kropotkin saw no good whatever in the state, and suggested that ancient societies were destroyed at the very point at which they became nation-states. He declared (in *The State, its Historic Role*, p. 56) that there was a clear choice for humankind:

'*Either* the State for ever, crushing individual and local life, taking over in all fields of human activity ... *or* the destruction of States, and new life starting again in thousands of centres on the principle of the lively initiative of the individual and groups, and that of free agreement.'

The power of language

Linguistics

Linguistics was once taken to indicate the study of the grammatical properties of language, which include:

- **morphology** – the structure of words;
- **syntax** – the structure of sentences;
- **phonology** – the 'sound-structures' of human utterance;
- **semantics** – the formal elements of meaning.

However, many academics found the concerns of mainstream linguistics restrictive. The established tradition seemed to be preoccupied with the search for those abstract rules which supposedly lay beneath the surface of human utterance. Part of the reason for this tendency to abstraction may perhaps be found in the division of language into *langue* and *parole* (mentioned in Chapter 1), made by Ferdinand de Saussure.

Language: langue and parole

Saussure divided the study of language into **langue**, the system or structure underlying speech, and **parole**, the speech of individuals, regarded as the infinitely variable expression of the abstract form. Langue is a collective system, true expression of which is found in societies rather than in the utterances of individual speakers. These utterances are perhaps accorded a less exalted place than the underlying structures upon which they are thought to depend.

Developments in linguistics

As an increasing number of linguists made studies of the relationship between language and power, and a greater interest was shown in actual speech events, newer 'branches' of linguistics were founded. These included **sociolinguistics**, **pragmatics**, and those approaches which grew from discourse analysis and became known as '**critical linguistics**'.

Sociolinguistics was an approach to the social dimension of language which, in its early forms, proved rather limited in its conceptual range. It made comparisons between the social location of speakers, the forms of speech they employed during exchanges with others, and the access to power achieved by each group studied. It did not examine the question of movement between genres of speech, or the more general question of power and language in society as a whole.

One study included under the heading of sociolinguistics was the concept of the **speech community**. This was a human aggregate defined according to its frequent internal communication, using shared verbal signs which showed *significant difference* to other groups. 'Speech community' is a catch-all concept which refers to everything from nation-states and regional groups to gangs and subcultures. The concept of a speech community is not particularly useful unless it is qualified by the use of example.

As linguistics became increasingly concerned with social context, the general field of sociolinguistics became too small to support the new inquiries which were being made, and discourse analysis moved centre stage. At the same time, some branches of sociolinguistic inquiry grew in strength, partly because mainstream linguistic studies had failed to assimilate their findings.

Women, men and language

In 1986, Jennifer Coates produced the first edition of *Women, Men and Language*. A second edition followed in 1993. Coates investigated the relationship between language and gender, where gender means (p. 3) 'socially constructed categories based on sex'. The point of such a project is not really to identify patterns of sexism in language use, but rather to investigate the whole range of difference evident in the verbal interactions which take place *between* men and women as distinct social *groups*. Early forms of sociolinguistic inquiry did not recognise women as a distinct group, concentrating instead upon ethnicity, class, or age.

However, we saw earlier in this chapter that a number of feminist academics object to the concept of women as a unified social group. G.M. Breakwell, for example, argued that there is no agreed view of women's identity. Therefore, women suffer the experience of marginalisation.

Coates described the two main approaches which are used to explain the 'structured social variation' found between the speech of men and women; these are the **dominance** approach and the **difference** approach. The first theory promotes the idea that women are an oppressed group, and that male power is (p. 13) 'enacted through linguistic practice'. The second theory proceeds from the view that men and women belong to different subcultures. Coates argues that (p. 84):

> 'Social groups need to assert their distinctiveness, and language is one way of doing this. It looks as though there are strong cultural pressures on men and women to distinguish themselves from each other, even though other groupings (such as social class, ethnic group, age) notionally place them together.'

Male verbiage

Studies of girls and boys below the age of 4 years show that girls talk more and with greater fluency than their male counterparts. However, when we consider classroom analysis of 9- to 11-year-olds, the results demonstrate that boys dominate conversation. Contrary to received wisdom, adult males talk considerbly more than females. A wide variety of research has demonstrated that men talk more (p. 115):

> 'in settings as diverse as staff meetings ... television panel discussions ... experimental pairs ... e-mail discussion via computer ... and also husband-and-wife pairs in spontaneous conversation'.

Research from 1975 discovered that, asked to describe three pictures, male subjects spoke for more than four times longer than females.

Spender (1981) explains that there are different expectations of male and female speakers in our society. Coates sums up this viewpoint by noting that (p. 12):

> 'while men have the right to talk, women are expected to remain silent – talking at any length, then, will be perceived as talkativeness in women'.

Women and men: competition vs. co-operation?

Coates also devotes time to examining research carried out into the different styles and purposes which exist in male and female language use. She notes that men (p. 10):

> 'typically adopt a competitive style in conversation, treating their turn as a chance to overturn earlier speakers' contributions and to make their own point as forcibly as possible'.

In contrast to this style, women tend to use a more co-operative approach. They add to rather than demolish other speakers' contributions. Whereas women's co-operative style was once regarded as tentative or weak, some recent approaches have emphasised the positive aspects of such discursive practices. In conclusion (p. 203), Coates finds that:

> 'women's conversational style is based on solidarity, while men's is based on power, a difference arising directly from women's and men's membership of a patriarchal society'.

Other differences account for what Coates calls 'miscommunication', where men and women fail to communicate properly because they have learned different rules for conversation during childhood and adolescence. Coates identifies eight 'problem areas' which cause miscommunication. These are:

- **minimal responses**, where forms like 'yeah' or 'mhm' are used by women to show that they are listening, though men take them to indicate agreement;
- **questions**, employed rhetorically by women to assist the flow of conversation, while men believe they are being asked for information;
- **links between speaker turns**, in which women refer to the contribution of the previous speaker, while men have a tendency to ignore previous speech acts;
- **topic shifts**, multiple in the case of men and much rarer in women's conversation;
- **self-disclosure**, avoided by men and used co-operatively by women;
- **verbal aggressiveness**, supposedly enjoyed in all-male groups but disliked by women;
- **listening**, important to women but less so to men;
- **simultaneous speech**, which in male speech means a high degree of interruption, and in female speech is used to offer briefer and more supportive remarks.

Disciplinary boundaries

It would appear that, on occasion, there is a need to depart from the standard aims of academic research in order to assist the overall development of a subject. Linguistics has to some degree incorporated new aspects into the main body of its concerns. This is a welcome development, since the point of academic inquiry is to seek truths about the world and human perception in general, not to defend an area merely because it happens to be the field one understands best. Hodge and Kress made a similar point in *Language as Ideology*, where they note that (p. 3):

> 'disciplines exist for the sake of their subjects, not the other way round. If the boundary that has been drawn round a discipline proves a hindrance to the proper study of that subject matter, then it is the boundary that must change.'

Language: capacity, use and prohibition

It is possible to investigate the **capacity** of language, in the sense that its range of capabilities may be explored. The aim would be to define the *boundaries* of the social power of language. It would then be possible to examine the degree of power found in intentional language use, including 'ordinary' speech and the employment of persuasive systems like rhetoric.

It is important to recall that the full range of language is sometimes circumscribed by various **prohibitions** over its **use**. Foucault noted that 'the prohibitions' surrounding language revealed 'its links with desire and power' (see Crowley, *The Politics of Discourse*, p. 1). At the same time, the prohibitions set on language use have never produced complete conformity.

Language, power and structure

When the question of **power** is introduced into the study of language, some writers still seem to think that it is a specialist study of some sort, devoted either to examining the utterances made by individuals who possess social power (politicians and so on), or to the study of 'types' of language which are considered to have powerful effects ('the language of power').

While it is true that both these aspects are important, the study of power and language should really be concerned with how the **structures** and *use* of linguistic expression allow various individuals, groups and classes to organise social existence. This must mean that the power of language emerges from *material* requirements, from the necessity to operate successfully in the natural and social environments we inhabit.

This does not mean, however, that it consists of only a handful of functional commands and responses. The reason why most studies of power concentrate upon either formal speeches, statements or short speech events is, according to Ng and Bradac (*Power in Language*, p. 6), because the study of 'sequential interaction between individuals is much more difficult than [studying] a monologue'.

Language and social power

If language is the primary vehicle for organising human affairs, whether those affairs are structured in competitive or co-operative ways, and power is quite simply the organised capacity of human individuals and groups to affect their environment, then the use of language is, according to Ng and Bradac (p. 1), 'inevitably an instrument for enacting, recreating, or subverting power'.

Language is the *expression* of **social power**, in all its forms. In *Language and Power*, Norman Fairclough explains why theories of the 'social' uses of language cannot form a specialist area of study, but must instead occupy a central position in linguistic inquiry (p. 23):

'Language is a part of society; linguistic phenomena *are* social phenomena of a special sort, and social phenomena *are* (in part) linguistic phenomena.'

Ordinary competencies

I indicated above that theorists who study the power of language as a specialised form often look at polished examples of public speech. However, their investigations may in fact have identified a number of effects which are part of the **competencies** of **ordinary discourse**. If speech is social, and *constructs* social reality, then the ordinary interactions made in the course of daily existence will reflect this connection, and will form the most valuable basic evidence of the workings of power in language. It may therefore be best to begin our inquiries into the everyday exchanges people experience, and not into public rhetoric.

Innate abilities

If the abstract structures of language (*langue*) may be deduced from studying speech events, then we will also find that these structures will reflect the 'in-built' capability of the human organism to produce speech. To this extent, the biological structures of the brain help to create and structure the discursive aspects of society.

Some may argue that each human being is unique, and that theories of **innate language ability** (such as Chomsky's) tend to downgrade the notion of a free and independent human nature. This is not the case. Within each *dialect* there is an *idiolect*, a personal use of language which will not be reproduced exactly in any two individuals, but which grows none the less from the fact that we are all 'programmed to speak', yet all uniquely situated in the social environment. To paraphrase Marx, the human subject makes its own destiny, but in circumstances which are not of its choosing.

Performative utterances

In 1962, J.L. Austin (see Coulthard, *An Introduction to Discourse Analysis*, p. 13) observed that philosophers had assumed that 'the business of a "statement" can only be to describe some state of affairs or to "state some fact", which it must do either truly or falsely'. Austin showed that this was not always the case. There are **constatives**, utterances that are not intended to produce information about facts. Another type consists of **ethical propositions**, which are intended to produce emotion or proscribe conduct. Then there are **performatives**, which match the performance of an action at the same time as the words themselves are spoken. Austin used the example of the performative statement 'I name this ship', where this is not merely a description of what is being done, but also the actual *performance of the act* of naming the ship. An example of a performative given by Coulthard is 'passengers are requested to return to their seats', where the statement is also an action entailing an effect.

Performatives and power

One of the features of power must be, as Austin says, the fact that the utterance must be delivered by the **appropriate person**. For example, if a child has misbehaved, only adults holding a position of authority *vis-à-vis* the child (such as the parent or teacher) will usually be recognised as standing in an appropriate relation to enable them to discipline the child. A stranger or another child would not be regarded as an appropriate figure. Coulthard provides the example of a blacksmith, who might be able to read the words of a marriage ceremony perfectly well, but will not have the power to make the words socially significant. By 'the appropriate person' we mean the individual who is allowed to take the appropriate **role** in a suitable context.

Austin noticed that the concept of a performative speech act extended to statements like 'I warn you' and 'I apologise', where the act of warning or apologising is actually *performed* in speech. This type of performative does not depend on the status of the person doing the warning or apologising; anyone is allowed to utter the words. Where material circumstances (and therefore roles) begin to change, individuals will be able to challenge received ideas about who is an appropriate source for various types of public and private communication.

Status and solidarity

The concept of **status**, as explained by Ryan and Giles (1982), indicates a person's position in a hierarchy, whether that hierarchy is based on strength, or learning or some other form of prestige. The idea of **solidarity** indicates a person's proximity to, or degree of inclusion in, a group. The idea of competence and attractiveness are self-explanatory, and these work in conjunction with the first two categories (Figure 3.8).

Status

|

Solidarity

|

Competence

|

Attractiveness   *Figure 3.8*

Status and competence can be seen as working either together or independently. Ng and Bradac argue that, in forming an impression of the power of a communicator in a group context, people attend to the dimension of status, while in private contexts they are more likely to pay attention to the competence of a communicator. These authors believe that the most powerful type of communicator is one who is perceived to belong to a highly valued group, and is competent, effective, active and strong. The weakest type of communicator is supposed to be seen as belonging to a 'devalued' group, and to be incompetent or ineffective, passive and weak. We should remember that groups which are considered to be low in status in some quarters will be regarded very highly in others.

Rhetorical psychology

Rhetorical psychology is an approach to the public use of language. Although the idea of analysing rhetoric usually suggests inquiries into the public speeches of the powerful, a rhetorical approach deals also with the ideas and opinions expressed by 'ordinary' individuals.

In the preface to *Ideology and Opinions*, Michael Billig argues that:

'old insights about the rhetorical nature of argumentation can be used for exploring contemporary issues of ideology and opinion'.

According to Billig's approach, the holding of opinions is (p. 1) 'an essentially rhetorical and argumentative matter'. This may suggest that opinion is less 'deeply felt' than some believe, and reinforces the idea that it only becomes fixed when an argument or debate is in progress.

Billig argues that the 'processes of everyday thinking can be processes of "ideology"'. He notes that traditional approaches to ideology and common sense have supposed that, in using commonsense notions:

'people will find themselves repeating the assumptions of their times. Moreover ... they will be repeating assumptions which confirm existing arrangements of power. In this way, the continuing history of domination flows through the patterns of commensensical thinking.'

This model of domination is a stumbling block that needs to be overcome. Billig argues (p. 2) that the human subject is not 'a blind dupe, whose mind has been filled by outside forces and who reacts unthinkingly'. The human subject is instead 'a rhetorical being who thinks and argues with ideology'.

Ideology and the human subject

The term **ideology**, was first used in France at the end of the eighteenth century, and meant originally a 'study of ideas'. At the end of various transformations, it has now come to mean 'systems of belief'. In *The Power of*

Ideology, Gregor McLennan sets out three conditions which must be met before something may be regarded as *ideological*:

- The ideas concerned must be shared by a significant number of individuals.
- The ideas must form a coherent system, whose elements support one another to make a recognisable structure.
- The ideas must have some relationship to the use of power in society.

Billig argues that certain assumptions have been made, to the effect that ideology works simply by being 'transferred' from a powerful authority to a weak subject population. He believes that traditional theories of ideology have been used, on the one hand, to make common cause with the oppressed against the might of their rulers but, on the other, have also been employed to characterise the underdog as the dupe or victim of the 'ruling ideas' of a society. The paradox of ideology is in his view (p. 8):

'a variant of a general paradox of language, for the use of language involves both autonomy and repetition'.

The relationship between ideology and language is central to Billig's arguments. He argues that, despite the 'repetition' involved in language use (what we would call the *available discourses*), human subjects are the authors of their own actions. Billig is opposed to the idea that the real author of human action is ideology.

Opinion and the citizen

Billig is unhappy with those theories of ideology which assume that every public address made by the powerful succeeds in influencing the subject population. He believes that the approach of theorists like Althusser neglects (p. 11) 'the chatter and argument of everyday life', or the philosophising of the 'everyday'. He insists that, above all (p. 11):

'modern democracies are places of "opinion"; citizens are expected to "hold opinions", "have attitudes"'.

This is certainly true, but only certain *types* of opinion are deemed acceptable. Opinion is indeed widely sought, as Billig notes, but it is explored by market researchers and other forces of authority for reasons which have very little to do with the exercise of democracy. Many things are 'thinkable' but only a proportion of these things are 'sayable'. In other words, opinion operates within boundaries or constraints. It is also important to realise that 'opinion' itself is understood, by those who hold it, to be an individual and not a collective expression. This limits its power as a social force.

Retreat from the real

Billig's argument (p. 14) is that we should move away from focusing on the 'uncovering of mental structures within the individual' to 'social factors, especially those relating to language'. Billig does not set the two projects in opposition, but proposes the idea that 'mental states are themselves socially created'.

Some rhetorical theorists, however, have used the growing interest in studies of ordinary speech to deny that there is much point in investigating the real world beyond speech events. Writers like John Shotter have moved away from a concern with the reality of *speech reference* to concentrate upon what he calls 'conversational realities'.

Beyond the laboratory

Edwards and Potter, writing in *Discursive Psychology*, declare an interest in what they call (p. 3) 'the rhetorical construction of factual versions'. This means studying a variety of situations where individuals are in disagreement or dispute, and therefore produce 'typically contrasting versions' of events. This, according to these authors, suggests that attempts to compare real utterances with laboratory definitions of real events should be abandoned:

> 'rather than trying to explicate the nature of some factual account through considering its relation to an "external" reality as defined by the analyst, it can be more fruitful to consider its relation to versions that the participants treat as alternative'.

These authors have little faith in the idea of an accurate and purely descriptive account of events, which is somehow able to exist outside the versions of reality offered through human utterance. They are interested in speech as a *discursive action*, and turn away from cognitive psychology to investigate real speech events through the use of a 'discursive action model' of analysis.

Rhetoric in the political arena

Rhetoric means the art of using language to persuade or influence the human subject. It is usually applied to persuasive attempts directed at an audience, often in some formal or institutional setting.

In the early 1980s, Max Atkinson made a close study of modern political rhetoric (see *Our Masters' Voices*). He argued that the modern era has witnessed some important developments in the relationship between the subject population and authority (Preface, p. xiii):

> 'We are nowadays more familiar with our political masters than at any time since government passed out of the hands of village elders.'

This claim needs careful consideration. In the first place, there are a number of questions about who 'our political masters' really are. The elected politicians we see or hear make up only part of the alliance of interests known as the ruling class. It also seems clear that no direct comparison can be made between two quite different types of authority. The leadership of a village will exercise power in a more direct and personal way, than would the leadership of a large nation. This leads to the problem at the heart of Atkinson's description: the type of familiarity we have with 'our political masters' is largely based on our experience of the mass media, and as such has certain limitations. Although Atkinson does describe 'the mass penetration of television and radio', which has brought 'the sights and sounds of politicians directly into our living-rooms', these *sights and sounds* do not provide evidence of the kind of familiarity suggested in his first paragraph.

Presentation and policy

To argue that our knowledge of political figures falls short of familiarity does not mean that we receive only images or 'sound-bites' unconnected with real events. The content of the material offered to voters is more substantial than mere appearance, but it is not usually a detailed description of **policy** (where such policy exists). Although there is much to be gained from the study of broadcast material, it remains in most cases a series of **presentations**. These presentations are not entirely the responsibility of the media. Political parties will prepare material in the hope that it will be transmitted in the form they wish.

Closer, my candidate, to thee?

However, where politicians are allowed to respond to reasonably searching questions, then an audience will gain a number of insights into their characters and intentions. An audience will simply employ the interpretative methods it uses in *everyday situations*, making judgements about matters like honesty and truthfulness from the evidence of the interaction itself.

Atkinson appreciates that, while politicians are given more power to broadcast their views (p. xiii):

'these same technological developments have also enabled us, their audience, to look more closely at the politicians themselves'.

He believes that recording technology has made it possible to carry out studies of (p. xvi) 'actual *oral performances*', whereas previously it was possible only to rely upon '*written texts* of famous speeches'.

Television and radio are, however, in a contradictory position; they are an essential *part* of our restricted democracy, yet operate according to rules which mean that they are unable to strengthen the democratic base, at least in the sense that present structures discourage participation in the *production* of texts.

Vulnerable audiences?

Atkinson believes that certain oratorical techniques are particularly effective, and that in the face of these public ploys, an audience is (p. xvii) 'remarkably vulnerable'. Mass audiences are, in his words, susceptible to 'the rhetoric of demagogues'. What is the measure of this vulnerability? Atkinson notes that (p. 6):

> 'large numbers of people ... react to public speaking in a more or less identical way'.

Again, this begs the same question: does this 'identical' set of responses indicate the audience's tendency to believe what they are told? The evidence Atkinson presents is based on the idea of *interaction*. However, interaction between speaker and audience cannot, in the context of a public speech, include coherent verbal responses, so it must take other forms (p. 6):

> 'They [audio and video tape-recorders] permit access to the *interaction* between speakers and audience, by making it possible to examine displays of approval (such as laughing, cheering, and clapping) and disapproval (such as booing, jeering and heckling).'

So the evidence is of a simple type: noises, gestures, vocalisations.

Atkinson anticipates some criticism at this point, acknowledging that the practice of collecting such behavioural details (p. 7):

> 'might sound like the most tedious and pointless enterprise imaginable'.

In fact, Atkinson's research concerns itself with formal speech in the established context of party conferences, where there are *ritual* as well as *interactive* reasons for displaying certain forms of behaviour. Certainly, audience responses are not meaningless so much as *limited* in the range of meaning they are able to reproduce.

Playing at home

While Atkinson believes that the use of recorded speeches may be used to trace the course of a successful 'result' (applause) in much the same way as an action replay may reveal the moves which lead to a goal being scored, the context of party conferences may limit the usefulness of this comparison. It would be more accurate to call the conference leadership the political equivalent of a football team playing to a crowd exclusively made up of home fans, with no opponents in sight and an empty goal twice the usual size.

In contrast to political delegates at a conference, the public itself hardly ever watches a speech which is unmediated. It is presented with a series of 'highlights', in much the same way as an edited version of a football match dispenses with detail considered inessential.

Watching the human animal?

Atkinson justifies his study by arguing that (p. 6):

> 'it must be remembered that similar observational studies of animal behaviour have enabled zoologists to make many remarkable discoveries about regularities in the animal world. These include a good many findings about the patterns of dominance among different species of animals, from the pecking orders of farmyard chickens to life-and-death struggles between potential pack leaders in the jungle.'

He goes on to advocate a direct comparison between the animal and human examples:

> 'Given that so much can be learned about animal politics by observing animals in their natural habitats, it is reasonable to expect that a great deal may also be learned by adopting a similar approach to the study of human politics.'

The use of the phrase 'animal politics' is not encouraging, since we may be reminded of the once popular practice of comparing the behaviour of the 'human animal' with the social organisation evident in the lives of other creatures. A 'similar approach' to human politics cannot possibly take place under the conditions suggested by Atkinson. Animals are observed, according to Atkinson, 'in their natural habitats'. While a public rally or a party conference may become an *unremarkable* part of human life, it is not a *natural* event in the sense that Atkinson suggests. He goes on to admit that 'the natural habitats of human politicians are obviously much more varied'.

Displays of public behaviour

Atkinson sees cause for celebration in the fact that 'a great deal of the behaviour of politicians takes place in public'. This means that 'we do not have to wait permission to eavesdrop inside Downing Street or the White House before work can begin'.

The actual point here is missed. Instead of the politician displaying behaviour in public, what he or she is actually doing is displaying *public behaviour*. Political figures know what to expect from a certain context, and will deploy the neccessary attitudes in order to meet the expectations of mediator and audience. Of course, some politicians scorn to alter their mode of behaviour when in public. The notion of 'eavesdropping' is not appropriate in this context and would yield completely different insights; when the 'private' becomes public all sorts of interesting consequences may be observed.

Differences to interaction

The difficulty faced by all speakers, however loyal an audience they meet, is the knowledge that they might bore their listeners. Although **interaction** was first used by Atkinson as an unproblematic category, he goes on to make an important distinction between public speech and interaction proper (p. 9):

> 'such situations [passive attention to public speech] involve a general weakening of the basic incentives to pay attention that work perfectly well for most other types of verbal interaction'.

In conversation, turn-taking ensures that each individual will in most cases be provided with an opportunity to speak. This means, as Atkinson says, that (p. 11):

> 'it is necessary for a person to know not just exactly *when* it would be appropriate to start speaking, but also *what* would be a suitable thing to say when the moment comes'.

The absence of such structures during public speeches means that concentration is difficult, and that the substitute for interaction might be 'collective activities like clapping or booing'. Therefore, the opportunity to show approval or disapproval might provide the incentive neccessary for an audience's continued attention.

Rhetorical devices

It is worth reviewing the basic techniques employed in party political address. The various devices available to speakers (though they are often used unconsciously), include:

- the **rule of three** or the **three-part list**, where a politician makes three points in a row, the third of which is the culmination of the utterance, and which is intended to prompt applause;
- the use of **contrast** or **juxtaposition**, where two alternatives are presented to an audience, one of which clearly represents an undesirable state of affairs and is meant to be rejected in favour of the choice preferred by the speaker;
- the biased presentation of a rival's position for the purposes of ridicule, known as **paper tigers** or '**set them up and knock them down**' (the point being to show one's own policy as vastly superior);
- the **inclusive 'we'**, where an address attempts to represent the interests and opinions of speaker and audience as identical;

- **rhetorical questions**, whose answers are either supplied by the speaker, or meant to be so obvious as to require no response;
- **assertion** – the use of statements rather than argument;
- **repetition**, where a statement is repeated in the hope that it will eventually be accepted by an audience;
- **negative identification**, in which a rival is pinpointed and identified as the cause of various misfortunes.

Animal Farm

George Orwell's fable *Animal Farm* deals with the political development of the Soviet Union. Using different types of animal to represent a variety of classes and individuals, Orwell demonstrates how a class of bureaucrats achieves the gradual usurpation of power. Every abuse committed by the ruling group, made up of pigs, is justified in the speeches of its propagandist, Squealer.

An early departure from the principle of equality occurs when the pigs reserve for themselves the windfall apples and the farm's entire milk production. Squealer is used to placate the other animals. His diatribe contains a number of the techniques listed above:

' "Comrades!" he cried. "You do not imagine, I hope, that we pigs are doing this in a spirit of selfishness and privilege? Many of us actually dislike milk and apples. I dislike them myself. Our sole object in taking these things is to preserve our health. Milk and apples (this has been proved by Science, comrades) contain substances absolutely necessary to the well-being of a pig. We pigs are brain-workers. The whole management and organisation of the farm depend on us. Day and night we are watching over your welfare. It is for *your* sake that we drink that milk and eat those apples. Do you know what would happen if we pigs failed in our duty? Jones would come back! Surely, comrades . . . surely there is no-one among you who wants to see Jones come back?" '

Rhetoric in the public arena

In the 1992 election campaign, Ian Lang, speaking on behalf of the Scottish Conservatives, made this attack on the Labour Party:

'You can't trust a party which is committed to self-serving proposals for constitutional change. You can't trust a party which would reduce choice in health, in education, in housing. You can't trust a party which would make Scotland the highest taxed part of the United Kingdom.'

The repetition here constitutes a three-part list and, within that, a further example of the technique.

It should be clear that rhetorical tricks of this nature are not necessarily effective; no public utterance works merely by virtue of being well-constructed. The Conservatives' propaganda on tax backfired very badly, albeit after the election. Of more significance, however, Scotland's overall enthusiasm for Tory politicians was less than ecstatic.

Norman Lamont, speaking to a fringe meeting of Conservatives, also during the 1992 election, provides a succinct but very useful collection of many of the techniques described earlier:

> 'If we want to reduce borrowing more quickly (2) spending cuts (.) are better than increasing taxes (1.5). A billion pounds of spending is worth more than a billion pounds on taxes (1.5). Substantial further tax rises would retard recovery, slow growth, abort job creation, penalise success and stifle endeavour and we should reject them.'

Here, we witness assertion, two examples of contrast or juxtaposition, the use of a direct address ('you') and the employment of the inclusive 'we'.

Informal context

If we move away from the formal context of the public speech, we may find that a new context enables speakers to frame their discourses in more informal ways. Michael Billig studied the activities of two branches of the Young Conservatives, and found that there was a clear division between socialising and fun on the one hand, and the necessary but 'dull' political activity required at election times on the other. In contrast to branches of the Young Socialists Billig studied, which took politics very seriously, the young Tories were less inclined to treat political activity as a crusade.

Billig provides an interesting insight into the ideological tendencies of the young people who regularly attend branch meetings, and offers a theory of the *discursive* formation of belief (p. 97):

> 'it is ... a matter of picking up Conservative habits in a Conservative environment. Slowly, common turns of speech, and thereby common turns of thought, are adopted, and the member drifts into conservatism without having made a conscious political choice.'

It should be clear how different this is from the fiercely ideological nature of some Conservative activists on the right of the party. In addition, there are within the branch definite divisions between men and women on political issues, with female members tending towards more liberal positions; they remain, in addition, less assertive than the men.

Keep politics out of politics

Billig describes the visit of a ward chairman to one of the meetings. In the context of the local meeting, and in a situation where most of the audience know one another and are at least vaguely familiar with the speaker, the flights of rhetoric required at large conferences are unnecessary. The local speaker begins his talk with 'the almost obligatory words: "if I finish early, there'll be more drinking time"'.

The content of the visitor's speech is interesting, in that it purports to be 'non-political'. The concept of politics is here narrowed down to refer to party matters, while something of vast political import is treated almost casually (p. 97):

> 'Instead of boring you with yet more politics, I thought I'd talk to you about my recent trip to Southern Africa.'

Instead of being a *bona fide* tourist, however, the speaker had made the journey as the representative of a road-building company. The trip was to Lesotho, a pitiable state surrounded by what was then apartheid South Africa. The political message is, despite the disclaimer at the beginning, clearly in evidence by the end of the talk:

> 'We might hate South Africa's policies but it is tremendously important to the West.'

A speaker faced with having to articulate the same message on a public platform, i.e. with the knowledge that it would gain a wider circulation, would perhaps be more circumspect. More importantly, he or she might frame the message using a *rhetorical* construction, in which the subtleties of a coded delivery could allow the possibility of disclaiming uncomfortable interpretations. As the audience is thought to be of a like mind, and the message is not for wider consumption, the speaker is content to deliver the traditional condemnation of apartheid policy, before mentioning South Africa's strategic value to the Western alliance.

SUMMARY

LANGUAGE, POWER AND HUMAN GROUPS

Categorisation

One of the major ways in which people distinguish between the various perceptions they make is through the process of **categorisation**. This means that the 'sense data' collected by individuals is organised into systems of 'belonging'. Categorisation is, therefore, the process of placing objects, events or living things in a series of *classes* or groups.

Traditional views of categorisation

Traditional approaches to categorisation assume that it codifies human experience in terms of *similarity*, while the philosopher Wittgenstein used the concept of 'family resemblances', where there exists a series of relationships between the members, each sharing a number of features but none encompassing all the possible criteria for membership.

Another alternative to the 'classical' theory was also proposed by William Labov in 1973. In one experiment, he presented a series of pictures of various receptacles to a group of students. Labov wished to discover whether there would be variations in the way each pictorial representation was named once different *uses* of the objects were suggested to the students. This proved to be the case.

Types of category: superordinate and basic

The difference between **superordinate** and **basic** categories is set out. A superordinate category is one which refers to the *general* class of whatever is being described, whether these are concepts, objects, events or living things. A *basic*-level category is more specific. There is a *hierarchy* of descriptive classes. For example, the following list shows a hierarchical progression: *chair*, *furniture*, *artefact* and *entity*. As the list of categories grows, each in succession indicates a greater range of significance. Each is more *inclusive* than the previous category on the list. The *basic* level, however, is the most commonly used in everyday speech.

Innocent parts of language?

Basic-level terms may appear to be the most natural and innocent parts of language. However, some theories of ideology assume that it is exactly the *ordinary* names given to aspects of experience, and the *basic* divisions made between 'things in the world', which reflect a society's values and beliefs.

Categorisation and language acquisition

Learning about categories is a basic part of **language acquisition** and also, therefore, a feature of socialisation. As the infant learns how the world is described, it grows to understand the *value* attached to those descriptions. *Value* means the moral, social and political worth accorded to different things through language, and the strength or degree of *effect* likely to be achieved by the *use* of specific linguistic 'labels.'

The effectiveness of **appeals to shared values**, where authority makes an address to individuals or groups, is examined. There is a difference between understanding moral precepts and choosing to act in accordance with the values from which they emerge.

Making sense of experience?

Some writers argue that the human subject categorises perceptions in order to cope with all the different events which occur in life. Glass and Holyoak's view of representation is presented and various disagreements are laid out. Essentially, they see categorisation as a process which *limits* or *controls* the amount of mental processing humans are required to undertake. In response to this view, it should be noted that people are actually engaged in a great deal of 'processing' anyway; presented with a variety of experiences, which occur in a number of different contexts, individuals have constantly to update or re-evaluate their perceptions.

Recognising context

The importance of recognition of **context** is emphasised; individuals are often assisted in their identification of objects, events and persons by the general nature of the situation in which each phenomenon is found.

Collective perceptions

It is important to realise that categories are established in the material practice of language use, and are therefore an important part of the *social process*, providing evidence of *collective* rather than merely individual perceptions. Categories should be understood as part of the 'outlook' of an entire culture at any given moment in its history.

The theory of **prototypes** is evaluated, while importance is accorded to the fact that human expression remains essentially **creative**; when events cannot be explained through the available terminology, new labels and categories are invented. The **act of naming** includes the production of new terms for new phenomena. The discovery of the 'Vu Quang ox' provides an example of this kind of naming.

Categorisation of people

As soon as we turn to consider people, we are dealing even more obviously with concepts of *the social*. An insight into the way that 'labels' are attached to different groups will help towards understanding the **social power** which is exercised through language.

Typage in verse is described, through reference to Semonides, an early Greek writer of the seventh century BC. Other forms of classification are cited, including the types of discrimination once practised by the **apartheid state** in South Africa. Modern and historical employment of **scare tactics** using negative categorisation are given in the text.

Mutually exclusive categories

One of the consequences of placing people in a particular category is the difficulty faced when they are found to 'belong' to more than one. Semin and Fiedler argue that powerful social categories 'may dominate the psychological field' in a way that 'inhibits multiple classification'. Rothbart and Taylor found evidence for this tendency in a statement made by Raymond Barre, prime minister of France in 1980. A synagogue on the Rue Copernic in Paris was bombed as part of a terrorist campaign against the state of Israel. Barre declared that: 'the criminal attack killed Jews as well as innocent Frenchmen'. The implication was clear that, in Barre's mind, being Jewish placed some of the victims outside the categories 'innocent' and 'French'.

Research evidence: categories which clash?

Research undertaken by Saltz and his colleagues in the late 1960s and early 1970s showed that young children demonstrate what is called the 'strong form' of mutual exclusivity, which takes the form of denial that an individual can belong at one and the same time to certain types of category. In a survey conducted in 1967, it was found that 63 per cent of 5-year-old children reported that a father who studied until he became a doctor would no longer be a father.

The power of contrast

Social categories work by indicating what they are not,

as much as what they are. They are essentially **contrastive**, implicitly drawing attention to differences.

'Natural kind', 'human artefact' and 'social' categories

Rothbart and Taylor make a distinction between **natural kind** and **human artefact** categories. They also refer to **social** categories, and argue that people are inclined to view categories of natural kind as 'less arbitrary' than those of artefact kinds. Things in the natural world are treated as though they have essential attributes that *cannot be changed*, so that the distinction between each category is thought to reflect some unchangeable truth about the thing which is categorised. In contrast, the names attached to human artefact categories are thought not to express the *essence* or essential qualities of the things which are named.

Social categories

Social categories are in reality very close to human artefact categories (those reserved for the *things* people have made). Social and artefact categories are similar because both are used, by human subjects, to organise *social* reality. The problem is that social categories are treated by most people as though they have more in common with natural kind categories.

CATEGORISATION AND THE STEREOTYPE

Allport said that 'the human mind must think with the aid of categories'. Once they have been formed, categories become 'the basis for normal pre-judgement'. **Stereotypes**, also associated with pre-judgement, are generally regarded as a form of negative categorisation, and are thus most often understood as a type of *prejudice*. The *established* definition of stereotyping is:

- the practice of making simplistic and usually negative social identifications of certain groups, in which the supposed attributes of the group are applied to all those identified (rightly or wrongly) as group members.

In other words, the process of stereotyping is said to work by taking the traits and characteristics thought to belong to specific groups, and reapplying them to individuals.

Stereotyping: flawed understanding?

The traditional approach to the question of stereotyping not only regards it as negative but also embraces the idea that it is *inaccurate*, or in some way flawed or inadequate. The notion which lies behind this view is that the people who are 'labelled' do not really resemble their stereotypes. Many theorists continue to argue that our perception of *group characteristics* is by and large a distortion of reality.

Alternative views of stereotyping

A number of investigations have made a stand against the tide of 'deficiency' theorists. There is often an inequality of *power* between the groups, with the stronger being able to deploy negative characterisations with more effect. It is not the stereotype itself which is most dangerous, but the imbalance of power which allows the dissemination of negative views.

The idea that stereotyping is a 'malfunction' does indeed require some revision, but it would be a mistake to decide, just because stereotypes emerge from the 'natural' process of categorisation, that they should be exempt from close scrutiny into their *effects*.

Stereotyping as differentiation

If we accept the idea that stereotyping is really about **differentiating** between one group and another, then it is not surprising that much of it is, after all, at least *contrastive* and also on occasion negative. The purpose would seem to be the need to create distinctions between the group to which one belongs and other groups. Negative judgements about others would therefore be a kind of side effect rather than the primary objective of the process.

Stereotypes and group membership

One of the most enduring concepts used when group theory is applied to the process of stereotyping is found in the notion of 'in-groups' and 'out-groups'. An 'in-group' is the collective with which the subject identifies, while an 'out-group' is a body which possesses contrasting and supposedly less desirable characteristics. We may find that we characterise ourselves in certain ways at certain times in order to gain the best advantage from different situations.

The section on **descriptions of the self** follows the idea that individuals need to make a positive self-identification, and uses the example of the 1976 trial of Steve Biko. **The recuperation of negative categories** outlines the idea that the negative characterisation of groups by their rivals may result in unintended effects. The negative value of the label may be turned into a positive one. Ideas about **group solidarity** are also explored. It is noticeable that stereotypes are employed in some situations but not in others.

Displacement of aggression

Some approaches have stressed that stereotyping is the displacement of frustration and aggression from oneself to an 'out-group'. Such an approach is often applied to cases of racism or attachment to fascist ideology. In such instances, the rage felt against the subject's own social or economic deprivation is supposedly transferred to some innocent group, which is then characterised as having caused all the problems which are endured. There are, however, certain deficiencies in this approach.

GROUP COMMUNICATION
Criteria for identifying a group

In 1951, G.C. Homans (see *The Human Group*) defined a group as:

'a number of persons who communicate with each other often enough over a span of time and who are few enough so that each person is able to communicate with all the others, not at secondhand through other people but face to face'.

The central features here are **frequency** of contact over **time**, the idea that the group is manageable in size, and the importance given to direct **inter-personal** or 'face-to-face' communication. A comprehensive description of group communication usually includes some reference to the **goals** and **values** which are supposed to be shared by groups, and to the ways in which groups categorise themselves and others.

Group size: primary and secondary groups

A **primary** group is small in size and its members have frequent face-to-face contact. A **secondary** group is more extended in size and is less able to provide an opportunity for personal contact between all its members.

Group structure: formal and informal groups

Groups may also be either **formal** or **informal**. The first type includes groups which possess a formal set of aims and objectives, laid out in advance of any tasks it undertakes. Informal groups are those which arise more naturally and spontaneously, and include friendship and peer groups (Figure 3.3).

The question of **belonging** is also examined. Part of the problem in defining groups lies in the question of choice, since some groups are deliberately chosen, while in other cases individuals find that membership is less than voluntary.

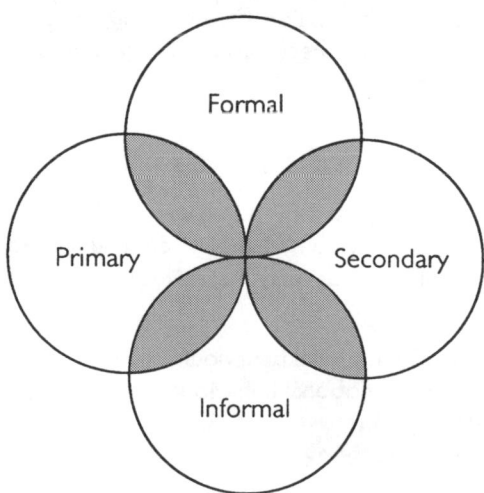

Figure 3.3   Possible composition of groups

Women as a social group

Jennifer Coates advocates the idea that women constitute a distinct social group. Although it is 'a very unusual social group', they seem to share a 'recognisable and distinctive sub-culture' and a positive social identity.

J.A. Williams and H. Giles see women as a *disadvantaged* gender group, whose social identity is constructed through *comparison* with men. They argue that the kind of remedial action taken by women may be either individual or collective in nature.

Skevington and Baker believe that Williams and Giles make the mistake of assuming that womanhood is perceived by all women in the same way. G.M. Breakwell suggests that there is in fact no agreed view of women's identity. If this is the case, it is unlikely that they could be described as a social group.

Class, sexuality and ethnicity in women's identity

Feminist writers in particular have helped to focus attention on the *subjective* elements of social research. They have asked how gendered individuals actually experience inequality in society. Just as it is misleading to treat the individual (the social subject) as 'neutral' in terms of gender, it is also a mistake to imagine that all the members of a particular sex will perceive their position and experiences in the same way. Gloria Joseph argues that: 'Both marxist and feminist analysis do gross injustice to Black women.'

Groups: ascribed and free

One problem faced in defining groups turns on the question of who does the 'labelling' or classification, and whether or not those described as members agree with the category ascribed to them. On many occasions, the use of a general category may obscure the very different types of conduct which occur within the 'group' itself.

Formation of groups

The reasons for the **formation** of a group emerge from two basic requirements: the need to achieve a *specific material goal*, and the desire to acquire or reinforce a *shared social identity*.

Development of groups deals with the theory of B.W. Tuckman, who proposed that the 'life' of a group goes through four stages before it reaches maturity.

THE GROUP AND THE INDIVIDUAL: SOCIAL IDENTIFICATION

Hogg and Abrams argue that groups have 'a profound impact on individuals' identity'. The groups they identify include national, religious, political, ethnic, sex, tribal and youth. They believe that 'the groups to which people belong will be massively significant in determining their life experiences'.

These authors are interested in how individuals express their own sense of belonging or *identification*. Hogg and Abrams search for evidence of how an individual's identity is acquired through membership of groups. Oakes, Haslam and Turner investigate the way that group character is created through the interaction of individual and group identity.

Social identity: a matter of choice

Social identity is a reference not simply to the fact that the individual knows that he or she belongs to a group, but also to the fact that the person concerned attaches some value to his or her membership of the group, feeling some emotional attachment to it. This means that **self-description** would be the most important aspect of the attachment an individual feels for a group. In such a case, group membership is chosen, and is not imposed or merely accidental. **'Psychological' groups** and **groups formed to combat a threat** are used to explore the idea of group membership.

Groups: goals and values

The extent to which goals and values are actually held in common depends on whether individuals:

- join a group willingly;
- have full knowledge of the aims and objectives of the group;
- sincerely accept the goals, values, and models of behaviour which the group appears to value.

The attitudes and values held by **gang members** are revealed in a study of the attitudes revealed by a gang leader in Los Angeles.

Group conflict

There has, in recent years, been much debate over the causes of inter-group conflict. A number of writers have emphasised the notion that conflict can arise for quite trivial reasons. This position is criticised in some detail.

ANALYSIS OF GROUP INTERACTION
Primitive models

One method for recording group interaction is to design a simple 'tally' system, in which each participant is represented by a labelled circle, and a mark is placed inside the appropriate circle each time a person speaks. This system is quite primitive, creating a record of frequency of intervention, but providing no insight whatsoever into duration, impact, style or form of the contributions made. For instance, a high degree of intervention will not necessarily indicate that the speaker will be influential.

Interaction process analysis

This system was proposed by R.F. Bales in 1950, and was built on the notion that all communicative behaviours within groups may be divided into four main areas:

- **positive** socio-emotional behaviour;
- **negative** socio-emotional behaviour;
- **information giving**;
- **information receiving**.

Discourse analysis and visual observation are described as a useful contemporary method of analysing group communication. The principles of discourse analysis are detailed. **Group speech events** and **formal exchange** also appear as a study, using examples of speech events. **Informal exchange** is featured as well.

COMMUNICATION AND POWER
Descriptions of power: capacity and use

Power means both the **capacity** to do something and the active **use** of that capacity. Communication research is usually devoted to calculating the effect of deliberate messages formed by individuals or collectives with the intention of attaining a specific result.

Power 'at rest?'

Power need not be always exercised, since it is also *structural* in nature.

Power: negative or positive effects?

Since power is both the capacity to affect the natural and social environment, and the exercise of dominance by societies, institutions, groups or individuals over any other social category, various writers have argued over whether power should be seen as generally **negative** or **positive** in its effects.

Distribution of power

There are a number of perspectives on the subject of power as it manifests itself in our society, but all commentators acknowledge the fact that there are certain inequalities in its distribution.

Theories of power are described, including **authoritarianism**, **pluralism**, **functionalism** and **leftism**. The section which follows this discussion explores the development of ideas which grew from the radical and Marxist perspectives on power, including **Gramsci's theory of hegemony**, the approach of the **Frankfurt School**, and the ideas of Nicos Poulantzas, David Coates, David Tetzlaff, Jurgen Habermas and Michel Foucault.

POWER AS A RELATIONSHIP

The approach advanced in this book is that power needs to be understood as a **relationship**. The relationships of power are numerous. Power can exist between individuals, between individuals and groups, and between groups and other collective forms such as whole societies.

The operation of power: authority and solidarity

The operation of power was represented in this chapter by the diagram in Figure 3.7.

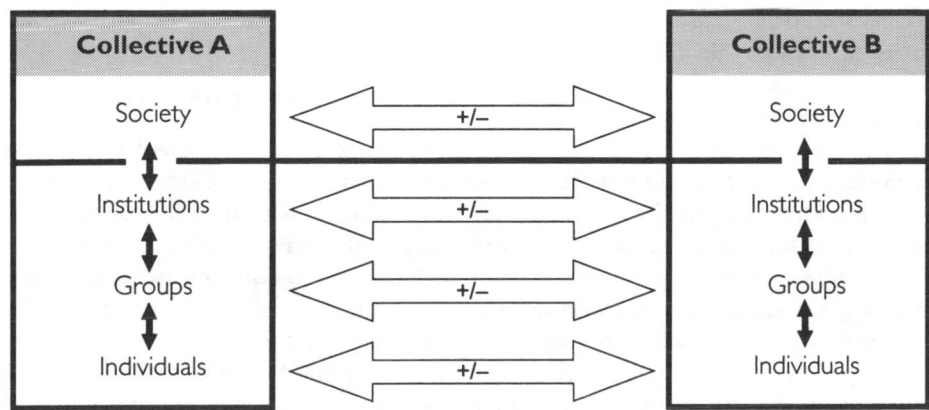

Figure 3.7   Operation of power

This diagram represents two collectives, where relationships of power are established internally between the components of each collective (seen in the vertical plane) and externally between elements of both collectives (shown in the horizontal plane).

Types of authority are described, including Max Weber's description of three types: **charismatic** authority, **traditional** authority, and **rational-legal** authority.

Reference to the **coercive power of the state** examines the use of power in early Bolshevik Russia. Other forms of Marxism, particularly those with a libertarian perspective, appear in this section.

THE POWER OF LANGUAGE
Linguistics

Linguistics was once taken to indicate the study of the grammatical properties of language, which includes:

- *morphology* – the structure of words;
- *syntax* – the structure of sentences;
- *phonology* – the 'sound structures' of human utterance;
- *semantics* – the formal elements of meaning.

Language: langue and parole

Saussure divided the study of language into **langue**, the system of rules underlying speech, and **parole**, the speech of individuals, regarded as the infinitely variable expression of those abstract rules. Langue is a collective system, the true expression of which is found in societies rather than individuals. The utterances of actual speakers are accorded a less exalted place than the underlying structures upon which they are thought to depend.

The section on **developments in linguistics** includes reference to sociolinguistics and Jennifer Coates's study of **women, men and language**. Coates's research into the different styles and purposes which exist in male and female language use is cited. She believes that 'women's conversational style is based on solidarity, while men's is based on power, a difference arising directly from women's and men's membership of a patriarchal society'.

Other differences account for what Coates calls 'miscommunication', where men and women fail to communicate properly because they have learned different rules for conversation during childhood and adolescence. Coates identifies eight 'problem areas' which cause miscommunication.

Language: capacity, use and prohibition

It is possible to investigate the **capacity** of language, in the sense that its range of capabilities may be explored. The aim would be to define the *boundaries* of the social power of language. It would then be possible to examine the degree of power found in intentional language use, including 'ordinary' speech and the employment of persuasive systems like rhetoric.

Language, power and structure

When the question of **power** is introduced into the study of language, it should not be merely as a specialist study of some sort. The power of language emerges from *material* requirements, from the necessity to operate successfully in the natural and social environments we inhabit.

Language and social power

If language is the primary vehicle for organising human affairs, whether those affairs are structured in competitive or co-operative ways, and power is quite simply the organised capacity of human individuals and groups to affect their environment, then the use of language is 'inevitably an instrument for enacting, recreating, or subverting power'.

Ordinary competencies

I indicated above that theorists who study the power of language as a specialised form often look at polished examples of public speech. However, their investigations may in fact have identified a number of effects which are part of the **competencies** of **ordinary discourse**. If speech is social, and *constructs* social reality, then the ordinary interactions made in the course of daily existence will reflect this connection, and will form the most valuable basic evidence of the workings of power in language.

Performative utterances

Performatives are statements which match the performance of an action at the same time as the words themselves are spoken. J.L. Austin used the example of the performative statement 'I name this ship', where this is not a merely a description of what is being done, but also the actual *performance of the act* of naming the ship.

Performatives and power

One of the features of power must be, as Austin says, the fact that the utterance must be delivered by the **appropriate person**. Austin noticed that the concept of a performative speech act extended to statements like 'I warn you' and 'I apologise', where the act of warning or apologising is actually *performed* in speech.

Rhetorical psychology

Rhetorical psychology is an approach to the public use of language. Although the idea of analysing rhetoric usually suggests inquiries into the public speeches of the powerful, a rhetorical approach deals also with the ideas and opinions expressed by 'ordinary' individuals.

Ideology and the human subject

The term 'ideology' was first used in France at the end of the eighteenth century, and meant originally a 'study of ideas'. At the end of various transformations, it has now come to mean 'systems of belief'. Three conditions must be met before something may be regarded as *ideological*:

- The ideas concerned must be shared by a significant number of individuals.
- The ideas must form a coherent system, whose elements support one another to make a recognisable structure.
- The ideas must have some relationship to the use of power in society.

Opinion and the citizen

Michael Billig is unhappy with those theories of ideology which assume that every public address made by the powerful succeeds in influencing the subject population. He believes that the approach of theorists like Althusser neglects 'the chatter and argument of everyday life', or the philosophising of the 'everyday'.

Rhetoric in the political arena

Rhetoric means the art of using language to persuade or influence the human subject. It is usually applied to persuasive attempts directed at an audience, often in some formal or institutional setting. Max Atkinson's study of modern political rhetoric is critically assessed.

Rhetorical devices

The basic techniques employed in party political address include:

- the **rule of three** or the **three-part list**, where a politician makes three points in a row, the third of which is the culmination of the utterance, and which is intended to prompt applause;
- the use of **contrast** or **juxtaposition**, where two alternatives are presented to an audience, one of which clearly represents an undesirable state of affairs and is meant to be rejected in favour of the choice preferred by the speaker;
- the biased presentation of a rival's position for the purposes of ridicule, known as **paper tigers** or **'set them up and knock them down'** (the point being to show one's own policy as vastly superior);
- the **inclusive 'we'**, where an address attempts to represent the interests and opinions of speaker and audience as identical;
- **rhetorical questions**, whose answers are either supplied by the speaker, or are meant to be so obvious as to require no response;
- **assertion** – the use of statements rather than argument;
- **repetition**, where a statement is repeated in the hope that it will eventually be accepted by an audience;
- **negative identification**, in which a rival is pinpointed and identified as the cause of various misfortunes.

Rhetoric in the public arena reproduces extracts from the speeches of two Conservative politicians. This is contrasted with the **informal context** which Billig recognises in local party politics.

STUDENT ACTIVITIES

CATEGORISATION OF PEOPLE
Revision: Physical appearance

Some of the most powerful acts of social categorisation are based on very simple aspects of human experience. This includes the idea (see Rothbart and Taylor in Semin and Fiedler, *Language, Interaction and Social Cognition*, p. 26) that 'deep, underlying attributes are inferred from appearance', implying that the presence of *physical* differences may 'have a . . . special status in intergroup attitudes'. Rothbart and Taylor argue that:

> 'the imposition of natural kind structure onto our thinking about social categories gives disproportionate strength to category differences correlated with physical appearance. This prediction seems consistent with what we know about the ubiquity and power of stereotypes based on race and gender.'

In this scenario, individuals' physical appearance leads to the creation of a great many assumptions about their character and category membership. The widespread power of the form of characterisation called 'stereotyping' is felt by these authors to grow from the tendency to regard the 'social' labels attached to people as though they reflect the essence of the individuals or groups concerned. G.W. Allport insisted that 'the human mind must think with the aid of categories' and that once they have been formed, categories become 'the basis for normal prejudgement' (see *The Nature of Prejudice*, p. 20).

CHARACTER AND APPEARANCE
Describing the villain of the piece – 1

Read the extract below from Ian Fleming's *Goldfinger* and answer the questions which follow:

> When Goldfinger had stood up, the first thing that struck Bond was that everything was out of proportion. Goldfinger was short, not more than five feet tall, and on top of the thick body and blunt peasant legs, was set almost directly into the shoulders a huge, and it seemed, exactly round head. It was as if Goldfinger had been put together with bits of other people's bodies.
>
> Nothing seemed to belong. Perhaps, Bond thought, it was to conceal his ugliness that Goldfinger made such a fetish of sunburn. Without the red-brown camouflage the pale body would be grotesque. The face, under the cliff of crew-cut carroty hair, was startling, without being as ugly as the body. It was moon-shaped without being moon-like. The forehead was fine and high and the thin sandy brows were level above the large light-blue eyes fringed with pale lashes. The nose was fleshily aquiline between high cheek bones and cheeks that were more muscular than fat. The mouth was thin and dead straight, but beautifully drawn. The chin and jaws were firm and glinted with health. To sum up, thought Bond, it was the face of a thinker, perhaps a scientist, who was ruthless, sensual, stoical and tough. An odd combination.

Questions

1   Why has the author chosen to describe Goldfinger's legs as 'blunt *peasant* legs'?

2   'It was as if Goldfinger had been put together with bits of other people's bodies.' At this point, of what exactly is the reader supposed to be reminded?

3   We see Goldfinger through Bond's eyes. Is it possible to make any judgements about *Bond's* character, through studying his attitude to Goldfinger?

4   Why are villains so often described as intelligent and strong, yet also sensual?

Describing the villain of the piece – 2

Read the following extract from Charles Dickens's *David Copperfield*, in which the narrator (Copperfield himself) describes an encounter with Uriah Heep, a villainous clerk. Comment on the following issues: character, physical appearance, the connotations of the villain's name, and the author's attitudes to social class.

> I found Uriah reading a great fat book, with such demonstrative attention, that his lank forefinger followed up every line as he read and made clammy tracks along the page (or so I fully believed) like a snail.
> 'You are working late tonight, Uriah', says I.
> 'Yes, Master Copperfield', says Uriah.
> As I was getting on the stool opposite, to talk to him more conveniently, I observed that he had not such a thing as a smile about him, and that he could only widen his mouth and make two hard creases down his cheeks, one on each side, to stand for one.
> 'I am not doing office work, Master Copperfield', said Uriah.
> 'What work, then?' I asked.
> I am improving my legal knowledge, Master Copperfield', said Uriah . . .
> My stool was such a tower of observation, that as I watched him reading on again, after this rapturous exclamation, and following up the lines with his forefinger, I observed that his nostrils, which were thin and pointed, with sharp dints in them, had a singular and most uncomfortable way of expanding and contracting themselves – that they seemed to twinkle instead of his eyes, which hardly ever twinkled at all.
> 'I suppose you are quite a great lawyer' I said, after looking at him for some time.
> 'Me, Master Copperfield?' said Uriah. 'Oh no! I'm a very 'umble person.'

Obsolete heroes: *Alamein to Zem Zem*

Read the following piece from *Alamein to Zem Zem* by Keith Douglas. The book is Douglas's account of a tank commander's war in the western desert in 1942. In this passage, Douglas describes one of his regiment's senior officers:

> Guy, the second-in-command of the regiment, . . . was older than Piccadilly Jim [the commanding officer] and had been in the regiment, I think, longer than anyone. He was fantastically rich and handsome, and appeared, as indeed he was, a figure straight out of the nineteenth century. He was charming and entirely obsolete. His ideas were feudal in the best sense – he regarded everyone in the regiment as his tenants, sub-tenants, serfs, etc., and felt his responsibilities to them as a landlord. Everyone loved him and I believe pitied him a little. His slim, beautifully clad figure remained among our dirty greasy uniforms as a symbol of the regiment's former glory. He seldom, if ever, wore a beret – on this particular occasion I remember he had a flannel shirt and brown stock pinned with a gold pin, a waistcoat of some sort of yellow suede lined with sheep's wool . . . on his head was a peaked cap with a chinstrap like glass, perched at a jaunty angle. His moustache was an exact replica of those worn by heroes of the Boer war, his blue eye had a courageous twinkle, and he had the slim strong hands of a mannered horseman. He chafed at having to keep out of the enemy's range when he might have charged the guns in line, and found the matter of writing a report afterwards very tedious. When it was done, six-figure map-references and all, he showed it proudly to Tom, and said 'Glance over that will you, Tom? See if it's all in order, you know, and all that'. Checking up on the map references, Tom found the actions reported taking place somewhere in the sea off Benghazi.

Questions

1   Identify the places where Douglas uses physical description to reinforce the judgements he makes of Guy's character.

2   'Everyone loved him and I believe pitied him a little.' Why is Guy 'pitied'?

STEREOTYPES: FLAWED UNDERSTANDING?

Revision: Categorisation and the stereotype

We saw above that Allport thought that once categories were formed they become 'the basis for normal pre-judgement' (see *The Nature of Prejudice*, p. 20). **Stereotypes**, also associated with pre-judgement, are generally regarded as a form of negative categorisation, and are thus most often understood as a type of *prejudice*. Prejudice may be defined as an extreme attitude which can be found in the *cognitive*, *emotional* and *behavioural* attributes of human subjects.

Although it is sometimes argued that the stereotype is a 'neutral' form of descriptive category, and that prejudice may be either 'positive' or 'negative' (prejudice *for* as well as prejudice *against*), most case-studies involving such theories concentrate upon their negative associations. As early as 1942, Zawadzski declared that (Oakes, p. 21):

> 'traits are selected, not because they are actually most found among members of the group, but because they serve best the malicious intent of ridiculing or discrediting the group'.

In everyday speech, terms like prejudice are nearly always employed to indicate the existence of negative values. I would therefore describe the *established* definition of stereotyping as:

- the practice of making simplistic and usually negative social identifications of certain groups, in which the supposed attributes of the group are applied to all those identified (rightly or wrongly) as group members.

In other words, the process of stereotyping is said to work by taking the traits and characteristics thought to belong to specific groups, and reapplying them to individuals.

The traditional approach to stereotyping

The traditional approach to the question of stereotyping not only regards it as negative but also embraces the idea that it is *inaccurate*, or in some way flawed or inadequate. The notion which lies behind this view is that the people who are 'labelled' do not really resemble their stereotypes. While there is no doubt, as Oakes, Haslam and Turner point out (see *Stereotyping and Social Reality*, p. 2), that 'groups are part of social reality', many theorists continue to argue that our perception of *group characteristics* is by and large a distortion of reality.

Doubts about the accuracy of perception of *groups*, and the tendency to regard group behaviour as somehow a distortion of true conduct, have been responsible for the belief that *interpersonal* communication and studies of individual psychology reveal a more accurate picture of human character. Evidence of this tendency may be found in those communication textbooks which dwell on interaction in 'dyads' and which make pleas for people to be appreciated as individuals, and not as 'members of a crowd'.

The fact that many researchers have taken the view that stereotyping arises from a warped process, resulting in a mistaken conception of both individuals and groups, has meant that vast efforts have been expended in trying to find what Oakes and her colleagues (see *Stereotyping and Social Reality*) call 'the psychological basis of that deficiency'.

Alternative views of stereotyping

A number of writers have made a stand against the tide of 'deficiency' theory. Fishman, writing in 1956, believed stereotypes to be valid to the extent that they reflected the actual *interactions* which take place between groups, both those groups which were categorised, and those which were responsible for applying the stereotype concerned. Sherif (1967) also argued that stereotypes reflected the reality of *inter-group relations*.

The idea that stereotypes reflect the *reality* of inter-group relations does not mean that the groups concerned are always *equally* responsible for the *use* of stereotypes. One aspect which is usually neglected or under-valued is the fact that there is often an inequality of *power* between the groups, with the stronger being able to deploy negative characterisations with more effect. It is not the stereotype itself which is most dangerous, but the imbalance of power which allows the dissemination of negative views.

The idea that stereotyping is a 'malfunction' does indeed require some revision. At the same time, we should exercise caution. It would be a mistake to decide, just because stereotypes emerge from the 'natural' process of categorisation, that they should be exempt from close scrutiny into their *effects*. If the difficulty with a 'negative' view of stereotyping is that it fails to examine the roots of the process, the problem created by 'neutral' approaches is that they are unlikely to provide a critical perspective on discriminatory forms of *behaviour*.

Stereotyping as differentiation

Tajfel argued that the negative and positive aspects of stereotyping grow from the process of categorisation itself (see his 1969 article 'Cognitive aspects of Prejudice'). The need to identify oneself in a reasonably positive way is therefore presumably a *social* need, involving the wish to find something in common with groups thought desirable. The group need not necessarily be physically present. Immediate physical proximity is not a prerequisite for categorising the self.

CATEGORISATION OF EVENTS
Research: Popular discourses

Read the material below and carry out the research activity which follows:

The investigation of ideology and power often concentrates on major political events and the 'large-scale' messages which are carried by the national media. In contrast, research into 'ordinary' forms of public communication is rarely concerned with ideological issues. In other words, catch-phrases, clichés, jokes and 'formulaic' exchanges are seen as part of socialisation and the 'social functional', whose purpose is to help 'affiliate' people to other individuals, institutions or societies. These types of communication are not always regarded as relevant to important public issues.

However, any idea which circulates in public discourse, whether part of a 'grand narrative' or taken from ordinary 'common sense', has to provide a *plausible* or attractive explanation of events. At certain periods, 'fashions of speech' are identifiable; individuals pick up and repeat phrases which are used regularly in certain contexts. Sometimes these achieve a significant degree of usage in a society. Certain terms, for instance, have attained considerable popularity in recent years: 'sad', for example, has come to mean not simply the condition of unhappiness, but also a state of severe social inadequacy. Or again, individuals (acting perhaps under the influence of American culture) exhort their acquaintances to 'get a life'.

Often, ideas which appear in the media are constructed on fairly simple lines, usually in the hope that they will be 'taken up' by media audiences, promoting a version of events that can prove advantageous to various establishment groups, especially at times like general elections. However, ideas are usually reinterpreted by groups and individuals in the light of their own experience. For example, the England rugby squad's defeat by New Zealand in the world cup semi-final on 18 June 1995 was attributed in some sections of the press to the commanding presence of Jonah Lomu, New Zealand's no. 11. While it is true that Lomu's contribution (four tries and a number of vital tackles) was central to his team's victory, such a simple and popular explanation could obscure other issues, including the deficiencies in England's style of play. Where an audience feels that their expertise equals or exceeds the quality of opinion found on television and in newspapers, media explanation of events may be treated with caution.

The media's role in the *circulation* of certain notions, contributing towards what I would call '**popular discourses**', can be seen in the way that events are *categorised*. Once a particular class of events has been established, it is quite easy to place similar incidents within the same broad category. For example, consider the following headline from a page of the *Somerset County Gazette* of 16 June 1995:

'Driver hit twice in "road rage" incident.'

The article goes on to read: '"Road rage" incidents of angry motorists attacking fellow drivers who annoy them are increasing in Taunton.'

Study of the article reveals that it is based on a court case in which one driver was accused of assaulting another at a set of traffic lights. This kind of incident is not particularly unusual, and at one time would perhaps have been described as an example of common assault. The article, however, has categorised the event differently; the reference to 'road rage' indicates the newspaper's awareness of a 'new' trend which has already achieved notice at a national level. The inverted commas around the term 'road rage' indicate its somewhat provisional status (in contrast, the long-established term *special needs* appears in another article on the same page, but without inverted commas.) Once this sort of category has been created, however, any further incidents may be attributed to the same cause, and used in turn as evidence of an increase in the 'road rage' phenomenon.

Research

1 Choose an issue which has 'made the headlines' and collect news reports from a number of different sources, including newspapers and television broadcasts.

2 Set up a debate on the issue concerned, using no more than three speakers, and record the event on audio tape.

3 Make a transcript of those passages in which individuals seem to use 'popular discourses', or in which they repeat well-known arguments in support of their point of view.

4 Examine the press and broadcast material and compare it to the transcripts. Are similar arguments, examples or even phrases in evidence?

5 Where similarity exists, discuss this question: does it indicate the dominance of mass media discourses over public expression, or does it show that the media attempt to reflect public opinion?

Example – extracts from a transcript

This debate on capital punishment was recorded on 27 April 1995. All three participants are female students:

1A: I don't actually agree with it at all though (1) like the Birmingham Six (.) they would be dead
B: Yeah (1) but if people re-offend after coming out of prison (2)
A: What about crimes of passion *everyone* would end up being killed wouldn't they? (laughter)

2A: Someone in the jury should have to do it [carry out an execution] (1) someone who's actually said he's guilty or she's guilty or whatever
B: In America who do they have doing it (.) is it three people?
C: Yes (.) all three pull the switch and no-one knows who's done it ...
B: If our children (1) if someone murdered my kids or something or someone from my family (.) I'd want them dead
A: You may not have the right person though (1) you have to think about that
B: You do if you watch them do it (.) yeah? ...

3A: I think it's more of a punishment to spend the rest of your life in prison
B: It isn't because it's not that bad any more (2) they've got golf courses on some of them (laughter) they have (.) you've seen it in the newspapers

THE ANALYSIS OF SPEECH
Revision: Women, men and language

Read the following edited extract from Chapter 3, then study the speech events which follow:

In 1986, Jennifer Coates produced the first edition of *Women, Men and Language*. A second edition

Figures 3.9–3.12   Debate in progress

followed in 1993. Coates investigated the relationship between language and gender, where gender means (p. 3) 'socially constructed categories based on sex'.

The point of such a project is not really to identify patterns of sexism in language use, but rather to investigate the whole range of difference evident in the verbal interactions which take place *between* men and women as distinct social *groups*.

A number of feminist academics, however, object to the concept of women as a unified social group.

Coates described the two main approaches which are used to explain the 'structured social variation' found between the speech of men and women: these are the **dominance** approach and the **difference** approach. The first theory promotes the idea that women are an oppressed group, and that male power is (p. 13) 'enacted through linguistic practice'. The second theory proceeds from the view that men and women belong to different subcultures. Coates argues that (p. 84):

'Social groups need to assert their distinctiveness, and language is one way of doing this. It looks as though there are strong cultural pressures on men and women to distinguish themselves from each other, even though other groupings (such as social class, ethnic group, age) notionally place them together.'

Women and men: competition vs. co-operation?

Coates also devotes time to examining research carried out into the different styles and purposes which exist in male and female language use. She notes that men (p. 10):

'typically adopt a competitive style in conversation, treating their turn as a chance to overturn earlier speakers' contributions and to make their own point as forcibly as possible'.

In contrast to this style, women tend to use a more co-operative approach. They add to rather than demolish other speakers' contributions. Whereas women's co-operative style was once regarded as tentative or weak, some recent approaches have emphasised the positive aspects of such discursive practices. In conclusion (p. 203), Coates finds that:

'women's conversational style is based on solidarity, while men's is based on power, a difference arising directly from women's and men's membership of a patriarchal society'.

Other differences account for what Coates calls 'miscommunication', where men and women fail to communicate properly because they have learned different rules for conversation during childhood and adolescence. Coates identifies eight 'problem areas' which cause miscommunication. These are:

- **minimal responses**, where forms like 'yeah' or 'mhm' are used by women to show that they are listening, though men take them to indicate agreement;
- **questions**, employed rhetorically by women to assist the flow of conversation, while men believe they are being asked for information;
- **links between speaker turns**, in which women refer to the contribution of the previous speaker, while men have a tendency to ignore previous speech acts;
- **topic shifts**, multiple in the case of men and much rarer in women's conversation;
- **self-disclosure**, avoided by men and used co-operatively by women;
- **verbal aggressiveness**, supposedly enjoyed in all-male groups but disliked by women;
- **listening**, important to women but less so to men;
- **simultaneous speech**, which in male speech means a high degree of interruption, and in female speech is used to offer briefer and more supportive remarks.

Exercise: discourse analysis

Read the four conversations printed below, and in each case answer the questions which follow (source: transcripts made by Fiona Jenkinson, Somerset College, 1995). Is it possible to use Coates's ideas about the difference between the speech of men and women to work out the sex of each speaker? The sex of participants is given at the end of this set of activities. Single capital letters indicate the first letter of an individual's name.

Conversation 1

A: But (.) well what does she do now
B: erm (.) i don't know she
A: does she go to college
B: no actually i think she's (.) like (.) working
A: oh yeah (.) din't she (.) ain't she a waitress or something like that
B: yeah i think you're right
    she still going with J
A: i 'spect so
B: oh yeah you seen C recently
A: no (.) why
B: nothin' i ain't seen her in ages

Questions

1 What sex was speaker A, in your opinion? Please explain your answer.

2 What sex was speaker B, in your opinion? Please explain your answer.

Conversation 2

A: T (.) T (.) T like your hair
B: it's nice in't it
A: like your hair
C: oh do you
A: yeah (.) it's really nice
B: suits her dun' it
A: makes you look really pretty
C: what
A: makes you look really pretty
C: does it (.) i like it then
A: like your earring too (.) it looks better than the stud

Question

What sex was each speaker (A, B, C and D), in your opinion?

Please explain your answer.

Conversation 3

A: yeah but you should play for the fun of it shun't you (.) not just to win
B: yeah (.) but see S tells me that's absolute rubbish (.) he says he plays to win (.) he's not just playing for the sport of it
A: I don't think that's completely true though
C: depends on the individual though don't it K
B: sorry
D: I don't think it's true (.) I hate playing competitively

Question

What sex was each speaker (A, B, C and D), in your opinion?

Please explain your answer.

Now compare your answers with those printed at the end of this section.

Were there any answers which surprised you? Did expectation or pre-judgement on your part, including your reading of Coates, lead you to believe that certain types of utterance were likely to be 'typically' male or female?

DISCOURSE AND IDENTITY : A CHILDREN'S NARRATIVE
Revision: Narrative, the representation of experience

Read the following material from Chapter 1, then the material from Chapter 2, then study the children's book reprinted below (*Not Now Bernard*).

Narrative is essentially a way of organising material. It consists of both the plot or story-line used by the storyteller, and the methods employed to tell that story. Narrative should not be seen as simply a 'fictional' practice. Human beings report everyday events and encounters in the form of narrative, often with the express intention of showing how 'true to life' their experiences are.

In *Narrative Comprehension and Film* (p.1), Edward Branigan explains how:

> 'making narratives is a strategy for making our world of experiences and desires intelligible. It is a fundamental way of organising data.'

Branigan believes that narrative is directly related to the way in which human beings perceive their environment: it is 'a perceptual activity that organises data into a special pattern which represents and explains experience'.

Narrative transformation

Todorov, a Russian critic, identified a process through which all narratives appear to pass. A simplified version of his method would be to note that, in all stories, there is usually some state of *equilibrium* – all in the social world is as it should be. This is followed by a *disruption* of this state, leading to *disequilibrium*. In turn, there must be some *recognition* that things are not as they were, followed by an attempt to repair the damage caused by the disruption. The final phase sees a return to some kind of *equilibrium*.

Why do so many narratives have the same structure? The theorist Wallace Martin (see Branigan, p. 10) writes that:

> 'Identification of universal narrative patterns would seem to tell us not just about literature but about the nature of the mind and/or universal features of culture.'

In other words, narratives are similar in structure because they all grow from human culture and reflect the ways in which the human mind operates when faced with the need to organise and represent experience.

Revision: Identity (from Chapter 2)

One tradition of communication research regards human identity as a phenomenon which is *confirmed* by social interaction. The question which remains to be examined is: how is identity *created*? Although an infant will be shaped in ways which the adults around it may regard as 'natural', its upbringing will entail many forms of **instruction** and **sanction** designed to ensure it follows the norms of the social group. *Instruction* is the issuing of direct orders, *sanction* is the system of rules which allows the application of penalties or rewards, while **affirmation** is the positive encouragement of certain actions which are regarded as beneficial or morally desirable.

'Not now, Bernard'

Read the children's book reprinted below and the comments made on certain sequences, and answer the questions which also appear.

This text, first published in 1980 by Andersen Press, and regularly reprinted since, displays a fairly traditional approach to representation. Roles and relationships within this white, middle-class family are shown to be divided, in time-honoured fashion, according to gender. Father attempts DIY (he tries to bang a nail into a wall), or sits reading the newspaper. Mother cooks and performs other chores, though she is a little more versatile than her partner, taking on a wider variety of activities (she paints a wall).

Despite, or perhaps because of, the conventional appearance and conduct of the family, some unusual events occur.

The first two sequences show Bernard attempting to gain the attention of his parents. The use of repetition in the text is supposed to assist the young reader in learning certain words, but also makes an important point in the narrative: Bernard is being ignored.

In the first sequence, Bernard's interruption has traumatic consequences. His father strikes himself with a hammer. Notice that Bernard does no more than utter a simple greeting, the phatic 'Hello, Dad', which actually fails to open the channel of communication. (We may remember that the *phatic* uses of communication encompass those apparently conventional or ordinary exchanges whose content is considerably less important than their function as the *reinforcement* of social contact and social status.)

The second event echoes the first. Bernard, apparently cheerful, tries to talk to his mother. She, too, is unwilling to listen. Bernard is then shown considering his options.

In the third sequence, Bernard makes what appears to be a ploy to gain attention. The vivid imaginative world of the child is here expressed in a measured and grammatical sentence: 'There's a monster in the garden and it's going to eat me.' The unfortunate crack in the vase which occurs immediately after the interruption seems to provide Bernard's mother, once again, with an excuse to ignore him. The next sequence is curious; Bernard finds someone who will pay him some attention.

Bernard goes into the garden and there is indeed a monster there, standing under a tree, with a fierce expression on its face.

"Hello, Dad," said Bernard.

"Not now, Bernard," said his father.

Figure 3.13   Not Now, Bernard: Sequence 1

"Hello, Mum," said Bernard.

"Not now, Bernard," said his mother.

Figure 3.14   Sequence 2

"There's a monster in the garden and it's going to eat me," said Bernard.

"Not now, Bernard," said his mother.

Figure 3.15   Sequence 3

Bernard went into the garden.

"Hello, monster," he said to the monster.

Figure 3.16   Sequence 4

The monster ate Bernard up, every bit.

Then the monster went indoors.

Figure 3.17   Sequence 5

"ROAR," went the monster behind Bernard's mother.

"Not now, Bernard," said Bernard's mother.

Figure 3.18   Sequence 6

Question

I   Why does Bernard remain polite and cheerful?

Suddenly, in sequence 5, the 'hero' has been killed. The apparent direction of the narrative has changed. This will not be about Bernard's attempts to persuade his parents of the monster's existence.

Question

2   Is part of the point of this story that Bernard is *too* well-behaved?

Sequence 6 shows the entry of the monster into the domestic environment. At this point, I will resist the temptation to talk about the transference of the alien 'other' to the realm of 'civilisation' setting, because such references have become the stock in trade of the lazy academic. Suffice it to say that instead of Bernard's innocent inquiry comes the monster's roar. But all to no effect. 'Not now, Bernard', says the mother. The monster looks suitably bewildered.

Question

3   Why is the monster ignored?

The monster bit Bernard's father.

Figure 3.19   Sequence 7

"Not now, Bernard," said Bernard's father.

"Your dinner's ready," said Bernard's mother.

Figure 3.20   Sequence 8

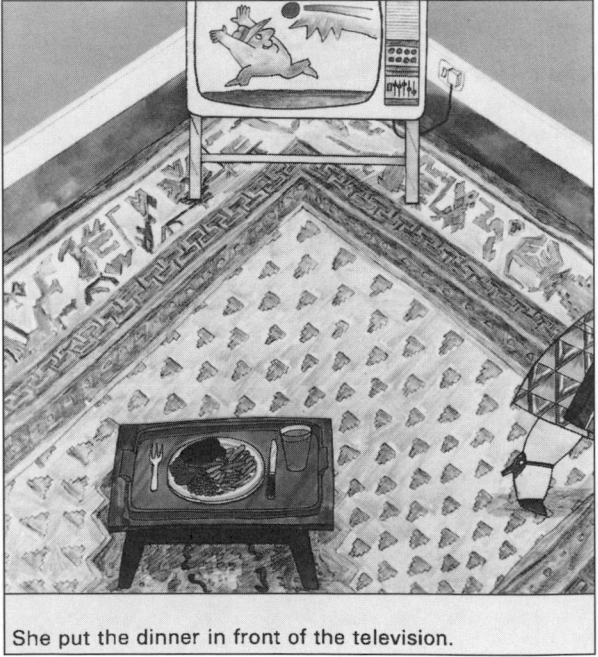

She put the dinner in front of the television.

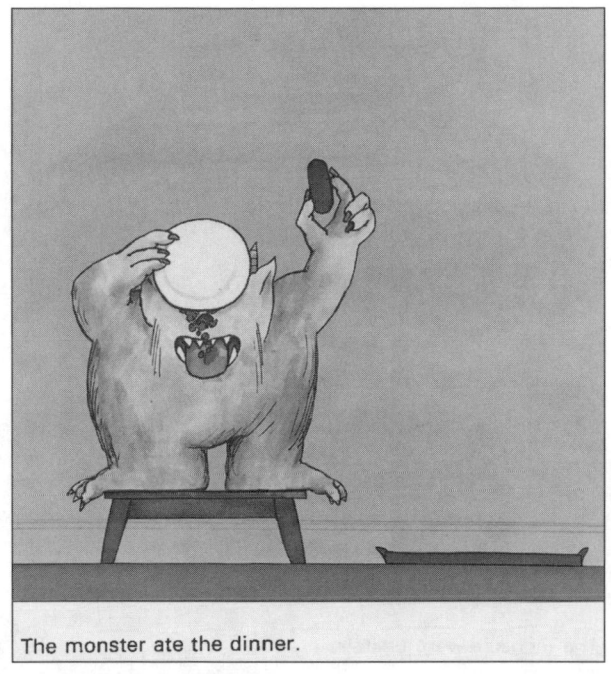
The monster ate the dinner.

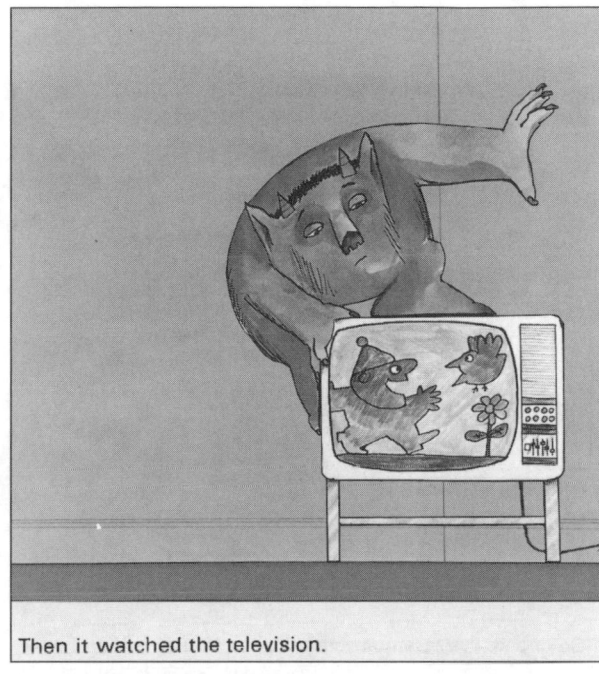
Then it watched the television.

Figure 3.21   Sequence 9

Then it read one of Bernard's comics.

And broke one of his toys.

Figure 3.22   Sequence 10

"Go to bed. I've taken up your milk," called Bernard's mother.

Figure 3.23   Sequence 11

The monster went upstairs.

"But I'm a monster," said the monster.

Figure 3.24   Sequence 12

"Not now, Bernard," said Bernard's mother.

The monster bites Bernard's father, but the same response is produced: it is ignored.

Question

4 Why does the bad behaviour of the monster go unpunished?

Question

5 Does Bernard always eat alone, in your opinion?

6 In sequences 9 and 10, in what sense is the monster's behaviour 'unsocialised'?

Bernard's mother announces bedtime.

Question

7 What has happened to the monster?

8 What is the moral of the story?

ESSAY TITLES

Questions

1 Some writers believe that true groups exist only where individuals consciously share a goal and a system of values.
On this basis, do *women* constitute a distinct social group?

2 'The process of stereotyping has *positive* as well as negative consequences.'
Discuss with reference to theories of subjectivity and self-identification.

3 'No name – no identity.'
True or false? Refer to theories of self and identity in your answer.

4 'Language is an entirely neutral tool; it is only when people *use* language that it becomes corrupt.'
To what extent is this a valid statement?

5 'An utterance is only meaningful when it is delivered in the appropriate context by the appropriate person.'
Discuss this statement, referring to at least two real speech events you have studied.

6 'If politicians use rhetorical devices in their public discourses, they are guaranteed a successful impact on their audiences.'

Discuss with reference to the form and content of public speech.

Answers to the questions on discourse and gender: in conversation 1, both speakers are female; in the second extract, A is male, while B and C are both female; in the final conversation, A and B are female, while C and D are male.

Communication and formal organisation

Formal organisations

Formal organisations: a definition

A **formal organisation** may be described as a human collective which is created in order to pursue an explicit purpose or goal. It is governed by rules and usually managed through a hierarchical system of control. The characteristics of a formal organisation may be listed as follows:

- It is established under material conditions by an individual or, more usually, a group of individuals.
- It has a set of official or public objectives, concerning which its members show different levels of awareness, and towards which they display varying degrees of commitment.
- It is commonly founded on a division of labour based upon set tasks.
- It allocates roles to individuals, often on the basis of preconceived notions concerning gender, ethnicity, age and other aspects of human subjectivity.
- It sets up specialised departments or sections.
- It develops formally structured relationships, as well as unofficial networks and working practices.
- It institutes methods of control over individuals and groups.
- It operates within broad 'areas' of influence, controlling part of a specific market, for example.
- It manages resources, successfully or otherwise.
- It uses both official and unofficial systems of communication.

The existence of organisations is a salient feature of life in industrial and 'post-industrial' communities. The school, the workplace, the hospital, the bank, the prison and the church all have the potential to exert some measure of influence upon the human subject. Some of these formal groups exercise greater power than others.

The *degree* of influence and the *kind* of power exerted depend upon the role of each organisation in society. A few will play a significant part in early socialisation – schools are the obvious example. Others have less direct or prolonged contact with their 'clientele', but have the potential to wield some power over the individual. Banks, for instance, are able to influence aspects of their customers' lives through the use of financial penalties or incentives, and require only a limited degree of communication to do so.

Formal entities

When Frederick Glen (see *The Social Psychology of Organisations*, p. 11) argues that 'it is people, not entities called organisations, who make rules, develop value systems, set goals and take decisions', there are two points worth making. First, people create organisations as **formal** and not personal **entities**, so that the results appear in some cases to have little of the 'humanity' sometimes attributed to the individual. Secondly, few people have an opportunity to create rules for the organisations in which they work. The working lives of most individuals are spent within structures which are not of their own making.

Alternative values?

Despite their conventional structure, formal organisations do not necessarily promote authoritarian *values*; and where they do, they do not always achieve success. At times, they may even find themselves opposed to central authority. The black Churches in South Africa are examples of organisations which helped defy the official system of government. It is also noticeable that many organisations which are founded on authoritarian principles nevertheless provide an opportunity for the development of **alternative values**. There is a marked contrast between the official procedures governing the organisation of prisons, for example, and the 'subcultures' which exist amongst prisoners themselves.

It could be argued that official structures inevitably give rise to unofficial systems. Instead of standing in opposition to each other, in many cases they prove to be interdependent. Some theorists have gone so far as to argue that the *official* goals set by organisations are more likely to be achieved by *unofficial* working methods and systems than through the formal structures laid out by authority.

Organisations and their relationships with outsiders

An organisation functions through a series of **relationships** with a number of distinct groups. In the first place, we might consider those groups which lie outside the organisation itself. In general, there are four types of 'out-group' which every organisation must take into account.

The first, as we have seen above, is the particular *section* of the public which must be *reached*; all organisations possess some idea of the groups they exist to 'serve' or hope to influence. The second type of external collective is made up of *other formal organisations*. These may be either rivals or allies, and will include groups like suppliers and retailers. The third kind consists of institutions which possess some kind of official or commercial remit to *oversee* or *review* the work of the organisation. Such institutions could be *regulatory bodies* or *commissioning agencies*. The fourth is made up of groups of *'visitors'*, a category which may encompass individuals who will be of some material use to the organisation.

The attitudes held by organisations towards the outsiders they meet can be very revealing. A police force may, for instance, think in terms of 'service' to the public, but will often use quite different categories to describe the groups it encounters in the course of everyday events. *Private citizens* who obstruct the building of a road, for example, may find themselves transformed into *protestors*, and as a result may experience a form of treatment the police think appropriate to that category.

Contact with 'out-groups': the advertising agency

A useful example of contact between an organisation and the types of 'out-group' described above may be found in the commercial activities pursued by an advertising agency. In the first place, there is always a *client*, an individual or more usually a company, which determines the overall brief for the campaign and to which the agency must answer. Within the agency, the point of contact for the client is the 'account handler', whose job it is to (see John Josling in Hart, *The Practice of Advertising*, p. 43):

> 'maintain contact with his [sic] client, building up a full understanding of that client's advertising and marketing situation'.

The *regulatory* function will be fulfilled by bodies like the Advertising Standards Authority or the Independent Television Commission, which in practice will have relatively little contact with advertising agencies, tending to intervene if at all when an advertisement has already reached the public domain. Finally, contact with *visitors* will be managed according to the purpose of each visit and the status of the visitor.

The agency will *conceptualise* the audience it has been asked to reach. In other words, it will attempt to imagine the defining characteristics of its market. It will probably have dealings with groups of people brought in to represent the *target market*, those consumers identified as the intended recipients of the advertising message.

These 'stand-ins' for the larger collective are sometimes organised into *focus groups*, small gatherings of individuals presented with a series of questions designed to reveal general social attitudes, which may then form the basis for the particular style of campaign directed at the consumer.

Finally, other bodies in the same line of work must be considered, whether allies or rivals. Some agencies hire out creative work to specialist companies, for example. At the same time, the advertiser will be anxious not to lose an account (a job of work) to a rival corporation. In December 1994, the Saatchi and Saatchi agency dispensed with the services of its founder, Maurice Saatchi. Despite the initial shock, Maurice Saatchi recovered sufficiently to set up the 'New Saatchi Agency'. A number of accounts previously held by the 'old' Saatchi group (including Dixons, Silk Cut, the Mirror Group and Private Patients Plan) remained loyal to the group's founder when he organised the new agency. British Airways, a vital customer, was won over to the New Saatchi Agency in early May 1995.

'Target' groups within the organisation

An important point to note is that a **'target'** or subject group is sometimes found, at various points in time, within the physical boundaries of the organisation itself. For instance, colleges have students on site and hospitals contain people who require treatment, while prisons hold a more long-term population.

In much of the commercial sector, however, customers remain outside the organisation and have usually a single point of contact with it. An ordinary customer, such as a person buying something from a shop, will usually find that the product is not manufactured by the retail outlet concerned; many companies therefore have contact with the customer only through the product, which is why most 'high-profile' firms are anxious that it should represent their corporate image successfully.

Authority and subordination

Besides the relationships which are established with outside bodies, organisations contain a series of 'internal' relationships. The most significant are those which exist between **authority** and various groups of **subordinates**. In some organisations, the workforce will be concentrated in one physical location, whereas in others it may be more widely dispersed. In all cases, it will be subject to authority, whether it is formal or informal, direct or indirect, despotic or enlightened. Authority is usually caught between what Therborn calls the requirements of *qualification* and the need for *subjection* (see Chapter 2).

Definitions of authority

Etzioni (1964) provides a classification of authority or power, which he divides into three separate types:

- the **coercive** form, based upon the use of compulsion;
- the **utilitarian**, which is exercised through a form of legalistic and rationalist authority;
- the **normative**, where relationships are based on the intrinsic value of the activities performed, or of membership itself.

According to Etzioni, the *coercive* form may include organisations such as prisons, concentration camps and custodial hospitals. The *utilitarian* form is supported by a system of economic reward, found in business, the armed services and the civil service. Finally, Etzioni believed that the *normative* form applied to hospitals, universities and voluntary bodies.

Authority: a more complex picture

In actual practice, all these forms will exist, to a greater or lesser degree, in every institution. Utilitarian approaches, for example, are quite easily reinforced by coercive features should the need arise. It is distinctly odd, for instance, that Etzioni does not regard the internal organisation of the armed forces as coercive. It seems clear that compulsion in an army exists alongside 'rational' forms of authority.

It is also the case that hospitals and universities are quite capable of employing coercive measures in particular instances, should those in power choose to exercise a more forceful approach. The point must be emphasised again: *all* powerful or ruling groups will possess the ability to mobilise any of the three types of authority, separately or in combination, depending upon what they perceive to be the requirements of the situation.

Feminist critiques of authority

Some strands of **feminism** argue that groups in authority share the same deficiencies because they are for the most part composed of men, or are controlled by men if they do not actually form a numerical majority. While there may be some disagreement about the origin of male authoritarianism (whether it is in-born or emerges from socialisation), the fact remains that male behaviour and attitudes often determine the precise *forms* in which authority manifests itself. It must be stressed that discrimination occurs as much through what authority believes women are actually *capable* of doing as through its prejudices about their 'shortcomings'. Women are given jobs which are supposed to suit their strengths, but the point is that such posts are often 'dead ends', lying outside the main structures of power.

Lindsay St Claire, writing in *The Social Identity of Women*, edited by Suzanne Skevington and Deborah Baker (see p. 130), argues that:

'a woman is handicapped by her gender when beliefs about her sex, and not her sex *per se*, account for limited opportunities and performances'.

St Claire believes that women's performances in a number of activities are judged 'subnormal' and attributed to some kind of female impairment, while in reality such failures arise because the principle of 'male as norm' is being applied (p. 135):

> 'the mechanical skills of a girl schooled in arts would most probably be subnormal judged against a distribution of scores derived from boys tutored in mechanics'.

In sum, St Claire believes that physical differences between men and women, inadequacies in women's performances, and women's failures to fulfil roles (p. 135) 'are frequently (mis)attributed to unchangeable biological givens like women's sex or "impairments" thought to reside therein'.

Some authors have noted that social science, which is supposed to interrogate authority and its role in the creation of social relations, has itself used methods which approximate to a 'masculine' approach. This does, however, depend upon accepting the idea that authoritarian structures are 'typically' male, or are at least one manifestation of male culture. Christine Griffin, for example (see Skevington and Baker, *The Social Identity of Women*, p. 176), believes that social identity theory (see Chapter 3) emphasises the role of 'agentic rather than communal modes of self-identification', the former being 'a prototypically masculine form'. 'Agentic' here refers to the role of *agency* or the active operation of some force – in our case, authority. The question we must ask is this: is authority itself a form of 'masculine' culture, or is the authority we *know* the masculine form of a phenomenon which might exist in any type of society, even if matriarchal forms of organisation were to flourish?

If we speak of authority, we must remember that it is exercised at a personal as well as at an institutional level. Sheila Rowbotham, writing in 1972 (see *Women, Resistance and Revolution*), recounts the story of Han Suyin, a woman of mixed Belgian and Chinese descent who, in the 1930s, married a right-wing officer in Chiang Kai-shek's anti-Communist army. Her husband tore up her books, lectured her on morality, and told her that 'a woman of talent is not a virtuous woman'. There are always individual casualties of authoritarian social attitudes.

Restructuring in education: the exercise of authority

The overall goals of an institution sometimes alter so radically that a form of authority which once seemed appropriate will be superseded by alternative models. An interesting example can be found in the public sector in Britain. The attempt to remodel the outlook of educational and other public bodies, along *competitive* and 'cost-effective' lines, led to a sharp conflict between the values originally held by such institutions, and the new types of conduct their members were supposed to accept.

In order to bring employees into line with '**restructuring**', more coercive forms of power were exercised. However, the workforce in further and higher education (to take one example) encountered forms of compulsion *alongside* appeals to normative standards and 'rational' values (see Etzioni, above). The introduction of what some called 'new' and others 'poorer' conditions of work was achieved in some cases because certain employees (particularly 'middle managers') were already used to responding to *utilitarian* and *normative* forms of authority. In many cases, one of the most useful persuasive devices was employed: the offer of financial incentives to move on to new contracts.

It is worth noting that the political rhetoric which supported forms of privatisation in education relied upon the idea that the public sector should not be 'protected' but should start to function 'in the real world', a world where competition was the norm. In fact, the notion that commercial reality consists of an arena of free and fair competition falls short of the truth. The huge variety of products available on the market should not disguise the existence of monopolies, cartels and other systems which guarantee that some will be assured an advantage before the commercial 'race' begins.

Authority and control in the workplace

All **workplaces** function through some form of coercion, even where this is largely paternalistic or benevolent. The behaviour of those individuals who 'belong' to the organisation is regulated in a variety of ways. In the first place, the existence of established working practices will ensure a basic level of discipline; people will usually have to carry out a number of functions, in a certain sequence, within a specified period in the working day or week. There are also a number of other forms of control available to those in authority, which are examined below.

Basic forms of control: work discipline, visibility, surveillance

The discipline imposed by the work itself can be quite effective, as noted above. In addition, theorists have examined the systems which are used to 'check up' on employees. Michel Foucault, for example, placed great emphasis upon the concept of employee **visibility** and the related category of **surveillance**.

Visibility is important, in the sense that a workforce must be seen to be engaged in the activities which are assigned to them. Foucault recognised that the architectural features of a building will either assist or frustrate management's attempts to gain sight of their subordinates.

He also investigated the connection between control in the workplace and the existence of prisons and other *carceral* organisations. Foucault studied the 'Panopticon', a prison design created by the philosopher Jeremy Bentham in the nineteenth century. In this system, the prison would be circular in shape, and all cells would radiate outwards from a central observation point. The guards would therefore be able, at all times, to observe the inmates.

Where a direct line of visual contact is impossible to establish, management may carry out inspections of various kinds. Anthony Giddens (see *Sociology*, p. 301) takes an example from Katherine Archibald's (1947) study of a shipyard in the United States. This extract clearly reflects the existence of full employment in a wartime industry:

'It was amusing to watch the sudden transformation whenever word got round that the foreman was on the hull or in the shop or that a front-office superintendent was coming by. Quartermen and leadermen would rush to their groups of workers and stir them to obvious activity ... where no work existed a pipe was busily bent and threaded, or a bolt which was already in place was subject to further and unnecessary tightening.'

Surveillance, on the other hand, means close and continuous observation. It takes more than one form, besides the direct visual scrutiny carried out by managers. There is also the maintenance of employee records, consisting of personal details, assessment of job performance, and in many cases information about political affiliation and trade union activity. Surveillance may sometimes include forms of spying, carried out by individuals who operate at approximately the same level as the ordinary worker.

Perhaps the most important form of control, however, is that type which depends upon the willingness of the employees to constrain or police their *own* behaviour. This form of control, particularly where it grows from a *positive* self-identification, will be examined below.

A slap on the wrist

In order to obtain the obedience of staff, managers may reproduce forms of discipline *already familiar* to the employee from his or her early socialisation, particularly from schooldays. Glen supports this viewpoint (p. 20), reminding us that:

'in the play situations of childhood and the controlled and contrived group situations of the classroom, we gain our first experiences of the results of success or failure in a social situation'.

These experiences come to form the basis for our public behaviours, though they are refined and even in some cases superseded. As we grow older, we may begin to select those situations in which we know that we are able to achieve some success, or else we may become more resilient to criticism.

Nevertheless, authority in organisations sometimes depends upon the simple mechanisms of 'adult' behaviour to get its own way. For instance, vocal opposition is often characterised as immature or petulant. Another familiar tactic is to call those who propose alternative systems 'unrealistic'; appeals to the 'way things really are' are widespread in institutional life. At times, individuals may be kept in line by patronising behaviour; women have, for example, often been the victims of condescension. The most clever form of authority uses the value systems of the employees themselves.

Work roles and the exercise of authority

The provision by organisations of **roles** and *identities* (what we have previously called 'subject positions') is a powerful form of influence over the employee. I do not mean to suggest that it ensures complete subservience; from the viewpoint of the organisation, however, the way that people *identify* with the roles they are given can provide a useful means of control.

It is often the case that individuals will take on the qualities that are part of their job description. The reason for this lies in the human tendency to define the self according to the social roles which are available. Supporting evidence is found in the considerable degree of psychological discomfort which may be experienced by someone who *does not* identify with the role he or she has been assigned. However, the individual *use* of institutional identity will differ, depending upon the people concerned and the situation in which they are placed. Promotion, for example, often entails a change of *attitude* in employees, since new responsibilities will usually entail some change in their relationship with other staff.

Involvement

Etzioni's work on the role of the individual in the workplace has been extended to show three types of **involvement** which characterise the role of individuals. In the first type, **alienative** involvement, the worker is obliged to remain with the organisation and has no commitment to it. In the second, **calculative** involvement, the individual may expect a reasonable return or exchange for his or her services. Finally, **moral** involvement sees a high degree of commitment from the individual to the organisation.

Like all models of human activity, this is a considerable simplification, as Etzioni recognised when he referred to the mixed forms that could be produced. Glen shows how individuals in organisations are often faced by conflicting values or 'involvements', where calculative and moral criteria come into play simultaneously. For example, a worker may have little or no respect for his or her immediate managers, or indeed for the whole ethos of the company, but may none the less feel great commitment to the product or the customer.

Group pressures

In *The Social Psychology of Organisations*, Frederick Glen notes that the **pressure** to accept social norms is part of daily existence (p. 20):

'The nature of society is such that external pressures upon the individual to conform – to fit in with the group – are central factors throughout the entire range of social experience.'

The essential point which should emerge from this observation is that people do not choose to 'fit in with society' as such. Instead, they choose to belong to groups which they regard as close to their own values. These groups *mediate* the wider values of the society.

Where people also belong to other groups by virtue of their membership of organisations, then they will be inclined to take note of their *colleagues'* opinions. The attitudes of colleagues, rather than those of managers, may ultimately prove effective in ensuring that outward behaviour, at least, conforms to the requirements of public scrutiny. On a practical level, the possibility that close acquaintances may suffer increased workloads if certain levels of efficiency are not reached may act as a major incentive to fulfil group norms. On the other hand, a strong group identity might provide its members with a base from which to defy the wishes of management.

Individual conformity?

The reasons for the existence of conformity given above indicate the power of group membership. Frederick Glen examined the basis of individual behaviour within formal and informal situations, finding that (p. 11):

'The behaviour of the individual is considerably influenced by group processes both informally and in organisational situations.'

Clearly, this group influence may benefit management or may, as noted before, provide a bastion against it. Cyril Sofer, writing in *Organisations in Theory and Practice*, supports Glen's perspective. He describes a series of major experiments in social psychology (p. 105) which point to:

'the profound influence which groups have on the judgements and behaviour of their members and to forces which influence members to adhere to group values and standards, sometimes against their spontaneous inclinations'.

However, there are certain reasons why caution must be exercised. The wholesale transference of the results of laboratory experiments to the workplace is a little problematic. Sofer notes (pp. 105–6) that:

'The average age of organisational colleagues is higher than that of laboratory subjects ... organisational colleagues usually know each other ... members of laboratory groups are strangers ... the tasks on which organisational groups are engaged are genuine tasks, not tasks contrived for the occasion or resembling games.'

In other words, the pressure to conform placed upon less mature individuals who do not possess strong interpersonal bonds, and who are engaged in laboratory tasks, will not necessarily represent the reactions of older people possessed of coherent group identity, who are working on tasks which have a 'real' outcome.

Group influence on judgement: Sherif's and Asch's experiments

The work of Sherif and Asch in the mid-1930s is usually seen as a landmark in social psychology research. Sherif used the *autokinetic* effect as the object of judgement in his experiments. The autokinetic effect refers to the fact that, if a subject observes a stationary point of light in a dark room, the point of light seems to move after a few seconds.

In the first part of the test, Sherif required individuals to make their own judgements about the amount of movement which appeared to take place. Each subject underwent the process a number of times, and then established an average *range* for the movement observed and a *norm* or standard for the amount of movement. In a situation where two or three subjects (whose estimates of range and norm differed widely) experienced the test simultaneously, each individual tended to alter his or her previous observations in order to move his or her estimates closer to the others'. When subjects were returned to the original conditions, as individuals, their responses were consistent with their first estimates. Sofer concludes (p. 107) that 'quite apart from the issue of moral rightness', Sherif's experiments.

> 'illustrate vividly the gestalt principle that perception of an item is influenced by its context. In this case, the perception of the amount of movement of the light is affected by the social context – the presence of others.'

However, Sherif's experiments used a test for which there was no right or wrong answer; they were ambiguous. In 1956, Asch used a number of college students (it is a wonder that American students ever found time to study), presenting them with a number of lines of different length. On one piece of cardboard, the researchers presented a single line, representing a 'standard' length. On another piece, three lines had been drawn, one of which was identical in length to the single line. The students were asked to identify which of the three lines matched the standard.

Each subject in turn had to call out the decision reached. For the first two phases of the experiment, the answers given were straightforward; all participants correctly identified the relationship between the matching lines. However, the third phase saw an odd occurrence; one member of the group of respondents, seated towards the end, found that he was out of step with all the others present. In fact, all members of the group, apart from the one who found he did not agree with the majority, had been primed to give answers which were obviously incorrect. The purpose of the experiment was to establish how an individual subject would respond to pressure. Of the sample used, one-third tended to conform to the deliberately misleading responses given by the researchers' stooges.

Male 'in-groups'?

Another form of group pressure exists where employees categorise *each other* in certain ways. This may take the form of 'labelling' *individuals*, but can also include the mobilisation of group attitudes. For example, it remains the case that, in many workplaces, male groups may form unofficial collectives which generate hostility to female 'out-groups'. This does not mean that every male group will demonstrate the *same* attitude towards their female colleagues, but it does mean that a similar range of prejudices may be found. In many cases, the inability of the system to deal fairly with women workers will be attributed to 'deficiencies' in the characteristics of the workers themselves (see St Claire's work, above).

Quite besides explicit or implicit forms of discrimination within the working environment, a male group intent upon maintaining a privileged position may be able to reinforce its position against the threat of 'equality', by organising exclusive social or sporting activities whose purpose is to strengthen male camaradarie in general.

Resistance: one consequence of positive self-identification

Identification with the work role, which I have argued may become a form of **positive self-identification**, may also, *at some stage* and *under certain circumstances*, allow the development of a critical perspective on the organisation itself. A clear example is found in those institutions which encourage a skilled workforce to behave in a *professional* manner. Head-teachers in schools, for instance, have typically made appeals of this kind to their staff. The concept of professionalism is, however, a notoriously dangerous weapon to wield, since it is 'double-edged'.

Widespread acceptance of professional standards may, for example, lead to demands for a truly professional *status*. Staff may develop alternative perspectives based on the perceived difference between management rhetoric and everyday reality. The roles individuals are given are also, to a certain degree, 'customised'. This means that people take the 'workable' elements of the job seriously, and alter those elements which are difficult to perform, substituting alternative systems which allow some degree of independence from the official culture of the workplace.

Persistent critics

In some organisations there are individuals who are recognised as *persistent critics* of the established order. Such critics may hold office in a union branch, or may use a particular post or department as a base, or may simply act in a personal capacity. The critic may act as a conduit for the dissatisfaction of staff, who might allow an individual to fulfil this role because it means that they themselves do not have to make their opposition public. Critics often find that they are then always expected to speak out and that, the more often they do so, the less likely it is that anyone else will feel inclined to make a similar contribution.

In the worst type of scenario, a persistent and *isolated* critic may be characterised as eccentric or abnormal. Glen (p. 20) makes the astute comment that:

> ' "normality" can be defined in terms of conformity with accepted modes of behaviour; failure to meet the criteria can earn for the individual at best a reputation for eccentricity, at worst a categorisation of his behaviour as deviant or plain mad'.

This is no exaggeration; the very fact that most employees are anxious to conform to behavioural norms points to the widespread fear of negative categorisation by work colleagues. To avoid isolation, it is better to operate from within a like-minded collective.

However, when Glen argues (p. 21) that 'the truly isolated individual is the psychotic', who 'cannot share in the group's perception of the world, nor they in his', there is actually no reason why the *group* should not prove instead to occupy the 'psychotic' position, in which case its judgement of individuals will be entirely unreliable. In some cases, such as Nazi Germany, a whole nation's system of values can become entirely distorted.

Individual responsibility?

Glen thinks that it is a mistake to attribute an individual identity to an organisation, which he believes leads to the displacement of (p. 35):

> 'personal responsibility for actions and events by blaming *the system*, *the rules*, *higher authority* (unspecified), rather than examining the psychological and social factors involved'.

It is quite plain that this perspective argues that people avoid responsibility by loading all their dissatisfactions onto the organisation. This may provide an explanation of some individual behaviours, but it may mean that we forget to analyse the power relationships within the organisation itself.

Responses to extreme repression

Certain types of organisation have been noted for systematic and extreme forms of repression. Institutions which have little contact with wider social values, and which function through secrecy and a specialised code of conduct, are often prone to internal corruption. Some organisations are actually founded on aims and objectives which ensure the complete distortion of human values and relationships.

The psychologist Bettelheim, who was at one time an inmate of Dachau and Buchenwald, noted how rapidly behaviour and personality were altered in the extraordinary context of camp life. Whereas many inmates were quickly destroyed, first psychologically and then physically, some of the prisoners began to identify with those who held complete sway over their fate; they modelled themselves on the camp guards, and even began to imitate aspects of their behaviour.

Bettelheim's description of this extreme form of identification should, however, be contrasted with the formation of resistance organisations inside the camps. One of the few British survivors of Buchenwald, the airman and secret agent Yeo-Thomas, formed a resistance group while a prisoner, and witnessed the existence of a variety of other organisations (see Bruce Marshall's war biography, *The White Rabbit*, published in 1952). In addition, numerous acts of violent defiance took place in a number of forced labour and concentration camps. In some cases, unpopular guards were killed, buildings destroyed with explosive, and escapes carried out.

Bureaucracy: a definition

Bureaucracy may be defined as the existence of established administrative practices; it also refers to the organised groups of officials which function on behalf of a government or other executive power. The social theorist Max Weber saw bureaucracy as the dominant form of organisation in modern society. He also described a general theory of 'social action', in which human beings perform actions because they are prompted by a series of motives. The types of possible action, each shaped by a specific underlying motive, include **affective**, **traditional** and **rational**.

Affective action is supposed to grow from an emotional state, *traditional* action is based upon established custom, and *rational* action comes from awareness of a goal and is thus directed towards its attainment. Once again, it can be argued that a writer has made an artificial demarcation between types of behaviour, when the real motivation for carrying out any activity may perhaps be more complex. It may consist, for example, of a mixture of emotional and intellectual factors.

Bureaucracy: rational action?

Weber also believed that bureaucracy is a system in which *rational* action is seen in an institutional form. Schein's (1965) definition of an organisation supports Weber's position:

> 'An organisation is the rational co-ordination of the activities of a number of people for the achievement of some common explicit purpose or goal, through division of labour and function, and through a hierarchy of authority and responsibility.'

Here, bureaucratic organisation is supposed to direct its collective energies towards achieving a clearly delineated goal, using rational, methodical approaches.

In practice, bureaucracies rarely attain Weber's or Schein's ideal of rationality. Indeed, the concept of bureaucracy has become a by-word for waste, inefficiency and cumbersome practices.

Formal processes, irrational outcomes

If we return to the concept of rationality itself, we should perhaps hesitate before applying the term (as Schein does) to all formal bodies. It may be helpful to make a distinction between the formal *systems* employed within organisations and an institution's capacity to make *rational* decisions.

There is, for example, a difference between rationality and those **processes** which are merely *logical*. Rationality is the possession or exercise of *reason* and good sense; logic is a process which begins with a proposition and moves through a chain of inferences to reach a conclusion. A logical truth is something which is true in a **formal** sense. In other words, its own internal structure is faultless, but it does not necessarily have any relationship to the material world.

A conclusion reached through a series of logical stages may in fact emerge from a completely false premise. Organisations often find that they have achieved some distinctly **irrational outcomes** as the result of a perfectly logical process.

In Chancery: *Bleak House* and bureaucracy

Charles Dickens examined the workings of legal bureaucracy in his novel of 1852–3, *Bleak House*. The background to the action of the narrative is the case known as 'Jarndyce and Jarndyce', a seemingly never-ending wrangle over an inheritance. The legal system symbolises the decay which Dickens saw at the heart of English society.

Bleak House begins with a description of an all-pervasive fog which covers the southern counties and the capital city itself. The obscurity of the dark November weather is matched by the muddle and delay for which the Court of Chancery is famous (p. 2):

'On such an afternoon, some score members of the High Court of Chancery bar ought to be – as here they are – mistily engaged in one of the ten thousand stages of an endless cause, tripping one another up on slippery precedents, groping knee-deep in technicalities ... making a pretence of equity with serious faces, as players might. On such an afternoon, the various solicitors in the cause, some two or three of whom have inherited it from their fathers, who made a fortune by it, ought to be – as are they not? – ranged in a line ... with bills, cross-bills, answers, rejoinders, injunctions, affidavits, issues, references to masters, masters' reports, mountains of costly nonsense, piled before them.'

This passage reveals an institution which has replaced meaningful communication with the *forms* of exchange, each form prompting a particular reply or inquiry, until eventually meaning is buried under a mountain of paperwork.

Criticisms of bureaucracy

In 1965, the American theorist Warren Bennis produced a ten-point critique of bureaucracy. The ten areas he identified were set out by Myers and Myers in *Managing by Communication* in 1982 (see p. 30), and may be summarised as follows:

- Bureaucracy does not allow for personal growth, nor does it encourage the development of mature personalities, presumably because relationships are distorted by the exercise of authority.
- It develops conformity and 'groupthink', a failure to use critical thinking because allegiance to the group over-rides free choice of alternative courses of action.
- It ignores the usefulness of 'informal' organisation.
- Its systems of control are outdated. (This idea may suggest that there are types of authority which are more enlightened or efficient, simply because they are reasonably 'modern'.)
- It has no juridicial process – that is, no ability to offer balanced or 'legal' forms of inquiry, and therefore no capacity to provide justice for those inside or outside the organisation.
- Related to the above, there is no adequate means for resolving conflict between different 'ranks' in the organisation.
- Communication, together with innovation, is frustrated by hierarchical structures.
- The full range of human resources is not used, because of mistrust and fear of reprisal. Instead, conformity and 'safe' behaviours are the order of the day.
- Bureaucracy cannot easily assimilate new technology.
- It modifies behaviour along conformist lines.

The liberal position which Bennis's work exemplifies is generally hostile to bureaucracy because that is thought inflexible and detrimental to healthy communication, particularly communication amongst peers. A liberal view of organisation does not, however, go so far as to suggest democratic control of production by the workforce. It argues for a more humane application of management principles, in which the ultimate *goals* of an organisation are in all essentials identical to the highly centralised model it criticises – efficiency and high levels of output. It is likely that the structure of all formal bodies is determined by the functions they must carry out, rather than simply by the model of internal organisation which is favoured.

Organisational structure and communication

In *Organisations*, March and Simon classify a series of *occasions* when **organisational communication** will take place (p. 183). Communication will occur to meet the following needs or eventualities:

- the presence of 'non-programmed' activity, i.e. that type of event which is not planned for or foreseen by the official system;
- the initiation, establishment and supervision of programmes;
- the provision of data to pursue a course of action;
- the focusing of attention on problems;
- the production of information about the results of activities within the organisation.

Communication *channels* are of course deliberately planned during the initial development of an organisation, but others will develop over time. It is often said (see *Organisations*, p. 189) that the greater the efficiency of the channel in communication terms, the more the particular channel will be used. This is why the 'grapevine', the informal channel of communication in an organisation, flourishes in those institutions which restrict the type of information which individuals are allowed to receive.

March and Simon describe the processes which should occur in a functional system:

- **Information** moves from *sources* to points of *decision*.
- **Instructions** move from points of decision to points of *action*.
- **Information about results** moves from points of action to points of **decision and control**.

Classifying events: established categories

March and Simon argue that organisations **classify** all the events which require a response. When an event occurs, the first question asked is supposed to be: 'What *kind* of event is this?'. March and Simon believe that organisations have a repertory of 'programmes', so that any occurrence can produce an automatic response, selected from the repertory.

This view may explain certain types of simple or mechanical response, but will not shed light on the ability of formal groups to produce *creative* solutions to the problems and challenges they face. March and Simon are, however, right to draw attention to the problems inherent in 'classification schemes' used by companies and other formal bodies. Where an organisation is inflexible or hide-bound, it may fail to see events in their true light.

The drawbacks of fixed interpretation

March and Simon note the dangers present in the types of categorisation used by some formal groups. If an event is thought to fall into an identifiable category, then it will be 'understood' and communicated according to set preconceptions. For example, an increase in sales is an indicator of a commercial firm's success, and will be communicated as such. The event appears to be easy to understand.

However, certain meanings may be neglected. For instance, the improved sales figures may once have been due to successful marketing policies. The danger is that the same event may in future be interpreted as meaning the same thing; unqualified success, based on good marketing, regardless of the precise nature of the evidence. Increased sales may simply be due to the demise of a rival firm.

Where an event does *not* fit easily into the established system of classification, then members of a dysfunctional organisation will find great difficulty in attributing meaning to it. It is not surprising that they will therefore find it hard to communicate any useful information. It is difficult to know which is worse: the 'pigeon-holing' of events and their subsequent misinterpretation, or the inability to make any useful sense of occurrences which fall outside the established system of categorisation.

Classical vs. behavioural approaches to organisation

Myers and Myers believe that it is possible to describe two types of organisational theory: **classical** and **behavioural**. Classical organisation is sub-divided into the **scientific management** of Frederick Taylor (see the section 'Against the "rationalisation" of leisure' below), the investigation of **bureaucracy** carried out by Weber (see the section on 'Bureaucracy: rational action?' above), and theories of **administrative management** associated with the work of practising managers like Chester Barnard (1938) and Henri Fayol (1915).

Behavioural attitudes to organisation have emerged from studies of sociology and psychology, and are discussed by Myers and Myers under three separate headings. These are **human relations**, **human resources** and **systems**.

Human relations is the title given to research carried out under the direction of Elton Mayo in the United States over a period of two decades, between the 1930s and the 1950s. The *social* rather than the *physical* environment of work was studied. *Human resources* was an approach based on the ideas of Douglas McGregor and Rensis Likert. McGregor (1960) emphasised the creativity and imagination of individual workers, and their powers of motivation and self-direction. McGregor labelled classical organisational theory as 'theory X' and his own approach as 'theory Y'. Theory X is based on coercion, while theory Y argues that organisations can utilise the natural desire for responsibility which exists within a workforce; threats and rigid central direction are therefore unnecessary. Likert (1961 and 1967) concentrated upon alternatives to hierarchical organisation, suggesting that managers facilitate communication by linking workers from different areas, rather than merely issuing instructions.

Systems theory emerged from the work of Daniel Katz and Robert Kahn (1978), who used the concept of 'boundaries' to argue that an organisation is separate from, and yet dependent on, the environment in which it exists. In **open systems**, energy comes into the organisation and is then transformed and returned to the environment. **Closed** systems of management do not have this positive relationship with their social and physical surroundings, expending more energy upon internal communication.

Communication in classical and behavioural systems

Most organisations will employ elements of both 'classical' and 'behavioural' approaches in dealings with staff. In some cases, each type of structure will be applied to *different* groups of employees; typically, those who have attained a certain degree of status will be allowed more autonomy than those who are regarded as mere functionaries. The type of system chosen to implement work may also depend upon the circumstances in which the organisation finds itself. A worker-centred outlook may flourish more readily during those periods when the economy is growing or when it is at least in a stable condition.

Communication is treated differently in the two systems. Classical theory is mainly interested in communication as it pertains to the successful transmission of orders from senior management. In other words, a process model of communication is regarded as perfectly adequate, in which managers set up a plan to be directed by 'foremen' and carried out by workers. The role of informal communication is thus either ignored or regarded as disruptive. What Myers and Myers (p. 30) call 'the complexity of human motivation and the richness of human resources' is neglected. Within this tradition, however, Henri Fayol envisaged some degree of contact between peers, although only when it was allowed by line managers.

Chester Barnard pointed out that one could not assume that communication had been received as its originators had intended. This leads directly to consideration of the opposing school of thought – the behavioural model. This sees the *work group* as the centre of decision making, in the sense that instructions which are received by ordinary workers are reinterpreted and made manageable.

Of course, the idea that employee motivation is central to successful production is not necessarily a progressive notion, since a behavioural model can allow employers a greater insight into the workings of small groups and may lead the manager to use fear (of redundancy, for example) as a means of motivating workers. In communication terms, behavioural approaches represent a recognition of the small-scale interactions which will always exist in formal bodies, and constitute an attempt to harness these energies. McGregor's 'theory Y', for example, emphasises the need for employees to exercise more control over their work. Once subordinates feel that they are being kept informed, behavioural theory assumes that they will make better decisions and will help to create an organisation founded on trust.

Once again, it is possible to argue that the two systems we have studied are not in fact diametrically opposed to one another, but are actually *strategies* which are available to managers, with the ultimate goal remaining the maximisation of profits, rather than the welfare of workers.

Power: communication in hierarchical systems

As we have seen, writers on organisational communication often insist that formal bodies cannot function without effective communication. It is, however, quite rare to discover an organisation of any scale which disseminates information or facilitates interaction with complete success. Published studies of a variety of organisations appear to identify the same problem – the *dysfunctional* state of the communication systems which are found in most formal groups.

Management consultants and communication theorists seem to agree that what is required are better systems, well-informed staff, managers who have a genuinely progressive outlook and, of course, more efficient lines of communication. However, there are few commentators who go further than simply arguing for more successful communication within a hierarchical system. For example, Bernstein, in *Company Image and Reality*, reproduces the definition ACAS (the Advisory, Conciliation and Arbitration Service) uses for workplace communication (p. 85):

'The provision and passing of information and instructions which enable a company ... to function efficiently and employees to be properly informed about developments.'

Here, the goal is efficiency. Employees are to be kept 'properly informed' about developments, but these developments *originate* elsewhere.

Many authors fail to recognise that it is precisely the fact that hierarchies exist, that sets limits on the possible range and content of official internal communication. In all formal organisations, information is 'graded' and some types are thought unsuitable for general circulation. With the increase in the number of institutions which have become 'corporate' (hospital trusts and colleges, for example), it is inevitable that new attitudes to information handling will arise.

The power structure

Some studies of organisational communication recognise the structural elements which prevent the free dissemination of ideas and information. In *The Reality of Organisations*, which was written as 'a guide for managers', Rosemary Stewart argues that (p. 95):

'The dominant factor in managerial relations ... is the existence of a power structure.'

This structure will govern the possible range of interaction not just between managers but between all the employees of a company.

The power structure is not exactly synonymous with the official organisational hierarchy, since it will also include groups and individuals who have achieved influence through informal means. Stewart goes on to note that the existence of a power structure is:

'rarely acknowledged ... many managers talk of decision-making as if it were a wholly rational choice between alternatives'.

She insists that rational decision making is unlikely to occur where other criteria operate; because decisions are made according to the balance of power inside the organisation, the most rational proposal will not be judged according to its merits. If, for example, the idea emerges from a weak group, or if it threatens the power base of an influential faction, then it may fail to receive support.

Social power and the workplace

The concept of **social power** expresses the idea that there are *general relationships* of power in society as a whole. The workplace is a good example of a place where social power operates. Collins and Raven produced an analysis of the concept in an article dating from 1969. They identified social power as:

> 'The potential influence of some influencing agent "O" over some person "P". Influence is defined as a change in cognition, attitude, behaviour or emotion of "P" which can be attributed to "O".'

These authors identify six different types of power:

- reward power – P sees that O has power to reward him or her;
- coercive power – P sees that O has power to punish him or her;
- referent power – P wishes to identify with O;
- expert power – P attributes greater knowledge to O;
- legitimate power – P accepts norms that O should have;
- informational power – based upon information which is independent of the nature of the source.

Power vs. authority: an artificial division?

Weber (1946) makes a distinction between **power** and **authority**. Power is exercised, he believes, when one individual is in a position to exert his or her will in a situation, regardless of any resistance from others. Authority, by contrast (see Glen, p. 37), 'implies voluntary compliance with demands that are essentially perceived as legitimate'.

We should be very careful before accepting this definition. As we have seen before (Chapter 3), power includes two elements, *capacity* and *use*, where the second is 'power over' some aspect of our social reality. Authority cannot function without the exercise of both types. The point is that some forms of authority may be regarded as more legitimate than others, but the 'voluntary compliance' is never in fact completely voluntary. In fact, there are many cases where there is no conscious *act of compliance* at all.

For instance, we might imagine a case where authority has been established over time, or where it is exercised at some remove from its subjects. Individuals will find that they inhabit a particular *status quo*, which requires no act, voluntary or otherwise, to make that authority legitimate. Certainly, a leader who is *chosen* by a group of people because he or she displays some great virtue or ability is clearly able to exercise a different form of authority from that observed in someone who simply inherits such a position. However, Weber's division between power and authority bears little resemblance to the actual exercise of domination, and may easily be used by apologists for corrupt forms of leadership.

Direct pathways?

Most of the formal organisations with which we are familiar are organised as hierarchies. That is to say, they are institutions which depend upon graded levels of status, related to a variety of functions. A diagram of a hierarchy will show **direct pathways** from, for example, the managing director of a company, down to the individual workers in any one of a number of departments. This makes communication appear straightforward.

However, in general terms decisions are passed down, while requests are passed upwards. Many of the representations made by a workforce, especially where they take the form of dissension or protest, will be 'sanitized' as they are passed upwards through the system. For example, where there is a meeting of middle managers in any organisation, the minutes produced for the event may paraphrase or even excise critical remarks. It is interesting to note that the more strident forms of censorship may actually be the most successful, since employees are so surprised by the audacity of the action that they feel too bewildered or embarrassed to protest.

Departmentalisation

Although many diagrams illustrate 'line management', where communication seems to proceed in stages from the 'lowest' to the 'highest' level, most large organisations create distinct departments (Figures 4.1 and 4.2). In most cases,

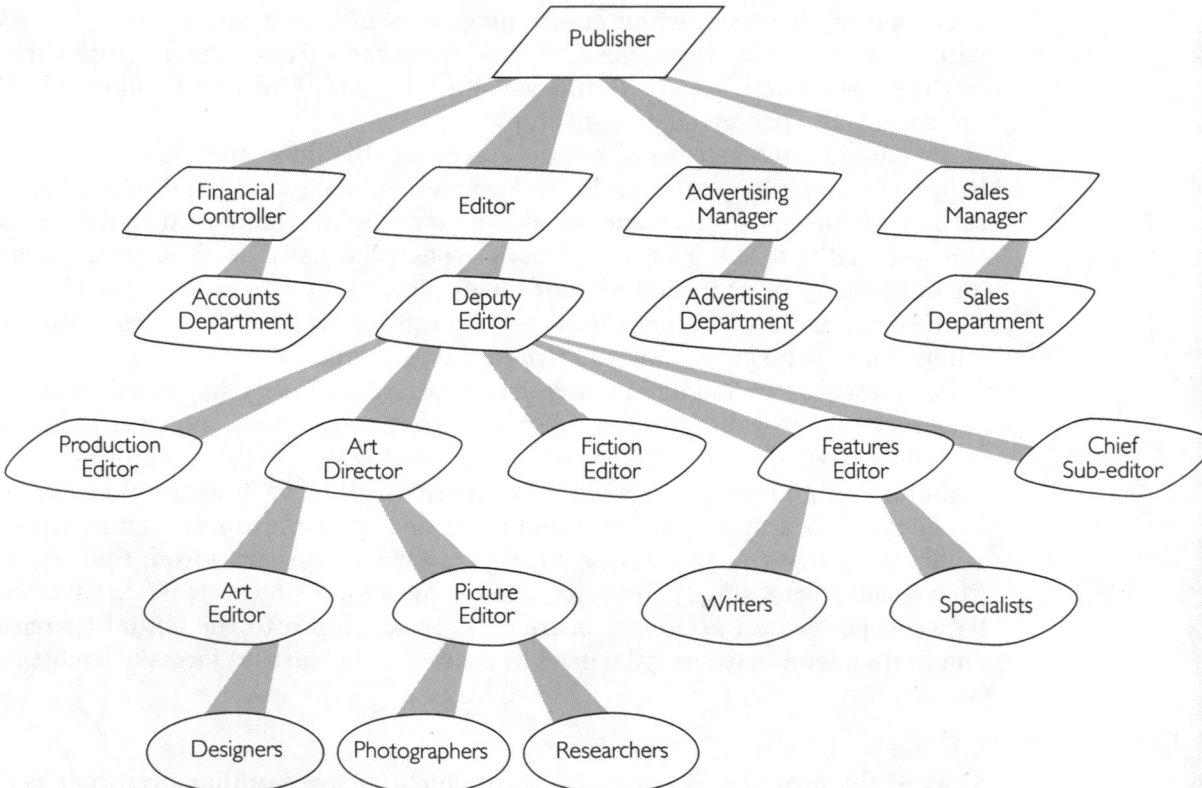

Figure 4.1   Typical 'chain of command' on a magazine (after Anthony Davis, Magazine Journalism Today)

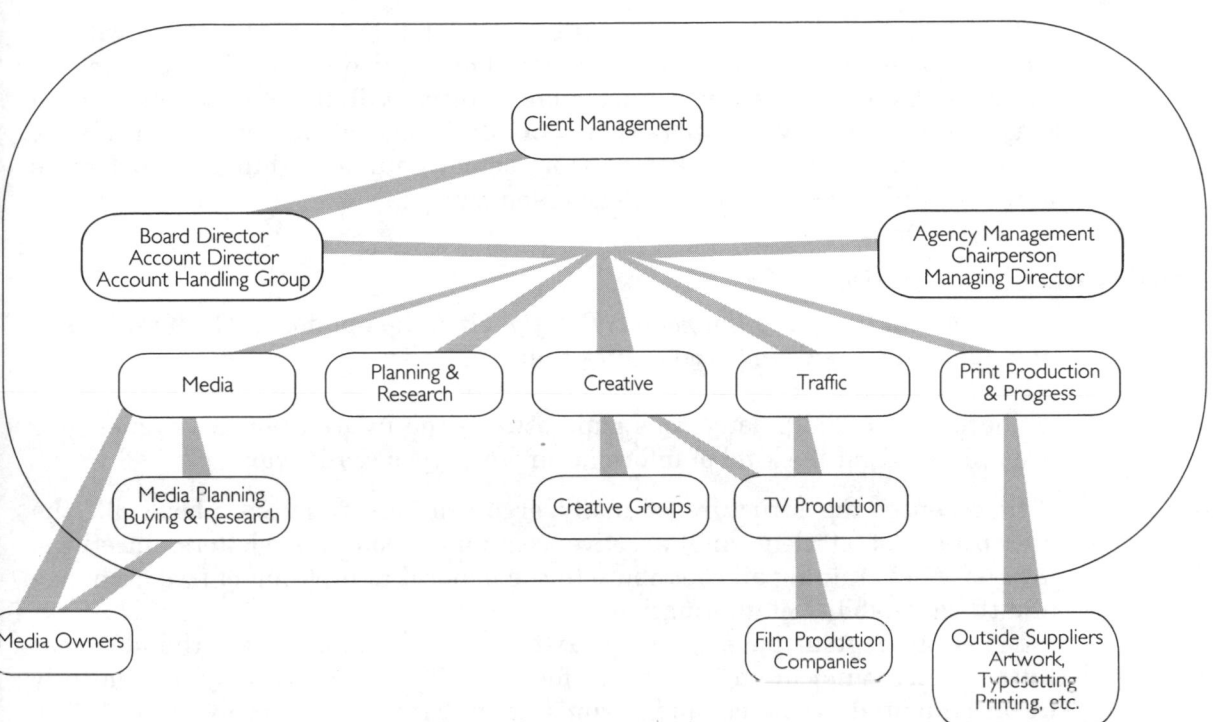

Figure 4.2   Departments in an advertising agency: after Hart, The Practice of Advertising

this reflects the degree of specialisation required in the organisation. For example, a manufacturing company may contain *production*, *finance*, *sales* and *marketing* departments. Hierarchical control may still be exercised through the directors of each department, though the same system is sometimes used to provide a high degree of autonomy.

In *functional* departmentalisation, individuals who perform the same tasks are grouped together. Departmentalisation may also be organised on the basis of *product lines* and according to *geographical location*.

Levels of responsibility

Departmentalisation encourages the proliferation of **levels of responsibility**. For example, a number of levels may be found in the academic divisions of a further education college. Within each department there will be a series of levels, with a head and deputy head of department, a number of heads of school (the schools being distinct areas such as science, mathematics, English and so on), followed perhaps by heads of section (smaller specialist units), and then the main body of lecturers. A parallel structure will exist for pastoral care. Departments will be represented by a group of senior managers, but will be placed under the overall direction of a principal, assisted by one or two vice-principals, whose decisions will in turn be reported to a board of governors.

The *types* of decision it is possible to take in this structure will be circumscribed by the position the individual or group occupies. Decisions about which syllabus to use for a particular subject will usually be made at a reasonably 'low' level, whereas major decisions about overall academic direction will probably be taken by more senior figures, within the constraints of the overall plans set out by college management.

The quality of communication

Bernstein, in *Company Image and Reality*, cites the opinion of Graham Cole, a management consultant, who argues that:

> 'there's a startling, dangerous gap between the information companies give employees and the kind of information employees really want'.

In essence, the structure of many organisations requires, above all, the *appearance* of efficient and effective communication. Newsletters, meetings, internal staff training all contribute to the general impression of free exchange and the availability of information.

In reality, regular bulletins may exist merely to communicate the idea that lines of communication are open for use. The content may be entirely inconsequential. Debates and forums may be opened merely in order to circulate an agenda already established by those in authority. Agendas will be presented late, or only tabled when a meeting begins, ensuring that individuals have no time to present an alternative case. Meetings will run over time, squeezing out space reserved for 'any other business'.

Bernstein takes an uncompromising line on the causes of inadequate communication (p. 84):

> 'Internal company communication is notoriously bad. There are many reasons. The fault lies entirely with management. If the receiver gets it wrong the fault must lie with the transmitter.'

Notice that Bernstein blames management for poor communication, but also that this reveals his assumption that communication should originate with management. To explain how communication works, he uses a straightforward transmission or process model, which is not really capable of explaining all the complexities inherent in real examples of organisational communication.

Networks of communication

In the 1950s, a number of theorists advanced the idea that there were distinct types of communication structure, each of which was suited to a particular type of task. These might be set up deliberately in order to cope with some aspect of work, but might also arise without formal control. Various types of group network would therefore exist within organisations. The following diagrams emerged from the researches of Bavelas (1950), Leavitt (1951) and Shaw (1954), and illustrate the variety of structures it is possible to find within task-orientated groups.

In the **circle network** (Figure 4.3), communication flows between pairs of individuals, allowing the production of a number of comments and opinions, though each individual communicates with only two others. In practice, it is inevitable that a greater number of 'crossovers' will take place between people than this network appears to allow.

The **wheel** network (Figure 4.4), reveals that one individual has a dominant role, since he or she controls the flow of communication between all the others, who receive instructions from, and report back to, the centre. This system is supposed to be useful for the completion of routine tasks. This conclusion is unsurprising, since the tasks set by H.J. Leavitt to test the networks were in fact very simple.

It may be seen immediately that the **multi-channel** network (Figure 4.5) implies a much more democratic exchange between the members of the group. Such an 'all-channel' net may be set up formally, or may arise spontaneously, if the conditions are favourable. In either case, a great deal of forbearance and goodwill is required if such a system is not to break down. When the multi-channel network is used in a formal situation, communication usually proceeds through a chairperson.

The **chain** network (Figure 4.6), communication takes place rapidly and with little interaction between members of the group. The person at the top of this chain network receives information. It may be seen that this approach to communication does not allow free interchange between subordinate positions in the chain. This system helps to reinforce the formal authority of the person at the summit.

In the **Y-shaped** network (Figure 4.7), the person at the conjunction of the separate parts of the figure holds power, because he or she is able to receive

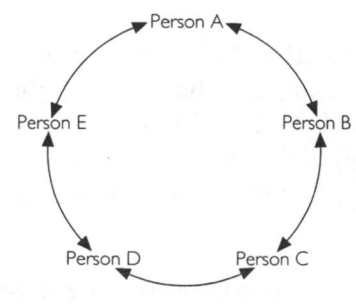

Figure 4.3   Circle network

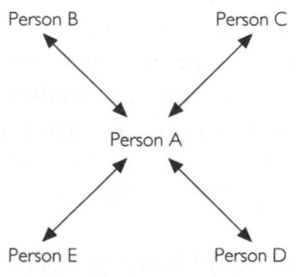

Figure 4.4   Wheel network

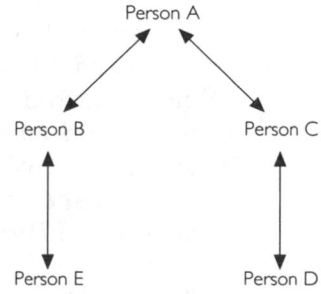

Figure 4.5   Multi-channel network

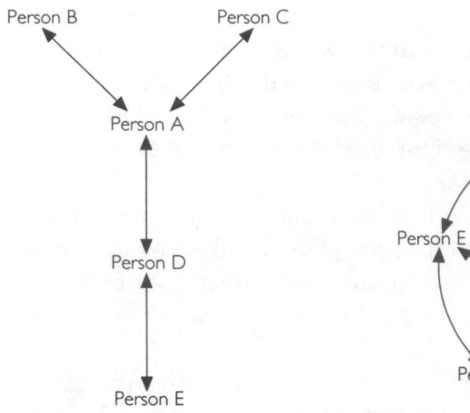
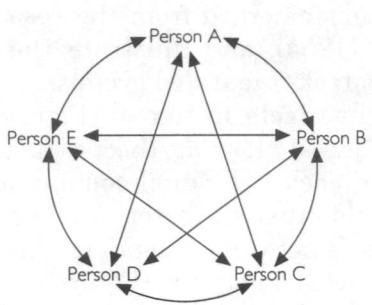

Figure 4.6   Chain network   *Figure 4.7   Y-shaped network*

information from the other individuals. A process of filtration may take place without any of the other participants being able to check the accuracy of the information passed through the network. This network might be found where an editor A receives information from two different sources, B and C, and then passes on a version to an audience D, which in turn might pass on the knowledge gained to another group E, which is at yet another remove from the original sources.

Informal systems of communication

We have already gained some insight into the concept of **informal communication**, but its uses may be further explored by reference to empirical research. During the 1960s and 1970s, the American researcher Peter Blau carried out an investigation into a federal bureau working in Washington, DC. The role of this bureau was to investigate a variety of businesses, to find out whether employment laws had been broken. The agents were assigned to various cases, with half their time devoted to looking through company books and interviewing employers and workforce, and the rest spent in their own office, processing the individual cases.

The application of employment law to the conduct of each firm was difficult and involved many complexities. The rules stated that any problems which manifested themselves should be brought to the attention of the supervisor. Since, however, this same supervisor was known to evaluate the work of the agents, and since their employment prospects depended upon his judgement, they sought advice from one another, in direct violation of the established rules.

The upshot of this practice is described by Haralambos (see *Sociology: Themes and Perspectives*, p. 423):

'Blau claims that this unofficial practice served to increase the agents' efficiency. Information and experience were pooled and problem solving facilitated. Knowledge of the complex regulations was widened and the various ways in which the law could be interpreted were shared. Considerable time was saved since, rather than searching through a thousand-page manual of regulations and two shelves of books on court cases, agents simply asked each other about a regulation or a reference.'

Blau himself came to the conclusion that (Haralambous, p. 423) 'unofficial practices that are explicitly prohibited by official regulations sometimes further the achievement of organisational objectives'.

Sometimes, however, unofficial structures of communication are actively detrimental to the functioning of the organisation, usually where they exist in secret amongst powerful groups. On occasion, unofficial management structures by-pass the very sub-committees they have set up; the sub-committee may in fact be no more than a 'talking shop'. This may remind us of the 'power structure' mentioned by Rosemary Stewart.

In other instances, informal structures are relatively harmless. Dimbleby and Burton discuss the existence of informal contacts (*More than Words*, pp. 116–17):

'networks of friendship and social contact ... can to some extent cut across these matters of status, so that at lunch times, tea breaks or at gatherings like those at churches or sports clubs, people from all levels and sectors of an organisation may have personal communication.'

These authors clearly regard this as a positive step, and note that 'a criticism of some industries has been the separation of canteen and other facilities according to status within the company'. The advantage of such a separation, from the workers' point of view, is that it fosters no illusions about the real relationship between manager and employee.

Dimbleby and Burton are really concerned to establish a more equitable form of communication within organisations, using co-operative structures which will allow efficiency without significantly disturbing power relationships. In fact, employers often rely upon more 'social' relationships, and the limited exchanges these allow between 'leaders' and 'led', to deflect criticism; this works because some employees will actually worry that criticism will be taken personally. Indeed, a very effective management ploy is to treat an unwelcome proposal as a personal affront.

Limits of a liberal agenda

Ultimately, Dimbleby and Burton see unofficial systems as undesirable. In their opinion, 'an active grapevine is present when people are kept ill-informed through official channels of communication'. They argue that (p. 122):

'from a communication perspective it does seem that if people are kept well-informed and involved in the issues and changes facing an organisation then there is less distrust and conflict between "us" and "them" '.

This liberal agenda becomes on occasion a little over-optimistic. On the same page they declare that, 'if the sources of conflict can be defined and communicated then there's a chance that the problem can be "managed" with both sides "winning" '. The larger context of employment relations should be considered; that is, the economic and political constraints found in society as a whole. During times of recession, and at the end of a period which has seen mass redundancy and the deliberate reduction of trade union influence, the balance of overall power has moved in favour of employers. The chances of both sides 'winning' under present conditions are extremely slim.

Some writers, by contrast, believe that corporate communication should either be completely overhauled, or left well alone. David Bernstein takes the view that (p. 89):

> 'a comprehensive change in communications policy is worthless if management's model (actual or implied) is unchanged. If management still sees communication as a one-way process nothing will happen other than a surface show of activity which, by raising then dashing hopes, may in fact leave the situation worse than before.'

Likert: four systems of management

The secrecy apparent in many companies is very different to the practice instituted in some firms and public bodies, where open criticism is encouraged through the use of 'quality circles' of employees, and where ideas sent upwards to management come to form the agenda for a programme of action carried out by the workers themselves. The drawback is that such programmes may be limited to specific departmental issues.

Rensis Likert (see the section above on 'Classical vs. behavioural approaches to organisation') described four systems of management, a theory which emerged from extensive research into the ways in which managers perceived the structural dimensions of their organisations. He set out the four types as follows:

1 **exploitative-authoritarian**;
2 **benevolent-authoritarian**;
3 **consultative**;
4 **participative**.

Here, system 1 closely resembles McGregor's theory X, while system 4 is similar to his theory Y. In Likert's description, different approaches to communication make up the key element which determines the character of each management system. In system 1, there is little reciprocal communication; orders are transmitted and acknowledged. System 2 allows some communication to be initiated by subordinate groups, but this is limited in nature.

System 3 actively encourages interaction between management levels, within certain constraints. In system 4, communication is general and widespread, taking place within an atmosphere of trust. This does not necessarily mean that the *structure* of the organisation has changed, however.

Japanese management systems

In recent years, some writers have referred positively to the types of management found in Japanese corporations. In the second edition of his textbook *Sociology*, Anthony Giddens provides a summary of the distinctive features of Japanese management and communication systems (see p. 293). These, which resemble those of Likert's system 3, are as follows:

- consultation of workers by management, so that decision making is founded upon a variety of perceptions;
- generalisation rather than specialisation of employee experience;
- the guarantee of a job for life;
- the provision of benefits such as company loans, housing and leisure activities.

Despite its surface rationality, there have been a number of attacks on this approach. Giddens (see *Sociology*, p. 294) describes the experiences of Satoshi Kamata, a freelance journalist who worked for Toyota. Kamata wrote a book in which he deplored working conditions and the organisation of the factory:

'Workers are urged on to production, day and night ... through it all the conveyer belts are kept running, with the minimum number of men necessary ... workers are forced to work on Sundays and holidays.'

The consequences for communication are quite obvious; certain types of communication will cease to occur.

The pressure of work on communication was explored in a 1968 study made by Goldthorpe. It showed that some parts of a workforce are isolated because they are unable to participate freely in communication with their colleagues. Goldthorpe and his associates asked workers in a factory to calculate how much they talked to their workmates. Owing to the type of the work they carried out, setters and assemblers were able to communicate with one another, while process workers were much more fragmented and therefore unable to make the same degree of contact. The contribution of some workers to the communicative life of the company was therefore limited by the work itself.

Against the 'rationalisation' of leisure

Some theorists see the onset of a benign but 'total' management as extremely detrimental to the political development of a society. Ed Androw, in *Closing the*

Iron Cage (1981), sets out a critique of all forms of **scientific management**, which he feels attempt to manage not just the working lives of individuals but their leisure activities as well. 'Scientific management' is the term used to describe the results of Frederick Taylor's time and motion studies, in which he sought to control and improve the output of the industrial worker by rationalising every movement and action required to perform a specific function. Many aspects of 'Taylorism' were taken up by Lenin in his campaign to discipline the Soviet industrial worker.

Ed Andrew notices similarities between the 'scientific' breed of manager and the sociologists of leisure, who, he argues, 'conceive of leisure activities under the category of time'. Andrew argues that (p. 13):

> 'The unit-time approach to leisure is similar to that which Taylor applied to production; time-budgets of leisure activities correspond to Taylor's use of the stop-watch in production.'

The conception of leisure time as something to be *used* is, according to Andrew, merely the obverse of working time as another form of directed activity.

Andrew's criticism of the tendency to characterise leisure as a 'compensation' for having to work includes the suspicion that we have come to regard leisure as something to be 'managed' just as efficiently. Developments in the leisure industry have borne out some of Andrew's remarks. In his 1993 study, *The McDonaldization of Society*, George Ritzer sets out a similar case against the fast-food and leisure conglomerates that have produced standardised restaurants and shopping malls throughout America. Ritzer argues that (p. 33):

> 'McDonald's and the process of McDonaldization did not occur in a historical vacuum; it had important precursors ... these precursors provided the principles (of the assembly line, scientific management and bureaucracy) on which the chains of fast-food restaurants were built.'

Revolutionary forms of organisation: France, 1968

The belief that capitalism must be uprooted, rather than merely 'softened' in its effects, rarely gains wide support in industrial societies. When it does, the consequent social upheaval can be considerable. The movements which arose in 1968, the 'year of revolutions', produced a number of different models of organisation. In *French Revolution 1968*, written at the time of the May events in France, Patrick Seale and Maureen McConville described the leading form of organisation set up by the student militants and adopted by large numbers of the populace:

> 'The *comité d'action* was the vehicle chosen by the revolutionary leadership to mobilise mass support for its aims. It was ... an old idea, a variant of the 'councils' which mushroom in most revolutions, basic self-governing units

diametrically opposed to the top-heavy bureaucratic apparatus of the modern state ... they sprang up with incredible speed, in schools, universities, government offices, professional organisations, and firms, but also spontaneously in residential areas on the basis of a network of streets.'

Feminist and libertarian critiques of 'authoritarian' left-wing groups

One of the unfortunate features of some *formal* organisations which oppose the authoritarianism of the state and of capitalism in general is their own allegiance to internal structures which reproduce similar relations of power. In 1979, an attempt was made to reappraise the values held by 'the far left'.

Sheila Rowbotham, Lynne Segal and Hilary Wainwright produced a **feminist and libertarian** perspective on the problems which were thought to plague certain left-wing groups. Their book, which received enthusiastic support from a variety of socialist and feminist groups, was called *Beyond the Fragments*. It examined Trotskyist and Leninist principles of organisation and the 'ghetto' mentality of revolutionary politics. Lynne Segal, then a member of the libertarian socialist group 'Big Flame', explored the principles which were common to libertarian and feminist thought (p. 164):

'the *autonomy* of the women's movement was the central issue for women. Though left groups saw this as divisive, we were aware that their programmes of formal equality for women could conceal the actual subordination of women in their own organisations. Feminists always emphasised the importance of *the personal* and *the subjective*, the need for a total politics.'

Informal and libertarian principles of organisation were used when the Greenham Common and Upper Heyford peace camps were set up in the early 1980s, in an attempt to prevent the deployment of American cruise missiles. Maggie Lowry, writing in *Over Our Dead Bodies* (Thompson, 1983), described the networks of support which sustained mass direct action at the military bases. Caroline Blackwood (1984) examined the internal organisation of the Greenham camp itself, where systems had been set up to distribute the gifts of food and other basic necessities left by well-wishers. The organisation of the camps allowed for different levels of commitment (see *On the Perimeter*, p. 26):

'Because of the floating in and out nature of the camps it was impossible to gauge how many women were actually protesting at the base at any given moment. There was one solid coterie of Greenham residents, then there were the semi-residents who only camped part-time ... then there were the campers from abroad who only came a short time in order to make a gesture of support.'

Models of informal, community-based organisation were revived in the mid-1990s, when 'Alarm UK' co-ordinated the movement against the road-building programme, and the 'Advance Party' mobilised the rave culture in opposition to the Criminal Justice Bill.

The development of communication

Communication is often described as the transmission of information, and should include the concept of an established *route* or connection between places separated by physical distance. Roads, for example, form routes of communication between human settlements.

The 'spatial' aspect of the subject is often neglected. We often assume, when we examine media techniques and systems, that distance is indeed no object. However, it is inevitable that the notion of geography will come to the fore when we consider communication in pre-industrial Europe. In that period, communication depended upon the movement of people, animals and goods along roads and sea-routes which, however well established, were subject to the moods of climate and the predatory attentions of outlaws.

Communication in feudal society

In the first **feudal age**, which began in the ninth century AD, public routes in Europe were in a state of decline. Marc Bloch (an historian and member of the French Resistance who was killed in 1944) notes that the collapse of the Carolingian empire meant that no central power existed to institute public works (see his *Feudal Society*). The Roman roads which spread across Europe were still usable, but were not being maintained, and bridges were no longer kept in good repair. Bloch provides an overview of communication in this era (p. 62):

> 'Compared with what the world offers today, the speed of travel in that age was extremely slow. It was not, however, appreciably slower than it was at the end of the Middle Ages, or even the beginning of the eighteenth century ... On land, the normal distance covered in one day amounted, it seems, to between nineteen and twenty-five miles – for travellers who were in no hurry ... A courier or a handful of resolute men could by making a special effort travel at least twice as fast.'

Awareness of the forces which *motivate* communication is essential; commerce and trade have always been at the centre of the process. In *A History of Medieval Europe* (1970), R.H.C. Davis describes early ninth-century trade carried out by merchants from the south of France, who, according to a Muslim writer (p. 178):

'speak Arabic, Persian, Greek, Frankish, Spanish and Slavonic. They travel from west to east and from east to west, by land and sea. From the west they bring eunuchs, slave-girls, boys, brocade castor-skins, marten and other furs, and swords. They take ship from Frankland in the western Mediterranean Sea and land at Farma ... whence they take their merchandise on camel-back to Qulzum, a distance of twenty-five parsangs.'

It is significant that these traders had to speak a variety of languages, though it is not clear whether such knowledge was possessed individually or collectively within the group.

Despite the obstacles which people faced, some remarkable feats of communication could be performed during the medieval era. Bloch (p. 62) gives the example of a letter written by Pope Gregory VII at Rome on 8 December 1075, which arrived 'at Goslar, at the foot of the Harz, on the 1st January following'. This meant that its bearer had covered approximately 29 miles a day, or over 690 miles in some 24 days, across uneven terrain.

Types of communication in pre-industrial society

Bloch's study of feudalism argues that 'no institution or method could take the place of personal contact between human beings'. In other words, interpersonal communication, conducted face to face, was the only system which guaranteed a reliable exchange of meaning. Kingdoms could only be governed by the *personal* authority of kings. Bloch argues that (p. 62):

'It would have been impossible to govern the state from inside a palace: to control a country, there was no other means than to ride through it incessantly in all directions.'

Communication was therefore always spurred by some pressing need. Many travellers made religious pilgrimages, some wished to supervise far-flung estates, while others searched for an environment free from the scourge of war.

In such a society, the main instruments of communication were:

- word of mouth;
- proclamations;
- sermons;
- letters;
- handwritten books;
- narrative and verse forms;
- religious and secular iconography.

We must not imagine, however, that these forms were equally available to all members of a society. A proclamation, for example, would only be taken seriously if the individual intending to make a formal announcement was recognised as having the authority to do so. Literacy was not universal; the French historian Toussaert (1963) claimed that illiteracy was widespread until the eleventh century, and that the great lords of Flanders took exceptional pride in their ignorance.

The attitudes to learning held by ruling elites partly depended upon which social groups they thought worthy of education. The Church and the ruling class of various European states had, for example, mixed feelings concerning the literacy of women. Sophia Menache (see her essay in Crowley and Heyer, *Communication in History*, p. 77) examines this issue, finding that:

> 'the Church favoured the education of women in the basics of morality and religion, [though] some writers such as the knight of La Tour Landry wanted women to be able to read but thought it unnecessary for them to write. Philippe de Navarre, furthermore, was against the idea of education for women of all classes, since once women could read, he argued, they would be able to receive letters from their lovers.'

It seems clear that these reservations were founded on dissatisfaction with the thought that women would gain independence; the knight who proposed that women be taught to read but not to write appears to object to the *activity* associated with writing.

While letters in later medieval Europe became a recognised method of private communication, it is important to realise that, for the bulk of the population, all aspects of culture were transmitted orally. Authors wrote from within oral traditions, and knew that their work would usually be read aloud in a communal setting. Culture was therefore noticeably *social*. In addition, travelling poets and entertainers brought stories and news, often using verse forms to aid memory. James Burke, writing in Crowley and Heyer, *Communication in History* (p. 85), recounts the practice, common to many great households, of using a servant to read letters aloud. Even where members of the gentry were capable of reading, the task was allocated to a trusted underling. The idea of a silent perusal of text was regarded as unusual. Burke goes on to note that:

> 'those who could read silently were regarded with some awe. St. Augustine, speaking in the fifth century about St. Ambrose, said: "... a remarkable thing ... when he was reading his eyes glided over the pages and his heart sensed out the sense, but his voice and tongue were at rest".'

This provides strong testimony to the public and *discursive* nature of medieval culture.

The early Church: communicating an ideology

One central issue in communication is how elites establish and sustain themselves through the control of various systems of **ideological** reproduction; in other words, how they maintain their position through public forms of address and public actions. Menache (Crowley and Heyer, *Communication in History*, p. 73) writes that:

> 'Mediaeval ruling classes ... had the strongest imperative to develop a communication system. Their purpose was both to manipulate large masses of people ... and to receive and transmit information as an integral part of their rule.'

An early example of a group which tried to achieve ideological hegemony may be found if we study the growth of the Catholic Church. James Curran, writing in 1977 (see *The Media: Contexts of Study*), drew attention to the fact that Church liturgy reached a very wide audience throughout the medieval period. From this, we may realise that the use of modern technology is not the only means of achieving a significant *impact* in terms of communication.

Curran asks (see p. 10) how the See of Rome, which was 'merely a local bishopric' in the early fourth century, became 'the undisputed sovereign head of the Western Christian Church'. Part of the explanation for this extraordinary transformation comes from the initial advantages enjoyed by the state, which was:

> 'situated in the capital of the old Roman Empire, and was thought to have been founded by St. Peter ... it was assigned a special status by the Roman Emperors in the East'.

The ability of the early Church to act as a mediator between rival monarchs and other feudal leaders does not fully explain its rise to prominence. Curran (p. 11) attributes its success to 'its early dominance over institutional processes of ideological production that created and maintained support for its exercise of power'.

I would suggest that the papacy had the power to promote itself as an institution, through its exclusive right to promote the Christian religion as an *idea*. It used St Matthew's gospel to justify its sovereign power over the whole Church. The passage concerned came from a speech made by Christ to his disciple Peter: 'Thou art Peter and upon this rock I will build my Church.' Since the authority of Peter was thought to have passed to the bishops of Rome, the word of God could be mediated by the Roman See. The propagation of the Church's world-view was effected through the papal *curia*, a kind of headquarters office which communicated religious doctrine.

However, the assumption that the early Church relied chiefly upon the written or spoken word neglects the existence of other means of disseminating religious ideology. Icons and paintings reinforced a particular view of Christianity. Burke (Crowley and Heyer, *Communication in History*, p. 84) advances the idea that imagery was of central importance to the dissemination of religious doctrine:

'The great mediaeval theologian St. Thomas Aquinas particularly recommended the theatrical use of imagery for the recall of religious matters. "All knowledge has its origins in sensation", he said. The truth was accessible through visual aids . . . Church imagery took on the form of memory agent.'

Curran speaks of the role of 'religious magic'. He advances the idea that (p. 15):

'the whole paraphernalia of ecclesiastical sorcery and ritual was of crucial importance in mediating a . . . construction of reality . . . the medieval Church acted as a repository of magical power which it dispensed to the faithful . . . the rites of passage (baptism, confirmation, marriage, purification after childbirth, last unction and burial) administered by the Church invested religious significance into each stage of the life cycle'.

Mass communication

The concept of mass communication

The concept of **mass communication** requires careful handling. The term is employed to describe a number of features of public communication, suggesting perhaps that each possesses the same qualities. It is used to refer to media **institutions**, to the scale of **production** supposedly achieved by the media, to the **distribution** of media 'products', and to the **audiences** which receive or 'consume' media content. While it is probably acceptable to talk about 'mass' institutions, this must not obscure the existence of small-scale production companies which 'feed' the larger bodies with material. It would also be a mistake to ignore the growth in the number of outlets for the **distribution** of media (including satellite television and cable networks); at the same time, the increase in the number of outlets is matched by the *concentration* of media power, and the tendency to create monopolies (BSkyB is a well-known example).

Another important point is that it would be wrong to characterise the audience as a uniform mass, either in terms of the subject positions of the people who compose it, or with regard to the attitudes and values held by such individuals. John Corner (see *Television Form and Public Address*, p. 14) cites Raymond Williams's insistence that 'there are in fact no masses, only ways of seeing people as masses'.

Despite the dangers of a blanket application of the term 'mass' to the study of the media and their relationships, it remains a valid description. Corner makes a similar point about television (p. 15):

'the "mass" nature of broadcast television still seems to me to be widely evident as a feature of its economy and institutional structure'.

The birth of mass communication

The majority of theorists date the beginning of mass communication from the invention of movable type in the middle of the fifteenth century. However, as we saw above, Church services represent a form of communication notable for their 'mass' reproduction of a specific ideology.

Print was the leading force in the expansion of knowledge, but it depended upon the existence of what Crowley and Hayer (*Communication in History*, p. 91) call 'receptive conditions'. The growth of a 'vernacular literacy' (the ability to read and write in one's own language, as opposed to knowledge of Latin), together with improvements in technology, helped prepare the ground for the expansion of written forms of communication.

An example of 'receptive conditions' is the use of paper as a replacement for parchment, and the consequent rise in the production of handwritten manuscripts, from the thirteenth century onwards. The manufacture of paper originated in China, developing between the second and third century BC. By 1500, every major European city had a paper mill and, as Elizabeth Eisenstein writes (Crowley and Heyer, *Communication in History*, p. 105), 'the reproduction of written materials began to move from the copyist's desk to the printer's workshop'. Ecclesiastical control of the dissemination of ideas ceased to be a foregone conclusion.

A secular interpretation of the world grew to challenge the hegemony of the Church; in other words, human beings were seen increasingly as responsible agents, actors in a lay community whose values were no longer dictated by a priesthood possessed of a monopoly on education. As Curran puts it (*The Media: Contexts of Study*, p. 23):

'The effect of a book and pamphlet culture in the later middle ages was to shrink the space universe, to extend collective knowledge of people and events through the medium of the written word.'

Inside the Church, however, the use of copyists continued during the early years of the printing revolution, partly because it was seen as a useful device for encouraging monks to be diligent in their religious duties (see Eisenstein, in Crowley and Heyer, in *Communication in History*, p. 109).

The distribution of the Bible: the road to free interpretation?

In many walks of human life, various forms of authority seek to monopolise the **interpretation** of information and doctrinal matters. This is made a great deal easier when those in power maintain control of the seminal texts associated with their particular religion or creed. When literacy increased and the Bible began to circulate amongst the middle-class citizenry of Europe, individuals could quite easily assume, on the basis of what they had been told by the Church itself, that they had direct access to the word of God. The role of a priesthood as a class of interpreter might therefore be of less and less importance. Direct access to scripture implied that Christianity was both accessible and personal. This caused a proliferation of sects, which adopted a radical approach not simply to religion but to the political sphere as well.

The rise of print

The form of printing press which utilized metal type appeared in a number of different centres in and around the year 1450: Haarlem, Avignon and Mainz all contributed to the 'invention' of this phase of printing. McQuail, however, argues that the printed book was (p. 9) 'initially only a technical device for reproducing the same ... range of texts that was already being extensively copied'.

It is indeed true that much of the early output of the European press did not consist of new or original works, but met only the demand for the standard products of the time. Nevertheless, the increased scale of output was significant. In the mid-fifteenth century, one copyist might produce perhaps two volumes a year. By comparison, it is estimated that a Venetian printer active in the period 1481–1501 could produce nearly 350 volumes per annum. Of course, this is an average estimate of output produced by organised print shops, and does not refer to individual titles. Nevertheless, a massive increase in productivity had taken place, at the cost of a drastic reduction in the number of copyists.

A revolution in print?

Curran argues that print made possible 'an educational revolution' in Protestant countries in early modern Europe. The growth of literacy ran alongside the proliferation of printed books. It was the Protestant faith in particular, together with increased commercial activity, which appeared to act as a spur to the extension of oral and written political discourse. Christopher Hill, writing in *The World Turned Upside Down* (a study of radical ideas during the English revolution), identifies religious ideas as a central force in the rebellions of the sixteenth century (p. 161):

> 'Printing had made protestantism possible because it facilitated the rapid spread of popular theology among the literate, especially in towns. Where the Lollard Bible circulated in tens of copies, Tyndale's New Testament circulated in hundreds and the Geneva Bible in thousands. But printing also ruined protestantism as a single coherent creed because the reading of books is even less possible to control than the reading of manuscripts.'

In the 1640s, ordinary English people began to form their own congregations, and so relied less upon clerical authority. As soon as the exercise of direct religious power was avoided or abolished, people began to investigate the possibility of a more personal form of salvation. The political philosopher Thomas Hobbes (see Curran, p. 37) noted with revulsion that:

> 'Every man, nay, every boy and wench that could read English thought they spoke with God Almighty, and understood what he said.'

Radical ideas were also circulated in plays and other popular forms. Robert Greene's tragedy *Selimus*, for example, contained lines which suggested that heaven and hell were 'mere fictions', while religion was simply 'a fable' designed to keep the poor in a state of fear. It was but a short step to questioning the validity of all forms of authority.

Winstanley: against the 'hearsay' of the establishment

Gerard Winstanley, the leader of the radical political sect called the Diggers, published a number of tracts which argued against the established powers of church and state. He had an interesting perspective on the human perception of reality. Since he believed that the external world was the manifestation of God, it seemed to him desirable to achieve the most direct experience of reality possible. This meant that the human subject must trust the five senses, or immediate physical experience, rather than books, or doctrines, or vague imaginings. Hill selects this passage from Winstanley to illustrate the creed he espoused (see p. 149):

> 'Oh ye hearsay preachers, deceive not the people any longer by telling them that this glory shall not be known and seen until the body is laid in the dust. I tell you, this great mystery is begun to appear, and it must be seen by the material eyes of the flesh: and those five senses that is in man shall partake of this glory ... all outward glory that is at a distance from the five senses ... is of a transient nature; and so is the heaven that your preachers tell you of.'

Notice that Winstanley characterises the knowledge of the priests as 'hearsay;' in other words, as part of conventional belief and lacking the purity and truth of direct experience. Hill, examining Winstanley's doctrines, notes that if God 'is everywhere, if matter is God, then there can be no difference between the sacred and the secular'.

For many, the demise of religious belief altogether was an unavoidable consequence of the upheavals of the English revolution. Some of these individuals fell into despair. In 1649 Isaac Penington the younger (see Hill, *The World Turned Upside Down*, p. 171) declared that 'everything is darkness, death, emptiness, vanity, a lie'. Others felt liberated from what they came to see as superstition. Overall, the decay of old and the growth of new forms of belief was a major factor in the radicalisation of Parliamentarian soldiers and civilians alike, and allowed the formation of political organisations like the Levellers.

Print-based media

The development of the newspaper

The **newspaper** began its existence in the form of the newsbook or news-sheet, which appeared in the late 1640s (see 'Print and advertising' below. McQuail believes that (p. 9) the newspaper's 'chief precursor seems ... to have been the letter rather than the book'. Letters were sent through the nascent postal service in order to communicate intelligence about commercial developments. Some writers believe that the earliest newspapers were really therefore concerned with politics only where it related to trade. In fact, the revolutionary period saw the publication of a number of newsbooks which attempted to agitate for king or Parliament.

Nevertheless, it would appear that the commercial paper was the form which most closely determined the future development of what became the newspaper industry. The establishment of a flourishing press was not without incident; censorship occurred throughout the seventeenth century.

Restrictions on the press

Restrictions on what it is possible to print continue to the present day, and have taken different forms throughout the history of newspapers. Where direct force was effective, it was employed. The Printing Act was in force from 1662 to 1669, but financial rather than legal control has often proved more useful, from the establishment's point of view.

In Britain, financial restriction took the form of 'Stamp Duty', first imposed in 1712 but containing inconsistencies which allowed longer newspapers to avoid the tax by registering themselves as pamphlets! Between 1714 and 1725, twenty-two provincial newspapers were in circulation. Unstamped newspapers were sold in the streets throughout the first half of the eighteenth century, but an Act of 1743 ensured that such outlets were removed. However, nothing could halt the growth of the press; there were some thirty-five extant local papers in 1760. In London, there were nearly ninety titles available in the same year.

The suppression of political content may have been partly responsible for the limited service which some late eighteenth-century newspapers were able to provide. Public announcements, news from abroad, excessive data on the latest royal occasion, and commercial news remained the staple diet until the rise of the radical press of the early and mid-nineteenth century.

The Public Ledger of September 1761, for example, carries a detailed running order for the Coronation of George III under the heading 'Plan of the Procession at the Coronation', and goes on to print a 'patriotic' poem on the event, a letter to the printer, a compendium of shipping movements and an announcement of a 'National Lottery'. It is odd to think that this dismal feature is likely to be the most obvious connection with the content of modern newspapers.

Dissent and the radical press

In *The Making of the English Working Class* (1968), E.P. Thompson argues that the deference and political quietism once shown by the working class had begun to dissipate as the result of two forces: the influence of Methodism and the industrial system of labour, which brought workers together in close proximity. The growth of working-class self-organisation was accompanied by the flowering of a **radical political press**. Government legislation against the formation of *national* organisations led to the establishment of local political groups, which often took their lead from the radical newspapers of the time. The largest circulation was achieved by *The Black Dwarf*, which was founded by T.J. Wooler in 1818. Other notable publications included *The Gorgon*, and *The Political Register*, which was edited by the 18-year-old Thomas Sherwin and later became renowned as *The Republican*.

Meanwhile, the growth of interest in newspapers, and the security offered to the commercial press by advertising revenue, made all publications, whatever their political affiliation, difficult to control. Increased revenue also allowed the middle-class press to retain full-time journalists.

The second wave of radicalism took place in the early 1830s, revealing the beginnings of a political analysis which saw the interests of labour and capital as diametrically opposed. *The Poor Man's Guardian*, in a front-page address of 1831, called upon its readership to support its campaign against the 'tyrants' who had summoned its editors to appear in court:

> 'Again, let us firmly declare that we dispute the power of any one man, or any set of men ... to make "laws" for affecting life and liberty ... they can have no *moral right* to subject an unwilling and adverse party to rules which suit their own interests; we object to, and dispute all their "laws".'

The attempt to discipline such newspapers through legal action became, however, increasingly ineffective. Juries were reluctant to convict editors and journalists of the crime of 'seditious libel'. The middle-class press was also often opposed to such laws, because its own freedoms could decline as a result of general repression. By 1843, the laws against libel were moderated.

The power of the bourgeois press

Eventually, the suppression of the radical press was seen as counter-productive. A current of argument began to circulate amongst middle-class editors and other commentators to the effect that it was more desirable to encourage the growth of a conservative outlook amongst the working class itself. This might be achieved, they thought, by allowing the greater circulation of 'quality' newspapers. Thus, the abolition of press taxes was due to what Curran (see p. 51) calls the 'social imperialism' of the bourgeoisie, rather than 'a principled commitment to anarchic freedom of expression in the press'.

By 1854, *The Times* had achieved a circulation of 40,000 copies per issue, and was efficiently and legibly printed. *The Daily Telegraph* was one of the first newspapers to take advantage of the abolition of the press tax, displaying a cover-price of a penny and moving from a radical stance to a right-wing position (which it still seems reluctant to abandon). Giles and Hodgson, in *Creative Newspaper Design*, argue that the *Telegraph*, long before the rise of the tabloid press, was fond of using stunts and promotions:

> 'In 1873 it discovered the "Loch Ness Monster", in 1877 it gave a Jubilee party for 30,000 children in Hyde Park ... and claimed to be the first newspaper to treat prostitution boldly and plainly.'

In the light of these events, it is remarkable that the *Telegraph* did not foresee more recent developments in publicity; though perhaps the discovery of a headline reading 'Queen Victoria Ate my Hamster' is too much to hope for.

Despite the frivolities of the period, Curran describes the outlook of the bourgeois press in this era as an essential ideological preparation for the triumphant imperialism of the British state (p. 51):

> 'these newspapers presented a very different construction of reality from that mediated by the early popular radical press. A view of society as a system of class exploitation gave way to a new definition of reality in which different sections of the community were portrayed as being interdependent, with shared interests in common ... the early stress on class solidarity gave way to a stress on the individual ... the internationalist perspective of the early radical press ... dissolved into an increasingly nationalist and imperialistic coverage of foreign affairs.'

Lord Northcliffe: shaping the popular

Alfred Harmsworth began his career in journalism as a writer on the magazine *Titbits*, which pioneered the concept of small and inconsequential 'snippets' of information, designed to entertain rather than inform. In 1894, Harmsworth bought *The London Evening News* and took it down market. With the launch of his own title in 1896, *The Daily Mail*, he began to consolidate his approach to newspaper publishing. He concentrated upon tales of human interest and adventure, calculating that there was a mass readership eager to consume such a product. In 1900, the *Mail* became the first newspaper to exceed a million readers. Increased circulation led to more advertising revenue; the paper was thus able to keep its cover price low.

Harmsworth was granted a barony in 1905 and became Lord Northcliffe. Giles and Hodgson (p. 49) present him as the 'father' of the popular press:

'The effect of Northcliffe's ideas on the newspapers of the period was two-fold: it spawned a new growth of down-market dailies . . . [and] . . . spelt a decline in fortune of the more conservative Victorian dailies . . . the battle for readers had begun, a battle in which some old and influential titles would go to the wall.'

Northcliffe's influence was on popular journalism; photojournalism was reserved for *The Daily Mirror*, founded in 1903 (also by Northcliffe) and intended primarily as a paper for women.

The 1930s: raising the temperature

The Daily Mirror gained an extensive readership by the mid-1930s, by making itself as distinctive as possible. Headlines were cast in thick black type, of a size then quite uncommon. On occasion its editors used a combined headline of poster size which covered both front and back pages. Other changes are described by Giles and Hodgson:

'The length of the news items shrank, foreign news almost disappeared, pictures became bigger, a page of comic strips appeared . . . human interest stories abounded.'

Meanwhile, *The Daily Mail's* pole position as cheerleader of the political right was held against all comers. The growth of far-right groups, such as Mosley's 'British Union of Fascists', was supported by Associated Press titles, which controlled the *Mail*, the *Evening News* and *The Sunday Dispatch*.

In overall command of these newspapers was Lord Rothermere, another of the twentieth century's press tycoons. Rothermere was in the habit of writing his own leading articles, and on 8 January 1934, he demonstrated his commitment to political extremism by producing one entitled 'Hurrah for the Blackshirts!'. This was a reference to the uniformed supporters of Mosley's fascist party. The article began (see Colin Cross, *The Fascists in Britain*, p. 96) with praise for Nazi Germany and Fascist Italy, and continued:

'At this next, vital election, Britain's survival as a Great Power will depend on the existence of a well-organised Party of the Right, ready to take over responsibility for national affairs with the same directness of purpose and energy of method as Mussolini and Hitler have displayed.'

The article ended with a list of addresses at which readers could enrol in the British Union of Fascists. A number of mainstream and even aristocratic right-wing figures were seduced by the apparent power of the new movement. Thomas Moore, the Tory MP for Ayr, claimed that fascist ideals were 'largely derived from the Conservative Party'. However, other Tories took care to distance themselves from Mosley.

Although widespread outrage greeted Rothermere's press campaign, it continued for some time and in a variety of curious forms. In a book called *Fascism Inside England* (published in 1946), Frederick Mullally described the competition run by the *Evening News* in March and April 1934 (see p. 57):

> 'the *Evening News* invited its readers to join in a 'Why I like the Blackshirts' feature. Reasons had to be submitted on a post card. They were published, a score or so at a time, in successive issues of *Evening News* and the best 250 entries were rewarded with – double tickets to the Albert Hall [a mass fascist rally held on 22 April 1934].'

The fascist 'propaganda' supremo, William Ivens, took the opportunity of ordering his members to encourage at least a dozen letters to be sent in from each branch! However, Rothermere's relationship with fascism became strained as it grew increasingly obvious that Mosley was committed to a policy of anti-Semitism. Curiously, Rothermere had expended some energy denying, in the pages of the *Mail*, that Hitler had any policy which discriminated against Jewish people.

The much-advertised Blackshirt meeting at the Albert Hall was followed by one at Olympia, where Mosley's stewards overplayed their hand. The left infiltrated the meeting and settled amongst the crowd. As the meeting proceeded, person after person got to their feet to interrupt. They could not easily be heard above Mosley's amplified voice, but he stopped speaking on each occasion to allow stewards to identify the hecklers. The vicious beatings doled out to scores of people, and their violent ejection from the hall, was widely reported in the press and cost Mosley a great deal of support.

News: selection at work

Roger Fowler, in *Language in the News* (p. 110), examines the question of **news values** and declares: 'the world of the Press is not the real world, but a world skewed and judged'. In this case, reference to the real world is intended to show that the press is **selective** and that 'the vast majority of events are not mentioned'. Since most events are never reported, 'selection ... gives us a partial view of the world'.

However, it is a physical impossibility to report every event that occurs. All human understanding and judgement is based upon selection. The point Fowler is trying to make is that there are social and institutional *principles* at work in those selections which are made by the press. Readers of newspapers are then dependent on a narrow field of information from which to make, in turn, their own selections.

Not found but created

Greg Philo (Fowler, p. 13) argues that the usual picture of journalistic activity is mistaken: 'news is not "found" or even "gathered" so much as made. It is a *creation* of a journalistic process, an artifact, a commodity even.' This is not to argue that events are 'fictions' with no relationship to the truth. Real events occur and the results have material consequences. The purpose of analysis is to discover the ways in which such events are presented. This moves beyond selection to the **creation** of news and meaning.

Analysis: 'The John Smith choice'

The death of the Labour leader John Smith in May 1994 led to a leadership contest in which the opinion of news journalists played a significant role. The right-wing press, particularly the tabloids, had for many years campaigned against any form of socialist argument. It had made a point of vilifying institutions and individuals responsible for implementing left-of-centre policies. In effect, an agenda was set which the Labour party was forced to recognise. In the case of the Labour leadership election the Conservative press, in the guise of reporting the prospects of the candidates standing for the leadership, made what amounted to a direct intervention. David McKie, writing in the *Media Guardian* of 15 August 1994 (see his article 'Five heads with a single mind'), argued that the papers controlled by Rupert Murdoch were hedging their bets in anticipation of a Labour General Election victory:

> 'Apart from *Today*, the Murdoch editors seem by a happy coincidence to be saying much the same thing as Rupert ... The Murdoch hierarchy has to calculate now that a Labour win next time is more than likely. Murdoch's message [that he could envisage supporting Blair] holds out the hope that the kind of vicious media assault usually turned on Labour at election time might be spared – if Labour acts acceptably.'

Blair's success in replacing the party's historic Clause Four, achieved on 29 April 1995, was an important signal to would-be allies that Labour was indeed prepared to act in an 'acceptable' manner.

Blair surge?

The following analysis is based on material which appeared in *The Sunday Express* of 15 May 1994. The headline carried on the front page concerned the contest for the leadership of the Labour party, and read:

'BLAIR SURGE SINKS BROWN'.

This was a reference to the dramatic increase in support for Tony Blair, at the expense of one of his rivals, Gordon Brown. Above this headline appeared the words 'Sunday Express weekend poll exclusive'. On the following day, 16 May, under the headline 'Blair's lead stirs doubts', *The Guardian* reported that:

'Some Labour supporters are concerned about being bounced by a quick summer election into a Blair succession, particularly as his case is already being proclaimed by newspapers not normally friendly to the party.'

Amongst these newspapers was *The Sunday Times*, which had run a poll giving Blair a 32 per cent lead, and *The Sunday Telegraph*, which reported its own finding that Blair was 27 per cent ahead of his nearest rival.

Categorising the rivals

The article which followed *The Sunday Express* headline used a number of phrases which described Blair in positive terms. Blair was the 'rising star' and 'the leading party moderniser'. By contrast, another candidate, John Prescott, is described as 'firebrand employment spokesman'.

Thus two of the eventual contenders were **categorised**, one as *modern* and the other as a *firebrand*. The description of Prescott is not necessarily negative, but the categories used here create meaning because they carry *implicit opposites*. The opposites here are not Blair and Prescott, but rather the opposing qualities suggested by what each is not. Thus Blair, by being modern, is not old-fashioned, or out of date, or yesterday's man. Equally, he is not a *traditionalist*, a category which is sometimes used positively. Prescott, as a firebrand, is not gentle, or retiring or self-effacing – nor is he a wimp. Ultimately, however, the qualities which are accorded to each man depend for their meaning on the *context* in which they are found.

Rise of the new man

Inside the paper, an article by Julia Langdon sets out Blair's qualifications in a headline and supporting blurb:

'Opponents have called him Mr Blur but Oxford-educated socialist high-flier knows exactly where he is heading

THE JOHN SMITH CHOICE: RISE OF THE NEW MAN.'

The entire article is positive in tone, carrying a picture of Blair with his wife and offspring over the caption, 'Happy family man'. The descriptions of Blair are telling; he is an 'Oxford-educated socialist high-flier'. The term 'socialist' is used so often to denigrate an individual that its function here is unusual. It is qualified, even overwhelmed, by the surrounding phrases, 'Oxford-educated' and 'high-flier'. (It may be Blair's own policy to use the word 'socialist' in the context of policies which voters will identify as refreshingly 'undogmatic', in order to take the sting out of the term when it is applied to his party by its enemies.)

The article itself is written in a relatively informal style, and begins:

'It was John Smith, of course, who picked him out, almost as soon as he arrived in the House of Commons. He was bright and clever and going somewhere. Smith asked for Tony Blair.'

This could be the beginning of an adventure narrative, or perhaps a species of light romance. The exact time and place of the encounter is vague, so the event may be no more than the whim of the writer. The story-line is simple, and structurally comparable to the plot of a fairy-tale; arrival at the Commons, recognition, then the elevation to power.

However, the need to express the idea that Blair is somehow extra-special leads to some contradictions, chiefly centred on the clash between this idea and his lack of experience. While it 'seems incredible' that Blair was picked out only eleven years ago, it is nevertheless 'inevitable' that 'someone as able as Blair was going to rise with a resurrected, new look Labour party'.

Blair's supposed vagueness over policy is presented as a positive asset: 'he has been wise enough ... not to be too specific'. He is described in positive terms as:

'a New man, not only according to the customary definition – he changed the nappies of his three children when they were babies – but because he is a New Socialist, too'.

The typical proof of the 'new man's' credentials has long been cited as the willingness to change children's nappies, and is part of the convenient 'short-hand' that is used as a substitute for evidence or extended argument.

Another common theme emerges in the discourse which insists that real leftists are motivated by envy, while Blair is above such emotions: 'he describes himself as a socialist, formed not from the unhealthy motivation of guilt, but from instinct and reason'. Blair is contrasted here with those unknown others who became socialists for entirely the 'wrong' reasons. A simple opposition is set up, between political belief which derives from guilt or envy, and that which emerges from purer motives; this kind of contrast is a device taken from rhetoric (see Chapter 3). It is a 'loaded' choice, between alternatives which exclude other possibilities.

Print and advertising

Advertising has always had a public character and usually a commercial intention. As a type of address which is 'carried' by the mass media, some commentators argue that it does not qualify as a form or medium in its own right. However, the danger in such a view is that it could lead us to underestimate the importance of advertising's place in society as a whole. Armand Mattelart (see *Advertising International*, Preface, p. ix) is one of a number of writers who point to the widespread influence of advertising as an institution:

'Advertising has become an essential actor within public space. It has overflowed the cramped frame of the commercial break in order to consitute itself as a mode of communication.'

Andrew Wernick's *Promotional Culture* advances a similar argument. Wernick describes how he (Preface, p. vii):

'began to see that advertising was not just a commercial phenomenon, nor ... just the product of a specific communications apparatus. Promotion (my term for advertising and its practices taken in the widest and most generic sense) was a rhetorical form diffused throughout our culture.'

In Wernick's opinion, advertising had 'come to shape not only that culture's symbolic and ideological contents', but also its 'ethos, texture and constitution as a whole'.

As a 'rhetorical form', advertising employs a number of different modes of **address**. An *address* (mentioned in Chapter 1) is the deliberate direction or delivery of a message (an utterance, written passage or public display) from an individual, group or institutional source to any type of recipient, whether an individual person or an established collective.

Types of advertising

Advertising can be divided into the following types:

- **consumer advertising**, directed at the mass market and carried by the mass media, or directed at a local market and carried by smaller outlets;
- **sponsorship**, where the advertiser seeks to keep its name in public view, and/or seeks to enhance its reputation through association with an event or an activity, or even where it seeks to control the object of its patronage;
- **trade and specialist** advertising, usually addressed to other manufacturers or client groups;
- **state** advertising, where the state seeks compliance from the population: this may take the form of public information campaigns (wearing

seatbelts, driving responsibly) or appear under the guise of information but actually may have a commercial or political purpose (advertising shares in public utilities);

- **charitable appeals**, where the exchange between advertiser and audience is not 'goods for money', but an appeal to the practical exercise of socially acceptable forms of conscience.

Closely related forms of public address are found in public relations and other promotional forms:

- **corporate advertising**, intended to enhance the reputation of a company or conglomerate, with a general view to the promotion or consolidation of its social or symbolic power;
- **public relations**, a form of promotion or news management closely related to commercial advertising but more concerned with producing acceptable, attractive or innocuous images of individuals or institutions;
- **party political broadcasts**, concerned to achieve a political objective.

The development of modern advertising

Commercial activity has always entailed the promotion of raw materials, finished articles, or services. The most primitive form of advertising consists of a symbol or word either inscribed directly upon or affixed to a building or site where a commercial activity takes place and a certain product is available. The next stage is the circulation of a form of symbolic content at some distance from the point of sale. Pre-industrial advertising consisted of these forms, supplemented by the sending of newsletters and the use of public announcements.

Gillian Dyer (in *Advertising as Communication*) places advertising in its context (p. 15):

'In order to understand advertising as a form of communication and as an influential social institution, it is important to see it as part of an historical and social process firmly linked to the economies of western industrialised nations.'

In the pre-industrial era, advertising was, in Dyer's words (p. 15), 'a relatively simple system of proclamation and announcement on the periphery of the national economy'. Mattelart, on the other hand, thinks that (*Advertising International*, p. ix) 'the question of advertising has long ceased to be a national question' and refers to its 'transnational dimension'. The history of advertising, both national and global, is clearly an important aspect of any study of its social power.

Dyer argues that the origins of advertising lie in the rise of seventeenth-century news-sheets or 'mercuries', the early forms of what we now call newspapers. In the middle of the seventeenth century, advertisements resembled the 'small ads' which still appear in various journals. These were cast in the form of 'announcements'. By 1658, however, Dyer detects a new development, reflected in an advertisement which appeared in the *Mercurius Politicus* of that year. Instead of a plain description of services or products, there is a *rhetorical* flourish in the address which is made (p. 16):

> 'That excellent, and by all Physicians, approved China drink, called by the Chineans Tcha, by other nations Tay, alias Tee, is sold at The Sultaness Head Cophee-House, in Sweetings' Rents, by the Royal Exchange, London.'

Dyer also cites an advertisement for toothpaste, which appeared in 1660. This, she believes, demonstrates an even greater commitment to techniques of persuasion (p. 16):

> 'Most excellent and approved Dentifrice to scour and cleanse the Teeth, making them white as ivory, preserves from the Tooth-ach; so that being constantly used, the Parties using it are never troubled with the Tooth-ach; It fastens the Teeth, sweetens the Breath, and preserves the Gums and Mouth from cankers and Impothumes; . . . and the right are only to be had at Thomas Rookes, Stationer.'

'Small ads' in eighteenth- and nineteenth-century American newspapers

'Small ads' are regarded by some as 'amateur' versions of the large corporate advertising seen in industrial societies. However, study of such forms of public address reveal the principles which lie behind the construction of all types of advertising. The following examples are taken from early American advertisements of the eighteenth and nineteenth centuries.

The Worcester Gazette, based in Massachusetts, carried a number of advertisements for the sale of land, goods and services. Notice that there is no specialist agency involved in the mediation of a client's message in these cases; the client's product is mediated by the typographical abilities of the compositor and the available space in the newspaper itself. In its issue of 5 September 1792, the following display appeared:

> 'Hoſpital for the Small Pox.
> The ſubsſriber hereby in–
> forms his friends and the publick, that his
> Hoſpital is now open for the reception of patients
> for INNOCULATION with the SMALL POX, on
> as low terms as it can poſſibly be done, viz. *eight*
> *dollars* for three weeks, and ſix ſhillings for every
> week, if longer detained.
>   ISRAEL ATHERTON.

N.B. House Room and Attendance for three
dollars.
Lancaster, September 5, 1792.'

The essential elements of this particular address are clearly apparent. The
first part is designed to draw attention to the *existence* of the product. Most
advertisements draw attention to the product in some way, though some
modern advertisers use more abstract references.

The first line of the address is printed large to make an impact, but there is
only the most tenuous connection between the size and the content, so that it
becomes clear that the printer has selected large type here in order to obey a
convention. It is a convention which does not always help the reader understand
the message.

The second line reveals an attempt to *establish a relationship* with the
prospective customers. The next part of the address is concerned to reinforce
audience perception of the product, while the insistence that inoculation will
be carried out 'on as low terms as it can possibly be done' is intended to
persuade the consumer of the reasonable cost of the service. Here, the need for
medical assistance has been turned into a commodity.

Some advertisements confine themselves to more or less simple statements,
but all will contain some element designed to impress or persuade; adverts are
never purely 'informational' in character. Even the following brief display
includes the word 'cheap' to draw the customer:

'*FOR SALE*,
A FEW hundred weight of
good RUSSIA FEATHERS, cheap for
CASH at the Store of
WILLIAM CALDWELL, 2d.
Worcester, January 9, 1801.'

Where an advertiser is sure that his or her service will be regarded as
essential by a group of consumers, then it is less important to go to great
lengths to persuade the target audience to respond. A display from 1839
advertises the *Great Western* steamship, essentially through a wood-cut of the
ship, a few introductory remarks, and the list of the year's sailings between
Bristol and New York. Children under 13 years and servants go for half price,
but there are 'no second class or steerage passengers taken'.

Slavery in print

In the 1840s, American newspapers carried a great many notices devoted to
tracing the whereabouts of runaway slaves. This represented the concern of

owners to protect their investment, and was one consequence of the dismal trade in human beings. The following is taken from *The Washington Intelligencer*:

> '200 DOLLARS REWARD. – Ran away from the
> subscriber's residence, about 4 miles from Bryantown,
> Charles county, Maryland, on Thursday morning, the 11th of June
> my negro man CHARLES, calls himself Charles Dyson, about
> 23 years old, 5 feet 6 or 7 inches high; a bright mulatto, and has
> a scar on the right or left side of his lower jaw bone, occasioned
> several years ago by a burn. The above reward will be paid if
> taken in a non-slaveholding State, and fifty dollars if taken within
> the states of Virginia and Maryland, or the District of Columbia.
> july 10–2awcptf   J. ED. KEECH'

It is interesting to note that the facial expressions of another escaped slave are described in some detail, but that the owner has no conception that he is actually describing the effects of a lifetime of stress and servitude, rather than the simple evidence of character:

> 'His voice is coarse, and when spoken to his eyes, though generally turned towards the ground, are rolled suddenly upwards, so as to display the balls considerably.'

Advent of 'the new social self'?

In the 1990 edition of *Social Communication in Advertising*, Leiss and his co-authors suggest that the destruction of older forms of community by the concentration of urban labour led to a '**new social self**', characterised by individualism.

In the later part of the nineteenth century, and the early years of the twentieth, Leiss advances the idea that the advertiser paid increasingly greater attention to the promotion of goods and services which were not part of the *essential* requirements of life. In other words, various types of social need were catered for. From the 1920s, visual representation became more prominent in advertising, but the printed text remained of great importance.

Address to the consumer

The addresses made by advertisers often exploit the fear of rejection and social stigma. A 1928 advertisement produced in America for Paris garters (a device intended to keep up men's socks) pictures a young man and a young woman sitting on a chaise longue. The young woman has turned away and the man appears upset. The copy (see Marchand, *Advertising the American Dream*, p. 215) reads:

'Could he have read her thoughts he would not have lost her. A picture of neatness herself, she detested slovenliness. And not once, but many times, she had noticed his ungartered socks crumpling down around his shoe tops. To have to apologise to her friends for her husband's careless habits was too much to ask. So she had to say 'NO' – and in spite of his pleading couldn't tell him WHY.'

The unsuccessful suitor has committed a social gaffe which is so embarrassing that the object of his affections is unable to tell him the truth. The disapproval of others, which grows from the sense of belonging to a group whose values one is reluctant to transgress, is presented as a major feature of an individual's consciousness.

However, it is doubtful if even the sartorially challenged of the time would find this particular example convincing. In fact, such advertisements might appear to employ a 'psychological' approach to selling, while in reality they are 'dramatisations' of events which the onlooker may actually find amusing. The real effect is to draw attention to a particular *brand*.

'Shifting relationships'

Roland Marchand describes the 1920s in particular and early consumer society in general as (*Advertising the American Dream*, p. 214) 'an age of shifting relationships', in which (p. 215):

> 'individuals had to be prepared to transform themselves for new roles and new opportunities, thus making them peculiarly vulnerable to shifting definitions of themselves by others'.

This theory is useful, since it draws attention to the techniques of the advertiser, but it cannot confirm that people were more 'vulnerable' than before to social pressures. It does appear, however, that Americans in this era were under pressure to (p. 216) 'create their own identities' in the face of 'superficial and unsympathetic judgements by impersonal others'.

In the process of analysing American films of the period 1920–40, Wolfenstein and Leites (see Marchand, *Advertising the American Dream*) noticed a common parable in which the central character is an innocent who is ostracised from society. These victims of an unfeeling or hostile world eventually triumph over adversity and gain acceptance. Advertisers, in contrast, had a commercial interest in maintaining the nervous self-doubt they believed was prevalent in their audiences. Marchand sees inter-war advertising as eager to emphasise (p. 217):

> 'the power, validity, and pervasiveness of the world's judgemental scrutiny'.

Public scrutiny is the factor which was, and still is, supposed to induce guilt and self-accusation. The way individuals feel they are regarded by others is certainly important, but they care more about the opinions of some groups than others. It also seems clear that the power of social conformity is considerably reduced when it is used artificially in a form we know is really a commercial address.

Advertising and narrative

Marchand divides the different techniques of personal address into *parables* or moral tales. In doing so, he recognises the heavy reliance of advertising on **narratives**, either explicit or implicit. The parables are:

- the parable of the **first impression**, turning largely on the 'tragedy of manners,' where first impressions bring success or failure;
- the parable of the **democracy of goods**, in which modern production enables all individuals to enjoy the luxuries favoured by the elite, or where the wealthy use the same remedies in which the ordinary person finds relief (the 'democracy of afflictions');
- the parable of **civilisation redeemed**, showing how the drawbacks of living in a civilised world (the decline in vigour because of 'soft living') can nevertheless be overcome by products supplied by modern production; products will restore natural or primitive values;
- the parable of the **captivated child**, an idea based on an address to parents, advising them not to force their offspring to eat the right foods, but to encourage them to consume products which the child will find more palatable.

Visual imagery and implicit narrative

What Marchand calls the 'persistent patterns or clichés' of visual advertising may reveal the myths and established narrative formulas offered to the popular imagination. Successful advertising does not impose a 'view of the world', but has instead some understanding of the shared fantasies of a society. It seems to be true that there are indeed stories, fantasies and scenarios which animate the interest of all groups and classes in a society. The problem with advertising is that it makes links between collective myths and commerce. Universal needs and motivations, such as those outlined by Maslow and Schutz, are turned into decisions about what to purchase.

If it is true that the dominant mode of thought used during fantasy is **visual**, then it is only natural that advertisers should use this mode when they wish to appeal to the pleasurable aspects of the consumer's imaginings. One psychologist advised advertisers to 'short circuit' the consumer's mind through the use of images which might appeal to the basic emotions (*Psychology of Advertising*, Poffenberger, 1926).

In fact, some regarded the stimulation of *intellectual* processing as altogether a bad idea. Such views may remind us of the starring role the image is allowed in many theories of human cognition. Here, the image was thought to reinforce non-critical responses. The other advantage of using images was that a message put into words might sound grossly inflated or offensive. A similar approach given a broader, thematic treatment in images might escape the charge of inappropriateness. Marchand provides a useful example (p. 236):

> 'a copywriter might well have hesitated to advertise a product as just the thing for the man who lusted after power over others. But an illustration with a man standing in a commanding position, perhaps overlooking an impressive urban vista, might convey the same message.'

One of the most frequent images used in the early twentieth century is that of a commanding male figure who looks out over a landscape which includes factories, dwellings, and sometimes distant mountains. This genre is called by Marchand 'Master of all he Surveys' (Figure 4.8). This representation associated the businessman with (p. 242) 'control over an independent and autonomous domain'.

Figure 4.8   Master of all he surveys

Figure 4.9   'Towards the Heavenly City.'

By contrast, the domestic sphere produced an ideal image of another type. Using in most cases a 'soft-focus' illustration, the man was pictured sitting in a comfortable chair with his wife by his side and children playing on the floor. All members of the family appear in close proximity.

It is always a question as to how far actual life corresponds to the pictures deployed by the advertiser. The point is that advertisers are in the business of circulating ideas which will produce profit, but placing the profit motive at the centre of a message is unlikely to have much appeal. Therefore, the social subject must be placed at the centre of the campaign, in a recognisable situation. These subjects must represent individuals and collectives whom the population in general, or the target market in particular, are able at least to recognise, even if they do not ultimately identify with them.

Progress and prosperity are represented in advertisements which show people gazing into a distance filled with light. In most of these examples, the future is represented by a gleaming city (Figure 4.9).

Mass communication: questions of address

The concept of **address** is central to the study of communication. To make an 'address', as we saw above with reference to advertising, means to direct a form of speech or writing or other type of message to an individual or audience.

The term implies that a concentration of attention and effort has been made by the communicator. The linguistic and other powers and techniques at his or her disposal are focused on the act of communication. An alternative definition of 'address' reflects this concentration of powers: the *Oxford English Dictionary* refers to 'readiness, skill and dexterity'.

Audience: anybody there?

The intention behind address in general is to deliver a message which will make an impact on a particular **audience**. An address must consider both form and content. If the address which is delivered does not have meaning or relevance for the intended audience, then it is bound to fail.

The common assumption that an audience must be known to the person, group or institution responsible for initiating the act of communication is not strictly true. A good number of those messages which make a significant impact are created without any *personal* knowledge of the 'target' audience. In fact, language is always addressed to some 'other', even where that other is only imagined.

The communicator who wishes to create some material change must, however, have access to certain types of information. In the first place, something must be known about the general range of values held in a society; this is not too difficult, since everyone involved in the process of communication both inhabits, and contributes to the social. Secondly, the communicator or 'addressor' must know something about the *particular* values he or she wishes to mobilise. Finally, an idea of the general subject position held by the target audience is often supposed to be useful, especially where the address has a commercial intention behind it (though a unified 'mass' of people sharing the same subjectivity is unlikely to exist). The conception of audience and the intention of the communicator together influence the particular *form* of the message.

Media: definitions

In 1968, Janowitz produced an influential description of the **media**. James Curran, writing in 1977 (see *The Media: Contexts of Study*, p. 9, unit 2), adapted Janowitz's original view and proposed the following definition:

> 'The mass media comprise the institutions and techniques by which specialised social groups disseminate symbolic content to large heterogeneous and geographically-dispersed audiences.'

The 'specialised social groups' mentioned here are the *formal organisations* purposely set up to disseminate information, entertainment, instruction, aesthetic forms of expression and so on. The BBC would be one example, the News International group another.

Media institutions employ certain techniques, or 'modes of delivery', to reach their audiences, and the techniques used are usually included in any definition of the mass media. A mode of delivery is quite simply the form used to 'carry' the content. The BBC will use radio and television broadcasts, News International will use the newspaper format.

A *symbolic code*, as we saw in Chapter 1, refers to those systems (spoken language, for example) which are used by human beings to refer to their experience of the world, and to create meaning within specific contexts. 'Symbolic content' therefore means the signs, pictures, gestures and so on which are used by human beings to refer to experience. 'Heterogeneous' audiences are those which are made up of different groups.

Commercial motives and social power

Curran's definition is accurate so far as it goes, but there is little sense of what **motivates** media organisations to make contact with their audiences. There is always an **industrial** and a **political** aspect to mass communication activities, and therefore a **commercial** motive which drives individual media corporations.

Corner and Hawthorn (see the 1993 edition of *Communication Studies: An Introductory Reader*) emphasise the 'policies and professional routines' of media organisations, which are 'located within the political, economic and legal structures of the societies in which they operate'. This means that media organisations function within a society which accepts the legitimacy of financial gain, regards the profit motive as 'natural' and allows the media to generate quite extensive **social power**.

Denis McQuail, writing in the second edition of *Mass Communication Theory*, is aware of the fact that the media message is 'a commodity with an exchange value as well as being a symbolic reference with a *use* value'. He also points out that the 'message' sent out by the mass media is (p. 31):

> 'not unique, variable and unpredictable, but often "manufactured," standardised, always multiplied in some way'.

Presumably, McQuail means to imply that human communication consists of messages which *are* 'unique, variable and unpredictable'. This is only partly correct; everyday communication events also contain a number of routine exchanges, and the human subject often tries to 'standardise' a message so that a particular point is clearly understood.

The need for standardised output in the *mass media* arises because all capitalist enterprises must depend upon *recognisable* products which, wherever purchased, reflect the same level of quality and generate as far as is possible the *same broad range of meanings*, and will thus be able to generate a constant level of return on investment.

A comprehensive definition

A comprehensive definition would have to include the social, financial and political issues outlined above. Based on Curran's adaptation, it could be summarised as follows:

- The mass media comprise the institutions and techniques by which powerful, specialised social groups disseminate standardised commodities (in the form of units of symbolic content) to large, heterogeneous and geographically dispersed audiences.

The use of personal address

In an attempt to reach their desired audiences or markets, a number of groups and individuals, including politicians, advertisers, celebrities and private corporations, use a 'personal' mode to frame messages. The purpose of this is obvious: a direct appeal using the second-person singular is supposed to make a greater impact on the recipient than would a more general discourse.

Here, for example, is a message sent in 1993 from a building society to its investors. It concerns an offer to take out personal insurance against the possibility of decreased income. Ostensibly in the form of a letter, it carries the name of the addressee, but also uses separate headings, special boxes, heavy type and underlining to emphasise its message. It begins as follows:

'Have you ever asked yourself how you'd cope if you lost your income due to unemployment, sickness or accident?'

Although the question which begins this letter appears to require no more than a simple answer, the real intention is to make the recipients ask themselves the question as they read it. The individual is addressed as 'you', although this letter is one of many and the sender has only limited knowledge of each recipient. The address intends to work on the fears of the reader. Advertisements and other sales pitches often work in this way, using economic insecurity to persuade people to take a variety of measures which will supposedly help to secure the future.

The letter continues:

'It may not be a situation you like to think about – but don't make the mistake too many people make, thinking it will never happen to you.'

If the reader remains sceptical, there is another appeal which, although worrying, paints a slightly less dramatic picture:

'Have you also considered how even temporary loss of income through illness or accident could severely stretch your finances?'

The direct address, the urgency (later, the letter announces 'we may not be able to make such an offer again'), and the suggestion of hard times all attempt to motivate the reader.

More motivation?

There has been a substantial market in home exercise videos since public figures like the actress Jane Fonda made the 'workout' fashionable. In two successive years, 1993 and 1994, GMTV's 'Mr Motivator' (a fitness trainer called Derrick Evans) had best-selling exercise videos called, respectively, *Mr Motivator's BLT Workout* and *Mr Motivator's Body Conditioner*. In these videos, 'Mr M.' uses the second person singular to address his followers.

The purpose of this is encouragement, and takes the form of exhortations to 'get wicked' and follow the various sequences in the fitness programme. This is in marked contrast to the types of address which are designed to worry the addressee. Mr Motivator seeks to reassure his viewers; of course, he does not know them personally, but he does know that they wish to make an attempt to improve their fitness. He also intends his exercise programme to appeal to those who might not previously have engaged in such activity.

This extract is taken from the closing sequence of *Mr Motivator's Body Conditioner*, with the exercises still in progress:

> 'you've really done well ... I'll see you in a moment. Hey listen, you should be really proud of yourself, you've done well ... listen – make each day your masterpiece ... oh-oh ... find peace in who you are ... yeah go huh! – alright now, come on, take it over the head – take care and time for yourself – you're important, remember that – go huh! ... be positive ... here we go, circle it up and down, that's good ... what you have done is the best insurance policy – you know why? It pays up while you're still alive.'

This rather intimate form of address also suits the private realm in which the exercise video is used.

Could you be an SAS superman: inclusive or exclusive address?

On the 20 July 1982, *The Sun* newspaper carried an article, accompanied by a still from the 'forthcoming film, *Who Dares Wins*', which used a direct form of address to its readership:

> 'COULD YOU BE AN SAS SUPERMAN?'

In this case, *The Sun's* female readership is completely excluded by the initial question.

Underneath the headline, the sub-heading reads: 'Only a few pass the test of terror.' The article goes on to ask:

> 'Could you join the SAS? It's the dream of every young fella who fancies his chances playing football in the park or pushing weights around in the local gym.'

Implicit within the assertion that this dream is shared by 'every young *fella*' (*The Sun*'s special code for youthful males) is the idea that old 'fellas' are not part of the target group to which the address is made; and yet, by the end of the first paragraph, the answer to the original question is given. 'Could you join the SAS ... almost certainly ... no.' So we are faced with a curious outcome. Hardly anyone amongst the readership is in fact suitable. A number are addressed only to be excluded from the substance of the article.

In fact, the point of this particular address is to create mystique about and reverence for the 'bravest of the brave'. The long list of horrible tasks and gruelling tests faced by prospective recruits is intended to show that the 'dream' of joining will remain exactly that. However, the *form* of the address (to 'you') is maintained throughout the article:

> 'A three-week combat survival course on Exmoor ends with volunteers being left to live rough for several days and nights while other soldiers hunt you.'

Here, grammar comes adrift as the 'volunteers' become 'you'.

Near the end, this form of address is still maintained, when the reader is told:

> 'You are not fully trained until you can be dropped into a room held by several armed men and kill or maim every one.'

Why these armed men all wish to retain possession of one room is not revealed. It is certain, however, that *The Sun's* article has been a tease, a device to gain and hold attention, attention which is always in danger of slipping away.

Address and interpellation

Interpellation means an address with a 'will to power' behind it. It could be explained as a form of address which intends to exert control over an individual. The Marxist Louis Althusser's description of the way that interpellation works relies on the idea that the human subject is 'hailed' by authority, and furthermore that the individual who is addressed will recognise that it is him or her who is called (almost 'called to attention') and will respond to the address which is made. It is supposed to be the subject's own recognition of his or her *subjection* to authority which makes interpellation so powerful.

The example Althusser uses, as we have seen above, is that of a citizen who is hailed by a police officer: 'Hey you!'. Although this does reveal an important insight into the power of language, it is too dramatic an example to apply to the way that the mass media operate. The media offer a number of 'subject positions' in the full knowledge that they are often forced to operate 'blind', that they do not always quite know their audience, and that the audience's use of media texts is a complex issue.

Broadcast media: radio and television

Radio: sounds in the air

Raymond Williams (*Television: Technology and Cultural Form*, p. 29) characterised both **radio** and television as systems 'primarily designed for transmission and reception as abstract processes, with little or no definition of preceding content'. These forms were therefore 'derivative' or 'parasitic', relying upon existing events and unable, in their initial stages, to provide innovative materials of their own. Andrew Crisell (see *Understanding Radio*) emphasises the fact that radio was first envisaged as a means of 'point-to-point communication'. Asa Briggs, in his 1961 *History of Broadcasting in the United Kingdom*, revealed that the political establishment regarded the concept of *broadcast* radio as a somewhat inferior version of telegraphic communication between individuals.

The development of radio

The first broadcast of music and speech was made by an American called Fissenden in 1906. By 1916, the American Radio and Research Company was broadcasting concerts two or three times a week. The Marconi company, licensed by the Post Office, began its first British broadcasts from Chelmsford in 1920, a year after the removal of a ban on the private use of radio, which had been in force since the outbreak of the First World War. It was not until 1922, however, that regular broadcasts were allowed to be made. Marconi set up a London broadcasting station called '2LO'.

The leading groups involved in broadcasting, and those which manufactured equipment like wireless receivers, were brought together in 1922 to form a consortium called the British Broadcasting Company. Under its first general manager, John Reith, the company began to lay the foundations of a national network. By 1925, reception was available to 85 per cent of the population. The numbers of people using radio sets increased with great rapidity, from some three to four hundred thousand receivers in 1923 to around five million in 1924.

As the new technology spread, the price of receivers fell, but during the 1920s remained beyond the means of most sections of the working class. It was not until the latter part of the Second World War that wireless sets became generally affordable.

Restrictions on broadcasting

The BBC was not allowed to broadcast news until after 7 p.m. in the evening, in order to safeguard the circulation of newspapers. It also had to rely upon the output of the established news agencies. These restrictions lasted until 1938, except for the brief period of the General Strike in 1926. During this episode, the broadcasters were under threat of government requisition.

Although Reith avoided direct government control, the careful censorship he exercised in order to avoid a complete takeover meant that the company's position was largely in support of the establishment. The strike, which began when the miners refused to accept increased hours and lower pay, lasted nine days before the trade union leaders capitulated. The miners carried on for another six weeks, but were eventually forced back to work by extreme privation.

In the following year the BBC became a corporation, with Reith as the first director-general. It had to conform to a charter, based upon the central obligation to 'inform, educate and entertain', but was able to secure a guaranteed income through the licence-fee system. In the US, by contrast, radio was dependent upon advertising, a system that appeared utterly repugnant to the patrician outlook of Reith. The BBC underwent a significant expansion and by the mid-1930s had well-established national and regional programme networks. Scannell and Cardiff, writing in 1982, described the 'mixed programming' provided by both networks as offering:

'a wide and diverse range of programme materials over the course of each day and week ... news, drama, sport, religion, music ... variety or light entertainment'.

A single 'Home Service' was created in 1939, and by 1944 the BBC had begun to employ its own foreign correspondents. Crisell describes the excellence of the BBC's radio broadcasts during the war (p. 25):

'radio at last came into its own as a rapid news medium ... the BBC's 9 pm news bulletin commanded huge and avid audiences ... it was under pressure of the war that the techniques of news broadcasting evolved from the early days of straight bulletin delivery to something like the blend of reading, correspondents' reports and sound actuality that we are familiar with today'.

A new rival

By 1946, the BBC had divided its radio network into the Home Service, the Light Programme, and the Third Programme, which Crisell calls 'an unashamedly "highbrow" network devoted to the arts, serious discussion and experiment'. Radio broadcasting by the BBC found itself challenged by the post-war popularity of television. The coronation of Elizabeth II in 1953 was one of the turning points in the competition between radio and television. The coronation, which had to be improvised to some extent because there was confusion over how it should be conducted, was nevertheless a visual event. Over 20 million people watched the event, far outstripping the number of radio listeners, though television sets were relatively few. People crammed into the houses of their neighbours to see the new queen, which probably added to the sense of togetherness engendered in the early part of this new 'Elizabethan' era.

Television came to be regarded as an essential device whenever history was 'in the making'. Some readers of this book will still retain images of the newsflash of the Kennedy assassination, of Churchill's coffin brought by barge down the Thames, and of the first moon landing.

The birth of commercial radio

The BBC had struggled for a number of years against the growing popularity of pirate stations, until in 1967 it created Radio One to cater for a youth audience. It was about to face greatly increased competition. Local commercial radio was established under the Sound Broadcasting Act of 1972, which was then consolidated and became the Independent Broadcasting Authority Act of 1973. The first two stations came on the air in 1973 – Capital and LBC. Initial prospects did not look good. The advertisers believed the market to be too small, while costs inside the companies were high.

In 1977, the Annan Report on Broadcasting suggested that both the BBC and IBA (Independent Broadcasting Authority) should surrender 'their local radio stations to a new 'Local Broadcasting Authority' (which was never created). The IBA controlled the nineteen local radio stations which had been established by 1979. In 1977–8, all of these stations made a clear profit. Capital Radio made £1.8 million in 1978 (*Labour Research Department*, August 1979). During the late 1970s, about 8 per cent of broadcast time on commercial radio was taken up by advertisements (a 15 per cent ceiling had been set). In 1977, a survey made by the Joint Industry Committee for Radio Audience Research discovered that independent local radio had an audience of 13.6 million adult listeners. By 1980, there were twenty-six stations on the air.

There was, however, some resistance to the new network. The Local Radio Workshop in London was particularly critical of Capital radio, arguing that it did not cater for its listeners and that (see *Nothing Local About It*):

'the only people who seem to benefit are the advertisers, the record companies and the shareholders'.

In some areas, local community groups had become involved in the radio network, with the result that it did respond more readily to community needs.

Twenty-one years of independent radio: the key to the door?

The year 1994 marked the twenty-first anniversary of commercial radio broadcasts in Britain. Nearly a hundred local and regional commercial stations were in operation by that time. An improvement in the fortunes of independent radio took place in the mid-1980s, when stock-market investors began to take an interest in radio. Capital Radio's share flotation was oversubscribed some sixty-two times. Programme sponsorship increased and new stations in the bigger cities were granted licences. Specialist radio stations began to appear. Commercial radio seemed to be on the brink of overtaking the combined audience total of the BBC's various radio outlets.

Private operators appear to believe that their future will be increasingly profitable. In a supplement to *Media Week* of October 1994, Richard Branson declared that 'the only stations we [Virgin and Classic] are interested in taking audiences from are BBC stations'. Branson remains aware of the need to keep the advertiser happy. For him, the advertiser is central to the prospects of commercial radio. The listener, he feels, has a certain loyalty to radio, a loyalty which will produce high margins of profit:

> 'Listeners have a relationship with radio stations, quite unlike any other medium. They feel radio is their friend and they relate to it on a personal level. It's this special relationship which makes radio a unique medium for advertisers to reach their target audience.'

Writing in the same magazine, Paul Kavanagh argues for the greater use of scientific testing of audience and product: 'like jeans or baked beans, radio needs to be marketed, and marketing requires research'. Kavanagh lists the research methods available to the advertiser. The extent of the commercial broadcaster's intrusion into the psychology of the audience makes for interesting reading:

> 'Focus groups help identify the key motivations for listening; auditorium music tests enable programmers to measure the popularity and durability of older songs; call-out tests the popularity of new releases; image association gauges listeners' perception of the station; and strategic market studies identify trends.'

Radio and the youth market

One of the most difficult markets for advertisers to penetrate is the youth market. A recent trend has been to target pirate radio stations, in an attempt to reach this group. In 'Reaching the right ears' (see *Media Week* radio supplement, October 1994), Richard Benson describes how pirate radio is regarded as having 'street credibility'. Noting that 'Johnny Student doesn't interact with any one advertising medium and is therefore difficult to target', Benson draws attention to what he calls 'college radio'. Although this is, in his words, 'prone to amateurism and haphazard quality', he sees it as a valuable outlet for the advertiser.

An interesting detail is found in a reference to the Fresh FM station in Bristol. Benson notes that:

> 'Fresh FM broadcasts to 20,000 students and is run by media studies students of the University of West England [sic], Bristol University and

South Bristol College. Advertisers include the local Sprint Pizza restaurant, Bristol Brewhouse, Guinness and Barclays Bank.'

Even more revealing is the piece Benson writes on 'restricted service' radio stations which operate under licence. One such station was provided with equipment by Sony in return for what he calls 'subtle plugging'. This is clearly a 'covert' form of advertising.

Television

In January 1926, a Scottish engineer called John Logie Baird appeared before the Royal Institution to demonstrate the mechanical transmission of an image by means of a primitive camera. Baird's apparatus depended upon the use of the photo-electric cell, a device which converted light into electric current. Baird scanned the object he wished to transmit and produced a picture composed of thirty lines.

Despite this success, Baird's system had certain drawbacks. An experienced research team from the company EMI soon developed a rival system based on electronic scanning. The two systems, electronic and mechanical, were tested against one another. Baird's system required strong lights to illuminate the subject and was prone to mechanical failure. The EMI team, under Isaac Shoenburg, was selected by the British government to set up the world's first high-definition television service, in 1936. Transmission continued until the outbreak of war, which clearly delayed the development of television. It was not resumed until June 1946. Three years later, the whole of the BBC came under scrutiny by the Beveridge committee, set up to examine the state of broadcasting. Although it gave its approval to the corporation, it was alive to the dangers of a BBC monopoly. US-style commercial broadcasts were strongly opposed.

A search for technology?

In *Television, Technology and Cultural Form*, Raymond Williams describes television as 'a complex of inventions', arguing that all **technology** is actively sought with purposes in mind, rather than being merely stumbled upon. It became, in Williams's view, a *technological* enterprise only in the 1920s, the decade which saw early experiments in making television systems. In effect, technology had preceded content, so that television was forced to search for pre-existing materials. Eventually, television content was a combination of earlier forms of public communication and the innovative forms which television itself promoted. Pre-existing material included films, sport, advertising, news, and argument and discussion. As time went on, television changed each form to suit its own purposes.

Commercial television

The new Conservative government of 1951 turned its attention to the broadcasting monopoly of the BBC. With the Television Act of 1954, it created the Independent Television Authority. The **commercial** channel was allowed a first 'term' of ten years, which was subsequently renewed.

A number of inquiries have been held into British television. The first of these, the Pilkington committee of 1962, was highly critical of the standards which had been achieved by independent television. McQuail (see *Media Performance*, p. 57) reproduces an extract from the report which indicate its attitude to the commercial sector:

> 'Triviality is not necessarily related to the subject matter ... [it] resides in the way the subject matter is approached and the manner in which it is presented. A trivial approach can consist in failure to respect the potentialities of the subject matter ... or in a too-ready reliance on well-tried themes.'

The 1977 Annan committee was responsible for establishing Channel 4, a commercial channel which was set up specifically to encourage cultural diversity but which, unlike other stations, did not produce its own programmes. Instead, it was to act as a commissioning agent for independent producers. It also allowed the introduction of the first breakfast television programmes. The Peacock committee of 1986 looked into the question of public service broadcasting, examining the possibilities of alternative sources of finance for the BBC.

Deregulation

The Broadcasting Act of 1990 dispensed with the services of the IBA in favour of the ITC (Independent Television Commission), which was to exercise a 'lighter touch' which meant in effect the exercise of reduced powers. In the ensuing franchise battle, in which companies had to convince the government that they had satisfied a 'quality threshold' before submitting sealed bids for a licence to broadcast, four television companies lost their tenure to new consortiums. The quality threshold consisted of three key requirements: to provide regional programmes, to broadcast high-quality news programmes at peak viewing times, and to provide a wide diversity of programmes to cater for 'a variety of tastes and interests'.

Channel 5: bids

In 1987, the Conservative government commissioned a feasibility study into the provision of additional terrestrial television services. The following year saw a broadcasting White Paper which proposed that a third commercial channel should be set up; called '**Channel 5**', this new service would broadcast material to between 50 and 75 per cent of the British population, though video recorders would have to be retuned in order to eliminate interference from the new channel. The 1990 Broadcasting Act set the Independent Television Commission the task of preparation, and two years later applications were invited, overseen by the ITC.

Only one application was received, from a group calling itself 'Channel 5 Holdings', backed by Thames Television and Time Warner. The bid itself amounted to no more than a thousand pounds. In December 1992, when the deadline had been twice extended, the ITC announced that it would not award the franchise.

In November 1994, the offer of the franchise was resurrected. The deadline for the new set of bids was set as 2 May 1995. By the deadline, the following bids had been received:

- *New Century Television – £2,000,000.* This group is backed by Rupert Murdoch's BSkyB, Granada, the Really Useful Group, TCI International (an American cable company), Polygram, Goldman Sachs, Hoare Govett and a Swedish group called Kinnevik.

  Programmes proposed by New Century included a new soap opera from the makers of *Coronation Street*, the showing of a nightly feature film, a 90-minute current affairs programme, and a general emphasis on live broadcasts. New Century intended to use satellite and cable to reach some of those consumers unable to receive direct broadcasts.
- *Channel Five Broadcasting – £22,002,000.* Pearson, the owners of Thames and the publishers of *The Financial Times*, the MAI Group (which runs Anglia and Meridian), and a company called CLT (based in Luxembourg) make up Channel Five Broadcasting.

  The channel would concentrate upon entertainment, with a new soap opera scheduled for five nights a week, a drama series about trainee police officers, a courtroom drama in which viewers deliver the verdict on individual cases, a Saturday night entertainment show, current affairs, news bulletins from ITN, children's programmes, and a substantial amount of educational material backed by the Open University.
- *Virgin TV – £22,002,000.* The partners in this consortium are Virgin Communications, Associated Newspapers (publishers of *The Daily Mail*), HTV, Philips, Electra and Paramount.

  Films and drama would feature prominently in the output of this consortium, including 1,000 hours of British-produced drama per year. Reuters would supply news bulletins, while some 30 hours of children's programmes would be produced. The general emphasis would be on entertainment or, as the group itself claimed, 'viewer-friendly' television.
- *UKTV – £36,261,158.* Despite its title, this group is composed of Canadian, Australian and Scandinavian interests – CanWest, Network 10, and Scandinavian Broadcasting Systems respectively. Also included is SelecTV, which produced a number of successful British sitcoms such as *Lovejoy* and *Birds of a Feather*.

Sixty per-cent of programmes would be original, including comedy and drama.

Two of the competitiors for the Channel 5 franchise, in what Andrew Culf (*The Guardian*, 3 May 1995) called 'an extraordinary coincidence', had produced identical bids of £22,002,000. The Channel Five Broadcasting group had brought their bid to this figure by adding £1,000 a few hours before submission. The other oddity was the very low figure offered by New Century.

Channel 5: issues and disputes

In an *Observer* article which appeared on 30 April 1995, Richard Brooks and Emily Bell argued that 'Channel 5 is being created primarily because television companies want to make money, not because there is any public demand for it'. In addition, Brooks and Bell believed that 'this is the last chance for the foreseeable future to get a stake in a major terrestrial channel with reasonable prospects of a return from advertising'. This is echoed in an article by John Dugdale (see *The Guardian*, 24 April, 1995):

> 'Major media players feel they have to apply ... to confirm their status as major media players, on the basis that you must be seen on the pitch if there's a game on.'

The eventual winner of the franchise would have to commit between £80 million and £120 million a year on programmes, ensuring that at least 40 per cent of total output in the first two years is original British or European material, rising to 65 per cent by the sixth year of operation. However, the commitment to reach some 70 per cent of the British population must be seen in the light of the ITC's decision to allow Channel 5 a smaller initial target of a million viewers. The attainment of 70 per cent is supposed to occur after some five years of operation.

The apparent diversity of interests which the various consortia represent can be misleading. The Pearson group is a shareholder in BSkyB, while Philips, part of the Virgin bid, controls 80 per cent of Paramount, involved in the BSkyB consortium. The concentration of power in so few hands has not gone unnoticed, particularly where the media empire of Rupert Murdoch is concerned. Michael Grade, the chief executive of Channel 4, declared that (see *Observer*, 30 April 1995):

> 'If Murdoch's tentacles now attach themselves to a national terrestrial network, he will take an unbreakable stranglehold on our entire broadcasting system. Unless Parliament acts, he will be unstoppable.'

Suspicion was excited when Murdoch's group submitted a 'suicide' bid of only two million pounds for Channel 5. Had he merely 'lost his political bottle' as some of his competitors believed (see Andrew Culf's *Guardian* article of 3 May 1995), or was the low bid part of a deal struck between Murdoch and the British government, in which the Conservatives would avoid a political storm by letting BSkyB fall on its sword, in return for favourable treatment in other spheres?

This very question was put to Murdoch in a BBC 2 *Money Programme* interview, broadcast on 21 May 1995. The chair of BSkyB gave an unequivocal reply:

> 'That's absolute nonsense, and just another example of paranoia and craziness. No one ever spoke to me, nor did I speak to anybody about Channel 5.'

The real reason for the submission of such a bid, according to Murdoch himself, lies in the uncertainty of Channel 5's commercial future:

> 'I think it's going to be very very hard for Channel 5 to be commercially successful ... Channel 5 just can't reach ... all the homes in Britain, and I think you start off crippled, when you try to compete.'

Rupert Murdoch cannot be understood unless his own perception of his role is taken into account. Asked to comment on the fact that there are so many parts of the world in which his empire has a dominating presence, Murdoch argued (see the transcript of the BBC interview in *The Guardian* of 22 May 1995) that 'we are not monopolies ... I mean, if we succeed somewhere and become a leader that doesn't make you a monopolist'. The idea of government regulation is clearly something that irritates Murdoch. Pressed on the question of regulation of media ownership, he replied:

> 'I don't care if you say "get out of Britain", give the world to the BBC, what sort of society do you really want? You know we got rid of that stuff when the Berlin Wall came down.'

Murdoch's utterances are characterised by constant reference to the free market, in the belief that his critics should show they are in earnest by entering the field of competition. The following extract from the BBC 2 interview shows this tendency to confuse his critics in the media with potential competitors:

> 'Anybody could set up Sky Television, anybody, and we started it and people are still free to start against us, but they'd rather write articles, bitch and moan, lay [*sic*] around and say no, we'd rather just keep our lazy way of life, we don't want to compete.'

In one sense, Murdoch is adept at using the ambiguities of language. When asked on the *Money Programme* to characterise his relationship with British ministers, he stated that this was neither very bad nor very good, in the sense that he did not know them personally.

Changing the rules of ownership

On 23 May 1995, the procedures governing the **ownership** of media in Britain were 'liberalised' or relaxed in order to sweep away what Conservative minister Stephen Dorrell called the 'complex, myriad' rules facing media groups. Many leading figures in the newspaper and television industries greeted the changes with enthusiasm, while Murdoch's News Corporation and the Mirror Group found that the scope of their expansion had been limited.

The change affecting newspaper ownership of television stations, and by the same token broadcasters' possession of newspapers, was based on the use of a 'circulation threshold' below which groups are able to own other media outlets. So, for example, any group attaining less than a 20 per cent market share of national newspaper circulation is allowed to own up to 15 per cent of the total television market, defined by audience share. In addition (see Andrew Culf's *Guardian* article of 24 May 1995):

> 'National newspaper groups owning regional papers, or regional papers wishing to control a regional TV licence, will have to prove their local titles account for no more than 30 per cent of circulation in the relevant area.'

In the case of newspapers and radio stations, groups below the 20 per cent threshold can apply to the Radio Authority to control radio stations, while only one national licence will be awarded where newspapers have more than 30 per cent circulation in a locality. The limit on the number of radio licences which can be acquired has been raised from twenty to thirty-five.

Restrictions on television companies owning radio stations will be scrapped. Terrestrial television's ownership of cable and satellite stations is permitted where each individual group has no more than 15 per cent of audience share. The same principle operates in the case of those satellite or cable groups which express an interest in terrestrial television. Companies which have more than 20 per cent of their interests controlled by newspapers are in turn unable to gain more than a 20 per cent holding in an ITV company or the Channel 5 licence.

From protest to democracy?

Objections to the new rules came from a number of sources, and reflected a variety of concerns, from the possible detrimental effect on local and regional newspapers to the reduction of quality in journalism and the sacrifice of smaller journals as larger commercial interests gain control of the marketplace. Overall, the changes must be seen within the framework of a capitalist or market-driven philosophy, in which 'diversity' is supposedly assured through allowing established organisations to create an interlocking structure based on political power and commercial strength.

Normative theories or models of media structure, which argue for a complete revolution in the relationship between institution and its audience, are usually neglected. Denis McQuail, for example, identifies 'democratic-participant' theory as a challenge to other models of media organisation. This approach was prompted (see *Mass Communication Theory*, 1987, p. 122) as a:

'reaction against the commercialisation and monopolisation of privately-owned media and against the centralism . . . of public broadcasting institutions'.

The much-vaunted 'free press' theory has, according to this approach, failed 'because of its subversion by the market'.

The whole point of democratic-participant theory lies in its adherence to (p. 122) 'the needs, interests and aspirations of the active "receiver" in a political society'. It implies not only that individuals and groups have the right to be 'served' by the media, but also that they should work to establish their own media based upon local and group-centred requirements. The most committed advocates of this approach are libertarian socialists, environmentalists, and some feminist thinkers.

Satellite and cable

Satellite: from theory to practice

In October 1945 a magazine called *Wireless World* published an article by an airforce employee called Arthur C. Clarke (Clarke went on to become a famous author of science fiction). His short paper demonstrated the possibility of placing a communication **satellite** in a constant position above the earth. The idea was that a satellite placed at the correct distance from the planet, 35,786 kilometres above the Equator, and matching the speed of its rotation, would in effect hold a *geostationary* or *geosynchronous* orbit.

Other types of satellite orbit are also possible, but the first geosynchronous satellite was Early Bird, launched by the Intelsat agency in 1965. It had the capacity for 240 voice telephony circuits, the equivalent of one television channel. This type of satellite was not designed for the transmission of television signals for direct reception by viewers, but was appropriated for such use.

Non-geosynchronous satellites were launched from the 1950s, and were used to relay television signals, but usually required large and expensive earth stations in order to track their movement through space. Telstar, launched in 1962, orbited the earth every 157 minutes and was able to relay television signals for eighteen minutes at a time. The first live transatlantic programme exchange occurred on 23 July 1962, and included the transmission of views of well-known landmarks in America, followed by a series of images of Europe broadcast two-and-a-half hours later, upon Telstar's reappearance.

The knowledge that one of his press conferences was being transmitted by satellite prompted President Kennedy to claim that 'the understanding which will inevitably come from this speedier communication is bound to increase the well-being and security of all people'. Whenever technological advances are made, public figures often emphasise the positive potential for human progress. Overall, geosynchronous satellites were established throughout the 1960s and 1970s. With the advent of more powerful satellites in the 1980s, the size and cost of earth stations was reduced and, as Richard Collins explains (see *Satellite Television in Western Europe*, p. 14):

> 'For the first time, the antenna and electronics necessary for direct-to-home reception of satellite television were available to individuals in Western Europe at reasonably affordable cost.'

Entrepreneurs and the growth of cable

Although satellite technology became increasingly sophisticated, and a 'second generation' of direct satellite television became available (with no need for the intervention of a terrestrial broadcaster), the distribution of material from earth stations relied in the main on the use of **cable** networks.

Early enthusiasts for the use of cable in America were anxious to maintain some independence from the major broadcasters and the telephone companies. In 1970, the US Federal Communications Commission (FCC) banned phone companies from owning cable systems in their locality, and banned television networks from owning cable networks altogether. The pressure of market forces, however, proved too great to maintain such a blanket ban. In 1981, the FCC granted the CBS television network permission to buy a cable network serving 90,000 homes. In 1982, the FCC announced its intention to establish a series of regulations to replace the ban.

One of the most successful of the cable entrepreneurs was the American Ted Turner, whose 'Superchannel' began its broadcasts in 1976 from Atlanta in Georgia. Interviewed on a Thames Television programme in 1978 (see William Shawcross's 1995 Channel 4 series, *Satellite Wars*), Turner explained that:

> 'We stress entertainment more than we do information here, we feel that the other networks do enough to depress everybody, we try to cheer everybody up.'

Asked by a Thames journalist to explain what would happen if all the networks simply broadcast entertainment, Turner replied 'I'd put on the news, you dummy.'

This remark proved to have more significance than a mere quip. On 1 June 1980, Turner was the first to produce a 24-hour news programme, under the aegis of his Cable News Network (CNN). This service provided news to a variety of nations, but some questioned the validity of Turner's conception of news. *The Listener* of 16 October 1986 carried an article by Richard Gilbert which announced (see Andrew Boyd's *Broadcast Journalism*, p. 105):

'What CNN means by news is very different from what the BBC and ITN mean. On CNN, news, as well as politics, current affairs, and the "and finally" stories, means Hollywood gossip, sport, cookery hints, business, more business and Fitness Breaks with Jake. Muscle-bound Jake exercises on a sandy beach and exhorts viewers, "Don't Quit!" Shadowed by a bikini'd blonde, he demonstrates his "one-arm dumb-bell triceps extension workout".'

Turner's desire to provide a positive alternative to run-of the-mill broadcasting has not changed, but his current attitude to news and information could not be further from his original position. From 1987, through his CNN network World Report, Turner provided uncensored news stories from around the world, using local journalists. Don M. Flournoy, writing in *CNN World Report* (see p. 1), recounted his own experience of watching Turner's cable channel:

'There were news items from Zimbabwe, Thailand, Venezuela, Poland, Guam, Grenada, Switzerland, Portugal and Cyprus – places you only hear about in America if there is some disaster, an earthquake or a terrorist bomb, a US invasion, or a visit from the US Secretary of State.'

What had prompted this change in Turner's practice? He had always seen himself as 'a good person' (see Flournoy, p. 19), but found during a trip to Cuba that 'most of what I thought was wrong'. During a trip to India, he met leaders who complained that little of significance in Indian society ever reached the West, and that anything that was reported conformed to Western news values. This was, apparently, the point at which the idea for World Report began to take shape. Another moment of revelation came when Turner observed the scientist Carl Sagan describe the giant receiving antennas directed towards space, whose purpose is to listen for messages sent from extraterrestrial civilisations. Turner declared (see Flournoy, p. 18):

'My God. We didn't have a system to even find out what was going on from the various nations of the world until the World Report came around.'

Satellite wars

In 1982, the first European satellite programme was broadcast from a small studio in London's Soho. Two female presenters, in lamé jackets, introduced the first transmission in English, with a few sentences of welcome from other languages thrown in for good measure. Brian Haynes, responsible for the new satellite company, sought backing from Thames Television, but was turned down. 'Satellite TV Ltd' selected material which it thought might be palatable for a variety of countries, concentrating upon comedy and items that would make a visual impact.

In 1983, the company received visitors from Australia who seemed anxious to mask their identity; they were in fact envoys from Rupert Murdoch.

Murdoch took over the company and went through its programme schedules with one of its executives. A series called *Window on the World* caught his attention; finding that this consisted of various stock material bought from overseas broadcasters, he declared (see William Shawcross's series *Satellite Wars*) that the company had 'bought a load of crap and given it a good title', a device which the Satellite TV executive claimed Murdoch understood and had practised. Murdoch called his new acquisition 'Sky Channel'.

The next important move in Murdoch's campaign to establish himself in the satellite marketplace was the acquisition of broadcasting space on a European satellite, since Sky was available to only a few thousand homes. In the 1980s, Candice Johnson made a business proposition to the Luxemburg government. At a time when satellite broadcasting was strictly regulated, she advanced the idea of making a private investment in a European satellite (which came to be known as Astra). In 1985, the Societé Européene des Satellites (SES) attained a 22-year franchise on the operation of a satellite system.

In 1986, the British government, through the Independent Broadcasting Authority, orchestrated bids for the British satellite contract. It was won by a company called British Satellite Broadcasting. BSB, under a European Community Directive of 1986, was informed that it would not be allowed to use the established PAL transmission system, as this was thought inferior in terms of picture quality; instead, it had to invest in a high-quality system called MAC. In the belief that only high-powered satellites and the MAC transmission system could provide the standards required, BSB was saddled with a financial disadvantage.

Sky, on the other hand, invested in the Astra satellite and the PAL system. In November 1988, the Astra satellite was launched. Murdoch was ready to transmit his programmes in early 1989. When he did so, picture quality seemed perfectly acceptable, even though a shortage of satellite dishes meant that the majority of viewers relied upon cable transmission; BSB felt cheated, their investment in MAC having caused a serious delay. Sky delivered four channels before BSB had even launched its satellite. Although BSB hoped that Sky would be prosecuted for breaking the satellite monopoly it held, Murdoch seemed to be immune because he was based in Europe and because, in the words of BSB's chief executive (Anthony Simmonds-Gooding in Shawcross's series *Satellite Wars*), 'the Tory party felt that Rupert was a useful ally'. Murdoch declared, in populist mode, that (see *Satellite Wars*) 'BSB preferred fine buildings and big cars, but we worked out of pre-fabs and spent the money on creating a market, on selling the idea of television choice.'

BSB embarked on a £20-million advertising campaign for its autumn launch, claiming that it had over two thousand first-run feature films lined up for transmission. In the ensuing battle between the two companies, both were nearly destroyed. A mere six months after BSB went on air, a merger was announced. To many commentators, it seemed like a Sky victory. The new company was called BSkyB. The award of the franchise to the original group had become, along with the dream of a system belonging to the 'British tradition' of broadcasting, quite meaningless. Murdoch, with some connivance from political allies, had out-manoeuvred his opponents. By December 1992, BARB calculated that, out of 22,237,000 television homes, 10.3 per cent had satellite dishes, and some 2.7 per cent cable (see *BFI, film and Television Handbook 1994*). By 1995, BSkyB had established itself in four million homes in Britain.

In 1993, Murdoch purchased a 63 per cent share in Star TV, a company launched in Hong Kong in 1991, using a satellite called Asiasat which could reach fifty-four Asian countries. Finding that the blanket broadcasting of Western programmes would not achieve a mass market, Murdoch put greater emphasis on local and regional elements. Included amongst the nations in receipt of Star's programming was China, with a population of over a billion people. One of the channels which formed part of Star's output was BBC World Service Television.

In 1989, during the growth of the pro-democracy movement in China, the Chinese government viewed Western news agencies with suspicion. BBC coverage of the suppression of the democracy movement, and in particular its reports on the Tiananmen Square massacre, was never forgiven by the Chinese authorities. In September 1993, Murdoch made a speech in which he argued that (see Shawcross's series *Satellite Wars*):

'Advances in the technology of telecommunication have proved an unambiguous threat to totalitarian regimes everywhere.'

Once Star began broadcasting, the Chinese government wasted little time in complaining to Murdoch about the output of the BBC. In March 1994, Murdoch renegotiated his agreement with the BBC, terminating its lease of the northern beam covering China. Murdoch's declaration that technology threatened totalitarianism now appeared in a very different light. In reality, technology did not seem unequivocally progressive, or even merely neutral; once again, its benefits were seen to be closely tied to political expedience and the profit motive.

The 'new' media

Information technology and 'computer literacy'

The concept of **'new' media** has emerged from the growth of **information technology** and the 'convergence' of various delivery systems. *Information technology* is a term which refers to the electronic storage and use of knowledge, and was employed extensively in the 1980s to describe the existence of computer-based word-processing. Shortened to 'IT', it was regarded as an essential component of public education. 'Computer Studies' was another variant found in schools and colleges. It was often said of this period that schools would always find money for a computer, and many did indeed invest in complete IT suites, though few institutions had enough hardware to cover the number of students on their courses.

In contrast, the growth of student familiarity with computer culture in the 1990s was due to the explosion of interest in computer games. The concept of **'computer literacy'** became outdated with the advent of simpler access and 'user-friendly' systems like the Apple Macintosh computer. It was no longer necessary to know and use a separate 'language' in order to give commands and produce text. 'WYSIWYG' ('What you see is what you get') also helped break down the distance between user and computer, with the production of software that could create on-screen graphics and typefaces that approximated closely to the final, printed result.

Information technology: industrial determinism?

An important text, which brought together many of the late-1980s debates on technology, was produced by the Open University in 1987. This was Finnegan *et al.*'s *Information Technology: Social Issues*. Faced with the need to explain technical change, a number of authors proposed a variety of approaches. Christopher Freeman, an academic from Sussex University, advanced a **'deterministic'** argument. Unimpressed by theories which emphasised the idea that technological advance was achieved through rational, 'goal-directed' effort, and by explanations which stressed the gradual modification of existing systems, he declared that the adoption of new technology was simply a necessity (p. 5):

> 'Such "new technological systems" can offer such great technical and economic advantages in a wide range of industries and services that their adoption becomes a necessity in any economy exposed to competitive economic, social, political and military pressures.'

Freeman's perspective is 'deterministic' in the sense that he regards the role of human willpower in shaping the future as less important than technological forces. He softens this perspective by arguing that technology has a 'limited' autonomy (or independence of action) and that we should not become fatalistic about the future. What comes across most strongly, however, is Freeman's belief in abstract forces of change (p. 5):

> 'Increasingly this century, the world-wide diffusion of such new techno-economic paradigms dominates the process of technical change for several decades.'

This does not sit easily with Freeman's claim that technology has only a 'limited' independence from other spheres of existence.

The idea that any new technological or economic force dominates the process of change in an entire society is also questionable. Marx used the concept of the 'uneven' development of capitalism to explain how some nations were less 'advanced' than others, an idea which may also be applied to the internal development of a nation. In other words, new technology is likely to be concentrated in certain industries and geographic areas, leaving other places at an 'earlier' stage of development.

Brian V. Street, whose essay on the new technology appears in the same book as Freeman's work, takes issue with the idea of determinism, especially the notion that technology and the qualities it is supposed to represent are somehow 'neutral' or 'value free'. For example, Street attacks the notion of 'computer literacy' as it is used by most commentators (p. 34):

> 'Many representations of . . . "computer literacy" rest on the assumption that it is a neutral technology that can be detached from specific social contexts.'

Street prefers a view of literacy which (p. 35) 'depends upon the social institutions in which it is embedded'. Kevin Robins and Frank Webster go further, arguing that 'IT education' was in effect a 'myth', offering students a practical but limited introduction to some aspects of computer operation, but revealing nothing about (Finnegan *et al.*, *Information Technology: Social Issues*, p. 153):

> '[the] major shapers and users of computer-communications such as the military . . . nothing of the role or significance of transnational corporations'.

The 'information age': greeting the Millennium?

The prospect of life in a new technological environment has always prompted the expression of high hopes. From the Festival of Britain in 1951, and the 'white heat' of technology announced by Harold Wilson in the 1960s, to more recent celebration of the 'superhighway', the idea of a revolution in science has inspired great optimism. Steven Barnett, writing in *The Times* of 16 March 1994, described the 'technological miracles' which had been announced in the 1980s:

> 'Rewind to 1982, when Kenneth Baker was minister for information and technology and offered his vision for the next ten years: "By the end of the decade the multi-channel cable television will be commonplace in-home countrywide" . . . in the late eighties, it was satellite: different technology, same reaction. Here was another breakthrough which would . . . revolutionise our viewing lives . . . now there's multimedia, and the euphoria starts again.'

However, the coincidence of advanced technology with the advent of a new century has proved even more exhilarating for those commentators who see only the positive side of technology. For example, the American businessman Dan Mapes, speaking on Channel 4's *Cyberville* (transmitted on 11 December 1994), paid particular attention to the approach of the twenty-first century:

'I think it's no accident ... the tremendous speed that we're seeing in the development of this new cyber culture ... an amazing neural layer which is evolving right in front of our eyes, right around this Millennium time. Why is that? Well, Carl Jung would say it's not happening by accident, it's the actual Millennium itself making this happen, it's like an energy ... it's like a magnet that the closer you get to it, the more it speeds up, it's almost like a black hole, so as you hit right on the year 2,000, the culture is moving at almost maximum speed.'

One characteristic response to the new media is an enthusiasm which seems to overwhelm the ability to make critical or even coherent remarks. Some commentators oppose this kind of 'free association' of ideas, like Fred Dewey (see Channel 4's *Cyberville*), who argues that:

'Instead of dealing with the growing problems of society, and [US] government cutbacks ... people are focusing instead on this future Utopia of cyberworld and cyberville'.

Terms and definitions

In recent years, a whole vocabulary has grown from the general concept of the new technology. In many cases, this terminology has become assimilated into youth culture, where general meanings have attached themselves to a whole range of ideas, and specific explanations seem unnecessary; the culture itself appears to use terms to signify its own attachment to the fashionable connotations of technology.

The following passage is taken from a 'Merlin' sticker album published in 1995, called *The Adventures of Mighty Max*. Max is a character who started life in a collection of miniature toys, and is now marketed through videos and stickers. In this adventure, Max gets too closely involved in a video game, in which his opponent is a robot called Cyber Skull:

'suddenly, as he hit a hidden target, the screen transformed and Cyber Skull morphed into a high resolution 3D image. Max had been so intent on playing the game that he hadn't noticed he had been drawn into a different dimension – a Virtual Reality Doom Zone! ... "Woah", gasped Max, "This dude just got digital on me!" Megacorp had created the ultimate net surfer. It was designed to digitalise everything in its path and feed the information back to Megacorp's central brain.'

The author of this material relies upon the range of associations which are prompted by the use of key words. 'Morphing' was popularised by the Power Rangers series, and means simply a change, here a dramatic transformation from one state to another; in recent years, 'morphing' has been used in computerised film technique, to change one object into another. It was employed to some effect in the film *Terminator 2*. The reference to 'virtual reality' is intended to remind the reader that Max has entered the world of the computer. 'Digital' is used imprecisely, but calls forth the idea of compressed signals representing data. 'Net surfer' refers to those who move freely around the Internet. Notice that Cyber Skull is the servant of an evil corporate power of inestimable size – Megacorp.

In many ways, this new vocabulary has a dual ability: to provide a precise reference where necessary, but also to mobilise cultural references which indicate a general type of experience. The definitions given below are intended as a guide to the range of meanings these terms create.

Cyberspace

'Cyber' is taken from 'cybernetics', a word invented by Norbert Wiener in the 1940s, meaning the science of control and communications in animals and machines. Since 'cyber' came to indicate anything to do with computers and 'machine intelligence', the prefix has acquired a range of fashionable uses.

Cyberspace is a term originally coined by the American author William Gibson to refer to the 'interconnected web of databases, telecommunication links and computer networks', which, in the words of *The Cyberspace Lexicon* (p. 56), 'seem to constitute a new space for human communication and action'. Some definitions call cyberspace the 'invisible' space occupied by a phone call or credit-card transaction. The great preoccupation in fiction, in films like *Tron* and *Lawnmower Man*, and in the virtual reality industry, is to experiment with the idea of human 'interaction' with or within this 'environment'.

Digital technology

Digital technology forms the basis for the revolution in telecommunications. A digital signal, made up of binary digits (0 and 1), can be compressed and stored on optical discs like CD-ROMs. *The Cyberspace Lexicon* (p. 62) states that 'all of the principal elements of media – graphics, text, music, video, animation, photographs and so forth – are available in digital form'.

Digital signals are capable of 'clean' reproduction of sound, image or text, with little interference of the kind experienced with **'analog'** systems. 'Analog' refers to those modes of reproduction possessing a form similar to that of their source. *The Cyberspace Lexicon* (p. 16) uses the example of 'the grooves on a gramophone record' which are 'similar to the soundwaves they reproduce'.

The Internet

'**The Internet**' is the term used to describe the network of computer users linked through the telephone system. Modems, devices which translate digital information to analog data, are used to send messages between computers. The Internet allows individuals to log into a variety of programmes run by other users. Files may be copied and other forms of data, including pictures, may be exchanged.

Networking originated amongst the players of 'fantasy' games, who collaborated on versions of 'dungeons and dragons' but soon moved on to experiment with a form of group communication. Angus McIntyre (*The Guardian*, 24 November 1994) explained that, to a novice, the kind of group interaction produced 'can appear bewildering, like a kind of radio play being written in real time by multiple authors'. The freedom of multi-user exchange has come under scrutiny, and a variety of 'scares' has drawn attention to the fact that attempts may one day be made to 'police' the Internet through government regulation.

Opinions as to the true significance and usefulness of 'the Net' vary. In *Being Digital* (1995), Nicholas Negroponte greets the new age of 'information' with open arms, emphasising the idea that there will be a complete conversion from all analog and paper-based systems to digital technology. Negroponte even sees an end to business meetings, which in his opinion will be replaced by 'virtual conferencing'. By 2005, in this scenario, one 'box' will integrate all the functions of computer, television and telephone.

Clifford Stoll's *Silicon Snakeoil* (1995), by comparison, written from the perspective of someone who was 'wired' to the Arpanet (the Internet's ancestor) in the 1970s, insists that the digital age is over-rated and over-blown. Stoll's opinion is important, not simply because it is based on extensive experience, but because he makes the essential distinction between **data** and **information**. He is one of the few to point out that 'information has content, context, accuracy, pedigree and timeliness'. It is possible to take this further and argue that the quality of material received through the Internet is actually rather poor, and does not provide a sound basis for a resurgence of democracy; so far, it has posed very little threat to state or corporate power.

Joseph Gallivan, weighing up the merits of these two authors in a *Guardian* article of 1 June 1995, writes of Negroponte: 'he does not predict the social consequences of the technocracy he describes'. His rival Clifford Stoll seems to have realised that the concept of an 'information' revolution may be a misapplication of terminology, and could well disguise a far more mundane reality.

Virtual reality

Virtual reality is a project which makes the 'leap' into cyberspace, providing a complete experience in which the human senses are manipulated into taking their cue from computer-generated imagery. Stereo-optical visors and position sensing gloves are used to move through an environment and 'grasp' computer-generated 'objects'. Barrie Sherman and Philip Judkins, writing in *Glimpses of Heaven, Visions of Hell*, give a simple explanation of 'VR' (p. 17):

'Instead of looking at a screen you are enclosed in a three-dimensional graphic universe where you can affect what happens to the virtual world.'

VR's applications are well suited to the exploratory nature of some programmes of education, but its most intensive use has been in battlefield simulation. The American military in particular have used it for air-crew and infantry training.

Multi-media: an interactive form?

A literal definition of the term '**multi-media**' would imply that the process involves the use of more than one media form. This is correct, but the essential feature of multi-media is that the different elements are brought together to form an integrated, *computer-based* programme. Sound, word-processed text, the graphic image and video are all incorporated into a system which can be manipulated by the user to produce a variety of possible 'interactive experiences'.

For example, a travel guide may display a choice of destinations, and a list of options for each choice. By using the mouse to move the cursor (the 'I' bar), an area of the screen (usually called a 'button') may be selected. When this is activated, information will appear on screen. For example, a short digitalised video image may be played, while a voiceover provides additional guidance. Two-dimensional images and animated sequences may also appear. The user is able to decide which aspect of the presentation to run first.

In the diagram in Figure 4.10, it is possible to see the various systems which are used to design and run full-blown multi-media programmes.

New synthesis?

Frank Rickett, writing in *Future Visions: New Technologies of the Screen* (see p. 89), believes the significance of the union of 'television with word-processing, desktop publishing with high-fidelity stereo, computer-based training with graphical arcade adventure' lies in the **new synthesis** which is produced. The new system has certainly allowed greater flexibility in film and broadcasting, and has proved successful when applied to the production of 'interactive' books.

However, when the multi-media synthesis is promoted in the consumer marketplace, it sometimes has the tendency to appear as yet another pastime for a leisured clientele. The advocates of multi-media, none the less, are anxious to stress the wide variety of serious tasks it is able to master.

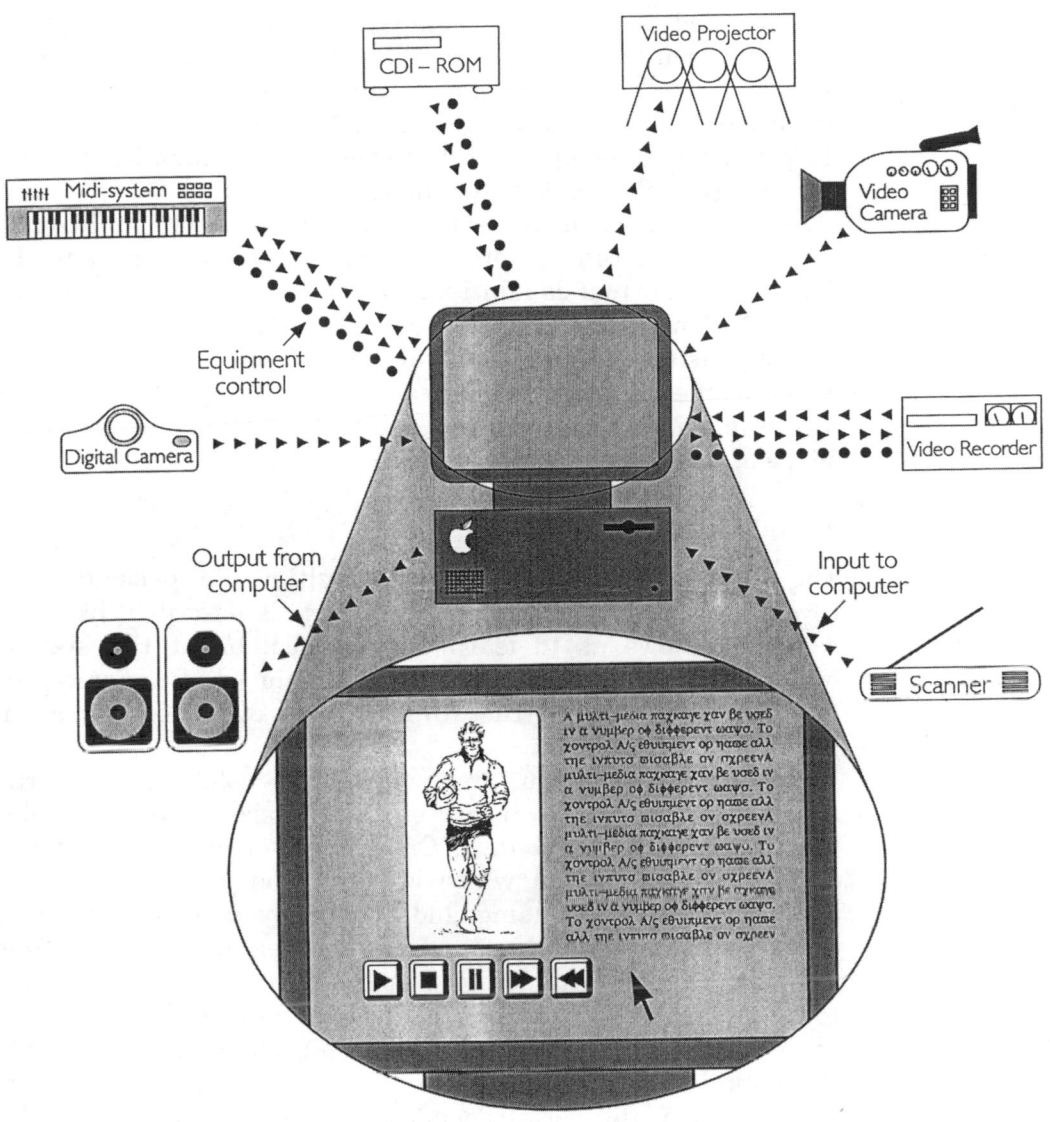

Figure 4.10   Multimedia

True interaction?

In some quarters, the rise of multi-media has been greeted with breathless enthusiasm. Much of the positive response which has been generated comes from the conviction that the technology is **'interactive'**; in other words, that it is significantly different to the model of 'passive' reception which characterises television and film. The problem here is that the term *interactive* is usually applied without a great deal of precision. As we saw in Chapter 1, a precise definition of interaction would be an exchange between *people*, which must be accompanied by some sort of impact and response. No true interaction takes place between the machine and the human subject, since a machine is not an independent entity and cannot initiate communication. However technologically advanced it may be, no real change of state occurs in the machine as a result of its 'contact' with an operator. It responds to commands, according to the range of response built into its programme.

Although we could argue that, strictly speaking, multi-media is not truly interactive, the concept of interaction has become a central feature of the 'hype' which surrounds multi-media systems.

The systems are often marketed through an appeal to *individual* use despite the emphasis on the *multiple* purposes which they may fulfil. If we study the way that the consumer is addressed, then we might gain a fuller picture of the future imagined by advertisers and the 'social engineers' who plan the future shape of public life.

Social landscaping

The concepts used in selling many multi-media 'packages' are actually very revealing. The way that multi-media *use* is described in advertisements, for example, allows us to learn a great deal about the **social landscaping** undertaken by governments and by a number of major corporations. 'Social landscaping' is the restructuring of social existence through intervention in work and leisure.

Multi-media systems are not offered solely as 'entertainment': they are conceptualised in terms of their place in and possible contribution to a *changing social context*. One recent television advertisement showed a family using a system which converts and extends their suburban house, creating an office building and eventually a whole cinema complex. Such advertisements often begin with the idea of 'working from home'. This reference cannot be understood unless it is seen as part of the general trend towards 'flexibility' in employment; the middle and lower middle classes have in recent years been forced to undergo a profound reassessment of their role in the workplace.

In addition, the social agendas followed by authority in both public and private sectors have moved closer together. 'Downsizing' is the term used to describe the extensive reduction of permanent posts which has taken place in both sectors, achieved through early retirement, part-time working and job cuts. This has been a deliberate policy, involving the use of specialist agencies to identify individual workers who fall short of the company's ideal. Questionnaires produced by a firm called Saville Holdsworth were used in the mid-1990s by a wide range of companies (like Anglia TV and Boots) to discover which employees were least attuned to corporate goals. Such individuals could easily find themselves 'released' from their posts.

Multi-media: hierarchies of use?

There is, of course, the obvious distinction between those who can and those who cannot afford to purchase the equipment. However, there is an additional point worthy of our attention. This is the difference between the role taken by the designer or specialist user of multi-media and the consumer of the product. As time goes on, it is possible that this gap will become narrower, but at present the most ardent enthusiasts for multi-media are those who are involved in its design and production. These individuals experience a high degree of active involvement in the production of multi-media, while the *model of use* offered to the consumer is a rather pale imitation of the creative 'interaction' experienced by the designer.

It is worth looking at how the use of multi-media is envisaged in the present and the near future. Victor Burgin, writing in a 1991 issue of *Ten-8*, argued that:

> 'One of the nice things you can do with the technology as it's advanced now, on your own desk-top, is you can take a videotape or a laser disk of a film, and you can send the signal to the computer and watch the film on the screen. You can stop it, reverse it, put it in slow-motion and so on ... The computer gives you the power to shift everything around in the film. I can take a character from one scene, store the character in the attitude I've selected, and then I can move that character into any one of the other scenes.'

The purpose of this simple kind of manipulation is unclear, and may strike some as rather lacking. The model of activity proposed by Burgin offers the consumer little more than the scraps from the multi-media table.

The virtues of passive forms?

It is also the case that stopping a sequence and moving characters around within the narrative is unlikely to produce the kind of entertainment which film is best suited to provide. The point is that film narrative is valued exactly because it is to some degree a **passive** experience, in which an audience witnesses an unfolding story-line in a setting which usually allows mental activity without the expense of significant physical effort.

It seems likely that the basic principles of film will remain the same, because there are already established 'hybrid' forms which cater for the home-computer games market.

Some argue that 'interactive' films are already in production. The first was supposed to be *Thunder in Paradise*, an adventure shot in the summer of 1994, starring Hulk Hogan and John Lemmon. However, *Thunder in Paradise* did not so much integrate film and interactive forms as recognise their essential differences. The action was recorded by one crew for the television/film audience and by another for the games market, requiring the actors to repeat scenes, sometimes with minor variations, for the benefit of each crew.

The style of the two forms, television/film on the one hand and computer games on the other, will certainly create innovations, but the forms themselves will remain separate, and will be viewed/consumed in different settings and for different purposes.

Future comforts?

As we saw at the beginning of this section, there has been a tendency to seize upon technology as the harbinger of an age of freedom or leisure. Perhaps it is difficult for some to 'go overboard' about the new technology, because, in the words of Michael Brady (see *The Times Higher Education Supplement* of 4 February 1994) 'information science and technology' have already been recognised as 'the most important scientific advance this century.'

The one prospect which multi-media enthusiasts most savour is the ability to gain access to *more information*. Rickett, for example, looking even further forward to a time when 'molecular' and 'bio' computers will become available, argues that (*Future Visions*, p. 89):

> 'with such machines we could ... download vast amounts of information from a network of centralised databases'.

There are two interesting points here. The first is the use of the first person; the 'we' employed here must refer, at least in the present stage of development, to a reasonably small number of affluent individuals, concentrated in universities, big corporations, and so on. The second point concerns the *type* of information available to the multi-media user. If we do inhabit an 'information' age, then it is clear that information will be valuable and that it will increasingly resemble other types of commodity available on the market. Yet, at the same time, certain types of information have always been regarded as more valuable than others. To imagine that access will be possible to 'sensitive' data would perhaps be too optimistic.

A dream of privilege?

The cultural assumptions behind the future visions of multi-media use are relevant to an understanding of the class which at present has most experience of its use. This passage is taken from Aston and Schwarz's *Multimedia*, and reflects a mixture of fantasy and the lived experience of a specific class of social actors:

> 'It is January 15, the year 2010, and as you awake to your morning toast and coffee, a personal digital "accountant" on your computer TV appliance informs you via voice response that a tax refund has been credited to your account and the annual surplus was transferred to the retirement fund.'

The following very similar vision is the work of David Bowen, in *Multimedia: Now and Down the Line*. He describes 'an ordinary day' (p. 5):

'Wilbur takes no notice [of his sister Amanda's interruption]. He is concentrating on the screen in the sitting room. It hangs on the walls five feet wide and half that in height. It is a top-of-the-range model: when not in use it turns itself randomly into different old masters, or sometimes a mirror. Like all the screens in the house, it is also a computer, and is connected both to the BT Multi Com network and to most of the electrical appliances in the house.'

As usual in such scenarios, the whole house is 'wired'. At this point, we may expect the narrative to take a turn for the better in the manner of Spielberg, with a rogue electronic signal, a crackle of electricity and the sudden malevolence of previously docile food-mixers, percolators and other gadgets. Bowen, however, is in deadly earnest.

Social roles and new technology

Wilbur behaves as we might expect, exercising a certain freedom to choose forms of entertainment. When he decides to play a computer game, the computer itself asks him what he wishes to select. After Wilbur presses a button on his handset, it announces:

' 'You have chosen Super-Mario 239. Now searching for a suitable partner ... Angus in Aberdeen ... would you like to play with him? ... He will be ready in two minutes. Please put on your videospecs and data glove.'

Most parents would expect at this point an anguished cry: 'Where's my data glove?'.

If we cast a glance at Wilbur's sister Amanda, however, we may notice that some gender roles appear to have survived intact into the twenty-first century. She goes upstairs:

'to finish her Japanese homework. Her teacher has given her a flash memory card – a wafer of silicon about three inches by two – which she slots into the front of her screen.'

It 'contains her entire year's course, tailored for her by her teacher'. If Amanda makes a mistake, 'an electronic "tutor" pops up to explain what she has done wrong'.

This scenario may reflect the day-dream of the technocrat, but it seems to have little connection to the immediacies of life as they are presently known. When Steven Barnett (*The Times*, 16 March 1994) tells us not to be surprised, 'if the media world in five and even ten years' time looks uncannily similar to today', he might also have been referring to the fact that social relationships, such as that between teacher and pupil, are likely to remain intact, despite their 'mediation' by technology.

SUMMARY

A **formal organisation** may be described as a human collective which is created in order to pursue an explicit purpose or goal. It is governed by rules and usually managed through a hierarchical system of control. The characteristics of a formal organisation may be listed as follows:

- It is established under material conditions by an individual or, more usually, a group of individuals.
- It has a set of official or public objectives.
- It is commonly founded on a division of labour based upon set tasks.
- It allocates roles to individuals.
- It sets up specialised departments or sections.
- It develops formally structured relationships, as well as unofficial networks and working practices.
- It institutes methods of control over individuals and groups.
- It operates within broad 'areas' of influence, controlling part of a specific market for example.
- It manages resources, successfully or otherwise.
- It uses both official and unofficial systems of communication.

The existence of organisations is a salient feature of life in industrial and 'post-industrial' communities. The school, the workplace, the hospital, the bank, the prison and the church all have the potential to exert some measure of influence upon the human subject. Some of these formal groups exercise greater power than others.

● Formal entities

When Frederick Glen (see *The Social Psychology of Organisations*, p. 11) argues that 'it is people, not entities called organisations, who make rules, develop value systems, set goals and take decisions', there are two points worth making. First, people create organisations as **formal** and not personal **entities**, so that the results appear in some cases to have little of the 'humanity' sometimes attributed to the individual. Secondly, few people have an opportunity to create

rules for the organisations in which they work. The working lives of most individuals are spent within structures which are not of their own making.

● Alternative values?

Despite their conventional structure, formal organisations do not necessarily promote authoritarian *values*; and where they do, they do not always achieve success. At times, they may even find themselves opposed to central authority.

● Organisations and their relationships with outsiders

An organisation functions through a series of **relationships** with a number of distinct groups. In general, there are four types of 'out-group' which every organisation must take into account.

The first, as we have seen above, is the particular *section* of the public which must be *reached*. The second type of external collective is made up of *other formal organisations*. The third kind consists of institutions which possess some kind of official or commercial remit to *oversee* or *review* the work of the organisation. The fourth is made up of groups of '*visitors*', a category which may encompass individuals who will be of some material use to the organisation.

Contact with 'out-groups': the advertising agency

A useful example of contact between an organisation and the types of 'out-group' described above may be found in the commercial activities pursued by an advertising agency. These relationships are described in some detail.

● 'Target' groups within the organisation

An important point to note is that a '**target**' or subject group is sometimes found, at various points in time, within the physical boundaries of the organisation itself. For instance, colleges have students on site and hospitals contain people who require treatment, while prisons hold a more long-term population.

AUTHORITY AND SUBORDINATION

Besides the relationships which are established with outside bodies, organisations contain a series of 'internal' relationships. The most significant are those which exist between **authority** and various groups of **subordinates**.

Definitions of authority

Etzioni (1964) provides a classification of authority or power, which he divides into three separate types:

- the **coercive** form, based upon the use of compulsion;
- the **utilitarian**, which is exercised through a form of legalistic and rationalist authority;
- the **normative**, where relationships are based on the intrinsic value of the activities performed, or of membership itself.

According to Etzioni, the *coercive* form may include organisations such as prisons, concentration camps and custodial hospitals. The *utilitarian* form is supported by a system of economic reward, found in business, the armed services and the civil service. Finally, Etzioni believed that the *normative* form applied to hospitals, universities and voluntary bodies.

Authority: a more complex picture

In actual practice, all these forms will exist, to a greater or lesser degree, in every institution. Utilitarian approaches, for example, are quite easily reinforced by coercive features should the need arise. It is distinctly odd, for example, that Etzioni does not regard the internal organisation of the armed forces as coercive. It seems clear that compulsion in an army exists alongside 'rational' forms of authority.

Feminist critiques of authority

Some strands of **feminism** argue that groups in authority share the same deficiencies because they are for the most part composed of men, or are controlled by men if they do not actually form a numerical majority. While there may be some disagreement about the origin of male authoritarianism (whether it is inborn or emerges from socialisation), the fact remains that male behaviour and attitudes often determine the precise *forms* in which authority manifests itself.

Some theorists believe that physical differences between men and women, inadequacies in women's performances, and women's failures to fulfil roles are frequently misattributed to unchangeable biological givens like women's sex.

Some authors have noted that social science, which is supposed to interrogate authority and its role in the creation of social relations, has itself used methods which approximate to a 'masculine' approach. This does, however, depend upon accepting the idea that authoritarian structures are 'typically' male, or are at least one manifestation of male culture.

Restructuring in education: the exercise of authority

The overall goals of an institution sometimes alter so radically that a form of authority which once seemed appropriate will be superseded by alternative models. An example of this can be found in the public sector in Britain. The attempt to remodel the outlook of educational and other public bodies, along *competitive* and 'cost-effective' lines, led to a sharp conflict between the values originally held by such institutions, and the new types of conduct their members were supposed to accept.

Authority and control in the workplace

All **workplaces** function through some form of co-ercion, even where this is largely paternalistic or benevolent. The behaviour of those individuals who 'belong' to the organisation is regulated in a variety of ways. These ways are described.

Basic forms of control: work discipline, visibility, surveillance

The discipline imposed by the work itself can be quite effective, as noted above. In addition, theorists have examined the systems which are used to 'check up' on employees. Michel Foucault, for example, placed great emphasis upon the concept of employee **visibility** and the related category of **surveillance**.

Foucault studied the 'Panopticon', a prison design created by Jeremy Bentham in the nineteenth century. In this system, the prison would be circular in shape, and all cells would radiate outwards from a central observation point. Surveillance, on the other hand, means close and continuous observation. It takes more than one form, besides the direct visual scrutiny carried out by managers.

A slap on the wrist

In order to obtain the obedience of staff, managers may reproduce forms of discipline *already familiar* to the employee from his or her early socialisation, particularly from schooldays. Authority in organisations sometimes depends upon the simple mechanisms of 'adult' behaviour to get its own way. For instance, vocal opposition is often characterised as immature or petulant. Another familiar tactic is to call those who propose alternative systems 'unrealistic'; appeals to the 'way things really are' are widespread in institutional life.

Work roles and the exercise of authority

The provision by organisations of **roles** and *identities* (what we have previously called 'subject positions') is a powerful form of influence over the employee. I do not mean to suggest that it ensures complete subservience; from the viewpoint of the organisation, however, the way that people *identify* with the roles they are given can provide a useful means of control.

Involvement

Etzioni's work on the role of the individual in the workplace has been extended to show three types of **involvement** which characterise the role of individuals. In the first type, **alienative** involvement, the worker is obliged to remain with the organisation and has no commitment to it. In the second, **calculative** involvement, the individual may expect a reasonable return or exchange for his or her services. Finally, **moral** involvement sees a high degree of commitment from the individual to the organisation.

● Group pressures

In *The Social Psychology of Organisations*, Frederick Glen notes that the **pressure** to accept social norms is part of daily existence (p. 20):

> 'The nature of society is such that external pressures upon the individual to conform – to fit in with the group – are central factors throughout the entire range of social experience.'

The essential point which should emerge from this observation is that people do not choose to 'fit in with society' as such. Instead, they choose to belong to groups which they regard as close to their own values. These groups *mediate* the wider values of the society.

Individual conformity?

The reasons for the existence of conformity given above indicate the power of group membership.

Group influence on judgement: Sherif's and Asch's experiments

The work of Sherif and Asch in the mid-1930s is usually seen as a landmark in social psychology research. Sherif used the *autokinetic* effect as the object of judgement in his experiments. These used a test for which there was no right or wrong answer; they were ambiguous. In 1956, Asch used a number of college students in an experiment designed to establish how an individual subject would respond to pressure.

● Resistance: one consequence of positive self-identification

Identification with the work role may also, *at some stage* and *under certain circumstances*, allow the development of a critical perspective on the organisation itself. A clear example is found in those institutions which encourage a skilled workforce to behave in a *professional* manner. Widespread acceptance of professional standards may, for example, lead to demands for a truly professional *status*.

Persistent critics

In some organisations there are individuals who are recognised as **persistent critics** of the established order. The critic may act as a conduit for the dissatisfaction of staff, who might allow an individual to fulfil this role because it means that they themselves do not have to make their opposition public. Critics often find that they are then always expected to speak out and that, the more often they do so, the less likely it is that anyone else will feel inclined to make a similar contribution.

However, when Glen argues (p. 21) that 'the truly isolated individual is the psychotic', who 'cannot share in the group's perception of the world, nor they in his', there is actually no reason why the *group* should not prove instead to occupy the 'psychotic' position, in which case its judgement of individuals will be entirely unreliable. In some cases, such as Nazi Germany, a whole nation's system of values can become entirely distorted.

● Responses to extreme repression

The psychologist Bettelheim, who was at one time an inmate of Dachau and Buchenwald, noted how rapidly behaviour and personality were altered in the extraordinary context of camp life. Whereas many inmates were quickly destroyed, first psychologically and then physically, some of the prisoners began to identify with those who held complete sway over their fate; they modelled themselves on the camp guards, and even began to imitate aspects of their behaviour.

Bettelheim's description of this extreme form of identification should, however, be contrasted with the formation of resistance organisations inside the camps. One of the few British survivors of Buchenwald, the airman and secret agent Yeo-Thomas, formed a resistance group while a prisoner, and witnessed the existence of a variety of other organisations.

● BUREAUCRACY: A DEFINITION

Bureaucracy may be defined as the existence of established administrative practices; it also refers to the organised groups of officials which function on behalf of a government or other executive power. The social theorist Max Weber saw bureaucracy as the dominant form of organisation in modern society. He also described a general theory of 'social action', in which human beings perform actions because they are prompted by a series of motives.

In Chancery: *Bleak House* and bureaucracy

The Chancery dispute in Charles Dickens's novel *Bleak House* is used as an example of bureaucracy. The passage cited reveals an institution which has replaced meaningful communication with the *forms* of exchange, each form prompting a particular reply or inquiry, until eventually meaning is buried under a mountain of paperwork.

● Criticisms of bureaucracy

In 1965, the American theorist Warren Bennis produced a ten-point critique of bureaucracy. The ten areas he identified are set out in the text.

● ORGANISATIONAL STRUCTURE AND COMMUNICATION

In *Organisations*, March and Simon classify a series of *occasions* when **organisational communication** will take place. Communication will occur to meet the following needs or eventualities:

- the presence of 'non-programmed' activity, i.e. that type of event which is not planned for or foreseen by the official system;
- the initiation, establishment and supervision of programmes;
- the provision of data to pursue a course of action;
- the focusing of attention on problems;
- the production of information about the results of activities within the organisation.

Classifying events: established categories

March and Simon argue that organisations **classify** all the events which require a response. When an event occurs, the first question asked is supposed to be: 'What *kind* of event is this?'. March and Simon believe that organisations have a repertory of 'programmes', so that any occurrence can produce an automatic response, selected from the repertory.

These authors note the dangers present in the types of categorisation used by some formal groups. If an event is thought to fall into an identifiable category, then it will be 'understood' and communicated according to set preconceptions.

Classical vs. behavioural approaches to organisation

Myers and Myers believe that it is possible to describe two types of organisational theory: **classical** and **behavioural**. Classical organisation is sub-divided into the **scientific management** of Frederick Taylor (see the section 'Against the "rationalisation" of leisure'), the investigation of **bureaucracy** carried out by Weber (see the section on 'Bureaucracy: rational action?'), and theories of **administrative management**, associated with the work of practising managers like Chester Barnard (1938) and Henri Fayol (1915).

Behavioural attitudes to organisation have emerged from studies of sociology and psychology, and are discussed by Myers and Myers under three separate headings. These are **human relations, human resources** and **systems**.

Human relations is the title given to research carried out under the direction of Elton Mayo in the United States over a period of two decades, between the 1930s and the 1950s. The *social* rather than the *physical* environment of work was studied.

Human resources was an approach based on the ideas of Douglas McGregor and Rensis Likert. McGregor (1960) emphasised the creativity and imagination of individual workers, and their powers of motivation and self-direction.

Communication in classical and behavioural systems

Most organisations will employ elements of both 'classical' and 'behavioural' approaches in dealings with staff. In some cases, each type of structure will be applied to *different* groups of employees; typically, those who have attained a certain degree of status will be allowed more autonomy than those who are regarded as mere functionaries.

POWER: COMMUNICATION IN HIERARCHICAL SYSTEMS

As we have seen, writers on organisational communication often insist that formal bodies cannot function without effective communication. It is, however, quite rare to discover an organisation of any scale which disseminates information or facilitates interaction with complete success. Published studies of a variety of organisations appear to identify the same problem – the *dysfunctional* state of the communication systems which are found in most formal groups.

The power structure

Some studies of organisational communication recognise the structural elements which prevent the free dissemination of ideas and information. In *The Reality of Organisations*, which was written as 'a guide for managers', Rosemary Stewart argues that (p. 95):

'The dominant factor in managerial relations ... is the existence of a power structure.'

Social power and the workplace

The concept of **social power** expresses the idea that there are *general relationships* of power in society as a whole. The workplace is a good example of a place where social power operates. Collins and Raven produced an analysis of the concept in an article dating from 1969. They identified social power as:

'The potential influence of some influencing agent "O" over some person "P". Influence is defined as a change in cognition, attitude, behaviour or emotion of "P" which can be attributed to "O".'

These authors identify six different types of power, which are reproduced in the text.

Power vs. authority: an artificial division?

Weber (1946) makes a distinction between **power** and **authority**. Power is exercised, he believes, when one individual is in a position to exert his or her will in a situation, regardless of any resistance from others. Authority, by contrast (see Glen, p. 37), 'implies voluntary compliance with demands that are essentially perceived as legitimate'.

The point is, however, that some forms of authority may be regarded as more legitimate than others, but the 'voluntary compliance' is never in fact completely voluntary. In fact, there are many cases where there is no conscious *act of compliance* at all.

Direct pathways?

Most of the formal organisations with which we are familiar are organised as hierarchies. That is to say, they are institutions which depend upon graded levels of status, related to a variety of functions. A diagram of a hierarchy will show **direct pathways** from, for example, the managing director of a company down to the individual workers in any one of a number of departments. This makes communication appear straightforward.

However, in general terms decisions are passed down, while requests are passed upwards. Many of the representations made by a workforce, especially where they take the form of dissension or protest, will be 'sanitized' as they are passed upwards through the system.

Departmentalisation

Although many diagrams illustrate 'line management', where communication seems to proceed in stages from the 'lowest' to the 'highest' level, most large organisations create distinct departments. A typical 'chain

of command' on a magazine is reproduced, together with an illustration showing the departments within an advertising agency.

NETWORKS OF COMMUNICATION

In the 1950s, a number of theorists advanced the idea that there were distinct types of communication structure, each of which was suited to a particular type of task. These might be set up deliberately in order to cope with some aspect of work, but might also arise without formal control. Various types of group network would therefore exist within organisations. Illustrations are provided for the study of each type of network.

Informal systems of communication

During the 1960s and 1970s, the American researcher Peter Blau carried out an investigation into a federal bureau working in Washington, DC. Blau came to the conclusion that (Haralambous, p. 423) 'unofficial practices that are explicitly prohibited by official regulations sometimes further the achievement of organisational objectives'.

Sometimes, however, unofficial structures of communication are actively detrimental to the functioning of the organisation, usually where they exist in secret amongst powerful groups. On occasion, unofficial management structures by-pass the very sub-committees they have set up; the sub-committee may in fact be no more than a 'talking shop'.

Likert: four systems of management

Rensis Likert (see the section on 'Classical vs. behavioural approaches to organisation') described four systems of management, a theory which emerged from extensive research into the ways in which managers perceived the structural dimensions of their organisations. He set out the four types as follows:

1 **exploitative-authoritarian**;
2 **benevolent-authoritarian**;
3 **consultative**;
4 **participative**.

Japanese management systems

In recent years, some writers have referred positively to the types of management found in Japanese corporations. Despite its surface rationality, there have been a number of disagreements with the Japanese approach.

Against the 'rationalisation' of leisure

Some theorists see the onset of a benign but 'total' management as extremely detrimental to the political development of a society. Ed Andrew, in *Closing the Iron Cage* (1981), sets out a critique of all forms of **scientific management**, which he feels attempt to manage not just the working lives of individuals but their leisure activities as well.

Revolutionary forms of organisation: France, 1968

The belief that capitalism must be uprooted, rather than merely 'softened' in its effects, rarely gains wide support in industrial societies. When it does, the consequent social upheaval can be considerable. The movements which arose in 1968, the 'year of revolutions', produced a number of different models of organisation.

Feminist and libertarian critiques of 'authoritarian' left-wing groups

One of the unfortunate features of some *formal* organisations which oppose the authoritarianism of the state and of capitalism in general is their own allegiance to internal structures which reproduce similar relations of power. In 1979, an attempt was made to reappraise the values held by 'the far left'.

Sheila Rowbotham, Lynne Segal and Hilary Wainwright produced a **feminist** and **libertarian** perspective on the problems which were thought to plague certain left-wing groups. Their book, which received enthusiastic support from a variety of socialist and feminist groups, was called *Beyond the Fragments*.

THE DEVELOPMENT OF COMMUNICATION

Communication is often described as the transmission of information, and should include the concept of an established *route* or connection between places separated by physical distance. Roads, for example, form routes of communication between human settlements. The 'spatial' aspect of the subject is often neglected.

Communication in feudal society is described, together with **communication in pre-industrial society** in general. Bloch's study of feudalism argues that 'no institution or method could take the place of personal contact between human beings'. In other words, interpersonal communication, conducted face to face, was the only system which guaranteed a reliable exchange of meaning. In pre-industrial society, the main instruments of communication were:

- word of mouth;
- proclamations;
- sermons;
- letters;
- handwritten books;
- narrative and verse forms;
- religious and secular iconography.

The early Church: communicating an ideology

One central issue in communication is how elites establish and sustain themselves through the control of various systems of **ideological** reproduction; in other words, how they maintain their position through public forms of address and public actions. An early example of a group which tried to achieve ideological hegemony may be found in the growth of the Catholic Church.

MASS COMMUNICATION
The concept of mass communication

The concept of **mass communication** is employed to describe a number of features of public communication, suggesting perhaps that each possesses the same qualities. It is used to refer to media **institutions**, to the scale of **production** supposedly achieved by the media, to the **distribution** of media 'products', and to the **audiences** which receive or 'consume' media content.

The birth of mass communication

The majority of theorists date the beginning of mass communication from the invention of movable type in the middle of the fifteenth century. However, as we saw above, Church services represent a form of communication notable for their 'mass' reproduction of a specific ideology.

Print was the leading force in the expansion of knowledge, but it depended upon the existence of what Crowley and Hayer (*Communication in History*, p. 91) call 'receptive conditions'. The growth of a 'vernacular literacy' (the ability to read and write in one's own language, as opposed to knowledge of Latin), together with improvements in technology, helped prepare the ground for the expansion of written forms of communication.

When literacy increased and the Bible began to circulate amongst the middle-class citizenry of Europe, individuals could quite easily assume, on the basis of what they had been told by the Church itself, that they had direct access to the word of God.

The rise of print

The form of printing press which utilized metal type appeared in a number of different centres in and around the year 1450. Haarlem, Avignon and Mainz all contributed to the 'invention' of this phase of printing. McQuail, however, argues that the printed book was (p. 9) 'initially only a technical device for reproducing the same ... range of texts that was already being extensively copied'.

Curran argues that print made possible 'an educational revolution' in Protestant countries in early modern Europe. The growth of literacy ran alongside the proliferation of printed books. It was the Protestant faith in particular, together with increased commercial activity, which appeared to act as a spur to the extension of oral and written political discourse.

PRINT-BASED MEDIA
The development of the newspaper

The **newspaper** began its existence in the form of the newsbook, which appeared in the late 1640s. McQuail believes that (p. 9) the newspaper's 'chief precursor seems ... to have been the letter rather than the book'. Nevertheless, it would appear that the commercial paper was the form which most closely determined the future development of what became the newspaper industry. The establishment of a flourishing press was not without incident; censorship occurred throughout the seventeenth century.

Dissent and the radical press

The growth of working-class self-organisation was accompanied by the flowering of a **radical political press**. Government legislation against the formation of *national* organisations led to the establishment of local political groups, which often took their lead from the radical newspapers of the time. Meanwhile, the growth of interest in newspapers, and the security offered to the commercial press by advertising revenue, made all publications, whatever their political affiliation, difficult to control. Increased revenue also allowed the middle-class press to retain full-time journalists.

The power of the bourgeois press

Eventually, the suppression of the radical press was seen as counter-productive. A current of argument began to circulate amongst middle-class editors and other commentators to the effect that it was more desirable to encourage the growth of a conservative outlook amongst the working class itself.

Lord Northcliffe's role in shaping popular journalism is explored, together with the role of *The Daily Mail* as cheerleader of the political right and ally of fascism.

NEWS: SELECTION AT WORK

Roger Fowler, in *Language in the News* (p. 110), examines the question of **news values** and declares: 'the world of the Press is not the real world, but a world skewed and judged'. In this case, reference to the real world is intended to show that the press is selective and that 'the vast majority of events are not mentioned'. Since most events are never reported, 'selection ... gives us a partial view of the world'.

Not found but created

Greg Philo (Fowler, p. 13) argues that the usual picture of journalistic activity is mistaken: 'news is not "found" or even "gathered" so much as made'.

Analysis: 'The John Smith choice'

An analysis of a *Sunday Express* article is made.

PRINT AND ADVERTISING

Advertising has always had a public character and usually a commercial intention. As a type of address which is 'carried' by the mass media, some commentators argue that it does not qualify as a form or medium in its own right. However, the danger in such a view is that it could lead us to under-estimate the importance of advertising's place in society as a whole.

Types of advertising

Advertising can be divided into eight types, which are set out in the text.

The development of modern advertising

In the pre-industrial era, advertising was a relatively simple system of proclamation and announcement on the periphery of the national economy. Gillian Dyer argues that the origins of advertising lie in the rise of seventeenth-century news-sheets or 'mercuries', the early forms of what we now call newspapers. In the middle of the seventeenth century, advertisements resembled the 'small ads' which still appear in various journals. These were cast in the form of 'announcements'. By 1658, however, Dyer detects a new development: a *rhetorical* flourish in advertising address.

A series of '**small ads**' which appeared in eighteenth- and nineteenth-century American newspapers is studied and analysed.

Advent of 'the new social self'?

In the 1990 edition of *Social Communication in Advertising*, Leiss and his co-authors suggest that the destruction of older forms of community by the concentration of urban labour led to a '**new social self**', characterised by individualism.

In the later part of the nineteenth century, and the early years of the twentieth, Leiss argues that the advertiser paid increasingly greater attention to the promotion of goods and services which were not part of the *essential* requirements of life. In other words, various types of social need were catered for. From the 1920s, visual representation became more prominent in advertising, but the printed text remained of great importance.

Roland Marchand describes the twenties in particular and early consumer society in general as (p. 214) 'an age of shifting relationships', in which (p. 215):

> 'individuals had to be prepared to transform themselves for new roles and new opportunities, thus making them peculiarly vulnerable to shifting definitions of themselves by others'.

Visual imagery and implicit narrative

What Marchand calls the 'persistent patterns or clichés' of visual advertising may reveal the myths and established narrative formulas offered to the popular imagination. Successful advertising does not impose a 'view of the world', but has instead some understanding of the shared fantasies of a society. One of the most frequent images used in the early twentieth century is that of a commanding male figure who looks out over a landscape which includes factories, dwellings, and sometimes distant mountains. This genre is called by Marchand 'Master of all he Surveys'.

MASS COMMUNICATION: QUESTIONS OF ADDRESS

The concept of **address** is central to the study of

communication. To make an 'address' means to direct a form of speech or writing or other type of message to an individual or audience. The term implies that a concentration of attention and effort has been made by the communicator. The linguistic and other powers and techniques at his or her disposal are focused on the act of communication. An alternative definition of 'address' reflects this concentration of powers: the *Oxford English Dictionary* refers to 'readiness, skill and dexterity'.

Audience: anybody there?

The intention behind address in general is to deliver a message which will make an impact on a particular **audience**. An address must consider both form and content. If the address which is delivered does not have meaning or relevance for the intended audience, then it is bound to fail.

Media: definitions

In 1968, Janowitz produced an influential description of the **media**. James Curran, writing in 1977 (see *The Media: Contexts of Study*, p. 9, unit 2), adapted Janowitz's original view and proposed the following definition:

> 'The mass media comprise the institutions and techniques by which specialised social groups disseminate symbolic content to large heterogeneous and geographically-dispersed audiences.'

The 'specialised social groups' mentioned here are the *formal organisations* purposely set up to disseminate information, entertainment, instruction, aesthetic forms of expression and so on.

Commercial motives and social power

There is always an **industrial** and a **political** aspect to mass communication activities, and therefore a **commercial** motive which drives individual media corporations. Media organisations function within a society which accepts the legitimacy of financial gain, regards the profit motive as 'natural', and allows the media to generate quite extensive **social power**.

A comprehensive definition

A comprehensive definition would have to include the social, financial and political issues outlined above. Based on Curran's adaptation, it could be summarised as follows:

- The mass media comprise the institutions and techniques by which powerful, specialised social groups disseminate standardised commodities (in the form of units of symbolic content) to large, heterogeneous and geographically dispersed audiences.

The use of personal address

In an attempt to reach their desired audiences or markets, a number of groups and individuals, including politicians, advertisers, celebrities and private corporations, use a 'personal' mode to frame messages. The purpose of this is obvious: a direct appeal using the second person singular is supposed to make a greater impact on the recipient than would a more general discourse.

A *Sun* newspaper article, 'COULD YOU BE AN SAS SUPERMAN?', is discussed in terms of the address it makes to its audience.

BROADCAST MEDIA: RADIO AND TELEVISION

The **development** and history of **radio** is set out. **Restrictions on broadcasting** are also discussed, together with the **birth of television and commercial radio. Radio and the youth market** is also investigated. The section moves on to describe the **technical development of television**.

Deregulation

The Broadcasting Act of 1990 dispensed with the services of the IBA (Independent Broadcasting Authority) in favour of the ITC (Independent Television Commission), which was to exercise a 'lighter touch' – which meant in effect the exercise of reduced powers. In the ensuing franchise battle, in which companies had to convince the government that they had satisfied a 'quality threshold' before submitting sealed bids for a licence to broadcast, four television companies lost their tenure to new consortiums.

Channel 5: bids

In November 1994, the offer of the Channel 5 franchise was resurrected. The deadline for the new set of bids was set for 2 May 1995. Each of the bids is described.

Changing the rules of ownership

On 23 May 1995, the procedures governing the **ownership** of media in Britain were 'liberalised' or relaxed in order to sweep away what Conservative minister Stephen Dorrell called the 'complex, myriad' rules facing media groups. Many leading figures in the newspaper and television industries greeted the changes with enthusiasm, while Murdoch's News Corporation and the Mirror Group found that the scope of their expansion had been limited.

From protest to democracy?

Objections to the new rules came from a number of sources, and reflected a variety of concerns, from the possible detrimental effect on local and regional newspapers to the reduction of quality in journalism and the sacrifice of smaller journals as larger commercial interests gain control of the marketplace. Overall, the changes must be seen within the framework of a capitalist or market-driven philosophy, in which 'diversity' is supposedly assured through allowing established organisations to create an interlocking structure based on political power and commercial strength.

Normative theories or models of media structure, which argue for a complete revolution in the relationship between institution and its audience, are usually neglected. Denis McQuail, for example, identifies 'democratic-participant' theory as a challenge to other models of media organisation. This approach was prompted (see *Mass Communication Theory*, 1987, p. 122) as a:

'reaction against the commercialisation and monopolisation of privately-owned media and against the centralism . . . of public broadcasting institutions'.

SATELLITE AND CABLE
Satellite: from theory to practice

The history and development of satellite are examined in detail, together with the growth of **cable. Satellite wars** are also investigated in depth, particularly the commercial struggle between British Satellite Broadcasting and Rupert Murdoch's Sky television, which ended in a merger that many saw as a Sky victory. Murdoch's speech, in which he argued that:

'advances in the technology of telecommunication have proved an unambiguous threat to totalitarian regimes everywhere',

is contrasted with his decision effectively to suspend BBC broadcasts to China after the Chinese government's suppression of the democracy movement.

THE 'NEW' MEDIA

The concept of **'new' media** and **information technology** is studied in detail. The prospect of life in a new technological environment has always prompted the expression of high hopes. From the Festival of Britain in 1951, and the 'white heat' of technology announced by Harold Wilson in the 1960s, to more recent celebration of the 'superhighway', the idea of a revolution in science has inspired great optimism.

Terms and definitions

In recent years, a whole vocabulary has grown from the general concept of the new technology. A number of definitions are given, including those for **cyberspace**, **digital technology**, the **Internet** and **virtual reality**.

MULTI-MEDIA: AN INTERACTIVE FORM?

A literal definition of the term **'multi-media'** would imply that the process involves the use of more than one media form. This is correct, but the essential feature of multi-media is that the different elements are brought together to form an integrated, *computer-based* programme.

True interaction?

Much of the positive response to multi-media which has been generated comes from the conviction that the technology is '**interactive**'; in other words, that it is significantly different to the model of 'passive' reception which characterises television and film. The problems with this conception are described.

Multimedia: hierarchies of use?

At present the most ardent enthusiasts for multi-media are those who are involved in its design and production. These individuals experience a high degree of active involvement in the production of multi-media, while the *model of use* offered to the consumer is a rather pale imitation of the creative 'interaction' experienced by the designer.

The virtues of passive forms?

'**Passive forms**' like film narrative are valued exactly because they allow mental activity without the expense of significant physical effort.

A dream of privilege?

The cultural assumptions behind the future visions of multi-media use are relevant to an understanding of the class which at present has most experience of its use. The social roles ascribed to male and female users are an interesting case in point.

STUDENT ACTIVITIES

INSTITUTIONS AND ADDRESS

Chapter 4 began by describing the attributes and practices of formal organisations. This section looks at examples of corporate *address*. When large private institutions try to create a positive public image, they usually adopt the method known as 'corporate advertising'.

This is not the marketing of products, but the promotion of a company and its functions, which requires the use of various communication devices. There is no point in hoping that a 'good name' will be acquired simply through product quality or through contributions to charitable organisations. Nor is it enough to expect consumers to find out information for themselves; an active policy of communication must be pursued.

There are many ways of making the individual corporation seem virtuous. Slogans and logos can be created and events stage-managed. In pursuing the aim of 'image management', a company must consider what kinds of public address it ought to make, not simply in terms of content, but also with regard to form.

The edited extract from Chapter 4 printed below describes the concept of formal organisation and the types of 'out-group' with which relationships may be established; the extracts taken from David Bernstein's *Company Image and Reality* give examples of corporate slogans; finally, the passages from Donn J. Tilson's article 'The shaping of "eco-nuclear" publicity: the use of visitors' centres in public relations' reveal the measures taken by the nuclear power industry to promote itself.

Revision: Communication and formal organisation

A **formal organisation** may be described as a human collective which is created in order to pursue an explicit purpose or goal. It is governed by rules and usually managed through a hierarchical system of control. The existence of organisations is a salient feature of life in industrial and 'post-industrial' communities. The school, the workplace, the hospital, the bank, the prison and the church all have the potential to exert some measure of influence upon the human subject. Some of these formal groups exercise greater power than others.

The *degree* of influence and the *kind* of power exerted depend upon the role of each organisation in society. A few will play a significant part in early socialisation – schools are the obvious example. Others have less direct or prolonged contact with their 'clientele', but have the potential to wield some power over the individual. Banks, for instance, are able to influence aspects of their customers' lives through the use of financial penalties or incentives, and require only a limited degree of communication to do so.

Organisations and their relationships with outsiders

An organisation functions through a series of **relationships** with a number of distinct groups. In the first place, we might consider those groups which lie outside the organisation itself. In general, there are four types of 'out-group' which every organisation must take into account.

The first, as we have seen above, is the particular *section* of the public which must be *reached*; all organisations possess some idea of the groups they exist to 'serve' or hope to influence. The second type of external collective is made up of *other formal organisations*. These may be either rivals or allies, and will include groups like suppliers and retailers. The third kind consists of institutions which possess some kind of official or commercial remit to *oversee* or *review* the work of the organisation. Such institutions could be *regulatory bodies* or *commissioning agencies*. The fourth is made up of groups of 'visitors', a category which may encompass individuals who will be of some material use to the organisation.

The attitudes held by organisations towards the outsiders they meet can be very revealing. A police force may, for instance, think in terms of 'service' to the public, but will often use quite different categories to describe the groups it encounters in the course of everyday events. *Private citizens* who obstruct the building of a road, for example, may find themselves transformed into *protestors*, and as a result may experience a form of treatment the police think appropriate to that category.

CORPORATE ADDRESS
Reading: extracts from David Bernstein's *Company Image and Reality*

Bernstein takes a wry look at corporate address and image making, but with a serious purpose. He notes the 'interchangeability ... and vacuous quality' of corporate advertising slogans, and clearly prefers plain language and accuracy to the overblown claims of many institutions. Read the following and answer the questions which follow.

'When the Independent Television Contractors Association commissioned The Creative Business [an advertising agency] to write and produce a film documentary on how the television companies regulated the content of commercials, the audience was a little over 600 ... the target audience was the House of Commons and the objective was equally clear: to convince MPs that the self-regulatory system of advertisement vetting is effective, in the public interest, and more efficient – because less bureaucratic – than a state system. (p. 92)

A politician, influential in a major decision affecting a corporate advertiser, may see a television commercial for which he is a prime target. However, seeing it simultaneously with some 16,000,000 others alters the nature of the communication and the importance of the message. It is both more important and more public.

Furthermore, the use of a public medium may prove a more successful way of communicating since there is less of a feeling of being got at. He may feel less of a target. He may choose to identify with the issue rather than react to it. He may behave, initially, like a member of the public. This could be an essential first step towards understanding and subsequent action. He is more likely to act on behalf of the public if he has become involved as one of its members. (p. 93)'

There are hundreds of product fields and countless brands. Yet when we come to the corporate advertising of the companies who labour in those fields and market those brands, somehow different considerations apply. The advertisements look and sound like each other ... Companies find it difficult to arrive at a single-minded proposition ... so they select a clichéd approach. They appropriate a thought. Unfortunately, it's equally appropriate to competitors and to companies in unrelated areas. Here is a basic selection compiled by Graham Barnes [of typical corporate themes]:

(a) How our products make life richer, more agreeable for the masses.
(b) How we spend huge sums on, and are very successful in, technological development.
(c) Despite our colossal size, we're terribly human really.
(d) How concerned we are for the environment and other social/human relations problems.
(e) How we are helping the country by exporting, exploiting North Sea oil/gas, etc. (p. 192)

The corporation is big, human, innovative, conscious of its duty, a setter of standards and, above all,

a leader ... Should you ever be called upon to compose a baseline for a company — any company — you could do worse than use my colleague Rex Audley's patent baseline kit. It consists of four components:

TODAY
TOMORROW
NEEDS
SATISFYING

Rearrange and add your own seasoning of apostrophes, full stops, commas ... Here are a few combinations to start you off.

SATISFYING TOMORROW'S NEEDS TODAY.
TODAY, TOMORROW. SATISFYING NEEDS.
SATISFYING TODAY TOMORROW'S NEEDS.
SATISFYING NEEDS: TODAY, TOMORROW.
TOMORROW NEEDS SATISFYING TODAY.
(pp. 192–3)

Questions

1 (First extract) Why would advertisers wish to convince MPs that the 'self-regulatory' system of advertisement vetting should continue? What other reasons could there be for self-regulation, besides the conviction that it is 'in the public interest, and more efficient ... less bureaucratic – than a state system'?

2 (Second extract) Are messages always 'more important' when they are made public? Is it true that a

politician 'is more likely to act on behalf of the public if he [sic] has become involved as one of its members'?

3 (Third extract) Collect a series of corporate 'baselines' or slogans; can any of these be 'translated' into the 'basic selection' of corporate themes set out by Bernstein?

THE NUCLEAR INDUSTRY AND PUBLIC RELATIONS
Reading: Extracts from Donn J. Tilson's 'The shaping of "eco-nuclear" publicity'

Tilson, a lecturer in Miami University's School of Communication, carried out research into the way that the nuclear power industry 'has counted its losses, regrouped its forces and mounted a proactive campaign'

to advance the case of nuclear power. He uses the term 'advocational' to describe the blending of special pleading and education which characterises the public strategy of the nuclear companies. Read the extracts printed below and answer the questions which follow.

'In the wake of Three-Mile Island and Chernobyl, perhaps no other industry has had a more troubled history in recent years than the nuclear power industry. And yet, despite such disasters, not to mention scores of less dramatic, more localised incidents, the industry, particularly in the US and the UK, has ... mounted a proactive campaign to sell nuclear power to its key publics. The campaign, conceived, designed and directed by the industry's corporate public relations managers, is a classic exercise in issues management, albeit with two extraordinary twists. First, the approach, instead of being strictly one of hard-nosed advocacy, has incorporated elements of public education campaigns and, as such, can be considered uniquely 'advocational' in design. Second, and more important, the industry has increasingly wrapped itself in an 'eco-nuclear' mantle, distinctly promoting nuclear power as an 'environmentally friendly' energy source. The 'eco-nuclear' message represents a significant new interpretative package and, as such ... frames the nuclear power issue in terms of a societal commitment to environmental stewardship. (p. 419)

Pacific Gas and Electric Company (PG&E), a multibillion dollar utility in California and one of the largest power companies in the US, launched a major 'advocational' campaign in the late 1960s to persuade public opinion of the need to construct a nuclear power station at Diablo Canyon ... The centrepiece of the campaign was a visitors' information centre that served as an advocational magnet, drawing invited individuals and groups ... the centre ... included an 'overlook' area, where visitors could view the site and the adjacent offshore sea, and a picnic playground area. (p. 422)

The premier nuclear advocational campaign in Britain for many years has been that of British Nuclear Fuels Limited (BNFL), focused on its visitors' centre at Sellafield ... The company launched its advertising campaign in July 1986 – just six weeks after Chernobyl

– with a 50-second television commercial, broadcast throughout the UK, and a double-page spread advertisement with a stuck-on invitation in the colour supplements of a number of Sunday newspapers. The advocational campaign had a substantial effect on visitor traffic to Sellafield – increasing it from 30,000 visitors in 1985 to 104,000 in 1987 – so much so that BNFL built and opened a new, larger, £35-million centre in 1988.

In building its new visitors' centre, BNFL included a full array of working models, computer games and quizzes, multi-screen presentations, displays, interactive exhibits, a walk-through 'Fission Tunnel' simulating a chain reaction and a life-size walk-in model of a nuclear reactor core presenting 'an atmospheric voyage of discovery' that would be 'both exciting and educational' in a 'futuristic style' setting. (p. 423)

In an attempt to persuade political opponents, and achieve what SNL [Scottish Nuclear Limited] Public Relations Manager Dick Marshall characterises as 'political control', SNL has been making constant offers of visits and talks ... 'in relaxed, hospitable environments ... dinner etc.' to key Members of Parliament. (p. 427)

In November 1991, SNL launched the first of its 'progressive' programmes with the introduction of 'Talkabout', a public talks service. Interested groups are encouraged to invite an SNL speaker to address their next meeting by calling a special 'Talkabout' Freephone number. The service is offered without charge ... 'Talkabout' represents yet another communication forum in which SNL can present the case for nuclear power directly to key publics without mediation by the press or other external 'gatekeepers'. (p. 429)

Questions

1 (*First extract*) What are the advantages, to the nuclear industry, of using 'educational' programmes and portraying itself as 'eco-friendly'?

2 (*Second and third extracts*) Why do visitors' centres include games, working models, and other activities? Such 'gimmicks' seem to be used to reinforce a certain message – but what is the message?

3 (*Fourth and fifth extracts*) Bernstein's material included reference to advertisers 'targeting' Members of Parliament. SNL is engaged in the same practice, while the 'Talkabout' programme is also aimed at 'key publics'. Why do institutions make *direct* appeals to certain groups, instead of using press releases and other outlets provided by the media?

CONFORMITY AND NORMS

Revison: Read the edited material (below) from Chapter 4, then study the role-play exercises which follow.

Authority and subordination

Besides the relationships which are established with outside bodies, organisations contain a series of 'internal' relationships. The most significant are those which exist between **authority** and various groups of **subordinates**. In some organisations, the workforce will be concentrated in one physical location, whereas in others it may be more widely dispersed. In all cases, it will be subject to authority, whether that it is formal or informal, direct or indirect, despotic or enlightened. Authority is usually caught between what Therborn calls the requirements of *qualification* and the need for *subjection* (see Chapter 2).

Authority and control in the workplace

All **workplaces** function through some form of coercion, even where this is largely paternalistic or benevolent. The behaviour of those individuals who 'belong' to the organisation is regulated in a variety of ways. In the first place, the existence of established working practices will ensure a basic level of discipline; people will usually have to carry out a number of functions, in a certain sequence, within a specified period in the working day or week. There are also a number of other forms of control available to those in authority, but perhaps the most important is that type which depends upon the willingness of the employees to constrain or police their *own* behaviour. This form of control sometimes grows from *positive* self-identification.

A slap on the wrist

In order to obtain the obedience of staff, managers may reproduce forms of discipline *already familiar* to the employee from his or her early socialisation, particularly from schooldays. Glen (*The Social Psychology of Organisations*, p. 20), reminds us that:

'in the play situations of childhood and the controlled and contrived group situations of the classroom, we gain our first experiences of the results of success or failure in a social situation'.

These experiences come to form the basis for our public behaviours, though they are refined and even in some cases superseded. As we grow older, we may begin to select those situations in which we know that we are able to achieve some success, or else we may become more resilient to criticism.

Nevertheless, authority in organisations sometimes depends upon the simple mechanisms of 'adult' behaviour to get its own way. For instance, vocal opposition is often characterised as immature or petulant. Another familiar tactic is to call those who propose alternative systems 'unrealistic'; appeals to the 'way things really are' are widespread in institutional life. At times, individuals may be kept in line by patronising behaviour; women have, for example, often been the victims of condescension. The most clever form of authority uses the value systems of the employees themselves.

Work roles and the exercise of authority

The provision by organisations of **roles** and *identities* (what we have previously called 'subject positions') is a powerful form of influence over the employee. While it does not ensure complete subservience, the way that people *identify* with the roles they are given can provide a useful means of control.

It is often the case that individuals will take on the qualities that are part of their job description. The reason for this lies in the human tendency to define the self according to the social roles which are available. Supporting evidence is found in the considerable degree of psychological discomfort which may be experienced by someone who *does not* identify with the role he or she has been assigned. However, the individual *use* of institutional identity will differ, depending upon the people concerned and the situation in which they are placed. Promotion, for example, often entails a change of *attitude* in employees, since new responsibilities will usually entail some change in their relationship with other staff.

Group pressures

In *The Social Psychology of Organisations*, Frederick Glen notes that the **pressure** to accept social norms is part of daily existence (p. 20):

> 'The nature of society is such that external pressures upon the individual to conform – to fit in with the group – are central factors throughout the entire range of social experience.'

The essential point which should emerge from this observation is that people do not choose to 'fit in with society' as such. Instead, they choose to belong to groups which they regard as close to their own values. These groups *mediate* the wider values of the society.

Where people also belong to other groups by virtue of their membership of organisations, then they will be inclined to take note of their *colleagues'* opinions. The attitudes of colleagues, rather than those of managers, may ultimately prove effective in ensuring that outward behaviour, at least, conforms to the requirements of public scrutiny. On a practical level, the possibility that close acquaintances may suffer increased workloads if certain levels of efficiency are not reached may act as a major incentive to fulfil group norms. On the other hand, a strong group identity might provide its members with a base from which to defy the wishes of management.

Persistent critics

In some organisations there are individuals who are recognised as **persistent critics** of the established order. Such critics may hold office in a union branch, or may use a particular post or department as a base, or may simply act in a personal capacity. The critic may act as a conduit for the dissatisfaction of staff, who might allow an individual to fulfil this role because it means that they themselves do not have to make their opposition public. Critics often find that they are always expected to speak out and that, the more often they do so, the less likely it is that anyone else will feel inclined to make a similar contribution.

In the worst type of scenario, a persistent and *isolated* critic may be characterised as eccentric or abnormal. Glen (p. 20) makes the astute comment that:

> ' "normality" can be defined in terms of conformity with accepted modes of behaviour; failure to meet the criteria can earn for the individual at best a reputation for eccentricity, at worst a categorisation of his behaviour as deviant or plain mad'.

This is no exaggeration; the very fact that most employees are anxious to conform to behavioural norms points to the widespread fear of negative categorisation by work colleagues. To avoid isolation, it is better to operate from within a like-minded collective.

Analysis: Role-play exercises

In *The Dynamics of Human Communication*, Myers and Myers present a number of situations designed to encourage role-play. Many of these are based on the assumption of identities which allow the student a sense of responsibility, power or achievement. Here are some examples (pp. 377–8):

> 'The President of the United States greets the prime minister of a foreign nation in the Rose Garden of the White House (one person should be the President, and the visitor's role may be either imagined or played by another member of the class).

You have been elected Miss Universe, and you step forward to the microphones to deliver your acceptance speech.

You have been selected to meet the governor of your state at the airport and act as official escort to the annual Chamber of Commerce dinner.

You are the dean of students confronting a student leader in an attempt to get help in finding out who has been responsible for recent vandalism on the campus.'

These exercises might prove useful if the speeches/ interactions are recorded and then studied to see what types of discourse are used by the students playing each role. Notice, however, that the identities and situations set out seem to suggest fairly conformist responses, as well as appearing to construct specific gender roles. More significant still, is the fact that these roles (with the exception of the Miss Universe example) involve the possession of social power. The exercise is conducted, therefore, from the vantage point of authority.

In subsequent material, Myers and Myers concentrate on the idea of motivation, describing a workplace scenario in which the role assigned to the student is again based on the exercise of authority. The following is taken from pp. 379–80:

'Sally has been coming to work late mornings. Because other men and women in the office depend on her to assign their work, her lateness holds up the functioning of several people. You as her supervisor have found out that Sally received a good raise just six months ago in recognition of the fact that she had been a good worker for three years in the office. You want to have her become more punctual,

to arrive at least on time with the others in her section. What do you say to her?'

Perhaps it would be useful to ask what type of address Myers and Myers expect students to produce. It is quite likely, taking into account their general outlook, that they envisage a sensitive but firm approach to the problem. However, the viewpoint offered in Chapter 4 of this book is somewhat different; it starts from a critical perspective on authority, in which workplace relationships are seen in terms of the unequal distribution of power. Myers and Myers are clearly interested in workplace scenarios because they provide the opportunity to test the communicative sensitivity of students. However, this goal means that students are always provided with roles which conform to models of *liberal management*; the next extract supports this point (p. 380):

'Harry is clerking in the sports department of the store where you are a personnel counselor. You have received a complaint from the billing office that Harry's charge slips have been made out incorrectly, causing losses of money and time for the store. Harry was also accused by a customer of "not paying attention" when asked questions about exercise bicycles ... you are talking to Harry about his performance and hope to retain him, since he's been a very productive employee for six years.'

Role-play exercises

The following exercises are designed to allow questions of power and argument to emerge during role-play. When a group has become familiar with the principles involved, individual exercises may be recorded on audio tape or, in special circumstances, on video tape.

Questions

1 One student is asked to take the part of a manager who has helped to formulate a programme of savings, including compulsory redundancies, and is now faced by a strike. Another student is assigned the role of a union representative who works in the same institution and who has been instrumental in preparing for the strike. A third is given the role of a local union

official who wants to use the threat of a strike to reduce the number of compulsory redundancies. The three are each given half an hour to prepare for a confrontation to be witnessed by the rest of the group, which has decided in advance the context of the debate, including the type of industry represented, the history of its industrial relations, and the mood of workers and management.

2 One person assumes the role of a candidate in a local election, another the position of a reporter on the local newspaper, who is sent to interview the candidate about the following issues; employment, the environment, and central government cuts in the funding of education. The rest of the group will produce a 'profile' for the town in which the election is to be held, including its location, economy, patterns of employment, and current political allegiance. The two students 'playing' the parts are each given half an hour to prepare their contributions to an interview lasting fifteen minutes.

ROLES AND PORTRAITURE
Study: photographs

Certain types of portraiture are known as 'environmental', showing an individual in his or her workplace or home environment; others depend for their effect upon the use of 'references' to the occupation or social role of the sitter. Study the portraits in Figures 4.11 and 4.12. Notice that some aspect of the individual's role is revealed in each photograph through, respectively, the inclusion of the bill-hook and the child.

Figure 4.12   Traveller with child: photo by Mick Garland

Figure 4.11   Somerset basket-maker with bill-hook: photo by Mick Garland

Production: the portrait

Use a 35mm camera loaded with monochrome film to produce a set of portraits of one individual. The photographs should include:

1 a picture where the subject is allowed to control every aspect of his or her appearance, dress, and expression, together with the lighting conditions, angle, distance and pose taken within the frame;

2 a shot of the subject, in which the photographer controls every aspect of the portrait including the pose taken;

3 an 'environmental' photograph, showing the subject in either a domestic or occupational context;

4 a picture which includes the 'tools' of the subject's trade or some other objects closely associated with the sitter.

THE EARLY HISTORY OF COMMUNICATION
Revision: The development of communication

Read the following edited extracts from Chapter 4.

Communication is often described as the transmission of information, and should include the concept of an established *route* or connection between places separated by physical distance. Roads, for example, form routes of communication between human settlements.

The 'spatial' aspect of the subject is often neglected. We often assume, when we examine media techniques and systems, that distance is indeed no object. However, it is inevitable that the notion of geography will come to the fore when we consider communication in pre-industrial Europe. In that period, communication depended upon the movement of people, animals and goods along roads and sea-routes which, however well established, were subject to the moods of climate and the predatory attentions of outlaws.

Communication in feudal society

In the first **feudal age**, which began in the ninth century AD, public routes in Europe were in a state of decline. Marc Bloch (an historian and member of the French Resistance who was killed in 1944) notes that the collapse of the Carolingian empire meant that no central power existed to institute public works (see his *Feudal Society*). The Roman roads which spread across Europe were still usable, but were not being maintained, and bridges were no longer kept in good repair.

Awareness of the forces which *motivate* communication is essential; commerce and trade have always been at the centre of the process. Despite the obstacles which people faced, some remarkable feats of communication could be performed during the medieval era. Bloch (p. 62) gives the example of a letter written by Pope Gregory VII at Rome in December 1075, which arrived 'at Goslar, at the foot of the Harz, on the 1st January following'. This meant that its bearer had covered approximately 29 miles a day, or over 690 miles in some 24 days, across uneven terrain.

Types of communication in pre-industrial society

Bloch's study of feudalism argues that 'no institution or method could take the place of personal contact between human beings'. In other words, inter-personal communication, conducted face to face, was the only system which guaranteed a reliable exchange of meaning. Kingdoms could only be governed by the *personal* authority of kings.

Communication was always spurred by some pressing need. Many travellers made religious pilgrimages, some wished to supervise far-flung estates, while others searched for an environment free from the scourge of war.

In such a society, the main instruments of communication were:

- word of mouth;
- proclamations;
- sermons;
- letters;
- handwritten boks;
- narrative and verse forms;
- religious and secular iconography.

The birth of mass communication

The majority of theorists date the beginning of mass communication from the invention of movable type in the middle of the fifteenth century. However, Church services represent a form of communication notable for their 'mass' reproduction of a specific ideology.

Print was the leading force in the expansion of knowledge, but it depended upon the existence of what Crowley and Hayer (*Communication in History*, p. 91) call 'receptive conditions'. The growth of a 'vernacular literacy' (the ability to read and write in one's own language, as opposed to knowledge of Latin), together with improvements in technology, helped prepare the ground for the expansion of written forms of communication.

An example of 'receptive conditions' is the use of paper as a replacement for parchment, and the consequent rise in the production of handwritten manuscripts, from the thirteenth century onwards. The manufacture of paper originated in China, developing between the second and third century BC. By 1500, every major European city had a paper mill and, as Elizabeth Eisenstein writes (Crowley and Heyer, *Communication in History*, p. 105), 'the reproduction of written materials began to move from the copyist's desk to the printer's workshop'. Ecclesiastical control of the dissemination of ideas ceased to be a foregone conclusion.

A secular interpretation of the world grew to challenge the hegemony of the Church; in other words, human beings were seen increasingly as responsible agents, actors in a lay community whose values were no longer dictated by a priesthood possessed of a monopoly on education.

NEWS: DISCOURSE AND DEBATE
Revision: Selection and creation of news

Roger Fowler, in *Language in the News* (p. 110), examines the question of **news values** and declares 'the world of the Press is not the real world, but a world skewed and judged'. In this case, reference to the real world is intended to show that the press is **selective** and that 'the vast majority of events are not mentioned'. Since most events are never reported, 'selection . . . gives us a partial view of the world'.

However, it is a physical impossibility to report every event that occurs. All human understanding and judgement is based upon selection. The point Fowler is trying to make is that there are social and institutional *principles* at work in those selections which are made by the press. Readers of newspapers are then dependent on a narrow field of information from which to make, in turn, their own selections.

Not found but created

Greg Philo (Fowler, p. 13) argues that the usual picture of journalistic activity is mistaken: 'news is not "found" or even "gathered" so much as made. It is a *creation* of a journalistic process, an artifact, a commodity even.' This is not to argue that events are 'fictions' with no relationship to the truth. Real events occur and the results have material consequences. The purpose of analysis is to discover the ways in which such events are presented. This moves beyond selection to the **creation** of news and meaning.

Analysis: A front-page story

Study the reproduction in Figure 4.13 of the *Daily Express* front page of 29 November 1993, 'Why we had to talk to the IRA'. Then answer the questions which follow.

Note: The political context of the headline and article was the argument over long-standing government contacts with the Irish Republican Army. Most of the Conservative tabloids condemned the secret links, while the *Express* tried to represent the secret talks as necessary.

Major and Mayhew on the spot over contact with terrorists

WHY WE HAD TO TALK TO THE IRA

By JON CRAIG Political Editor

NEW BOYS ARE HEROES OF ENGLAND VICTORY

A FULL account of secret British contacts with the IRA will be unveiled by the Government today after it was dramatically revealed that links had been forged over a number of years.

Ulster Secretary Sir Patrick Mayhew will put his credibility — and that of the Prime Minister — on the line when he publishes the documents and makes a statement in the Commons in face of angry demands for their resignation by some Unionists.

Sir Patrick will explain the high-risk strategy as he faces claims from MPs that he misled them by denying that talks were going on.

MPs will also tackle John Major over his claim that face-to-face talks with Sinn Fein President Gerry Adams "would turn my stomach".

The decision to tell all follows the disclosure of a secret communication chain between

> **Double agents silenced: Page 4**
> **Opinion: Page 8**

the Government and the IRA. It followed a message from the Provisional IRA that the "conflict is now over" and the Provos were seeking ways of extricating themselves from their campaign of violence.

Sir Patrick and Mr Major will say nothing happened that could be described as negotiations. They will argue that no government could ignore a chance for peace — with public revelation certain to wreck any hopes of ending the killing.

But hardline Northern Ireland Unionists, led by Ian Paisley, immediately demanded the resignation of both men.

William McCrea, an MP from Paisley's Democratic Unionist Party, admitted he had leaked the links between the Government and

Page 2 Column 1

TASTE OF GLORY: Jon and wife Gail, left, relaxing with Kyran and his girlfriend Victoria yesterday   Picture: JACK KAY

IT WAS their finest hour — and England glory boys Jon Callard and Kyran Bracken were making the most of it yesterday as they relaxed happily after their team's triumph over the mighty All Blacks.

For both it was a debut match at international level — and both were greeted as heroes of the 15-9 victory at Twickenham on Saturday.

Bath full-back Callard was joined by his wife Gail as the couple celebrated with Bristol scrum-half Bracken and his girlfriend Victoria Fay.

The two, praised by captain Will Carling

for their performances, helped the England side to their first win over the All Blacks since 1983 — and only their fourth ever.

Penalty kicker Callard proved the match winner, scoring 12 of England's points.

Twickenham Special:
Pages 46, 47, 48, 49 and 52

INSIDE: Weather 2, Opinion 8, Foreign News 10, Ross Benson 25, TV 29 - 31, Letters & Stars 32, Radio, Crosswords & Target 34, Business 35, Sport 41 - 52

Figure 4.13   From The Daily Express, 29 November 1993

2 DAILY EXPRESS Monday November 29 1993

NEWS

Why we had to talk to the IRA

From Page One

the IRA. He claimed he had confronted Mr Major at a meeting at 10 Downing Street last week.

"The Prime Minister, across the table, and very genuinely as you would have thought at that moment, looked into our eyes and said that he and his ministers were not in contact with Sinn Fein and the IRA," he said.

"At that moment he was telling a downright lie. The big question in this whole thing is — when can you believe them again?"

Tory MPs solidly backed the Government's peace effort. But some admitted that the handling of first the denials and then the disclosures was clumsy.

Sir Patrick confirmed there had been contact with Sinn Fein's Martin McGuinness at the request of the IRA.

He said there was "a chain of communication" going back years, not just months.

The first communication from the IRA this year had been received in late February. Then British officials met Sinn Fein representatives two days after the March 20 Warrington bomb blast that killed two children.

"It said the conflict was over," said Sir Patrick. "It said they needed advice, that is to say British advice, as to how it could be brought to a close."

Gerry Adams disputed that. "This particular phase of the contact was initiated by the British Government," he said. "Mayhew is telling lies from beginning to end."

Sir Patrick said latest communication had come from the IRA as recently as November 2. A reply was sent on November 5.

He said that in every reply the IRA

WHEN MAYHEW DENIED IT ALL

SIR PATRICK: No violence

ULSTER Secretary Sir Patrick Mayhew had repeatedly denied suggestions the Government has been in contact with Sinn Fein or the IRA.

"We have always made it perfectly clear that there is going to be no negotiating with anybody who perpetrates or justifies the use of violence," he told BBC's Breakfast Time this month. "That's been our public policy and we have stuck to it."

Sir Patrick repeated on BBC's Today programme this month: "Nobody has been authorised to talk or negotiate on behalf of the British Government with Sinn Fein.

"We have always made it clear that there will be no talking or negotiating with Sinn Fein or any other organisation that justifies violence."

was told there could be no dialogue until they ceased violence and were seen to have ceased. "The Government's position has long been made perfectly clear by the Prime Minister and myself," said the Ulster Secretary.

"Nobody has been authorised to undertake talks or negotiations on behalf of the Government with the IRA, with Sinn Fein, with any organisation that undertakes violence for political purposes. That has remained the case and it is the case today.

"I have certain responsibilities as a Government Minister. First and foremost among those is the responsibility for every single life in Northern Ireland.

"I do not believe — had I made no response, had the Government made no

response — that if subsequent bombs were exploded and life taken and people injured, as indeed was the case, I would have been readily forgiven by the people of Northern Ireland."

Sir Patrick said the advice given to the IRA in private was the same as the Government had been saying in public — that there could be no dialogue until they had given up violence for good and been shown to do so.

He insisted there could be no bargaining with terrorists. "Nothing of that kind has taken place at all."

Martin McGuinness claimed that contacts were continuing "even now" at a high level, weekly or even daily, with the full knowledge of Mr Major. Interviewed on BBC TV's On the Record, he

said the first contact with a Government official happened in October 1990.

"The meeting which took place three years ago, in October 1990, was a meeting between a representative of the Foreign Office and myself.

"It was just a discussion. It was a meeting at their request which I agreed to after consultation with my colleagues."

Sir Patrick and Mr Major came under fire from senior Opposition MPs and from the DUP.

Dr Paisley said: "There has been deliberate bare-faced lying from the Secretary of State and Downing Street.

"Both the Prime Minister and the Secretary of State are involved in this and both of them should get out."

His deputy, Peter Robinson, added: "Sir Patrick has been found out to have been lying publicly and openly to the people of Northern Ireland.

"While he was saying this, he had given approval for contacts with that very organisation."

Liberal Democrat leader Paddy Ashdown accused the Government of "at best stupidity and at worst duplicity".

Shadow Northern Ireland Secretary Kevin McNamara said: "What is at stake is the question of the integrity and honour of the British Government.

"The main issue is not that there has been contact between the Government and Sinn Fein but that it has been denied."

The father of Warrington bomb victim Tim Parry said talks must go ahead with the IRA.

Colin Parry, 47, said he felt no bitterness that British officials met Sinn Fein leaders two days after the atrocity which killed his son.

AGENTS SILENCED: Page 4 ● OPINION: Page 8

Figure 4.13 (Continued)

Questions

1 Who is the 'we' referred to in the headline?

2 (*Front page, paragraphs 1 and 2*) Comment on the use of phrases like 'dramatically revealed' and 'angry demands'. What effect are they meant to create?

3 (*Front page, paragraph 6*) 'Sir Patrick and Mr Major will say nothing happened that could be described as negotiations.' In what sense is 'talk' different from 'negotiation'? Does negotiation inevitably occur between two sides, when talk begins?

4 (*Page 2, paragraph 1*) Why does the phrase 'looked into our eyes' so often appear when someone is reported to have told a lie?

5 (*Page 2, paragraph 3*) Why do some Tories admit that the 'handling of first the denials and then the disclosures' was 'clumsy', rather than accept the idea that Major was lying?

6 (*Page 2, paragraph 8*) Gerry Adams also accuses the British government of lying – over what?

7 (*Page 2, paragraph 11*) When Mayhew says that 'nobody has been authorised to undertake talks or negotiations with the IRA', is there any aspect of this statement which could be read in an ambiguous way?

Note: There are no quotation marks around the main part of the large headline. It is therefore not a direct quotation from a recognised source. The use of an apparently inclusive 'we' to make an address is one of the tools used in rhetorical speech. However, it is unclear to whom the 'we' refers. Is this a statement made on behalf of the government or of the country? Perhaps it is meant to refer to the position of the two named individuals who appear above the headline, 'Major and Mayhew', who are 'on the spot' over 'contact with terrorists'. In contrast to the highly critical coverage the talks had received in most of the tabloid press, the *Express* offers a headline which is based more on explanation than on condemnation.

NEWS: BIASED PRESENTATION?
Research: An extract from GMTV news

Television, while it may not have proven effects, is certainly involved in the presentation of ideas, incidents and discourses. The familiar idea of 'agenda-setting' may be explored in any number of news reports. The entry for *agenda-setting* given in *Key Concepts in Communication* (O'Sullivan *et al.*, p. 6) reads 'a term used to describe the ways in which the media wittingly or unwittingly structure public debate and awareness'. The definition goes further, explaining that:

> 'In the first instance agenda setting refers to the question of what topics the media present to the audience, and secondly how information on these topics is presented.'

The example given here is taken from GMTV coverage of Gerry Adams's visit to America in 1994, broadcast at 7.00 a.m. on Thursday 3 February 1994. GMTV introduced the report with a 'phone-in poll, asking for viewers' opinions on Adams's "propaganda visit to America"'. The result was some 60 per cent against John Major talking to Adams, and 30 per cent in favour. This is hardly surprising, considering that the context of the exercise clearly indicated the programme's opposition to Sinn Fein. The report itself began as follows:

'The government's set to press ahead with new plans for a political settlement in Northern Ireland in the next two weeks. The proposals, including a new assembly, are an attempt to win back the initiative from Sinn Fein. Their President Gerry Adams has just arrived back in Ireland and is expected to make an announcement on the peace process. We have two reports, the first from Maxine Malwinny in New York.

Kisses and hugs of farewell for Gerry Adams as he left New York, but not before squeezing in yet another television appearance. Now we hear from Gerry Adams, the President of Sinn Fein. Analysts say that the visit was not only a propaganda victory for Sinn Fein, but a victory for IRA fundraisers in America, who have been given a veneer of respectability and are now waiting for donations to flood in.

Question

Describe the function and possible effect of the following comments made by the GMTV reporter: 'yet another television appearance'; 'analysts say that the visit was not only a propaganda victory'; 'IRA fundraisers in America, who have been given a veneer of respectability'.

Assignment

Record a number of early morning news bulletins and make transcripts of major news stories. Describe the form in which these stories are presented, including choice of words, intonation, and visual elements. Compare them with transcripts of Ceefax and other news services. How are events represented by television news?

TRUTH AND FALSEHOOD
Reading: Lies and communication

In his Introduction to *The Penguin Book of Lies* (p. 3), Philip Kerr refers to Chomsky's 'belief that we are genetically pre-programmed to master the use of language'. The capacity to lie, according to Kerr, must be inherent in the growth of the language function. Kerr believes that human beings learned to lie at the same time as they learned to speak; 'thus the capacity for lying is essential to the speech function'. He maintains, however, that truth is a moral concept that has to be taught, since children in his opinion have only 'the vaguest dividing line between true and false reporting'. (Perhaps they understand precisely the difference between truth and falsehood, but their sense of the real allows for more ambiguous and fanciful utterances.)

Lies can be *active*, taking the form of deliberately crafted falsehoods, or *passive*, involving the practice of omission. Deliberate lies, rather than mistakes or misunderstandings, are believed to be harmful in a variety of situations. In contrast, nearly all communicative exchanges involve the omission of some information; the point is that it should still be possible to reproduce accurately the essential truth of an event.

Ng and Bradac's theory of Propositional Communication

In *Power in Language* (1993), Ng and Bradac examine the internal elements of a statement intended to reproduce either a *truthful* or a *false* description of an event or state of mind. They use truth-telling as their 'baseline' for this study, describing it as combining a series of *positive* elements. According to these authors, a true statement would require the following series of elements (the plus sign here indicates a positive act):

+ accuracy + relevance + utterance + accountability

Bradac's (1986) theory deals with *intended* messages, rather than messages which are actually produced by speakers. Actual messages would be difficult to interpret without some knowledge of context; deception, for example, cannot be identified simply from studying a statement. In addition, I would argue that if we accept an *unambiguous* intention on the part of a speaker, then we will avoid (for the moment) the complication of having to investigate ideology and the unconscious influence on individuals of 'available discourses'.

Each of the categories described above must be explained in turn. **Accuracy** is first on the list because a speaker telling or intending to tell the truth (p. 125):

'intends to produce in hearers an accurate belief regarding the speaker's belief X, when X is the topic at issue'.

Notice that the speaker is concerned to express a statement which he or she *believes* to be reliable. Any truthful expression must also be **relevant** to the topic X, otherwise the recipient of the message will not understand why the information is being offered. **Utterance**, which seems obvious at first sight, is included because truth-telling involves *expression*, and is clearly not a form of silence, omission or disguise. **Accountability** means the speaker believes that the statement he or she offers will be one for which he or she will be held accountable. Ng and Bradac note that, if the positive value of an *utterance* changes to a negative (in other words, if a truthful statement is not expressed), then a *secret* ensues. A secret is the intention to withhold an utterance that would be accurate, relevant and understandable in a clearly defined way. This does not constitute a lie, but a suppression of the truth. Consider this statement as an expression of events which are thought by a speaker to be true:

'The Prime Minister is unable to attend tonight's screening because his laundry requires urgent attention.'

It is possible to use Ng and Bradac's criteria in the following analysis. Once expressed for an audience, the statement above may be accepted as an *utterance*. The speaker concerned has made a positively *accurate* statement (+ Accuracy) if he or she truly believes that the Prime Minister is indeed unable to attend the event and is indisposed because he needs to wash or otherwise process his laundry. It is a *relevant* statement (+ Relevance) because it explains to an expectant crowd why they will be severely disappointed in their expectation of seeing the Prime Minister. *Accountability* is the expectation by the speaker that he or she will be associated with the statement and may in future be judged on the basis of its accuracy.

These authors go on to show that, by altering the condition of either accuracy or relevance (that is, by changing the 'positive charge' to a negative one), and allowing utterance and accountability to remain the same, the status of the entire statement will be changed to that of a **falsehood**.

Falsehood

According to Ng and Bradac, falsehood is the intention to produce an utterance that is inaccurate, relevant, and unambiguously interpretable (− Accuracy + Relevance + Utterance + Accountability). Consider this statement.

'Britain is on the mend; green shoots of recovery may now be seen everywhere.'

This utterance will be used to illustrate a falsehood, though in the right circumstances it may be used to demonstrate a truth. The statement may be regarded as *inaccurate* but *relevant*, if it can be taken to refer to a state of affairs of which an audience already has knowledge, or uttered in a context which refers to politics.

The system begins to look like a series of random messages in an obscure code, as different combinations of falsehood are presented. If the speaker intends to avoid the consequences of presenting a falsehood (the value of accountability changing to −), this may be described as a *devious falsehood* (−++−). If the value of the utterance changes to −, the statement becomes one of *falsehood avoidance* (−+−+) which is the withholding of a relevant utterance that would produce a false belief about a speaker belief. A fourth and rare member of what these authors call the 'falsehood family' is *devious falsehood avoidance* (−+− −).

The Homeric hymns

The Homeric hymns (by an unknown author and not the great pre-classical poet Homer) contain a passage in which Hermes, still an infant, is accused of stealing the god Apollo's cattle. Apollo threatens to cast Hermes into Hades, where, because he is so young, he will have to be content with being the leader of mere babies. Hermes' reply is an interesting example of deceptive speech:

> 'I have not seen the cattle: I have not heard of them: no one has told me of them ... Am I like a cattle-lifter, a stalwart person? This is no task for me ... I care for sleep, and milk of my mother's breast, and wrappings round my shoulders, and warm baths ... I was born yesterday, and my feet are soft and the ground beneath is rough ... I will swear a great oath by my father's head and vow that neither am I guilty myself, neither have I seen any other who has stolen your cows − whatever cows may be; for I know them only by hearsay.'

This is accompanied by other contextual elements which indicate that Hermes may be lying:

> 'So then said Hermes, shooting quick glances from his eyes: and he kept raising his brows and looking this way and that, whistling long and listening to Apollo's story as to an idle tale.'

Apollo picks up the little thief, who immediately breaks wind and sneezes.

MASS COMMUNICATION AND ADVERTISING
Revision: Mass communication − questions of address

The concept of **address** is central to the study of communication. To make an 'address', as we saw

with reference to advertising, means to direct a form of speech or writing or other type of message to an individual or audience. The term implies that a concentration of attention and effort has been made by the communicator. The linguistic and other powers and techniques at his or her disposal, are focused on the act of communication. An alternative definition of 'address' reflects this concentration of powers: the *Oxford English Dictionary* refers to 'readiness, skill and dexterity'.

Audience: anybody there?

The intention behind address in general is to deliver a message which will make an impact on a particular **audience**. An address must consider both form and content. If the address which is delivered does not have meaning or relevance for the intended audience, then it is bound to fail.

The common assumption that an audience must be known to the person, group or institution responsible for initiating the act of communication is not strictly true. A good number of those messages which make a significant impact are created without any *personal* knowledge of the 'target' audience. In fact, language is always addressed to some 'other', even where that other is only imagined.

The communicator who wishes to create some material change must, however, have access to certain types of information. In the first place, something must be known about the general range of values held in a society; this is not too difficult, since everyone involved in the process of communication both inhabits and contributes to the social. Secondly, the communicator or 'addressor' must know something about the *particular* values he or she wishes to mobilise. Finally, an idea of the general subject position held by the target audience is often supposed to be useful, especially where the address has a commercial intention behind it (though a unified 'mass' of people sharing the same subjectivity is unlikely to exist). The conception of audience and the intention of the communicator together influence the particular *form* of the message.

A dog's not just for Christmas.
(It comes free with a pair of shoes.)

FORM AND CONTENT IN ADVERTISEMENTS
Form and content: 'A dog's not just for Christmas'

Study the advertisement reproduced in Figure 4.14. Answer the question and complete the assignment below.

Figure 4.14   Hush Puppy. 'A Dog's Not Just for Christmas.'

Question

What references does this advertisement use in order to influence a potential audience? Is the joke in bad taste?

Assignment: advertisement design

1   Select three advertisements and describe in each case the:

- type of content;
- form;
- target audience or market.

2   Design an advertisement for inclusion in a particular type of magazine (lifestyle, music, 'domestic', political, etc.) Consider *content* – what elements the advertisement contains; the *form* – or the arrangement of content; the *audience* – the group to whom the address is made; the *address* – or the way that an audience is 'spoken to'; the *register* – this means the 'level' at which an address is pitched.

ESSAY TITLES

1 Etzioni (1964) provides a classification of authority or power, which he divides into three separate types: the *coercive* form, based upon the use of compulsion; the *utilitarian*, which is exercised through a form of legalistic and rationalist authority; and the *normative*, where relationships are based on the intrinsic value of the activities performed, or of membership itself.

Using at least *two* examples of familiar institutions (college, family, company, etc.), describe the ways in which they maintain control over their members. Which of Etzioni's forms of power do they appear to favour? Mention any other theories of authority and control which might be useful (Likert's 'four systems of management', Therborn's theory of subjection/ qualification, feminist critiques of authority, and so on).

2 'Mass communication imitates the modes of address used in interpersonal exchange; therefore it is merely extends the reach of human communication.'
Discuss, using examples to support your argument.

3 What models of behaviour do the mass media offer their audiences? You may wish to refer to representations taken from any two of these areas: television, film, display advertising, and the press.

4 Is the overall quality of television declining because of the influences of 'trash TV', deregulation, and 'new' technologies such as cable and satellite?

In your answer, give a definition of quality and refer to a variety of texts in support of your argument.

5 'The shortage of schools, teachers, equipment and buildings is chronic in most Third World countries. Satellites have the capacity to multiply these meagre resources at a fraction of their terrestrial costs.' (Neville D. Jayaweera, in Finnegan *et al.*, *Information Technology: Social Issues*).

What other problems, besides finance, may prevent the world's poor from using satellite as an educational tool?

6 Some authors fear: 'the creation of a new kind of information, *transactional information*, generated every time we use electronic terminals, not just in the home, but also on the phone, in banks, shops and restaurants ... it becomes possible to pinpoint the location of an individual at a particular moment, indicate his daily patterns of work and sleep, and even suggest his state of mind'. (Robins and Webster, 'Dangers of information technology', in Finnegan *et al. Information Technology: Social Issues*)

How real are such fears in the 'electronic age'?

CHAPTER 5

Critical theory and the study of communication

This chapter begins by re-examining the definition of communication given in Chapter 1 and asks, on the basis of that definition, what kinds of event *qualify* as communication. It also returns to the concepts of address and identity, before moving on to study written communication and literature, the discourses of art, and the portrayal of human interaction in film. It ends by considering communication in the context of a number of influential social and critical theories, including modernism, postmodernism, structuralism and post-structuralism.

Communication: problems of definition

Chapter 1 offered a definition of communication, describing it as **an activity in which symbolic content is not merely transmitted but exchanged between human agents, who interact within a shared situational and/or discursive context**. However, all descriptions or models suffer from a tendency to abstraction. In other words, while they might be useful for summing up the process of interaction, they often seem removed from our everyday experience of communication. It is also the case that, as society undergoes change, the meaning of various terms alters.

At the very least, a good definition of communication should help to explain events as they are encountered. Where events do not 'fit' the general description offered, falling outside its range, it is worth asking whether there is a shortcoming in the definition itself.

What events qualify as communication?

If we accept that communication is an activity in which symbolic content is not merely transmitted but exchanged between human agents, who interact within a shared situational and/or discursive context, then this description will cover the following events: a telephone conversation, a group discussion, an argument between two people, an exchange of messages on the Internet, an exchange of letters in the post, a public lecture in which questions are answered, and a 'video conference' made through a satellite link. In some cases, there may be a delay between address and reception, or address and response, but an act of communication will nevertheless have taken place.

The problem is, however, that our definition excludes a large number of other events which are normally studied under the heading of communication. For example, a sermon, an announcement, a radio talk, a television advertisement, an exhibition of sculpture, public graffiti, or the reading of a book would all fail to qualify.

According to the terms of our definition, the reason why the first set of events would be accepted as examples of communication, and the second would be rejected, is found not in the *distance* or difference between participants, but in the fact that an *exchange of meaning* occurs in the first group and not in the second. Therefore, a telephone conversation would qualify as an interaction, while a television advertisement would fall outside this category.

So, what is the solution? Is it to exclude some events from study altogether? Before we separate 'real' communication from other public events, we should remember that any one of the second set has the *potential* to qualify as a collection of 'real' communication events, if and when a response is made (within a shared context) to the initial address. For example, the screening of a controversial film may lead eventually to a 'reply' by an audience (taking, perhaps, the form of a public protest), a response which may in time make an impact on the film maker responsible for the original message. Here, the context of the event is *discursive* and not situational. This means that the controversy is discussed and circulated in the public sphere and is not confined to an immediate exchange between two parties.

Alternatively, a piece of graffiti would only count as communication if two or more social actors (not necessarily including the author of the original statement) were engaged in and aware of an *exchange of meaning*. In this case, situational as well as discursive context is important; the exchange cannot be conducted at any great distance. A good stretch of accessible wall is required.

In essence, while the examples in the second group do not amount to interaction between 'sender' and 'receiver', they may lead to more generalised exchanges of meaning within 'social spaces'. In other words, they are part of the social process from which communication is drawn, and as such will probably encourage exchanges within and between social groups.

Mass communication: secondary exchange

Some of the problems surrounding the idea of **mass communication** were raised in Chapter 4. The idea that the 'audience' makes up a uniform mass, either in terms of the subject positions of the people who compose it, or with regard to the attitudes and values held by individuals and groups, was found to be unconvincing. The alternative view is that audience is not a single, 'mass' collective, but is instead composed of a multiplicity of groups.

This question apart, it is important to appreciate that most media events, and indeed many other examples of communication, do not involve what I would call a direct or *primary* exchange between the producer and receiver of a message, but usually only an indirect or **secondary exchange** between audiences and other social agencies, creating in some cases a general *cultural impact*. This idea was outlined above.

Media events are probably the most obvious examples of phenomena which are not, strictly speaking, 'interactive'. Despite the lack of real interaction between institution and audience, it is undoubtedly the *impact* the media have on our culture, rather than the mistaken notion that they facilitate direct communication between media producers and consumers, which must account for their place within Communication Studies. (It is worth noting, however, that the media do use real groups of people as stand-ins or *symbolic represen-tatives* for the wider audience they intend to address. The physical presence of 'audience as witness' is essential to programmes like *The Oprah Winfrey Show*.)

The concept of address

The concept of **address**, mentioned in Chapters 1 and 4, may be explained as the *delivery* of a communication (statement, request, admonition and so on) to a specific person or group of people, taking into account the suitability or *register* of the symbolic form used.

As we saw in Chapter 1, most forms of expression, even those usually regarded as private, are produced with a sense of audience in mind. This results in a certain degree of 'dramatisation' of the communicative act. It is worth repeating the idea that the natural instinct of all individuals and groups is to frame a message in a way which will have an impact on those they intend to address. The cartoon in Figure 5.1 provides an excellent illustration of this point.

Dennis's first address, 'You look like my pet pig, missus', produces a decidedly negative response, shown in the Duchess's body language (crossed arms, the sideways presentation of the body) and her angry facial expression. The second approach, 'You look like my pet pig, your graciousnesship', receives a positive reaction, demonstrated by the open stance and smiling face. Of course, the joke lies in the fact that the insult remains identical in both cases.

This cartoon presents the idea that it is *form* rather than *content* which is the major factor in securing the acceptance of a message. The use of the 'correct'

Figure 5.1   *'Dennis the Menace': how to address a duchess*

title makes the message palatable, though 'graciousnessship' is over-blown, a reference which draws attention to the ludicrous conventions of speech applied to the aristocracy.

While it is unlikely in reality that an individual would be quite so ready to accept this kind of affront, however it is dressed up, this extract from *The Beano* provides a very useful insight into the importance of an initial opening which recognises the *identity* of the addressee (the recipient of the 'message'). In most examples of mass media address, it seems that a common aim is to treat audience members as though they have *individuality*. It is notable that, in a mass society, the appeal to individuality is used exhaustively in advertising and other forms of public address. Even where people are addressed as members of a group, the group is often presented as having some special qualities.

Modes of address and reception: media and audience

Chapter 1 argued that the public and private bodies involved in 'mass' communication often imitate *personal* modes of address. This is not meant to suggest that the media threaten to replace interpersonal communication, a popular supposition found in remarks such as 'television has killed the art of conversation'. My argument is rather that the media regularly, though not exclusively, 'speak to' their audiences in ways which resemble the opening gambits of public speech. Such types of address are thought to be effective and constitute an *established practice*; ultimately, however, they are simply a natural way of making an impact on an audience.

In one of a collection of essays on the subject of the relationship between human and mass communication (see Gumpert and Cathcart, *Inter/Media*, p. 185), Donald Horton and Richard Wohl (1956) describe 'the illusion of face-to-face relationship with the [mass media] performer', in which the appearance (p. 186) of 'conversational give and take may be called *para-social interaction*'. Here, for example, the experience of watching television is thought to mimic real exchanges. These authors see the creation of a kind of 'intimacy' between performer (chat-show host, newscaster, etc.) and audience member, based upon (p. 187):

'direct observation and interpretation of his appearance, his gestures and voice, his conversation and conduct in a variety of situations'.

Leaving aside the limits of such 'intimacy', it is clear that all forms of media imitate 'direct' address, but that much of the repertoire available to a speaker is lost when the message appears in print. The need to attract and retain attention, especially in two-dimensional advertising, forces the use of modes of address which are more directly **interpellative** (where an attempt is made to create a power relation between 'speaker' and audience member) than **interactive** (where a message is constructed so that it resembles the initial part of a conversational exchange). The two types may in fact be combined in one message.

Examples of second-person address

It is relatively easy to discover examples of address which use the second-person singular; in one edition of *The Times*, for example (7 June 1995), most advertisements contained a direct address to the newspaper's readership. The following are taken from that day's advertising copy; each extract comes from a different advertisement:

'No private medical insurance? If your family falls ill it's you who'll feel sick.'

'We plan to send you all the reports listed opposite if you reply within 7 days.'

'So put your feet up, phone your credit card details and look forward to receiving your phone in five working days.'

'The key to your advertising will be found in the 21st Century.'

'Are you causing your workers unnecessary suffering?'

'Stretch out your legs in a seat that has 44% more legroom.'

A 'profile' of the typical *Times* reader may begin to emerge from these examples. The advertising seems to suggest an individual who is the head of a household, who must consider the welfare of employees, whose firm probably requires a strategy for advertising its products or services, and whose other needs include information, tools of communication, and 44 per cent more 'legroom' on aeroplane flights. Of course, each address will not necessarily reach or represent every reader.

It is also worth noting that, in each case, the advertisers concerned are engaged in the *mediation* of a general message about the desirability of certain goods and services; behind the advertiser stands the client, which makes the 'we' used in many advertisements less than straightforward.

At this point, it has probably become clear that address depends greatly upon a sense of the 'receiver's' identity. A return to the concept of identity would therefore be useful.

The concept of identity

Identity is often defined as *individuality*, or those qualities which mark out one person from another. Individual identity, however, seems to emerge from a sense of *belonging* and attachment to others, rather than simply from the possession of 'unique' attributes.

Chapter 2 investigated Harré and Gillett's view that, in order to have a sense of self, a human subject must also have an appreciation of *place*. This is a sense of 'location' in *space* and *time*, together with an awareness of moral status and of subjective qualities like class and gender. The chapter also examined the idea that the particular meaning of a verbal exchange depends on the identity of the participants.

Chapter 3 set out Hogg and Abrams's notion that groups have 'a profound impact on individuals' identity'. These authors are particularly interested in how individuals *express* their own sense of belonging through a process called *identification*. Overall, the idea that human beings *acquire* an identity through their experience of social processes, rather than beginning life with one which is ready-made, has become widely accepted.

We also saw that some authors believe that the process of *self-identification* depends upon an ability to contrast oneself with 'out-groups', thought to be different or in some way undesirable. A number of writers use the concept of 'the other' to acknowledge the existence of difference, whether between (for example) mainstream Western civilisation and the 'exotic' practices of other cultures, or between the sexes.

There are a number of arguments to the effect that identity in the modern or 'postmodern' age is actually subject to fragmentation. A related approach is founded on the notion of 'shifting' identity. In this theory, the precise configuration of identity *alters* according to the positions in which individuals are placed (in which case we see the exercise of 'circumstantial' influence over the individual), or because individuals attempt to attain certain types of status (the use of 'free will' in the process of self-identification). Chapter 4 mentioned the human tendency to define the self according to the social roles which are available.

Identity and address

The next task is to investigate the function of audience **identity** in the construction of an **address**; or, to be more accurate, how a **sense** of audience identity is used by a communicator to form a message. When a deliberate act of communication is initiated, the individual or group responsible for framing the address will act under a number of conditions. These conditions will include the following elements:

- the **context** in which the communicative act is to be made;
- the **audience** (group or individual) intended as the recipient of the address;
- message **content**;
- the consequent message **form**.

The 'addressor' (whether an individual or a group) will not necessarily have to know everything about the target audience in order to produce a suitable message. The values which circulate within the target group, as well as those shared within the wider society, may provide the basis for action.

In the front page article shown in Figure 5.2, *The Daily Mail* acts within the discursive *context* of public debate on crime, showing an awareness of an *audience* or readership which favours 'right-wing' rhetoric. The journalists involved in the construction of the report take the basic *content* (information about an annual Conservative party conference), and give it a particular *form* (that of a public pronouncement or 'warning').

The title across the top, known as the 'strap line', reads 'Tories get tough over law and order – and benefits'. This is a reference to conference speeches announcing changes in government policy. Yet most readers will suspect that this is more than the mere provision of information. The headline underneath confirms that the whole front page is in fact both a *dramatisation* and a *celebration* of one part of the conference proceedings. It is an attempt to reinforce and to increase the *circulation* of the Conservative party's message.

Daily Mail

THURSDAY, OCTOBER 7, 1993

32p

FEMAIL *Magazine*

Margaret, the last Princess

PAGES 36, 37

ROYAL SPECIAL

Serena & Linley: The A-Z of love

PAGES 29, 34 & 35

Tories get tough over law and order — and benefits

CRIMINALS AND CHEATS BEWARE

By PAUL EASTHAM and GORDON GREIG

THE Tories acted decisively to crack down on crime and social security scroungers yesterday.

Both Michael Howard and Peter Lilley brought the party conference to its feet with hard-hitting speeches outlining tough action.

It was a sharp Right turn for John Major's government, moving firmly back to traditional Tory values.

The wide-ranging moves delighted delegates, who had worried that their leaders were losing their way. It also distracted attention from the arrival in

Conference Special
— PAGES 4, 5 & 6

Blackpool of Lady Thatcher and the debate over what she does or does not say about her successor in her memoirs.

Home Secretary Mr Howard unveiled what he called 'the most comprehensive programme of action against crime that has ever been announced'.

His 27-point package aims to deter, catch, convict and punish the 'tidal wave' of criminals and tilt the justice system back in favour of their victims.

Radical measures include scrapping a suspect's historic right to silence — exploited by terrorists and experienced crooks — setting up a national DNA bank to store criminals' genetic fingerprints, tightening the rules on allowing bail to those accused of rape, murder or manslaughter, and building four more prisons, to be run by private firms.

Tougher punishments, a crackdown on young hooligans and plans to put more police back on the beat meant his moves went much further than the Royal Commission recommendations last July.

Mr Howard's forceful reassertion that the Tories are the party of law and order was rewarded with a two-minute standing ovation. But Social Security Secretary Mr Lilley won even longer cheers with a

Turn to Page 2, Col.1

Maggie towers in Blackpool

WITH a mass of pressmen and party workers fighting for the best view, Lady Thatcher swept into Blackpool's Imperial Hotel last night to prepare for her conference appearance today.

Figure 5.2   From The Daily Mail, 7 October 1993

Such an address is couched in terms quite different from the direct personal mode studied earlier. It is impersonal, and general in its application. The readership of the *Mail* will hardly imagine that it is being 'interpellated' by the headline. 'CRIMINALS AND CHEATS BEWARE' seems to be a public warning directed at others, but in reality is part and parcel of a political campaign designed to identify an 'enemy' against whom the right wing can unite. There is little doubt that this particular 'out-group' may help the *Mail's* readers to achieve positive self-identifcation, but these 'criminals and cheats' are unlikely to be affected by the warning, even if they see it.

Exactly who does the *Mail* consider these 'criminals and cheats' to be? Study of the article reveals that the category of 'criminal' is straightforward enough; but the 'cheats' are 'social security scroungers', rather than financiers practising 'insider dealing' in the City of London, or politicians making money by representing the interests of major corporations. The mention of 'undesirable' groups is used to justify measures like the abolition of the right to silence:

'Radical measures include scrapping a suspect's historic right to silence – exploited by terrorists and experienced crooks.'

Reference to 'terrorists' and 'crooks' creates just the sort of 'out-group' which can be used to help suggest the curtailment of civil liberties. In the last analysis, considerable dramatic licence is being exercised; the headline tries to create a simple distinction between groups in society.

Meaning alters, however, when a new context is applied to an event, or when a different audience is in receipt of a message. In the light of the misconduct seen amongst politicians, reference to 'criminals and cheats' may produce connotations which the *Mail* journalists did not intend to suggest.

Investigating written and literary expression

The handwritten vs. the printed text?

Written and 'literary' expression has been somewhat neglected within the study of communication, probably because it is regarded as the property of other subject areas, such as English language and literature. The category which appears in the AEB syllabus called 'written communication' is not as straightforward as it might appear.

First, it is important to recognise the difference between the **printed text** and the **handwritten text**. The printed text is employed as part of an *industrial* process, and is necessary in order to produce large quantities of material. Handwriting, by comparison, is used for personal and informal communication. Quite often, a 'system' of handwriting is taught in the early years of a child's school career, but an individual 'hand' remains distinctive at any stage of an individual's life. Handwriting is said to have a 'character' and is sometimes thought to reveal personality.

It is interesting to note that a person's signature, as a unique handwritten 'sign', is taken to be binding and to carry legal force. A printed fascimile of a name would never be regarded as an adequate substitute, since printed text is 'impersonal' and has become standardised. The standardised typefaces or fonts have evolved from designs originally based on handwritten italicised script.

As far as the study of communication goes, little investigation of the differences between handwriting and word-processing as *methods* of expression has taken place. Communication Studies as a discipline has in general concerned itself with the meaning generated by texts, rather than with the methods used to produce or reproduce them.

The immediate advantage of the printed text over some expressive forms is that it is 'democratic'. Great numbers of written texts can be reproduced mechanically, so that they appear as exact replicas of the symbolic form originally set out by the author. Of course, the original handwritten text (if there is one) is usually thought to possess unique value, but the copies are usually reasonably cheap.

Communication Studies and literature

Two approaches might help to focus on the relationship between communication as a study and written/literary expression. We could first ask: 'Does Communication Studies have anything to contribute to the study of the written/printed word?'. This means finding out if the various 'models' of communication as they presently exist, whether graphical or wholly theoretical, are able to provide useful insights into the different categories of written expression. (By 'categories', I mean the variety of types such as handwritten notes, printed books, essays, the content of personal documents like diaries, and so on.) The second approach might be to look at the problem from a different angle, and ask what kinds of *analysis* different types of writing appear to require.

Transmission models

If we begin with established communication theory, the most straightforward at our disposal is the concept of **transmission**. Transmission is concerned with 'sending messages' and is expressed diagramatically through *linear* models. In these, a message is sent from a source to a receiver, along a suitable channel, with the purpose of making an unambiguous impact upon the receiver, who is then at liberty to reply. The illustrations provided in Chapter 1 demonstrate theories of linear process.

There are indeed some examples of written expression which suit the sender/receiver theory. A note which is sent across a classroom from one pupil to another fits the idea of transmission; this particular method is appropriate for simple requests or the passing of essential information, especially where open verbal exchange is likely to be restricted. In another context, such as a conversation during lunch, the act of passing a note between two pupils would be interpreted in a different light, because *other channels* are available.

There are occasions when it is essential that a message take a written rather than a verbal form. When a doctor prescribes a certain drug, for example, he or she does not ask the patient to remember the name of the substance; a prescription is provided so that the pharmacist is able to find the correct medicine.

Uses and purposes

It is not as easy to apply transmission models to acts of communication which possess a more complex purpose or structure. As Chapter 1 explained, communication has a variety of **uses** and **purposes**. Use refers to how communication, in whatever form, is employed, while *purpose* means the end result intended when a communication takes place. The list of uses and purposes appeared as follows:

- socialisation;
- the social functional or ritual;
- the instrumental;
- the persuasive;
- the expressive.

It should be clear that there is a difference between *consuming* a text and *producing* one. Production, broadly speaking, involves the concept of purpose; part of this purpose must involve the uses to which the author expects his or her work to be put. Consumption, on the other hand, though concerned with use, also produces meanings within the limitations set by the text itself.

Texts are not 'consumed' by their audiences in the way that the traditional models of mass behaviour suggest. First, such material is taken in in different places and at various times. Second, the ideological coherence of a text is considerably affected by the individual and collective subjectivities through which it is mediated. In other words, people get different things from the same texts. For example, it is clear that some people read what many regard as 'serious' newspapers for the sake of *entertainment*. Another instance occurs where researchers study the popular tabloids for *academic* purposes.

Of course, the real point is that all individuals are capable of gaining a variety of pleasures from any number of texts. In this sense, *use* and *purpose* are not determined entirely by the text itself. Some theorists take this a stage further, believing that meaning is really created by an audience and not a text.

In fact, the *text* and *audience* stand in a *relationship*. The relationship produces meaning, within certain cultural boundaries.

Socialisation

What functions do the various types of written communication perform? It is a fairly safe bet that each of the uses and purposes listed above will be found in a variety of genres of writing. The first item on the list is one of the most important. **Socialisation** refers to the process through which human subjects acquire values, roles and norms. If culture is mediated through language, as well as through other practices, then written as well as spoken forms must help to socialise the individual.

Such forms would have to be public in nature, and therefore widely disseminated, which would indicate the mass media as an important secondary source, including comics, magazines, newspapers and so on. We should not forget that any form is capable of a variety of uses and purposes, and that the most fundamental of these is the *instrumental*, which is simply that which attempts to achieve or obtain some identifiable outcome.

The social functional

Besides the mass media forms already mentioned, the production and distribution of literature could be seen as part of socialisation, but also of the **social functional**. Does literature, which is obviously *expressive* when produced by an author, help to 'affiliate' people to other individuals or to institutions when it is consumed by a readership? A novel, for example, will have a number of aims. It might be written for the private satisfaction of its author, but by virtue of its public form will inevitably intervene in the debates which circulate within a society.

Communication and the novel

In *The Novel as Communication* (see D.H. Mellor, *Ways of Communicating*), David Lodge explores the idea that the 'classic novelists' seemed to regard their activity as communication, in the most basic sense of imparting or exchanging information. Lodge (p. 97) uses an example from Henry Fielding's *Tom Jones*, in which 'a metaphor of social intercourse' draws the novel to a close:

> 'We are now, reader, arrived at the last stage of our journey. As we have, therefore, travelled together through so many pages, let us behave to one another like fellow-travellers in a stage-coach, who have passed several days

in the company of each other; and who, notwithstanding any bickerings or little animosities which may have occurred on the road, generally make up at last ... since after this stage, it may possibly happen to us ... never to meet more.'

This is an example of 'the intrusive authorial voice' and provides, in Lodge's view (p. 97), 'the most obvious signs that these writers saw themselves as engaged in an exchange with their readers'.

Prose forms before the novel

At this point, it is worth looking at an example of a form of writing which preceded the novel. The following is taken from *The Unfortunate Traveller*, written by Thomas Nashe in 1593. Much of Nashe's writing could be described as belonging to a *rhetorical* form, based upon religious, social and personal disputation. His prose occasionally appears to resemble the 'stream of consciousness' technique employed by some later writers. In this example, a statement becomes a piece of rhetoric (p. 284):

'Christ would have no followers but such as forsake all and follow him, such as forsake all their own desires, such as abandon all expectations of reward in this world, such as neglected and contemned their lives, their wives and children in comparison of him, and were content to take up their cross and follow him.'

Much of Nashe's writing intends to provide entertainment through a series of aggressively satirical tableaux. The next extract deals with the concept of meaness and greed, and uses a *personification* to make the point. In the apartments of 'Signor Greediness', there is nothing to eat, and even the household vermin become desperate for sustenance (p. 65):

'It were lamentable to tell what misery the rats and mice endured in this hard world; how, when all supply of victuals failed them, they went a boot-haling [looting] one night to Signor Greediness' bedchamber, where finding nothing but emptiness and vastity, they encountered (after long inquisition) with a cod piece, well dunged and manured with grease, which my pinch-fart penny-father had retained from his batchelorship, until the eating of these presents. Upon that they set, and with a courageous assault, rent it clean away from the breeches, and then carried it away in triumph, like a coffin, on their shoulders betwixt them.'

In such passages, the writer employs narrative devices and rudimentary characterisation, but there is less concern to establish mutual recognition or 'trust' between author and reader. Rather than the 'intrusive authorial voice', Nashe invites the reader to admire the *persona* he presents. This persona is adventurous, sophisticated and inventive. Nashe's work is not 'confidential'; it is a performance.

Origins of the novel and critical response

Most writers place the origin of the novel in the eighteenth century, but some argue that it evolved at least a century earlier. Juliet Mitchell, for example, writing in *Femininity, Narrative and Psychoanalysis* (see Lodge's *Modern Criticism and Theory*, p. 426), believes that the novel 'starts with autobiographies written by women in the seventeenth century'. Mikhail Bakhtin (1895–1975) saw the novel as a form which grew from the parodic genres of classical and medieval literature. Bakhtin (Lodge, p. 125) notes that the novel was not widely recognised as a separate form or genre until the nineteenth century, though a number of critical works which dealt with fictional narratives began to appear from the late seventeenth.

An object of suspicion?

David Lodge provides an account of the '**suspicions**' which the novel tended to arouse in some twentieth-century critics (see Mellor, *Ways of Communicating*, p. 100):

> 'the peculiarly hypnotic spell the novel casts upon its readers [has] always made it an object of some suspicion, both morally and aesthetically. Is there not something fundamentally unnatural and unhealthy about a form of art which suspends the reader's awareness of his own existence in real space and time? Is not the pleasure of the novelistic text akin to day-dreaming, wish-fulfilment fantasy?'

The summary which Lodge provides here is very much akin to the criticisms which virtual reality systems have faced. Some theorists avoid this 'moralistic' approach and focus instead on the question of the novel's status as communication.

Storytelling vs. the novel?

The Marxist critic Walter Benjamin described **storytelling** as a transaction between individuals in close physical proximity to one another, and contrasted this with the novel, produced in one place by a solitary author and consumed in another by an isolated reader. James W. Carey's 1988 book *Communication as Culture* also describes the gradual erosion of oral traditions of communication and their substitution by print, which he thinks cultivated (p. 3):

> 'distinctive habits . . . spending a lot of time alone, conversing over distances, composing in private . . . keeping up with the news'.

Benjamin saw the novel as distinctly *anti-social*, in the most precise meaning of the term (see Lodge, p. 100):

> 'The novelist has isolated himself. The birthplace of the novel is the solitary individual, who is no longer able to express himself by giving examples of his most important concerns, is himself uncounselled and cannot counsel others.'

Benjamin's belief that the novel is not 'social' seems both to under-value its role in society and to over-estimate the positive features of traditional oral narratives. A close proximity between storyteller and reader does not necessarily mean that the relationship will be more interactive or democratic. Storytelling is not the only way that 'the social' is reproduced. It is in fact quite surprising to find that a *materialist* critic like Benjamin fails to recognise the social functions which the novel fulfils. He went further than this, appearing to think that the novel should not be regarded as a form of communication at all (see the beginning of this chapter for a definition of communication and the concept of 'secondary' exchange).

A single drop of ink: authors, readers and address

As we saw above, one of the most significant abilities of literary communication is supposed to be its capacity to transport the reader to times and places beyond his or her common order of experience. The opening paragraph of *Adam Bede*, written in 1857 by the novelist George Eliot, makes this claim explicit (p. 49):

> 'With a single drop of ink for a mirror, the Egyptian sorcerer undertakes to reveal to any chance comer far-reaching visions of the past. This is what I undertake to do for you, reader. With this drop of ink at the end of my pen, I will show you the roomy workshop of Mr Jonathan Burge, carpenter and builder, in the village of Hayslope, as it appeared on the eighteenth of June, in the year of our Lord 1799.'

The relationship between author, reader and 'past' is a much more ordered, selective affair than the 'far-reaching visions' which the sorcerer presents. While the author implicitly lays claim to a vestige of sorcery, the reader's position entails a private and privileged view of this 'past'.

A sense of privilege is not an unusual feature of the Victorian novel, and owes much to the fact that literacy was not universal. Within the text itself, authors would often reveal their intention to **address** a particular class of readership. In *Adam Bede*, George Eliot speaks directly to her conception of reader. There is a sense of shared experience present in the author's early picture of pastoral Hayslope (p. 62):

'It was that moment in summer when the sound of the scythe being whetted makes us cast more lingering looks at the flower-sprinkled tresses of the meadows.'

The 'us' in this sentence is the author and her audience, the educated reader, both part of a class which is removed from the performance of labour, and thus able to interpret the scene as part of a pastoral universe.

Communication with an audience

The question of readership or **audience** might seem to complicate the process of literary interpretation. Justin Lewis (1994), for example, in *Viewing, Reading, Listening* (p. 19), argues that:

'If ... we want to evaluate the meaning of *Hamlet* for specific audiences (whether Elizabethan or contemporary), we find ourselves ... suddenly forced to play our literary game by the rules of social science.'

However, one would expect most critics to use methods of interpretation which go beyond the standard forms of literary criticism, to include consideration of audience. This does not necessarily require a strict adherence to sociological approaches.

In the case of *Adam Bede*, for example, it is obvious that a modern audience must exercise some imagination in order to place itself within the compass of the author's address. It is most likely that such an audience will read this version of the past, not as '1799' (the date in which the narrative is set), but as part of the experience of its author in 1857 (the year of the book's composition).

Class and audience

Adam Bede is a novel which deals with a number of issues, including class, religion, relations between the sexes, and the value of the rural environment. The central character is a carpenter called Adam Bede, who is unusual in having received some education, and who eventually takes over his master's business. At the time of its publication, the novel was renowned as an exercise in realism. However, when the labouring folk of George Eliot's fictional Hayslope are presented, the encounter is mediated by the observer on horse-back, for whom there is a choice between 'other beauties in the landscape' and the 'living groups' of villagers. It appears that Eliot places the rural workers in a 'natural' rather than a 'social' category. The 'slouching labourer' looks about with 'a slow bovine gaze'. The rural workers seem (p. 63) 'almost as incapable of an undertone as a cow or a stag'.

What is interesting here is that we are shown the scene both from the vantage point of a more 'advanced' age (that of the latter part of the mid-1850s) and also from the perspective of an elevated class – the view from the saddle. We are offered the author's as well as the horseman's perception of Hayslope and its inhabitants.

Tensions in the text

The tension in *Adam Bede* is between the 'timeless' picture of a Midland rural society and those references to historical movements and events, such as the rise of Methodism, which must be made in order to give the novel a convincing period flavour. The problem arises in the clash between these two perspectives. In order to maintain the image of a rural idyll, the author is forced to distort historical facts. However, the reader is still able to catch a glimpse of the historical impact of Methodism, when the horseman says (p. 60):

> 'I should have thought there would hardly be such a thing as a Methodist to be found about here. You're all farmers aren't you? The Methodists can seldom lay much hold on *them*.'

By questioning the impact of Methodism in Hayslope, its importance in the wider world is actually brought to our attention as a *social* and not simply a religious unorthodoxy. The muted version of Methodism in *Adam Bede* is used to present a dramatic counterpoint to traditional forms of society, but ultimately lacks the force of its historical counterpart.

Authorial values

A novelist has the power to demonstrate the desirability and correctness of one set of **values**, as compared to another. Hayslope is constructed as an 'organic' community in which the dominant forces of class and patriarchy overcome the challenge of religious dissent, and the spectre of female independence in both social and sexual spheres. (A character called Dinah is presented as a talented female preacher, while another called Hetty fulfils the role of 'fallen woman'.) The problem in *Adam Bede* lies in the fact that the author is unable to present these opposing viewpoints in anything like their historical vigour, since to do so would be to admit the ideas and challenges they offer.

Therefore, in distorting the nature of social dissent, another problem is created: if the opposition is so puny, then the 'moral victory' eventually established by the bourgeois community is worthless. This dilemma is not resolved in the text. This is not to argue that George Eliot was a poor historian, rather that her *uses* of the historical are loaded in favour of the established order.

Looking beyond the text

If we consult history as a *contextual* factor in the appreciation of Eliot's text, we find evidence of the strong antipathy directed towards Methodism by the rich. Methodists were convinced that all human souls were equally important. In some senses, this form of dissent paralleled the growth of the radical sects during the English Civil War. The inclusion of forms of *class* consciousness made Methodism particularly reviled amongst some ruling groups in society. The Duchess of Buckingham, for example, wrote to the Methodist Countess of Huntingdon (see E.P. Thompson's 1968 *The Making of the English Working Class*, p. 46):

'I thank your Ladyship for the information concerning the Methodist preachers; their doctrines are most repulsive and strongly tinctured with impertinence and disrespect towards their Superiors, in perpetually endeavouring to lead all ranks and to do away with distinctions. It is monstrous to be told that you have a heart as sinful as the common wretches that crawl on the earth.'

The year in which the novel is set, 1799, saw the Combination Acts, the suppression of the London Corresponding Society (a group dedicated to universal suffrage), and the birth of the underground group called the 'United Englishmen' (formed to establish a republic). A wave of arrests swept the country, while the end of the conflict with France brought war debts, higher rents, higher taxes, and game laws designed to protect the estates of the rich.

Some of the book's first readers actually took offence at the limited realism Eliot introduced. An unsigned review article in *The Saturday Review* of 1859 insisted that:

'there is no reason why a picture of village character and village humour should be made so painful as it is by the introduction into the foreground of the startling horrors of rustic reality'.

Class and communication

An interesting feature of middle-class Victorian England was the belief that the working class was unable to express itself. It was thought incapable of shaping its own discourses; in simple terms, it could not communicate. In his book *Chartism* (1842), Thomas Carlyle referred to the 'great dumb toiling class which cannot speak'. He sought to interpret the thought which 'torments these wild inarticulate souls', these 'dumb creatures in pain'. The novelist Elizabeth Gaskell also sought to 'give some utterance to the agony which, from time to time, convulses this dumb people'. This 'dumbness', however, was perceived by middle-class commentators because they were unfamiliar with the codes through which working-class concerns were expressed.

Working-class perceptions: *Mary Barton*

In *Mary Barton*, nevertheless, Gaskell allows her characters to speak in a way that is far from inarticulate; working-class speech is represented as vivid and direct. John Barton, one of the working-class characters in the novel, provides the following appraisal of the capitalist system (p. 104):

> 'You'll say they'n getten capital an' we'n getten none. I say, our labour's our capital and we ought to draw interest on that. They get interest on their capital somehow a' this time, while ourn is lying idle, else how could they all live as they do? . . . nor they're worth their tens of thousands, a' getten out of our labour; why the very land as fetched but sixty pound twenty year agone is now worth six hundred, and that, too, is owing to our labour.'

Barton refers here to no less an idea than the role of labour-power in the creation of wealth, an accumulation of 'value' which is stolen by the capitalist and justified as 'profits'. Barton cannot 'draw interest' on his labour, because it is merely a commodity in a market which, at this point, does not require it.

It is interesting to note, in the light of the debate over emotion and cognition, that Gaskell always empathises with the emotion expressed by this character, but has no sympathy with the perfectly logical reasoning he is allowed to express. One of the most revealing passages comes earlier, when Gaskell again attempts to get inside the heads of her working-class protagonists (pp. 59–60):

> 'Carriages still roll along the streets, concerts are still crowded by sub-scribers, the shops for expensive luxuries still find daily customers, while the workman loiters away his unemployed time in watching these things, and thinking of the pale, uncomplaining wife at home . . . the wailing children asking in vain for enough food . . . the dying life of those near and dear to him. The contrast is too great. Why should he alone suffer from bad times? I know that this is not really the case; and I know what is the truth in such matters: but what I wish to impress is what the workman feels and thinks.'

This is an extraordinary passage. Gaskell starts by describing the condition of a class which was at the time quite literally starving, then disagrees with her own observations by ascribing them to the 'workman'. If Gaskell does 'know what is the truth in such matters', she does not reveal this to her audience.

Close to events

Mary Barton bears all the marks of its closeness to the events it relates. Unlike *Adam Bede* it is not able to suppress the truth. The 'documentary' elements of the novel lie side by side with the 'romance' of ordinary lives. Gaskell focuses on the family, apparently in the belief that it is the domestic existence of the working class which will gain sympathy, not its understanding of politics. Barton's trade unionism is therefore represented as a 'fall' into bad company.

The focus on family is used in this novel as an alternative to a sense of community; the reader's sympathy need not be engaged with the class as a whole, only with those representatives which the narrative chooses to deploy. The absence of descriptions of family labour, and the emphasis placed on the male worker, is a telling one. The reports of the factory commissioners of 1833 showed that, out of every four factory workers, only one was an adult male (see Brian Inglis, *Poverty and the Industrial Revolution*, p. 352). In fact, *Mary Barton* reveals nothing about actual working conditions, since the whole action takes place during a recession in trade.

Individual dramas

Gaskell is interested less in the social and the group than in individual events and the internal 'psychological' life of hero and heroine. Major public events, such as the burning down of Carson's mill, act merely as a backdrop to the individual dramas. The crowd at the fire is simply the dramatic element through which attention may be drawn to Mary Barton herself. She is in fact a misplaced heroine, a conventional character taken from another fictional genre.

Eventually, Gaskell abandons the drama of 'real' lives and concentrates on those characters who have either escaped from, or are otherwise set apart from, the working class. With these characters, a blind girl, a sailor, a young foreman and Mary Barton herself, Gaskell turns the novel into a melodrama. John Barton becomes a murderer, assassinating the mill-owner's son.

Although both Gaskell and Charlotte Brontë (in *Shirley*) use the theme of murder to extinguish or qualify the reader's sympathy for the oppressed, the first half-century of industrial struggle in England saw only two employers killed through the actions of radical workers. In the first case, in 1812, state reprisals resulted in the deaths of twenty-nine Luddites (see Thompson, *The Making of the English Working Class*, p. 612). It appears ultimately as though the working-class characters must remain 'dumb' or 'inarticulate' in order to retain the approval of a middle-class audience. Once they act for themselves, that action is characterised as irresponsible.

Thomas Hardy and the representation of female labour

One of the most striking differences between a novel like *Tess of the d'Urbervilles* and the moral tales written by Eliot and Gaskell is the attitude displayed to physical labour. In *Adam Bede*, Eliot is less interested in the process of labour than in the effect she wishes to achieve through its representation. The carpenter's shop in the novel is a case in point (p. 49):

'the slanting sunbeams shone through the transparent shavings that flew before the steady plane. On the heap of those soft shavings a rough grey shepherd-dog had made himself a pleasant bed, and was ... occasionally wrinkling his brows to cast a glance at the tallest of the five workmen who was carving a shield in the centre of a wooden mantelpiece.'

This rather charming but vacuous picture characterises labour as skilful but somewhat mysterious. It represents the work of the artisan, fully integrated into the community and the society.

Hardy's characterisation of labour in *Tess of the d'Urbervilles* is quite different. There are certainly symbolic elements, and a suggestion of the idyll, but also close observation of the conditions of 'unskilled' labour. Thomas Hardy appears to understand the process he describes (p. 138):

> 'Her binding proceeds with clock-like monotony. From the sheaf last finished she draws a handful of ears, patting their tips with her left palm to bring them even. Then stooping low she moves forward gathering the corn with both hands against her knees, and pushing her left gloved hand under the bundle to meet the right on the other side, holding the corn in an embrace like that of a lover, she brings the end of the band together and kneels on the sheaf while she ties it, beating back her skirts now and then when lifted by the breeze.'

Hardy shows how the female worker is alienated from work (the 'clock-like monotony') rather than assimilated by it into society. Women workers were actually employed at extremely low rates throughout the nineteenth century. In 1851, average wages for women working in the countryside stood at seven to eight pence a day. In 1893–4, some forty years later, the Royal Commission on Labour in Dorset discovered that the wage for female labourers was only nine or ten pence a day (see G.E. Mingay, *Rural Life in Victorian England*, p. 79).

Hardy himself held an ambiguous place within the Victorian social formation, and was a relentless editor of his own past. Robert Gittings (in *Young Thomas Hardy*) argues that Hardy eliminates all reference in the *Life* he wrote to relatives who occupied lowly positions in the social order. Hardy's attitude to his origins is revealing, and may help to explain his 'materialist' view of society and his 'deterministic' view of character. Throughout his career, he encountered many patronising references to his status as a 'provincial' writer, able to pen convincing rural scenes but out of his depth when it came to representing educated people and their speech. The attitude taken by many reviewers to *Tess* is revealing. *The Speaker* of 26 December 1891 expressed the opinon that:

> 'there are whole chapters of the book [so] steeped in the sunny atmosphere of Wessex that the reader feels himself to be one of the personages of whom Mr Hardy writes, falls to their level and sympathises with them in their wants and woes'.

Andrew Lang, writing in the *New Review* of February 1892, recognised, albeit in hostile form, the radical implications which Hardy's vision may have for some of his readers:

'That we should be depressed is very natural . . . and indeed, I suppose we shall be no better till, we have got the Revolution over, sunk to the nadir of humanity, and reached the middle barbarism again.'

A novelist like Hardy would seem to disprove Walter Benjamin's belief that the novel is somehow removed from the social, and that the novelist is unable to 'counsel' others.

Visual communication: the discourses of art

This section, which examines the subject of art, gives an account of the way in which 'modern art' is described and argued over. In other words, it looks at the discourses which various individuals and groups mobilise to talk about art.

Fine art and elitism?

One of the charges laid against **fine art** has been **'elitism'**. It has been attacked for holding itself aloof from common experience, and for spawning a class of expert which reserves to itself the task of translating an artist's intention. It does so, according to this view, for an audience which is imagined to have no specialist training in or knowledge of art. The traditional role of the art critic is that of someone who appears to have the required expertise and refinement of aesthetic taste needed to explain to others the worth of paintings or artefacts.

Aesthetics

A definition of the original meaning of aesthetics is supplied by O'Sullivan and his colleagues in the 1987 *Key Concepts in Communication*, where it is described as (p. 4):

'a concept inherited from idealist philosophy, referring to principles of taste, especially good taste, and hence of beauty'.

The object of study for aesthetics is 'the art-object itself, taken out of its historical, cultural and means-of-production context'. Here, expertise would be used to isolate 'those textual properties' which make an art-object beautiful.

A new aesthetics: changing the guard?

The revolt against elitism in artistic taste led to a new conceptualisation of beauty and new standards of worth. Instead of a pure 'aesthetics', where the art-object itself carries value, artistic production came to be recognised as carrying an aesthetic code, which could be interpreted once its historical context and mode of production (mechanical or artisanal, for example) were taken into account. The movement away from a notion of 'pure' value in art, towards an appreciation of less traditional forms, has certainly encouraged greater freedom of expression. However, some may suspect that one orthodoxy has merely been replaced with another.

For example, the idea that semiology, as one element of this revolt, has moved towards what O'Sullivan calls (p. 5) 'a value-free' description of aesthetic codes must be questioned; if we realise that all forms of expression and analysis incorporate values, then semiological approaches will certainly also do so. In addition, the reputation of image-based semiology as theory (see Hodge and Kress's *Social Semiotics* of 1988 and Price's *Media Studies* of 1993) and as critical methodology (see Barker, *Comics: Ideology, Power and the Critics*, 1989) has been rather down-graded in recent years.

We may, nevertheless, be returning full circle to the notion that there is an expert group of critics and theorists who hold keys to understanding – only this time the members of the group may call themselves 'semiologists'. Unless 'the public' seizes the chance provided by a turn to more democratic forms of criticism, then we may have witnessed no more than the changing of the guard.

The response of the 'public'

In fact, the expansion of critical interest in what O'Sullivan calls 'the output of mass commodity and mass production' has led to some wholly negative public reactions. Where the object of critical interest has turned to texts produced through advertising, graffiti, video and so on, the audience encountering many such artefacts, far from appreciating its liberation from traditional values, appears instead to resent what is perceived as 'junk' masquerading under the title 'art'.

It appears that some of the discourses used by the old art establishment to confer status on fine art seem to a large extent to have become part of what we may call the popular consciousness. Notions of 'quality' remain high on the popular agenda.

Notions of quality

Part of the problem is the way in which our society tends both to categorise and subsequently to value a range of creative activities. In *Art in the Age of Mass Media* (1983), John Walker recognises the values which operate through the categories used and the 'agendas' which are set, before we even consider any individual examples of expressive communication (p. 15):

'In the west, culture is categorised in various ways: we speak of "high" and "low" culture, we distinguish between fine art, craft, industrial design and mass media ... these categories are not merely mental phenomena: they have material effects in terms of the policies and practices of educational institutions, cultural organisations and the contents of galleries and museums.'

Walker notes that an application made in 1979 to the Arts Council for the repair of trade union banners was refused. Banners were regarded by the Council as *craft*, not art. The individual work had fallen into the wrong *category*.

Such inequalities in status were questioned by the artist Lynn Malcolm, who used a series of 'domestic' items such as samplers and cakes, which, when viewed as one piece, formed the question: 'Why have there been so few great women artists?'. Malcolm recognises also (in a 1992 Open University programme) that fine art was always 'hierarchically the most important'. She does not, however, argue for new hierarchies, asking instead:

'is it more important to use our creativity around us or to take an object worth eleven million pounds and put it in the vault of a bank where no-one will ever see it?'

A pile of bricks

In 1974, at a cost of £4,000, the Tate Gallery bought a work of art from an American called Carl Andre. The piece was called *Equivalent VIII* and consisted of a set of 120 bricks laid two deep in a rectangle. It was not until 1976, however, that the public became aware of the event; the response which followed was one of outrage, with the agenda for the ensuing furore set by the popular press. For example, *The Daily Mirror* of 16 February 1976 carried a front-page article with the same photograph of the bricks printed from three different angles. The headline read:

'Whichever way you look at Britain's latest work of art ...
WHAT A LOAD OF RUBBISH. How the Tate dropped 120 bricks.'

The article, by Philip Mellor, opened by attacking the Tate in the following terms:

'A top art gallery was under fire last night for spending taxpayers' cash on ... a pile of bricks. It was all done in the name of art. The 120 loose firebricks go under the heading "low sculpture". They are under lock and key at London's Tate Gallery, which gets a £500,000 Government handout every year.'

Here we may recognise a number of devices designed to make the reader complicit in the address being offered. He or she is taken along a narrative path which, if accepted (and the point is that it is very difficult to disengage from a convincing narrative), may well involve absorbing the discursive position offered by the writer. Notice also that familiar phrases are used as points of identification in the text; for example, 'it was all done in the name of art', where 'done in the name of' is the key sequence of words which the reader will recognise. Here, clearly, we are meant to think that something questionable is being performed, some low act is being committed in the name of a practice which is usually regarded as more exalted.

The writer appears to find the category used by the Tate to describe the bricks ('low sculpture') quite ludicrous. One of the most telling words used is 'handout', which is clearly negative and which was to be used extensively when the 'undeserving' recipients were identified.

The article ends with a direct, second-person address to the reader:

'You can buy ordinary household bricks for between £40 and £80 a thousand.'

Here we see an appeal to 'common sense'. The 'true' value of the bricks is established – except that it is not. All commodities, however cheap, carry an inflated price designed to ensure a profitable return on investment.

The shock of the new?

In an interesting study of public perceptions of the 'avant-garde', Ian Ground (see the 1989 *Art or bunk?*, p. 2) insists that:

'what the public at large found so outrageous was simply *the fact that "Equivalent VIII" could be considered to be a work of art at all*'.

This is certainly the primary response, but I would argue that such outrage is inextricably linked with the idea that the 'bunk' concerned often fetches an indecent amount of money in a marketplace made up of the rich and gullible. Walker (*Art in the Age of Mass Media*) stresses that the response to the event must be seen in the context of a series of stories which appeared throughout the tabloid press attacking wasteful public expenditure.

However, Ground correctly identifies our old friend *categorisation* as chiefly responsible for the public response to the material status of Andre's work (p. 3):

'They [the public] knew that what he had produced was not a work of art in the same way that a glass of water or someone's auntie or a pile of old newspapers lying in a cupboard are not works of art. Such things are not wors of art in the sort of way that animals are not astronomical events and cauliflowers are not kings. They belong to entirely different categories.'

How then are we to judge objects or artefacts which are presented as art? It seems to turn on the intention of the artist, the relationship of the artefact to immediate and historical context, and the expectation of critics and audience.

Intention, context, expectation

In order to investigate the status of the 'art-object', Ian Ground uses the example of a hypothetical sculpture by Henry Moore, which he calls 'Recumbent Figure', and a meteorite which has fallen from outer space. The meteorite is, remarkably, exactly similar to the sculpture in all respects. Ground then presents a series of terms of negative and positive value, like *elegant, balanced, dramatic, vulgar, crass*, which the reader is encouraged to mark if the term could possibly be applied to both sculpture and meteorite.

It seems that, where a term expressing value (negative or positive) is able to be applied to the sculpture, it is less likely to seem appropriate to the meteorite. Ground uses this to support the idea that we are not interested in the work of art as an *object*, but are more concerned with (p. 25) 'the appearance of the object as meant by someone'. The key words here are 'meant' and 'someone'. There is human **intention** and personality working behind any artefact that is produced for an expressive or aesthetic purpose. Ground points out that (p. 27):

> 'What we attend to is not just the physical appearance of the stone or the visual appearance of the paint on the canvas … we must … attend to the intended appearance.'

While Ground says that people must have a *notion* (an idea) of a work of art to use as a guide to what they might see in an object, the problem remains that this guiding notion is quite often fairly narrow. The attempts to broaden public *expectation* of what constitutes art serve really only to confirm the idea that there is an awful lot of rubbish being produced, and that this material gains respectability only because it is placed in the *context* of a gallery.

Public expectations?

The public still seems to expect art to require some measurable effort on the part of the artist. It still clings stubbornly to the idea that the artist must be talented, that he or she must have some artistic ability, such as being able to draw, sculpt or paint. Above all it holds firmly to the belief that the end product should be recognisable as having a commercial value which at least meets its market price. By contrast, the critics seem to be less interested in old-fashioned notions of quality than in the impact a piece has on those who experience it.

A brief content analysis of the terms used by contemporary writers on art will show that the word 'work' is used when the art-object is discussed, followed closely by the term 'exciting'. Put the two together and we have 'exciting work'. This is not an assessment of artistic standards, or a judgement of skill. Meanwhile, the 'public' still seems to suspect that many artists are prepared to challenge the establishment, as long as that challenge brings in a substantial financial reward.

Two discourses: more on context and intention

By contrast to 'the public', the type of critic who supported Carl Andre's *Equivalent VIII*, and who may be expected to champion the output of someone like Michael Landy or Damien Hirst, seems anxious to stress that modern artists force us all to look again at what is traditionally *accepted* as art.

The idea of challenging preconceptions is, of course, central to those strategies which attempt to institute new or more diverse standards in taste. However, artefacts have to be displayed within a context which will enable them to be discussed as 'works'. Michael Landy's installation of a flower stall in the Royal Academy was one example where context was all-important.

'That's what it's about': talking about art

There seems always to be a tension between the idea that such 'work' can speak for itself and the necessity which some feel to explain and defend its aims and purposes. The two descriptions of the flower stall (called *Costermonger's Stall*) which follow are taken from the television programme *Arena*, broadcast on 21 February 1994. The first is a transcript taken from remarks made by the artist, Michael Landy, and the second comes from comments made by an art critic:

> 'This is called *Costermonger's Stall* and we're at the Royal Academy . . . what it's about? . . . erm . . . it's about what it is, really . . . I can't really say it's anything else but what it is, it's a Costermonger's stall, with some lights and some flowers on it. So, erm, that's what it's about.'

> 'It's about somehow . . . a kind of err . . . *memento mori* of er of you know, the world of the consumer . . . this is the kind of thing that he's done very very successfully, these extraordinary pieces that remind one of being in those shops in, I don't know, in South London or wherever, you know with the vegetable markets . . . the kind of giving or drawing attention to their formal qualities and you know we might forget that everything has formal quality too, as well as it were inherent subject quality.'

So, according to the artist, it is what it is and there is no point in attempting to achieve some other kind of status. In the second extract, the installation is a reminder of the demise of a certain type of consumer culture, presumably one which was once an authentic part of life in the capital city.

The idea of art being a matter of context and point of view was expressed by the same critic in the *Arena* programme mentioned above:

> 'All those strange objects that Duchamp as it were transformed into art . . . he was doing exactly the same thing. It's a kind of extension of the possibility of art . . . the bus that you ride to work in the morning is a work of art too, it depends how you look at it.'

If art depends simply upon the perspective of an audience, and thus everything is art, there may be no need to recognise the special calling of 'artist', which these critics appear anxious to do.

A dead cow

The objections raised to Andre's bricks have been more than matched by the disquiet which has grown over the artistic practices of Damien Hirst, who began with various photographic experiments in a morgue and progressed to the celebrated 1991 'assemblage' called *Isolated Elements Swimming in the Same Direction for the Purpose of Understanding*. This consisted of thirty-eight dead fish in separate containers of formaldehyde. The title was, according to a remark made by Hirst in August 1991 (see *The Independent Magazine* of 3 August 1991), an attempt to explain, which ends up by 'making matters worse, leaving huge holes for interpretation'.

Hirst's most famous works to date have been the dead animals which have been cut in half, preserved with injections of formaldehyde and then displayed in transparent cases. *Mother and Child Divided* was one example of this practice, consisting of a dead cow and a dead calf which had each been cut in two along their length, using a chain-saw. This process, in keeping with the tradition which allows much of the labour to be carried out by someone other than the artist, was performed by a worker at a knacker's yard. A sheep, likewise divided into two parts, appeared in the Serpentine Gallery in 1994, and was attacked with black ink by a man who described himself as a struggling artist.

Art and commerce: the Turner Prize

In 1993, a series of full-page advertisements appeared in the broadsheet press. The first read 'Abandon All Art Now', and 'Await Further Instructions'. The second, which appeared some time later, announced that:

> 'It has been brought to our attention that you did not Abandon All Art. Serious Direct Action is therefore necessary. The K foundation will award £40,000 to the artist who has produced the worst body of work in the last twelve months.'

On 23 November 1993, the night of the award of the Turner Prize, twenty-five journalists were driven by the K Foundation to an isolated location, and each presented with £1,600 in cash. This they were asked to nail to a pallet in order to make up the total of £40,000. This money was then driven back to London and presented to the winner of the Turner Prize, Rachael Whiteread. Whiteread refused to accept until the very last moment, when it was about to be burned. She then donated the money to good causes.

The K Foundation also put up another pallet for sale as a work of art. This was called *Nailed to the Wall*, and consisted of a pallet covered in banknotes to the value of one million pounds. Its reserve price stood at exactly half that amount, £500,000. The catalogue which accompanied the pallet included the following explanation:

> 'the face value will be eroded by inflation, while the artistic value will rise and rise. The precise point at which the artistic value will overtake the face value is unknown. .... the point is simple: art as a speculative currency, and vice-versa. To put it more bluntly: Art equals Money and Money equals Art.'

The K Foundation's point about commerce is expressed through its readiness to destroy vast sums of money; it appeared to regard this as more radical than redeploying the money on constructive social projects.

Art as commodity

In *Promotional Culture* (1991) Andrew Wernick provides a number of useful insights into the commodification of art-objects (the production of art as items for sale in the marketplace). Wernick describes how the eighteenth-century potter Josiah Wedgwood was commissioned to make a copy of a Roman vase called the 'Portland vase'. The original vase was regarded as a wonder of the ancient world, but it remained a commodity, an item which could be exchanged for cash in the marketplace.

From Wedgwood's point of view, its value as a commodity was significantly increased, because the copy he made was used to enhance his reputation. The original vase therefore had (and in fact still retains) an 'exhibition' value, since it was used to sell other items. In his book *Ways of Seeing* (1977) John Berger goes so far as to argue that the art object which generates copies undergoes a change in status (p. 21), and that 'the uniqueness of the original now lies in it being the original of a reproduction'.

Handwritten manuscripts are quite different, having no exhibition value, though it is true that illuminated texts and books which rely upon elements of 'craft' in their production form an exception to the rule. While there *is* a direct relationship between the symbolic content of a manuscript and a printed book, there is usually no such link between the two when they are considered as *physical artefacts*.

Hierarchies of value

Creating copies of paintings is generally quite straightforward, since the printing of colour reproductions is relatively cheap. In order to create a more exclusive market, some copies are issued with the artist's signature and are numbered and sold as 'limited editions'. The copying of certain types of art is, however, a little more complicated; some sculptures, for example, are almost impossible to reproduce in a material form. Value will therefore reside only in the original work and the interest or controversy it is able to arouse, as we have seen above.

Feminist interventions

In *Vision and Difference* (1988) Griselda Pollock asks (p. 1): 'is adding women to art history the same as producing feminist art history?'. Pollock's answer is that the inclusion of women not only changes what is studied, but challenges the existing disciplines in political terms. The reason that women were excluded in the first place seems to Pollock neither forgetfulness nor mere prejudice, but:

> 'The structural sexism of most academic disciplines ... [which] ... contributes actively to the production and perpetuation of a gender hierarchy.'

One of the most important points she makes is that 'women's studies' are not just about women, but also:

> 'about the social systems and ideological schemata which sustain the domination of men over women within the other mutually inflecting regimes of power in the world, namely those of class and those of race'.

Rather than accept the pre-defined criteria of 'greatness' set out by the male art history establishment, Pollock argues for a new paradigm or set of objectives through which artistic activity may be judged. She rejects the concept of the gifted individual whose work is uniquely formed and then launched into a world of appreciative art lovers. She turns instead to Marx's *Grundrisse*, which analyses the relations between *production*, *consumption*, *distribution* and *exchange*. Marx sets out his approach as follows (Pollock, p. 3):

> 'Production not only supplies a material for a need, but also supplies a need for the material ... the object of art – like every other product – creates a public which is sensitive to art and enjoys beauty.'

The idea here is that production produces consumption, by first creating the material for it, then determining the manner of consumption, and finally creating the products in 'the form of a need felt by the consumer'. This mode of production has traditionally excluded female artists.

Inside the frame

The dominant male tradition in art is not just an academic question; it is actually made visible in choice of subject and the representation of the sexes in painting and sculpture. In *Women, Art and Power*, Linda Nochlin notes that the opposition between strength and weakness is used as one of the dominant paradigms in the representation of men and women. She examines Jacques-Louis David's *Oath of the Horatii*, in which three brothers in Ancient Rome take an oath of loyalty to the state, swearing on swords held before them by their father. The women and children of the family appear seated on the right of the picture, overcome by feeling, heads lowered, in stark contrast to the upright and energetic stance of the men, whose arms are outstretched in the act of allegiance. Nochlin believes that:

> 'The striking effectiveness of the visual communication here depends in the most graphic way possible upon a universal assumption: it is not something that needs to be thought about. The ... division here between male energy, tension, and concentration, as opposed to female relaxation, flaccidity, and relaxation, is ... clear.'

Changing representation

In an Open University programme of 1992, the artist Lesley Sanderson talked about her efforts to alter traditional gender roles as they are portrayed in fine art. Working within a representational tradition (rather than an abstract one) in order to make the clearest impact on her audience, Sanderson used a self-portrait as an example, calling it 'a very austere portrait ... a strong representation as well as a sensitive representation'.

This artist was motivated by the belief that 'it's time that women represented themselves rather than have representations made for them'. Opposing the tradition which portrays ethnicity in women as 'exotic and passive', Sanderson's self-portrait challenges the voyeuristic gaze which many artists encourage:

> 'The work is very much a social commentary. I've always worked in a very representational academic way because I want the images to be easily read. I don't want there to be any misunderstanding of the construction of the imagery.'

Other women artists, like Roxanne Permar and Françoise Dupré, feel that feminist art does not have to be figurative, and that 'the most important aspect is to create work collectively'. Co-operation and collective working methods have long been regarded as an alternative to the concept of the artist as an 'isolated genius'. This kind of practice is clearly different to Berger's description of 'that art [which] makes inequality seem noble and hierarchies seem thrilling'.

Communication and democracy

The work of critics like John Berger encouraged leftist perspectives in a number of art colleges in the late 1970s and early 1980s. However, attempts to use art as a weapon for democracy have often foundered when faced with the 'commodification' of artistic production.

Some forms of communication, nevertheless, have encouraged the growth of democracy and free expression. Print, for example, has always been an important feature of a democratic society. Film is one form which has contributed immensely to the shaping of *popular* though perhaps not *democratic* culture, since the institutional power of the Cinema has become concentrated in the hands of a small number of corporations.

One of the advantages of film remains its ability to represent both the fantastic and the mundane. The ordinary human subject, from the time of the silent melodramas produced by Harold Lloyd, Buster Keaton and Charlie Chaplin, has been elevated to a position of considerable importance. Cinema-goers are presented with narratives which *re-present* people and events belonging to a world with which they are closely familiar.

The portrayal of human interaction in film

Although there have been some doubts about the theory of representation, in the sense that it is not entirely convincing as a picture of the mental process (see Chapter 2), the distinction between *presentation* and *representation* is still useful. It is the difference between these two concepts which needs to be explored in any attempt to understand the cinematic portrayal of human interaction.

Social actions: presentation

The roles we 'play' within the context of everyday interaction can vary quite significantly. A private exchange between two people is clearly quite different to an interaction involving a number of individuals within the context of a public forum. It would be too easy, however, to declare that the public context is inherently more 'dramatic' than the private one.

In fact, expression requires *some sort of performance* whatever the prevailing circumstances. In other words, the human subject has to **present** the best 'case' whenever it wishes to pursue an instrumental or persuasive purpose, as well as the best 'self' when it is engaged in social, phatic or indeed any type of interpersonal communication.

Social actions: re-presentation

So far, we have discussed the concept of *presentation*; however, any exchange which is scripted in advance and then presented for public consumption may be described as a **re-presentation** of the themes or ideas which the script makes concrete. It is still the case that, in performance, actors will use the same techniques of presentation that are employed in everyday existence.

These techniques may of course be magnified and formalised, in order to meet the requirements of emotional projection and the need to repeat a standard performance (in Theatre) or the attributes of a standard character (in mainstream Cinema). While the 'magic' of Theatre may be partly explained by the fact that each performance, though necessarily 'standardised', is also in some sense unique, the repeated viewing of a film produces a sense that screen interaction remains timeless.

A 'virtual' exchange?

In *Theatrical Presentation*, Bernard Beckerman describes *presentation* as both the act of giving and 'the force of being'. The meaning of 'presentation' in the theatre turns on the 'symbolic value' of the performance. Beckerman sees the performance not as an 'actual exchange' (p. 4) but as 'a **virtual** one'. As communication theorists, we might understand it as a virtual rather than a real exchange because there is usually no exchange of discourse or speech between actors and audience.

Theatrical performance

An actor is a performer, making contact with an audience through the expression of ideas in a temporal space. Behind the actor, however, are other individuals who contribute to the play's impact, including writer, director, designer and so on. Beckerman lists the elements which give each **performance** its particular structure: performer, audience, act and context.

In many cases, critics have concentrated on the performer and the personal, rather than the social function he or she must perform. John Harrop writes that an actor has (see *Acting*, p. 4) 'to be both himself [sic] and someone else at the same time'. Harrop is fond of the paradox. The actor is 'both present on stage and yet at the same time absent, replaced by the illusion he or she creates'. Later, he contradicts himself (p. 6), arguing that 'no matter how actors act, they cannot expunge themselves from the performance'. He describes the actor's task as 'the adoption of otherness'. At one point, the actor is (p. 5):

> 'replaced by the illusion he or she creates. If the actor "appears," it is usually through a break in the illusion – a stumble, the forgetting of a line, a missed entrance.'

(An audience may find it difficult to notice an actor who 'appears' through a missed entrance.)

Actors are often applauded for their ability to reproduce *character*, and that character is quite often already formed in the mind of an audience, if the role

Figure 5.3   Actors in a performance of Lorca's Blood Wedding

portrayed is well known. Harrop tries to distinguish between different kinds of performer, where at 'the simplest level' (p. 5):

> 'the muscleman, the Miss Universe contestant and the stand-up comedian are projecting themselves'.

From these quaint examples, we might decide that all performances, of whatever kind, involve the presentation of some aspect of the self.

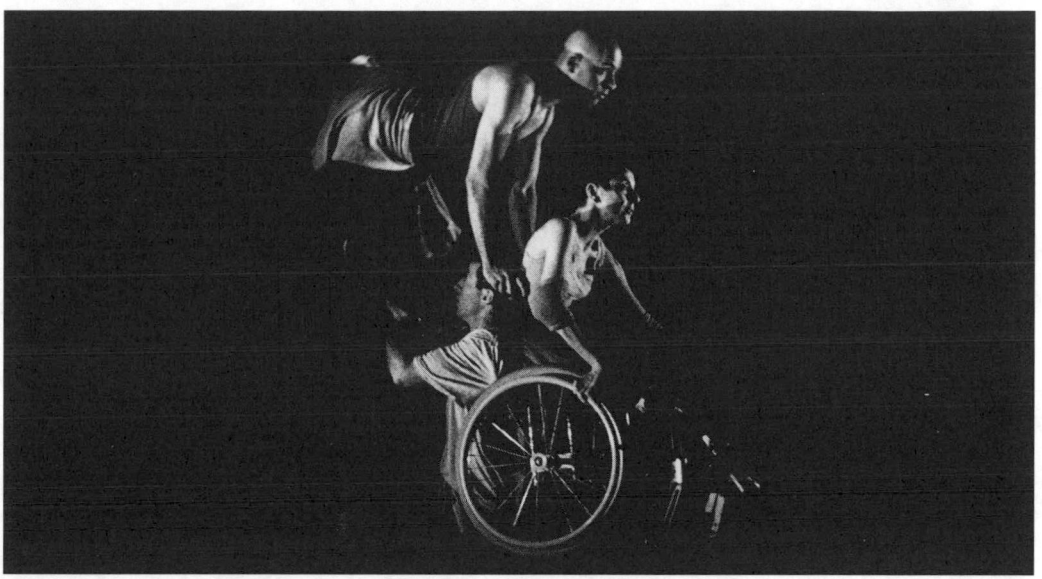

Figure 5.4   The CandoCo Dance Company in performance

The re-presentation of human interaction in film

Television and film create episodes in which individuals carry out actions and are involved in verbal exchanges. Whether these are fully 'scripted' or partly improvised, an analysis of such presentations would need to take account of a number of factors:

- In the first place, we should examine *physical characteristics* and *stereotypes* in the Cinema, and how these are linked to *behavioural* patterns as they are represented on the screen.
- All the elements which constitute human *subjectivity*, including age, gender, class, ethnicity and so on, would be encompassed by this kind of investigation.
- *Dress codes* and *codes of speech* (including accent, intonation, dialect and pitch) could also be considered.
- So could the typical *spatial arrangement* of characters and their *physical proximity* to one another. This would necessitate a study of the social implications of *mise en scène* (what is actually observed on the screen at any one time).
- One of the most important factors would be the apparent *physical* and *social* context in which the narrative places the characters.
- *Discourse analysis* would need to be carried out, as would some consideration of *non-verbal* communication, including *body posture* and *gesture*.

The analysis of interaction

The aim of investigating interaction in the Cinema is not to decide how 'realistic' a particular speech event seems, because 'acting' of a sort takes place in all ordinary interactions. Social subjects are also *social actors*, already engaged in *conscious self-presentation*. Erving Goffman, in *The Presentation of Self in Everyday Life* (p. 30), believed that:

> 'It is probably no mere historical accident that the word person, in its first meaning, is a mask. It is rather a recognition of the fact that everyone is always and everywhere, more or less consciously, playing a role ... It is in these roles that we know each other, it is in these roles that we know ourselves.'

This point of view is noticeably different to those approaches which argue that the playing of roles *distorts* the freedom people have to interact.

Some actors and directors attempt to make cinematic 'exchanges' as convincing as possible, especially through improvisation. However, poor improvisation betrays certain repetitive features which indicate that the actors are attempting to get from one place in the narrative to another (the endless challenge 'You lookin' at me?' in minor imitations of the 'mafia' genre would otherwise be hard to explain).

Two speech events

At times, ordinary exchanges can read as though they have been deliberately scripted, especially where the participants know one another and are accustomed to turn-taking and the roles which are habitually played. The conversation below is taken from an exchange which occurred between a married couple, who are presented with the possibility of allowing their two children to attend a half-term theatre group:

A: That was Lorraine
B: Who's Lorraine?
A: Lee's mum (.) She told me there's a scheme next week, 9.30 to 12.30 every day (1) Unfortunately it's run by a Sunday school (.) They take about a hundred children () Theme of Gideon (.) They make up a play during the week and show it on the Friday night
B: Fantastic! (1) I can't make it on the Friday by the way
A: You bugger! (laughs)

Here, A is female, B male. The man's exclamation ('Fantastic!') at first appears to be an enthusiastic response to the proposal; in fact it seems that he is simply pleased to get the children out of the house, which his wife recognises in her final remark.

While everyday speech events can resemble scripted exchanges, film actors sometimes reproduce all the features (hesitancy, changes of direction, incoherence) which are ordinarily supposed to be a feature of real speech. The following extract is taken from Spike Lee's biopic *Malcolm X*:

[Malcolm X is seen walking onto a university campus with three other men, all Muslims].

[White female student runs towards them. A bell chimes].

Student: Excuse me (.) Mr. X? Um (.) Hi (.) I've read some of your speeches and I honestly believe that a lot of what you have to say is true () and I'm a good person in spite of what my ancestors did and I wanted to ask you what can a white person like myself who isn't prejudiced (.) What can I do to help you and further your cause?

Malcolm X: (Nods) Nothing (walks off)

Speech genres in film: *Southern Comfort* and the representation of the male

Walter Hill's 1981 film *Southern Comfort* examines the misfortunes of a platoon of part-time soldiers (National Guardsmen) on exercise in the swamps of Louisiana. When one Guardsman decides to scare a group of Cajun trappers by firing blank rounds from a machine gun, they respond by killing the sergeant leading the patrol. What follows is a struggle between the two groups, the Guardsmen hampered by an incompetent leader, internal disputes and unfamiliar terrain. The themes which emerge most clearly in the course of the narrative concern masculinity, power and the nature of group leadership, while the question of intra-group racism is suggested but not developed.

One of the most interesting features of this action thriller is the clear distinction made between formal and informal speech. After the death of Sergeant Poole the group's corporal, Caspar, takes over command. Caspar struggles to assert his authority through the use of a formal mode of address which he thinks suited to the predicament in which they find themselves. Its failure to impress grows partly from its closeness to the 'military bullshit' which, from past experience, the men have come to distrust. This is revealed at the beginning of the excursion, where Spencer (later to assume a leading role) reveals that he has provided his colleagues with an incentive to complete the exercise; a group of prostitutes will be waiting to entertain them once they reach their objective. Spencer parodies official speech when, accompanied by the sniggers of his comrades, he tells the sergeant that 'these women are expecting some small-unit military penetration'. The one thing the men do not expect is a real battle, one which really does test their cohesion and prowess as a military group.

Military jargon

In the following transcript from the film, hierarchies within the group have begun to break down. An alternative leader is soon to emerge, while Caspar's discourse oscillates between a fairly effective mixture of informality and instruction, and the straightforward military jargon which signals his failures of imagination. In this scene, the men have just buried two of their dead:

Coach: We give this prayer as dead men (2) asking for our salvation (1)

Caspar: I don't wanna hear anymore of that kind of talk (2) Now we're at war and that's all there is to it (1) I want you men to start looking like soldiers and not like mail men (.) weapons carried at the ready (.) Now we only got about a half hour of daylight left (.) So this is it, we'll bivouac here (.) the clearing is big, it'll make it tough for those bastards to sneak up on us (4)

Spencer: Right, hey Caspar wait a second (2) let's talk a few things over, huh (2) Tomorrow morning the helicopters'll be out looking for us (.) Damn good chance they'll find us too, if we stay in clear ground like this (.) So all we have to worry about until then is the Cajuns, right?

Caspar: We don't know the enemy's strength or his disposition and while he may have the advantage of familiar terrain we have the advantage of military training

Spencer: That's a terrific speech Caspar but I wanna improve our odds a little bit

Caspar is more effective when he uses colloquial terms and when his words have a genuine link with the practical business of survival: 'we only got about a half hour of daylight left – so this is it, we'll bivouac here – the clearing is big', and so on. Where he relies upon formulaic responses, he fails to make a connection with the real conditions of the crisis: 'while he may have the advantage of familiar terrain we have the advantage of military training'. The words carry no useful meaning.

Spencer remains convinced that Caspar is leading them all to disaster, calling him 'a dumb asshole'. The corporal's reply marks a break from formal modes of address, moving to the direct assertion of authority:

Caspar: Now you listen to me Spencer and you listen good (.) now tomorrow morning we're heading North with the prisoner (1) the man who killed Crawford Poole (.) the man whose buddies killed Tyrone Cribbs (.) in case you've forgotten Spencer they were friends of ours (4) Now let's all get unpacked and bedded down (1) No fire tonight

The course of action Caspar selects is not based on a logical appraisal of their common dilemma. He selects instead an emotional reinforcement for his decision: 'in case you've forgotten Spencer they were friends of ours'.

In *Southern Comfort*, military genres of speech are shown breaking down very early in the narrative. It is significant that the sergeant is more willing to speak in the 'language' of the patrol members, while the corporal, who has less authority, finds refuge in more formal expression.

Resolution: the rejection of speech

When the two survivors, who are unable to speak French, find a temporary and precarious refuge in a Cajun village, the barriers of language mean that they are only able to guess at the meaning of the events around them. Our sense that the two men should flee the village with all possible haste is expressed by the initial difference which exists between Hardin and Spencer. Spencer, enjoying the Cajun party, assumes that they have found safety. Hardin comes to the right conclusion, that they are in grave danger, but only because he misinterprets the significance of two nooses, brought out to hang up the pigs which are about to be killed. (The pigs symbolise the peril which faces the men.) Hardin responds to the emotional 'atmosphere' which he senses, and this feeling proves more reliable than a purely rational assessment of their situation.

At the end of the film, the efficient military action which had constantly eluded the patrol is acted out by the two survivors. The fact that these two combine their efforts so effectively is an interesting comment on the worth of the verbal interaction and instruction which went before. It is also a comment on the value of the military outlook: they only survive by abandoning military pretension and resuming their role as intelligent civilians. In the last struggle, Spencer and Hardin communicate without speaking, relying, it seems, on a sort of sixth sense. Argument is finally unnecessary, and they kill their tormentors without exchanging a word.

Speech cultures?

Where discourse fails to reflect the reality of events, it becomes redundant. In cases where no immediate or dire consequences grow from incompetence, discrepancies between what is said and what is really going on may simply be the cause of humour, encouraging the growth of subcultures (the workplace is a good example). Official language may remain an irritant, but without either alternative structures of power or the kind of breakdown which follows a dire emergency, different 'speech cultures' will simply continue to exist side by side, as indeed they do in the early parts of *Southern Comfort*.

Social attributes of 'stars'

There have been many attempts to explain the '**star**' phenomenon, in which an actor attains an exalted status and a persona which is recognised across the globe. In 1960, Morin described how the function of film stars changes over time. At the beginning of the sound era, Morin argued that stars were transformed from an embodiment of society's ideals to 'identification figures', representing the more ordinary or typical aspects of individual behaviour. Tyler, writing in 1970, decided that they provided a point of religious identification, in an age when traditional religious belief had declined.

Writing in 'Social attributes of American movie stars', Emanuel Levy argues that this kind of explanation is inadequate. Using the 'Motion Picture Herald Poll', a survey of the top stars in the American film industry which has appeared yearly since 1932, Levy examines the 'social attributes' of American movie stars. The *physical appearance, age, acting abilities* and *screen image* or *persona* are all taken as indicators of the **social attributes** of a total of 129 actors over the period 1932–84. Using these indicators, Levy discovered a great deal about the values espoused by US society.

For example, male actors were usually possessed of dark looks, while the preferred image of female stars was blonde. Only two male stars in the entire period studied were blond, and they attempted to offset this 'disadvantage' by taking roles which emphasised their toughness and masculinity. Overall, however, physical attractiveness is only one element which goes to make 'star quality'. A distinctive screen image is of great importance in establishing individuals as stars.

Levy uses the concept of 'statements' to explore the durability of individual actors. Within the film narrative, certain 'statements' of a social nature are made. These must be recognised as socially relevant by an audience. Where an actor appears in a role which suits his or her persona, in a film whose 'statement' seems apposite to the values of the age, the status of 'star' is often attained.

Social values and the Cinema

The **values** of certain sections of society are reflected in mainstream Cinema. The 'strong individual protagonist' (Levy, p. 259) is a central feature of all Hollywood productions. The representation of the events of a single individual's life form the major concern of such narratives. In addition to *individualism*, the most important 'cultural qualities' which characterise the most important stars are described by Levy (p. 259) as follows:

- **common sense** – practical as opposed to theoretical knowledge;
- **pragmatism** – a realistic attitude to life;
- **resourcefulness** – the ability to mobilise resources to accomplish goals;
- **self-assurance** – explained as a strong belief in one's powers of survival and self-improvement;
- **determination** – the capacity to fight for one's values;
- **control over individual fate** – the ability to direct the course of one's own life;

- **optimism** – Levy believes this includes a willingness to defer immediate rewards for the sake of the achievement of future goals.

It is usually the case that the male American screen hero possesses a set of values which run counter to those held by his on-screen rivals. He also enjoys some freedom from conventional forms of behaviour. The 'anti-establishment' stance of many cinematic characters is, however, rather more complex than Levy suggests.

The hero is often in a position of authority; quite often he is a police officer or someone else who has access to power and information. His 'anti-authoritarianism' is often defined through a clash with higher ranks. He is usually 'taken off the case', or he 'turns in his badge' and pursues the villain on his own. His actions towards those he perceives as villainous, which are entirely authoritarian, marks out the contradictory nature of his position and the confused message offered to the audience.

Despite their shortcomings, however, these roles do allow the exploration of a common feature of our society. The bureaucratic constraints placed upon the population are symbolically broken in cinematic narrative. The problem lies in the fact that rebellion is shown to be individual, chiefly masculine, and confined to the ranks of those who have some power to affect the destinies of others.

Narrative in the Cinema

The word '**narrative**' has more than one meaning; it may refer to either the end product of storytelling and the comprehension of a story, or to its process of construction. In *Narrative Comprehension and Film* (1992) Edward Branigan advances the theory that narrative is 'one of the important ways we perceive our environment'. This involves (p. 1):

'telling ourselves mini-stories about that environment based on stories already told. Making narratives is a strategy for making our world of experiences and desires intelligible. It is a fundamental way of organising data.'

He puts forward a strong argument that narrative should not be seen as exclusively *fictional* but instead should be contrasted to other non-narrative ways of assembling and understanding data. For Branigan, narrative does not belong merely to the Cinema, or to fiction, but to every aspect of daily life. It appears in his view as another form of cognitive processing (p. 3):

'a perceptual activity that organises data into a special pattern which represents and explains experience'.

Narrative concerns not just 'space', in the sense that things are identified as belonging to a particular context, but also time. It is therefore also 'a way of organising spatial and temporal data into a cause–effect chain of events with a beginning, middle, and end'. Wallace Martin (Branigan, *Narrative Comprehension and Film*, p. 10) believed that:

> 'Identification of universal narrative patterns would seem to tell us not just about literature but about the nature of the mind and/or universal features of culture.'

Logical transformations in narrative

In all narratives, some person, object, or situation (Branigan, *Narrative Comprehension and Film,* p. 4) 'undergoes a particular type of change'. Branigan insists that narrative is a way of *experiencing* an event, whatever that event may be; a group of sentences, pictures, gestures or dance movements. The structure of narrative, which Branigan describes as 'beginning, middle, and end', is 'not contained in the discrete elements, say, the individual sentences of a novel'. Instead, it is 'signified in the overall relationships established among the totality of the elements, or sentences'.

According to this theory, the first sentence of a novel is not itself 'the beginning' but only acquires that status in *relationship* to other sentences. This may sound odd; after all, the words which form the start of a novel do appear at the beginning of the narrative. Branigan, however, wishes to emphasise the idea that the elements themselves are *not* the pattern. The essential part of a narrative is, according to this theory, that part which provides the most vital information, which allows one to read forwards and backwards from that point. The beginning of a narrative sequence does not provide this type of information.

Existents and Processes

Existents are those elements which assert the existence of something, while **processes** are elements which indicate a change or process. According to Branigan, typical existents are 'characters and settings' while typical processes 'are actions of persons and forces of nature'. He notes that (p. 6):

> 'the *actual process* of moving from ignorance to knowledge will be of central importance to our experience of narrative'.

What qualifies as a narrative and what does not? An understanding of narrative seems to be quite easy to obtain. Narratives require a link between one element and another, where one event is caused by another. The following are cited by Branigan as examples of narrative:

(1b) The king died, and then the queen died of grief [causality].
(2b) Shirley was good and then she drifted into a life of crime.

It is perhaps more difficult to imagine a 'non-narrative' form. Examples of 'non-narratives' given by Branigan are (p. 11):

(1a) The king died and then the queen died [chronology].
(2a) Mary ate an apple.

Another example given is the rhyme 'Roses are red', which is described as a *catalogue* rather than a narrative, because no temporal (time-based) logic works in the elements of the verse. It reads more like a statement than a story:

'Roses are red
Violets are blue
Sugar is sweet
And so are you.'

This does not mean to say that catalogue systems do not exist within narrative texts.

Branigan speaks of narrative as possessing a 'dual focus', where one focus is composed of a chronological and causal progression (the 'syntagmatic') while the other is composed of a multitude of binary oppositions among elements that are 'static' and that exist outside the time of the causal progression (the 'paradigmatic'). Any textual element (a shot, an attribute of character, a theme, and so on) which works in a paradigmatic way makes a pair by suggesting a *parallel* with something else, either through a similarity or in contrast.

Hidden processes

Stephen Heath (see Branigan, p. 10) demonstrated how some elements of a film 'escape' the narrative structure and become what he calls a *residuum*, a sort of left-over which reveals the 'hidden psychic and ideological processes at work in the text'. Narrative is the result of these processes, and is yet also an explicit attempt to master them and to cast them into a formal order. For Heath, the causality of narrative events in a plot is a pretext for larger transformations which point to *everyday beliefs* about the social world.

Heath is less interested in discovering a stable logical structure than in uncovering systems of belief, modes of persuasion and values which are not 'logical' in the way conceived of by theorists like Tzvetan Todorov. Todorov argued that the structure of the fictional environment is marked by a series of stages, from a state of equilibrium, through disruption, to recognition of the disruptive event, to an attempt at 'repair' or recovery, to a final phase in which a return is made to some kind of equilibrium (see Chapter 1).

The limits of logic

Branigan attempts to provide a description of narrative which avoids a strictly 'logical' perspective but which does not jettison the aim of making an analysis of the *cognitive* processes, which he believes are (p. 12) 'active in a perceiver during his or her comprehension of narrative in an actual situation'. He searches for an 'overall pattern' in such perception, choosing to study two types of memory: **intermediate-term** memory, known as 'working' memory, and **long-term** memory. These two categories are supposed not to be directly experienced by the perceiver. He goes on to assert that human subjects' memory of narratives is dictated by what he calls 'specific methods' which are used in the hunt for 'global properties'.

Cognition and access: back to schemas

The classifications which a person imposes on material at the time of its processing appear to limit the ways in which the material can be subsequently accessed. The full-blooded attachment to a cognitive model may be seen when Branigan describes a schema as (p. 13):

> 'an arrangement of knowledge *already possessed* by a perceiver that is used to predict and classify new sensory data'.

Here, emotional approaches to communication and knowledge retention are not investigated.

Branigan goes on to argue that one of the most important facts about narrative is (p. 14):

> 'that perceivers tend to *remember* a story in terms of *categories of information stated as propositions, interpretations, and summaries* rather than remembering the way the story is actually presented or its surface features'.

This would seem reasonable, until he argues that 'it requires great effort to recall the exact words used in a novel or the exact sequence of shots, angles, lighting, etc. used in a film'. The reason he advances for this belief is that features of the 'surface structure' of texts are stored only in so-called 'push down' stacks, where new elements are continually being added at the boundary, 'pushing the older elements farther away'. This attachment to a strict separation between 'working memory' and 'long-term memory' leads Branigan to under-estimate the ability of an audience to remember the precise details of narrative exposition:

> 'When we say that we remember a film, we do not normally mean that we remember the angle from which it was viewed in the movie theatre, or the exact angles assumed by the camera in a scene.'

This is exactly what we do at times remember. While it is true that we tend to recall 'clusters' of scenes in a film, rather than the sequential order in which they *occurred*, we often recall quite detailed aspects of those scenes. The idea that a perceiver will attempt to create 'logical' connections among data in order to match the general categories of the 'schema' seems to move too closely to a cognitive, 'information-processing' view of film.

Critical theory and communication

The latter part of Chapter 1 provided an introduction to the major currents or traditions of inquiry which have affected the study of communication. Types of social and critical theory reviewed in that section included *functionalism*, *interactionism*, *Marxism*, *feminism*, *structuralism*, *post-structuralism* and *post-modernism*. Perhaps the key to understanding these different (yet often related philosophies) is the study of **modernity**.

Modernity

The term '**modern**' refers to an era which began around 1500. Some social theorists think that modern times include the present, while others believe that we have recently entered a new period, the 'postmodern'.

What marks the modern era from earlier periods of history? Peter Wagner (*A Sociology of Modernity*, p. 3) notes that it is actually:

'immensely difficult to both exactly define the characteristics of modern societies and to show when they actually broke with traditional social formations'.

The growth of technology of many different kinds, from the printing press to the internal combustion engine, is clearly one important factor which has shaped the modern world. Such change does not simply alter the 'efficiency' of machinery or the speed at which events take place; it affects the way whole societies function. This, in turn, means that human beings must adapt to the challenge of new *ideas* about the world. In this sense, the condition of modernity is a shared *state of mind*.

Berman, writing in 1982 (see Harvey, *The Condition of Postmodernity*, 1990), called modernity (p. 10):

'a mode of vital experience – experience of space and time, of the self and others, of life's possibilities and perils – that is shared by men and women all over the world today . . . to be modern is to find ourselves in an environment that promises adventure, power, joy, growth, transformation of ourselves and the world – and at the same time threatens to destroy everything we have, everything we know, everything we are'.

It is clear from this passage that change has both good and bad effects. It is important to remember that, with every new wave of change, some groups or classes of people are called upon to pay the 'social price' for the consolidation of the new order. To take an obvious example, industrial 'restructuring' appears to cause widespread job loss. Furthermore, some groups of people (sometimes referred to as the 'underclass') seem to have become permanently excluded from the full benefits of 'modernity'. We should realise that development is always uneven, in the sense that new technologies may be concentrated in specific social or geographical areas, while elsewhere other, less 'advanced' modes of life may prevail.

Modernity as a contradictory force

All things considered, modernity exists in a state of contradiction. For example, Goran Therborn's theory of subjection/qualification, examined in Chapter 2, demonstrated the problems caused by the state's need for subjects who are capable of independent work, yet who will remain under the ultimate control of authority. Anthony Giddens, writing in *The Consequences of Modernity* (1993), also contrasts the positive and negative features of the modern condition (p. 7):

> 'The development of modern social institutions and their worldwide spread has created vastly greater opportunities for human beings to enjoy a secure and rewarding existence than any type of pre-modern system. But modernity also has a sombre side, which has become very apparent in the present century.'

Peter Wagner, in *A Sociology of Modernity* (p. xiii) expresses the ambivalence of modernity in the following terms:

> 'it is becoming less possible for individuals or groups of human beings to escape the reach of modern institutions. At the same time, everybody who makes successful use of these institutions can expect to extend his, or more rarely, her reach.'

Here, Wagner recognises that the benefits of modern life are not equally available to men and women. In Wagner's view, the (p. xiv) 'transformation of the human self during modernity should be seen as a . . . process of both liberation and disciplinisation'.

In sum, many commentators argue that modernity has produced a world whose pace and scope of change have far outstripped that found in earlier societies, creating new opportunities for some groups and individuals, at the expense of restrictions on human freedom. In many ways, the extent of 'progress' has also outstripped the ability of human subjects to understand how their society functions. The complexity of modern institutions is often used to hide processes which are distinctly undemocratic.

Modernism

Modernism refers to a variety of social, political, economic and cultural 'movements' and ideas which began in the seventeenth century and which continue to exert vast influence upon life. Modernist movements depend upon the existence of an 'advanced' society with an industrial base and great productive power. In such a society, there will be highly developed (if unequal and distorted) relations between people. Some currents of modernism, such as futurism, celebrated the energy and power of the machine age, while others – Dada is one example – attacked the militarism which re-emerged in Europe after the First World War.

Capitalism and modernism

David Harvey (*The Condition of Postmodernity*) finds in the work of Karl Marx one of the most thorough descriptions of the creation of modern society. Marx described how **capitalism** had reforged the material conditions of life, uprooting communities, concentrating resources and overcoming material obstacles, in order to produce new social forms. The eventual consequence was a new international order, in which certain nations dominated the globe.

It is, however, the advent of a 'money community' which Marx identifies as the difference between the modern and pre-industrial eras. 'Real communities' were dissolved, while the money system made all relations between individuals impersonal and objective. Human exchanges became market exchanges, with the money system standing outside human relations yet masking the true nature of social relationships. Marx describes this as the 'fetishism of commodities'.

'The scientific domination of nature'

Harvey (p. 103) points to capitalism's 'highly organised technical and social division of labour', which is one of the 'founding principles of capitalist modernisation'. He goes on to describe modernism as '**the scientific domination of nature**' and 'the development of rational forms of social organisation'. Although *rational* forms of social life were brought about, this does not mean that they were fair or equitable.

The positive side of the modernist project appeared in the form of enlightened thinking, freedom from superstition, and movements towards social and political equality. The French revolution clearly emerged from the modern or rationalist project. The disadvantage, identified amongst others by writers who belonged to the Frankfurt School (see Chapters 1 and 3), was the tendency of some forms of rational organisation, particularly those employed by nation-states, to provide the conditions for the increasing domination of the human subject.

Culture and modernism

In **cultural** terms, modernism is not necessarily a complete or coherent philosophy so much as a general description of a number of movements and tendencies which emerged in the industrial age. David Harvey calls it (see *The Condition of Postmodernity*, p. 116) 'a troubled and fluctuating aesthetic response to conditions of modernity'.

The idea of a modernist *response* to prevailing conditions is important. In the world of art and aesthetics, the influence of feverish industrial innovation was particularly marked, but as David Harvey argues (p. 23):

'the modernism that emerged before the First World War was more of a reaction to the new conditions of production (the machine, the factory, urbanization), circulation (the new systems of transport and communications), and consumption (the rise of mass markets, advertising, mass fashion) than it was a pioneer in the production of such changes'.

Modernist movements have occurred within religion, art, architecture, literature, politics and a number of other social and expressive forms. These 'modernisms' are often described as being devoted to progress, and are usually thought to display some degree of allegiance to rationality and the benefits of a technocratic society. However, the concept of modernism in aesthetics is sometimes attractive simply because it suggests opposition to retrogressive or old-fashioned ideas. In modernism as a whole, we witness the standardisation of knowledge and production, and the forging of new conditions of life which have the *appearance* at least of progress and improvement.

Critical voices

Some writers, like Anthony Giddens and Peter Wagner, have criticised the construction of over-simplified accounts of modernism. Others have noticed the tendency to confuse modernism as 'critical theory' with modernism as 'historical epoch'. Joanna Hodge, for example, in an essay called 'Feminism and Postmodernism' (see *The Problems of Modernity*, p. 89), argues that as:

' "structuralism" and "modernism" are primarily terms picking out respectively particular kinds of theoretical enquiry and particular kinds of artistic practice, it is far from self-evident that they can be used ... as terms designating temporal epochs, which can then be deemed to have come to an end'.

Hodge's point is of great importance: it can be confusing to use a single term to describe critical theory and artistic production, while also using it to refer to a period of history.

Postmodernism

The prefix 'post', as we saw in Chapter 1, refers to an event or thing which comes *after* something else. **Postmodernism** would therefore appear, at first sight, to be a period of history which has followed and perhaps even replaced modernism. However, Joanna Hodge's argument (quoted above) that terms are often used to refer to both critical movements and historical epochs should make us question the wisdom of allowing 'postmodernism' to be used as a temporal 'marker', especially if it suggests that other currents of development have somehow come to an end.

Occasionally, postmodern theory seems to encourage a rather arrogant attitude amongst its proponents, based upon its claim to be the 'latest' (and even 'the last') development in social thought. At the same time, the issue is further complicated by the fact that the postmodernist outlook is generally opposed to the construction of theories which recognise distinct or historical 'eras'; this implies that a 'postmodern era' is a contradiction in terms!

Anthony Giddens (see *The Consequences of Modernity*, p. 1) describes the 'dazzling variety of terms' which are used to describe the so-called 'transition' from modernity to 'postmodern' or 'post-industrial' society. There is a strong case, in fact, for arguing that it makes no sense to set modernism and postmodernism against each other, as though they are two opposing forces. David Harvey (*The Condition of Postmodernity*, p. 116) sees the latter 'as a particular kind of crisis within the former'.

The postmodernist critique

While some writers doubt there is such a thing as the 'postmodern condition' and hold that, if it does exist, it is (in the words of Kuan-Hsing Chen's essay in Corner *et al.*, *Postmodernism*, p. 37), 'plural, disunified, multiple and contra-dictory', the main features of the postmodern **critique** of established philosophical thought are quite easy to describe.

In the first place, despite the diversity of postmodernist theory, a major preoccupation of its adherents has been the rejection of the legacy of the Enlightenment. The Enlightenment was that period in history, beginning in the seventeenth century, which saw the growth of rationalism and a belief in progress, free will and human equality. The philosophical traditions associated with this era include all those which accept the idea that it is possible to create a reasonably accurate picture of the social world.

Some Enlightenment thought comes from the political left, while other currents tend more to the right. According to the postmodern perspective, however, all shared a tendency to construct 'grand narratives' or 'overall conceptions of history' (Giddens, *Sociology*, p. 665), which are ultimately misleading since they ignore the fractured and provisional nature of social formations.

The postmodern critique also involves the notion that the human subject has suffered an assault from the vast amount of information which is produced by the mass media. According to this view, instead of helping to enlighten people, such information tends to destroy meaning; at the same time, the code used for transmission becomes of more interest than its reference to the real. This aspect of the postmodern outlook ultimately suggests that human subjectivity is invaded and becomes 'objectified'.

Such an idea relies entirely upon accepting the notion that the audience for media messages is both passive and susceptible to the supposed machinations of the mass media. Jean Baudrillard, for example, in an essay of 1980 (*The Implosion of Meaning in the Media*, p. 142), argued that 'the objective of information is always to circulate meaning, to subjugate the masses to meaning'. In philosophical terms, postmodernism is known for its opposition to theories of knowledge which propose a clear distinction between subject (the aware or 'thinking' human individual) and object (the non-aware external thing which is 'thought about'). The 'pervasive' nature of the media message seems to provide a convenient reason for such a development.

Like modernism, however, postmodernism appears in a variety of guises. In the long run, we should remember that the thinkers who contribute to postmodern theory hold a variety of views and do not form an organised 'school' as such. In fact, a number of 'post-structuralist' thinkers, such as Derrida and Foucault (see Chapter 1 and the section on 'Post-structuralism' below), are often described as belonging to the postmodernist project.

Lyotard and 'meta-narratives'

Postmodernism's distrust of '**meta-narratives**' may be explored through the work of Jean-François Lyotard, once a professor of philosophy in France, who produced a book called *The Postmodern Condition* in 1979. In this volume, he used the concept of 'meta-narratives' to describe those public discourses which provide 'credible' reasons for the continued existence of the social order. 'Meta-narratives' might consist of those internally consistent 'stories' which seek to persuade people to have faith in science or religion or some form of political conservatism. In Lyotard's opinion, the use of 'meta-narratives' in the postmodern 'age' have become irrelevant because the conditions of life no longer support them; such discourses boil down, therefore, to no more than 'language games', where no single theory is capable of explaining language in its totality.

Anthony Giddens (*The Consequences of Modernity*, p. 5) argues that the most influential 'narrative' of the modern age is the 'evolutionary narrative', which he believes Lyotard has not fully considered. According to Giddens, a revision of the evolutionary narrative should not lead us to argue that history has 'ended', nor should it (p. 6):

'imply that all is chaos or that an infinite number of ... "histories" can be written. There are definite episodes of historical transition ... whose character can be identified and about which generalisations can be made.'

The puzzling issue here is why postmodernism itself did not appear earlier in the century, since the conditions appeared favourable. Perhaps the real reason for the rise of the movement lies in the collapse of political optimism which followed the winding-down of 1970s radicalism.

Baudrillard: free from logic?

Jean Baudrillard, who began his writing career in 1968, has had a considerable impact on contemporary thought. His books are not 'academic' as such (he has never held a full-time academic post) but have proved influential, probably due to the boldness of the claims they have made.

Baudrillard began by making a departure from Marx's distinction between the 'use value' and the 'exchange value' of an object, where 'use value' is the extent to which an object can satisfy human needs, and 'exchange value' is the market value placed on the object. Baudrillard advanced the idea of 'sign value', where the object has the power to *signify* or mean certain things to people. We might say, for example, that a Coca-Cola bottle has acquired a 'sign value', that it signifies a certain lifestyle over and above its use as a drink or its value as a commercial product.

By the mid-1970s, Baudrillard had taken this further, arguing that the 'code' (whether semiotic, digital or binary) for any real object had become so pervasive that the code, and not the thing itself, had come to dominate social life. The end result was a state of 'hyper-reality', where the code seemed to appear more 'real' than the real itself.

Opposed to what Stuart Sim calls 'the supposedly constraining effects of logic' (see p. 33 of *Beyond Aesthetics*), postmodernism's chief theorists have produced texts which are either epigrammatic or notoriously complex. An example of the first tendency is certainly found in the writings of Baudrillard, who remains uninhibited by the demands of conventional scholarship. John Lechte, for example (in *Fifty Key Contemporary Thinkers*, p. 235), notices that Baudrillard:

'rarely defines his key terms in anything like an exhaustive fashion, the sense being largely derived from the context, and from the view that Baudrillard accepts the developments in semiotics and other fields as given'.

Accepting anything in the field of semiotics as 'given' is probably a risky business.

Baudrillard is chiefly concerned to provide 'insights' into the 'simulated' reality we supposedly inhabit. This is a fairly typical example (see *Cool Memories*, 1987):

'Snow is no longer a gift from on high. It falls precisely at those places designated as winter resorts.'

Where Baudrillard is celebrated, it is often for his 'poetic' use of language, though the statements he produces appear to lack both the coherence of good prose and the emotional force of the best poetry. However, Baudrillard's theories of 'hyper-reality' and the 'simulacra' (which depend on the idea that postmodern society, especially the American version, has lost sight of the real) are likely to experience a new lease of life if they are taken up by the advocates of new technologies like 'virtual reality' (see Chapter 4).

Baudrillard: the final act?

Christopher Norris's hostility to Baudrillard in *What's Wrong with Post-modernism?* may be explained partly as an attempt to disassociate more serious writers like Derrida (see the section on 'Post-structuralism' below) from the suspicion that Baudrillard represents the logical outcome of postmodernist thought.

Reviewing his *Cool Memories* of 1990, Ruth Barcan (see *Textual Practice*, summer 1993), argued that his observations, while 'falling short of being evocative and provocative', remain 'at best distasteful'. Some openly misogynist attitudes seem to run through Baudrillard's later work. Paragraphs like the following may serve as an example (p. 68 of *Cool Memories*):

'Women can get together in their millions, but they will never produce that image which can only come from elsewhere. If women don't accept being dreamt of any more, including the phantasm of violence, then they will lose even their sexual pleasure and their rights ... Man must continue to decide what is the ideal woman.'

Baudrillard employs what Barcan calls a 'tactical use of rhetoric', distancing himself from his own statements and thus pre-empting criticism. If language is only self-referential, and we get no closer to the real meaning behind it, then Baudrillard is able to slip away from our judgement. In other places, he makes a stand against explanation (p. 201):

'They say that stupidity is a crime, but it seems to me that explanation is the real crime.'

His attitude to the state of contemporary life always stresses the stupe-faction and defeat he appears to finds within himself and which he obviously considers general (p. 44):

'We are becoming like cats ... enjoying an indifferent domesticity. Nice and snug in the "social" ... our half-closed eyes now seek little other than the peaceful parade of television pictures.'

We may ask if this picture really matches our experience of the social.

In Baudrillard's hands, postmodernism seems to celebrate its own confusions while still wishing to retain all the benefits of a privileged academic discourse. Michael Billig, in an essay on Baudrillard (see *After Postmodernism*, p. 164), argues that his writing has become 'de-populated', that his style:

> 'resembles that of much contemporary cultural and ideological analysis … the cultural artifacts are portrayed, but not the lives of those who use, purchase and are affected by such artifacts'.

Barcan, also writing from a critical perspective, concludes her review by referring to the realities which Baudrillard denies: 'despite the death of Meaning, meanings are still produced and still have consequences in a world that doggedly insists on existing'.

Postmodernism: positive uses?

Chapter 1 acknowledged that postmodernism has the potential for creating positive effects, based upon what David Harvey (*The Condition of Postmodernity*, p. 113) calls its 'concern for difference, for the complexity and nuances of interests, cultures, places'. Stuart Sim in *Beyond Aesthetics* argues that postmodern theory is useful in that it demonstrates the weakness of 'total' systems of thought.

Joanna Hodge (in *The Problems of Modernity*, p. 87) identifies 'a strong connection between radical feminism and the postmodernist … rejections of time, narrativity and historical process'. Hodge notes that women are not encouraged to identify with the social subject which lies at the centre of much political and social theory, and are thus excluded from the traditional but sham concept of (p. 99) the 'sexually undifferentiated human being'.

Hodge believes that established 'Enlightenment' theories in fact retain (p. 87) 'a male figure at their centre'. Some aspects of postmodernism therefore provide an opportunity for the 'de-centred' female subject to be heard, though Hodge acknowledges that, in other ways, postmodernism still remains locked within the established system of patriarchal philosophy.

Chen (see Corner *et al*. *Postmodernism*) also believes that a 'critical postmodernism' has developed, which offers, in common with cultural studies, the potential to challenge the establishment through postmodernism's willingness to listen to (p. 37) 'the oppressed voices of history'.

In other words, postmodernism's criticism of various philosophies may allow the development of alternative versions of history which were previously suppressed. David Tetzlaff (see 'Divide and conquer') notes that it is nevertheless difficult to find (p. 14) 'any concrete ideas about how postmodern culture might be brought to aid a progressive challenge to dominant social structures'.

The limitations of postmodernism?

It is clear that postmodernist polemicists have been particularly concerned to attack liberal and leftist outlooks, but seem to have failed to mount a coherent challenge to the 'new world order', which exerts far greater influence upon contemporary existence. In fact, many writers have argued that the 'postmodern project' actually supports the 'post-industrial' strategies of governments and large corporations. Harvey describes the situation as follows (*The Condition of Postmodernity*, p. 116):

> 'Postmodernism has us accepting the reifications and partitionings, actually celebrating the activity of masking and cover-up, all the fetishisms of locality, place, or social grouping, while denying the kind of meta-theory which can grasp the political/economic processes (money flows, international divisions of labour, financial markets, and the like) that are becoming ever more universalising in their depth, intensity, reach and power over daily life.'

This passage suggests that increasingly powerful forces are able to disguise their operations by encouraging the fragmentation of social life, while postmodernism celebrates the state of disorder.

The postmodern interest in diversity is certainly very different to the practice of those left-wing political movements and parties, such as Lotta Continua in late 1970s Italy, which sought to unite the 'fragments' of various social groups in a common programme. It is not surprising, therefore, that theorists like Sim (see *Beyond Aesthetics*) are convinced that postmodernism posesses only a 'surface radicalism'.

The weakness of postmodern theory

One of the interesting contradictions which lie at the heart of the 'postmodern project' is the tension between its hostility towards 'grand narratives' of all kinds (Marxism, liberalism, socialism and so on) and the choice it faces once it has attacked Enlightenment thinking. What is the next step: Derrida's call to 'write', Lyotard's advocacy of individual 'svelteness' (a sort of small-scale, ironic resistance – see below), or Baudrillard's retreat into misogyny and the 'hyper-real'?

Postmodernists are certainly correct when they draw attention to the fact that the great philosophies of liberation have often ended in outright repression. This has happened partly because philosophies like Marxism, which oppose 'individualism', were taken up by authoritarian groups which repressed individual and collective aspirations in the name of a greater good which never materialised. Some postmodernists, however, appear hostile not only to theories of collectivity, but also to collective action itself. This provides the starkest possible contrast between postmodernism as a critique of 'grand theory', and other movements which have shared some of its antipathy to centralised power.

Libertarian critics of authoritarianism

It is quite common to read criticisms of postmodernism's weakness as coherent theory (which it, in turn, claims not to attempt), but no one seems to have noticed that its attack on the negative tendencies of 'grand theory' and its hostility to authoritarianism have actually come very late in the day. The earliest twentieth-century attacks on centralist politics, inflexible theory and the dehumanising scale of modernism began among a number of political activists who are now all but forgotten. These people went under a variety of titles – anarchists, syndicalists, socialist-feminists, left-communists, **libertarians**, and so on – but taken together they provide an alternative intellectual tradition which stands apart from both Leninist doctrine and the rhetoric of capitalism.

As early as April 1918, for example (see Brinton, *The Bolsheviks and Workers' Control*, p. 39), the Bolshevik Osinsky criticised Lenin for his increasingly centralist attitude to workers' control in the newly 'liberated' factories:

> 'Socialism and socialist organisation will be set up by the proletariat itself, or they will not be set up at all: something else will be set up – state capitalism.'

A year before this was written, a rank-and-file worker called Belushov attacked the centralised planning carried out by the Bolshevik leadership, on the grounds that it destroyed local initiative. Real workers' control was the only solution (p. 31):

> 'The only way out remaining to the workers is to take the factories into their own hands and manage them.'

Spain and Germany in particular offered models of left-wing organisation which contrasted strongly with the Leninist orthodoxy and its highly manipulative use of the working class as a 'stage army'. Spanish anarchism and the growth of parties like the POUM (Workers' Party of Marxist Unification) in the 1930s allowed the creation of libertarian organisations in agriculture, industry and the armed forces. In Germany, a current of 'council communism' grew in strength, culminating in the foundation of the Left Radical Communist Workers' Party in 1920. Its leaders became convinced that the Russian state was soviet in name only, and that the workers had little control over their own destiny. Its most advanced theorist, Anton Pannekoek, declared that Lenin's historic function had been to change Russia from an agricultural state to an industrial one, through the use of dictatorship (see D.A. Smart, *Pannekoek and*

Gorter's Marxism). Pannekoek and his close associate Herman Gorter continued to agitate for 'council communism', which resulted in the foundation of the 100,000-strong General Workers' Union of Germany, an organisation which posessed a *federal* and not a centralist structure.

Postmodernism: wilful ignorance?

Postmodernism stands outside the libertarian tradition and remains suspicious of practical collectivity; many writers associated with this perspective seem to prefer individual resistance (Lyotard, for example). It is possible that a general neglect of the libertarian tradition has allowed some postmodernists to characterise all leftist philosophy as equally repressive.

For instance, Jean-François Lyotard's hostility to what he calls 'economic [and] political liberalism' and 'the various Marxisms' grows from his belief that these currents of thought are not free from 'the suspicion of crimes against mankind' (see Sim, p. 107). My argument here is that such a position is only possible because of the genuine or wilful ignorance shown towards alternative currents of thought.

Sim describes Lyotard's position as a 'kind of protest politics', but it appears to be resistance based upon the idea of the 'svelte' human subject. 'Svelteness' is a theory of subtle and 'decentred' resistance at the margins of the social world, in which the individual is able to give authority the slip, as it were, by (in Foucault's terms) not even knowing what he or she will do or think next.

Lyotard argues that (in Sim, p. 114):

'The intelligentsia's function should not be to tell the truth and save the world, but to will the power to play out, listen to and tell stories.'

Yet Lyotard's own patience even to tell his own stories seems exhausted (Sim, p. 3):

'When you're trying to think something in philosophy, you don't care less about the addressee, you don't give a damn. Someone comes along and says, "I don't understand a word of what you say, of what you write:" and I reply, "I don't give a damn. That's not the problem. You're not my judge in this matter." '

At this point, the study of communication ends; if the audience is irrelevant, why publish anything?

Structuralism

Chapter 1 introduced **structuralism** by describing it as a method of critical inquiry which investigates *structures* and the laws which govern them. Essentially, structuralism examines the *relationship* between the internal elements of any phenomenon or event: a text, a society, an equation and so on. Its appearance in the mid-1960s caused considerable controversy. As I indicated above, structures exist in a variety of social forms, but it seemed easier to accept their presence in scientific disciplines like mathematics than in the human sciences and the arts. Nevertheless, the work of critics such as Genette, Barthes, Levi-Strauss, Foucault and Althusser introduced structuralist thought into the study of literary and philosophical narrative, popular culture, anthropology, power and politics.

Structuralist analysis in operation

A useful example of structuralism in practice may be found in the analysis of the literary text. In Terry Eagleton's words (*Literary Theory*, p. 94): 'the [elements] do not have a 'substantial' meaning, only a 'relational' one'. This means that intrinsic significance is not attached to each event, but is reserved for the action of the whole story.

Eagleton outlines a simple narrative to demonstrate how a structuralist critique might work. A boy leaves home after quarrelling with his father, sets out on a walk in the forest and falls into a deep pit. His father searches for him, finds the pit and looks into it, but cannot see the child until the sun reaches a point directly overhead. The rays of the sun illuminate the boy and the father rescues him. Eagleton remarks that (p. 95):

'A psychoanalytical critic might detect definite hints of the Oedipus complex in it, and show how the child's fall into the pit is a punishment he unconsciously wishes upon himself for the rift with his father ... perhaps ... a symbolic recourse to his mother's womb. A humanist critic might read it as a poignant dramatization of the difficulties implicit in human relationships.'

A structuralist critic, however, would 'schematize the story in a diagrammatic form'. This idea might seem quite strange, but is really quite straightforward:

'The first unit of signification, "boy quarrels with father", might be rewritten as "low rebels against high". The boy's walk through the forest is a movement along a horizontal axis, in contrast to the vertical axis "low/high" and could be indexed as "middle".'

Equilibrium is restored between 'high' and 'low' at the end of the tale.

In structuralism, there is no need to go beyond the text to discover meaning, since it resides in the relationship between the units within the work itself. A strict structuralist approach would not need to concern itself with *content* so much as *form*. As Chapter 1 argued, an important feature of the structuralist approach is that it does not attempt to estimate the *value* of what is studied but only the structure; similar events or characters may be substituted for the original elements, and the same basic meanings will be generated.

Structuralism and language

The investigation of **language**, in the structuralist sense, is an *abstract* study, one concerned with systems and structures. We may remember the distinction made by Ferdinand de Saussure between the temporal and the spatial plane of language, the first of these being **diachronic** and the second **synchronic**.

In America, Leonard Bloomfield was as influential as was Saussure in Europe. Bloomfield was interested in grammar while Saussure was more concerned with the process of *signification*, the creation of meaning by individual linguistic units. One point in Bloomfield's favour was that he looked at larger units of meaning than Saussure did, though he still confined his investigations to the sentence. Bloomfield noted that there was a problem in trying to establish generalizations about language (see John Sturrock, *Structuralism*, p. 7):

'Features which we think ought to be universal may be absent from the very next language that becomes accessible ... the fact that some features are, at any rate, widespread, is worthy of notice and calls for an explanation.'

His conceptual range was, however, limited by his allegiance to behaviourism, a philosophy which (as mentioned in Chapter 1) confines itself to recording the recurrent patterns in human behaviour, in the belief that only observable phenomena have objective worth.

Langue and parole

Chapters 1 and 3, explained that Saussure divided the study of language into **langue**, the system of rules underlying speech, and **parole**, the speech of individuals. John Sturrock explains the link between this system and the diachronic/synchronic opposition (p. 8):

'This distinction [langue/parole] follows on from that between the synchronic and diachronic axes of language-study: *langue* is the term Saussure gives to the "system" or totality of language stored in the "collective consciousness". The grammar of language, obviously, makes up a large part of that system ... the *langue* thus comprises a full catalogue of the elements of a language together with the rules for their combination. *Parole* on the other hand is the use which individuals make of the total resources of the language they are born into ... If *langue* is structure, then *parole* is an event.'

Noam Chomsky's version of this distinction is *competence* and *performance*. However, Chomsky's 'competence' remains, unlike Saussure's 'langue', the possession of each individual. Chomsky advanced the cause of structural linguistics by suggesting that the human subject itself had an in-born ablty to generate language, and therefore that the mind itself possessed innate structure.

The sign in Saussure's structuralism

The **sign** is made up, in Saussure's system, of the **signifier** (a physical representation of something in the real world) and the **signified** (the mental concept called to mind by the signifier). It is unfortunate that this 'structural' division has led to the idea of a material reality as distinct from a 'non-material' world of concepts.

In Saussure's system, a signifier is something human beings are *able to perceive*, which suggests that it must have some recognisable external form, such as a photograph, drawing, spoken word, written word and so on. If we wished to refer to the mental concept 'tree', then a photograph, drawing, spoken or written word which makes a recognisable reference to the concept 'tree', would count as a signifier. A signifier always makes a reference to something besides itself. The tradition of treating single words as complete signs, sometimes found in linguistics, has definite limitations, since units of meaning or structure are usually much larger. Saussure did, however, recognise the complexity inherent in linguistic signs when he noted the difference between the phonetic and the semantic aspects of meaning.

On the whole, Saussure's approach is too abstract, partly because he is concerned more with systems than with individual usage of language. It is exactly in the individual, social expression of language that the links between signs and our understanding of the real are discovered. Language is meaningful not simply because it constitutes a system of rules, but also because the *form* of its expression, whatever that may be (intonation of speech, style of lettering, non-verbal communication, and so on), combines with the context of use to allow audiences to understand the complexity of the message.

In 1929, the Soviet theorist Voloshinov (see Hodge and Kress, *Language as Ideology*, p. 18), noted that Saussure had rejected the 'speech act – the utterance – as something individual ... [but] the utterance is a social phenomenon'. Voloshinov was concerned to show that 'the social organisation' of the participants in a speech exchange, and the 'immediate conditions of interaction', both contributed to the creation of linguistic or semiotic meaning. This is similar to the theory of *contextual* communication outlined in previous chapters.

Structures of meaning

Saussure did not attempt to 'match' individual linguistic signs and human apprehension of reality, turning his attention instead to **systems** or **structures of meaning**. This move to the study of meaning in general rescued linguistic philosophy from a rather arid project. It was an advance on the previous tradition of thought, which held that the proper study of language was the investigation of the correlation between words and the objects, events and people to which they were supposed to refer.

The long interest in the validity of signs (what I would call '**unit reference**') and the idea that language is a rational construct began with Plato (see Chapter 1), who sought to explain the origin of individual terms by inventing a mythical person called the 'name-maker' who gave everything a fitting and suitable name. Of course, this might seem ridiculous at first sight, but perhaps things have swung too far in the other direction. Modern theorists, as indicated above, are less interested in questions of validity; in fact, some are much more likely to declare that the sign and its referent have only an 'arbitrary' connection (see below).

Is it possible that individual signs have a verifiable connection with the world, emerging in a natural way from human expressiveness, based in turn upon human *response* to a real environment? One theorist who followed the idea of a real connection between language and the world it indictates is Gerard Genette, who accepted Plato's idea that names, in some fundamental but unexplained way, 'imitate' that to which they refer (see *Mimologiques*, 1976). It is quite possible that human expressiveness continually reinvents 'convention'.

The notion of the 'arbitrary'

The term '**arbitrary**' means that the connection between the sign and the thing for which it stands, is supposed really to be no more than a random or accidental event. In Saussurean linguistics, no sign which derives from language is thought to have a real connection with the thing it is meant to represent, whether that is a real object or the shared human *perception* of real objects. The sign is not supposed to be determined by the thing it calls to mind. Sturrock argues (p. 15) that 'the proof of this is the enormous variety of signs to be found in different languages for the same referent [the real thing itself]'. Sturrock notes that a 'horse' in one language is a 'cheval' in another.

In fact, this does not constitute any sort of proof. The term 'horse' in English may well be determined by some *historical* development of emotive or onomatopoeic language (linguistic elements which imitate sounds in the natural world). The fact that French has produced a word based upon a different historical development or *convention* does not imply that either language works upon an arbitrary connection.

The 'arbitrary' is a flaw in Saussure's approach. Calling it 'the first principle of language signs', he made it the centrepiece of his system, but then had to recognise that not all signs were *equally* arbitrary. Some seemed to be more arbitrary than others. His attempted solution is an embarrassment. He decided that some signs could be 'relatively' arbitrary and others 'absolutely' arbitrary. This unhappy compromise brings us straight back to the question of 'unit reference'.

The insistence upon the 'random' nature of the sign has produced a number of attempts at explanation. John Fiske, for example, writing in the first edition of *Introduction to Communication Studies* (1982), says that in Saussurean linguistics (p. 56):

> 'there was no necessary relationship between signifier and signified: the relationship was determined by convention, rule or agreement'.

We are first told that there was no *necessary* relationship. In the next clause, however, we find that convention, rule or agreement seems to provide exactly one type of the 'necessary connection' we have been told does not exist. Since Fiske describes convention as 'the social dimension of signs', why not admit that a form of social convention is a better explanation for the creation of meaning than theories which stress an arbitrary link betwen what is written and said on the one hand, and what is perceived and understood on the other?

Later in the same book, Fiske argues that (p. 60) 'signs with no conventional dimension are purely private and thus do not communicate'.

If 'private' signs do not communicate, they cannot be signs at all! The definition of a sign involves the idea that meaning can be, if necessary, communicated to a recipient or audience.

Peirce

C.S. Peirce, the nineteenth-century logician and the first to use the term 'semiotics' in its current form, believed that there were three types of sign. According to Peirce's scheme, an **icon** is a sign that bears a resemblance to its object, where the 'object' is an idea, artefact, person or event. An **index** is a sign which has a direct, material link with the thing or idea it represents. This suggests that there is some relationship in space and time between index and object, a factor often neglected in indexical theory. An index is usually taken to be 'natural', such as smoke as an index of fire, but the interpretation of an indexical sign depends on the cultural circumstances or context in which it is observed. It is interesting to note that neither icons nor indices are at all 'arbitrary' in their link to their objects or referents.

Finally, a **symbol** is that sort of sign whose connection with the real is a matter of agreement or rule (Peirce calls it a 'law'). In this case, the 'object' indicated by the symbol is not an object in the world, but part of language. This idea, that reference is made to other signifiers, may lead to the post-modernist concept of endless signification. We should also remember that signs established through *convention* are not necessarily static, that conventions are established over time, that they decay, or are broken, and are re-established in different forms by human subjects.

Althusser

Louis Althusser (1918–90) was a Marxist philosopher who, for some forty years, held an academic post at the Ecole Normale Supérieure. He used structuralist approaches in his reading of Marx, believing society to be composed of a number of semi-autonomous structures, including legal, political, cultural and ideological elements. These powerful forces are seen as possessing a degree of independence which is not, however, extended to the human subject. Althusser used the concept of the 'Ideological State Apparatus' to escape the economic determinism of Marxist thought, and to explain how the population could be forced to accept a kind of intellectual and cultural subjugation. At this point, a review of the concept of *ideology* must be undertaken.

Ideology

The traditional Marxist explanation of **ideology** is *forms of consciousness* (or types of understanding) which mould the outlook of human beings. There is a difference, according to Marx, between the interests of people and the 'form in which these interests are experienced'. In other words, this view of ideology concentrates on a split between ideas which influence people, and the 'true' or actual interests of various individuals.

Class is important here, because the working class is seen as the only group whose interests lie in overthrowing the social order. Ideology is seen as a set of ideas or beliefs to which the working class falls prey; it prevents the workers from seeing their 'true' interests. This idea, generally called the 'negative' view of ideology, has been distinctly unhelpful, because it tells human subjects that they are somehow deluded, and that their real interests lie in their class allegiance as described by the Marxist scholar.

An alternative view of ideology insists first that there are many ideologies or *systems of belief*, and that the real operation of ideology takes place in material actions, through acts which are expressed in physical and discursive forms. At the same time, it must be recognised that some discourses tend to dominate public expression and debate, while others struggle to be heard, or appear as alternatives within the frame of dominant discourses.

Ideology and address: leftist perspectives

The relationship of individuals to authority is interesting, because individuals are **addressed** by authority in many aspects of their everyday lives. The point Althusser tried to advance is that *having to reply* in itself constitutes a recognition of the power of authority. By contrast, those whom we regard as powerless are thought sometimes to merit only a perfunctory response, or no response at all. The fact that authority will allow individuals the 'right to reply' shows not enlightenment, but rather the eagerness of the powerful to make their subordinates recognise the relationship of power.

Who's there?

In *Essays on Ideology* (p. 46) Althusser attempted to explain that ideology works in what can only be described as a very *ordinary* way. Althusser uses the example of a friend who knocks at the door. When asked 'who's there?' the person will reply 'it's me'. The 'me' in this case is the rational subject who recognises him or herself as a distinct being.

Ideology is supposed to work at this very obvious level, since it is assumed that it seems natural to those who are subjected to it. Althusser writes that we 'constantly practise the rituals of ideological recognition'. This could be extended to include the idea of the psychological needs of individuals. Since people depend upon being recognised by others in order to maintain their sense of self, they require their place in the social order to be recognised, as this too is part of their identity. By the same token, authority is made up of individuals, and these individuals will need to assert their own position as real agents of the social order. The recognition they gain from their subordinates will work to support their notion of themselves, just as the recognition by authority will reinforce the individual. People require recognition from as many of those around them as possible, at a series of different levels, since there are rewards in recognition. Althusser notes that a person's name is a point of recognition of his or her status as a unique subject.

Interpellation

As we have seen above, Althusser's basic concept was that ideology (p. 47) 'hails or interpellates concrete individuals as concrete subjects'. Ideology 'recruits' its subjects by calling them, or **interpellating** them. I would describe the best translation of Althusser's meaning as 'calling the subject (to order)'.

Althusser, as we have seen above, gives the example of a police officer who hails an individual. The individual responds to the shout 'hey you' by turning around, which means in effect that he or she has recognised the call and has therefore accepted the state of subjectivity.

It is here that the problems start. Althusser has used a highly concrete example, and seems to believe that the response will always be of one kind. In fact, we need to question the whole process of recognition. Althusser's view of a *necessary* response in every case – the idea that the same response is bound to occur on every occasion – leads to the unlikely conclusion that the influence of the dominant ideology is inescapable.

The exercise of free will

When we are 'hailed' we may often *fail* to recognise that it is us that authority wants. We may, alternatively, resent the intrusion. Or again, we may recognise the call to order only when it suits us. What does this mean for Althusser's concept of interpellation?

In the first place, it implies that the subjects of the state do retain **free will** within certain constraints of the rational. Subjectivity is not merely imposed upon us. If our sense of self includes anti-authoritarianism, then we are uncomfortable subjects of the state. Since Althusser recognised the fact that ideology works through appearing to be natural and obvious, it should also be apparent that individuals are sometimes capable of questioning the obvious and the usual. If we cannot live outside ideology, because it is so clever, because it always appears 'natural', then how do manage to identify it?

It is Althusser's conception of ideology which is the problem. Ideologies, as *systems of belief*, create subjects who do more than accept conventional notions. Althusser insists (p. 49) that 'those who are in ideology believe themselves by definition outside ideology'. There appears to be no escape, but in fact our ability to describe the 'grand narratives' of ideology at work must mean that we are able to stand to one side, even if we attain this perspective through the use of other ideological systems. In the final analysis, if we seem to be able to act as though we are outside ideology, then to all intents and purposes we have retained some freedom of action.

Post-structuralism

A theory of deferred meaning

Post-structuralism is closely associated with the work of Jacques Derrida, whose *Of Grammatology* appeared in 1967. Chapter 1 explained Derrida's belief that meaning is always scattered or dispersed along the 'chain' of linguistic signification. The sign's relationship to a present reality is always deferred because reality is always *mediated* by language. In simple terms, we could say that reality is always at several removes from human perception. Since Derrida stands against the 'absolute' or final interpretation of any sign, it comes as no surprise to find that he considered structuralist interpretations of texts to be mistaken.

Structuralism was, in his opinion, concerned to establish a core of meaning (the 'centre') which can be reached once all the elements have been identified. In the course of investigating the concept of structure in the human sciences, Derrida refers to this 'centre' as an organising principle designed to ensure the stability of theory (see *Modern Criticism and Theory*). He regards such stability as a sham (p. 109):

> 'The concept of centred structure is in fact the concept of a play based on a fundamental ground, a play constituted on the basis of a fundamental immobility and a reassuring certitude, which itself is beyond the reach of play.'

For Derrida, the concept of stable references ignored the 'play' of meaning, allowing one interpretation a privileged position above all other possible readings. He was convinced that texts have no 'centre' as such, for the precise reason that they contain *structures*. In *Deconstruction and Criticism*, Derrida argued that (p. 84):

> 'a "text" … is … no longer a finished corpus of writing … but a differential network, a fabric of traces referring endlessly to something other than itself.'

In explaining Derrida's approach, particularly the idea that language is a *temporal* process (i.e. meaning is created within a certain period of time), Sarup (*An Introductory Guide*) uses the example of a sentence (p. 36):

> 'When I read a sentence the meaning of it is always somehow suspended, something deferred. One signifier relays me to another; earlier meanings are modified by later ones … each sign is somehow scored over or traced through with all the others, to form a complex tissue which is never exhaustible.'

In addition, Derrida displaces the author of a text, considering that he or she does not have absolute control over language and thus cannot ensure that the meaning *intended* is the meaning which readers will prefer. When he notes that writing 'does not know where it is going', Derrida is making a stand against what he sees as the dead hand of structuralism. In Stuart Sim's words (see *Beyond Aesthetics*, p. 35):

> 'Structuralism is pictured … as a totalitarian method of analysis whose essentialism arbitrarily delimits meaning and inhibits imagination and creativity.'

Presence and non-presence: the arrow's flight

Derrida is particularly opposed to the tradition in Western thought which regards human identity as 'fixed' or exclusive, an idea found in the writings of Aristotle. Derrida regards the apparently logical 'oppositions' in philosophy (*identity* versus *non-identity*, *fiction* versus *truth*, *internal* versus *external*) as exclusive, neglecting complexity and the possibilities of difference. Through *deconstruction*, Derrida attempts to show that philosophy is in a state of contradiction or paradox.

At the heart of much Western thought is the notion of '*presence*' or 'being'; something is either in existence or is not in existence. Jonathan Culler (see *On Deconstruction*) uses the example of an arrow's flight to explain how 'presence' is, in Derrida's terms, a paradoxical notion (p. 94):

> 'If reality is what is present at any given instant, the arrow produces a paradox. At any given moment it is in a particular spot; it is always in a particular spot and never in motion. We want to insist, quite justifiably, that the arrow *is* in motion at every instant from the beginning to the end of its

flight, yet its moment is never present at any moment of presence ... something can be happening at a given instant only if the instant is already divided within itself, inhabited by the non-present.'

The concept of presence can therefore be 'deconstructed', which would involve (p. 95) 'the demonstration that for presence to function as it is said to, it must have the qualities that supposedly belong to its opposite, absence'.

Writing and speech

Derrida believed that Saussure had granted speech a privileged position, while written language was relegated to being either a graphic *aide memoire* or an imitation of the phonetic qualities of spoken language. It is odd that Saussure should be thus accused, because his interest in real examples of *parole* or ordinary speech was not extensive.

As an alternative to traditional structuralist theory, Derrida offers a conception of writing which stresses its 'differance'. In Derrida's view, mainstream structuralism regards the written sign as standing for the absent 'thing' which it represents. He explains Saussure's system in the following way (see Peggy Kamuf's A *Derrida Reader*, p. 61):

'The sign is usually said to be put in the place of the thing itself, the present thing, "thing" here standing equally for meaning and referent. The sign represents the present in its absence. It takes the place of the present. When we cannot grasp or show the thing, state the present, the being present, when the present cannot be presented, we signify, we go through the detour of the sign ... The sign, in this sense, is deferred presence.'

In one sense, we may wonder why Derrida champions *writing* when he recognises that the creation of meaning through the use of the written word is notoriously unreliable. Sim (p. 41) notes that:

'Writing is simultaneously our only means of escape from a repressive authority, and a vicious circle that undermines our resistance at source.'

The reason for Derrida's attachment to the written word seems to emerge from his belief in the 'impurity' of writing; it challenges, in his view, the concept of a fixed identity, because it is neither fully present (it stands in for the 'thing' in the world) nor entirely absent (it is visible on the page as a graphic system).

Derrida appears to have gone some way towards making an assault on values and practices which seem to limit our freedom to interpret the sign, but ends by referring back to the same systems of expression which he thinks inadequate. One strategy he has recently adopted is to cross the boundaries between different written forms, such as rhetoric and academic writing. In Sim's words, Derrida's reluctance to go further may mean that the old systems he so distrusts have been shaken but have not fallen.

The suspicion must remain that Derrida is really interested in the challenge to established philosophy, and not in solutions to the problems he raises. In recent years, he appears to have disassociated himself from the more radical implications of the deconstructionist movement, declaring that (quoted in Sim, p. 140) he was never hostile to philosophy as such, and that:

'there is no such thing as a deconstructive *enterprise* – the idea of a *project* is incompatible with deconstruction'.

Derrida's agenda: a criticism

Although Derrida objects to the 'phonocentrism' of our attitudes to language, his belief that the 'abstract' work of Saussure represents a 'pro-speech' tendency is an indication of exactly how far removed he is from those writers working towards a discursive theory of human communication. In other words, it is exactly intonation and phonetics which may provide a fresh impetus to Derrida's project.

There is a hint of recognition of the disruptive power of intonation in Sturrock's assessment of 'linguistic aids' (*Deconstruction*, p. 88):

'The considerable extension to our powers of communication which semiotic systems such as those of gesture or intonation represent is one, interestingly, quite absent from our dictionaries. We have no authority to which we can refer to settle questions about which gestures or intonations are conventional and which are not.'

In fact, gesture and intonation are not merely linguistic 'aids' but informal systems which give contextual meaning to speech. In this case, the idea that we 'have no authority' to which we can refer seems to be a positive rather than a negative feature of systems like intonation! Derrida's rejection of such studies, and his preference for written forms, provides an interesting parallel to Saussure's preference for the study of structure.

Derrida also objected, as we saw in Chapter 1, to the notion that the human subject is able to interpret meaning *intuitively*, without recourse to signs. Yet there are some meanings which are not communicated through 'rational' systems (emotional responses to music, for example), and some states of mind (if we recall Gilbert Ryle's comments on panic) in which the individual does not have time to interpret meaning through sign systems. The prospect of intuitive understanding seems to run counter to the system-bound theories of the Western academic tradition; in refusing to consider such questions, we may see just how firmly entrenched Derrida remains within the tradition he has disrupted.

Context: the 'boundary' of signification?

Part of the problem with semiology has been the tendency to assume that signs can consist of very small elements, such as single words. Individual words are, however, unable to bear the weight of significance which is often placed upon them. Signification is more likely to emerge from larger units, though meaning is always *qualified* as the event (narrative, speech event, broadcast, etc.) proceeds. Meaning is *emergent*, because it depends upon the internal arrangement of elements (the relationship between units of meaning) and the external parameters of the event.

Derrida also argues that meaning is contingent, but that it depends upon what the individual sign is *not*, as much as what it is; this is the theory of 'differance'. To Derrida, all language is metaphorical, and cannot express literal truth. For this reason, fictional forms, which acknowledge their 'rhetorical' foundation, are in his opinion more 'honest' than texts produced by philosophy or other academic practices.

Communication Studies appears to be faced with a number of highly abstract alternatives. Whatever their strengths as academic theories, structuralism and post-structuralism seem unable to provide the tools for understanding the ordinary exchanges which make up the bulk of human interaction. On a practical note, we could ask if it is advisable to return to studies of *context*, where consideration of internal structure and external circumstance, including the activities of readers and other participants, may produce a more rounded appreciation of human exchange. In other words, would a *contextual* approach help to establish certain **boundaries of meaning** for communication events?

Derrida was once involved in a debate with the American philosopher John R. Searle, in which Searle used J.L. Austin's idea of *performatives* to suggest a contextual theory of communication. Performatives (see Chapter 3) are those utterances which perform or 'do' what they say; for example, the statement 'I name this ship' when it is made in the context of the launching of a ship, and when uttered by the appropriate person, can be described as a 'performative'. Derrida, however, pointed out that an 'infelicitous' performative can be made by any individual, as for instance when the 'wrong' person takes it upon him or herself to open a meeting. This ability to repeat an utterance in a different situation suggests that context has a greater influence in determining meaning than does the intention of a speaker.

Post-structuralists argue, however, that this is not enough to prove that context can be used as a general principle for deciphering meaning. Jonathan Culler, in *On Deconstruction*, sets out this argument (p. 123):

'A theory of speech acts must in principle be able to specify every feature of context that might affect the success or failure of a given speech act ... this would require ... a mastery of the total context ... but total context is unmasterable, both in principle and in practice. Meaning is context-bound, but context is boundless.'

Culler advances the idea that context is boundless in two senses (pp. 123–4):

'First, any given context is open to further description ... the historian brings new or re-interpreted data to bear on a particular event ... second ... any attempt to codify context can always be grafted onto the event it sought to describe.'

Post-structuralism: on the branch line to nowhere?

In common with the theory of deferred meaning, and the supposedly 'endless' chain of signification produced by language, this notion of 'boundless' context suggests once again a journey without a destination; endless branch lines but no terminus. In fact, post-structuralism appears to favour an essentially *linear* process, in which meaning is never reached.

However, at certain times and in certain places, meanings *are* constructed, circulated and above all *acted* upon. Agreements about meaning are sometimes achieved through consensus, are sometimes imposed, but it is certain that there are periods when attention is drawn to a single link in the 'chain' of references. At such a point, particular discourses may produce a material change in the lives of human subjects, for better or worse. As a practical inquiry, Communication Studies can choose to take sides.

Theories of 'differance' seem abstract and diffuse. Unlike the Marxist 'dialectic', in which meaning is produced through the difference or opposition between categories, there seems to be no productive tension in the category of 'differance', only a sort of drift into negation, as though the implied opposite of any sign cancels its ability to act in a material world.

The ambiguity inherent in language and the multiple meanings it is able to produce seem to have misled a number of philosophers into supposing that ambiguity is the only possible, or even the only proper, outcome of expression; but there is a vast difference between the productive capacity of a communicative act, where the complexity of reference helps to enrich and extend the range of meaning, and the postmodernist tendency to perceive and even to celebrate confusion. The existence of ambiguity does not prove that language is unreliable.

Earlier in this section, I mentioned the way that signification is often seen as a linear process, in which one provisional meaning is handed onto the next in a 'chain' of signifiers. Perhaps meaning is not passed down a chain; perhaps signification resembles an impulse rushing through the branches of a neural network. Or, to use a different metaphor, instead of 'multiple' meanings leading us away from understanding, they may act like a number of lights, each set up from a different angle, and each able to illuminate the subject of inquiry, so that for all practical purposes a reasonably full conception may be obtained.

SUMMARY

This chapter begins by re-examining the definition of communication given in Chapter 1 and asks, on the basis of that definition, what kinds of event *qualify* as communication. It ends by considering communication in the context of a number of influential social and critical theories, including modernism, postmodernism, structuralism and post-structuralism.

COMMUNICATION: PROBLEMS OF DEFINITION

Chapter 1 offered a definition of communication, describing it as **an activity in which *symbolic content* is not merely transmitted but *exchanged* between human agents, who interact within a shared situational and/or discursive *context*.**

What events qualify as communication?

Using this description, certain events qualify as communication: a telephone conversation, a group discussion, an argument between two people, an exchange of messages on the Internet, an exchange of letters in the post, a public lecture in which questions are answered, and a 'video conference' made through a satellite link. However, our definition excludes a large number of other events which are normally studied under the heading of communication. For example, a sermon, an announcement, a radio talk, a television advertisement, an exhibition of sculpture, public graffiti, or the reading of a book would all fail to qualify.

The reason why the first set of events would be accepted as examples of communication, and the second would be rejected, lies in the fact that an *exchange of meaning* occurs in the first group and not in the second. We should nevertheless remember that any one of the second set has the *potential* to qualify as a collection of 'real' communication events, if and when a response is made (within a shared context) to the initial address.

In essence, while the examples in the second group do not amount to interaction between 'sender' and

'receiver', they may lead to more generalised exchanges of meaning within 'social spaces'. In other words, they are part of the social process from which communication is drawn, and as such will probably encourage exchanges within and between social groups.

Mass communication: secondary exchange

Most media events, and indeed many other examples of communication, do not involve a direct or *primary* exchange between the producer and receiver of a message, but usually only an indirect or **secondary exchange** between audiences and other social agencies, creating in some cases a general *cultural impact*. This idea was outlined above.

It is the *impact* the media have on our culture, rather than the mistaken notion that they facilitate direct communication between media producers and consumers, which must account for their place within Communication Studies.

THE CONCEPT OF ADDRESS

The concept of **address** may be explained as the *delivery* of a communication (statement, request, admonition and so on) to a specific person or group of people, taking into account the suitability or *register* of the symbolic form used. A 'Dennis the Menace' cartoon is used to illustrate this point.

This extract from *The Beano* provides a very useful insight into the importance of an initial opening which recognises the *identity* of the addressee (the recipient of the 'message'). In most examples of mass media address, it seems that a common aim is to treat audience members as though they have *individuality*. It is notable that, in a mass society, the appeal to individuality is used exhaustively in advertising and other forms of public address. Even where people are addressed as members of a group, the group is often presented as having some special qualities.

Modes of address and reception: media and audience

The media regularly, though not exclusively, 'speak to' their audiences in ways which resemble the opening gambits of public speech. Such types of address are thought to be effective and constitute an *established practice*.

All forms of media imitate 'direct' address, but much of the repertoire available to a speaker is lost when the message appears in print. The need to attract and retain attention, especially in two-dimensional advertising, forces the use of modes of address which are more directly **interpellative** (where an attempt is made to create a power relation between 'speaker' and audience member) than **interactive** (where a message is constructed so that it resembles the initial part of a conversational exchange). The two types may in fact be combined in one message.

Examples of second-person address, taken from an issue of *The Times* newspaper, are given in the text. A 'profile' of the typical *Times* reader may begin to emerge from these examples.

THE CONCEPT OF IDENTITY

Identity is often defined as *individuality*, or those qualities which mark out one person from another. Individual identity, however, seems to emerge from a sense of *belonging* and attachment to others, rather than simply from the possession of 'unique' attributes.

The work on identity completed in Chapters 2 and 3 is set out. Overall, the idea that human beings *acquire* an identity through their experience of social processes, rather than beginning life with one which is ready-made, has become widely accepted.

Some authors believe that the process of *self-identification* depends upon an ability to contrast oneself with 'out-groups', thought to be different or in some way undesirable. A number of writers use the concept of 'the other' to acknowledge the existence of difference, whether between (for example) mainstream Western civilisation and the 'exotic' practices of other cultures, or between the sexes.

The notion of 'shifting' identity is also introduced.

Identity and address

When a deliberate act of communication is initiated, the individual or group responsible for framing the address will act under a number of conditions:

- the **context** in which the communicative act is to be made;
- the **audience** (group or individual) intended as the recipient of the address;
- message **content**;
- the consequent message **form**.

The 'addressor' (whether an individual or a group) will not necessarily have to know everything about the target audience in order to produce a suitable message. The values which circulate within the target group, as well as those shared within the wider society, may provide the basis for action.

A front-page article from *The Daily Mail* is analysed.

INVESTIGATING WRITTEN AND LITERARY EXPRESSION

Written and 'literary' expression has been somewhat neglected within the study of communication, probably because it is regarded as the property of other subject areas, such as English language and literature. The category which appears in the AEB syllabus called 'written communication' is examined.

Communication Studies and literature

Two approaches might help to focus on the relationship between communication as a study and written/literary expression. We might first wonder whether Communication Studies has anything to contribute to the study of the written/printed word. The second approach might be to look at the problem from a different angle, and ask what kinds of *analysis* different types of writing appear to require.

Various possible approaches to written communication are studied, including **transmission models**,

uses and purposes, **socialisation** and the **social functional**.

COMMUNICATION AND THE NOVEL

An extract from David Lodge's *The Novel as Communication* (see D.H. Mellor, *Ways of Communicating*) explores the idea that the 'classic novelists' seemed to regard their activity as communication, in the most basic sense of imparting or exchanging information.

Prose forms before the novel are studied, through Thomas Nashe's *The Unfortunate Traveller*. Much of Nashe's writing could be described as belonging to a *rhetorical* form, based upon religious, social and personal disputation. Nashe's writing intends to provide entertainment through a series of aggressively satirical tableaux. His persona is adventurous, sophisticated and inventive. Nashe's work is not 'confidential'; it is a performance.

Origins of the novel and critical response

Most writers place the origin of the novel in the eighteenth century, but some argue that it evolved at least a century earlier. Juliet Mitchell, for example, writing in *Femininity, Narrative and Psychoanalysis* (see Lodge's *Modern Criticism and Theory*, p. 426), believes that the novel 'starts with autobiographies written by women in the seventeenth century'. Mikhail Bakhtin (1895–1975) saw the novel as a form which grew from the parodic genres of classical and medieval literature.

David Lodge provides an account of the 'suspicions' which the novel tended to arouse in some twentieth-century critics. Walter Benjamin described **story-telling** as a transaction between individuals in close physical proximity to one another, and contrasted this with the novel, produced in one place by a solitary author and consumed in another by an isolated reader. Benjamin's belief that the novel is not 'social' seems both to under-value its role in society and to over-estimate the positive features of traditional oral narratives.

A single drop of ink: authors, readers and address

The opening paragraph of *Adam Bede*, written in 1857 by the novelist George Eliot, is used to demonstrate a point about the relationship between **author**, **reader** and 'past'. A sense of privilege is not an unusual feature of the Victorian novel, and owes much to the fact that literacy was not universal. Within the text itself, authors would often reveal their intention to **address** a particular class of readership.

Class and audience

Adam Bede and the issues it raises, including class, religion, relations between the sexes, and the value of the rural environment, is examined in some detail. The tension in *Adam Bede* is between the 'timeless' picture of a Midlands rural society and those references to historical movements and events, such as the rise of Methodism, which must be made in order to give the novel a convincing period flavour. The muted version of Methodism in *Adam Bede* is used to present a dramatic counterpoint to traditional forms of society, but ultimately lacks the force of its historical counterpart.

The power of a novelist to demonstrate the desirability and correctness of one set of **values**, as compared to another, is also explored. History is used as a *contextual* factor in the appreciation of Eliot's text.

Class and communication

An interesting feature of middle-class Victorian England was the belief that the working class was unable to express itself. It was thought incapable of shaping its own discourses; in simple terms, it could not communicate. In his book *Chartism* (1839), Thomas Carlyle referred to the 'great dumb toiling class which cannot speak'. The novelist Elizabeth Gaskell also sought to 'give some utterance to the agony which, from time to time, convulses this dumb people'.

Working-class perceptions: *Mary Barton*

The novel *Mary Barton*, written by Elizabeth Gaskell, is

used as an example of a narrative in which the author allows her characters to 'speak'. *Mary Barton* bears all the marks of its closeness to the events it relates. The 'documentary' elements of the novel lie side by side with the 'romance' of ordinary lives. Gaskell is interested less in the social and the group than in individual events and the internal 'psychological' life of hero and heroine.

Thomas Hardy and the representation of female labour

Hardy's characterisation of labour in *Tess of the d'Urbervilles* contains symbolic elements, and a suggestion of the idyll, but also close observation of the conditions of 'unskilled' labour. A novelist like Hardy would seem to disprove Walter Benjamin's belief that the novel is somehow removed from the social, and that the novelist is unable to 'counsel' others.

VISUAL COMMUNICATION: THE DISCOURSES OF ART

This section, which examines the subject of art, gives an account of the way in which 'modern art' is described and argued over. In other words, it looks at the discourses which various individuals and groups mobilise to talk about art.

One of the charges laid against **fine art** has been '**elitism**'. It has been attacked for holding itself aloof from common experience, and for spawning a class of expert which reserves to itself the task of translating an artist's intention. It does so, according to this view, for an audience which is imagined to have no specialist training in or knowledge of art. The traditional role of the art critic is that of someone who appears to have the required expertise and refinement of aesthetic taste needed to explain to others the worth of paintings or artefacts.

Aesthetics

A definition of the original meaning of aesthetics is supplied by O'Sullivan and his colleagues, in the 1987 *Key Concepts in Communication*, where it is described as (p. 4):

'a concept inherited from idealist philosophy, referring to principles of taste, especially good taste, and hence of beauty'.

The object of study for aesthetics is 'the art-object itself, taken out of its historical, cultural and means-of-production context'. Here, expertise would be used to isolate 'those textual properties' which make an art-object beautiful.

A new aesthetics?

The revolt against elitism in artistic taste led to a new conceptualisation of beauty and new standards of worth. Instead of a pure 'aesthetics', where the art-object itself carries value, artistic production came to be recognised as carrying an aesthetic code, which could be interpreted once its historical context and mode of production (mechanical or artisanal, for example) were taken into account.

The response of the 'public'

In fact, the expansion of critical interest in what O'Sullivan calls 'the output of mass commodity and mass production' has led to some wholly negative public reactions. Where the object of critical interest has turned to texts produced through advertising, graffiti, video and so on, the audience encountering many such artefacts, far from appreciating its liberation from traditional values, appears instead to resent what is perceived as 'junk' masquerading under the title 'art'.

Part of the problem is the way in which our society tends both to categorise and subsequently to value a range of creative activities. Walker notes that an application made in 1979 to the Arts Council for the repair of trade union banners was refused. Banners were regarded by the Council as *craft*, not art. The individual work had fallen into the wrong *category*.

A pile of bricks

The Tate Gallery's 1974 purchase of *Equivalent VIII*, a set of 120 bricks laid two deep in a rectangle, is used to study public perceptions of the 'avant-garde'. By contrast to 'the public', the type of critic who supported

Carl Andre's *Equivalent VIII* seems anxious to stress that modern artists force us all to look again at what is traditionally *accepted* as art.

The idea of challenging preconceptions is, of course, central to those strategies which attempt to institute new or more diverse standards in taste. However, artefacts have to be displayed within a context which will enable them to be discussed as 'works'. Michael Landy's installation of a flower stall in the Royal Academy was one example where context was all-important.

A dead cow

The objections raised to Andre's bricks have been more than matched by the disquiet which has grown over the artistic practices of Damien Hirst, who began with various photographic experiments in a morgue and progressed to the celebrated 1991 'assemblage' called *Isolated Elements Swimming in the Same Direction for the Purpose of Understanding*. This consisted of thirty-eight dead fish in separate containers of formaldehyde. Hirst's most famous works to date have been the dead animals which have been cut in half, preserved with injections of formaldehyde and then displayed in transparent cases. *Mother and Child Divided* was one example of this practice, consisting of a dead cow and a dead calf which had each been cut in two along their length, using a chainsaw.

Art and commerce: the Turner Prize

In 1993, a series of full-page advertisements appeared in the broadsheet press. The first read 'Abandon All Art Now', and 'Await Further Instructions'. The K Foundation's attack on standards in modern art is described.

Art as commodity

In *Promotional Culture* (1991) Andrew Wernick provides a number of useful insights into the commodification of art-objects (the production of art as items for sale in the marketplace).

Feminist interventions

In *Vision and Difference* (1988) Griselda Pollock asks (p. 1): 'is adding women to art history the same as producing feminist art history?'. Pollock's answer is that the inclusion of women not only changes what is studied, but challenges the existing disciplines in political terms. Rather than accept the pre-defined criteria of 'greatness' set out by the male art history establishment, Pollock argues for a new paradigm or set of objectives through which artistic activity may be judged. Other women artists, like Roxane Permar and Françoise Dupré, feel that 'the most important aspect is to create work collectively'. Co-operation and collective working methods have long been regarded as an alternative to the concept of the artist as an 'isolated genius'.

Communication and democracy

The work of critics like John Berger encouraged leftist perspectives in a number of art colleges in the late 1970s and early 1980s. However, attempts to use art as a weapon for democracy have often foundered when faced with the 'commodification' of artistic production.

THE PORTRAYAL OF HUMAN INTERACTION IN FILM

Although there have been some doubts about the theory of representation, in the sense that it is not entirely convincing as a picture of the mental process (see Chapter 2), the distinction between *presentation* and *representation* is still useful. It is the difference between these two concepts which is explored in this section.

Social actions: presentation

The roles we 'play' within the context of everyday interaction can vary quite significantly. A private exchange between two people is clearly quite different to an interaction involving a number of individuals within the context of a public forum. It would be too easy, however, to declare that the public context is inherently more 'dramatic' than the private one.

Social actions: re-presentation

Any exchange which is scripted in advance and then presented for public consumption may be described as a **re-presentation** of the themes or ideas which the script makes concrete. In *Theatrical Presentation*, Bernard Beckerman describes *presentation* as both the act of giving and 'the force of being.' The meaning of 'presentation' in the theatre turns on the 'symbolic value' of the performance. Beckerman sees the performance not as an 'actual exchange' (p. 4) but as 'a **virtual** one'. As communication theorists, we might understand it as a virtual rather than a real exchange because there is usually no exchange of discourse or speech between actors and audience.

The re-presentation of human interaction in film

Television and film create episodes in which individuals carry out actions and are involved in verbal exchanges. Whether these are fully 'scripted' or partly improvised, an analysis of such presentations would need to take account of a number of factors, which are given in the text.

Speech genres in film: *Southern Comfort* and the representation of the male

After analysing two extracts, one from ordinary speech and one taken from Spike Lee's *Malcolm X*, Walter Hill's 1981 film *Southern Comfort* is used to study the differences between formal and informal speech in the Cinema.

Social attributes of 'stars'

There have been many attempts to explain the '**star**' phenomenon, in which an actor attains an exalted status and a persona which is recognised across the globe. Writing in 'Social attributes of American movie stars', Emanuel Levy argues that this kind of explanation is inadequate. Using the 'Motion Picture Herald Poll', a survey of the top stars in the American film industry which has appeared yearly since 1932, Levy examines the 'social attributes' of American movie stars. The *physical appearance*, *age*, *acting abilities* and *screen image* or *persona* are all taken as indicators of the **social attributes** of a total of 129 actors over the period 1932–84. Using these indicators, Levy discovered a great deal about the values espoused by US society.

Social values and the Cinema

The **values** of certain sections of society are reflected in mainstream Cinema. The 'strong individual protagonist' (Levy, p. 259) is a central feature of all Hollywood productions. The representation of the events of a single individual's life form the major concern of such narratives. The most important 'cultural qualities' which characterise major stars are described.

Narrative in the Cinema

The word '**narrative**' has more than one meaning; it may refer to either the end product of storytelling and the comprehension of a story, or to its process of construction. In *Narrative Comprehension and Film* (1992) Edward Branigan advances the theory that narrative is 'one of the important ways we perceive our environment'. He puts forward a strong argument that narrative should not be seen as exclusively *fictional* but instead should be contrasted to other non-narrative ways of assembling and understanding data.

Hidden processes

Stephen Heath demonstrated how some elements of a film 'escape' the narrative structure and become what he calls a *residuum*, a sort of left-over which reveals the 'hidden psychic and ideological processes at work in the text'. Narrative is the result of these processes, and is yet also an explicit attempt to master them and to cast them into a formal order. For Heath, the causality of narrative events in a plot is a pretext for larger transformations which point to *everyday beliefs* about the social world.

CRITICAL THEORY AND COMMUNICATION

Perhaps the key to understanding the different social and critical theories is the study of **modernity**.

Modernity

The term '**modern**' refers to an era which began around 1500. Some social theorists think that modern times include the present, while others believe that we have recently entered a new period, the 'postmodern'.

Modernity as a contradictory force

Modernity exists in a state of contradiction. Peter Wagner, in *A Sociology of Modernity* (1994, p. xiii), expresses the ambivalence of modernity in the following terms:

'it is becoming less possible for individuals or groups of human beings to escape the reach of modern institutions. At the same time, everybody who makes successful use of these institutions can expect to extend his, or more rarely, her reach'.

Here, Wagner recognises that the benefits of modern life are not equally available to men and women. In Wagner's view, the (p. xiv) 'transformation of the human self during modernity should be seen as a ... process of both liberation and disciplinisation'.

In sum, many commentators argue that modernity has produced a world whose pace and scope of change have far outstripped that found in earlier societies, creating new opportunities for some groups and individuals, at the expense of restrictions on human freedom.

Modernism

Modernism refers to a variety of social, political, economic and cultural 'movements' and ideas which began in the seventeenth century and which continue to exert vast influence upon life. Modernist movements depend upon the existence of an 'advanced' society with an industrial base and great productive power. In such a society, there will be highly devel-

oped (if unequal and distorted) relations between people.

Capitalism and modernism

Karl Marx described how capitalism had reforged the material conditions of life, uprooting communities, concentrating resources and overcoming material obstacles, in order to produce new social forms. The eventual consequence was a new international order, in which certain nations dominated the globe.

It is, however, the advent of a 'money community' which Marx identifies as the difference between the modern and pre-industrial eras. 'Real communities' were dissolved, while the money system made all relations between individuals impersonal and objective. Human exchanges became market exchanges, with the money system standing outside human relations yet masking the true nature of social relationships. Marx describes this as the 'fetishism of commodities'.

Culture and modernism

In **cultural** terms, modernism is not necessarily a complete or coherent philosophy so much as a general description of a number of movements and tendencies which emerged in the industrial age. David Harvey calls it (see *The Condition of Postmodernity*) 'a troubled and fluctuating aesthetic response to conditions of modernity'.

Postmodernism

Postmodernism would appear, at first sight, to be a period of history which has followed and perhaps even replaced modernism. However, Joanna Hodge's argument that terms are often used to refer to both critical movements and historical epochs should make us question the wisdom of allowing 'postmodernism' to be used as a temporal 'marker', especially if it suggests that other currents of development have somehow come to an end.

There is a strong case, in fact, for arguing that it makes no sense to set modernism and postmodernism against each other, as though they are two opposing forces. David Harvey sees the latter 'as a particular kind of crisis within the former'.

The postmodernist critique

In the first place, despite the diversity of post-modernist theory, a major preoccupation of its adherents has been the rejection of the legacy of the Enlightenment. The Enlightenment was that period in history, beginning in the seventeenth century, which saw the growth of rationalism, a belief in progress, free will and human equality.

The postmodern critique also involves the notion that the human subject has suffered an assault from the vast amount of information which is produced by the mass media. According to this view, instead of helping to enlighten people, such information tends to destroy meaning; at the same time, the code used for transmission becomes of more interest than its reference to the real. This aspect of the postmodern outlook ultimately suggests that human subjectivity is invaded and becomes 'objectified'.

Lyotard and 'meta-narratives'

Postmodernism's distrust of '**meta-narratives**' may be explored through the work of Jean-François Lyotard, who used the concept of 'meta-narratives' to describe those public discourses which provide 'credible' reasons for the continued existence of the social order. Perhaps the real reason for the rise of the movement lies in the collapse of political optimism which followed the winding-down of 1970s radicalism.

Baudrillard: free from logic?

Jean Baudrillard began by making a departure from Marx's distinction between the 'use value' and the 'exchange value' of an object, where 'use value' is the extent to which an object can satisfy human needs, and 'exchange value' is the market value placed on the object. Baudrillard advanced the idea of 'sign value', where the object has the power to signify or mean certain things to people. We might say, for example, that a Coca-Cola bottle has acquired a 'sign value', that it signifies a certain lifestyle over and above its use as a drink or its value as a commercial product.

By the mid-1970s, Baudrillard had taken this further, arguing that the 'code' (whether semiotic, digital or binary) for any real object had become so pervasive that the code, and not the thing itself, had come to dominate social life. The end result was a state of 'hyper-reality', where the code seemed to appear more 'real' than the real itself.

The distasteful and misogynist attributes of Baudrillard's work are discussed. Baudrillard employs what Barcan calls a 'tactical use of rhetoric', distancing himself from his own statements and thus pre-empting criticism.

Postmodernism: positive uses?

Chapter 1 acknowledged that postmodernism has the potential for creating positive effects, based upon what David Harvey (p. 113) calls its 'concern for difference, for the complexity and nuances of interests, cultures, places'. Stuart Sim in *Beyond Aesthetics* argues that postmodern theory is useful in that it demonstrates the weakness of 'total' systems of thought.

Joanna Hodge (in *The Problems of Modernity*, p. 87) identifies 'a strong connection between radical feminism and the postmodernist ... rejections of time, narrativity and historical process'. Chen (see Corner *et al.*, *Postmodernism*) also believes that a 'critical post-modernism' has developed, which offers, in common with cultural studies, the potential to challenge the establishment through postmodernism's willingness to listen to (p. 37) 'the oppressed voices of history'.

The weakness of postmodernist theory

One of the interesting contradictions which lie at the heart of the 'postmodern project' is the tension between its hostility towards 'grand narratives' of all kinds (Marxism, liberalism, socialism and so on) and the choice it faces once it has attacked Enlightenment thinking. What is the next step: Derrida's call to 'write', Lyotard's advocacy of individual 'svelteness' (a sort of small-scale, ironic resistance), or Baudrillard's retreat into the hyper-real?

Some postmodernists appear hostile not only to theories of collectivity, but also to collective action itself. This provides the starkest possible contrast between postmodernism as a critique of 'grand theory', and other movements which have shared some of its antipathy to centralised power.

Libertarian critics of authoritarianism

An alternative, **libertarian** intellectual tradition, based on leftist and feminist currents in Europe, is described. Spain and Germany are cited as examples of countries in which left-wing organisations contrasted strongly with the Leninist orthodoxy.

Postmodernism stands outside the libertarian tradition and remains suspicious of practical collectivity; its only recourse appears to be individual resistance (Lyotard) or complete surrender (Baudrillard). It is possible that a general neglect of the libertarian tradition has allowed some postmodernists to characterise all leftist philosophy as equally repressive.

● Structuralism

Essentially, **structuralism** examines the *relationship* between the internal elements of any phenomenon or event: a text, a society, an equation and so on. Its appearance in the mid-1960s caused considerable controversy. The work of critics such as Genette, Barthes, Levi-Strauss, Foucault and Althusser introduced structuralist thought into the study of literary and philosophical narrative, popular culture, anthropology, power and politics.

Structuralist analysis in operation

A useful example of structuralism in practice may be found in the analysis of the literary text. In Terry Eagleton's words (*Literary Theory*, p. 94): 'the [elements] do not have a "substantial" meaning, only a "relational" one'. This means that intrinsic significance is not attached to each event, but is reserved for the action of the whole story.

Structuralism and language

The investigation of **language,** in the structuralist sense, is an *abstract* study, one concerned with systems and structures. We may remember the distinction made by Ferdinand de Saussure between the temporal and the spatial plane of language, the first of these being **diachronic** and the second **synchronic**.

Langue and parole

Saussure divided the study of language into **langue**, the system of rules underlying speech, and **parole**, the speech of individuals. Noam Chomsky's version of this distinction is *competence* and *performance*. However, Chomsky's 'competence' remains, unlike Saussure's 'langue', the possession of each individual. Chomsky advanced the cause of structural linguistics by suggesting that the human subject itself had an in-born ability to generate language, and therefore that the mind itself possessed innate structure.

The sign in Saussure's structuralism

The **sign** is made up, in Saussure's system, of the **signifier** (a physical representation of something in the real world) and the **signified** (the mental concept called to mind by the signifier). It is unfortunate that this 'structural' division has led to the idea of a material reality as distinct from a 'non-material' world of concepts.

In Saussure's system, a signifier is something human beings are able to perceive, which suggests that it must have some recognisable external form, such as a photograph, drawing, spoken word, written word and so on. If we wished to refer to the mental concept 'tree', then a photograph, drawing, spoken or written word which makes a recognisable reference to the concept 'tree', would count as a signifier. A signifier always makes a reference to something besides itself. The tradition of treating single words as complete signs, sometimes found in linguistics, has definite limitations, since units of meaning or structures, are usually much larger.

Structures of meaning

Saussure did not attempt to 'match' individual linguistic signs and human apprehension of reality, turning his attention instead to **systems** or **structures of meaning**. One theorist who followed the idea of a real connection between language and the world it indictates is Gerard Genette, who accepted Plato's idea that names, in some fundamental but unexplained way, 'imitate' that to which they refer (see *Mimologiques*, 1976). It is quite possible that human expressiveness continually reinvents 'convention'.

The notion of the 'arbitrary'

The term '**arbitrary**' means that the connection between the sign and the thing for which it stands is supposed really to be no more than a random or accidental event. In Saussurean linguistics, no sign which derives from language is thought to have a real connection with the thing it is meant to represent (whether that is a real object or the shared human *perception* of real objects). Objections to this view are outlined.

Peirce

C.S. Peirce believed that there were three types of sign. According to Peirce's scheme, an **icon** is a sign that bears a resemblance to its object (where the 'object' is an idea, artefact, person, event). An **index** is a sign which has a direct, material link with the thing or idea it represents. Finally, a **symbol** is that sort of sign whose connection with the real is a matter of agreement or rule (Peirce calls it a 'law').

Althusser

Louis Althusser (1918–90) was a Marxist philosopher who used structuralist approaches in his reading of Marx, believing society to be composed of a number of semi-autonomous structures, including legal, political, cultural and ideological elements. These powerful forces are seen as possessing a degree of independence which is not, however, extended to the human subject.

Ideology

The traditional Marxist explanation of **ideology** is *forms of consciousness* (or types of understanding) which mould the outlook of human beings. There is a difference, according to Marx, between the interests of people and the 'form in which these interests are experienced'. In other words, this view of ideology concentrates on a split between ideas which influence people, and the 'true' or actual interests of various individuals.

An alternative view of ideology insists first that there are many ideologies or *systems of belief*, and that the real operation of ideology takes place in material actions, through acts which are expressed in physical and discursive forms. At the same time, it must be recognised that some discourses tend to dominate public expression and debate, while others struggle to be heard, or appear as alternatives within the frame of dominant discourses.

In *Essays on Ideology* (p. 46) Althusser attempted to explain that ideology works in what can only be described as a very *ordinary* way. Althusser uses the example of a friend who knocks at the door. When asked 'who's there?' the person will reply 'it's me'. The 'me' in this case is the rational subject who recognises him or herself as a distinct being.

Ideology is supposed to work at this very obvious level, since it is assumed that it seems natural to those who are subjected to it. Althusser writes that we 'constantly practise the rituals of ideological recognition'.

Interpellation

As we have seen above, Althusser's basic concept was that ideology (p. 47) 'hails or interpellates concrete individuals as concrete subjects'. Ideology 'recruits' its subjects by calling them, or **interpellating** them. I would describe the best translation of Althusser's meaning as 'calling the subject (to order)'.

Althusser's view of a *necessary* response in every case – the idea that the same response is bound to occur on every occasion – leads to the unlikely conclusion that the influence of the dominant ideology is inescapable.

● Post-structuralism

A theory of deferred meaning

Post-structuralism is closely associated with the work of Jacques Derrida, whose *Of Grammatology* appeared in 1967. Derrida believed that meaning is always scattered or dispersed along the 'chain' of linguistic signification. The sign's relationship to a present reality is always deferred because reality is always *mediated* by language. Derrida is particularly opposed to the tradition in Western thought which regards human identity as 'fixed' or exclusive, an idea found in the writings of Aristotle. Derrida regards the apparently logical 'oppositions' in philosophy (*identity* versus *non-identity*, *fiction* versus *truth*, *internal* versus *external*) as exclusive, neglecting complexity and the possibilities of difference. Through *deconstruction*, Derrida attempts to show that philosophy is in a state of contradiction or paradox.

Writing and speech

Derrida believed that Saussure had granted speech a privileged position, while written language was relegated to being either a graphic *aide memoire* or an imitation of the phonetic qualities of spoken language. As an alternative to traditional structuralist theory, Derrida offers a conception of writing which stresses its 'differance'. In Derrida's view, mainstream structuralism regards the written sign as standing for the absent 'thing' which it represents.

Derrida's attachment to the written word seems to emerge from his belief in the 'impurity' of writing; it challenges, in his view, the concept of a fixed identity, because it is neither fully present (it stands in for the 'thing' in the world) nor entirely absent (it is visible on the page as a graphic system).

Derrida also objected, as we saw in Chapter 1, to the notion that the human subject is able to interpret meaning *intuitively*, without recourse to signs. Yet there are some meanings which are not communicated through 'rational' systems (emotional responses to music, for example), and some states of mind (if we recall Gilbert Ryle's comments on panic) in which the individual does not have time to interpret meaning through sign systems. The prospect of intuitive understanding seems to run counter to the system-bound theories of the Western academic tradition; in refusing to consider such questions, we may see just how firmly entrenched Derrida remains within the tradition he has disrupted.

Context: the 'boundary' of signification?

Derrida argues that meaning is contingent, but that it depends upon what the individual sign is *not*, as much as what it is; this is the theory of 'differance'. To Derrida, all language is metaphorical, and cannot express literal truth. For this reason, fictional forms, which acknowledge their 'rhetorical' foundation, are in his opinion more 'honest' than texts produced by philosophy or other academic practices.

Whatever their strengths as academic theories, structuralism and post-structuralism seem unable to provide the tools for understanding the ordinary exchanges which make up the bulk of human interaction. Would a **contextual** approach help to establish certain **boundaries of meaning** for communication events?

The ambiguity inherent in language and the multiple meanings it is able to produce seem to have misled a number of philosophers into supposing that ambiguity is the only possible, or even the only proper, outcome of expression. The existence of ambiguity does not prove that language is unreliable.

STUDENT ACTIVITIES

ADDRESS AND AUDIENCE
Revision: The concept of address

The concept of **address** may be explained as the *delivery* of a communication (statement, request, admonition and so on) to a specific person or group of people, taking into account the suitability or *register* of the symbolic form used.

Identity and address

It is important to investigate the function of audience **identity** in the construction of an **address**; or, to be more accurate, how a *sense* of audience identity is used by a communicator to form a message. When a deliberate act of communication is initiated, the individual or group responsible for framing the address will act under a number of conditions. These conditions will include the following elements:

- the **context** in which the communicative act is to be made;
- the **audience** (group or individual) intended as the recipient of the address;
- message **content**;
- the consequent message **form**.

Research: Clause 4

On 14 March 1995, the Labour Party's National Executive Committee endorsed the Labour leadership's draft replacement for the historic Clause 4 of the party's constitution. The problem faced by the leadership was how to appeal to a new constituency of voters while ensuring majority support within the Labour Party itself for 'modernisation'. On 29 April, the commitment to 'the common ownership of the means of production', first enshrined in the 1918 constitution, was finally ditched by a conference held in London.

The new clause was considerably longer, at three hundred words, than the original, which stood at sixty. An *Observer* correspondent (Andrew Rawnsley, 30 April) reported that he had failed to find a single delegate at the special conference 'capable of reciting a complete sentence' from the new clause. Part of the problem, according to Bernard Crick (*The Guardian*, 14 March 1995) was that the need to satisfy a very wide audience had reduced the clarity of the piece. Its first paragraph read:

> 'The Labour Party is a democratic socialist party. It believes that ~~by the strength of our common endeavour, we achieve more than we achieve alone so as to create for each of us the means to realise our full potential and for all of us a community in which~~ power, wealth and opportunity ~~are~~ *should be* in the hands of the many not the few. ~~where the rights we enjoy reflect the duties we owe, and where we live together freely, in a spirit of solidarity, tolerance and respect.~~'

The Guardian gave the speech to a former Fleet Street tabloid editor, Roy Greenslade, and asked him to sub-edit the entire clause. His version of the first paragraph cut out much of what he regarded as unneccessary verbiage:

> 'The Labour party is a democratic socialist party. It believes that ~~by the strength of our common endeavour, we achieve more than we achieve alone so as to create for each of us the means to realise our ful potential and for all of us a community in which~~ power, wealth and opportunity ~~are~~ *should be* in the hands of the many not the few. ~~where the rights we enjoy reflect the duties we owe, and where we live together freely, in a spirit of solidarity, tolerance and respect.~~'

It is interesting to note that the kind of language used in the new clause provides scope for comic imitation. The cartoonist Steve Bell produced a version in a cartoon of 14 March, which showed John Prescott as Moses, bringing the word of Tony Blair from the mountain-top:

> 'Thou shalt endeavour to secure for the many the choice for responsible partnership in casting out discriminatory unpleasantness to stand firm in solidarity against sin in a kind of fullish sort of work opportunity society just insofar and for so long as that's alright with the few.'

The second paragraph of the new clause covered the economy:

> 'To these ends we work for: a dynamic economy, serving the public interest, in which the enterprise of the market and the rigour of competition are joined with the forces of partnership and co-operation to produce the wealth the nation needs and the opportunity for all to work and prosper, with a thriving private sector and high quality public services, where those undertakings essential to the common good are either owned by the public or accountable to them.'

Greenslade's sub-editing reduced this to the following:

> 'To these ends ~~we~~ it *works* for: a dynamic economy, ~~serving the public interest~~, in which the enterprise of the market ~~and the rigour of competition are~~ is joined with the forces of partnership and co-operation to produce ~~the wealth the nation needs and the~~ opportunity for all to work and prosper ~~with a thriving private sector and high quality public services, where those undertakings essential to the~~'

479

~~common good are either owned by the public or accountable to them.'~~

Assignment: Investigating values and beliefs

Values are ideas about the relative worth of things, events and experiences, and are usually *applied to* things in the world, rather than being in the nature of things. Beliefs, on the other hand, express a *perceived link* between two aspects of a person's world. Beliefs operate as thoughts or statements about the relative truth or falsehood of a thing. Some beliefs are 'fundamental', such as belief in the existence of certain material objects.

Question a fellow student about his or her values and beliefs. One way to do this is to draw up a list of propositions about various issues, and to ask the individual concerned to supply a response on a scale from 'strongly disagree' to 'strongly agree'. For example, a proposition may state: 'The NHS in Britain should be privatised.' Comparing the responses to a list of statements, it is possible to build up a 'profile' of an individual's values and beliefs. A simpler approach is for each student to list five core values which he or she would defend in any argument. Once a coherent set of values and beliefs has been established, each person can present his or her ideas in the form of a political credo; he or she might be asked to produce his or her own 'Clause 4' as a blueprint for political action.

WRITTEN COMMUNICATION

This section begins with revision material and goes on to examine 'dramatic' prose in the novel and, more particularly, factual reportage.

Revision: Communication and the novel

In *The Novel as Communication* (see D.H. Mellor, *Ways of Communicating*), David Lodge explores the idea that the 'classic novelists' seemed to regard their activity as communication, in the most basic sense of imparting or exchanging information. Lodge (p. 97) uses an example from Henry Fielding's *Tom Jones*, in which 'a metaphor of social intercourse' draws the novel to a close:

> 'We are now, reader, arrived at the last stage of our journey. As we have, therefore, travelled together through so many pages, let us behave to one another like fellow-travellers in a stage-coach, who have passed several days in the company of each other; and who, notwithstanding any bickerings or little animosities which may have occurred on the road, generally make up at last ... since after this stage, it may possibly happen to us ... never to meet more.'

This is an example of 'the intrusive authorial voice' and provides, in Lodge's view (p. 97), 'the most obvious signs that these writers saw themselves as engaged in an exchange with their readers'.

The Marxist critic Walter Benjamin described **storytelling** as a transaction between individuals in close physical proximity to one another, and contrasted this with the novel, produced in one place by a solitary author and consumed in another by an isolated reader. Benjamin's belief that the novel is not 'social' seems both to under-value its role in society and to over-estimate the positive features of traditional oral narratives. A close proximity between storyteller and reader does not necessarily mean that the relationship will be more interactive or democratic.

One of the most significant abilities of literary communication is supposed to be its capacity to transport the reader to times and places beyond his or her common order of experience.

DRAMATIC VISUALISATION IN THE NOVEL
Research: *Martin Chuzzlewit*

Many nineteenth-century authors produced highly dramatic 'visual' representations in their novels. This is sometimes regarded as a remarkable achievement in a society which had yet to develop a cinematic art. However, it is in fact quite natural for a writer to convey the visual impact of a scene to his or her readers, as we shall also see in the section below on reportage. Here is a passage from *Martin Chuzzlewit* by Charles Dickens, in which two men are travelling by carriage in the midst of a thunder storm:

'Surrounded at one moment by intolerable light, and at the next by pitchy darkness, they still pressed forward on their journey ... the eye, partaking of the quickness of the flashing light, saw in its every gleam a multitude of objects which it could not see at steady noon in fifty times that period. Bells in steeples, with the rope and wheel that moved them; ragged nests of birds in cornices and nooks; faces full of consternation in the tilted waggons that came tearing past ...'

Film and television imitate the human ability to report on the visual integrity of events, yet have also produced a 'vocabulary' of their own, seen in the use of close-ups, over-shoulder shots, matches on action, and so on.

REPORTAGE
Reading: Introduction to and extracts from *The Faber Book of Reportage*

We saw above that writers are often able to convey the visual impact of an event. Read the following extract from John Carey's introduction to *The Faber Book of Reportage*. It argues that good factual descriptions rely upon the ability to present an occurrence in as vivid and visual manner as possible:

'Some definitions of reportage insist that it should have been written in the heat of the moment, reflecting the rush and compression and ignorance of what is going to happen next that all reporters have to put up with ... but to include only instant-response stories seemed too cramping ...

What makes good reportage good? ... The power of language to confront us with the vivid, the frightening or the unaccustomed is equalled only by its opposite – the power of language to muffle any such alarms. Either power is available for language-users, but bad reportage opts firmly for the second ... for example, hundreds of pages

of battle accounts filled with sentences like 'Our horse inflicted severe punishment on the enemy's right flank' or 'Four brigade did tremendous execution with the bayonet' – circumlocutions that ... are designed to neutralise and conceal experiences the writers felt too terrible or unseemly or too prejudicial to the future of good order and military discipline to record directly. Such euphemisms illustrate one major function of language, which is to keep reality at bay.

A distinguishing feature of good reportage is that it combats this planned retreat of language from the real ... the good reporter must do everything in his [sic] power to ... isolate the singularities which will make his account real for his readers – not just something written, but something seen.'

The following extracts are taken from Carey's book, and illustrate the ability of prose to reflect the immediacy and visual impact of an event. First, Xenophon's description of the retreat of a Greek mercenary army in Kurdistan, 401 BC:

'Soldiers who had lost the use of their eyes through snow-blindness or whose toes had dropped off from frostbite were left behind. It was a relief to the eyes against snow-blindness if one held something black in front of the eyes while marching; and it was a help to the feet if one kept on the move and never stopped still, and took off one's shoes at night. If one slept with one's shoes on, the straps sank into the flesh and the soles of the shoes froze to the feet. This was more likely to happen since, when their old shoes were worn out, they had made themselves shoes of undressed leather from the skins of oxen that had just been flayed.'

Second, Pliny the Younger's account of the eruption of Vesuvius, 24 August AD 79:

'By now it was dawn, but the light was still dim and faint. The buildings around us were already tottering, and the open space we were in was too small for us not to be in real and imminent danger if the house collapsed. This finally decided us to leave the town. We were followed by a panic-stricken mob ... who hurried us on our way by pressing hard behind in a dense crowd ... We also saw the sea sucked away and apparently forced back by the earthquake: at any rate, it receded from the shore so that quantities of sea creatures were left stranded on dry sand. On the landward side a fearful black cloud was rent by forked and quivering bursts of flame, and parted to reveal great tongues of fire, like flashes of lightning magnified in size.'

Third, William Howard Russell's report on the Charge of the Light Brigade, 25 October 1854:

'They advanced in two lines, quickening their pace as they closed towards the enemy ... At the distance of 1200 yards the whole line of enemy cannon belched forth, from thirty iron mouths, a flood of smoke and flame, through which hissed the deadly balls. Their flight was marked by instant gaps in our ranks, by dead men and horses, by steeds flying wounded or riderless across the plain. The first line was broken – it was joined by the second, they never halted or checked their speed an instant ... Through the clouds of smoke we could see their sabres flashing as they rode up to the guns and dashed between them, cutting down the gunners as they stood. The blaze of their steel, as an officer standing near me said, was "like the turn of a shoal of mackerel".'

Assignment: Reportage

Choose a topic for investigation. This may be anything in the public realm, perhaps a national or local issue, or some controversy which has become part of everyday consciousness. For example, students at Somerset College investigated the effects of the 'recession' on retail traders in their area. *Task One* is to carry out background research into the subject using secondary sources, and to formulate questions for in-depth interviews. *Task Two* is to select interviewees, and is followed by *Task Three*, which is the execution and recording of the interviews. Finally, the results are to be transcribed and the information used to produce an article which includes quotation from the subjects concerned.

In *The Newspapers Handbook* (1994) Richard Keeble devotes a chapter to the practice of conducting interviews (p. 63):

'An interview is intentional conversation. The journalist should always be aware of its specific purposes: they may be seeking information, opinion or evidence of someone's state of mind. They may be investigating a subject and seeking to expose a lie or a wrong-doing.'

Keeble also describes the points which must be remembered when dealing with the interviewee or 'source' (p. 64);

- the source may be confused, yet afraid to admit this
- they may be afraid to speak their true opinion; they could lose their job; they could face social or professional isolation
- the source may be lying; conveying misinformation, propaganda
- they may be intimidated by the presence of the reporter and so not express their true feelings
- the source may be flattered by the attention of the journalist and be more 'extrovert' and colourful than they usually are
- they may forget or hide important details
- the source may be speaking in a foreign language and so be unable to express what is meant [presumably, Keeble means that English may not be the mother tongue].

Assignment: Magazines

Glancing through the pages of a popular magazine or journal, a reader may notice that the various articles, features and displays which appear seem to 'belong' to a number of distinct genres or types. This is no accident, because the division of material into categories is part of the stock in trade of the magazine journalist. The content of a magazine is designed (in the fullest sense of the word) to meet the expectations of an audience which is *already familiar* with past examples of popular journalism. It is, therefore, the *balance* between different material which is essential to the creation of a magazine's character. For example, it is conceivable that a Sunday supplement issued with a popular tabloid might carry material which can also be found in a mainstream women's journal.

Creating a magazine

Carry out the following instructions:

1 Select three magazines and describe in each case the:
   - type of content;
   - form;
   - target audience or market.

2 Select one article, one advertisement, and one other example of
   - design
   - address.

3 Comment on the general outlook or perspective of the magazine.

4 Choose an *audience* and a *theme* and design a front cover. Write an article for a contemporary magazine.

In the creation of a magazine, the most important elements to understand are as follows:

1 *content* – this means what the magazine contains; the articles, advertisements, contents page, advice column, letters page, and so on. If we are talking about the general type of content, we are referring to *generic* content.

2 *form* – this is the arrangement of content; it refers to the *individual* arrangement of an article, advert, and so on, as well as to the *juxtaposition* of these individual elements.
In the first case, a letters page may include photographs which illustrate the themes concerned. In the second case, an advertisement for a third-world charity might appear next to an article on cookery. Typefaces, design and the use of space are all aspects of form.

3 *audience* – all magazines have a sense of audience; the audience is, to some degree, known by the institution which produces an individual magazine. Market research is carried out, so that data about an audience's class and age and region is gathered.

4 *address* – this refers to the way that an audience is 'spoken to'. Individual audience members respond to an address, sometimes by assuming the role that is offered to them, although perhaps only for a short period of time.

5 *register* – this means the 'level' at which an address is pitched, and the suitability of the address to the target audience.

BROADCAST TALK
Reading: Studio talk

In his Introduction to *Broadcast Talk*, Paddy Scannell describes studio talk shows, game shows, discussion programmes, quizzes and musical performances as 'live' media. Of course, a great deal of this material is recorded, and is therefore only live in the sense that it is originally *recorded* under live conditions. The recordings are made, however, without the use of extensive editing. As Scannell observes (p.1):

> 'Recorded programmes are just that: Wogan and Blind Date, for instance, are not constructed shot by separate shot, but in one continuous take.'

This gives such programrnes a 'sense of existing in real time'. They are also produced in 'actual institutional settings' and the talk they contain is therefore *intentionally* communicative, a public discourse designed not simply as an interaction between individuals, but

APRIL 18 1994

Figure 5.5   The Guardian: front cover from a magazine exercise (Zoe Watson)

also to be heard by what Scannell calls 'absent audiences'.

Analysis: *Have I Got News for You*

An example of 'broadcast talk', where a number of individuals engage in group communication for the sake of entertainment, is given below. In some studio events, such as political interviews, drifting away from the point of the exchange would be unacceptable. In a comedy programme of this nature, however, such digression can be permitted if it appears to make the

audience laugh. (There are two audiences in this case, the studio audience and the 'absent' audience – the viewers – which it represents.)

The ostensible purpose of *Have I Got News for You* is for one team to gain enough points to win the contest. However, the real purpose is an exercise in political satire, allowing the regular contestants and their guests to make amusing remarks. Where the material concerned is unpromising, it is still necessary to keep the audience and the panel entertained. The contestants are Ian Hislop, Hugh Dennis, Paul Merton and John Stalker, with Angus Deayton in the chair. Here, one member of the two teams is asked to supply the background and context to a newspaper headline:

Deayton:	... with Paul (.) a tricky one for you to decipher (1.5) 'Personnel Officers are a waste of time' (2)
Merton:	Well (,) Personnel Officers are a waste of time (2)
Hislop:	We all know that
Merton:	If you (,) if you sort of send a Personnel Officer down the shops to get you some fags or something they'll come back with a lawnmower or something (1,5) and they are a waste of time (1)
Deayton:	You don't know the answer to this one do you
Merton:	It's self-evident (1.5)
Deayton:	Er – not as such (.) er well it's a good (.) I was gonna say a good answer it's actually the same as the question isn't it really (1.5) um any idea over here
Hislop:	Is it a survey
Merton:	Well it's obviously a survey (,) a study that's decided that Personnel Officers are a waste of time (1.5) I don't really know any other way of putting it really
Deayton:	No (.) no evidently not because
Merton:	They are not um as good as they could be (1.5) they take a certain amount of time but the bit of time they take (.) is wasted (2)
Hislop:	Is this the one about the parrot on um amphetamines (4)
Deayton:	This is er reading between the lines somewhat isn't it um

Merton:	It's a parrot on amphetamines and the only thing it can say is Personnel Officers are a waste of time (.) but very quickly (1)
Hislop:	And the neighbours are totally fed up of this boring parrot saying Personnel Officers are a waste of time yeh (.) a huge court case
Deayton:	It's not a hundred per cent true (1)
Merton:	Yeah but then what is (3)
Deayton:	It's getting rather philosophical now um (1) Ian any ideas as to what this might be
Hislop:	We reckon that the people in offices designated to deal with (1.5) the problems of their staff are on the whole not really working at 100% efficiency (3)
Merton:	In fact there's a very good phrase that would sum up what you've just said (7)
Deayton:	It is (,) it is a new study by the LSE (.) which has revealed that uh companies which employ a Personnel Officer actually perform worse than those which don't (.) or to put it another way they're a waste of time (,) apparently there are now so many Personnel Officers in Britain that they outnumber coal miners ten to one (,) If only you could convert power stations to run on bullshit
Merton:	Ironically you'd be in constant demand, wouldn't you
Deayton:	Yes
Merton:	You haven't ever been a Personnel Officer have you
Deayton:	My brother has been (.) well he is actually
Merton:	Really
Hislop:	Is he a waste of time (1.5)
Merton:	What's your brother's name

Deayton:	Bill
Merton:	Bill um (1.5)
Deayton:	Sorry (,) we have to be getting on (1) Ironically the Government is employing thousands of Personnel managers in hospitals (2) and uh
Hislop:	Oh are we still on this one (1.5)
Merton:	Oh we were right when we said it was a waste of time weren't we (4) have you got any pictures of him (1.5)
Deayton:	No (.) well I have (,) at home
Hislop:	This is the most boring round we've ever had on this show (3)
Stalker and Merton (together):	It's a waste of time (2)
Dennis:	Would you have been Bill if you'd been the oldest (2) or not
Deayton:	I probably would actually Hugh yeah (.) you're not actually called Hugh are you Hugh
Dennnis:	No I'm not called Hugh
Deayton:	What's your real name
Dennis:	Pete
Merton:	Pete (1)
Dennis:	I thought about Bill but I didn't like it (2)
Merton:	Have you got a brother called Dennis (1)
Dennis:	Denis Dennis
Merton:	Yeah (.) cos Duran Duran had sort of the same thing (3)
Hislop:	Sorry (1) are we still doing the show (2)
Merton:	So anyway I think the answer is that Personnel Officers are a waste of time
Deayton:	Thankyou

Questions

1 'We reckon that the people in offices designated to deal with the problems of their staff are on the whole not really working at 100% efficiency.' How is Hislop's answer intended to be humorous?

2 How does the following digression come about?

Dennis:	Would you have been Bill if you'd been the oldest (2) or not
Deayton:	I probably would actually Hugh yeah (.) you're not actually called Hugh are you Hugh
Dennis:	No I'm not called Hugh
Deayton:	What's your real name
Dennis:	Pete

Merton:	Pete (1)
Dennis:	I thought about Bill but I didn't like it (2)
Merton:	Have you got a brother called Dennis (1)
Dennis:	Denis Dennis
Merton:	Yeah (.) cos Duran Duran had sort of the same thing (3)

3 William Labov (1970) used the following structures for conversation analysis:

- question and answer;
- challenge and response;
- invitation and acceptance.

Identify and record any examples of these structures in the exchange above.

4 Was this whole speech event a waste of time?

THE DISCOURSES OF ART
Revision: Aesthetics

One of the charges laid against **fine art** has been '**elitism**'. It has been attacked for holding itself aloof from common experience, and for spawning a class of expert which reserves to itself the task of translating an artist's intention. It does so, according to this view, for an audience which is imagined to have no specialist training in or knowledge of art. The traditional role of the art critic is that of someone who appears to have the required expertise and refinement of aesthetic taste needed to explain to others the worth of paintings or artefacts.

Aesthetics

A definition of the original meaning of aesthetics is supplied by O'Sullivan and his colleagues in the 1987 *Key Concepts in Communication*, where it is described as (p. 4):

'a concept inherited from idealist philosophy, referring to principles of taste, especially good taste, and hence of beauty'.

The object of study for aesthetics is 'the art-object itself, taken out of its historical, cultural and means-of-production context'. Here, expertise would be used to isolate 'those textual properties' which make an art-object beautiful.

The revolt against elitism in artistic taste led to a new conceptualisation of beauty and new standards of worth. Instead of a pure 'aesthetics', where the art-object itself carries value, artistic production came to be recognised as carrying an aesthetic code, which could be interpreted once its historical context and mode of production (mechanical or artisanal, for example) were taken into account. The movement away from a notion of 'pure' value in art, towards an appreciation of less traditional forms, has certainly encouraged greater freedom of expression. However, some may suspect that one orthodoxy has merely been replaced with another.

Research: Abstract art

If representation is the re-presentation of things known in the real world, how does abstract art work as a form of expression? Language and other sign systems consist of *symbolic content*, but no system always produces exact correspondences between symbol and reference. Abstract art appears to make direct reference to emotions and ideas, and does not appear to refer first to objects or artefacts.

One method of studying the meaning of abstract or non-figurative art is to present fellow students or another suitable audience with a series of paintings and ask audience members to write down their immediate response to what they see. Sean Scully's paintings, which consist of lines, squares and blocks of colour, are a useful example. A class was shown two of his paintings from the videotape of the Turner prize programme (Channel 4, November 1993), but were given no explanation of the pictures. The group was then asked to comment on the meanings created by the paintings (all responses were written down without discussion).

Of course, if one asks people to look for meaning, this will effect how they report what they see. However, within the range of written answers, there were a number of similar responses. The comments below were based on studying Scully's *Vita Duplex*:

'Anger, repressed emotions and feelings.'
'Jail on one side, freedom on the other.'
'Prison – entrapment. The stripe signifies that the left-hand side is bad.'
'Contrast, segregation. Black and cold.'
'Liquorice allsort.'
'Everyone going in different directions. Looks troubled.'
'All muddled. Squares are the path through it.'
'You don't know which you want to look at – bright or grey. Repressed feelings.'
'A maze, life – lots of points not leading anywhere.'
'Orange is the happy side, the other is sadder.'
'Black and white is confusion. Orange and grey is the path you should take.'

There are some aspects of human understanding which seem to bypass 'rational' systems like language; emotional responses to music provide one example. Images also appear capable of creating meaning through a form of *graphical communication*. These meanings are sometimes difficult to put into words. What meanings or responses are generated by the image reproduced in Figure 5.5A (p. 188)?

REPRESENTATION
Revision: Social attributes of 'stars'

There have been many attempts to explain the '**star**' phenomenon, in which an actor attains an exalted status and a persona which is recognised across the globe. In 1960, Morin described how the function of film stars changes over time. At the beginning of the sound era, Morin argued that stars were transformed from an embodiment of society's ideals to 'identification figures', representing the more ordinary or typical aspects of individual behaviour. Tyler, writing in 1970, decided that they

provided a point of religious identification, in an age when traditional religious belief had declined.

Writing in 'Social attributes of American movie stars', Emanuel Levy argues that this kind of explanation is inadequate. Using the 'Motion Picture Herald Poll', a survey of the top stars in the American film industry which has appeared yearly since 1932, Levy examines the 'social attributes' of American movie stars. The *physical appearance*, *age*, *acting abilities* and *screen image* or *persona* are all taken as indicators of the social attributes of a total of 129 actors over the period 1932–84. Using these indicators, Levy discovered a great deal about the values espoused by US society.

For example, male actors were usually possessed of dark looks, while the preferred image of female stars was blonde. Only two male stars in the entire period studied were blond, and they attempted to offset this 'disadvantage' by taking roles which emphasised their toughness and masculinity. Overall, however, physical attractiveness is only one element which goes to make 'star quality'. A distinctive screen image is of great importance in establishing individuals as stars.

Levy uses the concept of 'statements' to explore the durability of individual actors. Within the film narrative, certain 'statements' of a social nature are made. These must be recognised as socially relevant by an audience. Where an actor appears in a role which suits his or her persona, in a film whose 'statement' seems apposite to the values of the age, the status of 'star' is often attained.

Analysis: TV 'trailers'

One neglected area of media study is the way that 'trailers' for television series, together with the retelling of story-lines at the beginning of each episode, are used to capture the attention of viewers. Such introductions often make up complete narratives in their own right. Study the example below, taken from the second episode of the police series *Grushko*, before recording a series of trailers and introductions. An oblique symbol /, indicates a cut between those shots from the first episode which are used to illustrate the voiceover.

Figure 5.5A   Photo by Andrew Parker

'Two bodies are found in a Russian forest. A Georgian gangster identified as Vager and / Mickan Milukin, the acclaimed television journalist / Investigating this double murder is Colonel Grushko, Chief of Police in St Petersburg, a city ravaged by rival factions / fighting for control of the black market / Grushko's inquiries reveal two leads, a golden carved trophy stolen from the journalist's apartment on the night of the murder / and the KGB was tapping his phone / the Georgian's gang demands vengeance / for Vager's death; one suspect is Sultan the Chechen gangboss. While Grushko / was under pressure to solve the murder of a /public figure, the gangs pursue their murderous vendettas.'

EDITING VIDEO TAPE
Production: Using an editing suite

Figure 5.6 shows a remote control unit with two monitors. Two VHS tapes are required for editing. The master tape containing the source material is placed in the source unit, usually the top one, while the edit tape is placed in the editor unit, usually the lower machine (the units are not shown in the diagram). Images from the master tape are displayed on the left-hand screen, while the edit tape is viewed on the right. The purpose of editing is to transfer an image electronically from the source or master tape to the edit tape. The edit tape must carry a signal at the beginning, lasting at least 30 seconds, so that the electronic image may have something to 'hook' onto at the start of the tape.

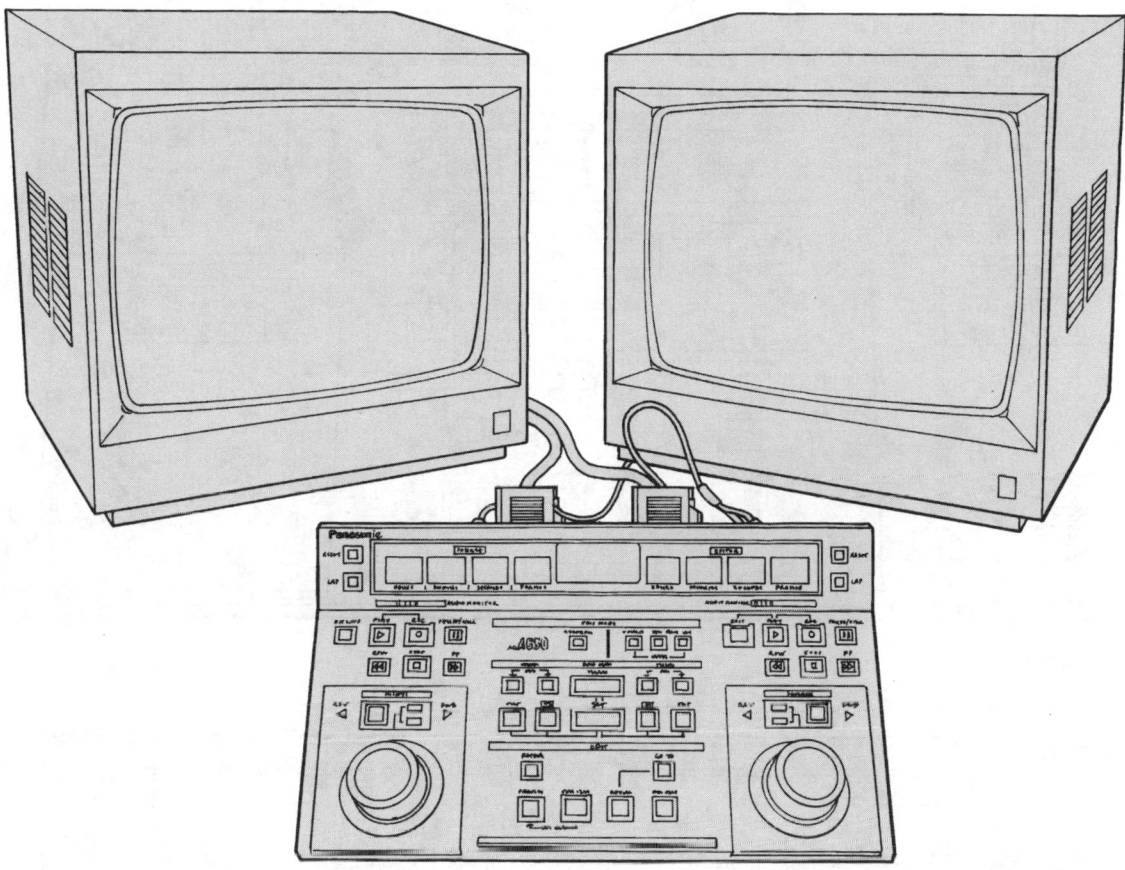

Figure 5.6   Monitors and control unit

Figure 5.7 shows a close-up of the control unit. The two edit machines are controlled by this unit, its left-hand side controls the source, while the right-hand side controls the editor unit.

The large circular dials at left and right are the control knobs (Fig. 5.8). When video cassettes are played, these are used to find the correct place on the tapes. The left-hand knob controls the source tape, while the right-hand dial controls the editor tape. Moving the control knob to the centre position brings the tape to a halt. If the tape is to be rewound (RW), the dial is turned anti-clockwise. If it is to be advanced, the dial is turned clockwise (FF). The further a dial is turned, the faster the tape will move. With care, the tape can be moved in either direction, frame by frame.

Notice that there is a 'window' which shows the time settings for both source and editor units (Fig. 5.9). These are used so that a note can be made of the exact place where an edit is to begin and thus where the image is to be transferred.

The place at which an edit is to be made is known as the 'edit-in point'. Once you have found the start of the scene on the source tape which you want to transfer, the IN and SET buttons are pressed simultaneously for the source unit (Fig. 5.10). When you have located the position on the editor tape at which you want the transferred scene to begin, press the IN and SET buttons for the editor unit. The scene will be transferred from master or source tape to the edit tape.

Once the edit-in points have been selected, press the two EDIT START buttons, shown in Figure 5.11. Both tapes travel backwards for about five seconds, then

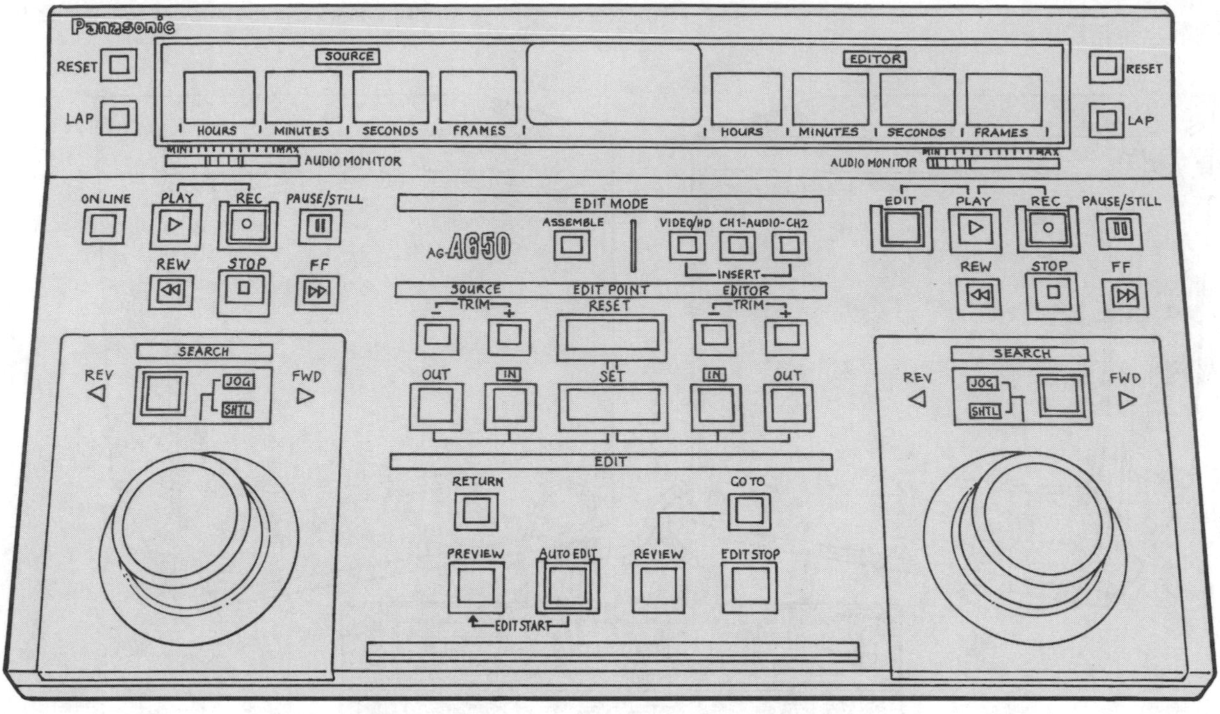

Figure 5.7   Control unit

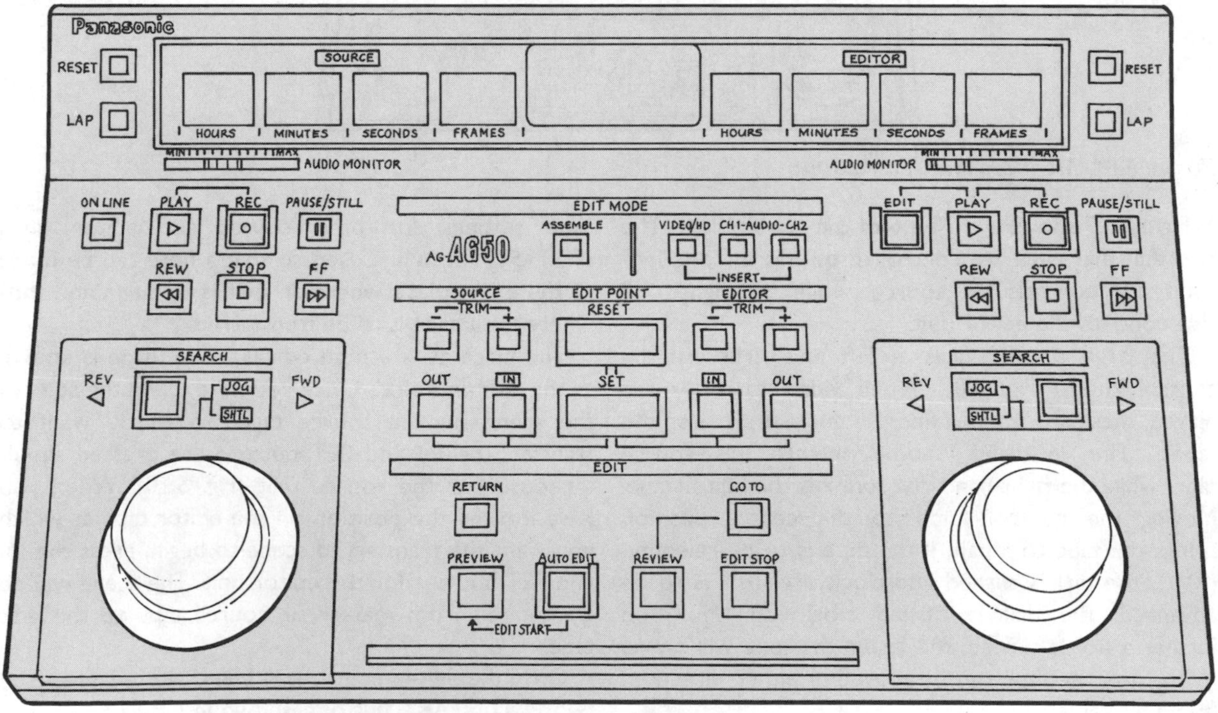

Figure 5.8   Control unit showing control knobs

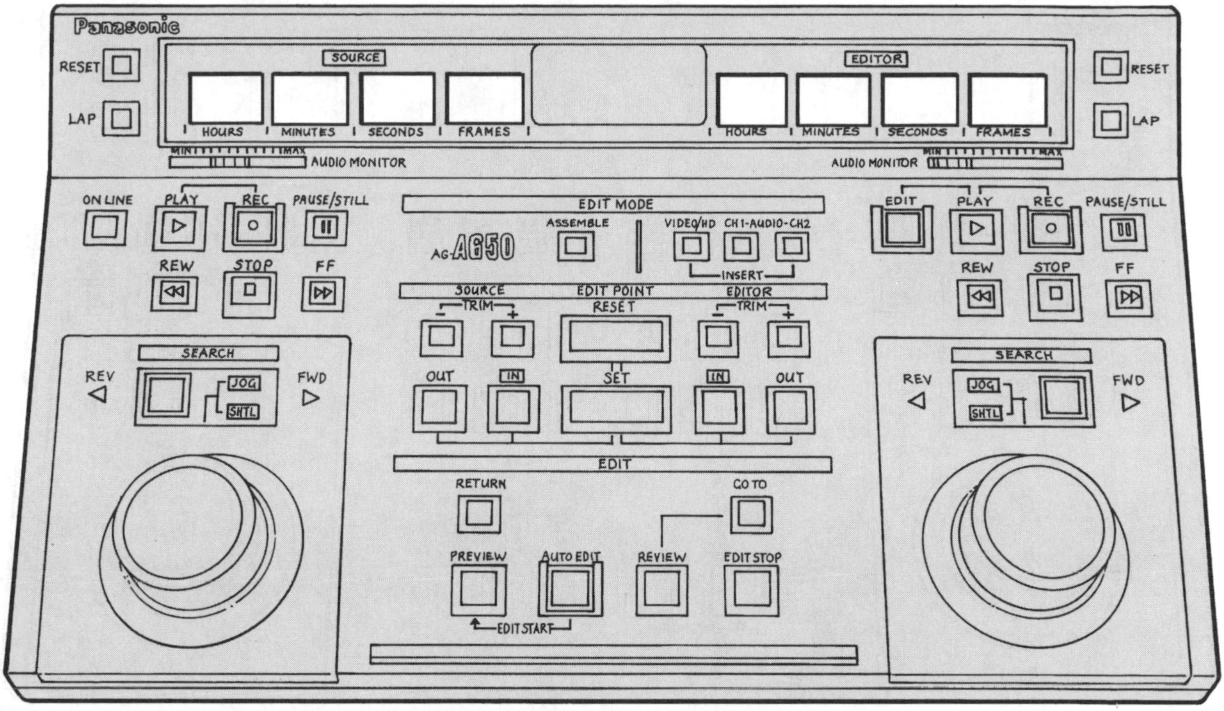

Figure 5.9   'Windows' from which time settings are read

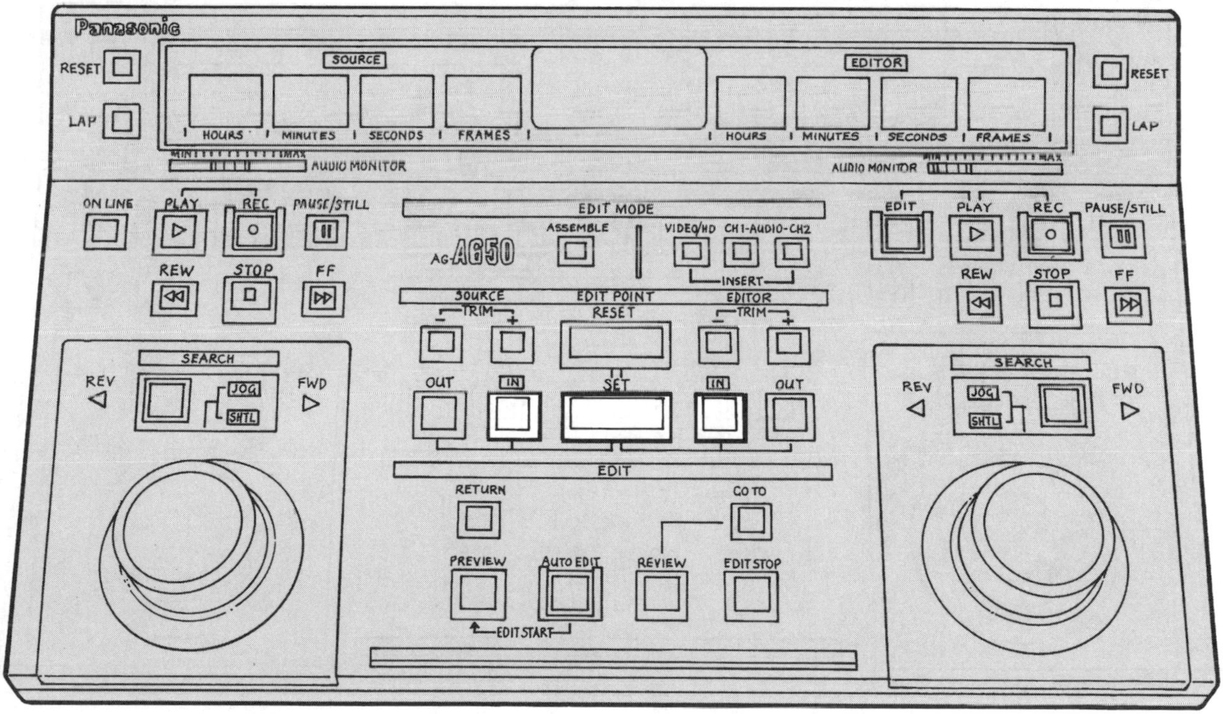

Figure 5.10   IN and SET buttons for source and editor

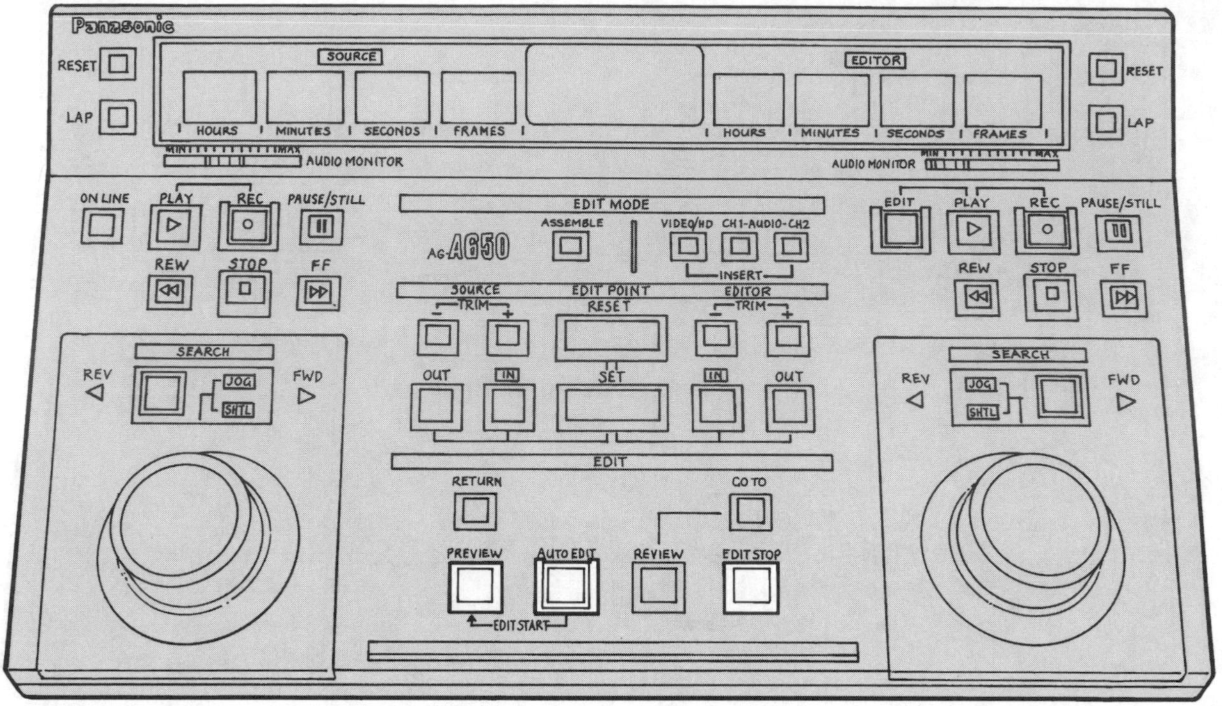

Figure 5.11   EDIT START and EDIT STOP buttons

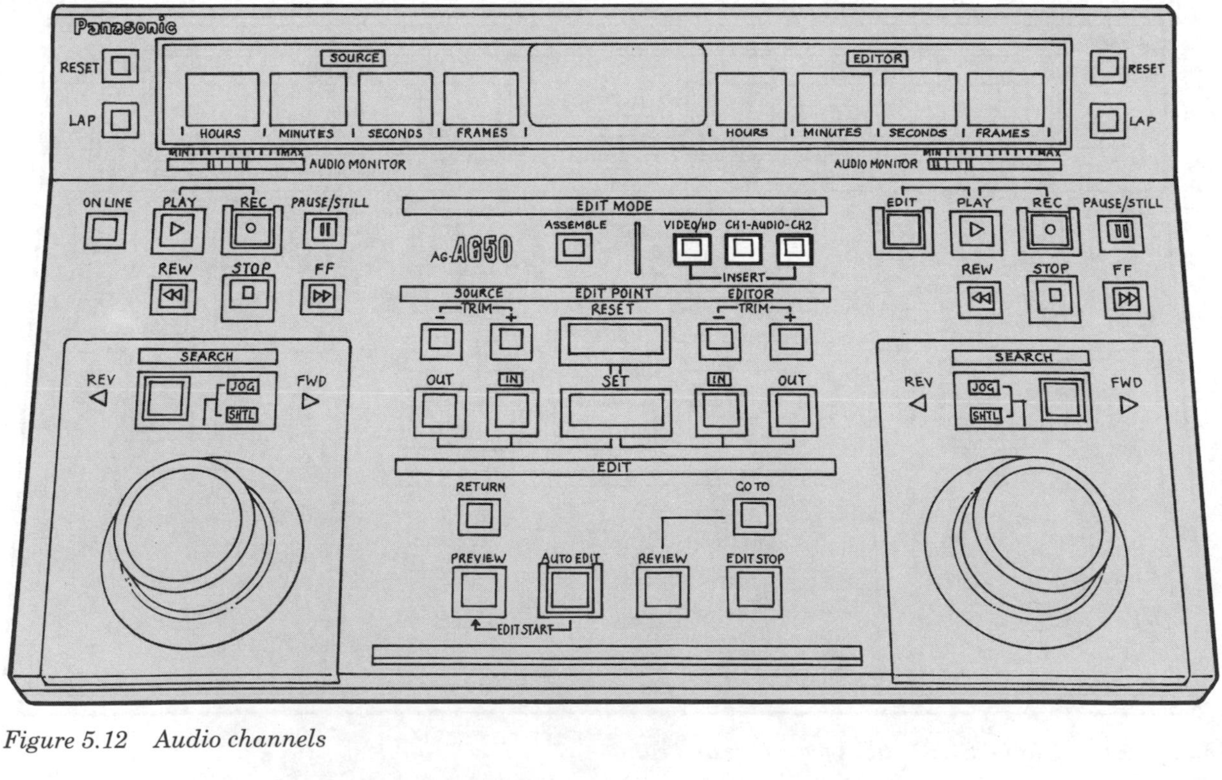

Figure 5.12   Audio channels

move forward to the points set previously. Allow the tapes to go a little further than required, then press the EDIT STOP button and wait for the edit to stop.

The process may be repeated any number of times, until the task is completed. Sound may also be transferred from source to edit tape (Fig. 5.12). Three lights may appear in the centre of the control unit, When these lights are switched on, they show that a signal is being transferred. It is possible, for example, to transfer only one audio channel onto the edit tape. It is also quite easy to lay a soundtrack over an existing image, or a new picture over existing sound.

ESSAY TITLES

Questions

1 'Is there not something fundamentally unnatural and unhealthy about a form of art which suspends the reader's awareness of his own existence in real space and time? Is not the pleasure of the novelistic text akin to day-dreaming, wish-fulfilment fantasy?' (David Lodge)

Is the novel an unhealthy distraction from real life, or does it serve more positive functions? Refer to examples from your own reading.

2 'The point is simple: art as a speculative currency, and vice-versa. To put it more bluntly: Art equals Money and Money equals Art.' (The K Foundation)

Have painting and sculpture become simply another commodity, or are they still able to raise significant and important issues?

3 'Despite its shortcomings the typical cop thriller does allow the exploration of a common feature of our society; the bureaucratic constraints placed upon the population. The problem lies in the fact that rebellion is confined to the ranks of those who have some power to affect the destinies of others.'

Discuss with reference to at least *two* 'cop movies' you have seen.

4 Select *three* scenes from any mainstream films and provide an account of actions performed and dialogue spoken. Where possible, choose different

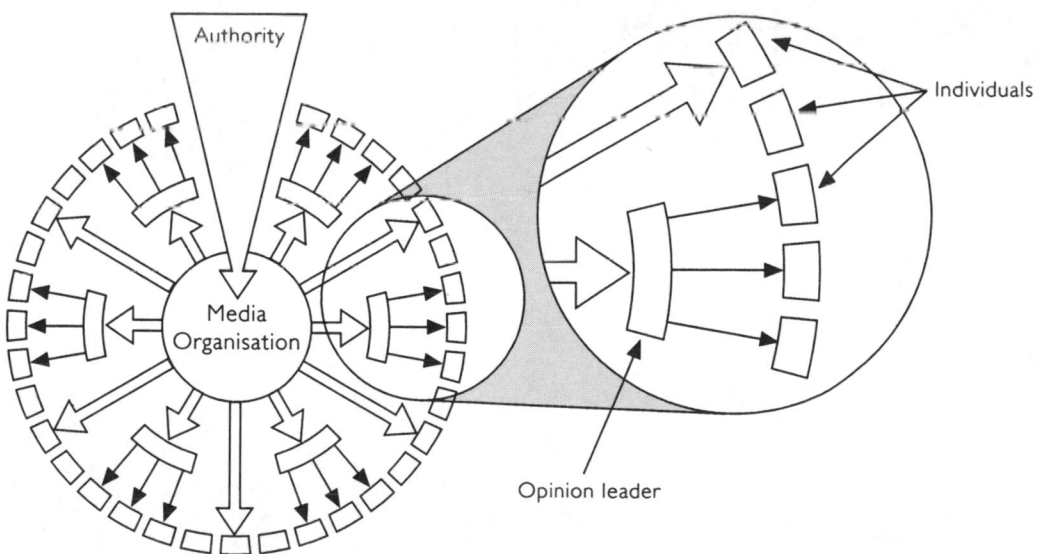

Figure 5.13   Two-step flow theory (see Question 5)

films and select encounters where the number of characters is limited to two or three. In addition, record or write down examples taken from ordinary interactions where the participants are unaware of your presence (you will, however, need to seek permission for the use of this material once recorded).

5 Study Figure 5.13, which illustrates *two-step flow theory*. This is the idea that the media make an impact on their audiences by first making an impresison on an 'opinion leader', who passes his or her response to a message (whether favourable or unfavourable) on to other individuals.

How useful is this model in analysing the process of influence involved in *either* party political broadcasts, *or* advertisements, *or* controversial cinema films?

6 'Postmodernism has us accepting ... actually celebrating the activity of masking and cover-up, all the fetishisms of locality, place, or social grouping.' (David Harvey, 1990)

To what extent is this a fair assessment of the influence of postmodernism? Are there other points which may be presented in its favour?

CHAPTER 6

Research and project work

Theory and research

Theory should not be seen as a necessary evil, the 'abstract' component of Communication Studies, endured because candidates must pass written papers or because the subject needs to maintain credibility in the eyes of other disciplines. Where it is valued, theory is too often presented as purely *academic*, with all the negative connotations suggested by a term once defined by the *Concise Oxford Dictionary* as 'Scholarly (and by implication) abstract, unpractical, cold, merely logical'.

In the study of communication, theory must be applied in a practical context if it is to make sense. The role of **research** and project work is therefore one of the most important areas of study in the whole subject. When research is undertaken, teachers and students are faced with a series of problems which are never purely conceptual, nor exclusively practical; they are a combination of the two. As Tim May writes in his book *Social Research* (1993, p. 20):

'Social theory is not something that can be separated from the process of social research. Theory informs our thinking which, in turn, assists us in making research decisions and sense of the world around us. Our experiences of doing research . . . in turn, influence our theorising.'

If we take this idea to heart, work in communication theory should benefit from research, showing how ideas are relevant to ordinary life. As early as 1959 (see May, p. 21), authors like C. Wright Mills (in *The Sociological Imagination*) disparaged those 'grand theorists' who were unable to understand the problems which are important to real people in real contexts. May takes this point seriously, emphasising the difference between (p. 22) 'grand' and 'grounded' theory. The former attempts a complete description of the social world, while sometimes losing sight of the real conditions of life, while the latter is based on research into lived experience.

The concept of science

The **concept of science** has played a central role in the development of modern social theory. The debate about the exact status of the 'scientific' remains an important issue for investigation. 'Science' means systematic and supposedly *objective* inquiry into the world. The basic assumption usually made about scientific investigation is that it is primarily concerned not with *ideas* but with *facts*, which are directly observed from reality and are then presented in a rational and ordered fashion. The traditional view of scientific activity sets great store upon rationality and the reliability of the data which scientists produce.

One fundamental criticism of the 'objective' view of science is that the scientific community creates meaning *within* the models of reality available at the time; information is always classified according to the prevailing notions of knowledge. When such models have to be revised, the conclusions based on them may also be called into question.

In fact, there are times when a particular 'fashion' for certain types of investigation encourages major errors in scientfic practice. Marten Shipman, in *The Limitations of Social Research* (1988) recalls Blondlot's 1903 discovery of 'n-rays' which (following Röntgen's 1896 breakthrough in establishing the existence of X-rays) seemed plausible because it was in keeping with the expectations of the age. However, attempts by scientists outside France to reproduce Blondlot's experiments failed, and the 'n-ray' disappeared from history. The 'discovery' had been encouraged by the 'world-view' held by scientists; in other words, by what seemed probable at the time. In Shipman's words, Blondlot was (p. 10): 'a victim of his own expectations', an 'extreme, unfortunate but understandable occurrence given the way scientists go about their work'.

This leads to another basic criticism of the 'infallibility' of science. Shipman takes issue with the idea of objective method in research, arguing that the scientific paper is (p. 10): 'a fraud because it suggests observation and experiment followed by discussion of the results obtained'. In Shipman's opinion:

'that is to reverse the actual process which starts with the expectations built into models that guide the observations made and their interpretation'.

Shipman goes on to distinguish between two competing views of science (p. 11):

'First, there are those who have held that science is indeed concerned with the collection and interpretation of raw data impinging on an open mind. Second, there are more recent approaches that incorporate the idea of a scientific community influencing members and sharing conceptual frameworks that influence observation and interpretation.'

In other words, the differences are between a view of science which sees it as entirely objective, and one which regards it as an activity partly determined by the ideas and discourses of the age in which it operates. The latter view does not necessarily mean that science inevitably produces a distorted picture of reality.

Traditions of research

Early social science

Once nineteenth-century academics had become interested in social issues, it was inevitable that active forms of research would be carried out. The 'early' period of research, identified by Jensen and Jankowski (see *A Handbook of Qualitative Methodologies*), took place from approximately 1890 to 1930. Early work in the **social sciences** tended to be qualitative in nature, because of the influence of the humanities. The scientific paradigm, involving the 'objective' measurement of social phenomena, was not at first applied to the social sciences.

However, the belief in an objective science of *nature* led some thinkers to believe that there could also be a rational and scientific study of *society*. This development was not surprising since, as Shipman points out (p. 19), 'scientific method was seen as free of mystery, superstition and religious obscurity'. It is nevertheless ironical that at a time when the science of nature had to adjust to an unpredictable, *atomic* basis for inquiry, the social sciences became engaged in the struggle to find the 'laws' of human development and behaviour. Of course, the identification of any 'law' must consist in part of what Shipman calls (p. 21) 'an oversimplification'.

From the Chicago School to the modern period

Sociological investigations carried out by the famous '**Chicago School**' were characterised by their adherence to first-hand observation. This did not, however, extend to modern practices of participant observation. By the 1930s, quantitative methodologies (following a tendency to imitate the approaches favoured by the scientific community) had increased in popularity at the expense of the qualitative approach of the early period (see above).

The years from 1930 to 1960, identified by Jensen and Jankowski as the 'middle' period of inquiry, saw the establishment of the survey as a form. The aim of quantitative sociology seems to have been (Jensen and Jankowski, p. 49): 'to elevate the status of sociology to a science'.

The current period, from about 1960 to the present, has seen extensive dissatisfaction with the 'scientific' approach. In words reminiscent of postmodernist critiques, Gouldner (1970) attacked the idea of 'grand theory', while Blumer (1954) expressed disagreement with the tendency to 'reduce social existence to variables'. The return to qualitative methods put greater emphasis upon empathy with the human subject. Weber described this process of understanding as *verstehen,* and this became a byword for a certain type of interpretative sociology. Blumer (1969) argued that people behave according to the *meanings* they attribute to their own experience of events and other material phenomena. This means that the sociologist must understand the perspective of the individual subject on the events or experiences under investigation, suggesting in turn that the relationship between researcher and subject will inevitably be reasonably close.

A brief survey of less 'interventionist' methods would include *participant observation* (see below) and *symbolic interactionism* (see Chapter 1), an approach which tries to avoid making judgements about the individuals and groups studied. In the words of Cuff and Payne (in Hugh Chignell's *Data in Sociology*, p. 7), symbolic interactionism depends upon:

> 'describing the competing and conflicting claims men [sic] make about what is "real" and "what is happening"'.

Ethnomethodology is another form of interpretative enquiry which (Jensen and Jankowski, p. 53) 'seeks to identify the rules people apply in order to make sense of their world'. No single research method is associated with this current, but participant observation, in-depth interviews and investigation of everyday conversation feature prominently in the range of approaches at its disposal.

Research: new paradigms?

The concern with audience is not an entirely recent phenomenon, but one that appears in communication research at various points throughout the twentieth century. For example, a celebrated article by Katz and Foulkes, published in the *Public Opinion Quarterly* of 1962, suggested a move from studying 'what the media do to people' to a focus on 'what people do with the media'. It is, however, important to stress that an interest in *reception* did not always mean that *audience studies* took a more humane form than the study of public institutions or the 'grand narratives' of social theory. In 1981, for example, Peter Reason and John Rowan argued against the dominant models of social research, which they believed alientated the human subject at the centre of study (see *Human Inquiry: A Sourcebook of New Paradigm Research*).

Reason and Rowan's '**New Paradigm** research' is based on the idea that the two established methods of research, the 'naive inquiry' and the 'scientific method', are both inadequate. In the first place, *naive inquiry* is thought to be too subjective, while the second category of research is regarded as creating an entirely clinical view of the human subject. While the naive paradigm is (p. xiii) 'very prone to error' it has at least the virtue of being 'involved, committed, relevant, intuitive; above all it is *alive*'. 'Objective' research, on the other hand, appears to clear up many of the faults of the subjective model, but in so doing 'kills off everything it comes into contact with, so what we are left with is dead knowledge'. It is against the 'scientific' model that Reason and Rowan protest (p. xii):

'Through our balanced cool appraisal there comes an undercurrent of hatred and horror about what traditional research does to those it studies, those who do the research, and about the dreadful rubbish that is sometimes put forward as scientific knowledge.'

The rigidly 'objective' model used by social science produces, in their opinion, a series of outcomes which treat human responses as (p. 93) 'emitted behaviours' and 'variables'. The aim of the 'New Paradigm' model is to allow the subject greater involvement in setting the parameters of research. It also pays closer attention to the motives of the researchers who initiate the inquiry.

A turn to audience and the 'everyday' does not, however, solve all the problems inherent in studying human and 'mass' communication. Issues of influence and power, whether personal or institutional, will always remain a vital part of the communication agenda. The solution, as these authors see it, is to opt for an 'objectively subjective' approach, one which draws upon (p. xvii):

'ethnomethodology, and participant observation [which], while not totally beyond reproach, at their best show that a researcher may get to grips with the messiness and confusion of everyday life ... [emerging] with some reasonably valid understandings'.

Values and ethics in research

One view of research and scientific inquiry states that it is possible to separate *positive* findings (factual data about what really happens in the world) from *normative* theories (ideas about what the world ought to be like). Some writers, on the other hand, argue that it is impossible to create a social science which is 'value free'. This debate is essentially similar to the one on the natural sciences, mentioned above. Tim May (*Social Research*, p. 33) thinks that a 'value-free' science, whether social or natural, is unlikely to exist, citing 'the constant interaction between ideas within society and the ideas within science'. May gives an example of this interaction (p. 33):

'some religious groups in the nineteenth century believed that the world was only a few thousand years old. Subsequent advances in the science of geology demonstrated that some rocks were a million years old and others considerably older. In the face of such findings these religious groups had several choices; to deny the validity of the scientific findings; to modify their religious beliefs accordingly; or perhaps even to hold on to both belief and evidence at the same time.'

An example of the incorporation of scientific evidence into the religious 'world-view' is given by May when he refers to 'Big Bang' theory. This does not disturb the beliefs of some Christians because they imagine that it was God who lit the blue touch-paper. It is worth noting that a number of popular science books, such as Stephen Hawking's *A Brief History of Time*, talk about the role of scientific inquiry in reaching an understanding of God.

Research: origins and purposes

The question of values and ethics in communication inquiry must extend to examining the origins and purposes of research. Whenever research is initiated, it is important to ask which institutions or individuals provided the funding, what intention lay behind the study, how the research was designed and conducted, and how the findings were interpreted and then used.

It is clear, for example, that social power is not distributed evenly amongst all groups; the relationship of the researcher to some sections of his or her 'target' group is therefore worth exploring. Feminist researchers have noted that the values held by many male academics colour the entire research process, and therefore its ultimate outcome. In *Managing Sociology Coursework*, Peter Langley also identifies the tendency for values to influence results (p. 25):

'A research project concerning images of women in the media may well use content analysis as a method. A content analysis frame can be drawn which only includes counting instances where women are portrayed in stereotypical ways. A significant degree of strereotyping will inevitably be found.'

Research: ethics

The question of **ethics** is also of major significance when research is being conducted. The term 'ethics' refers to the set of standards which a group or larger collective uses to regulate the behaviour of its members. May (in *Social Research*) cites Barnes's (1979) definition of ethics in research as those standards which (p. 42):

'arise when we try to decide between one course and another not in terms of expediency or efficiency but by reference to standards of what is morally right or wrong'.

This means that more is at stake than simply the success of the research or the well-being of the researcher. The well-being, both physical and moral, of all the participants in the research process should be of the utmost importance. May writes of social research carried out during the Vietnam War, when social scientists conducted surveys into the moral and political allegiances of the Vietnamese people. The results were allegedly used by the US military to select targets for bombing (see May, p. 37). If true, this example clearly demonstrates the failure to carry out research in an ethical framework.

Some researchers have argued, in contrast, that the development of a 'professional' ethics can lead to restrictions on freedom of information and freedom of speech. However, it is possible to discover considerable differences between those who are genuinely concerned with public morality, and those who use 'the public interest' as an excuse for secrecy.

Communication projects: purpose and choice

To argue that science and social science are not entirely objective should not lead us to suppose that nothing of value is ever produced through academic research, nor should it discourage anyone from making a success of project work. A number of small-scale investigations have produced material of outstanding originality and considerable accuracy.

The **purpose** of projects has often been described as the creation of links between the 'classroom' and 'the real world' (see Neil McKeown, *Case Studies and Projects in Communication*). This is a valid point, but might give the impression that education has somehow been a 'protected' sphere of experience, while in fact it has always been subject to the pressures of political and economic change. Many of my readers do not need to be introduced to 'the real world', because they already inhabit it. Choosing an area of research is therefore often a case of exploring issues which have already been experienced, both within the boundaries of the course and outside it.

The best approach to project work is to get involved in *research* and in *presentation* of that research from the outset. Ideally, small-scale research projects should be attempted well before any externally assessed work is required. (At A-level a project might run over a period of six months; at degree level a study or dissertation might form one of a series of modular components).

The project proposal

The **proposal** form can appear quite daunting, but the intention is to help clarify ideas. The AEB includes the following areas, each of which must be submitted before the project is allowed to begin:

- a brief description of the intended project, including the format proposed;
- intended readership or audience;
- aims of the finished project;
- a list of available resources;
- a plan of action;
- a provisional plan for testing the effectiveness of the communication itself.

This form cannot be filled in until a viable 'title' has been selected for investigation.

Choosing research and project topics

Developing a viable **project/research brief** must involve progression through the following initial stages:

1 identification of a topic, together with a suitable audience or readership;
2 construction of a problematic, hypothesis or brief;
3 identification of sources of information;
4 evaluation of available methods of research;
5 execution of a feasibility test.

These first five stages are important preparatory steps. If any one of them cannot be fulfilled, then a new topic will need to be chosen and investigated. For the benefit of readers, each of these five steps will be examined below.

Choice of topic

The selection of a research **topic** is not an easy process. The initial difficulty in making a choice arises because a balance must be achieved between personal interest, course content and the challenges of delivering a project to a specific *audience*. In Communication Studies, the project is not aimed at an 'imaginary' readership; it is intended to make a verifiable impact on a group of people identified at the beginning of the study. This group will then form a real audience for a final 'validation' of the work.

In some courses, productions or 'texts' are supposed to reveal their intended audience by virtue of their structure. Assumptions are made about what kind of form and content will be 'suited' to a particular group of people. It is not unusual to find certain 'techniques' of production being employed in the belief that a specific audience will always respond favourably to the same ploys. For example, students will sometimes declare that 'I made it colourful because I wanted to attract a young audience.' In communication projects, all such assumptions must be tested.

Finding an idea: extracts from project work

The following extracts are taken from student projects submitted for the AEB A-level, and reveal how individuals grapple with the problem of choice. Student A is male, and writes about his initial project idea in his 'self-assessment':

'When I first started thinking about my project I was trying desperately to link it to football or sport. After a while, I realised the reasons for doing that kind of project were too personal.'

A balance must be achieved between personal interest and the needs of an audience. If the project topic is simply an obsession on the part of the writer, or if there is existing material which more than adequately fulfils the purpose of communicating with the intended audience, then the project will find it impossible to fulfil its objectives. The project is not a scrapbook of items: it is at best an original contribution to the study of communication.

Student B (male, like the previous subject) describes his initial idea as follows:

'Thinking back to my GCSE revision and also considering the revision I would have to undertake for my A-levels ... I considered ways in which I could produce an artefact as a revision aid to overcome problems of motivation and boredom ... I tried to think of ways of livening it up and making it more sociable.'

Here, the student has identified a personal interest which has also a universal application; how revision may be made more tolerable. In this sense, the student may well have identified a real need which a good project will be able to answer.

Finding an idea: questions

At this stage, it is worth exploring the kinds of question which might help to focus attention upon the variety of possible *areas* of investigation:

- Is there a particular theory which is felt to be relevant to individual experience, or which appears to contradict that experience?
- Is there a theory or piece of research which could be tested for the first time, or tested in a new way, or on a new audience?
- Are there particular *methods* of research which seem interesting?
- Do different areas of the course suggest that they could shed light on one another? Could they be combined or contrasted in a study?

- Are there 'communication issues' which could be investigated?
- Does a certain locality provide any 'ready-made' communication issues?
- Does the researcher have any contacts which either may lead to a commission, or might be able to provide useful information?

Finding an idea: 'brainstorming' and 'spidergrams'

Some of those looking for project ideas begin by listing their interests, often in the form of a '**spidergram**'. This is a diagram which puts the subject to be investigated at the centre of a page, and proceeds by drawing a series of lines which radiate outwards, making the spider's 'legs'. Each leg of the diagram leads to an area which is related to the central 'body'. It is essentially a form of '**brainstorming**', where the mind is allowed to range freely across a wide series of initial possibilities.

Student C is female, and is initially uncertain as to her choice of topic. Her spidergram (Figure 6.1, taken from a log submitted to the AEB) begins at the centre with 'hobbies and interests' and radiates out to include 'social life, college, shopping, interior design, advertising, travelling, art, music'. Each of these areas then produces another series of ideas. For example, 'shopping' leads to 'fashion', and 'art' leads to 'exhibitions' and 'life drawing'.

Student D is male and makes a list of initial ideas, but approaches the problem by concentrating on the possible *artefacts* which he might produce:

'Environmental Study Package/Teaching Pack aimed at children aged 10–12 years old, focusing on global issues ... could be expanded to include posters, videos ... A video showing life for young people in Exeter which doesn't use any speech, just contemporary musical soundtrack and on-screen writing ... Radically and completely (re)inventing a college magazine.'

This is, strictly speaking, the wrong approach; it is only once a range of ideas has been explored, and the suitability of various audiences outlined, that we should begin to think about the kind of artefact or product which will most usefully bring the topic to the attention of an audience. (Student D rejected all of the ideas listed above.)

Striving for originality

It is not unusual to choose a topic and then to find that it has already been explored by one's contemporaries; projects on the representation of women in advertising, the audience for soap opera, and the environmental package aimed at the young may all seem to have been 'done to death'. However, a little originality of approach can provide a new impetus for the project inquiry. For example, groups of female viewers can be assembled to watch certain advertisements, and then encouraged to talk in general about images and products, before any suggestion of sexism in stereotyping is applied. In this

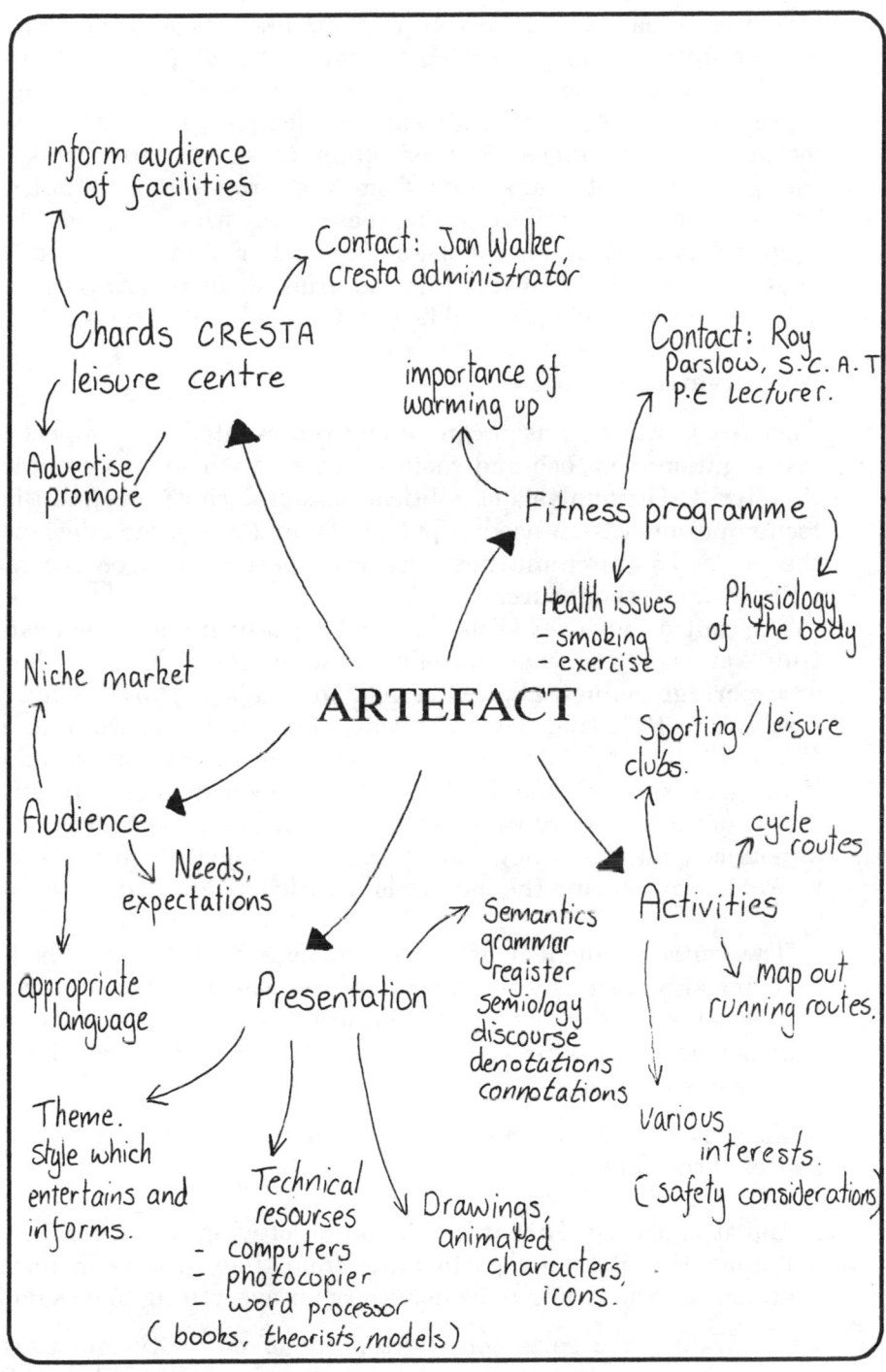

Figure 6.1   Spidergram for the Cresta Leisure Centre

way, the researcher can discover what interests and concerns the audience sample, rather than presenting the term 'stereotype', which in itself tends to trigger certain responses. Or again, it might be interesting to study the representation of inter-group communication in soap opera, perhaps by focusing on exchanges between different age groups; this would involve the production of transcripts from the programmes studied. Finally, the environmental project could be based on what individuals are actually prepared to sacrifice for the sake of a cleaner planet; one student produced a questionnaire which moved from inquiries about recycling to questions which asked if the respondent would be prepared to break the law.

Investigating speech

One area which has been under-represented in project work is the investigation of speech and rhetoric, an area which was covered at the end of Chapter 3. The analysis of political discourse can provide an insight into the techniques of evasion used in public life, and offers the opportunity to analyse the power of communication. Political speeches can be recorded from news bulletins and other sources.

The controversy over arms sales to Iraq, which made the headlines after the Gulf War, is only one example of many which could be used. The secret revision of export guidelines allowed a company called Matrix Churchill to export machine tools to Iraq. On the twenty-seventh day of the inquiry into Matrix Churchill, led by Lord Justice Scott, the Conservative minister William Waldegrave denied that Parliament had been deliberately misled about the export of military hardware. He argued that, because there had been no public announcement, the policy had not really changed. Sir Richard Scott's question to Waldegrave during the inquiry is recorded as follows:

> 'The outrage about what was happening to the Kurds [attacked with chemical weapons by the Iraqi military] was a proper and natural response. Is it not a healthy feature of a mature democracy that issues of this sort can be debated, and they certainly cannot be debated if the subject-matter of the debate is not made known.'

Waldegrave's reply is interesting because it concentrates on one particular aspect of the question:

> 'But it is also Sir Richard, a definition of what a *mature* democracy means. I think that it knows particularly from time to time in relation to foreign affairs, it is not going to be necessary for everything to be said in detail.'

Here, Waldegrave seizes on the concept of maturity and uses it differently from the way in which it is employed in Scott's question. Scott refers to the need to conduct political affairs in a becoming and seemly fashion. Waldegrave means that a democracy which is 'mature' will be grown-up enough to accept the reality of secrecy. A subsidiary term is highlighted and then turned to the advantage of the Tory politician.

Geoffrey Howe performs a similar linguistic trick in the passage below. He is asked two questions by a television interviewer, one about public disquiet over the chemical attack on the Kurdish people, and one about the change of government policy which allowed weapons to be exported to Iraq:

'at the time there was considerable public disquiet about the gassing of the Kurds and I think the point that Lord Justice Scott is making, is given public disquiet on what amounted to a change of policy, there should have been some debate about it'.

Howe makes an interesting response:

'well, there *was* debate about it, we answered questions about the gassing of the Kurds in Parliament on a number of occasions. But there is a limit to the extent to which one can discuss changes in policy of this kind.'

Howe's reply treats the question about 'debate' as though it refers to debate about the Kurds, when in fact the interviewer's suggestion was that there should have been debate about the *change of policy* which allowed the provision of war material to Saddam Hussein. (Matrix Churchill had supposedly been exporting machines for 'general engineering' when in fact it was known that they were intended for the manufacture of sophisticated fuses and artillery parts. Although the government allowed the licences, and allegedly had intelligence reports on the intended use of such machinery, Matrix Churchill was prosecuted.)

The problematic/hypothesis

Once an issue has been decided upon, the inquiry needs to be made *manageable*. Projects which do not have a carefully worked-out perspective or set of aims will waste time on a field of research which is too wide to be successful. It is important to work to a specific *brief*. A small-scale but in-depth study of the discourses used during one political controversy, like the example cited above, is better than an attempt to study the entire traffic of a year in Parliament. One way in which careful focus may be attained is to work out either a **problematic** or a **hypothesis**.

A *problematic* is a question which is used to focus an inquiry. It may be, for example, 'How are men in the 18–35 age group represented in television advertising?'. The ability to frame a question is useful when someone is interested in a particular area, but perhaps uncertain as to his or her own position on the issues he or she might encounter.

A *hypothesis*, by contrast, is an idea or proposition which must be investigated or tested. In this case, the same basic idea might read: 'Men are represented in advertising in ways which were once reserved for women.' Hypotheses are useful if the investigator has a strong feeling about a particular topic, and wishes to investigate the soundness of that perception.

Whichever is chosen, problematic or hypothesis, attention is focused upon a specific issue within a wider topic.

Variables

Once the project has been established in the way described above, the 'abstract' ideas which may have begun the inquiry (such as, for example, the idea of 'representation' in 'mainstream Cinema') need to be made more concrete and specific. The task is therefore to find 'measurable' **variables** for the concepts which have been selected. The process is known as **operationalisation**. Frankfort-Nachmias and Frankfort, in *Research Methods in the Social Sciences* (1992), provide these examples of operationalisation (p. 54):

> '*social class* is a variable because it can be differentiated by at least five distinct values: lower, lower-middle, middle, upper middle, and upper. Similarly, *expectations* is a variable because it can be assigned at least two values: "high" and "low".'

If we take the example of *representation*, this concept needs to be turned into a series of descriptive categories which can be measured. The 'variables' involved are all linked to human subjectivity and the ways in which it is presented by the media. Therefore, the measures are age, class, gender, ethnicity, and so on, but also the technical and dramatic devices used to construct these aspects of individuality. *Mainstream Cinema*, on the other hand, is a set of institutional practices which produces certain types of 'realist' narrative, together with a conventional exposition of events. Once the range of variables has been established it is then possible to look at the relationship between the main concepts which are being studied. It is clear, however, that the selection of certain concepts, such as *representation* and *mainstream Cinema*, suggest an agenda from the start.

Sources of information and types of data

Once the topic has been chosen, the issue identified, and the audience selected, it is important to ensure that there is free access to sufficient **sources of information**. Information or data may be described in the following ways:

- **Primary** data is information which the researcher must generate; it is material which is produced to meet the specific requirements of the chosen area of study. It may be collected using questionnaires, interviews, or by either *direct* or *participant* methods of observation (see below).

- **Secondary** data is information which is already in the public domain, but which was assembled with aims or objectives in mind that are almost certainly different to those held by the researcher. It consists of books, articles, CD-ROMs, statistics, and video, audio and film material.
- **Quantitative** data is produced on a large scale, using surveys and questionnaires; it provides insight into broad social trends and simple preferences.
- **Qualitative** data is the result of in-depth studies, including the use of personal interviews and the gathering of documentation which reveals the attitudes and beliefs of individual subjects; it is sometimes regarded as providing insight into psychological as well as social phenomena.

Data may be a combination of these categories. The best way to demonstrate this is through the use of a diagram (Figure 6.2).

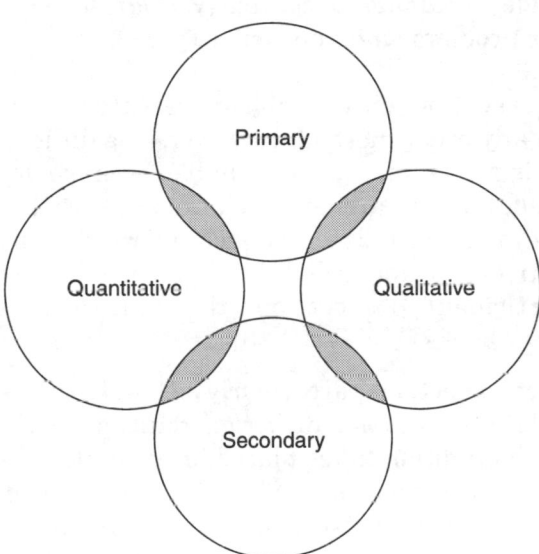

Figure 6.2   Sources of information

Thus, information may be both *primary* and *quantitative*. In such a case, the data may be gathered using large numbers of questionnaires which have been issued. Alternatively, information may be *primary* and *qualitative*. For example, an in-depth interview would qualify as an example. It could also be *secondary* and *quantitative*, where published statistics, surveys and investigations taken from various sources are consulted in order to support project research. Information described as *secondary* and *qualitative* appears in the form of personal memoirs, letters, and other (often autobiographical) material.

Evaluating research methods

Research methods are identifiable *approaches* to the collection of data. They include audience sampling of various kinds, and all the types of secondary inquiry which are available. The methods used in research will depend upon a number of factors.

In the first place, some organisations and groups may not welcome the kinds of investigation which good communication research wishes to pursue. For example, it would be very difficult to obtain co-operation from a government office if the stated aim of the researcher was to discover how ministers manipulate statistics to disguise unemployment. In addition, types of research which require participant observation to be carried out (which some people regard as the equivalent of going 'under cover') are rarely manageable; a great deal of time is required before an individual can become established in a group – time which the project does not always allow.

The use of any *single* method on its own is also inadvisable, because each approach requires another 'angle' on the isssue in order to see the results in perspective. Peter Langley (*Managing Sociology Coursework*, 1993) gives a useful breakdown of this problem when he writes (p. 19):

'using participant observation may enable a researcher to gain insights unobtainable through any other method. However, it is difficult to argue that the data collected using this method is reliable because it is the unique product of the particular researcher's relationship with the group in question. Surveys are often criticised for lacking validity but if a survey, strong in representativeness and reliability, was used to check the data gained from the participant observation, then the advantages of each method offset their drawbacks.'

If a number of project 'objectives' are clearly set out, this should help to establish which methods are suitable. If *factual* data is required (times and places in which media consumption takes place, for example), then an in-depth study is not necessary. If the *perspectives* of respondents are required, it may be a mistake to give such people a list of categories which they have to 'fit' their responses into. This implies that an *in-depth* or *qualitative* approach is suitable; the terms and concepts used by the individuals concerned may then become part of the project's own descriptive categories. If individual responses are thought sufficient, then *unstructured* qualitative interviews might be suitable. No single method is inherently superior to another; each should be used for different purposes and to reinforce the findings of the various approaches. Published studies which are similar to the concerns of the project should be read carefully, in order to ascertain whether the study of other work would be instructive.

These are summaries of the basic types of research method:

- **Direct observation**: the attempt to observe social interaction in an unobtrusive manner. This is easy to do where an event has observation built into its structure (Parliament, or a court of law, for example), but difficult where it is not part of the event. This is a method for the gathering of *primary* information.
- **Participant observation**: an attempt is made to participate in the activities of the group under scrutiny. This can mean that the observer ceases to observe and becomes lost in the events themselves. This is another *primary* method.
- **Structured interviews** and **questionnaires** (see below): basic *primary* data is collected from quite a large number of respondents, allowing broad trends and developments to be studied and compared.
- **Unstructured interviews**: the researcher uses a set of pre-prepared or extempore questions in order to elicit in-depth *primary* data.
- **Content analysis**: a form of textual study and assessment, often based on categorisation and numbering. It might try, for example, to discover which characters in a soap opera are shown carrying out certain types of action. This is a type of *secondary* research.
- **Semiological analysis**: another form of *secondary* textual interrogation, based on a system which supposes there is a relationship between the appearance/structure of a text and the meanings it produces within a specific culture.
- **Narrative analysis**: the relationship between the spatial and temporal nature of a *secondary* text is investigated.
- **Discourse analysis**: in the case of the study of conversation, this is based on either *primary* or *secondary* transcripts, while the printed or electronic text encourages a broader ideological approach founded on what is usually *secondary* material.
- **Statistical analysis**: government and other data, some of it 'raw', is analysed according to the principles of *secondary* inquiry.
- **Study of theory**: based on the search for useful *secondary* perspectives on the social world or on textual material.
- **Analysis of documents**, personal or otherwise: a line of research based on data which is either already in the public domain and therefore *secondary* or, if generated specifically for the purposes of the project (such as the maintenance of a diary by respondents), of a *primary* nature.

Approaches to textual analysis

When a text is being analysed, the following areas must be considered, where appropriate: the **semiology of the image**, **discourse**, **design**, **form**, **content** and **register/address**.

Register and *address* refer to the level at which a certain text is pitched, and the way that certain techniques are mobilised in order to 'speak' to a target audience. In each case, the aim is to establish the range of possible meanings which might be generated in an audience; the next step would be to discover the actual response of individuals and groups.

If a researcher investigates the *semiology of the image*, for example, he or she might be able to discover a number of associations which are prompted by various images (especially those which are not supported or 'anchored' by text), but should test material on the target audiences. Researchers should not imagine that each system is able to reveal the entire range of possible interpretation. *Discourse* analysis, for instance, may allow an understanding of the more straightforward semantic elements of conversation or text, but the use of the same text in a variety of contexts is likely to result in the production of a number of meanings. *Design*, to take another example, refers to the way that all types of content are placed in relation to one another, within a particular space; but the actual impact of this element must be measured rather than merely suggested.

Content analysis is, in the words of Arthur Asa Berger (see *Media Analysis Techniques*, p. 92):

'a research technique based upon measuring (counting) the amount of something . . . in a random sampling of some forms of communication'.

However, the analyst may find that his or her initial *identification* of types of content is quite different from the elements perceived by an audience.

All the analytical techniques above may be deployed in attempting to understand the structure of 'texts', whether they are articles, radio broadcasts, musical scores, public speeches, or whatever. A full critical analysis of each text used as research, including all the approaches listed above, must appear in the project file.

The feasibility test

This idea is quite straightforward, and grows partly from the process detailed above. A number of practical questions must be posed, the answers to which will establish how relevant or successful the project is likely to be. A **feasibility study** means a kind of 'pre-testing' of the project's concerns. The questions to be answered must have a practical as well as a theoretical basis. These are some examples:

- Will it be possible to complete the project within the time available?
- Does the project show some originality or does it reproduce existing material?
- Is there an accessible audience which can be tested?
- Is a reasonable amount of secondary data available?
- Are the advantages and disadvantages of the methods to be used understood?

Each of these questions suggests a *practical inquiry* which can be carried out. A feasibility study implies beginning an investigation; the material which follows is based on each of these questions in turn.

In the first place, other projects of a similar scale can be studied in order to discover how much *time* is required. Part of the actual project inquiry can be conducted in order to establish the time spent on one element. It is also important to investigate the extent to which specific communication theories can be mobilised in support of the project.

The question of *originality* can be tested by looking at the approaches taken in the past to the same kind of topic. In order to find out more about *audience*, a questionnaire can be circulated which establishes basic information about individual members, including how they may be reached. The availability of *data* must be tested in advance, by visiting libraries, bookshops, archives and other sources. The suitability of *method* to the aims of the project can be discovered by carrying out a small-scale survey of audience, for example, using the preferred approach, and then reviewing the results.

Evaluative diaries or logs

Each stage of investigation must be recorded in the evaluative diary or log book. The purpose of keeping a diary lies in the fact that it:

- emphasises the importance of *process* instead of merely the end result of the work undertaken;
- helps the writer to focus on his or her own communicative practices;
- assists in the evaluation of research;
- provides a record which may be used for final assessment;
- allows theory to appear in relation to a practical exercise.

Every decision made with regard to the project must be evaluated, first in the simple sense that it needs to be contrasted with alternative decisions which were not taken, and then in terms of its impact on the overall direction taken by the project work.

The appearance of theory in diaries or logs always seems to create problems. How does 'abstract' or academic inquiry relate to the practical activity of creating an artefact for a specific audience?

One solution is the use of communication models, based upon the idea that they can be applied to the interaction between target group and researcher. However, this can be quite an artificial exercise unless it actually helps to place the particular situation in the context of general theory (see below, under 'Applied theory'). Sometimes, it is tempting to include reference to communication concepts on the smallest pretext. This also leads to a rather unnatural or forced appreciation of the conceptual field. The following example is cited in *Case Studies and Projects in Communication*, by Neil McKeown (p. 116):

> 'I have today met parents for and against the college ... I have realised exactly how strongly people feel about Countesthorpe and how their attitudes would not be changed by discussion. They seemed to have a barrier to the sort of communication I was putting forward, probably through previous experience governing the interpretation of the message; therefore there would seem to be an incompatibility of schemas preventing acceptance of my ideas.'

Here, the idea that a 'barrier' is preventing reception of the student's ideas is attributed to 'previous experience', but this is not investigated; instead, an 'incompatibility of schemas' is held ultimately responsible. It explains nothing about the reasons which might be given for resistance to the student's message, and which might be suggested through even a small sample of qualitative interviews.

An alternative approach would be, therefore, to record audience response to established communication and media concepts; in other words, the log might be used to record the result of experiments which test the validity of theory. For example, a researcher undertaking specialist work on audience 'spectatorship' in the cinema might begin by using the log to record the established approaches to this theory. The log could then describe the general nature of audience response, with reference to media *effects*. Precise details and transcripts could then appear in the research section of the project.

The diary/log as a record of work accomplished

McKeown suggests that certain pages of the diary should be reserved for a record of work accomplished. He uses Richard Hare's work (1970) as the basis for this scheme, which encourages the maintenance of a critical analysis of progress under these headings (p. 123):
a) Work done on project last week
b) Evaluation of work done last week
   i) *skills learned / developed*
   ii) *principles of communication to which work relates*
   iii) *models of communication to which work relates*
c) Work planned for next week
d) Work planned in the long term
e) Detail of work
f) Aspects of project that need revision
g) Equipment and resources needed for work planned

A sense of audience

It is one thing to 'conceptualise' an **audience**, but quite another to find ways of reaching it. Student C took the next step, which follows the search for a topic. This was to list the audiences to which she had ready access. These included art students, elderly people at a day centre, and other groups within the local community. It is always wise to select an audience which may be reached with relative ease, since testing of the final artefact must be carried out using a representative sample of the chosen group. This should not, however, distort the way that the artefact is constructed. At times, good ideas are wasted because a researcher decides to take the line of least resistance, using friends as an audience without thinking about their suitability to the inquiry being undertaken.

Student A, initially attracted to the idea of investigating sport, spoke to a relative in the building trade who suggested that there was very little information concerning safety on building sites. This lead was followed, but the student was at first unable to find an audience:

'I only had a vague idea who my audience was. I thought that they would be "casual workers", but I was not sure precisely what the general definition of a "casual worker" was ... I had very informal chats with friends I knew had worked on building sites and got the impression that they had never got any information about safety.'

The term 'casual workers' requires much more careful exploration, in the sense that there are difficulties inherent in using such a category. Although such an audience is by its very nature difficult to locate, a working definition must be provided. Careful reading of the self-assessment reveals that this individual's audience research remained quite personal, and was initially based on people who had had experience of building sites at some stage, but who were not at the time of interview engaged as casual labour.

Student C had initially (and quite sensibly) decided to list those audiences to which she had ready access. In the final analysis, however, her requirements were for a specific age group, since she decided that there was no adequate guide to her home town aimed at young people. As a result, she had to go to places where she knew members of the 'target' age group could be found:

'Having perfected the questionnaire I presented it neatly ... I then approached the youth hostel ... they were extremely helpful and interested ... a major problem I encountered in this process was knowing how to find out if the people fitted into my 16–30 age bracket.'

In most cases, this should not have been too difficult, but the solution chosen was to ask individuals if they would agree to participate in a questionnaire aimed at the age group concerned.

Audience: practical/theoretical problems

Many difficulties which arise when studying audiences are due to the fact that it is hard to make a 'dividing line' between practical problems and theoretical ones. Individual examples of audience research often seem to present a combination of the two. This may be seen most clearly in the field of Media Studies, because the audience for most products is not found in a single place at the same time. It is not only separated from the source of the 'message' (the institutional forces which produce texts), but is sometimes thought not to exist as a coherent entity at all. In other words, audiences are partly 'concepts' used to justify the production of a particular product and, where actually tangible, have often been brought together specifically for the purposes of research. Where this happens, it is not surprising that such groups are described as 'artificial'.

Shaun Moores, in *Interpreting Audiences*, notes that the reason for the 'naturalisation' of the category 'audience' (p. 2):

'has undoubtedly been the vested interests of media institutions (as well as many academic researchers) in imagining the existence of such a fixed object to measure or monitor'.

Moores, however, argues that there are real audiences as well as 'discursively constructed' ones which exist in the social world. Ien Ang's 1991 study of the 'television audience', *Desperately Seeking the Audience'* showed her that (p. 18):

'Television audience membership is not a matter of compulsion or necessity, but is principally voluntary and optional. Therefore, the television institution is ultimately dependent upon people's unforced appetite to continue watching day after day.'

We should realise that, as we investigate a specific audience, we are also to some degree 'constructing' it.

Selecting a sample

Before we examine the writing of questionnaires, it is worth considering who will receive them. This is an immediate and practical investigation of the concept of audience. In *A Handbook of Social Science Research* (1987), Dixon, Bouma and Atkinson explain the need for **sampling** an audience (p. 134):

'A carefully drawn sample not only makes the task possible, it often produces more accurate results [than large-scale but unfocused investigation] ... We use sampling and we generalise from the samples we draw in our everyday life. If we want to check the weather we look out of the window and judge the weather as a whole from the sample that we can see through the window. Other forms of sampling and generalization follow the same logic ... in the case of the weather, we may look out of windows on different sides of the house before drawing a conclusion (i.e. generalising our findings from our sample).'

One of the most important points about this process is that the approach used in selecting the sample will determine to what extent generalisations can be made from it. If the sample is in some way unrepresentative, then the conclusions which are produced will apply only to the sample itself, and will have no bearing on the wider population. It may be, of course, that the researcher has no desire to draw wider conclusions; where such conclusions are required, Dixon *et al.* point out (p. 135):

'if you had selected a sample of twenty people which accurately reflected the views of a larger group of two hundred (for example, all the sixth-formers in a particular school) you could draw conclusions about the two hundred from the results'.

Questionnaires

Most communication projects will begin by establishing a link between the researcher and his or her intended audience. This is usually carried out by means of an initial **questionnaire** which will generate quantitative information. There are two basic ways in which these may be answered.

In the first case, the questions can be read to the respondent by an interviewer who ticks off or writes down their answers. This is called a **structured interview**. The respondent is encouraged to develop points and is sometimes allowed to talk at length. (Alternatively, it can be filled in by the respondent and collected by, or sent to, the researcher).

The advantage of a structured interview is that it allows questions to be explained, should the need arise, while its disadvantage is that the presence of the interviewer may affect the usefulness of the material. On the other hand, the issuing of large numbers of questionnaires without personal contact of any sort can quite easily result in a low rate of response. In some cases, particularly where research is carried out in educational institutions, the interviewer may be able to use the class groups into which the respondents are already organised. A large number of responses may then be obtained during the course of one session. If a questionnaire has been coded (so that particular answers correspond to a series of numbers), the process of sorting results into categories is made easier. An unstructured interview allows the interviewer to alter the direction or nature of the questions, as he or she sees fit.

Designing questionnaires

The point about using questionnaires is that they should provide the opportunity to compare the answers of respondents, with a view to the rational presentation of useful but *general* information about the issue being studied. There are many problems inherent in the design of questionnaires. If these can be avoided, then the production of meaningful data is more likely.

In the first place, a very simple approach would be to ask oneself a list of straightforward questions:

- What questions will be asked?
- Who will be addressed by the questions?
- How will the answers be recorded?
- What will be done with the results?

Many questionnaires begin by asking for personal detail, such as age, sex and ethnicity. These are known as **classification questions**. However, it has been suggested (Oppenheim, 1992) that such questions are best placed at the end of a questionnaire, because respondents may be more prepared to disclose even such apparently 'neutral' detail once they know what other information is required of them. Most approaches to design provide a series of alternatives for simple classification questions, such as a series of boxes for people to tick. For example, a number of boxes may be provided for the age of a respondent, as follows:

Under 19 ☐   20–34 ☐   35–44 ☐   45 and above ☐

This might also encourage individuals to answer the question, since it is usually thought easier to make this kind of general request than to ask for a person's exact age.

Besides classification questions, there are other basic types. **Knowledge questions** are designed to elicit responses which reveal the extent of individual knowledge on a specific topic or issue. The aim of **opinion questions**, is to establish what is thought about a certain issue. Through **motivation questions** the reasons for opinions or actions are sought.

A question which aims to discover the amount of time individuals spend watching television per week should either set out the different 'periods' in advance (5–10 hours, 11–20 hours, and so on) or allow the respondent to calculate the time based on his or her own judgement. In the latter case, when the information is returned, the researcher will have to identify the 'average' amount of time devoted to the activity, in order to decide whether individual results are above or below the average for the sample concerned. It is probably a good idea to make the respondents list the names and duration of individual programmes before a request is made for an overall figure, as this will ensure greater accuracy.

Common mistakes in design

One of the most common mistakes may be identified as **overlapping categories**. In such a case, there is no clear distinction between the alternatives given in the text of the questionnaire. For example, if the question on age was presented as below, overlapping categories would result in confusion and would render the data acquired useless:

Under 19 ☐   20–35 ☐   35–45 ☐   45 and above ☐

Where would any respondent who is 35 or 45 mark his or her age?

Another problem is encountered when interviewees are presented with **non-exhaustive categories**. If, for instance, we wish to know how many times the respondent has visited the cinema in the last year, the following approach will not cover all possibilities:

1–4 times
5–9 times
10–20 times

How would someone who has attended the cinema on more than twenty occasions be expected to respond?

Common difficulties also include asking **two questions in one**. For example, the question printed here conflates two distinct enquiries:

'Do you think that sex and violence should be censored on television?'

Here, the person filling in the questionnaire is prevented from giving an opinion on issues which might well be regarded as separate.

The tendency to produce **leading questions** must be avoided. For instance, the kind of question which asks 'Do you agree that all decent people should condemn violence on television?' makes it difficult to answer in the negative.

Questions which **presume some knowledge or state of affairs** are notorious for their ability to cause offence. A question which asks:

'How much money do you spend on holidays abroad?'

has neglected to discover whether the subject is able to take any holidays at all. Alternatively, an enquiry which poses the question:

'Do structuralist theories allow a flexible interpretation of textual meaning?'

assumes that an audience will share the strange vocabulary of critical theory.

Finally, **lack of clarity** can produce contradictory information. Where a researcher asks 'How often do you watch TV?' and supplies the alternatives 'regularly, occasionally, or obsessively', it is clear that the different values which each respondent may ascribe to these alternatives are likely to vary.

Factors which influence response

Marten Shipman (*The Limitations of Social Research*, pp. 80–7) lists all the factors which can distort a response to a question, whether that question is printed or delivered during an interview. These factors are as follows:

- The *difficulty* of the questions: wary of displaying ignorance, individual respondents may guess the answer. Terms like 'the establishment' or 'violence' may produce an emotive response (useful to some researchers), but there is no guarantee that each person interviewed interprets such vague terms in the same way.
- The danger of *the question suggesting the answer*, illustrated by Shipman with a question once posed to students undergoing teacher training: 'If you were quite free to choose, and could obtain the qualifications necessary, what field of employment would you ideally like to enter?' The results of this survey indicated that 53 per cent of trainees were 'reluctant' entrants to the profession. Shipman notes that, considering the question, it is surprising that any of the students elected teaching as their preferred choice.
- *Prestige and emotion*, which may be involved in the response to certain questions. Admitting that one reads certain popular newspapers, for example, may seem inappropriate in the formal context of social research.
- *The environment*, which itself may have influenced the answers, especially where that environment is 'closed' or has an official 'line' which people feel they must reproduce while they are 'on site'.
- The *pre-coding* of answers, which can mean that the responses given are sometimes squeezed into the categories which have been decided upon by the interviewer.

All these factors, as well as the level of training received by interviewers, may lead to the distortion of results.

Attitudinal scale and direct techniques

When a chosen audience is asked to explain its attitudes, it may be difficult to obtain a useful answer. The strength of an opinion will not always be revealed if the respondents are merely asked how they feel about a certain issue. One solution is to produce an **attitudinal scale**, where there are clearly marked alternatives. This provides a quantifiable (though some would argue essentially distorted) measurement of the differences in attitude displayed by various individuals. The scale would be preceded by a question:

'Please state your response to the following statements, on a scale of 1 (Strongly Agree) to 5 (Strongly Disagree). Please tick one box only.

The leadership of the student union has failed to communicate with its members.

1 (Strongly Agree) ☐   2 (Agree) ☐   3 (Neither Agree nor Disagree) ☐
4 (Disagree) ☐   5 (Strongly Disagree) ☐

A new student magazine is required.

1 (Strongly Agree) ☐   2 (Agree) ☐   3 (Neither Agree nor Disagree) ☐
4 (Disagree) ☐   5 (Strongly Disagree) ☐

Other **direct techniques** (where a respondent is asked for an evaluative judgement of the object or issue under study) include **semantic differential** tests, where subjects rate the issue on a seven-point scale. At each end of the scale, a term possessing a clear 'value' is found. The words used are sometimes called **bipolar**; they are exact opposites. This type of test might, for example, take the following form:

'Object under study: the tabloid press.

Please indicate your opinion of the tabloid press on the following scale

Good - - - - - - - Bad
Powerful - - - - - - - Weak
Energetic - - - - - - - Unenergetic

The 'neutral' value in such tests lies at the centre of the scale. The first pair constitutes the **evaluative** factor, the second illustrates the degree of **potency**, while the last pair makes up the factor of **activity**. At least nine different pairs are used to provide the semantic differential test.

Questionnaire layout

The physical layout of a questionnaire is important, and must provide a clear series of stages through which a respondent may pass. The questionnaire reproduced in Figure 6.3 is taken from Student C's project and includes her evaluation of the layout.

→ *No focus for eye*

CRITICISMS...

My name is Ellen Jones and I am currently a student at Exeter College studying for my Communication Studies A-level.
My coursework project is to produce an alternative guide to Exeter for people between 16 and 30 visiting the city.
The guide will, as well as providing general infromation, aim to give the user an "insiders" knowledge of Exeter in order for them to enjoy their visit to the full.
I should be very grateful if you would assist my research by completing the following questionnaire. Thank you for your help.
You need only complete the questionnaire if you are between 16 and 30 years old.

1) What is your age? ....
2) What is your sex? ....
3) What is your nationality? ....
4) Is this your first visit to the Exeter area?

↖ register too formal ?

gap should be smaller

↖ Looks very squashed up

should line all boxes up

    Yes [ ]
    No [ ]

5) How long are you planning to stay in the Exeter area? ....

6) Where are you staying during your visit to the Exeter area?

Questions 1 → 7 hard to follow, higgly piggledy!

Youth Hostel [ ]   Hotel [ ]
Y.MCA [ ]   Student Hostel [ ] ←
Bed and Breakfast [ ]   Friends [ ]

Other (please specify) ....

7) Would you find a leaflet designed for 16 to 30 year olds, containing information about this age group's needs and interests when visiting the city of Exeter useful?

    Yes [ ]
    No [ ]

8) Which of the following things would you be interested in having information about when visiting the Exeter area:
    ("1" = no interest;   "2" = slight interest;   "3" = definite interest)

	1	2	3
Accommodation			
Eating out			
Pubs			
Nightclubs			
Public Conveniences			
Clothes Shopping			
Public Transport			
Car Hire			
Bike Hire			
Sports Facilities			
Places of Interest			
Local History			
Guided Tours			
Museums			
The Arts Centre			
Local Art & Crafts (exhibitions and shops)			
Theatres			
Live Music			
Shopping Centres			
Others (please specify)			

Too much white space, could have used it to spread out question 8.

↑ lack of obvious instruction eg. 'Please tick box'

1, 2, 3 is a confusing method

Type face is too boring

9) Would you find information on the prices of accommodation, places to eat out, etc., useful?

    Yes [ ]
    No [ ]

10) Are there any general questions that you would like to ask a resident of Exeter about the city if you had the opportunity e.g. Are there any areas to avoid at night?

....
....

Figure 6.3   Student C's questionnaire

Attitudes vs. facts?

The material in this section is taken from Student D's questionnaire, which was produced as a way of finding out more about the subject he eventually chose to investigate. The title of the project was 'Smash fascism'. Student D realised that he was dealing with a difficult inquiry (it was aimed at fellow students):

> 'The nature of the area I had chosen to base my project around was one in which it was difficult to write questions that did not ask, in a thinly disguised form, "are you a racist or hold racist views?" '

The idea was, in this candidate's words, to 'create questions that would reveal people's attitudes towards race, racism and fascism in a subtle way'.

The approach taken, however, does have certain flaws. Many of the questions seek to find out how far 'the myth[s] perpetuated by ... Nazi organisations' have become commonly accepted. These myths, as identified by the student, include ideas about the proportion of Britain's population made up by ethnic minority groups, the extent to which such groups are composed of recent immigrants (rather than of individuals born in Britain), and the degree to which council housing is or is not made available to ethnic groups over and above the requirements of other groups. One example reads:

> 'What percentage of the British population are from ethnic minorities? Circle the percentage you feel is nearest to the true figure.
>
> 1%   5%   10%   15%   25%   50%'

This approach can be quite revealing, but may have its dangers, in that it is possible to encourage negative perspectives by the actual introduction of certain questions. It is certainly not possible to characterise a selection from this kind of multiple choice (in the case above, the selection of any percentage higher than the true figure, which is 5 per cent) as evidence of racist belief.

The notion that negative outlooks are 'myths' rather than social constructions also needs some investigation. In addition, it is clear that Nazi organisations alone do not have the power to disseminate racist ideas. Sections of the press and other sources, including certain communities, must also contribute to such views.

The ultimate aim of this project is to counter the 'bizarre and false way of thinking' found amongst racists. Thus, it aligns itself firmly with the 'false ideology' school of thought. According to this outlook, the cause of many unsavoury beliefs may be traced to a 'distorted' perception of reality, and the solution lies in providing information which will reveal the 'true' picture to the subject. It is not necessarily the case, however, that providing facts will ever be enough to alter certain types of perception.

The perspective taken by Student D led him to suppose that he had discovered 'racist ideas' in his sample group, while he believed that 'significant anti-fascist ideology' was not present. In this case, the beliefs held by the researcher may have resulted in the neglect of other possible explanations for the results obtained. Alternatively, had the student made reference to the widespread racist attacks and murders taking place throughout Europe, and the strength of far-right organisations in many countries (both of which are noted in the student's synopsis), more urgent material might have been provided for use in the questionnaire. The attempt to investigate belief is laudable, but the method used is inadequate.

A variety of methods

All research methodologies have advantages and disadvantages, so it is most advisable to use a variety of approaches, each of which may be used to check or supplement the others. This process is known as **triangulation**. It does not mean that there will be an absolute guarantee of accuracy, but rather that the researcher will be able to answer any challenges to his or her research in a more reasonable manner.

In the case of the research undertaken above, it would have been useful to have selected members of the sample for more in-depth questioning. The fear when pursuing the question of racial prejudice is often that the researcher will end up 'reinforcing' negative attitudes. This concern sometimes leads to the conduct of research 'at arm's length'. In fact, the discovery of the exact form in which unsavoury belief manifests itself is probably more useful than the reproduction of a researcher's own assumptions.

An 'unstructured' and in-depth interview may provide an insight into the general nature of the opinions held by the interviewee, and might, in the case of the research undertaken by Student D, have suggested that the whole range of a respondent's beliefs would have provided an insight into the racist component. This would also have helped avoid the conflation of racism with fascism.

An historical example may illustrate the point I am trying to make: although it is about the practical strategies of opposing fascism, it is based on the ability to think creatively about the complex issues of belief and allegiance in general. During the struggle against fascism in the East End of London in the 1930s, a leading Communist called Phil Piratin became curious to see what kind of people would attend one of Mosley's marches (see Colin Sparks', *Never Again!*, 1980). Watching from the sidelines, Piratin noted the scene (p. 78):

'The fascist band moved off, and behind them about fifty thugs in blackshirt uniform. Then came the people. About 1,500 men, women (some with babies in arms) and youngsters marched behind Mosley's banner ... while we would fight Mosley's thugs, what do you get by fighting the people? ... above all these people, like most in East London, were living miserable, squalid lives ... the Communist party should help people improve their conditions of life, in the course of which we could... get them to fight their real exploiters.'

The campaign against eviction and poor housing, which the Communist party supported, attacked the wider causes of disillusion, founded on a *variety* of beliefs about the circumstances in which these 'ordinary working-class folk' (Piratin's term) lived, and this eventually made significant inroads into the fascist 'base'.

Research for artefact production: form and content

It is probably clear that the **artefact** lies at the centre of the communication project. This is a specially designed production which carries the intended message of the project to its audience. It may be a video, a short film, a series of promotional materials, a lecture, a magazine article, a display, a radio talk or programme, a comic and so on.

During the process of designing the artefact, research must include close examination of any material which bears some relationship to the final production. If, for example, a leaflet is being produced, then *any* leaflets intended to make a public impact may be examined, irrespective of the subject they cover. In addition, other materials which treat the same topic, including video programmes, audio tapes and so on, should be used to investigate how that content is *shaped*.

In other words, texts which contain the *same* **content** as the project artefact, but which organise that content in a *different* **form**, should be investigated. Equally, texts which exhibit *identical* **form** to the artefact, but contain *different* **content**, must also be examined. So, for example, if the purpose of the project is ultimately to produce a study booklet on visual communication for art students, the researcher will need to examine the form taken by booklets in general, while also investigating the specific content relevant to the artefact. The interplay between form and content is an important part of analysis. An understanding of the relationship between the two is essential for the production of a successful artefact.

For example, Student D produced a public display board which carried a dramatic anti-fascist message (Figure 6.4). He examined a wide range of artefacts in order to find the most suitable form for his message. The power of the finished artefact owes as much if not more to the way in which the information is displayed (the form) as to the images and text it reproduces (the content).

Figure 6.4 *'Smash fascism': part of the display*

Once research has been carried out, and the investigation of form and content is complete, then an artefact may be designed and a protoype tested on the target audience. It is permissible to use the talents of other individuals to assist in some aspects of production, but the number of reasonably accessible techniques means that each person should attempt to execute the work him or herself.

Applied theory

The idea of an **applied theory** often causes uneasiness. Readers may find that they are 'grafting' theory onto a project which they feel is essentially practical. The use of theory should, however, arise naturally from two areas of project work: the status of the project itself as an *exercise in communication*, and the communication concepts which apply to the *particular* study being undertaken. The first two headings below discuss the project itself as an exercise or event, while the third refers to theory as it is applied to the specific studies made within the project.

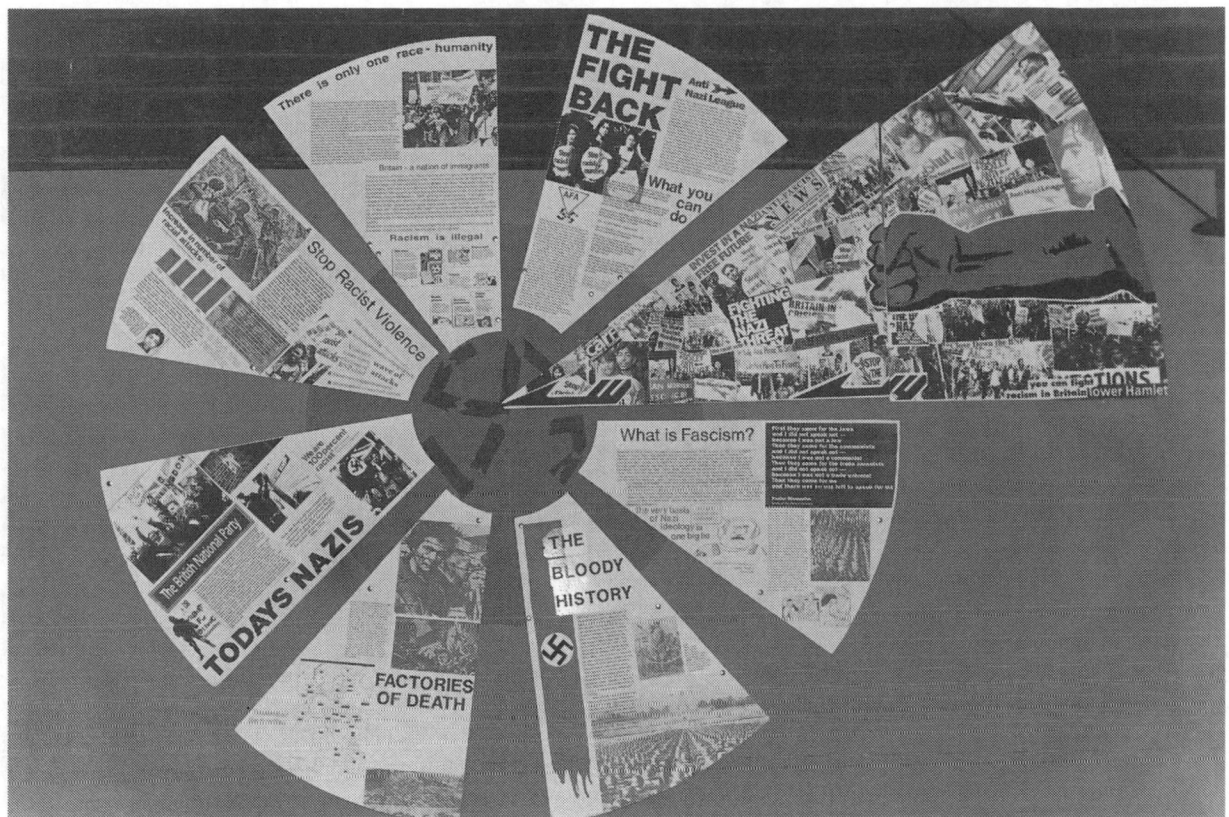

Figure 6.4 *'Smash fascism': the finished display*

The project and the use of models

Treating the project as an example of communication is a popular method of introducing theory, in which the artefact can be seen as a 'message' aimed at a particular audience. Models of communication (see Chapter 1) are often used for this purpose.

There are certainly limitations to this approach, as we saw in a previous section (see 'Evaluative diaries or logs'); the uncritical application of models to the project 'event' can be misleading, especially if it suggests that the creation of a project is a purely objective process, unaffected by the pressures and influences which surround all social research. Nevertheless, it is important to be aware of a number of models, exactly because the project provides an opportunity to test them within a practical context.

Lasswell's formula of 1948, described in Chapter 1 (who says what, in which channel, to whom, with what effect?), is often used for the purpose of illustrating how the project message is shaped and delivered. The *who* is the student, the *says what* is the project message, the *channel* is the form of

Figure 6.4   'Smash fascism': part of the display

the artefact, the audience forms the group *to whom* the message is addressed, while the *effect* is only gauged when the final artefact is tested.

Shannon and Weaver's model, which also appeared in the first chapter, provides another diagram which regularly turns up in communication log books. The *information source* in this model is the researcher and his or her interpretation of research material; the content of the artefact is the *message*; the form of the artefact (video, booklet, poster, display, etc.) is the sender or *transmitter*; the code in which the message or content is sent (images and sound, printed words, two-dimensional images, and so on) makes up the *signal*; the *noise source* refers to all the factors which may interfere with the clarity of the original message or its reception; and the audience stands in the position of *receiver*, though it is possible that it may obtain a *received signal* which is different from the original message.

The project in perspective

Theories of *transmission*, *exchange*, the *generation of meaning*, *context* and *discourse*, all explained in Chapter 1, may help to provide what a straightforward use of simple models fails to supply: a sense of the social context in which the project 'event' takes place.

What other areas of theory might be applied to the project as an *act* of communication? We might refer back to some of the traditions outlined in earlier chapters. If the project is seen not as the simple formation and delivery of a message but as an example of social *interaction* between researcher and audience, then it may be possible to use Mead's theory of symbolic interactionism, which emphasises the 'collective' actions of individuals and the creative aspects of human behaviour. As we saw, this tradition emphasises the idea that the individual, through acts of communication (such as the creation of a project), is able to gain an objective view of his or her own social role. This whole approach would suggest a much closer involvement with audience, together with awareness of the place of 'intrapersonal' communication in the formation of messages.

Indeed, the whole notion of *audience* provides another instance of a category which demands close examination. The very difficulty involved in locating target groups and measuring audience response should help to underline the idea that the concept of audience is not a simple one. Some writers (see in particular Ien Ang, *Desperately Seeking the Audience*) have argued that 'audience' is an imaginary entity, constructed for the benefit of academic or commercial research. *Media Studies* (Price, 1993) includes an entire chapter on 'constructing the audience'. No one can assume that 'audience' exists in a 'stable condition': not only is there constant change and flux in the composition of particular audiences, but they can be *described* in different ways depending upon the agenda set by individual research projects.

A sound knowledge of theory can alert the researcher to the provisional nature of some of the traditional social and critical perspectives. For example, Chapter 1 argued that certain traditions, including some feminist, Marxist and postmodernist currents, have called into question the use of a variety of established concepts. Feminism, in particular, questions the point of making references to an apparently 'abstract' social subject, which, it argues, ignores the social differentiation between women and men.

When we consider the issue carefully, *any* aspect of communication theory can be applied to the project as an 'event'. For example, the whole notion of the 'split' between *internal processes* and *external expression*, examined at the start of Chapter 2, could be tested by studying the effects of audience response on the researcher, and thus on the project's conceptual 'shape' and overall direction.

Specific issues

Once we have grasped the idea that the project itself is an example of communication, it will be possible to consider the use of theories which apply to the specific subject matter of the project. Earlier in this chapter, I used the example of a researcher working on audience 'spectatorship' in the cinema. This study would of course demand knowledge of the different perspectives on identity, would suggest that the concept of 'the male gaze' must be understood, and might also require familiarity with the technical codes of film which allow the 'gaze' to be constructed for an audience.

Similarly, a project dealing with language acquistion would need to examine the whole concept of thought and language, including reference to Piaget, Vygotsky, Sapir, Chomsky and Pinker. Arguments about nativism would clearly be important. In all cases, speculations on theory must appear in the log. This extract, for example, is taken from a student diary produced at Somerset College. The student concerned demonstrates an awareness of how theory may be applied to his own investigations:

> 'I wish to produce a study that will incorporate my interest in comics and their art work ... [I] have decided upon a comic that will convey the increasingly popular environmental message ... Communication theories, such as address and role, plus Vladimir Propp's models of story-telling, could be utilised in the production of the artefact.'

In this case, theory is not seen as something remote which deserves only passing reference; it is employed in an active framework. A study of how address is used in communication helps to shape the message in an appropriate way, while Propp's ideas about character and function provide a model for the construction of the comic. Of course, the theories chosen will depend upon what has first been selected as a topic for study, but inventiveness on the part of the researcher is always required.

Creative use of theory means looking for different ideas which will shed light on the project's hypothesis or problematic. An example may be the study of violence in 'cult' films like *Reservoir Dogs,* where the usual approach seems to involve content analysis, in which acts of brutality are counted without reference to their treatment. In *Reservoir Dogs*, the film's much-vaunted 'realism' actually seems to disguise a highly charged fantasy, suggested by the dialogue, the pseudonyms used by the robbers (Mr Black, Mr Pink and so on), the story spun by the undercover cop, and the rather stagey stand-off at the end. An investigation of realism might therefore be balanced by reference to those authors like Propp and Todorov who studied the structure of the fantastic.

In the case of advertising and film, stereotyping is one concept which is widely employed, but usually within the tradition which treats the process as entirely negative. It is possible, however, to explore the use of stereotyping as a dramatic device, based on theories of differentiation and the idea that it reflects the *reality* of intergroup relations. If an individual is specifically interested in film, it may be possible to set up a study of the difference between cinematic representation and the 'natural' behaviours found in everyday interaction, using studies of acting and Goffman's theories of self-presentation.

Writing up and presenting results

Once data has been assembled, the results of each stage of investigation must be presented in a recognisable form. Both quantitative and qualitative material should appear in the *research* section of the project, while the *log* should be used to record the process of research.

Some material is best presented in a written form; this would certainly be the case with qualitative data, where quotation from primary research interviews or secondary document analysis must be used to illustrate the conclusions reached by the researcher (see below). Quantitative information, on the other hand, may appear in a variety of guises, discussed below. No chart or diagram, however, should appear without a key to each element, so that the user is able to make sense of the information.

Forms of quantitative presentation

The variety of forms used for presenting quantitative data can be summarised as follows:

- **Tables**: a table is the presentation of figures in columns and rows. The reader can see the evidence of precise numbers – how many working-class households, for example, have satellite television.
- **Bar graphs**: the advantage of a bar graph is that information can be seen at a glance, and that the relative size or extent of each type of factual data or response is easily noticeable. Figure 6.5 shows an example.
- **Line graphs**: in this case, lines are presented on a grid to show features like change over time.
- **Pie charts**: these are particularly useful in showing proportions which are relative to the whole. For example, the percentage of students capable of operating a certain desk-top publishing programme, out of an overall total, is best displayed in a pie chart. See Figure 6.6 for two examples.

Student B, who was engaged in research for a revision guide in the form of a board game, not only produced a pie chart to illustrate the response of each age group, but also written analysis to explain these responses, and a bar graph comparing types of revision and their relative effectiveness.

There is a very important point to be made about the gathering and presentation of data: not only should we form suitable questions, we must appreciate the *significance* of what has been discovered in response to those questions.

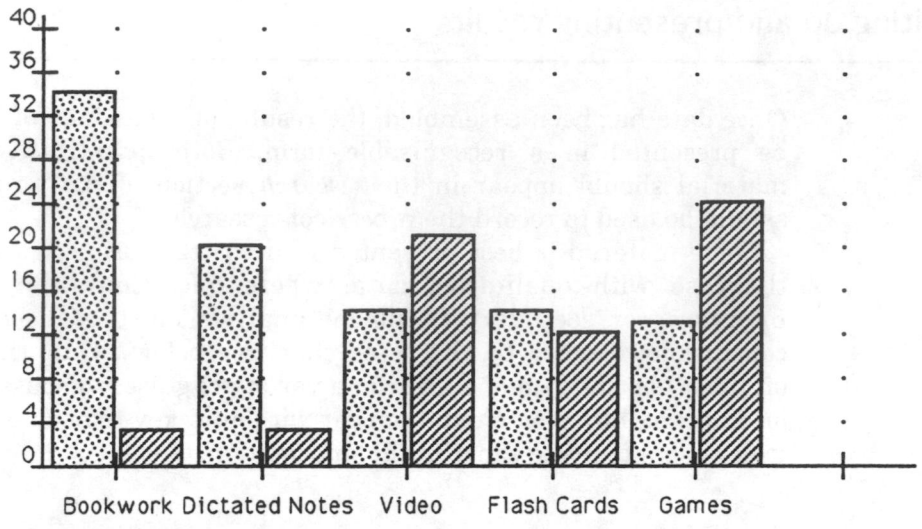

Figure 6.5   Bar chart showing a comparison between 'effectiveness' and 'enjoyability' of types of revision

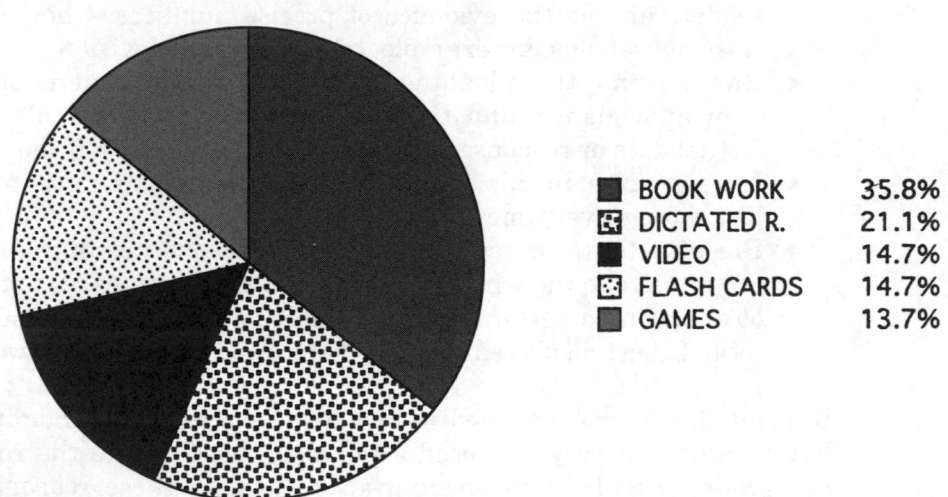

Figure 6.6   Pie chart showing effective revision techniques used by all in sample group

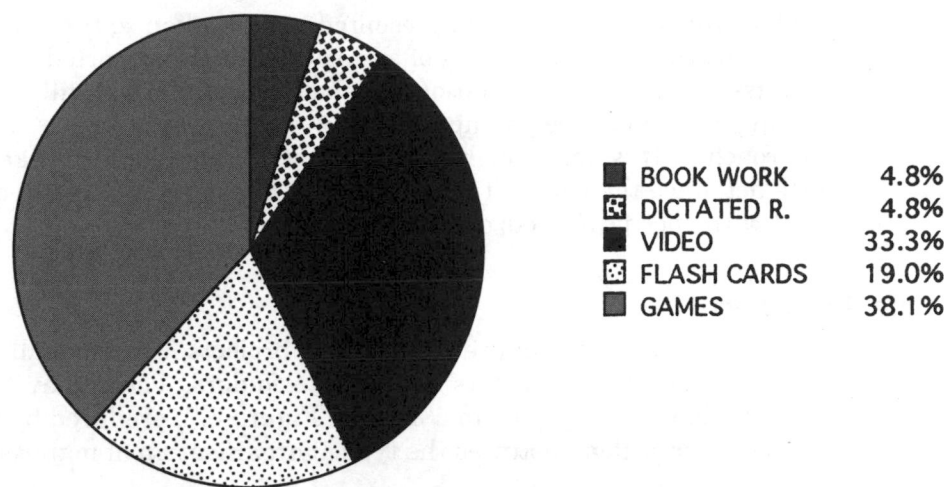

■	BOOK WORK	4.8%
▦	DICTATED R.	4.8%
■	VIDEO	33.3%
▨	FLASH CARDS	19.0%
▨	GAMES	38.1%

Figure 6.6   Pie chart showing enjoyable revision techniques used by all in sample group

The presentation of qualitative data

The challenge of using qualitative data lies in understanding what is relevant to the project, and therefore by implication realising what is not essential. This is a matter of editing the sources which have been assembled, and of knowing where they should appear in the body of the project.

Where unstructured interviews have been carried out, relevant material will have to be **transcribed** from audio tape, and the quotations used in one of two ways. Each interview could be presented with introductory remarks, or, more usually, a particular topic could be used as a heading and all pertinent material, from a variety of respondents, could appear under that heading. In most cases, qualitative data will be written up as a continuous report, in a narrative form, since narrative is one of the basic ways of representing experience.

There is one important difference between communication work and mainstream sociology. Unlike sociology coursework, or media research, Communication Studies does not involve the production of a research report as the central or end product. The intention of the whole exercise is to produce an *artefact*, or set of materials, which make a measurable impact on the chosen target group. This means that the *process* of research and artefact design must be described in the log, together with an account of those *ideas* and *theories* which seem relevant to the project. Separate research and design files will also be produced, again with the intention of demonstrating the process involved in the planning and execution of a *practical* exercise.

Once the artefact has been presented to an audience, the whole process must be **validated**, and the results of audience response reported in a file devoted to self-assessment and evaluation (see below). Validation will again involve the testing of audience samples using both quantitative and qualitative approaches. It is not enough merely to ask an audience if it liked or enjoyed an artefact; once the whole of the production has been presented, questions which deal with specific aspects of the artefact should be posed.

Presenting the project

The standard method of presentation for projects is to label all material and to place the different elements in separate folders. These may then be labelled and numbered and placed in a box file. Figure 6.7, produced by a student on an A-level course, demonstrates the typical organisation of material.

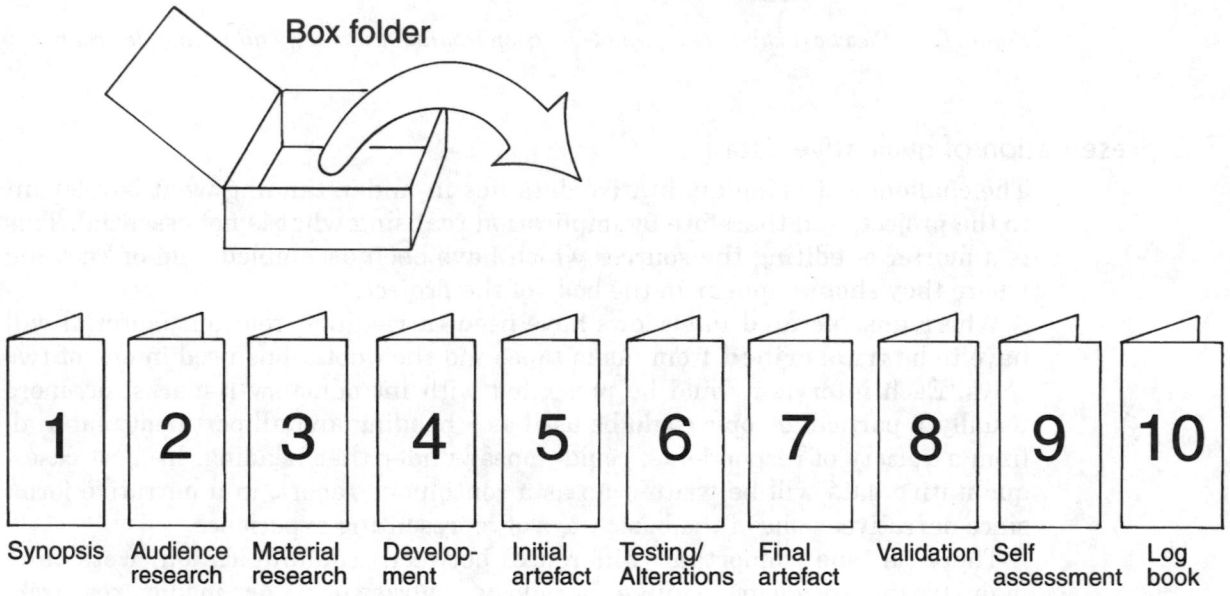

Figure 6.7   Organisation of a project file

Self-assessment and evaluation

Evaluation consists of a critique of one's own work, including consideration of the suitability of form, content and address to the chosen audience. **Self-assessment** covers all aspects of an individual's work during the course of the project. Some of the questions which should be posed for a successful self-assessment could be listed as follows:

- Was a productive project topic chosen?
- Did it have relevance to a particular audience?

- Was the project enquiry focused through the use of a problematic or hypothesis?
- Were the most suitable methods of textual research employed?
- Were the most appropriate forms of audience research selected?
- Had all relevant sources of information been identified?
- Had all useful information been collected?
- Was all relevant information edited?
- Were appropriate methods of design selected and utilised?
- Was communication theory used in the diary?
- Were all alternative decisions and courses of action analysed?
- Did the practical nature of the task mean that communication concepts were neglected?
- Was the social and ideological context of the communication process understood?
- Was the project tested on its audience?
- Was a validation produced?
- Was a synopsis provided for the guidance of the reader?

Ultimately, a good project depends upon a number of factors. The most important are the identification of a productive title, an understanding of audience, the use of appropriate research, the ability to evaluate work as it proceeds, and above all originality of approach. At its best, the project is an original contribution to communication research.

Case-studies

At A-level, the **case-study** is presented at the end of a two-year course as the second part of the final external examination. It consists of two sets of papers taken from any number of sources: holiday brochures, newspaper and magazine articles, books, promotional material, advertising, reports, letters, job descriptions and so on. Usually, the number of sources for each study will be limited in scope and will not cover all the examples given here. For instance, a brief survey of case-study work published from 1980 to 1991 includes the following:

1980
Case-study A: a school prospectus, a letter from a parent criticising the prospectus, a leaflet describing the area in which the school is located
Case-study B: a letter in a magazine devoted to the maintenance of a local steam railway club; the accounts of the club

1987
Case-study A: an illustrated guide for prospective engineering employees, called 'Engineering your Communications'; a leaflet on the 'Communication Needs of Working People'
Case-study B: a United Nations leaflet on a 'Water Fund' project; a four-page Oxfam leaflet called 'Hungry for Change'

1990
Case-study A: a careers booklet and a recruitment leaflet produced by Sainsbury's
Case-study B: two articles, on 'Representation' and 'A Woman's Place', aimed at teachers

1991
Case-study A: a series of listeners' letters to a community news radio station; a variety of news reports; a number of news releases from various sources, written for the station; a piece on the value of community radio; a model showing the various community groups in contact with the local broadcaster
Case-study B: a set of briefing notes on television soap operas; a piece on *Dallas* penned by Clive James; an article and a letter on the educational value of soap opera; an interview with three teenagers on the relevance of soaps to their lives

This 'raw material' is given to each candidate a number of days before the examination, so that individuals are faced with the task of preparing to answer a set of questions which can only be inferred from the content of the case-study.

One thing of which candidates can be certain is that they will be required to turn the *content* provided for them into a different *form*. There would be no point, for example, in presenting a series of newspaper articles on crime with a view to the candidate writing another batch of news stories in the same form. The usual practice is to set a task which demands a change in form. A script synopsis and storyboard intended for a 'Crimestoppers' television programme, based on the newspaper material, would be a possibility, because this represents a significant movement between forms.

The purpose of case-studies

The AEB syllabus carries the following information on the purpose of the case-study as an exercise:

> 'Questions will test the ability to adapt theories and/or models to practical situations, to adopt a mode or modes of communication appropriate to a particular role or roles, and to evaluate the case study materials.'

The first point requires candidates to adapt *abstract* ideas to *practical* situations. The second advances the notion of communicating in a way which is suited to certain *roles*. The last point calls for the *evaluation* of the material set by the Board.

In practice, the final piece of advice needs to be considered first. The ability to 'detect and describe inconsistency, inaccuracy, redundancy, or incompleteness in verbal, graphical, statistical material' (Neil McKeown, *Case Studies and Projects in Communication*, p. 28) is obviously an essential prerequisite for any process which requires the re-presentation of the content of a case-study. However, as McKeown notes:

'Analysis is always easier if there is a known *purpose* to the analysis. The problem here is that at this stage the student does not know this purpose.'

The solution is to make notes on those features which appear most significant. When the outstanding elements are all identified, it is possible that some pattern may emerge. The task is then to imagine what principle lies behind the selection of the material. The next stage in this process is the construction of a list of questions which are thought most likely to be presented in the examination itself; these must be answered in order to help the candidate become familiar with the principles of 'content manipulation'.

However, just as a project cannot be produced without considering the audience for which it is intended, a case-study cannot be answered unless the question of role is considered. This final requirement is vital for an exercise in communication, because it shapes the way in which content is handled; it reproduces the *intention* which lies behind all purposeful communication. The adoption of a specific role is a regular feature of Paper Two work.

Questions and roles

A school prospectus

The published case-study work listed at the beginning of this section can be used to reveal the range of questions found in the examination. Two selections will be made: 1980 and 1991. The first section of the 1980 study was summarised as follows:

'Case-study A: a school prospectus, a letter from a parent criticising the prospectus, a leaflet describing the area in which the school is located'

The role given to candidates was that of 'a reporter on the local paper'. Four questions were set for Case-study A:

1 The production of a set of ten questions in preparation for an interview with the school Principal (25 marks)

2 A 300 word article on the advantages, from the pupils' perspective, of such a booklet (30 marks)

3 A reply to the 'worried parent' letter, carried in the diary column of the paper (20 marks)

4 An assessment in note form, of the booklet *as an example of communication* (25 marks)

The role of local reporter may perhaps be regarded as rather uninspiring. It seems to have been assigned because it is a plausible way of introducing a range of activities, from the production of interview material to textual analysis. As a position from which to evaluate or articulate the various points of view on the issue (those of headteacher, pupils, and worried parent), the role is convenient rather than challenging. In other words, the role itself is not 'problematised'; issues surrounding reporting and the question of news values (the ideological 'agenda' supposedly internalised by journalists) do not form part of this case-study's overall approach.

Each of the tasks does, however, provide an opportunity to demonstrate skills which should have been acquired on the Communication Studies course. The preparation of interview questions, the ability to compose a piece of writing of a set length for a specific purpose, the marshalling of an argument, and the use of analysis are all important areas requiring practice. We have studied, in previous chapters, the various approaches to textual analysis, including semiological and discourse analysis, and these methods would need to be applied to the final question.

Railway club

The second section of the 1980 paper was set out earlier in this section, as follows:

'Case-study B: a letter in a magazine devoted to the maintenance of a local steam railway club; the accounts of the club'.

The role offered for Case-study B is a volunteer publicity officer. As in the last example, the role is not intended to be a contentious issue. The tasks set were:

1 a) an outline draft for a membership drive (25 marks)

   b) a draft for a fund-raising campaign (25 marks)

2 The use of *two* of the following approaches in support of either a) or b) above;

   i) a photographic display for a library foyer
   ii) a short video piece based on the ideas generated for the photos
   iii) a brief tape–slide presentation using transparencies of the prints selected (50 marks)

The first question requires one to establish which elements in the original material are essential. Once this is done, the next task concerns the type of campaign which needs to be run. In the case of (a) it may be that a membership drive is required either because there are simply not enough people in the club, or because the proportion of active members is low. The first problem may require a somewhat different strategy to the second.

When we consider (b), it is clear that the difficulty of obtaining voluntary donations must be overcome through the use of a strategy based on deliberate attempts at persuasion, but which ideally fall short of being manipulative. O'Keefe, writing in *Persuasion: Theory and Research* (1990), distinguishes between persuasion and manipulation by arguing that the social actor who attempts to persuade an audience (pp. 14–16) 'acts in good faith'. Manipulation is, according to O'Keefe, 'managing a person by unfair influence'. Such descriptions may not seem particularly objective, but they serve at least to remind the candidate that the solutions they propose to the funding problem must be realistic and founded on a basic level of honesty. Outlandish descriptions of the consequences which face the club should the appeal fail, or any exaggeration of the difficulties which must be overcome, may produce a negative response in an audience.

With regard to the second question, it is immediately clear that the apparently free choice offered depends in reality on concentrating on two-dimensional imagery and its role in public communication: all three approaches are based on the visual representation of social reality. Having said this, a display must carry some linguistic elements in order to inform the public about the benefits of membership, or the desirability of contributing funds. In addition, a video creates meaning through the context of sound, while a tape–slide presentation will obviously require the use of the human voice to provide explanation. It is the combination of image and words which provides the challenge in this paper. Notice that the principle underlying this exercise turns on the movement between *forms*.

A turn to the media: community radio

The eleven years between 1980 and 1991 saw some movement away from 'socially useful' though usually uncontroversial tasks and towards a greater preoccupation with the workings and products of the media. The 1991 case-study is a good example of this trend, the cause of which was quite possibly a conviction that the subject needed enlivening, and the suspicion that it might be outflanked by Media Studies if more attention were not paid to popular culture. In case we need reminding of the first part of the 1991 paper, it was summarised earlier as follows:

'Case-study A: a series of listeners' letters to a community news radio station; a variety of news reports; a number of news releases from various sources, written for the station; a piece on the value of community radio; a model showing the various community groups in contact with the local broadcaster'.

The role allocated is similar to the one already studied – an applicant for a post as trainee news editor/reporter with 'New Town Community Radio Station'. The type of role offered is often set at a fairly basic level, because this is intended as a realistic reflection of the circumstances likely to be encountered by a person of approximately the candidate's age. Applicants for jobs are also more likely to find themselves in the position of having to perform tasks to order.

Considered as a limited form of role-identification, the task may encourage the candidate to enter into the spirit of the exercise, producing a more lively and committed handling of the material. Its main purpose, however, is to ensure that the appropriate register is used by the person sitting the examination. Most of those involved in the study of communication will already understand what kind of address and discourse should be employed in order to achieve specific ends; revision could concentrate on the different responses made by fellow students.

Three tasks were set for Case-study A:

1 the writing of a treatment for a ten-minute 'Community Roundup' programme, based on an in-depth study of four or five stories, and presented in a lively and entertaining manner

2 the production of a presenter's script for the programme, marking where music, sound effects and interviews occur, and establishing the duration of each element

3 the writing, in note form, of a four-minute public talk on the importance to local communities of Community Radio Stations; the use of illustrations to be specified

The range of skills and the variety of modes of address belonging to these tasks is quite extensive.

If we consider the detailed breakdown of the work set under Task 1, we will find they include: a declaration of the general principles which would be applied to the programme; a detailed account of its structure and format; a list of reasons for the choice of stories; an indication of extra information required; a list of interviews to be arranged; and even a breakdown of the general direction such interviews would be expected to take.

The second task (which deals with scripting) requires some knowledge of established convention. The radio-script format may be illustrated by this extract from Andrew Boyd's *Broadcast Journalism* (1988), although the case-study question demands a rather more complex and detailed treatment of more than one story. The bulletin concerns a fictitious rail crash at Guildford station, involving the collision of two trains. Square brackets indicate where I have added information:

'ALLECK/OWN   19.8   16.38   CRASH/NETWORK U.D.

British Rail say points failure may have been to blame for this afternoon's rail crash outside Guildford which claimed four lives and injured twelve. This report from Julian Alleck at the scene of the crash ...

> REEL: CRASH/NETWORK U.D.
> IN: The crash happened ...
> OUT: SOC
> DUR: 40 seconds

[Journalist]: The crash happened after the Waterloo train was accidentally routed on to the same line as the train from Portsmouth Harbour. Mrs Petra Cavanagh saw it happen.

[CLIP/INSERT]

"There was a frantic squealing of brakes and a simply dreadful noise. The two front coaches were crushed together; I pity anyone inside ..."

[Journalist]: Six passengers were trapped and had to be cut free, but two were already dead. Chief fire officer Tony Stims was in charge of the rescue.

[CLIP/INSERT]

"Several were quite seriously hurt. Lucky to be alive. I'm surprised only two died in the impact and more weren't badly injured."

[Journalist]: British Rail are investigating. Their spokesman John Turbot:

[CLIP/INSERT]

"It could only really be points failure, but it's for the inquiry to make the final decision."

[Journalist/SOC]: This is Julian Alleck, Network Radio, at the Guildford train crash.'

The surname of the journalist responsible for compiling the report (Alleck) appears at the top left of the page, followed by the date and the time (19.8 and 16.38) and the title of the piece (CRASH), which is for Network distribution to other radio stations in the same group. The reel used for the broadcast is identified, together with the introductory sentence and the point at which the bulletin ends, the Standard Outcue (SOC). The abbreviation DUR stands for 'duration' of the entire item. I have shortened the eyewitness report and have added [CLIP/INSERT] to refer to those quotations regarded as most 'newsworthy' and which are extracted from longer interviews. When compiling this kind of script, one should also give, in minutes and seconds, the precise duration of each item. In addition, the use of sound effects and music is encouraged in this case-study.

The final task requires the production, in note form, of the text of a four-minute talk to be delivered to a public meeting. The subject is the importance of community radio to the community itself. A summary of the guidance provided in the original case-study material includes ideas about community needs, the obligations of the radio station, and the operating procedures governing its work. The talk itself should be 'punchy and different', but it is never an easy task to make something 'different' if no insight is provided into the established practices of public speech.

Soap opera

Once again, it is probably worth reproducing the outline given earlier for Section B of the 1991 paper:

'Case-study B: a set of briefing notes on television soap operas; a piece on *Dallas* written by Clive James; an article and a letter on the educational value of soap opera; an interview with three teenagers on the relevance of soaps to their lives'.

From the experience of case-studies gained so far, it is clear that roles are an essential part of the exercise. It is also important to realise that these roles are put together within specific **scenarios** – 'dramatised' situations which give context to the work undertaken. In this instance, the candidate is supposed to respond to a request from a publisher of audio-visual material who wishes to use students in the preparation of his or her product. This includes the following work:

1 a) writing the first four minutes of a script for a tape–slide presentation on 'Television, Drama and Society', concentrating upon soap opera within the period of time set

  b) sketching out and describing ten of the slides used in the first four minutes of the presentation

2 a) writing biographies for each of four characters who are to appear in a new soap opera, which avoid stereotyping

  b) producing the story-line for the first episode of the proposed programme

The first area of work encourages the candidate to use the case-study's critical and informative pieces as guidance and inspiration for a *creative* response. Information from the briefing notes, such as 'world events are looked at through the microcosm of the family', could be used as the basis for a scene which dramatises the relationship between the 'global' and the 'local'. Of course, soap operas which attempt to educate their audiences can sometimes allow their didactic intentions to dominate the narrative.

Some of the comments made in the briefing notes are somewhat questionable. For example, the assertion that 'American soaps are less true-to-life than British soaps' needs to be handled with care. Although the definition of 'realistic' may be quite straightforward, it is notoriously difficult to reach agreement on which soap operas, or which aspects of the soap format, create a realistic impression. It depends on established convention, the expectations of audience, and the particular cultural 'location' of the groups which receive the material. We could ask, for example, whether the various sub-groups which form British and American audiences really categorise programmes in such a simplistic manner.

The suspicion that case-study material might actually be inaccurate in some way need not cause alarm, because its purpose is to provide a stimulus for the production of ideas. This means that any departures from the Board's outline are acceptable, as long as a positive response is made to the questions which are set.

Question 1(b) helps to focus attention on visual meaning. However, the importance of elements which support the use of sketches (captions or other contextual material) is acknowledged in the requirement for a *description* of content.

Perhaps the most interesting challenge emerges in Question 2, the first part of which calls for the creation of characters for a proposed soap opera. The Board is anxious to 'avoid stereotyping', but there are two points which need to be made. In the first place, much popular drama offers boldly drawn characters, in order to attract and hold the attention of viewers. This means that stereotyping is difficult to avoid. The second point concerns the nature of stereotyping as a process, a central theme of Chapter 3. The form of the question reproduced above suggests that the examiners see the whole process as undesirable. If this attitude is taken to heart and one attempts to avoid negative representation, the outcome may be a series of unconvincing portraits, created merely to satisfy the 'correct' balance of individual traits and attributes.

The invitation to construct a story-line for the first episode of the programme, set out in 2(b), demands a careful balance between reproducing the familiar elements of soap opera as a genre and offering some novelty in order to convince an audience that this soap has a distinctive character. What elements would need to be covered in a candidate's response to this question?

First, the location or *setting* of the programme would need to be considered. This is often closely linked to the *title* of the drama, a practice which can be seen in the examples of *EastEnders*, *Brookside* and *Coronation Street*. The story-line is therefore partly structured through references to place and community. The difference between cinematic representation and the world of the soap opera lies in the greater attention paid to community in the latter.

The soap must also provide, as we have seen in the previous question, clearly identifiable *characters*, individuals who can be followed through a number of episodes. In addition, the detail of family and community life must be balanced by wider reference to *issues* in the society as a whole. In *Brookside*, for example, the trial and imprisonment of the Jordaches, and the subsequent campaign for their release, echoed public disquiet over the legal system's treatment of women found guilty of killing violent partners.

The chief elements mentioned here – location, characterisation, and the use of issues – help the writer to form the major themes of the soap opera. However, this exercise also requires some reference to specific *events*, incidents which drive forward the various plots and sub-plots. Ideally, these events should be interesting without falling into sensationalism. A number of soap operas have used highly melodramatic incidents in order to maintain audience share.

'The Thomas Eslopp Trust'

In 1988, the AEB produced two case-studies for the 1988 examination. Case-study B was called 'The Thomas Eslopp Trust'. The first part, given out two days before questions were issued, contained six handwritten applications with supporting recommendations from tutors (see Figure 6.8). The questions are reproduced after the first section (see Figure 6.9). The best approach to this study would be to complete the exercise before reading the comments that follow it in the text. The time set for completion is three hours.

Comments on 'The Thomas Eslopp Trust'

In this scenario, there are five committee members who meet to allocate the trust funds every year; the college's vice-principal, the local MP, a college counsellor, a trustee of the fund, and a representative of the student body (the role assumed by the examination candidate). The tasks allocated to the student demand that close attention be paid to the original purpose of the fund, because only this will ensure that competing views will be seen in perspective.

The fund's trustee, therefore, provides the best guidance in this respect; a working-class couple made the bequest in appreciation of the college's efforts on behalf of their son. In order to meet 'the spirit of the award', the trustee reccomends that 'we should be looking for a working-class young person who is going places'. Responses from the other committee members should be seen in the light of this comment, bearing in mind that the Trust also stipulates that the award should go to the student who has 'made best use of his/her last year in the college'.

The vice-principal's statement emphasises 'academic achievement' but does so only in relation to the college's reputation and a possible increase in student

THOMAS ESLOPP TRUST

APPLICATION

FULL NAME (Surname first): MATTHEWS, Amanda Sarah
TERM-TIME ADDRESS: 19, Mayhew Drive, Orford
TERM-TIME PHONE NUMBER: 0259 - 842591
COURSE: A-levels
PERSONAL TUTOR: Mr. W. Monteiro

DETAILS OF APPLICATION:

I am just completing my A-Level course and am expected to get at least Grade B's in my three subjects — Maths, Physics, and Chemistry. I want to go on to university to read computing and have offers from all my university choices. When I have finished my degree, I will have a job waiting for me in my father's engineering firm.

SIGNED: A. Matthews   DATE: 21 : 5 : 1988

TUTOR'S ENDORSEMENT:

Amanda has been the only girl in all of her classes and has, therefore, demonstrated great resolve in sticking to her studies. She will do well.

SIGNED: Willie Monteiro   DATE: 23/5/1988

Figure 6.8A   'The Thomas Eslopp Trust': handwritten applications

THOMAS ESLOPP TRUST

APPLICATION

FULL NAME (Surname first): RICHARDS, Gary Martin
TERM-TIME ADDRESS: 64 WELBECK AVENUE, LONGBARN
TERM-TIME PHONE NUMBER: 0259 663921
COURSE: MOTOR VEHICHLE MAINTENANCE
PERSONAL TUTOR: MR. A. HENRY

DETAILS OF APPLICATION:

I AM JUST FINISHING THE BASIC MOTOR VEHICLE COURSE AND I HAVE SAT THE FINAL CITY & GUILDS EXAMINATIONS.

I WANT TO GO ON TO DO THE HIGHER COURSE BUT I HAVE TO BUY MY OWN TOOLS. THEY ARE VERY EXPENSIVE AND MY PARENTS CANNOT AFFORD THEM AS WELL AS SUPPORTING ME.

I CAN'T TELL HOW WELL I'VE DONE IN MY EXAMS BECAUSE THE RESULTS AREN'T OUT YET, BUT I HAVE COME TOP OF MY YEAR IN NEARLY ALL THE COURSE ASSESSMENTS.

SIGNED: G. Richards   DATE: 22-5-1988

TUTOR'S ENDORSEMENT:

Gary has worked very well on his course, showing real potential in this area of work. He should go on to the Higher Course. An interesting feature has been the way he has supported and encouraged the few girls who have been brave enough to enrol on this course.

SIGNED: DATE:

Tony Henry   24.5.1988

Figure 6.8B   'The Thomas Eslopp Trust': handwritten applications

THOMAS ESLOPP TRUST

APPLICATION

FULL NAME (Surname first): Ellery, Heather AND Foreman, Jane
TERM-TIME ADDRESS: 124 Burleigh St, Tunstelth
TERM-TIME PHONE NUMBER: 0259 - 893143
COURSE: CPVE
PERSONAL TUTOR: Mr G. Popular

DETAILS OF APPLICATION:

Dear Sirs,

We have just completed the C.P.V.E. course at college and we took painting and decorating as our vocational option. We really liked it and when we did our work experience we found there are lots of people, like old people, who need this kind of work done for them and they can't find people who will do it for them. We think we can find enough work to do and we can do it well enough for people to be satisfied. So, we need the £500 so that we can apply to join the M.S.C. enterprise scheme for self-employed people, and we hope you will be able to help us.

SIGNED: H. Ellery + J. Foreman   DATE: 21/5/1988

TUTOR'S ENDORSEMENT:

Jane and Helen have shown considerable initiative during their course, particularly in going out and finding their own work experience opportunities. We would be very pleased to arrange a one day per week support course for them. They have indicated that they would welcome that, to improve their skills. I salute them and wish them well.

SIGNED: Giles Popular   DATE: 22.5.88

Figure 6.8C   'The Thomas Eslopp Trust': handwritten applications

THOMAS ESLOPP TRUST
APPLICATION

FULL NAME (Surname first): Willoughby, Jon
TERM-TIME ADDRESS: 'The Haven', Strauen Close, Orford
TERM-TIME PHONE NUMBER: 0259 59 2319
COURSE: AO levels
PERSONAL TUTOR: Caroline Stokes

DETAILS OF APPLICATION:

I have been doing an A level and some O level resits at college and I knew I would have lots of spare time so I decided to do something gratifying and I volunteered to help man the college telephone helpline. Some of the things I have heard have been fascinating and disturbing — you'd never guess what problems some people have. I could tell you some things, but I am, of course, bound by confidentiality. The £500 would be very useful next year when I do some more examinations.

SIGNED: J. Willoughby   DATE: 23/5/88
(JOHN WILLOUGHBY)

TUTOR'S ENDORSEMENT:

Jon has spent quite a lot of his time manning the college help-line, but it is unfortunate that any calls of real importance have had to be referred to other helpers. I am sure the Chaplain has valued his services.

SIGNED: Caroline Stokes   DATE: 24/5/88

Figure 6.8D 'The Thomas Eslopp Trust': handwritten applications

THOMAS ESLOPP TRUST

APPLICATION

FULL NAME (Surname first): : STRECKER, Jason.

TERM-TIME ADDRESS: Flat 1B, Elton Tower, Fore St., Orford

TERM-TIME PHONE NUMBER: 0259 - 113289

COURSE: Basic Engineering Skills

PERSONAL TUTOR: T Davies

DETAILS OF APPLICATION:

I have been doing the basic engineering course this year, with some problems, because I am confined to a wheelchair. However I do feel that I could cope with the computer-assisted engineering course at the Poly and I want to do this, just to show that I can do it, and so can other disabled people.

This would mean travelling and I would have to buy a car and have conversions done to it before I could drive it.

This is why I need the £ 500 and I hope you can help. I ~~expect~~ hope to be able to get a DHSS grant for the conversion to supplement any help the trust might be able to give

SIGNED: Jason Strecker   DATE: 21. 5. 1988

TUTOR'S ENDORSEMENT: Jason has shown remarkable tenacity in meeting the demands of the basic engineering course and should do well on a computer-assisted engineering course. I query whether the D.H.S.S. would keep with his car conversion.

SIGNED: Terry Davies   DATE: 22. 5. 88.

Figure 6.8E 'The Thomas Eslopp Trust': handwritten applications

THOMAS ESLOPP TRUST

APPLICATION

FULL NAME (Surname first):   JOHNSON, Alvard
TERM-TIME ADDRESS: 16 Carson Way, Longbarn
TERM-TIME PHONE NUMBER: 0259-112469
COURSE: Pre-nursing
PERSONAL TUTOR: Mrs. Evans

DETAILS OF APPLICATION:

Dear Sir,

I have been doing the pre-nursing course and want to go on to a university degree in nursing. I have done all the exams that I need and my tutor thinks I will manage to get a place. My dad is a qualified male nurse in Jamaica but his qualifications don't count here so he works as a hospital porter. He can't afford to send me to university without some help.

SIGNED: A Johnson   DATE: 23.5.1988.

TUTOR'S ENDORSEMENT:

Alvard has worked very hard on the pre-nursing course, demonstrating a truly caring attitude towards the sick and infirm. I am sure he has the ability to secure a place on a nursing degree course and he will be a truly professional nurse.

SIGNED: Grace Evans   DATE: 24. 5. 1988.

Figure 6.8F   *'The Thomas Eslopp Trust': handwritten applications*

CASE STUDY B

'THE THOMAS ESLOPP TRUST'

Some years ago the parents of an ex-student of your college established a Trust Fund – named the Thomas Eslopp Trust, after their son – from which a prize of £500 is awarded each year to the student deemed to have "made best use of" his/her last year in the college. Under the terms of the Trust, each year a specially constituted committee has to meet to select the successful applicant, or applicants, for the prize. The selection committee consists of:

> The Vice-Principal of the College (Chairperson)
> The local Member of Parliament
> A College Counsellor
> A Trustee of the Fund
> A nominated representative of the student body.

This year, you are the nominated representative of the student body.

Each member of the committee has been asked to define the criteria s/he feels should be applied in the selection process. Their responses were:

Vice-Principal: I feel that we have to put greatest emphasis on academic achievement. After all, this award is given publicity in all the local papers and on local radio and we have to do all we can to enhance the reputation of the College and boost student numbers.

Local M.P.: In these days of growing unemployment, we must emphasise the crucial importance of personal enterprise and give the award to someone who is going to 'have a go'.

College counsellor: It would be very wrong to think that academic prowess is the be-all and end-all of what education is about. More importance should be placed on the personal roles students have played in relation to their colleagues.

Trustee of the Fund: The original bequest was made by Mr. and Mrs. Eslopp because they were so pleased that although Mr. Eslopp was a factory worker with little formal education, their son did so well that he was successful in obtaining a place at University. To meet the spirit of the award we should be looking for a working-class young person who is going places.

You are to perform all the following tasks:

Task 1: Draft a brief memo to the Chairperson of the selection committee, setting out clearly the criteria which you, as the representative of the student body, feel should be applied in selecting the successful applicant. *(10 marks)*

Task 2: Draft a letter, to accompany the application forms, explaining the purpose of the award, suggesting the kinds of achievements/activities which would qualify people to apply and outlining the timetable and procedure for selection of the successful applicant. *(20 marks)*

Task 3: You have been given six completed applications to read **(Documents B1)**. Select **three** applications to go forward to final interview. Give clear and concise reasons why you have selected each of the final three and why you have rejected each of the others. *(30 marks)*

Task 4: (a) Draft **four** standard questions to be asked in all the final selection interviews. *(16 marks)*

AND

(b) Draft **two** extra open-ended questions for each specific interview (i.e. **six** extra questions), indicating clearly in which interview each pair of questions is to be used. *(24 marks)*

Figure 6.9 "The Thomas Eslopp Trust': exam questions

numbers. In this instance, the award is seen as a means to this end, as an opportunity to generate publicity. The political allegiance of the local Member of Parliament is not specified. He or she speaks of 'growing unemployment' and the need for 'personal enterprise', which also seems to indicate some divergence from the original purpose of the award. The college counsellor points out that the 'personal roles' of the applicants must be considered; this means that any support provided to other students should be regarded as a point in any applicant's favour. This is a worthy aim, though it too has no formal basis in the remit set out by the Trust. However, it is clear that the student representative has some freedom of action, because he or she is instructed to describe the criteria felt most appropriate for the selection of candidates. Therefore, if they follow its spirit, ideas need not always obey the 'letter' of the exercise. At the same time, the success of a candidate's answer depends on the ability to select *relevant* details from the applications received. Finally, we should remember that the first two tasks, the drafting of a memo and a letter, will provide an opportunity to set out other attributes which one feels it is important to reward.

The applicants

Amanda Matthews's tutor notes that she has 'demonstrated great resolve' in continuing her studies in subjects dominated, numerically at least, by male colleagues. However, the student herself writes that 'when I have finished my degree, I will have a job waiting for me in my father's engineering firm'. Matthews, hardly a working-class 'striver', does not need the award and should therefore be rejected.

Gary Richards, on the other hand, is in the process of completing a Basic Motor Vehicle course, and requires money to purchase tools because his parents cannot afford them. He has clearly achieved high standards in his course assessments and is also reasonably modest, because his tutor notes that 'he has supported and encouraged the few girls who have been brave enough to enrol on this course'. In all respects, Richards appears to be an ideal candidate and should go through to the shortlist.

Heather Ellery and Jane Foreman, two students on a CPVE course, demonstrate a clear sense of direction. If their application is successful, they intend to use the £500 offered by the Trust to join an MSC scheme for the self-employed. As working-class youth, they qualify for support, and many will appreciate the fact that two young women intend to make headway in an occupation usually favoured by males. Their determination to start as painters and decorators is not in doubt, and their sense of initiative is commendable, but their description of the types of client they have in mind should be treated with caution: 'we found there are lots of people, like old people, who need this kind of work done for them and they can't find people who will do it for them'. The reference to 'old people' may be a ploy designed to attract a favourable response to what is essentially a commercial venture. The fact that this is a joint application may suggest to some that only *one* other person from the list will be able to be interviewed, but these two would probably be treated as a single candidate. The primary aim of Ellery and Foreman is to set up a business; whether they are called for interview depends on how the criteria are interpreted. It is worth noting that, if these students are rejected, there will be no females on the shortlist.

There is no doubt that Jon Willoughby has ensured his own rejection with references to his work with the college help-line: 'some of the things I have heard have been fascinating and disturbing – you'd never guess what problems some people have'. His declaration that 'the £500 would be very useful next year when I do some more examinations' is also unlikely to impress. His unsuitability for the award is confirmed by his tutor, who notes that help-line calls of 'real importance' had to be taken by other volunteers.

Jason Strecker's application reveals his tenacity and determination, and it seems that he would make a very worthy recipient of the award. However, he appears not to have worked out how best to use the money on offer. If the DHSS is unable to supplement the award with its own support, as the course tutor suspects, the car conversion will not be viable and the award will have been misdirected. Strecker should be interviewed in order to find out if there are other ways in which he could usefully employ the Trust's money.

Another deserving case is Alvard Johnson, who receives praise from his tutor for his 'truly caring attitude towards the sick and infirm'. He mentions that his father's qualifications as a male nurse are not recognised in Britain, so that he must work as a hospital porter. Although at first sight this might seem irrelevant, it bears directly upon the applicant's request for support, since his father cannot afford to contribute to the cost of sending him to university. The fact that Johnson is pursuing a career essentially similar to his father's original occupation in Jamaica helps to suggest the seriousness of his intentions. He should probably be offered an interview.

If these comments are examined, it will become clear that the three candidates called for interview are Richards, Strecker and Johnson. It is possible, however, that one of these three could be replaced with the joint application made by Ellery and Foreman, on the grounds that they show the enterprise and initiative favoured by some committee members. The final decision on who to call will depend on the criteria used in the memo to the chairperson of the selection committee (Task 1).

The oral presentation of project work

The AEB course includes an oral component in which the candidate is required to present research findings and the project artefact. This is delivered in two phases; the **presentation** phase and the **discussion and questioning** phase.

In rehearsing the *presentation* phase, the candidate must consider two areas (this material is based on the AEB project and oral mark scheme of 1987):

- **verbal and non-verbal skills**: skills in oral presentation (intelligibility, clarity, fluency) and appropriate use of non-verbal communication (this phase lasts no more than 10–15 minutes);
- **register**: the idea that there is an appropriate level at which any presentation is set, including prior selection of appropriate language, arrangement of the room, use of support material, style, and sensitivity to the present state of the audience (support material is best limited to examples and extracts).

In the *discussion and questioning* phase (lasting 10 minutes at most), members of the audience are allowed to put questions. The following areas must be taken into account:

- **verbal and non-verbal skills**: skills in answering questions with intelligibility, clarity, and fluency;
- **rapport**: the ability to establish a successful relationship with audience and with individual questioners;
- **ability**: to develop and expand ideas.

The two phases of the oral are marked by lecturers (acting as examiners), and sometimes observed by outside moderators. In addition, there is an **evaluation** which the examiners must apply to the performance of each candidate. It consists of three distinct areas.

Under the heading **verification**, candidates must demonstrate that they have planned the project in terms of (AEB project and oral mark scheme, 1987): 'concept, design and execution in relation to audience/readership' and with regard to 'completing, testing and assessing the project'. The next area for assessment is **method**, in which the student concerned must demonstrate what he or she has learned about (AEB):

'the design of a project, the comparative success of the method or treatment chosen, his or her skills, any problems of communication [and] communication principles involved'.

Although many people are nervous during oral presentations, the audience for the event will ideally consist of some half dozen or so contemporaries who belong to the same course, together with two examiners and a small number of first-year students.

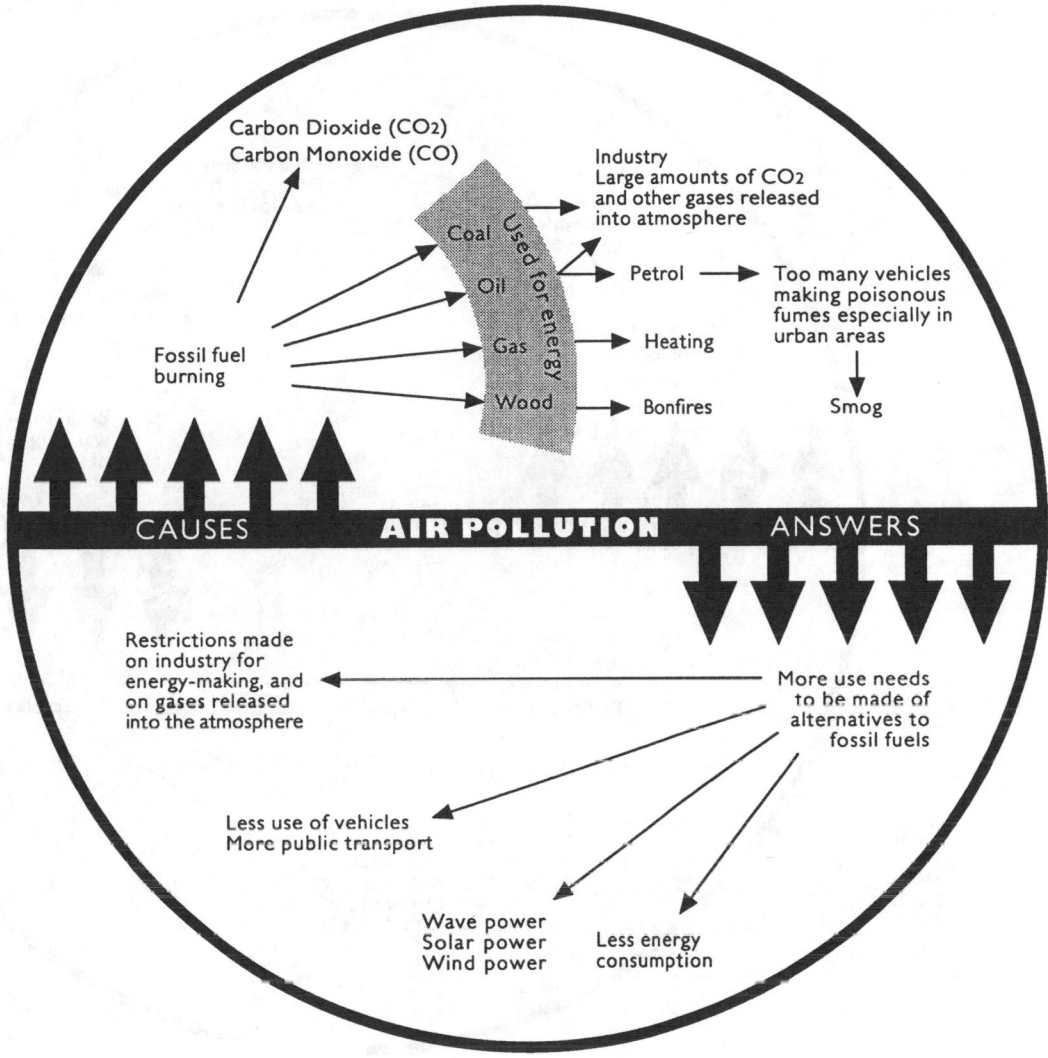

Figure 6.10 Display material for an oral presentation on air pollution

Scripting and delivering oral presentations

Although the oral should not be *read* aloud, it must be carefully prepared. The main points should be learned and rehearsed. Everything one wishes to say must be **scripted**, with information written out under a series of headings. Once a script has been produced, a series of 'prompt' cards should be made, which can be glanced at when necessary and then turned face down once each has been used. In this way, eye contact with an audience can be maintained and the whole speech will appear more natural. The length of sentences should be kept relatively short, so that points are easy to understand. In *Case Studies*

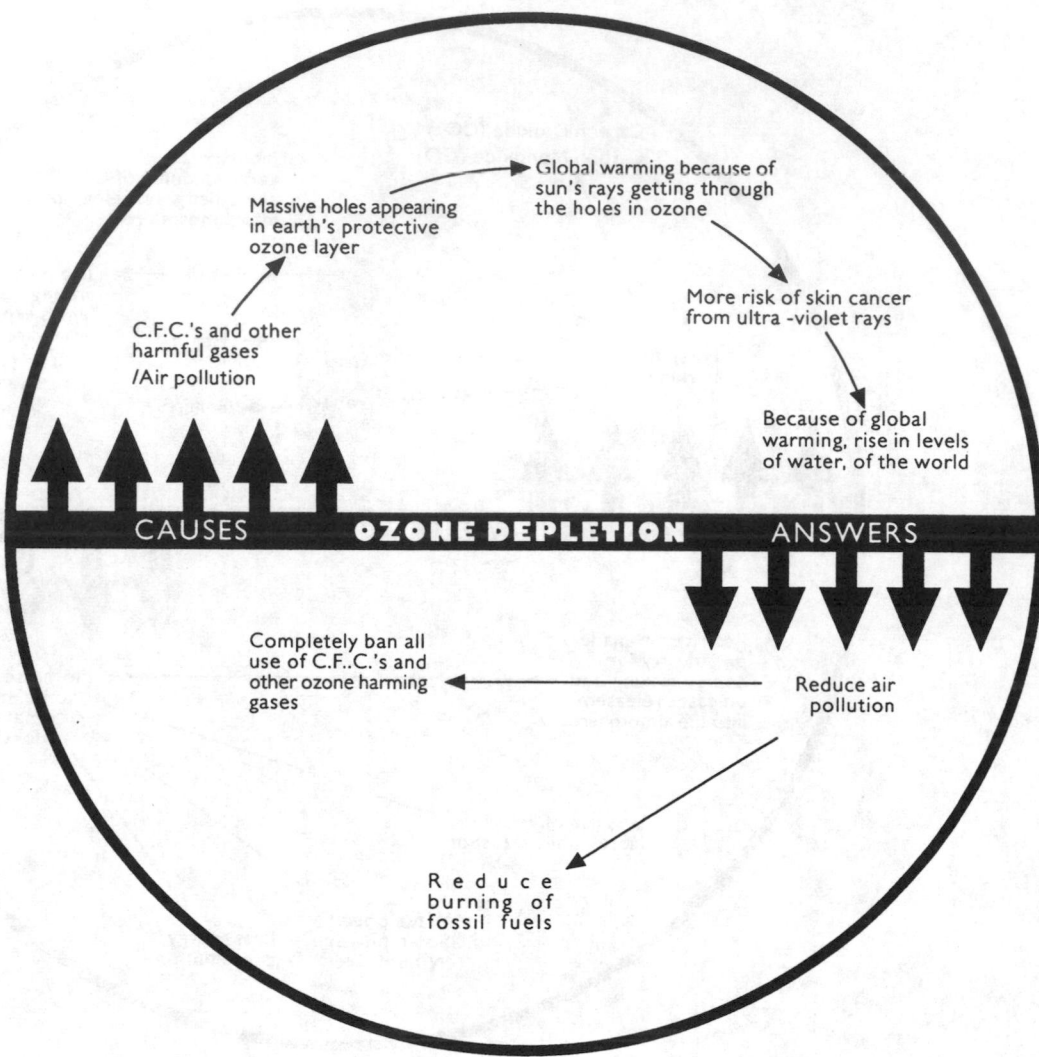

Figure 6.11 Display material for an oral presentation on ozone depletion

(p. 154) Neil McKeown recommends that 'a reasonable speaking speed ... is about 150–180 words per minute'. Individuals will need, however, to discover a pace with which they feel comfortable.

At the start of the presentation phase, a clear structure for the whole procedure must be laid out. Although a very firm structure can sometimes make a talk seem monotonous, McKeown (p. 155) advises that the following approach is useful: 'saying what you are going to say, saying it, and finally saying what you have said'. In other words, it is sometimes helpful if the overall direction of the speech is outlined, before the main body of research is described; at the end, a summary may be given. Another method may be to secure the audience's attention with a bold description of a major research finding, before the supporting evidence is provided. Athough dramatic and a little risky, such an approach can help to involve an audience in the investigation.

During **delivery** of the speech, some candidates use rhetorical devices (see Chapter 3), but the disadvantage is that audiences usually notice and resist such ploys. Although the straightforward reading of a script is, as I mentioned above, to be discouraged, it is quite permissible to read specific extracts from research findings aloud, in order to demonstrate certain points. Support material (such as extracts from videos, examples taken from a display and so on) is useful because it can also be used to illustrate the main arguments advanced during the presentation. The diagrams reproduced in Figures 6.10 and 6.11 are versions of support material used by an A-level student during the spoken examination to illustrate research findings for an environmental project.

SUMMARY

THEORY AND RESEARCH

Theory should not be seen as a necessary evil, the 'abstract' component of Communication Studies, endured because candidates must pass written papers or because the subject needs to maintain credibility in the eyes of other disciplines. In the study of communication, theory must be applied in a practical context if it is to make sense. The role of **research** and project work is therefore one of the most important areas of study in the whole subject. Communication problems are never purely conceptual, nor exclusively practical; they are a combination of the two.

The concept of science

The **concept of science** has played a central role in the development of modern social theory. The debate about the exact status of the 'scientific' remains an important issue for students to investigate. 'Science' means systematic and supposedly *objective* inquiry into the world. The traditional view of scientific activity sets great store upon rationality and the reliability of the data which scientists produce. A criticism of the 'objective' view of science is that the scientific community creates meaning *within* the models of reality available at the time; information is always classified according to the prevailing notions of knowledge.

TRADITIONS OF RESEARCH
Early social science

Once nineteenth century academics had become interested in social issues, it was inevitable that active forms of research would be carried out. The 'early' period of research, identified by Jensen and Jankowski, took place from approximately 1890 to 1930. The belief in an objective science of *nature* led some thinkers to believe that there could also be a rational and scientific study of *society*.

The years from 1930 to 1960, identified by Jensen and Jankowski as the 'middle' period of inquiry, saw the establishment of the survey as a form. The aim of quantitative sociology seems to have been (Jensen and Jankowski, p. 49): 'to elevate the status of sociology to a science'.

The current period, from about 1960 to the present, has seen extensive dissatisfaction with the 'scientific' approach. In words reminiscent of postmodernist critiques, Gouldner (1970) attacked the idea of 'grand theory', while Blumer (1954) expressed disagreement with the tendency to 'reduce social existence to variables'. The return to qualitative methods put greater emphasis upon empathy with the human subject.

Research: new paradigms?

The concern with audience is not an entirely recent phenomenon, but one that appears in communication research at various points throughout the twentieth century. Reason and Rowan's '**New Paradigm** research' is based on the idea that the two established methods of research, the 'naive inquiry' and the 'scientific method', are both inadequate. In the first place, *naive inquiry* is thought to be too subjective, while the second category of research is regarded as creating an entirely clinical view of the human subject. While the naive paradigm is (p. xiii) 'very prone to error' it has at least the virtue of being 'involved, committed, relevant, intuitive; above all it is *alive*'. 'Objective' research, on the other hand, appears to clear up many of the faults of the subjective model, but in so doing 'kills off everything it comes into contact with, so what we are left with is dead knowledge'.

VALUES AND ETHICS IN RESEARCH

One view of research and scientific inquiry states that it is possible to separate *positive* findings (factual data about what really happens in the world) from *normative* theories (ideas about what the world ought to be like). Some writers, on the other hand, argue that it is impossible to create a social science which is 'value free'.

Research: origins and purposes

The question of values and ethics in communication inquiry must extend to examining the origins and purposes of research. Whenever research is initiated, it is important to ask which institutions or individuals provided the funding, what intention lay behind the study, how the research was designed and conducted, and how the findings were interpreted and then used.

It is clear, for example, that social power is not distributed evenly amongst all groups; the relationship of the researcher to some sections of his or her 'target' group is therefore worth exploring.

Research: ethics

The question of **ethics** is also of major significance when research is being conducted. The term 'ethics' refers to the set of standards which a group or larger collective uses to regulate the behaviour of its members. May (in *Social Research*) cites Barnes's (1979) definition of ethics in research as those standards which (p. 42):

> 'arise when we try to decide between one course and another not in terms of expediency or efficiency but by reference to standards of what is morally right or wrong'.

COMMUNICATION PROJECTS: PURPOSE AND CHOICE

The **purpose** of projects has often been described as the creation of links between the 'classroom' and 'the real world' (see Neil McKeown, *Case Studies and Projects in Communication*). This is a valid point, but might give the impression that education has somehow been a 'protected' sphere of experience, while in fact it has always been subject to the pressures of political and economic change. The best approach to project work is to encourage *research* and *presentation* of that research from the outset of the whole study. Small-scale research projects should be undertaken well before any externally assessed work is required.

The project proposal

The AEB **proposal** form is described, before the choice of project topic is considered.

CHOOSING RESEARCH AND PROJECT TOPICS

Developing a viable **project/research brief** must involve progression through the following initial stages:

1 identification of a topic, together with a suitable audience or readership;
2 construction of a problematic, hypothesis or brief;
3 identification of sources of information;
4 evaluation of available methods of research;
5 execution of a feasibility test.

These first five stages are important preparatory steps. If any one of them cannot be fulfilled, then a new topic will need to be chosen and investigated. Each of these five steps is examined in the text.

Choice of topic

The initial difficulty in making a choice arises because a balance must be achieved between personal interest, course content and the challenges of delivering a project to a specific *audience*. In Communication Studies, the project is not aimed at an 'imaginary' readership; it is intended to make a verifiable impact on a group of people who will be identified at the beginning of the study. This group will then form a real audience for a final 'validation' of the work.

Finding an idea

Extracts taken from student projects are analysed in this section, before a series of questions is provided in order to assist in the process of choice, as follows:

- Is there a particular theory which is felt to be relevant to individual experience, or which appears to contradict that experience?
- Is there a theory or piece of research which could be tested for the first time, or tested in a new way, or on a new audience?
- Are there particular *methods* of research which seem interesting?
- Do different areas of the course suggest that they could shed light on one another? Could they be combined or contrasted in a study?

- Are there 'communication issues' which could be investigated?
- Does a certain locality provide any 'ready-made' communication issues?
- Does the researcher have any contacts which either may lead to a commission, or might be able to provide useful information?

The notion of '**brainstorming**' and the use of '**spidergrams**' are also investigated.

The problematic/hypothesis

Once an issue has been decided upon, the inquiry needs to be made *manageable*. It is important to work to a specific *brief*. One way in which careful focus may be attained is to work out either a **problematic** or a **hypothesis**.

A *problematic* is a question which is posed in order to focus an inquiry. The ability to frame a question is useful when someone is interested in a particular area, but perhaps uncertain as to his or her own position on the issues he or she might encounter.

A *hypothesis*, by contrast, is an idea or proposition which must be investigated or tested. Hypotheses are useful if the investigator has a strong feeling about a particular topic, and wishes to investigate the soundness of that perception.

Variables

Once the project has been established in the way described above, the 'abstract' ideas which may have begun the inquiry need to be made more concrete and specific. The task is therefore to find 'measurable' **variables** for the concepts which have been selected. The process is known as **operationalisation**.

Sources of information and types of data

Once the topic has been chosen, the issue identified, and the audience selected, it is important to ensure that there is access to sufficient **sources of information**. Information or data may be described in the following ways:

- **Primary** data is information which the researcher must generate.
- **Secondary** data is information which is already in the public domain.
- **Quantitative** data is produced on a large scale, using surveys and questionnaires.
- **Qualitative** data is the result of in-depth studies, including the use of personal interviews and the gathering of documentation which reveals the attitudes and beliefs of individual subjects.

Evaluating research methods

Research methods are identifiable *approaches* to the collection of data. They include audience sampling of various kinds, and all the types of secondary inquiry which are available. The methods used in research will depend upon a number of factors. If a number of project 'objectives' are clearly set out, this should help to establish which methods are suitable.

Summaries of the basic types of research method are given in the text:

- **Direct observation**: the attempt to observe social interaction in an unobtrusive manner.
- **Participant observation**: an attempt is made to participate in the activities of the group under scrutiny.
- **Structured interviews** and **questionnaires**: basic *primary* data is collected from quite a large number of respondents.
- **Unstructured interviews**: the researcher uses a set of pre-prepared or extempore questions in order to elicit in-depth *primary* data.
- **Content analysis**: a form of textual study and assessment, often based on categorisation and numbering.
- **Semiological analysis**: another form of *secondary* textual interrogation, based on a system which supposes there is a relationship between the appearance/structure of a text and the meanings it produces within a specific culture.
- **Narrative analysis**: the relationship between the spatial and temporal nature of a *secondary* text is investigated.

- **Discourse analysis**: in the case of the study of conversation, this is based on either *primary* or *secondary* transcripts.
- **Statistical analysis**: government and other data, some of it 'raw', is analysed according to the principles of *secondary* inquiry.
- **Study of theory**: based on the search for useful *secondary* perspectives on the social world or on textual material.
- **Analysis of documents**, personal or otherwise.

Approaches to **textual analysis** are described. When a text is being analysed, the following areas must be considered, where appropriate: the **semiology of the image, discourse, design, form, content** and **register/address**.

The feasibility test

This idea grows partly from the process detailed above. A number of practical questions must be posed, the answers to which will establish how relevant or successful the project is likely to be. A **feasibility study** means a kind of 'pre-testing' of the project's concerns.

EVALUATIVE DIARIES OR LOGS

Each stage of investigation must be recorded in the evaluative diary or log book. The purpose of keeping a diary lies in the fact that it:

- emphasises the importance of *process* instead of merely the end result of the work undertaken;
- helps the writer to focus on his or her own communicative practices;
- assists in the evaluation of research;
- provides a record which may be used for final assessment;
- allows theory to appear in relation to a practical exercise.

The diary/log as a record of work accomplished

McKeown suggests that certain pages of the diary should be reserved for a record of work accomplished:

a) work done on project last week
b) evaluation of work done last week
   i) *skills learned/developed*
   ii) *principles of communication to which work relates*
   iii) *models of communication to which work relates*
c) work planned for next week
d) work planned in the long-term
e) detail of work
f) aspects of project that need revision
g) equipment and resources needed for work planned

A SENSE OF AUDIENCE

It is one thing to 'conceptualise' an **audience**, but quite another to find ways of reaching it. It is always wise to select an audience which may be reached with relative ease, since testing of the final artefact must be carried out using a representative sample of the chosen group. This should not, however, distort the way that the artefact is constructed. At times, good ideas are wasted because a researcher decides to take the line of least resistance, using friends as an audience without thinking about their suitability to the inquiry being undertaken.

AUDIENCE: PRACTICAL/ THEORETICAL PROBLEMS

Many difficulties which arise when studying audiences are due to the fact that it is hard to make a 'dividing line' between practical problems and theoretical ones. Individual examples of audience research often seem to present a combination of the two. This may be seen most clearly in the field of Media Studies, because the audience for most products is not found in a single place at the same time. It is not only separated from the source of the 'message' (the institutional forces which produce texts), but is sometimes thought not to exist as a coherent entity at all. In other words, audiences are partly 'concepts' used to justify the production of a particular product, and, where actually tangible, have often been brought together specifically for the purposes of research. Where this happens, it is not surprising that such groups are described as

'artificial'. However, there are real audiences as well as 'discursively constructed' ones.

Selecting a sample

This is an immediate and practical investigation of the concept of audience. One of the most important points about this process is that the approach used in selecting the sample will determine to what extent generalisations can be made from it. If the sample is in some way unrepresentative, then the conclusions which are produced will apply only to the sample itself, and will have no bearing on the wider population.

QUESTIONNAIRES

Most communication projects will begin by establishing a link between the researcher and his or her intended audience. This is usually carried out by means of an initial **questionnaire** which will generate quantitative information. **Structured** and **unstructured interviews** are examined.

Designing questionnaires

In the first place, a very simple approach would be to ask oneself the following questions:

- What questions will be asked of the audience?
- Who will be addressed by the questions?
- How will the answers be recorded?
- What will be done with the results?

Common mistakes are examined, for the purpose of helping students to avoid certain pitfalls in questionnaire design.

Factors which influence response are listed, and **attitudinal scale and direct techniques** are investigated.

Questionnaire layout

The physical layout of a questionnaire is important, and must provide a clear series of stages through which a respondent may pass. A questionnaire is reproduced from a student project, including her evaluation of the layout.

Attitudes vs. facts?

The material in this section is taken from another student questionnaire, which was produced as a way of finding out more about racism and organised right-wing groups. The ultimate aim of this project is to counter the 'bizarre and false way of thinking' found amongst racists. Thus, it aligns itself firmly with the 'false ideology' school of thought.

A VARIETY OF METHODS

All research methodologies have advantages and disadvantages, so it is most advisable to use a variety of approaches, each of which may be used to check or supplement the others. This process is known as **triangulation**. It does not mean that there will be an absolute guarantee of accuracy, but rather that the researcher will be able to answer any challenges to his or her research in a more reasonable manner.

RESEARCH FOR ARTEFACT PRODUCTION: FORM AND CONTENT

It is probably clear that the **artefact** lies at the centre of the communication project. This is a specially designed production which carries the intended message of the project to its audience. It may be a video, a short film, a series of promotional materials, a lecture, a magazine article, a display, a radio talk or programme, a comic and so on.

During the process of designing the artefact, research must include close examination of any material which bears some relationship to the final production. Texts which contain the *same* **content** as the project artefact, but which organise that content in a *different* **form**, should be investigated. Equally, texts which exhibit *identical* **form** to the artefact, but contain *different* **content**, must also be examined.

APPLIED THEORY

The idea of an **applied theory** often causes uneasiness. Students may find that they are 'grafting' theory onto a project which they feel is essentially practical. The use of theory should, however, arise naturally from two areas of project work: the status of the project itself as an *exercise in communication*, and the communication concepts which apply to the *particular* study being undertaken.

The project and the use of models

Treating the project as an example of communication is a popular method of introducing theory, in which the artefact can be seen as a 'message' aimed at a particular audience. Models of communication (see Chapter 1) are often used for this purpose.

The project in perspective

Theories of *transmission*, *exchange*, the *generation of meaning*, *context* and *discourse*, all explained in Chapter 1, may help to provide what a straightforward use of simple models fails to supply: a sense of the social context in which the project 'event' takes place. Reference is made to some of the traditions outlined in earlier chapters.

Specific issues

Once we have grasped the idea that the project itself is an example of communication, it will be possible to consider the use of theories which apply to the specific subject matter of the project. Creative use of theory means looking for different ideas which will shed light on the project's hypothesis or problematic.

WRITING UP AND PRESENTING RESULTS

Once data has been assembled, the results of each stage of investigation must be presented in a recognisable form. Both quantitative and qualitative material should appear in the *research* section of the project, while the *log* should be used to record the process of research.

Some material is best presented in a written form; this would certainly be the case with qualitative data, where quotation from primary research interviews or secondary document analysis must be used to illustrate the conclusions reached by the researcher. Quantitative information, on the other hand, may appear in a variety of guises. No chart or diagram, however, should appear without a key to each element, so that the user is able to make sense of the information.

Forms of quantitative presentation

The variety of forms used for presenting quantitative data can be summarised as follows:

- **tables;**
- **bar graphs;**
- **line graphs;**
- **pie charts.**

There is a very important point to be made about the gathering and presentation of data: not only should we form suitable questions, we must appreciate the *significance* of what has been discovered in response to those questions.

The presentation of qualitative data

The challenge of using qualitative data lies in understanding what is relevant to the project, and therefore by implication realising what is not essential. This is a matter of editing the sources which have been assembled, and of knowing where they should appear in the body of the project.

Presenting the project

The standard method of presentation for projects is to label all material and to place the different elements in separate folders. These may then be labelled and numbered and placed in a box file.

Self-assessment and evaluation

Evaluation consists of a critique of one's own work, including consideration of the suitability of form, content and address to the chosen audience. **Self-**

assessment covers all aspects of an individual's work during the course of the project. Some of the questions which should be posed for a successful self-assessment could be listed as follows:

- Was a productive project topic chosen?
- Did it have relevance to a particular audience?
- Was the project enquiry focused through the use of a problematic or hypothesis?
- Were the most suitable methods of textual research employed?
- Were the most appropriate forms of audience research selected?
- Had all relevant sources of information been identified?
- Had all useful information been collected?
- Was all relevant information edited?
- Were appropriate methods of design selected and utilised?
- Was communication theory used in the diary?
- Were all alternative decisions and courses of action analysed?
- Did the practical nature of the task mean that communication concepts were neglected?
- Was the social and ideological context of the communication process understood?
- Was the project tested on its audience?
- Was a validation produced?
- Was a synopsis provided for the guidance of the reader?

CASE-STUDIES

At A-level, the **case-study** is presented at the end of a two-year course as the second part of the final external examination. It consists of two sets of papers taken from any number of sources: holiday brochures, newspaper and magazine articles, books, promotional material, advertising, reports, letters, job descriptions and so on. Various examples are given.

The 'raw material' is given to each candidate a number of days before the examination, so that individuals are faced with the task of preparing to answer a set of questions which can only be inferred from the content of the case-study. One thing of which candidates can be certain is that they will be required to turn the *content* provided for them into a different *form*.

The purpose of case-studies

The AEB syllabus carries the following information on the purpose of the case-study as an exercise:

'Questions will test the ability to adapt theories and/or models to practical situations, to adopt a mode or modes of communication appropriate to a particular role or roles, and to evaluate the case study materials.'

Questions and roles

Two selections are made, from the 1980 and the 1991 case-studies. Extensive guidance is offered with reference to a number of questions and other demands.

'The Thomas Eslopp Trust'

Another case-study from 1988, called 'The Thomas Eslopp Trust', is presented for study then analysed in detail. At the end of the analysis, suggestions are made for a solution to the problems posed.

THE ORAL PRESENTATION OF PROJECT WORK

The AEB course includes an oral component in which the candidate is required to present research findings and the project artefact. This is delivered in two phases: the **presentation** phase and the **discussing and questioning** phase. Oral presentations are discussed and advice is given.

Bibliography

Abbott, P. and Sapsford, R. *Women and Social Class* (Tavistock, 1987).

Allen, R.C. *Channels of Discourse, Reassembled* (2nd edn, Routledge, 1992).

Allport, G.W. *The Nature of Prejudice* (Addison Wesley, 1954).

Althusser, L. *Essays on Ideology* (Verso/NLB, 1984).

Andrew, E. *Closing the Iron Cage* (Black Rose Books, 1981).

Ang, I. *Desperately Seeking the Audience* (Routledge, 1991).

Argyle, M. *The Psychology of Interpersonal Behaviour* (3rd edn, Penguin, 1978).

Argyle, M. *Bodily Communication* (2nd edn, Methuen, 1988).

Aston, R. and Schwarz, J. *Multimedia: Gateway to the Next Millennium* (AP Professional, 1994).

Atkinson, M. *Our Masters' Voices* (Methuen, 1984).

Barker, M. *Comics* (Manchester University Press, 1989).

Barker, M. and Beezer, A. *Reading into Cultural Studies* (Routledge, 1992).

Barrett, E. *Text, Context and Hypertext* (MIT Press, 1988).

Bavelas, J.B., Black, A., Chouil, N. and Mullet, J. *Equivocal Communication* (Sage, 1990).

Beard, H. and Cerf, C. *The Official Politically Correct Dictionary and Handbook* (Grafton, 1992).

Beckerman, B. *Theatrical Presentation* (Routledge, 1990).

Benjamin, A. *The Problems of Modernity* (Routledge, 1989).

Bennett, R. *Organisational Behaviour* (Pitman, 1991).

Berger, J. *Ways of Seeing* (Penguin, 1977).

Bernstein, D. *Company Image and Reality* (Cassell, 1991).

BFI *Film and Television Handbook 1994* (BFI, 1993).

Billig, M. *Ideology and Opinions* (Sage, 1991).

Blackwood, C. *On the Perimeter* (Flamingo, 1984).

Bloch, M. *Feudal Society* (Routledge, 1965).

Bottomore, T.B. and Rubel, M. (eds) *Karl Marx: Selected Writings in Sociology and Social Philosophy* (Penguin, 1963).

Bowen, D. *Multimedia: Now and Down the Line* (Bowerdean, 1994).

Boyd, A. *Broadcast Journalism* (Heinemann Professional, 1988).

Branigan, E. *Narrative Comprehension and Film* (Routledge, 1992).

Breakwell, G.M. 'Women: Group and Identity?' (*Women's Studies International Quarterly, No. 2., 1979*).

Bremmer, J. and Roodenburg, H. *A Cultural History of Gesture* (Polity, 1993).

Briggs, A. *The History of Broadcasting in the United Kingdom* (Oxford, 1961).

Brinton, M. *The Bolsheviks and Workers' Control* (Solidarity, 1970).

Brontë, C. *Shirley* (Penguin, 1974).

Buckingham, D. *Children Talking Television* (Falmer, 1993).

Burgoon, M., Hunsaker, G. and Dawson, E.J. *Human Communication* (Sage, 1994)

Burke, E. *Reflections on the Revolution in France* (Penguin, 1968).

Carey, J. (ed.) *The Faber Book of Reportage* (Faber, 1987).

Carlyle, T. *Chartism* (2nd edn, Chapman Hall, 1842).

Carey, J.W. *Communication as Culture* (Routledge, 1992).

Chignell, H. *Data in Sociology* (Causeway Press, 1990).

Chomsky, N. *Aspects of the Theory of Syntax* (MIT Press, 1969).

Clark, A. *Diaries* (Weidenfeld and Nicolson, 1993).

Coates, J. *Women, Men and Language* (2nd edn, Longman, 1993).

Collins, R. *Satellite Television in Western Europe* (John Libbey, 1992).

Cooley, C.H. *Social Organisation* (Transaction, 1983).

Corner, J. *Television Form and Public Address* (Edward Arnold, 1995).

Corner, J. and Hawthorn, N. (eds) *Communication Studies: An Introductory Reader* (Edward Arnold, 1993).

Corner, J. (ed., *et al.*), *Media, Culture and Society Postmodernism* (1991).

Coulthard, M. (ed.) *Advances in Spoken Discourse Analysis* (Routledge, 1992).

Coulthard, M. *An Introduction to Discourse Analysis* (Longman, 1985).

Crisell, A. *Understanding Radio* (Methuen, 1986).

Cross, C. *The Fascists in Britain* (Barrie and Rockliff, 1961).

Crowley, D. and Heyer, P. (eds) *Communication in History* (2nd edn, Longman, 1995).

Crowley, D. and Mitchell, D. (eds) *Communication Theory Today* (Polity, 1994).

Crowley, T. *The Politics of Discourse* (Macmillan, 1989).

Cruz, J. and Lewis, J. *Viewing, Reading, Listening* (Westview Press, 1994).

Culler, J. *On Deconstruction* (Routledge, 1985).

Curran, J. *et al. The Media: Contexts of Study* (Open University Press, 1977).

Davies, K., Dickey. J. and Stratford, T. (eds) *Out of Focus* (Women's Press, 1987).

Davis, A. *Magazine Journalism Today* (Heinemann Professional, 1988).

Davis, R.H.C. *A History of Medieval Europe* (Longman, 1970).

Davis, S. *Emily Brontë: Heretic* (Women's Press, 1994).

Deleuze, G and Guattari, F. *Capitalism and Schizophrenia* (Viking Press, 1977).

Denzin, N.K. *Images of Postmodern Society* (Sage, 1991).

Derrida, J. *Positions* (Chicago University Press, 1972).

Dickens, C. *Bleak House* (Penguin, 1994).

Dickens, C. *David Copperfield* (Penguin, 1966).

Dimbleby, R. and Burton, G. *Between Ourselves* (Edward Arnold, 1988).

Dimbleby, R. and Burton, G. *More than Words* (Routledge, 1992).

Dimbleby R and Burton, G. *Teaching Communication* (Routledge, 1990).

Dines, G and Humez, J.M. *Gender, Race and Class in Media* (Sage, 1995).

Dixon, B.R., Bouma, G.D. and Atkinson, G.B.J. *A Handbook of Social Science Research* (Oxford University Press, 1987).

Douglas, K. *From Alamein to Zem Zem* (Faber and Faber, 1992).

Dyer, G. *Advertising as Communication* (Routledge, 1982).

Eagleton, T. *Literary Theory* (Blackwell, 1983).

Edwards, D. and Potter, J. *Discursive Psychology* (Sage, 1992).

Eliot, G. *Adam Bede* (Penguin, 1978).

Ellis, C. and Flaherty, G. (eds) *Investigating Subjectivity* (Sage, 1992).

Evelyn-White, H.G. *Hesiod, the Homeric Hymns and Homerica* (Harvard University Press, 1914).

Fairclough, N. *Language and Power* (Longman, 1989).

Finnegan, R., Salaman, G. and Thompson, K. (eds) *Information Technology: Social Issues* (Hodder and Stoughton, 1987).

Fiske, J. *Introduction to Communication Studies* (eds.) Methuen, 1986.

Fleming, I. *Goldfinger* (Coronet, 1989).

Flournoy, D.M. *CNN World Report* (John Libbey, 1992).

Foucault, M. *Power/Knowledge* (New York, 1972).

Fowler, R. *Language in the News* (Routledge, 1991).

Frankfort-Nachmias and Frankfort *Research Methods in the Social Sciences* (Edward Arnold, 1992).

Freeborn, D., French P. and Langford P. *Varieties of English* (Macmillan Educational, 1987).

Fromkin, V. and Rodman, R. *An Introduction to Language* (HBJ, 1993).

Gahagen, J. *Interpersonal Group Behaviour* (Methuen, 1975).

Gahagen, J. *Social Interaction and its Management* (Routledge, 1984).

Gaskell, E. *Mary Barton* (Penguin, 1970).

Genette, G. *Mimologiques: voyage en Cratylie* (Editions de Seuill, 1976).

Gerin, W. *Emily Brontë* (Clarendon Press, 1971).

Giddens, A. *The Consequences of Modernity* (Polity, 1993).

Giddens, A. *Sociology* (Polity, 1993).

Giles, V. and Hodgson, F.W. *Creative Newspaper Design* (Heinemann, 1990).

Giles, H. and Robinson, P. *Handbook of Language and Social Psychology* (John Wiley and Sons, 1990).

Gittings, R. *Young Thomas Hardy* (Heinemann, 1975).

Glass, A.L. and Holyoak, K.J. *Cognition* (2nd edn, McGraw-Hill, 1986).

Glen, F. *The Social Psychology of Organisations* (Methuen, 1975).

Goffman, E. *The Presentation of Self in Everyday Life* (Penguin, 1969).

Gramsci, A. *Selections from Prison Notebooks* (Lawrence and Wishart, 1971).

Graves, R. *Selected Poems* (Penguin, 1986).

Gray, J.A. *Psychological aspects of relationships between emotion and cognition* (Lawrence Earlbaum Associates, 1990).

Gross, R.D. *Psychology: The Science of Mind and Behaviour* (Hodder and Stoughton, 1992).

Ground, I. *art or bunk?* (Bristol Classical Press, 1989).

Gudy Kunst, W.B. *Bridging Differences: Effective Intergroup Communication* (2nd edn, SAGE, 1994).

Gumpert, G. and Cathcart, R. *Inter/Media* (3rd edn, Oxford University Press, 1986).

Haralambos, M. *Sociology: Themes and Perspectives* (Unwin Hyman, 1990).

Hardt, H. *Critical Communications Studies: Communication, History and Theory in America* (Routledge, 1992).

Hardy, T. *Tess of the d'Urbervilles* (Penguin, 1978).

Harré, R. and Gillett, G. *The Discursive Mind* (Sage, 1994).

Harris, D. *From Class Struggle to the Politics of Pleasure* (Routledge, 1992).

Harrop, J. *Acting* (Routledge, 1992).

Hart, N.A. (ed.) *The Practice of Advertising* (2nd edn, Butterworth Heinemann, 1990).

Hartley, P. *Interpersonal Communication* (Routledge, 1993).

Harvey, D. *The Condition of Postmodernity* (Blackwell, 1990).

Hayward, P. and Wollen, T. (eds) *Future Visions: New Technologies of the Screen* (BFI, 1993).

Hill, C. *The World Turned Upside Down* (Penguin, 1975).

Hodge, R. and Kress, G. *Language as Ideology* (2nd edn, Routledge, 1993).

Hodge, R. and Kress, G. *Social Semiotics* (Polity, 1988).

Hogg, M. and Abrams, D. *Social Identifications* (Routledge, 1988).

Homans, *The Human Group* (RKP, 1951).

Hopkins, G.M. *Poems and Prose* (Penguin, 1953).

Hughes, T. *The Hawk in the Rain* (Faber and Faber, 1968).

Jensen, K.B. and Jankowski, N.W. *A Handbook of Qualitative Methodologies* (Routledge, 1991).

Kamuf, P. *A Derrida Reader* (Harvester Wheatsheaf, 1991).

Kaplan, E.A. (ed.) *Women in Film Noir* (BFI, 1980).

Katz and Fodor *The Structure of Language* (Prentice Hall, 1964).

Kerr, P. *The Penguin Book of Lies* (Viking, 1990).

Kropotkin, P. *The State: its Historic Role* (Freedom Press, 1969).

Lacey, A.R. *A Dictionary of Philosophy* (RKP).

Langley, P. *Managing Sociology Coursework* (Connect, 1993).

Larrain, J. *Ideology and Cultural Identity* (Polity, 1994).

Latham, R. (ed.) *The Shorter Pepys* (Bell and Hyman, 1985).

Lattimore, R. *Greek Lyrics* (2nd edn, University of Chicago, 1960).

Lechte, J. *Fifty Key Contemporary Thinkers* (Routledge, 1994).

Leiss, W. Kline, F. and Jhally, S. *Social Communication in Advertising* (Routledge, 1990).

Leith, D. and Myerson, G. *The Power of Address* (Routledge, 1989).

Lenin, V.I. *Left-Wing Communism, an Infantile Disorder* (5th edn, Progress, 1968).

Lenin, V.I. *The State and Revolution* (2nd edn, Foreign Languages Press, 1976

Lenin, V.I. and Trotsky, L. *Kronstadt* (Monad Press, 1979).

Levy, E. 'Social Atributes of American Movie Stars' (*Media, Culture and Society*) (April 1990).

Lodge, D. (ed.) *Modern Criticism and Theory* (Longman, 1988).

Lukes, S. (ed.) *Power* (New York University Press, 1986).

Luxemburg, R. *The Russian Revolution* and *Leninism or Marxism* (University of Michigan Press, 1961).

Lyotard, *The Postmodern Condition: a report on Knowledge* (MUP, 1984).

March, J. and Simon, H. *Organisations* (2nd edn, Blackwell, 1993).

Marchand, R. *Advertising the American Dream* (University of California Press, 1986).

Marcuse, H. *One Dimensional Man* (Abacus, 1972).

Masterman, L. (ed.) *Television Mythologies* (Comedia, MK Media Press, 1984).

Mattelart, A. *Advertising International* (Routledge, 1991).

May, T. *Social Research* (Open University Press, 1993).

Maybury-Lewis, D. *Millenium: Tribal Wisdom and the Modern World* (Viking, 1992).

McAdams, S. and Bigand, E. *Thinking in Sound* (Clarendon Press, 1993).

McDowell, L. and Pringle, R. (eds) *Defining Women* (Open University, 1992).

McKee, D. *Not Now, Bernard* (Andersen Press, 1980).

McKeown, N. *Case Studies and Projects in Communication* (Methuen, 1982).

McQuail, D. *Communication* (Longman, 1975).

McQuail, D. *Mass Communication Theory* (2nd edn, Sage, 1987).

McQuail, D. *Media Performance* (Sage, 1992).

McQuail, D. and Windahl, S. *Communication Models* (2nd edn, Longman, 1993).

Mingau, G. E. *Rural Life in Victorian England* (Heinemann, 1977).

McLennan, G (ed.) 'Politics and Power' in *The Power of Ideology* (OUP, 1991).

Marshall, B. *The White Rabbit,* (Pan Books, 1955).

Mellor, D.H. *Ways of Communicating* (Cambridge, 1990).

Miller and Stiff, J. *Deceptive Communication* (Sage, 1993).

Moore, T. and Carling, C. *Understanding Language: Towards a Post-Chomskyan Linguistics* (Macmillan, 1982).

Moores, S. *Interpreting Audiences* (Sage, 1993).

Moravcsik, J.M. *Thought and Language* (Routledge, 1992).

Morgan, J. and Welton, P. *See What I Mean?* (Edward Arnold, 1992).

Mullally, F. *Fascism Inside England* (Claud Morris, 1946).

Myers, G.E. and Myers, M.T. *The Dynamics of Human Communication* (McGraw-Hill, 1985).

Myers, G.E. and Myers, M.T. *Managing by Communication* (McGraw-Hill, 1982).

Nashe, T. *The Unfortunate Traveller* (Penguin, 1972).

Negroponte, N. *Being Digital* (Hodder and Stoughton, 1995).

Newcomb T.M. and Hartley. E.L. *Readings in Social Psychology* (Methuen, 1958, 3rd edn).

Ng and Bradac *Power in Language* (Sage, 1993).

Nochlin, L. *Women, Art and Power* (Thames and Hudson, 1989).

Nofsinger, R.E. *Everyday Conversation* (Sage, 1991).

Norris, C. *Deconstruction* (2nd edn, Routledge, 1991).

Norris, C. *What's Wrong with Postmodernism* (Harvester Wheatsheaf, 1990).

Oakes, P.J., Haslam, S.A. and Turner, J.C. *Stereotyping and Social Reality* (Blackwell, 1994).

Orwell, G. *Animal Farm.*

Orwell, G. *Nineteen Eighty-Four* (Penguin, 1972).

O'Sullivan, T. Hartley, J. Saunders, D. Fiske, J. *Key Concepts in Communication* (Methuen, 1987).

Outhwaite, W. *Habermas: A Critical Introduction* (Polity Press, 1994).

Patton, B. R. and Giffin, K. *Interpersonal Communication in Action* (Harper and Row, 1981).

Pausanias, *Guide to Greece* Volume 1 (Penguin 1971).

Pinker, S. *The Language Instinct* (1994).

Pollock, G. *Vision and Difference* (Routledge, 1988).

Poulantzas, N. *State, Power, Socialism* (Verso, 1980).

Price, S. *Media Studies* (Longman, 1993).

Reason, P. and Rowan, J. (eds) *Human Inquiry: A Sourcebook of New Paradigm Research* (John Wiley and Sons, 1981).

Ritzer, G. *The McDonaldization of Society* (Pine Forge, 1993).

Rowbotham, S. *Women, Resistance and Revolution* (Pelican, 1974).

Rowbotham, S., Segal, L. and Wainwright, H. *Beyond the Fragments* (Merlin Press, 1979).

Ryle, G. *The Concept of Mind* (Penguin, 1973).

Sargent, L. (ed.) *The Unhappy Marriage of Marxism and Feminism* (Pluto Press, 1981).

Sarup, M. *An Introductory Guide to Post-structuralism and Postmodernism* (Harvester Wheatsheaf, 1988).

Scaff, A. *Language and Cognition* (McGraw-Hill, 1973).

Scannell, P. (ed.) *Broadcast Talk* (Sage, 1991).

Schutz, W. *The Interpersonal Underworld* (Science and Behaviour Books, 1966).

Seale, P. and McConville, M. *French Revolution 1968* (Penguin, 1968).

Sekuler, R. and Blake, R. *Perception* (McGraw-Hill, 1990).

Semin and Fiedler *Language, Interaction and Social Cognition* (Sage, 1992).

Shipman, M. *The Limitations of Social Research* (3rd edn, Longman, 1988).

Shotter, J. *Conversational Realities* (Sage, 1993).

Silverman, D. *Interpreting Qualitative Data* (Sage, 1993).

Sim, S. *Beyond Aesthetics* (Harvester Wheatsheaf, 1992).

Simons, H.W. and Billig, M. *After Postmodernism* (Sage, 1994).

Skevington, S. and Baker, D. *The Social Identity of Women* (Sage, 1989).

Smart, D.A. *Pannekoek and Gorter's Marxism* (Pluto Press, 1978).

Sofer, C. *Organisations in Theory and Practice* (Heinemann Educational Books, 1973).

Southern, R.W. *The Making of the Middle Ages* (Hutchinson, 1967).

Sparks, C. *Never Again! The Hows and Whys of Fighting Fascism* (Bookmarks, 1980).

Stewart, T. *The Reality of Organisations* (Macmillan, 1993).

Stoll, C. *Silicon Snakeoil* (Macmillan, 1995).

Sturrock, J. *Structuralism* (Fontana Press, 1993).

Tajfel, H. 'Interindividual behaviour and intergroup behaviour' *Differentiation between social groups* (Academic Press, 1978).

Tajfel, H. 'Cognitive Aspects of Prejudice' (*Journal of Social Issues*, No. 25).

Taylor, J.R. *Linguistic Categorisation* (Clarendon, 1989).

Tetzlaff, D. 'Divide and Rule' (*Media, Culture and Society*, 1991).

Therborn, G. *The Ideology of Power and the Power of Ideology* (Verso, 1980).

Thompson, D. (ed.) *Over Our Dead Bodies* (Virago, 1983).

Thompson, E. P. *The Making of the English Working Class* (Penguin, 1968).

Thucydides *The Peloponnesian War* (Penguin, 1972).

Tilson, D.J. 'The shaping of "eco-nuclear" publicity: the use of visitors centres in public relations' (*Media, Culture and Society*, vol. 15, no. 3, July 1993).

Wagner, P. *A Sociology of Modernity* (Routledge, 1994).

Walker, J. A. *Art in the Age of Mass Media* (Pluto Press, 1983).

Wardhaugh, R. *Investigating Language* (Blackwell, 1993).

Watson, J. *What is Communication Studies?* (Edward Arnold, 1988).

Watson, J. and A. Hill, *A Dictionary of Communication and Media Studies* (Edward Arnold, 1989).

Williams, R. *Keywords* (Fontana, 1976).

Williams, R. *Television: Technology and Cultural Form* (Fontana/Collins, 1974).

Weil, S. *Formative Writings, 1929–1941* (RKP, 1987).

Wernick, A. *Promotional Culture* (Sage, 1991).

Index